The Best of the
WINE COUNTRY

A witty, opinionated and remarkably useful
guide to California's vinelands

By Don W. Martin and Betty Woo Martin

DISCOVERGUIDES • **Las Vegas, Nevada**
A division of Pine Cone Press, Inc.

WARNING: When used as directed, wine enhances food, reduces stress, encourages camaraderie, enlivens conversation and kindles romance. Taken in moderation, it can aid digestion, promote good health and improve one's disposition. The recommended dosage is two glasses per day. Excessive usage is unwise, potentially unhealthy and decidedly uncivilized.

This book is dedicated—with deep gratitude—to the authors of the Twenty-first Amendment to the Constitution of the United States of America.

BOOKS BY DON AND BETTY MARTIN

Adventure Cruising ● 1996
Arizona Discovery Guide ● 1990, 1993, 1994, 1996, 1998
Arizona in Your Future ● 1991, 1993, 1998
The Best of Denver & the Rockies ● 2001
The Best of San Francisco ● 1986, 1990, 1994, 1997
The Best of the Gold Country ● 1987, 1990, 1992
The Best of the Wine Country ● 1991, 1994, 1995, 2001
California-Nevada Roads Less Traveled ● 1999
Inside San Francisco ● 1991
Las Vegas: The Best of Glitter City ● 1998, 2001
Nevada Discovery Guide ● 1992, 1997
Nevada In Your Future ● 2000
New Mexico Discovery Guide ● 1998
Northern California Discovery Guide ● 1993
Oregon Discovery Guide ● 1993, 1995, 1996, 1999
San Diego: The Best of Sunshine City ● 1999
San Francisco's Ultimate Dining Guide ● 1988
Seattle: The Best of Emerald City ● 2000
The Toll-free Traveler ● 1997
The Ultimate Wine Book ● 1993, 2000
Utah Discovery Guide ● 1995
Washington Discovery Guide ● 1994, 1997, 2000

Copyright © 2001 by Don W. Martin and Betty Woo Martin
All rights reserved. No written material, maps or illustrations from this book may be reproduced in any form, other than brief passages in book reviews, without written permission from the authors. Printed in the United States of America.

Library of Congress Cataloging-in-Publication Data
Martin, Don and Betty—
The Best of the Wine Country.
Includes index.
1. California—Description & Travel (California Wine Country)—Guidebooks. 2. California—History (California wine industry).

ISBN:0-942053-34-6
Library of Congress catalog card number 95-92024

MAPS ● **Dave Bonnot and Vicky Biernacki,** Columbine Type and Design, Sonora, Calif.
ILLUSTRATIONS ● **Bob Shockley**
PHOTOGRAPHY ● **Don** or **Betty Martin**

THE COVER ● *Tasting rooms convey much of the color and romance of California's wine country. Travelers can absorb the winery's atmosphere while sampling its products. The cover captures a portion of a stained glass window in the Sebastiani Cask Cellars tasting room in Sonoma.*

CONTENTS

MAPS

FOREWORD

Don Martin and I have been friends for three decades, and we have seen many changes in the wine industry through the years. However, one thing remains unchanged: an interest in visiting the Wine Country.

There was a time when this interest was focused mostly on the Napa Valley, when the only food available was from a few old family restaurants. If you wanted to stay overnight, you had better have a friend with an extra room, or be willing to put up with a second-rate motel.

Well, those were the not-so-good old days, as far as winery visitors are concerned. The number of places to eat and stay has multiplied and moved upscale dramatically. And the number of visitors has increased geometrically.

The Wine Country now offers everything from fancy resorts and convention facilities to some of the best restaurants in California. We now have our share of foreign ownership in the wine industry, which has brought wine and food flavors never dreamed of twenty years ago. And people have a choice of many wine producing regions, which offer not only interesting wineries but some great wines.

There was a time when I could boast of having been in the door of the great majority of California's wineries. Today there are wineries that I may have heard of, but I'd have to check a phone book to find them—even some in Sonoma and Napa. There were about 240 wineries in California in 1970; today there are more than 800.

With all of these changes, how can winery visitors find their way around without some help? This book takes an honest approach to the problem, giving people direction and choices as they visit the state's many Wine Countries. I live here, and I plan to keep it within reach.

By the way, here's another important thing about *The Best of the Wine Country.* The authors have kept the tempo light, and they poke a little fun at people who take wine too seriously. Wine should add enjoyment to a meal, not complicate it.

Life is complicated enough. A glass of wine, as well as Don and Betty's guidebook, will help ease the pressure.

Sam Sebastiani
Viansa Winery
Sonoma Valley, California

INTRODUCTION

"Fine fruit flavors over a steely base. It's a serious wine that secretly just wants to have fun."

—Winetaster's description of a Domaine de la Bousquette Blanc de Noir

Like that silly taster's description above, this is a serious book about wine that just wants to have a little fun. What you hold in your hand is the third completely revised version of the original 1991 edition, so it should be even more fun and—of course—more useful.

It was written for people who want to explore California's wine country and learn more about wine. It was not written for wine writers. In fact, it might offend some of those Colombard commentators, since it has a little fun at their expense. In flooding their tasting descriptions with silly adjectives, some of these Riesling reporters peddle more confusion than useful information. Really. Can you imagine a Cabernet that is "heavy on the tongue with a leathery finish and a slight hint of basil?" Try to picture a Pinot Noir with a big nose. (A late harvest Jimmy Durante?)

Betty and I chuckle when these writers try to bury us in a hailstorm of hyperbole. Many of them, it seems, get paid by the adjective. In fairness, however, these Sangiovese scribes *do* have a lot to tell us. By reading their newspaper columns or reviews in *The Wine Spectator* or other wine magazines, we can learn what interesting wines have been released, which vintner is winning all the medals and what dynamite Zinfandel is priced under fifteen dollars.

We *are* earnest about wine, incidentally. I've been a student of the California wine industry for forty-five years, and I've sipped Sirah with serious intent since the age of consent. Betty has taken several courses in wine appreciation and gourmet cooking. I was an active wine writer briefly, peddling my prose to *Vintage Magazine* and other publications. I soon tired of searching for the ultimate adjective to properly portray the pedigree of a Pinot. I decided that it was much more fun to drink wines than to talk about them.

And that's the subject of this book: discovering California wineries and drinking their wines—from Sonoma Sirah to Paso Robles Pinot.

There's no scarcity of books about the state's wine industry. However, some tell us more about the winemaker's relatives than we ever wanted to know. Others offer encyclopedic listings of every winery in the state, even those without tasting rooms. Many focus on the Napa and Sonoma valleys, although major California winelands stretch from Mendocino to Temecula.

This is a wine country *guidebook*, designed to steer you to more than 350 of the state's wineries and tasting rooms. Although our coverage is statewide, we focus on areas with wineries in reasonable concentration. We won't send you to a remote corner of the San Joaquin Valley for a sip of generic chablis.

Further, we include only wineries and tasting rooms that keep regular hours. Thus, you can toss this book into the glove compartment of your Belchfire V-Six and head for the nearest vineyard. We also suggest nearby restaurants and lodgings, and other area attractions.

In researching this book, we solicited nothing but information. We visited tasting rooms, sipped the wine, took the tours, asked a few questions to update our information and left. We dined covertly, made our own sleeping arrangements and paid our admission at attractions and museums. *The Best of the Wine Country* is full of opinions; however, they are all ours.

THE WINERIES

We offer a wide choice of wineries in each area, listing virtually all of those with tasting rooms that have set hours. Some smaller wineries that require an out-of-the-way drive may not be listed, and of course you may come across some that didn't exist when we researched the current edition of this book.

It goes without saying and therefore we'll say it: The wine business is in a constant state of flux. Some tasting rooms may change their hours, and some may charge for tasting where before they did not. Tasting fees are becoming more common, particularly in the Napa Valley, Sonoma Valley and the Santa Ynez Valley of the south central coast region. Often, the fees can be applied toward wine purchase, or they include a souvenir wine glass.

You'll note initials or little symbols beside each winery listing. They mean just what you think they mean:

T ● Tasting: the winery offers gratis sips of its product; a dollar sign following the symbol indicates a charge for tasting.

GT ● Guided tours are offered, generally on a specific schedule.

GTA ● Appointment needed for guided tours.

ST ● Self-guiding tours: Signs, arrows and/or graphics will guide you about the winery; or you're invited to take an informal peek.

☓ ● Picnic area is located near the winery. Most tasting rooms are licensed to sell and uncork a bottle of wine for your lunch. It is definitely *gauche* to bring your own from elsewhere.

📷 ● A **Gift shop** or a good selection of giftwares and/or specialty foods is located in or near the tasting room. Most tasting rooms sell a few wine related logo items, although we don't use the 📷 symbol unless the assortment is reasonably extensive.

Our **Tasting notes** at the end of each listing discuss the types and general style of wines produced. We attempt no in-depth critiques, since quality and style will vary from one vintage to the next. Also, the vintner may add new wines to the list and drop old ones. Under **Vintners choice,** we let the winemakers have their say, asking them to select their favorites. When they insist on saying "All of our wines are great," or they decline to make a choice, we omit this listing.

Since this book is about the *best* of the wine country, we have a little fun by listing wineries that offer the most interesting tasting rooms, nicest picnic areas, best gift shops, most informative tours and best wine values.

DINING & RECLINING

Since this is a winery guide, we list restaurants and lodgings that are near the vineyards, or in towns bordering the wine country. In areas where winery touring is secondary to other tourist pursuits, such as Monterey and Santa Cruz, we don't list specific lodgings or restaurants. Instead, we do refer readers to local visitors bureaus that can provide information.

Dining

Our intent is to provide a dining sampler, not a complete list. We used several methods to select café candidates for inclusion: inquiry among locals, suggestions from friends and from other guidebooks, and our own dining experiences. Comments are based more on overviews of food and service, not on the proper doneness of a specific pork chop.

Of course, one has to be careful about recommending restaurants. Obviously, people's tastes differ, and it's difficult to judge a café by a single meal. A chef might have a bad night, or a waitress might be recovering from one. Thus, your dining experience may be quite different from ours. Restaurants seem to suffer a rather high attrition rate, so don't be crushed if one that we recommended has become a laundromat by the time you get there. We grade restaurants with one to four stars, for food quality, service and ambiance.

☆ **Adequate**—A reasonably clean café with basic but edible food.

☆☆ **Good**—A well-run place that offers a fine meal and good service.

☆☆☆ **Very good**—Substantially above average; excellent fare, served with a smile in a fine dining atmosphere.

☆☆☆☆ **Excellent**—We've found heaven, and it has a great wine list!

Price ranges are based on the tab for an average dinner, including soup or salad (but not wine or dessert).

$—Average dinner for one is $9 or less
$$—$10 to $14
$$$—$15 to $24
$$$$—$25 and beyond

Reclining

We've checked most lodgings to ensure that they're reasonably neat, clean and well run. We often rely on the judgment of the California State Automobile Association (AAA) because we respect its high standards. We also include some budget places that may fall short of Triple A ideals, but still offer a clean room for a respite from wine sipping. Of course we can't anticipate changes in management or the maid's day off, but hopefully your surprises will be good ones.

Some of California's earliest bed and breakfast inns were established in the wine country, and their homey intimacy fits easily into the ambiance of the vinelands. We list only true B&Bs, not family homes with an extra room because the eldest son is out stomping grapes. Again, we reach for the stars to rate lodgings:

☆ **Adequate**—Clean and basic; don't expect anything fancy.

☆☆ **Good**—A well-run place with comfortable beds and most essentials.

☆☆☆ **Very good**—Substantially above average, usually with facilities such as a pool and spa.

☆☆☆☆ **Excellent**—An exceptional lodging with beautifully-appointed rooms, often with a restaurant and full resort facilities.

Price ranges reflect the cost for two people during high season. Specific prices were furnished to us by the lodgings and of course are subject to change. Use them only as a rough guide and call the facility for current rates.

$—a double for under $25
$$—$25 to $49
$$$—$50 to $74
$$$$—$75 to $99
$$$$$—$100 or more

"Quickly, bring me a beaker of wine, so that I may wet my brain and say something clever."　　　　　　　**— Aristophanes**

SURFING AND SIPPING

This latest revision of *The Best of the Wine Country* contains web sites for most of the listed wineries. They're handy for checking out the latest wine releases, news of the current crush and friendly gossip from the wineries. Some sites even offer "virtual tours" of the wineries, and many now put their newsletters online. Some vintners allow you to order wines from their sites, a rapidly growing practice. (One owner of a small winery said he now sells more than ninety percent of his wines via the Internet.) However, bear in mind that wines can be shipped only to a few states because of restrictive local regulations.

We've also included web sites the various winery associations, visitors bureaus and lodgings.

In addition to winery-specific web sites, you can get useful information from the sites listed below. (We lifted many of these from the Napa Valley's Beaucanon Winery newsletter, *Adventure Club*, and we express our thanks—particularly since we didn't ask permission.)

wines.com features winery listings, reviews of current releases and—for some wineries—ordering capabilities.

winetoday.com is a newsy site that discusses what's new at wineries around the world.

winespots.com offers reviews of new wines, information on wine club memberships and lists of recommended wineries.

napavintners.com obviously covers the Napa Valley, its wine history and its wineries.

smartwine.com features reviews of wineries, a directory of other wine websites and a tie to the industry publication, *Wine Business Monthly*.

foodandwine.com offers just what it says, focusing on wine with meals, recipes and tips on serving wine. It also has a wine-oriented book list.

winespectator.com is the website of one of the industry's most popular wine consumer magazines. We feel that it's too preoccupied with wine snobbery and uses entirely too many adjectives in its wine reviews. However, it is perhaps the most quoted magazine in the wine biz. For some winemakers, a 90+ rating from *Wine Spectator* is to die for.

epicurious.com is a great domain name for *Gourmet* and *Bon Appetít* magazines.

viavino.com covers wine regions, their wines varieties and wineries.

THANK YOU...

Through the years, many people have contributed to our interest and knowledge of wine and California's wine industry. In doing so, they have contributed directly or indirectly to the pages of this book. These folks are particularly deserving of our thanks:

Elizabeth Holmgren, director of research and education; **Gladys Horiuchi**, communications manager; and other staff members of California's **Wine Institute**. Their assistance was invaluable as we compiled data for this guide and our other grape-focused publication, ***The Ultimate Wine Book***.

Norm Roby, former West Coast editor of ***Vintage Magazine***, a contributing editor to ***The Wine Spectator*** and author of ***Guide to Winery Direct Wines***, for publishing some of my first wine articles.

Lindy Lindquist, who once hired me to write winery newsletters, thus convincing me that I wasn't cut out for that sort of thing.

Kathleen Elizabeth Martin, former wine and gourmet foods specialist for Macy's California, for sharing her wine knowledge.

Robert Mondavi for his efforts to convince America that wine should be regarded—not with awe or trepidation—but with simple respect. To quote Bob: "We view wine as an integral part of our culture, heritage and gracious way of life."

Justin Meyer, Napa Valley winemaker, for having the good sense to write a sensible book: ***Plain Talk about Fine Wine***.

Millie Howie, public relations representative for several northern Sonoma County wineries, for helping us discover that area's fine wines.

John and **Jim Pedroncelli**, northern Sonoma County winemakers, and their former tasting room host **John Soule**, for introducing us to the simple honesty of Zinfandel.

Sam Sebastiani of Viansa Winery for taking the time to sit with us on a ditch bank, bottle in hand, to talk about life, wine and the Sebastiani family legend. We thank him further for writing this book's foreword.

The **Ernie Fortino family**, the "new immigrants" of Gilroy, for sharing their friendship, their enthusiasm and their honest wines.

CLOSING INTRODUCTORY THOUGHTS
Nobody's perfect, but we try

This book is packed with thousands of facts, and a few of them are probably wrong. If you find an error, or discover a winery, restaurant or inn that deserves to be in the next edition, we'd like to know. We'd also like to hear your opinions of this book: What you liked and didn't like, what should have been included or ignored.

Address your cards and letters to:

DISCOVER**G**UIDES
P.O. Box 231954
Las Vegas, NV 89123

And now enough of this talk. Let's go out and find a decent Zinfandel.

THE CALIFORNIA WINE COUNTRY

Mendocino/Lake Counties
■ UKIAH

Northern Sonoma County
■ SANTA ROSA

Napa—Up Valley

SONOMA ■

Sonoma Valley

Napa— Down Valley
■ SACRA-MENTO

The Gold Country
■ PLACERVILLE
■ PLYMOUTH
■ MURPHYS
■ COLUMBIA

■ SAN FRANCISCO

LIVERMORE ■
South Bay Areas
■ SAN JOSE

Santa Clara County
■ SANTA CRUZ
■ GILROY
Southern Santa Clara

MONTEREY ■

■ GONZALES

■ MADERA
■ FRESNO

Monterey County

■ PASO ROBLES

■ SAN LUIS OBISPO

South Central Coast
■ BAKERSFIELD

■ SOLVANG

■ SANTA BARBARA

■ LOS ANGELES

■ TEMECULA
■ ESCONDIDO
Temecula

■ SAN DIEGO

"You ought to write a book On wines, count," I said.
"Mr. Barnes," answered the count, "all I want out of wines is to enjoy them."
— **The Sun Also Rises** by Ernest Hemingway

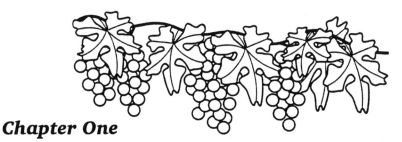

Chapter One

AMERICA'S WINELAND

It all started with vitis vinifera

By every measure, California is America's wineland. Several other states produce wine and we've heard rave reviews about Oregon Pinot Noir and Washington Chardonnay. Yet, more than eighty percent of America's wine is produced in California. Wineries are found in forty-five of the state's fifty-eight counties. Further, judging from national and international competitions, California's wines are among the world's finest.

In this book, we take you by the hand and lead you through the Golden State's fabled winelands, where you can meet the vintners and taste their wines. As you tour, you'll learn more about this noble beverage.

If you haven't toured one of California's wine regions in recent years, you'll find significant changes—as we did when we worked on the current revision of this book. When **The Best of the Wine Country** was first published in 1991, most premium vintners were preoccupied with producing varietals—wines made from specific grape varieties. And many worked from a rather short list—Chardonnay, Sauvignon Blanc, Chenin Blanc, Gewürztraminer and Semillon among the whites and such red standard-bearers as Cabernet Sauvignon, Pinot Noir, Merlot and of course that California classic, Zinfandel.

Today, more winemakers are doing what has been done for centuries in Europe—blending a variety of grapes to make styles distinctive to their winery. It began with the red and white Meritage movement as a few vintners started blending Cabernet Sauvignon and Chardonnay with other wines from their Bordeaux and Burgundy homelands. Other vintners began blending wines from these regions of France without using the lofty Meritage label.

(Gundlatch-Bundschu, the Sonoma Valley's good humor winery, came up with "Bearitage".)

Then came the "Rhône Rangers," employing a variety of Rhône Valley reds to make soft, full-flavored wines. The most recent trend is toward lesser-known Italian and French varietals. Thus, when you step into a tasting room you may encounter—in addition to the usual Cabs and Chards—Cinsault, Mourvèdre, Viognier, Sangiovese, Nebbiolo, Refosco and Aleatico.

Another change since our first edition is the continued growth of wineries, adding more variety to California's winelands. The first printing of **The Best of the Wine Country** featured more than 250 wineries with tasting rooms that kept regular hours. Now that list tops 350.

Where's most of this new activity happening? Not in the fabled Napa Valley. The fastest growing region—in numbers of wineries—is the south central coast of Santa Barbara and San Luis Obispo counties (Chapter Eleven). Other active growth areas are northern Sonoma County (Chapter Three) and the Gold Country (Chapter Twelve). The Livermore Valley (Chapter Seven) has stopped suburban intrusion with an agricultural protective zone and gained several wineries.

However, the Napa Valley remains the champion in total winery count, with so many that we needed two chapters—5 and 6—to hold them. A few wineries have closed while others have opened, for a small overall increase.

The accidental sipper

My affair with wine began by accident four decades ago. While handling publicity for U.S. Marine Corps recruiting in San Francisco, I was invited along with other public relations folks to a tasting sponsored by the Wine Institute. In my mind at the time, wine was just another beverage—something that occupied shelf space at the corner liquor store. My parents never drank alcohol, nor were they prohibitionists, so my attitude toward wine was neutral. I recall being a serious Scotch drinker at the time.

However, that wine tasting whetted both my appetite and my curiosity.

Although I couldn't tell a Chardonnay from a Charbono, I was intrigued by the almost reverent attitude that wine enthusiasts held for the stuff. With all that swirling and sipping and studied frowning, they seemed part of a

WINERIES OFFER CASE DISCOUNTS

mysterious cult. They used words like "nose", "finish" and "balance" in ways foreign to me. I wanted to learn more. Further, the idea of matching a particular beverage to food interested me, because I love good food.

My wife and I began visiting San Francisco Bay Area wineries, and we took wine study courses to learn more about this product. For a time, I was a freelance wine writer, but I ran out of adjectives long before I ran out of interesting wines.

The mystery is gone now, and we've learned to respect and appreciate this civilized beverage. And certainly, we've learned that the best place to become friends with wine is at the winery.

There, you can meet the winemaker, or at least a learned employee, who can discuss wine and unravel its mysteries. You can learn how they make the stuff, how and why they age it and how to best enjoy it with food. You'll also learn that most vintners are friendly, down-to-earth folk who don't worship their wines or drape them with descriptive adjectives. They merely respect and enjoy them.

Wineries like to sell their products at retail; thus the popularity of tasting rooms. Large wineries probably don't care where you buy their product, so long as you buy it. However, most of the smaller vintners' wines aren't available at liquor outlets or supermarkets, so you'd best do your shopping at the source. Some sell their wines only at their wineries. Besides, a tasting room nestled among the vines is a lot more appealing than a wine shelf nestled among the cabbages at Safeway.

The greatest advantage of touring is obvious—you can try a variety of wines and decide which are most agreeable to your palate and your budget. And where better to tour than in California, with its vast and widespread vineyards? Wine grapes rank sixth among the state's agricultural products. Grapes of all types comprise its second most valuable crop, exceeded only by dairy products. Wineries are a major tourist draw, as well. Some large Napa Valley establishments attract 300,000 sippers a year.

Overall, however, Americans are wimps when it comes to drinking wine. U.S. per capita consumption is less than three gallons a year, compared with about twenty in France and Italy. Wine drinking increased rapidly during the 1970s and 1980s as more Americans came to appreciate its value with food. Caught in the wave of an anti-alcohol movement, wine use dropped during the 1990s, although it's now enjoying a resurgence. Incidentally, per capita wine consumption in California is more than double the national average.

Where's the grapes?

And just where is California's wine country? Vineyards are scattered over most of the state, from the north coast to San Diego. However, premium grapes—those sensitive little fellows that require warm days, cool nights and well-drained soil—occupy more limited areas.

Historically, most of California's premier wines have been produced in vineyards encircling the San Francisco Bay Area. North bay counties of Napa, Sonoma and Mendocino, and the Livermore and Santa Clara valleys to the south offer the proper conditions.

The north bay counties are still major producers, although many south bay grapes have been squeezed out by the population crush, so vintners have sought new horizons. They're finding them in the Sierra Nevada foothills, in Monterey County, the south central coast area of San Luis Obispo and Santa Barbara counties, and the Temecula Valley, north of San Diego.

HOW TO APPRECIATE A FINE WINE

All that sloshing and sniffing practiced by wine-tasters isn't supercilious foolishness. Many subtleties lurk in a bottle of fine wine. Only by following these steps can you discern all of the nuances of the essence of the grape.

SEE ● Hold the glass up to the light and examine it for clarity. It should be—pardon the old Nixon cliche—perfectly clear. Don't panic if you detect minute particles, however. They're probably harmless bits of cork or, in the case of aged reds, some tannin residue that was stirred up when the wine was poured.

SLOSH ● Coat the inside of the glass by swirling the wine vigorously (being careful, of course, that you don't slosh it all over the individual next to you).

SNIFF ● Hold the glass up to your nose and inhale deeply, drawing in all the wine's smells—referred to as the *nose* by the pros. The fruity fragrance of the grape is described as the *aroma*, while the more subtle dusky smell is the *bouquet*—the essence of fermentation and aging.

SIP AND SLURP ● Your mother said this was bad manners, but it's the best way to taste wine. Take a sip, cradle it on your tongue, draw air over it, exhale through your nose, then swallow. This aeration—despite its odd sound—releases the wine's complex flavors. Your little taste buds can detect only sweet, sour, salty and bitter. All the nuances of taste are in your nose, and mixing air with the wine helps bring out its subtleties.

A young white wine should taste fresh, crisp and fruity, while reds will be more complex and berry-like, perhaps with hints of wood from barrel-aging.

Some wine writers insist that they can detect cedar, cigar boxes, licorice, pencil shavings, pineapples, apricots, cassis, chocolate, pears, peaches, plums, eucalyptus and—good grief—even the suggestion of a sweaty saddle. We suspect, however, that they've just run short of adjectives. Or, perhaps they sampled too many wines.

These so-called premium growing areas produce only about fifteen percent of California's total wine output. Most of the rest comes from the dry, hot and huge San Joaquin Valley. There, more hardy vines thrive to produce the large—and generally drinkable—flood of jug wines. A single winery, E. & J. Gallo of Modesto, bottles about half of America's total wine output. Neither Gallo nor most of the other valley giants have tasting rooms, so that region is not included in this book.

In the beginning, someone stepped on a grape

Historians debate which came first—wine or beer. Some scholars insist that beer was the first alcoholic beverage, since grain was cultivated before grapes. Others say wine came first because grapes are self-contained little alcohol factories. While beer has to be brewed from yeast and grain, grapes are coated with wild yeast and will ferment naturally when the skin is broken.

Stomp some grapes, step back, and you'll soon have wine. Most winemakers, however, use cultured yeast to better control fermentation.

"The wine industry certainly dates from at least 3000 B.C.," according to Maynard A. Amerine and Vernon L. Singleton's *Wine: An Introduction for Americans*. "Some housewife probably left crushed grapes in a jar and found, a few days later, that an alcoholic product had been formed."

A 1991 discovery of wine stains on the shards of a pre-Bronze Age Sumerian jar pushes the date back even further, to 3500 B.C. Fossilized grape seeds found in Stone Age middens suggest that folks may have been sipping wine 10,000 years ago. The Tigris-Euphrates Valley in Iran, Iraq and Turkey is regarded by historians as the cradle of agriculture and therefore of civilization. It's also the area where Noah supposedly parked his ark—on Turkey's Mount Ararat. According to Genesis 9:20-21, he "began to be a husbandman, and he planted a vineyard; and he drank of the wine and was drunken." Thus, the Bible may have recorded history's first hangover.

Grapes grew wild in California, although early-day padres found them unsuitable for wine making. They had to rely on unreliable shipments from New Spain (Mexico) for their essential altar wines.

Father Junipero Serra established the first mission in present day California at San Diego in 1769. However, some years passed before suitable grape vines, brought in from Mexico by way of Spain, were planted. The good padre wrote in 1781: "I hope that...the corn prospers and that the grape vines are living and thriving, for this lack of altar wine is becoming unbearable."

The vine in question, now called the mission grape, is a descendant of *vitis vinifera*, the mother of most European varieties. Although many popular French, Italian and German vines now flourish in California, the mission grape is relatively rare.

Many folks regard Sonoma and Napa as the root of California viticulture, although large scale winemaking actually began in Los Angeles. Plantings were so common early in the nineteenth century that it was called "The City of Vineyards."

California's first full time winemaker was Jean Louis Vignes, a Frenchman from Bordeaux. He arrived in Monterey by ship in 1831 and soon adjourned to Los Angeles, where he planted vineyards and established a major commercial operation. History reports that he was the first to import European wine grapes. Equally important, he is credited with planting some of the first orange trees in California. Vignes sold his orange and wine estate in 1855 to his nephews, Pierre and Jean Louis Sansevain. They became the state's lead-

THE TEN BEST REASONS
NOT TO BUY THAT BOTTLE OF WINE
With apologies to David Letterman

10. Some of the color has settled to the bottom.

9. The container is a mason jar.

8. It has a pull-tab opener.

7. It comes with a recipe for do-it-yourself Viagra.

6. The front label reads: "Shake well before using."

5. The back label reads: "For external use only."

4. It's approved by the Mormon Church.

3. It's labeled Lafitte Rothschild, although it's white Zinfandel.

2. The government warning label is in Arabic.

1. When you hold it up to the light to check for clarity, something swims past.

ing wine merchants and established its first commercial sparkling wine operation. Then in 1862, the brothers quit their business and California's pioneer vineyards disappeared under spreading Los Angeles suburbs.

While not the first, Sonoma was the most important seat of the state's early wine industry. The story involves an unlikely pair—an enterprising Mexican lieutenant and a flamboyant Hungarian of questionable lineage.

In the years following Father Serra's arrival, the missions became vast agricultural empires. They were governed by the padres and worked by native people who had been converted to Christianity—often unwillingly. Mexico won its independence from Spain in the 1820s and a few years later, it decommissioned the missions. Their great landholdings were parceled out to favored soldiers and politicians.

Lieutenant Mariano Guadalupe Vallejo was sent to the most northern of the missions, San Francisco de Solano in present-day Sonoma, to oversee its dissolution. The ambitious young officer established a military garrison and laid out a townsite. A good politician, he quickly attained the rank of military *commandante* of all northern California. And he picked up thousands of acres in Mexican land grants. The assertive Vallejo soon became a major producer of California wines.

The man from Hungary

Enter the visionary gentleman of dubious lineage. Agoston Haraszthy (*Har-RAS-they*) arrived in Sonoma in 1856, met Vallejo and purchased land to start a vineyard. He had come to America in 1840 after fleeing his native Hungary, perhaps for choosing the wrong side of a revolution. He was variously known as Colonel Haraszthy or Count Haraszthy, although the source of either title is vague.

He certainly was an ambitious fellow, and a gad-about promoter. In the sixteen years since touching American soil, he had founded the town of Sauk City, Wisconsin, crossed by wagon train to San Diego, dabbled in real estate, become a state assemblyman and later director of the U.S. Mint in San Francisco. He had attempted to raise wine grapes in Wisconsin, San Diego, San Francisco and San Mateo before finally finding the proper land and climate in Sonoma. The count and Vallejo became fast friends. Two Haraszthy sons, in fact, married two Vallejo daughters.

California's vinelands offer particularly pleasing vistas. Here, young vines dance over a steep ridge near the Silverado Trail in the Napa Valley.

Haraszthy's Buena Vista Farm became America's most prosperous wine empire. He lived regally in a Pompeiian villa cresting a knoll above his vineyards. His greatest contribution to California viticulture was the importation of hundreds of thousands of premium European grape cuttings. Many of these were made available to growers throughout the state.

The free-wheeling count's departure was appropriately bizarre. In 1868, restless for a new challenge, he went to Nicaragua to start a sugar cane plantation. Attempting to cross a stream, he fell into the water and vanished. Apparently, he was devoured by alligators.

The wine industry which Haraszthy helped set into motion had to struggle during its formative years. Over-production and the depression of the 1870s dropped wine prices to ten cents a gallon. Then the industry was nearly ruined by the invasion of *phylloxera*, a louse that destroys grapevine roots. Toward the end of the century, an ironic solution was found. The roots of wild American grapes, which the European varieties had replaced, were resistant to the little bug. By grafting *vitis vinifera* cuttings onto *vitis californica* root stock, the wine industry was saved. For the moment, at least.

The 1906 San Francisco earthquake dealt the business a serious blow, in and out of the wine country. Many Sonoma and Napa County wineries were ruined by the temblor, which in fact was centered north of San Francisco. The city was the production and distribution center for much of California's wine, and the fire following the earthquake destroyed millions of gallons.

Then on January 16, 1920, the infamous Volstead Act added further ruin to the industry. We know it as Prohibition, with a capital "P." Repeal, with a capital "R," came on December 5, 1933, when Utah became the thirty-sixth state to ratify the Twenty-First Amendment to the Constitution.

During that long dry spell, California wineries had struggled mightily, and two-thirds of them closed. The rest survived by making sacramental wines and by selling grapes, since home winemaking was still legal. Particularly popular was a product with the wonderful name of Vine-Glo. It was a barrel of grape juice, complete with instructions for converting it to wine. Another product, a brick of compressed grape pomace, could be dissolved in water to create grape juice. A warning label stated:

"This beverage should be consumed within five days; otherwise it might ferment and become alcoholic."

The industry recovered slowly after Repeal. Thousands of acres of premium vines had been torn out and replaced with common grapes better suited to the production of Vine-Glo and wine bricks. Many Americans had gotten out of the wine-and-food habit. Further, the country was in the middle of the Depression. In 1934, several growers led by Napa's Louis Martini formed the Wine Institute to improve the quality of wine and promote its use. It's still the industry's leading voice.

World War II brought some financial respite to vintners. European wines were no longer available and the price of California grapes went from $15 to $50 a ton. However a shortage of labor, containers and rail cars hampered growth. The industry didn't really get back on its feet until the Fifties. By the Seventies, it had become fashionable to serve wine with dinner and California's winemakers were off and running.

They haven't looked back, except to see if their competitor had somehow produced a better Chardonnay.

Types of wine, premium and otherwise
For a glossary of wine terminology, see Chapter Fourteen, page 336.

To give you an idea of what you'll be sipping at tasting rooms, we present a list of the more common wine types, both varietal (which just means a specific variety) and generic.

Aleatico (*ah-lee-AHT-TEE-co*) — Common Italian red grape of the Muscat family with that grapy Muscat aroma and flavor, now finding some favor in California.

Angelica — Sweet, ordinary dessert wine that originated in California, probably named for Los Angeles; sometimes made from the mission grape.

Barbera (*bar-BEAR-ah*) — A full-flavored red wine grape grown in northern Italy and now in California.

Beaujolais (*BO-sho-lay*) — In France, a wine from a specific district, near Burgundy. In California, the name refers to wine made from the Gamay grape, often labeled Gamay Beaujolais.

Burgundy — In France, it refers to a specific wine producing region, famous for the Pinot Noir grape. In California, it means anything red.

Cabernet Sauvignon (*cab-air-nay sou-vin-YAWN*) — Considered the noblest of red wine grapes; the primary wine of a fine Bordeaux.

Carignane (*car-reen-YAN*) — Commonly planted red grape of medium quality; of southern French origin. Sometimes spelled "Carignan."

Chablis — Generic term in the U.S., referring to any white wine. A specific growing region in France.

Champagne — A term describing sparkling wine in the United States. In the rest of the civilized world, it's applied only to effervescent wine produced in France's Champagne district. Some American winemakers honor this tradition and call their product sparkling wine. Sparkling wine was discovered by accident three centuries ago when monk Dom Pérignon's wine underwent a second fermentation in the bottle. "I am tasting stars!" he supposedly exclaimed.

Charbono (*shar-BO-NO*) — Red grape of Italian origin producing full bodied, sometimes rough wine.

Chardonnay (*SHAR-doe-NAY*) — One of the premiere white grapes, grown in the Burgundy region of France and extensively planted in California. A good Chardonnay is dry, yet rich and full, sometimes spicy or nutty and with a hint of wood, since it's often barrel-aged.

Chenin Blanc (*SHAY-nan blawn*) — White grape, producing a typically fruity wine.

Chianti (*kay-AN-tee*) — Italian red wine usually made from the Sangiovese grape (see below), typified by full, berry-like flavor; usually drunk young. In America, the term is loosely applied to any full flavored, low-tannin wine. Spaghetti wine, if you will.

Cinsaut (*SAN-so*) — Red grape producing full-bodied wine, common in France and South Africa, and now among the "new wines" of California.

Colombard (*COL-lum-bahr*) — A rather ordinary French white grape, producing a full-bodied, usually high-acid wine.

Fumé Blanc (*FU-may blawn*) — Literally "White Smoke," a name first used by Napa Valley's Robert Mondavi to describe a lush, subtly smoky-flavored white wine produced from the Sauvignon Blanc grape.

Gewürztraminer (*Ge-WURZ-tra-mee-ner*) The world's most difficult-to-spell wine grape. Common in Germany, France's Alsace district and California. It's typically fruity, spicy and sometimes a bit sweet.

Green Hungarian — An ordinary white wine of unknown parentage, once common in California but now deservedly falling from favor.

Grenache (*greh-NAHSH*) — Fruity southern French grape commonly used to make rosé wine in California. Sometimes labeled Grenache Rosé.

Gray Riesling — White wine grape of unknown parentage, since it isn't a Riesling. The first reference may have been at Wente Brothers Estate Winery in the Livermore Valley.

Johannisberg Riesling — German white wine grape from the Rhine Valley. Typically fruity, usually fermented dry. It's a true Riesling, while many other grapes bearing that name are not.

Meritage — A term adopted by a group of California wineries to designate red or white premium wines blended from classic French grape varieties. Red Meritage seems to be more common. A winery must join the Meritage Association to use the label, and must meet strict blending criteria. Fewer than thirty wineries qualify.

Merlot (*Mair-LOW*) — Red grape producing a lush, full-flavored wine; often blended with Cabernet Sauvignon to ease its tannic edge, both in California and Bordeaux.

Mourvèdre (*moor-VED-dre*) — Another of the newly popular grapes in California; a widely traveled medium-bodied French red with a nice berry nose; it may have its roots in Spain, where a similar variety is called Mataró.

Muscat (*MUS-kat*) — Grape commonly planted throughout the world, usually white although there are red versions within its more than 200 varieties. Muscat wines are noted for their "grapey" flavor, whether made dry or sweet. The grape often is used to produce dessert wines.

Nebbiolo (*ne-bee-OH-lo*) — Classic Italian red grape, now finding its place in California vineyards, either as a varietal or for blending.

Petit Syrah or **Sirah** (*Puh-TEE see-RAW*) — Rather high tannin red grape grown in California and Australia. Also grown in the Rhône Valley, although not related to France's Syrah; see below. It's often called Shiraz in Australia.

Pinot Gris (*PEE-no gree*) — A cousin of Pinot Noir, not as complex or robust; now being planted in California vineyards, mostly for blending.

Pinot Noir (*PEE-no nawahr*) — Classic French red grape; right up there with Cabernet; commonly grown in Burgundy. Thus in France, a great Burgundy is a great Pinot Noir.

Port — Sweet, fortified wine named for Orporto, the city in Portugal that is the center of the Port trade.

Riesling (*REESE-ling*) — Noble white German grape predominately grown in the Rhine Valley. The name has come to be loosely associated with an assortment of white wines.

Sangiovese (*sawn-jo-VAY-SAY*) — Full-bodied Italian red common to the Chianti region and used in the wines of that name; often called Sangioveto. Now gaining favor in California.

Sauternes (*saw-TAIRN*) — French white wine, often sweet and usually golden. The term also is used to describe any number of generic sweet California wines; often spelled "Sauterne" here.

Sauvignon Blanc (*SO-veen-yawn blawn*) — It ranks with Chardonnay as one of the great French white wine grapes. Full bodied with a distinctive fruity bouquet.

Sherry — Sweet or dry fortified wine whose name is derived from the Jerez district of Spain, where it originated.

Sirah or **Syrah** (*see-RAH*) Red grape with deep color and high tannin grown in France and Australia, becoming popular in California. It is no relation to Petit Syrah.

Sylvaner (*sil-VAN-er*) — Premium white grape originating in Germany or Austria.

Trebbiano (*treb-be-AH-no* or *treb-YAWN-no*) — The world's most universal producer of white wine; common to Italy and now gaining favor in California. It produces full-bodied wine with a rather light bouquet.

Viognier (*vee-ON-yay*) — Excellent white French grape producing wine with a complex fruity taste; another of the lesser-known wines that has become trendy in California.

Zinfandel — California's most widely planted premium red grape, called the mystery grape because no one is sure how it got to America. However, Italy's Primitivo is its clonal twin. (See box in Chapter Three, page 70.) The wine is typically fruity and can range from light and soft to complex and full-bodied. Zins usually have light to medium tannin, although those from older vines can be quite robust.

DECIPHERING A TYPICAL CALIFORNIA WINE LABEL

CHIPMUNK CELLARS

1999

ESTATE BOTTLED
Shenandoah Valley
ZINFANDEL
Pinecone Vineyard

Produced & bottled by Chipmunk Cellars, Ltd.
Plymouth, California

Alcohol 13% by volume ● contains sulfites

1999: A wine can be vintage dated only if ninety-five percent of the grapes were crushed in that year.

Estate Bottled means that all the grapes used in the wine came from vineyards owned or controlled by the winery.

Shenandoah Valley is an appellation or Approved Viticultural Area (AVA), an officially designated growing region; eighty-five percent of the grapes must be grown within that area.

Zinfandel: A varietal name can be used only if at least seventy-five percent of the wine came from that grape.

Pinecone Vineyard is a "designated vineyard." To be listed, at least ninety-five percent of the grapes must have come from that vineyard, which must be located in an AVA.

Produced and bottled indicates that at least seventy-five percent of the grapes were fermented by the bottling winery. "Made and bottled" requires that only ten percent of the grapes be fermented by that winery. Such terms as "Vinted and bottled" or "Cellared and bottled" are non-specific. They don't require the bottler to have produced any of the wine.

Alcohol 13% by volume: This can vary a percent and a half percent either way. To be sold as a table wine, the alcohol content must be between seven and fourteen percent.

Contains sulfites: This statement is required on U.S. wine labels if sulfite content (naturally produced during fermentation and/or added to prevent spoilage) exceeds ten parts per million. It does in most wines.

A Book of Verses underneath the Bough,
A Jug of Wine, a Loaf of Bread—and Thou
Beside me singing in the wilderness—
Oh, Wilderness were Paradise endow!
        — The Rubaiyat of Omar Khayyam

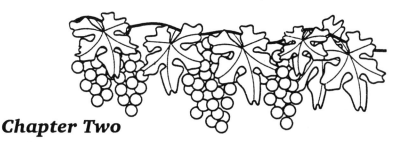

Chapter Two

MENDOCINO & LAKE COUNTIES
The wine country's northern rim

We begin our exploration of the California Wine Country at its geographic top, in Mendocino and Lake counties. A few wineries are scattered farther north; one even resides in the redwoods around Arcata, north of Eureka. However, that area is better known for clams and sawdust. For touring and tasting purposes, Mendocino and Lake counties offer California's northernmost grouping of vineyards and wineries. The two areas are particularly appealing, for many of the wineries are in some of California's prettiest pastoral settings. Further, wines here have won more than their share of medals. In fact, Lake County boosters insist that their wineries have gleaned more awards per vineyard acre than any other region in the country.

MENDOCINO COUNTY

Inland Mendocino has been creating wines for more than a century, although most of it was bulk production in the early days. However, one Charles Wetmore sailed off to the Paris Exposition of 1899 with some of his Mendocino wines and sailed away with *le grand prix.*

Tryfon Lolonis and Adolph Parducci were two other Mendocino wine pioneers. Greek immigrant Lolonis planted vineyards in the Redwood Valley in 1920; Italy's Parducci opened a Cloverdale winery in neighboring Sonoma County in 1916, then moved north to Mendocino's county seat of Ukiah in 1931. The Parducci Winery thrives as one the county's largest.

Winemaking didn't become a serious growth industry until the early 1970s. Initially, most growers sold fruits of their labors to established Sonoma County wineries. Then, realizing that the Sonoma vintners kept winning medals with Mendocino grapes, several growers began bottling their own wines.

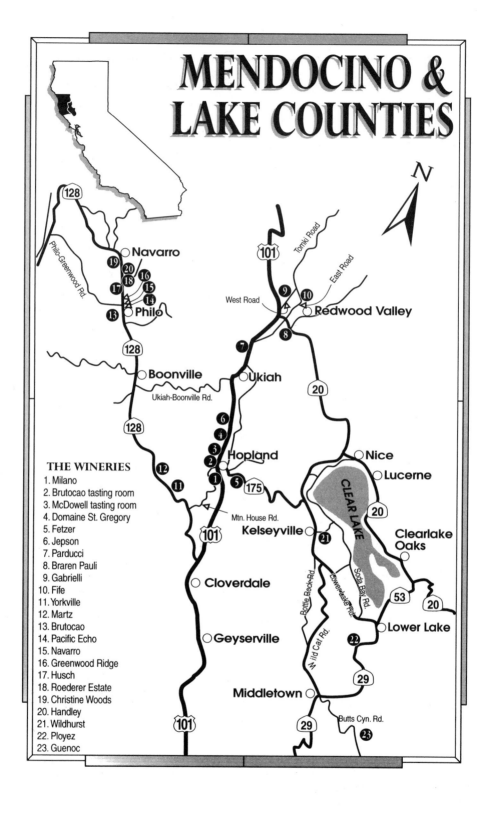

MENDOCINO & LAKE COUNTIES

N

128

Philo-Greenwood Rd.

Navarro

19
20
18 16
17 15
14
13 Philo

128

Tomki Road

101

West Road

East Road

9
10

Redwood Valley

8
7

128

Boonville

Ukiah

Ukiah-Boonville Rd.

20

128

6
4
3
2

Hopland

12

1 5

11

175

Mtn. House Rd.

101

Kelseyville

Nice

Lucerne

CLEAR LAKE

20

Clearlake Oaks

21

Bottle Rock Rd.

Lowerlake Rd.

Soda Bay Rd.

53

20

Cloverdale

Lower Lake

22

Geyserville

W. ild Cat Rd.

29

Middletown

29

Butts Cyn. Rd.

23

THE WINERIES
1. Milano
2. Brutocao tasting room
3. McDowell tasting room
4. Domaine St. Gregory
5. Fetzer
6. Jepson
7. Parducci
8. Braren Pauli
9. Gabrielli
10. Fife
11. Yorkville
12. Martz
13. Brutocao
14. Pacific Echo
15. Navarro
16. Greenwood Ridge
17. Husch
18. Roederer Estate
19. Christine Woods
20. Handley
21. Wildhurst
22. Ployez
23. Guenoc

Six simple steps to winery touring success

1 ● Plan your route in advance (which of course is why you bought this book) and set practical goals. Don't try to cover more than four or five wineries in a day. There is much to enjoy, to learn and to see in California's winelands. Why rush through them? Be selective. That's another reason you bought this book.

2 ● If possible, hit the wine country on weekdays. This should be no great trick if you're on vacation. If you're limited to weekend visits, get an early start. It may go against your grain to start sipping at 10 a.m., but you're here to sample wines, not engage in social drinking. Most tasting rooms—even in busy Napa Valley—are virtually empty in the morning. The crowds hit after lunch and build until closing time.

3 ● Plan for a picnic, since many wineries have picnic areas, often among the vines. Usually, you can find a deli in or near California's vinelands, and many tasting rooms sell picnic fare. And don't be a plebeian; buy your picnic wine at the winery.

4 ● Try to visit the wine country during the crush—again on weekdays. You can watch the proceedings and perhaps sample some of the grapes. At small wineries, you may even get to sip a little "must," the freshly crushed juice. The grape harvest ranges from late August through October, so call ahead to see what's being picked where. You'll find phone numbers with the winery listings in this book.

5 ● Limit the number of samples you try at each winery. If you taste too many wines, their differences will blur. So will your vision.

6 ● Although the small amounts of wine poured in tasting rooms shouldn't be a problem, it's still a good idea to select a designated driver. If that's your role, save the urge to party until you're safely back home, off the highway and close to the floor. Nationally, only about two percent of people arrested for driving while intoxicated were drinking wine. Please try to keep it that way.

Currently, about thirty Mendocino County wineries slap labels on their own bottles, and roughly half of these offer tasting to the passing public. Most wineries are clustered in three different areas—Ukiah-Hopland, Redwood Valley and Anderson Valley. All are in the central to southern reaches of the county.

Ukiah-Hopland

Ukiah is mostly a blue collar working person's town of about 13,000, although it offers a few items of interest. They include the excellent Sun House Historical Museum, a few fine old Victorians along tree shaded streets and some serviceable restaurants. Mendocino's county seat, it provides a good selection of shops and motels. Nearby Lake Mendocino is popular with boaters and campers.

Twelve miles south, tiny Hopland is turning its weathered storefronts into a charming tourist stop, offering several antique shops, tasting rooms and a few cafés. The Hopland micro-brewery and Thatcher Hotel and restaurant are particularly worth a visit. As you might imagine, hops were once the main crop here and one winery—Milone—occupies an old hop drying shed.

The town named for hops is now surrounded by vineyards. More vines are scattered among green and golden contoured hills between Hopland and Ukiah, presenting a rather pleasant picture. Hopland has several winery tasting rooms, two wineries are on U.S. 101 on either side of the town and another is just to the east.

UKIAH-HOPLAND WINERY TOUR ● Assuming you're driving north from the San Francisco Bay Area on U.S. 101, you'll encounter Hopland shortly after entering Mendocino County. Before you do, watch on your left for **Milone Family Winery,** a few miles beyond the end of the freeway.

From there, continue about a mile into the hamlet of Hopland which has become "Tasting Room Town," with five sipping parlors, all detached from their wineries. The most appealing and extensive is **Brutocao Cellars'** Schoolhouse Plaza. It's a tasting room and restaurant in the former Hopland high school building on your left as you enter town. Park here or nearby, and you can walk to the rest of the town's wine sipping parlors. On the same side of the street as Brutocao are **Going Vintage Antiques** which contains small tasting counters for Elizabeth Vineyards and Mendocino Hill Winery, and then **McDowell Wine & Mercantile** in a rustic barnboard false front store at the corner of Highway 101 and Center. Cross to the other side of the highway at Center Street, stroll northward and you'll soon encounter **Domaine Saint Gregory.**

Now, fetch your vehicle and take State Route 175 west for less than a mile to the new **Fetzer Vineyards** complex in a handsomely restored old ranch complex at the junction of Eastside Road. Return to Hopland and press northward; after about 3.5 miles, you'll see **Jepson Vineyards** on your left. From here, you have the option of passing through Ukiah on State Street or bypassing most of it on Highway 101, which returns to freeway status. If you choose to forsake Ukiah, take the Lake Mendocino exit at the town's northern edge and continue north briefly on State Street to Parducci Road. Turn left and follow it over the U.S. 101 freeway to—where else?—**Parducci Wine Cellars.**

Milone Family Winery ● T ✕

14594 S. Highway 101, Hopland, CA 95449; (707) 744-1396. (www.milonefamilywinery.com) Daily 10 to 5; MC/VISA, AMEX. Most varieties tasted. A few wine related gift and craft items. Picnic area under arbor.

The small Milone Family Winery is housed in one of the weathered hop kilns that once peppered this rural landscape. The winery dates only from 1977, although the family has been a part of this land for four generations. Jim's Milone's great grandfather Achilles Rosetti operated the area's first win-

---

WINERY CODES ● *T* = tasting with no fee; *T$* = tasting for a fee; *GT* = guided tours; *GTA* = guided tours by appointment; *ST* = self-guiding or informal tours; ✕ = picnic area; 🎁 = gift shop or a good giftware selection.

WINE PRICES ● *$* = average price under $10 per bottle; *$$* = $10 to $14; *$$$* = $15 to $19; *$$$$* = $20 or more

ery until it was closed by Prohibition. Meanwhile, Vincenzo Milone arrived here from Italy and married Achille's daughter Mary. They grew hops, pears, prunes and grapes, and the operation eventually included their son Frank. The hop business was booming in southern Mendocino in the 1940s, so family built the drying kiln. Eventually, the hopyards moved elsewhere and the old kiln was abandoned. Two decades later, Frank's son Jim began converting the old building into a winery.

Tasting notes: Milone wines are hearty and full bodied, with good varietal character. The list is short—a fruity and complex Chardonnay; full-bodied Zinfandel aged in French oak; a hearty table wine called Noble Blend with Zinfandel and Cabernet Sauvignon; and Echo, a premium Bordeaux style blend of Merlot, Cabernet and Petit Verdod. Prices: *$ to $$$*.

Brutocao Cellars' Schoolhouse Plaza ● T ✕ 🍴

13500 S. Highway 101, Hopland, CA 95449; (800) 433-3689 or (707) 744-1664. (www.brutocaocellars.com) Daily 10 to 5; MC/VISA, AMEX. Most varieties tasted. Large gift shop with extensive offerings of wine related items, crystal and gourmet foods. Deli, picnic area and restaurant.

Originally the Hopland High School, this handsome ivy shrouded facility served for years as the Fetzer Vineyards tasting room. After Fetzer moved to a new site on Highway 175, it was purchased by the Brutocao family, remodeled and expanded into an extensive 7.5-acre complex called Schoolhouse Plaza. It includes an attractive new tasting facility, several gift shops, the Crushed Grape Restaurant (see below on page 42), Zinfan Deli with light snacks, six bocce ball courts, kids' playground, lawn concert area, wedding and conference facilities and landscaped grounds with 2,000 imported roses. Old photos and regalia from early Hopland and the high school decorate the tasting room/gift shop complex.

The facility draws 100,000 visitors a year and comes close to being crowded on summer weekends. However, we had no trouble finding a spot at the large tasting bar on an October Sunday.

Tasting notes: The Brutocao list is mostly red, unusual for the cool Anderson Valley where most of the grapes are grown. The full bodied Zinfandel, Merlot, Cabernet Sauvignon and Pinot Noir—all unfiltered—were deeply flavored and complex. On the white side, a Chardonnay was lush, with a pleasing flowery nose and the Sauvignon Blanc had a nice fruity flavor and hints of oak. In addition to estate-bottle premiums, Brutocao produces two wines under the Bella Lona label—a Sauvignon Blanc-Chardonnay-French Colombard blend; and a mix of Zinfandel, Pinot Noir and Cabernet Sauvignon. Overall prices: *$ to $$$$*.

McDowell Wine & Mercantile ● T 🍴

13380 S. Highway 101, Hopland, CA 95449; (707) 744-8911. (www.mcdowellsyrah.com) Daily 10 to 5; MC/VISA. Most wines available for tasting. Good selection of wine related gift items and specialty food items.

This downtown Hopland tasting room is housed in appealing barnboard storefront with an island tasting counter and properly rustic décor. The source of its wines is McDowell Valley Vineyards, four miles away at 14100 Mountain House Road, and open by appointment only. The operation was established by Richard and Karen Keehn and Karen's son William Crawford. They sold their winery to Associated Vintage Group in 1993, but still make their wine there. Their specialty is Rhône style Syrah and Grenache from an-cient vines.

Tasting notes: Among the winery's Rhônes are a crisp white Viognier with tropical flavors, a white Marsanne with lots of fruit and a nice acidic nip, Mendocino Syrah with good berries and a light finish and a much heart-ier Reserve Syrah. Other wines are Western White and Rodeo reds, both blends; and Grenache Rosé. Prices: *$ to $$$$*.

Domaine St. Gregory • T

13251 S. Highway 101, Hopland, CA 95449; (707) 744-VINO. (www.do-mainesaintgregory.com) Daily 10 to 5; MC/VISA. Most varieties tasted. A few wine logo items.

Another of Hopland's storefront tasting rooms, Domaine St. Gregory is one of several wine lines produced by Gregory Graziano, a third generation Mendocino County vintner. His grandfather arrived here from Italy's Pi-emonte region in 1918 and planted vineyards. Because of Prohibition, they had to rely on grape sales and a bit of bootlegging to survive. Later, he joined other grape growers to form the Mendocino Vineyards Winery, which eventually was sold to Cresta Blanca. Those facilities are now gone, although Gregory has started a new tradition of winemaking. He was a founding part-ner at Milone Winery and served as winemaker at La Crema. Then he and his wife Trudi established Domaine Saint Gregory in 1988, followed by Monte Volpe Vineyards in 1991 and Fattoria Entoria Wines in 1998.

Tasting notes: Gregory's list is balanced between whites and reds and many—like Gregory himself—have Italian roots. Among the whites are Pinot Gris, Pino Blanc on the Saint Gregory label; Pinot Bianco, Pinot Grigio and Tocai Friulano in the Monte Volpe series and Arneis in the Enotria line. Among the reds are a soft and full Saint Gregory Pinot Noir, Sangiovese and an Italian-Rhône blend called Peppolino in the Monte Volpe series; and Bar-bera, Nebbiolo and Dolcetto in the Enotria label.

Fetzer Valley Oaks • T ✕ 🏮

13601 Eastside Rd. (P.O. Box 611), Hopland, CA 95449; (800) 846-8637 or (707) 744-1250. (www.fetzer.com and www.bonterra.com) Daily 9 to 5; major credit cards. Choice of four wines for free tasting. Extensive giftware and specialty foods selection, plus a deli. Self-guided tours of an organic garden complex. Large picnic area. B&B adjacent; see below on page 43.

A tree-shaded lane leads past vineyards to a the historic 1897 Foster Ranch, which has been carefully restored to become the Fetzer visitor center. The complex includes a large organic garden, picnic tables beneath an arbor, and a sizable tasting room, which has a good gift and specialty foods selec-tion and a well-stocked deli. Fetzer purchased this old stock farm in the mid-1990s and sold its former Hopland High School tasting complex to Brutocao Cellars. One of Mendocino County's largest wineries, Fetzer was established by the late Bernard Fetzer in 1968. Ten of his eleven children then took over, expanding the operation to more than 200,000 cases a year. They sold the operation to Brown-Forman of Louisville, Kentucky, although some family members still grow grapes for the winery.

Tasting notes: The large Fetzer list covers most of what's made any-where in California. Its roll call of wines includes the traditional Sauvignon Blanc, Chardonnay, white Zinfandel, Johannisberg Riesling, Gewürztra-miner, Zinfandel and Cabernet Sauvignon. Several Rhônes and other newly fashionable wines have been added, including Viognier, Sangiovese, Syrah, Marsanne and Rousanne. Prices are among the least expensive anywhere in the state, climbing into the twenties for limited releases: *$ to $$$$.*

Jepson Winery & Distillery • T & T$ GT & GTA ✕

10400 S. Highway 101, Ukiah, CA 95482; (707) 468-8936. (www.jepson-wine.com) Daily 10 to 5; major credit cards. Most varieties tasted free; fees for brandy tasting, which can be applied to purchase. Wine related gift items, picnic tables near the tasting room. Tours weekends 11 to 4 or by appointment on weekdays.

The first thing you will notice, after spotting the Jepson Vineyards sign on U.S. 101, is an imposing century old two-story farmhouse, now containing offices and meeting space for the facility. The winery, in a sturdy white painted stone and wooden structure, is a short distance away. The tasting room occupies a little bungalow fused to the main winery, looking something like a rustic New England cottage built into the side of a warehouse. Although small, the tasting room is spacious and light, accented by a gleaming brass chandelier. A couple of umbrella tables out front extend a silent invitation to picnickers to linger with lunches and newly purchased bottles.

The winery complex and more than 100 acres of vineyards were purchased virtually intact in the mid-1980s by Robert S. Jepson, Jr., former owner of Gerry sportswear. This is no mom and pop operation. Jepson obviously has invested generously to create an upscale, state of the art winery, which issues equally upscale premium wines.

Tasting notes: Jepson has expanded its list to include Alambic pot still brandy and sparking wine; it's the only winery in America that produces both. On the wine side, the list includes those sparkling wines, a lush yet crisp Sauvignon Blanc, a buttery and toasty Chardonnay, fruity Viognier and a full-flavored Merlot. Propriety wines are Feliz Creek Cuvée (French Colombard, Viognier, Chardonnay and Sauvignon Blanc), and Château d' Alicia (semi-sweet French Colombard) and a dessert wine called Mistelle of Viognier. Prices: *$ to $$$$.* The winery's brandy is distilled from French Colombard grapes in the classic French pot-still method.

Vintners choice: "Chardonnay, Sauvignon Blanc and Zinfandel—due to our access to some small but excellent Mendocino vineyards," says the winery's Toni Klein.

Parducci Wine Cellars • T GT ✕ ▥

501 Parducci Road, Ukiah, CA 95482; (707) 462-9463. Monday-Friday 10 to 5 and Sunday 10 to 4; MC/VISA, AMEX. Most varieties tasted. Gift shop with good selections of wine related items and some specialty foods. Guided tours hourly from 10 to 3. Picnic tables adjacent tasting room.

One of Mendocino County's two largest wineries, this venerable facility was founded by Adolph Parducci in 1931. It's now operated by second and third generations, with son John Parducci in charge, although a major interest has been sold to a teachers' retirement investment group. Several years ago, Parducci bought Hidden Cellars, a winery and vineyard complex just south of Ukiah. Both Parducci and Hidden Cellar wines are sampled and sold at this tasting room. The large facility backs into low hills above the northern end of Ukiah, a sanctuary from tract homes that march threateningly in its direction. The tasting room is California Mission eclectic—white stucco with Spanish arches and a shake roof. The interior is richly adorned with dark walnut, terrazzo tile and leaded glass. A gift shop specializing in crystal and china glitters from a room opposite the large tasting area. Outside, an arbor-shaded picnic area sits beside the vineyards. The hour-long tour through both vintage and modern facilities is quite thorough.

Tasting notes: The Parducci and Hidden Cellar lists cover most varie-tals, plus a range of jug and dessert wines; most are available for tasting. The Parducci series includes Chardonnay, Chenin Blanc and Sauvignon Blanc among the whites; and Pinot Noir, Sangiovese, Syrah, Zinfandel, Merlot, Cabernet Sauvignon and Petite Sirah on the red side. Hidden Cellar whites are Chauche Gris and Sauvignon Blanc; reds are Zinfandel, Petit Sirah, Mer-lot, Cabernet Sauvignon and Syrah. Prices are rather moderate: *$ to $$$.*

Redwood Valley

This is California's northernmost major wine producing area. The region is a rolling mix of oak thatched hills, shallow valleys and benchland ridges. Vineyards are scattered in the depressions and on those ridges, offering mi-cro climates where a surprising variety of premium wine grapes thrive. Among notable bottlings are Chardonnay, Sauvignon Blanc, Cabernet Sauvi-gnon and Zinfandel. Much of the foothill area is chopped into country abodes that range from rustically elegant to scruffy. The higher reaches of the valley offer pleasing visions of tawny hills, moss draped oaks and an oc-casional artistically rustic barn.

REDWOOD VALLEY WINERY TOUR • Only two wineries in this region have tasting rooms that keep regular hours, while another two offer their wines for tasting at a facility just off Highway 101. This portion of our tour is a logical extension of the Hopland-Ukiah safari. However, a bit of ma-neuvering is involved, since the tasting rooms form three points of a triangle.

From Parducci, return to State Street and drive north, paralleling the freeway. After a couple of miles, the route swings inland to pass through the scruffy hamlet of Calpella. Less than a mile beyond, as the road again swings alongside the freeway, you'll see the impressive spired tasting room of **Bra-ren Pauli** on your right. It's just beyond the hamlet of Capella.

From Braren Pauli, continue north on the aforementioned frontage road to a stop sign, turn right and you're on West Road, leading into the heart of Redwood Valley. It's a pleasant drive through a mix of vineyards, pasture-lands, ranchettes and rural homes. About three miles of this will deliver you to **Gabrielli Winery,** in an imposing brown structure on your left, uphill behind a vineyard. (If you hit a T-intersection of Tompki and East roads, you just missed it; look for the large mail box with the number 10950.) Now, re-turn to the freeway, head south and take the Highway 20 exit east. Follow it about a mile and a half to Road A, turn left and drive steeply and briefly up-hill to Road B and turn right. It makes a sharp left within a short distance, but continue straight ahead onto the lane marked "Private road; use at your own risk." It's more inviting than it sounds and leads you—within a few hun-dred feet—to **Fife Vineyards.**

Braren Pauli • T ✕ 🏠

7051 N. State Street, Redwood Valley, CA 95470; (707) 485-0321. Daily 9 to 5; MC/VISA. Most varieties tasted. Nice gift selection; picnic area.

This distinctive tasting room, with its upcurved laminated beams, suppos-edly forms an inverted champagne glass. Inside, a fountain bubbles appropriately as a centerpiece to a dramatic sweep of open space. A curved tasting counter occupies one side. Gift items and wine displays are placed about the roomy, circular tasting room. The grounds are equally attractive, featuring a picnic garden rimmed with grape vines and shaded by ancient oaks with white painted trunks. A burst of petunias emerges from an old barrel slat wine press. Once the Weibel tasting room, this facility, called Redwood Valley Cellars, now offers wines of two different Mendocino County vintners—Barra of Mendocino and Braren Pauli Winery.

Tasting notes: Braren Pauli wines include Sauvignon Blanc, Chardonnay, Semillon, Pinot Noir, Zinfandel, Merlot, Cabernet Sauvignon and Port. The Barra list is shorter: Pinot Blanc, a dry Muscat Canelli, Pinot Noir and Petit Sirah, Prices: *$$ to $$$$.*

Gabrielli Winery • T ST ✗

10950 West Rd., Redwood Valley, CA 95470; 485-1221. (www.gabrielli-winery.com) Daily 10 to 5; major credit cards. Most varieties tasted. Picnic area.

Shaded by mature trees on the brow of a hill above the vineyards, the Gabrielli facility occupies a straightforward wood frame winery building, with an attractive, airy cedar sided tasting room fused to the front. The tasting counter exhibits a rustic touch of class—two wine barrels topped by a cloth draped plank. The operation was started in 1989 by Sam Gabrielli, Bernadette Yamada-Gabrielli and Tom Yamada. They released their first wines and opened their tasting room in 1991. Their focus is on complex barrel fermented wines that are lightly processed to retain their strong varietal character. They have won considerable critical praise and numerous awards.

Tasting notes: The simplicity of handling comes through in the strong flavor of the fruit in the Gabrielli wines, all of which are unfiltered. Among the better offerings are a malolactic fermented Pinot Noir with spicy, berry-like flavor; an estate Syrah, full-flavored with a hint of wood; several fine Zinfandels with classic spice and berry flavors; and an excellent estate Sangiovese, Gabrielli's flagship wine. Prices: *$$$$.*

Vintner's choice: "One of our top priorities is to continue to be recognized as California's premium Sangiovese winery," said a winery voice.

Fife Vineyards • T GTA ✗

3620 Road B, Redwood Valley, CA 95470; (707) 485-0323. Daily 10 to 5 April-November and 10 to 4 the rest of the year; MC/VISA. Most varieties tasted. A few wine related gift items; lake view picnic area. Guided tours by appointment.

This winery, one of the northernmost in California, has gone through several nameplates, starting as Olsen Vineyards in the 1980s, then Konrad/Olsen and finally Konrad Vineyards. It's now the enterprise of Dennis and Karen MacNiel Fife, who have long careers in the wine world. Dennis was president of Inglenook, head of marketing for Beaulieu and the *consigliari* at Stag's Leap. Karen's background comes from a literary direction; she's a noted food and wine writer and lecturer, and author of *The Wine Bible*. In 1991, they established Fife Vineyards, consisting of vinelands but no winery. Then they purchased this facility in 1996.

The handsome wood sided winery sits atop a ridge, offering views of the Redwood Valley on one side and Lake Mendocino reservoir and the distant cloud capped Coast Range on the other. The small tasting room is as comfortable as a family living room. A pleasant garden offers picnickers a lakeview lunch site.

Tasting notes: The Fifes focus on vineyard-designated reds, particularly Zinfandel; a list of current wine releases may carry four distinct types. Other reds on the brief list are Carignane, Syrah and Cabernet Sauvignon. They also produce a couple of interesting proprietary blends—*L'Attitude* (Syrah, Carignane, Mourvèdre, Grenache and Cinsault) and Max Cuvée (a Rhône blend of Syrah and Petite Syrah. Prices: *$$$ to $$$$.*

Anderson Valley

This is exemplary rural northern California, a shallow valley rimmed by hills the color and shape of fresh baked rolls. It's garnished by shady clusters of oaks, madrones and pines and accented by sloping vineyards and emerald pastures.

Grizzled old Boonville is the best known of the valley's hamlets, popular for its grandly rustic turn of the century Boonville Hotel, the appealing Buckhorn Saloon brew pub and a couple of boutiques. Philo, with a population of 273, isn't much larger than some of the winery complexes surrounding it.

The valley is relatively new as a vineyard area. Although pioneers may have stomped a grape or two, current activity dates from 1971 when the Husch family established a winery near Philo. Most of the valley's vineyards and wineries line Highway 128 between Philo and Navarro. This is one of the cooler and wetter of California's vinelands, so grapes from northern Europe such as Chardonnay, assorted Rieslings and Gewürztraminers do best. However, we did encounter some good Cabernet and Pinot Noir.

ANDERSON VALLEY WINERY TOUR ● If you're returning south from the Redwood Valley or Hopland-Ukiah tour, you can take twisting Mountain House Road from Hopland; it starts beside Brutocao's Schoolhouse Plaza. Otherwise, pick up State Highway 128 just south of Cloverdale.

Touring Anderson Valley winery tasting rooms is no great trick. Although some of the wineries are on side roads, all of their tasting rooms are neatly aligned along Highway 128 between Yorkville and Navarro.

You'll first find **Yorkville Cellars,** on your right just after you've passed through that tiny town. A mile or so below, also on your right but easy to miss because the driveway is on the apex of a curve, is **Martz Vineyards.** It's up a long, twisting asphalt drive that snakes among trees and vineyards.

Now, settle down for a long and curving drive on Highway 128 through the Anderson Valley. Immediately outside the small town of **Philo** on the right is the strangely named **Pacific Echo Cellars.** Just beyond on the left, still maintaining its winery tasting room in addition to the Hopland facility is **Brutocao Cellars.** A bit farther along, you'll encounter a side-by-side pair of tasting rooms on the right: **Navarro Vineyards** and **Greenwood Ridge Vineyards. Husch Vineyards** is a short distance beyond on the left, and the imposing **Roederer Estate** is across the highway, on a vineyard upslope. Just down the highway, almost opposite one another, are **Christine Woods** on the left and **Handley Cellars** on the right. They're near the tiny town of **Navarro.** The brief stretch from Greenwood Ridge to Handley is one of the more appealing in all of California's wine country—a fetching blend of handsome wineries and sloping vineyards rising behind split rail fences, with softly rounded oak thatched hills on the horizon.

Yorkville Cellars • T ✕

25701 Highway 128 (P.O. Box 3), Yorkville, CA 95494; (707) 894-9177. (www.yorkville-cellars.com) Daily 11 to 6 in summer and 11 to 5 the rest of the year; MC/VISA. Most varieties tasted. A few wine giftwares, including wine-filled chocolates; picnic area.

British-born Edward and Debbie Wallo brought their English charm and love of French wines to ths area in 1988. They purchased land near Yorkville, with the intent of having a place to settle after their careers in international marketing. However, the wooded slope proved to be too tempting and they left their careers to establish their winery and tasting room in 1994. They produce about 1,000 cases of organically-grown wines from their tilted vineyards. Massive oak trees offer shade and charm to this pleasant setting. The tasting room occupies a handsome three-story, woodsy cottage bunkered against a steep slope. On chilly fall and winter days, a wood fire glows invitingly from a stove in the corner.

Tasting notes: Noted Mendocino County winemaker Gregory Graziano produces excellent, full-flavored wines for the Wallos. And since the English pair favors wines from *la belle France,* most are classic French varietals. The list includes a barrel fermented Sauvignon Blanc, a crisp and fruity Semillon, a very rich and spicy Cabernet Franc, a lush and full-bodied Malbec, a light yet nicely flavored Merlot and an outstanding Cabernet Sauvignon. Two proprietary wines reflect their British heritage—a Bordeaux style white called Eleanor of Aquitaine, and Richard the Lion-Heart which, of course, is a very authoritative red. Prices: **$$ to $$$$.**

Martz Vineyards • T ✕ ▥

20799 Highway 128, Yorkville, CA 94394; (707) 895-3001. (www.martzwine.com) Daily 10 to 5; MC/VISA, DISC. Most wines tasted. A few giftwares and specialty foods; picnic area.

Larry and Linda Martz make fine wines and shelter stray cats at their oak-cloaked winery high on a slope above Yorkville. They offer sanctuary to homeless cats of the Anderson Valley Animal Shelter, so you're likely to encounter a few felines after you follow a long, winding asphalt lane through woods and vineyards to their rustic farm-style winery. A permanent resident here is Corky, who claims to be the world's largest winery cat. You're also likely to see some Nubian goats and chickens—not in the tasting room, of course. A couple of picnic tables and an ancient, thoroughly rusted farm truck occupy the yard.

Inside the rustic tasting room you'll find, in addition to Corky, several specialty foods and dips, some of which are available for sampling.

Tasting notes: With all of their animal concerns, the Martz's find time to make fine wines. Among their offerings are a soft and cream Chardonnay with a slight hint of oak, a deeply flavored Merlot with lots of berries, a light and crisp Zinfandel and a full-bodied Cabernet Sauvignon. They also make dry and late harvest versions of Symphony, which is a cross between Grenache and Muscat. Prices: **$$ to $$$$.**

Brutocao Cellars • T ✕ ▥

7000 Highway 128 (P.O. Box 780), Philo, CA 95466; (707) 895-2152. (www.brutocaocellars.com) Daily 10 to 5; MC/VISA, AMEX. Most varieties tasted. Good wine related gift selection. Picnic tables adjacent to tasting room.

For decades, Anderson Valley grower Leonard Brutocao sold his grapes to producers such as Fetzer and Beringer, then he began making his own wine in the early 1990s. To reach the public, he purchased the attractive tasting room of the former Scharffenberger Cellars. The winery operation is a family affair, with sons David, Len Junior and Steve continuing the tradition. The Brutocaos have nearly 500 acres of vineyards under cultivation as a source for their estate bottled wines.

The Scharffenberger-turned-Brutocao tasting room is one of the more appealing in the Anderson Valley—an attractive sweep of space radiating out from a curved bar. A cathedral ceiling accents the facility's openness. The family expanded recently by purchasing the former Fetzer facility in downtown Hopland and creating an extensive wine-and-food complex. They've come full circle, since the family once sold grapes to the Fetzer winery.

Tasting notes: See "Brutocao Schoolhouse Plaza" above on page 27.

Pacific Echo Cellars ● T$ GTA ✕ 🍷

8501 Highway 128 (P.O. Box 365), Philo, CA 95466; (800) 824-7754 or (707) 895-2065. (www.pacific-echo.com) Daily 11 to 5; MC/VISA, AMEX. Most varieties tasted for a modest fee. Giftware and specialty food items; picnic area. Tours by appointment.

This attractive "American country" estate houses the Anderson Valley's only major sparkling wine facility. The tasting room dwells in a large two-story ranch-style cottage shaded by oaks. A couple of picnic tables occupy an old fashioned front porch and others are under a shady arbor. The facility was established in 1981 by the Scharffenberger family, among the first to produce sparkling wine in this area. It's now owned by Moet-Hennessey.

Tasting notes: True to the Scharffenberger tradition, sparkling wines dominate the list, and true to Moet-Hennessey tradition, they are not called champagnes because they are not made in the Champagne region of France. Among Pacific Echo's fine sparklers are a Pinot Noir and Chardonnay blend simply called non-vintage Brut, a rich Blanc de Blancs made of Chardonnay, Private Reserve Brut made from a Pinot-Chard blend, a Brut rosé and a non-vintage Crémant blend of Pinot and Chardonnay. The single still wine is a fine and spicy Eaglepoint Pinot Noir. Prices: *$$$ to $$$$.*

Navarro Vineyards ● T GTA ✕

5601 Highway 128 (P.O. Box 47), Philo, CA 95466; (800) 537-9463 or (707) 895-3686. Daily 10 to 6 in summer and 10 to 5 the rest of the year; MC/VISA. Most varieties tasted. A few T-shirts and such; picnic tables on a deck overlooking vineyard and under a trellis in the vineyard. Guided tours by appointment.

Only a few vines separate Navarro and Greenwood Ridge tasting rooms; both are surrounded by vineyards that sweep toward forested hills. We'd recommend either for fine picnicking views.

A cozy tasting room that might accommodate two dozen people (provided they're feeling friendly) occupies a corner of one of Navarro's modern, wood-faced structures. Visitors can adjourn to an outside deck to sip their wine while drinking in the vineland and mountain view. Upscale barn might be the proper architectural definition for this appealing complex. Ted Bennett and Deborah Cahn established the winery in 1975 to "focus on what Anderson Valley grows best—Gewürztraminer, Riesling, Chardonnay and Pinot Noir."

Tasting notes: At the risk of repetition, we found the whites to be typically Anderson Valley: lush, high in fruit, with a nice acid finish. Navarro's single red—Pinot Noir—is soft and well balanced. Prices: *$ to $$$*.

Vintners choice: Ted leans toward his dry, late harvest Gewürztraminer, late harvest Riesling and Chardonnay. The wineaker's newest interest is a Pinot Gris.

Greenwood Ridge Vineyards ● T ✕

5501 Highway 128, Philo, CA 95466; (707) 895-2002. Daily 10 to 6 in summer, 10 to 5 the rest of the year; major credit cards. Most varieties tasted. Picnic tables on deck overlooking vineyards and nearby hills.

Greenwood's tasting room is an intriguing hexagonal tepee, with a skylight to brighten the spacious interior. Picnic tables on a sheltered island are accessible by a footbridge, and a sign on a nearby pond advises visitors not to feed the alligators. The main winery is a few miles away, perched on a ridge above Greenwood Road. It's just six miles inshore from the coastal hamlet of Elk. Owned by Allan Green, the winery produces about 7,000 cases a year. His varietals have earned prestigious awards, including four "Best of Show" ribbons in recent years.

Green hosts the annual California Wine Tasting Championship the last weekend of July, with prizes for novice, amateur and professional sippers who can identify wines by varietal type. The weekend event also features live music, plus chocolate tasting and cheese tasting contests.

Tasting notes: Five wines appeared on Greenwood's list when we visited the tasting room, comprising four varieties—Sauvignon Blanc, Riesling, Pinot Noir and Cabernet Sauvignon. The whites were nicely balanced with good fruit flavor and a crisp acid finish. The Cabernet, mellowed by a hint of Merlot, tasted like a fine Bordeaux. Prices: *$$ to $$$$*

Husch Vineyards ● T GTA ✕

4400 Highway 128, Philo, CA 95466; (800) 55-HUSCH or (707) 895-3216. (www.huschvineyards.com) Daily 10 to 6 in summer and 10 to 5 the rest of the year; MC/VISA. Most varieties tasted. A few gift shop items; picnic area under a grape arbor. Tours by appointment.

Husch is the valley's only winery senior enough to offer a bit of rustic charm. Established in 1971, it occupies an old farm complex that predates the winery itself. The tasting room is in a cute, weather-beaten granary that could pass for a miner's shack. Here, amiable wine hosts pour from a fair sized list of ten wines. The H.A. Oswald family bought the winery from the Husch clan in 1979. They produce only estate bottled wines, drawing from the nearby Husch vineyards and their La Ribera Vineyards near Ukiah.

Tasting notes: The wines we tasted were pleasantly light—dry and fruity for the Chardonnay, Sauvignon Blanc, Gewürztraminer and Chenin Blanc; soft and herbal for the Pinot Noir and Cabernet Sauvignon. Some Chardonnay, Pinot Noir and Cabernet Sauvignon renditions were fuller and richer, as were the prices. Overall, wines are modestly priced: *$ to $$$$*.

Roederer Estate ● T$

4501 Highway 128 (P.O. Box 67), Philo, CA 95466; (707) 895-2288. (www.avwines.com) Daily 11 to 5; MC/VISA. Three sparkling wines sampled for a modest fee, which is applied toward bottle purchase.

The term "country elegance" may occur as you approach Roederer's sparkling wine facility, nestled into a knoll above the vineyards. The exterior of the low lying redwood structure is upscale American barn; inside, polished tile floors and brass chandeliers add touches of refinement. Visitors can—glass in hand—enjoy a fine Anderson Valley view from a sunny patio beside the winery. Most of the operational facilities are underground to maintain the structure's low profile.

Although relatively new to the Anderson Valley, the House of Roederer dates back to 1776, when it was established in France's Champagne district. Current company chairman Jean-Claude Rouzaud, a descendant of the founders, selected this area for an American expansion in the late 1970s. The climate and soils, he determined, were ideal for Chardonnay and Pinot Noir, the classic blend for Champagne. Vineyards were planted and the first wines were released in 1988.

Tasting notes: Three sparkling wines are tasted—a vintage L'Ermitage, a multi-vintage Brut and Brut rosé, plus a Pinot Noir still wine. All the Roederer wines were nicely complex, exhibiting subtle flavors of the fruit. To provide further complexity, some of the wines from each crush are held in reserve, aged in oak and added to later vintages. Prices: *$$$$*.

Christine Woods Vineyards • T ✕

3155 Highway 128 (P.O. Box 312), Philo, CA 95466; (707) 895-2115. (www.christinewoods.com) Thursday-Sunday 11 to 5; MC/VISA. Most varieties tasted; picnic area.

Don't look for Christine behind the tasting counter, or even in the winery. This small family-owned operation occupies an attractive slope of vines and woods that had been settled in 1855 by Swiss immigrants John and Elizabeth Gschwend. Their daughter Christine was born in 1857—the first white birth in the Anderson Valley—and they named their farm in her honor. Vernon and Jo Rose from Walnut Creek, California, purchased some of the property in 1966 and planted vineyards nine years later. They moved to the land in 1980, formed a partnership with their son Edward and his wife Lisa two years later, and established their winery in 1989. However, Vernon is no newcomer to the business; he had been a home winemaker for two decades.

The winery occupies a straightforward metal building, although the small tasting room is a bit more appealing. It's in a folksy little wood-sided shed, with a single picnic table out front.

Tasting notes: When we last tasted, the list featured just two varietals, each well crafted and with classic characteristics. Two different releases of Chardonnay and two versions of Pinot Noir were being poured. One was a gold medal winner that earned ninety points in a recent issue of *The Wine Spectator*. Prices: *$$$ to $$$$*.

Handley Cellars • T GTA ✕ 🏠

3151 Highway 128 (P.O. Box 66), Philo, CA 95466; (707) 895-2190. (www.handleycellars.com) Daily 11 to 6 in summer and 11 to 5 the rest of the year; MC/VISA, AMEX. Most varieties tasted. Some wine related gift objects; two picnic areas on a lawn and a garden courtyard. Tours by appointment.

Step into the Handley's comfortably stylish tasting room and admire its international art, folkcraft and Persian carpets; note particularly the carved tasting bar from England. You might think this to be the haven of a long established, much traveled winery dynasty. Yet all of this—and a list of premium wines—has been assembled in a few years by dynamic young Milla Handley and her husband Rex McClellan.

After graduating from the University of California at Davis in 1975, she worked for several other winemakers. Then she and Rex established this winery at an old ranch complex in 1987. Of course, Milla's heritage didn't hold her back. She's the great-great granddaughter of Oregon brewmaster Henry Weinhard.

Tasting notes: The busy Handley list ranges from dry table wines to sparklers. Among the whites are a fruity Sauvignon Blanc, several rich and creamy Chardonnays, Pinot Gris and a delicious double gold medal Gewürztraminer. Reds are Pinot Noir with full flavor and a hint of oak, and Pinot Meunier *Mystère*. A semi-sweet Brightligher White can serve as a good hot weather quaffing wine. Sparkling wines are Brut, Blanc de Blancs and several versions of Brut rosé. Prices: *$$ to $$$$*

Vintners choice: "Our barrel fermented Chardonnays have won many gold medals; and our Gewürztraminer is recognized as one of the best in California," a winery spokeswoman said.

Lake County

Wrapped around California's largest natural freshwater lake, touched by no freeway or railroad, Lake County is noted for its serene rural setting. One of the state's most thinly populated counties, it has barely enough residents to fill an average ball park—about 50,000. The county seat of Lakeport numbers fewer than 5,000.

Lake County would be an island in time, ignored by the world outside, except that the pale blue rough cut gem of Clear Lake draws thousands of summer visitors. They come to angle for bass, hurry across the lake's calm surface behind speedboat tow ropes and lie on its sandy shores. When summer ends, they leave the place to residents, who all seem to know one another as they go about their business in hamlets with ordinary names like Upper Lake and Kelseyville, or optimistic names like Lucerne and Glenhaven.

Viticulture here dates back to 1872 and more than thirty wineries once functioned. But the area's isolation made marketing difficult. Ironically, one of the county's early freight wagon roads led across the flanks of Mount St. Helena to the wine rich Napa Valley. Lake County's wineries began to falter during a turn of the century wine glut, then Prohibition closed the rest. Commercial crushing didn't resume until 1977. At last count, this rural enclave had only five wineries and just three offer tastings without prior arrangements. However, vineyard acreage is increasing rapidly, approaching 4,000 acres at the Millennium. Some are owned by notable out-of-county wineries such as Beringer, Louis Martini and Robert Mondavi.

A visit to Lake County's vinelands is certainly worth the brief right-hand detour from neighboring Mendocino, even with its limited tasting room selection. For one thing, the twisting drive over the Mayacamas Mountains that divide the two counties is a remarkably scenic one. For another, those few wineries are appealing and uncrowded, and the wines are excellent.

LAKE COUNTY WINERY TOUR ● Drive east from Hopland on State Highway 175 (Hopland Summit Road). It takes you through hillside vineyards, then up a corkscrew route to the crest of the Mayacamas Mountains. Enjoy views both east and west, then roller-coaster down to the Lake County floor. The scenery, a mix of wooded slopes, farmlands and vineyards, isn't as awesome as Mendocino County's vinelands, but it's pleasantly bucolic.

If you've taken the Route 175, swing south onto Highway 29 and follow it about five miles to the tiny town of Kelseyville. (En route, you'll pass **Steele Winery** on your left; it was open by appointment only when we last passed. Earlier visitors to this area will remember this as home to Konocti Winery. It's now owned by Jud Steele, once the winemaker for Kendall-Jackson, which got its start in Lake County.) Continuing past Steele Winery, follow signs from Highway 29 into Kelsyville and you'll see **Wildhurst Vineyards** tasting room on the right, housed in the skinny masonry 1926 IOOF building. Charmingly old fashioned Kelseyville, which was getting brand new sidewalks when we last passed, is worth a brief browse.

Continue southwest about fifteen miles to the dinky hamlet of **Lower Lake** and turn right (south) at a signal to stay with Highway 29. After just over a mile, you'll see **Ployez Winery,** set back off the highway on your right. Continue south on Highway 29 and turn right on Butts Canyon Road in **Middletown.** After about six miles, you'll happen upon the third Lake County facility that keeps regular visiting hours, **Guenoc.** The turnoff to the ridgetop winery is opposite a small lake.

Wildhurst Vineyards ● T 🎁

Tasting room at 3855 Main St., Kelseyville, CA 95451; (800) 595-WINE or (707) 279-4302. (www.wildhurst.com) Daily 10 to 5; MC/VISA. Good selection of giftwares and specialty foods.

Myron and Marilyn Holdenried planted their first vines in 1966 to become one of Lake County's earliest post-Prohibition vintner families. The family goes back considerably further; he's a sixth generation Lake County farmer. The Holdenrieds opened their winery and tasting room near Lower Lake in 1991, then later moved their tasting facility into Kelseyville's charming old 1926 social hall. It's a pleasing space, with high ceilings and original pine floors. Works of local artists adorn the walls.

Tasting notes: Wildhurst's winemaker Mark Burch likes to bring strong varietal character to his wines, focusing mostly on classic French varietals. The list includes Riesling, Sauvignon Blanc, Chardonnay, Zinfandel, Cabernet Franc, Cabernet Sauvignon and Merlot. Prices: **$$ to $$$$**

Ployez Winery ● T ✗

11171 Highway 29 (P.O. Box 1115), Lower Lake, CA 95457; (707) 994-2106. Daily 10 to 5; MC/VISA. Most varieties except sparkling wines tasted. A few wine logo items; picnic area.

Occupying the old Stuermer Winery (which had been leased by Wildhurst), Ployez is one of Lake County's newest wineries and the first to produce sparkling wine. And well it should; owner Gerald Ployez is a fourth-generation champagne maker from France. He and his wife Shirley moved to the county in 1997 and opened their winery shortly after. He'd made several visits here from France to help friends "fix" poorly made wines, and he met Shirley during one of these visits.

The winery occupies an old fashioned evergreen-shaded farmyard above pasturelands, not vineyards. The barnboard style tasting room sits beneath the Ployez' living quarters. However, they soon hope to build a house "at least ten miles away" so the can be more free of the winery.

Tasting notes: Although his specialty is sparkling wine, Ployez makes fine still wines as well, and all are 100 percent varietal. "I like to see what I can get out of a single variety. Sometimes when winemakers blend, it's because they screwed up." His table wines—none of them screwed up—include a lush and full-flavored Chardonnay, a light and crisp Sauvignon Blanc, a pleasantly tart Gamay Beaujolais, a nicely acidic medium bodied Zinfandel and a full-flavored Cabernet Sauvignon. He also produces a non-vintage sparkling Brut and he intends to add a Lake County Champagne to his list. "They say you aren't supposed to call it Champagne unless it's made in that district of France. But I'm going to call it that because I know what a good Champagne should be." Prices: *$$ to $$$*.

Guenoc Winery • T ST ✕
21000 Butts Canyon Road (P.O. Box 1146), Middletown, CA 95461; (707) 987-2385. Daily 11:30 to 5; major credit cards. Most varieties tasted. Picnic area beneath an arbor; informal winery tours.

"Am delighted. Words don't express my complete satisfaction. Join me in Paradise." Flamboyant British actress Lillie Langtry cabled this enthusiasm to her San Francisco attorney, W.H.L. Barnes, after inspecting vineyard property she'd purchased in Guenoc Valley in 1888. She imported a winemaker from Bordeaux with the intention of creating "claret of the finest quality known in the country." However, the operation was never a financial success, and she departed in 1906, leaving behind a stately Victorian home overlooking her vineyards. The winery was reactivated several years ago by Orville Magoon and his family, who created the first single-proprietor Approved Viticultural Area (AVA) in the state. To mark Lillie's passage, her cameo graces the Guenoc label.

The facility—an attractive rural rectangle—perches on a ridge, offering visitors views of vinelands, a small lake and tree-thatched mountains. Picnic tables under an arbor provide the same pleasing vista.

Tasting notes: The wine list embraces most classic varietals. We sipped a lush, buttery Guenoc Estate Chardonnay, a fruity Estate Sauvignon Blanc with a hint of oak and a gentle yet complex Zinfandel. Others on the list include a red Meritage (Cabernet Sauvignon and Merlot blend), Cabernet Sauvignon and Petite Sirah, plus Langtry red and white. Prices: *$$ to $$$$*.

THE BEST OF THE BUNCH

The best wine buys • Fetzer Vineyards and Parducci Wine Cellars in Mendocino County, Husch Vineyards in Anderson Valley and Wildhurst Vineyards in Lake County.

The most attractive wineries • Fetzer near Hopland, Roederer Estates, Navarro and Greenwood Ridge in Anderson Valley, and Guenoc in Lake County.

The most attractive tasting rooms • Brutocao and Fetzer in Hopland, Braren Pauli in Redwood Valley and Roederer Estates and Handley Cellars in the Anderson Valley.

The funkiest tasting room • Husch Vineyards in Anderson Valley.

The best gift shops • Brutocao Cellars and Fetzer Vineyards in Hopland, and Parducci Wine Cellars in Ukiah.

The nicest picnic areas • Brutocao and Fetzer in Hopland; Fife Vineyards and Braren Pauli in Redwood Valley; Navarro and Greenwood Ridge in Anderson Valley; and Guenoc Winery in Lake County.

Wine country maps and events

Winery maps and guides • *Lake County Wineries*, available from wineries or the Lake County Winegrape Commission, P.O. Box 877, Lakeport, CA 95453; (707) 955-3421. *(www.lakecountywinegrape.org) Mendocino Wine Country* flyer and map, available at area wineries or from Mendocino Winegrowers Alliance, P.O. Box 1409, Ukiah, CA 95482-1409; (707) 468-9886. *(www.mendowine.com) Hopland Winery Association* flyer and map available at Hopland area wineries. *(www.hoplandpassport.com)*

Wineland events • California Wine Tasting Championships, late July at Greenwood Ridge Vineyards; (707) 877-3262. Redwood Empire Fair and Wine Festival, August, (707) 462-4705; Lake County Wine Auction Gala in Middletown in early October, (707) 994-3600; Lake County Harvest Festival at the Steele Winery in mid-October, (707) 279-9475; Mendocino Wine & Mushroom Fest, mid-November, (866) 466-36367. Individual wineries also sponsor events throughout the year.

BEYOND THE VINEYARDS
Mendocino County

Escapees from the thickly populated San Francisco Bay Area flee to Mendocino to admire the bucolic land forms and play in the water. They fish in the Russian River, swim and boat in Lake Mendocino and scuff seaweed along the wild and handsomely rugged seacoast. A popular Mendocino tourist drive is Highway 128 from Cloverdale to the sea, which passes through the vinelands of Anderson Valley. In **Boonville,** check out the old **Boonville Hotel,** the **Buckhorn Saloon** brewpub and the **Anderson Valley Historical Museum** in the Conn Creek School just beyond town.

The Boonville area is home to a curious language called "Boontling," a rural slang developed by locals a century ago and still used by some. A tourist, for instance, is called a *brightlighter* and good restaurant food is *bahl gorms.* Some Boonville shops sell Boontling dictionaries, should you wish to converse with the natives.

In addition to funny talk and wineries, Anderson Valley offers a couple of hushed redwood groves. Twisting Fish Rock Road above Yorkville takes you to the solemnly beautiful **Mailliard Redwood State Reserve.** Beyond Philo, follow Greenwood Road to **Hendy Woods State Park,** with hiking trails, picnic areas and campsites.

If you persist along Highway 128 or Greenwood Road, you'll encounter the Mendocino coast, one of the prettiest stretches of seashore in America. Wind-graced meadows and redwood groves march down to a tumbled coastline of seastacks and hidden coves. Drive north to **Mendocino,** an old style New England town that somehow wound up on the Pacific Coast. The picture-perfect village is busy with galleries, antique shops, boutiques, bed and breakfast inns and some remarkably good restaurants.

Meanwhile, back in **Ukiah,** visit the **Grace Hudson Museum and Sun House** with Indian lore and changing historic exhibits. The town also is noted for its collection of Victorian homes; a tour map is available at the chamber of commerce. A launch ramp, campground, picnic area and hiking trail at **Lake Mendocino** can be reached by driving north on Main Street, then going east on Lake Mendocino Drive. Lake Mendocino camping facilities are just off westbound Highway 20, north of town.

From Ukiah, drive three miles east along Vichy Springs Road to **Vichy Springs Resort,** where Mark Twain, Ulysses S. Grant and ordinary folks have been soaking in mineral waters since 1854. You can rent a cozy cabin or ranch style room or pay a "use fee" and have the run of the springs and the 700-acre grounds. (See listing under "Wineland lodgings.")

If you head north on Highway 101 to **Willits**, you can ride the chuffing little **Skunk Train** through the redwoods to the old fishing village of **Fort Bragg,** home to a few decent seafood restaurants.

Lake County

Clear Lake is the largest freshwater pond entirely within California. Its shores are lined with marinas, fishing piers, swimming beaches and resorts. Check out the old fashioned resort towns of **Lower Lake** and **Clearlake,** and particularly cute little **Lakeport,** offering several restored Victorians, false front stores and a nicely groomed waterfront park.

Clear Lake State Park near Kelseyville offers hiking, swimming, a boat launch, camping and picnicking. **Anderson Marsh State Park** is a wetland on the lake's lower tip, encompassing a bird watching area and a pioneer farm complex.

Mendocino & Lake county attractions

Anderson Valley Historical Museum • *Highway 128, Boonville; (707) 895-3207. Friday-Sunday 1 to 4 (longer summer hours).* ☐ Historical exhibits of Anderson Valley and Boonville, including stuff on "Boontling" language; housed in the old Conn Creek School.

Grace Hudson Museum and Sun House • *431 S. Main St., Ukiah; (707) 462-3370. Wednesday-Saturday, 10 to 4:30 and Sunday noon to 4:30; donations requested.* ☐ Excellent museum focusing on Indian artifacts and area history.

Lake County Museum • *255 N. Main St., Lakeport; (707) 263-4555. (www.museum.lake.k12.ca.us) Wednesday-Sunday 11 to 4 in summer; closed on Sundays the rest of the year.* ☐ Native American and pioneer artifacts housed in the 1871 brick Lake County Courthouse.

WINE COUNTRY DINING

PRICE KEY: Dinner entrée with soup or salad, without drinks or dessert for under $10 = $; $10 to $14 = $$; $15 to $25 = $$$; over $25 = $$$$.

Bluebird Café • ☆☆☆ $$

☐ *13340 S. Highway 101, Hopland; (707) 744-1633. Breakfast through lunch Monday-Tuesday; breakfast through dinner Wednesday-Sunday. Major credit cards.* ☐ Cheerful little country style café with natural woods, ceiling fans, lace curtains and hanging plants. Busy menu ranges from sandwiches, soup and salad to grilled teriyaki chicken breast and vegetarian meals.

Boonville Hotel Restaurant • ☆☆☆ $$$

☐ *Highway 128 at Lambert Lane, Boonville; (707) 895-2210. California-American; wine and beer. Dinner Wednesday-Monday and lunch Sunday. MC/VISA.* ☐ Modern restaurant in the old fashioned Boonville Hotel, featuring *nouveau* fare on a frequently changing menu, plus creative pizzas. Locally done desserts are noteworthy. (Hotel listed below.)

Brick Grill ● ☆☆ $$$

□ *Main Street, Kelseyville; (707) 279-2213. American; wine and beer. Breakfast through midafternoon daily. MC/VISA.* □ Appealing café housed in an old vine-covered brick building, with wood wainscotting, ceiling fans and green and white tile floors. A handy breakfast or lunch stop, featuring typical American fare.

Broiler Steak House ● ☆☆ $$$

□ *8400 Uva Dr., Redwood Valley (just north of Ukiah; West Road exit west from U.S. 101, then north on Uva Road); (707) 485-7301. Basic American; mostly steaks; full bar service. Dinner nightly. MC/VISA, AMEX.* □ Noisy, friendly restaurant with steaks, accompanied by a huge salad and a melon-sized baked potato; also chicken, chops and seafood; good local wine list.

Buckhorn Saloon (Anderson Valley Brewing Co.) ● ☆☆☆ $

□ *14081 Highway 128, Boonville; (707) 895-BEER. Light pub grub; beer and wine. Lunch through dinner daily except Wednesday. MC/VISA.* □ Stylish Western saloon with natural wood and leaded glass, accented by a large brew kettle out front. The place serves light fare such as sausages, piroshki, teriyaki chicken and fish and chips. Anderson Valley Brewing Company's hearty beers are featured.

The Crushed Grape ● ☆☆☆

□ *In the Brutocao Schoolhouse Plaza complex at 13500 S. Highway 101, Hopland; (707) 744-2020. Italian-American; full bar service. Lunch through dinner daily and Sunday brunch. MC/VISA.* □ Attractive restaurant with indoor and outdoor seating. The menu features assorted pastas, pizzas and other typical Italian entrées, plus a few American steaks and chops.

El Sombrero ● ☆☆ $$

□ *131 E. Mill St. (Main Street), Ukiah; (707) 463-1818. Mexican; full bar service. Lunch through dinner Tuesday-Sunday with Sunday brunch. MC/VISA, DISC.* □ Appealing Mexican restaurant in a refurbished old farmhouse, with rough-hewn ceiling beams, high back chairs and wrought iron lamps.

Hopland Brewery ● ☆☆ $ to $$

□ *13351 Highway 101 South, Hopland; (707) 744-1015. Light pub grub; beer and wine. Lunch through late dinner daily. MC/VISA.* □ An old style brewpub serving beer sausages, seafood, salads and other light snacks. It occupies sturdy century-old red brick tavern with pressed tin walls and early American furnishings; beer garden shaded by a grape trellis. Opened in 1986 by Mendocino Brewing Company, it claims to be the oldest post-Prohibition brewpub in California.

Lotus Restaurant ● ☆☆ $

□ *403 S. State St. (Clay Street), Ukiah; (707) 463-2288. Chinese-Japanese; wine and beer. Lunch and dinner daily except Sunday. MC/VISA.* □ Storefront restaurant trimmed by an occasional paper lantern, serving huge portions at modest prices. Versatile menu lists both Chinese and Japanese fare; sushi bar.

The Maple Restaurant ● ☆☆ $

□ *295 S. State St., Ukiah; (707) 462-5221. American; wine and beer. Breakfast through lunch weekdays; lunch through dinner Saturday; closed Sun-*

day. MC/VISA. □ Simple American diner with a basic Formica interior; inexpensive fare in generous portions. It's the kind of place where the waitress approaches your table with a smile and a coffee pot.

Thatcher Inn Restaurant ● ☆☆☆☆ $$$

□ *13401 S. Highway 101 (Center Street), Hopland; (707) 744-1890. American-continental; full bar service. Breakfast, lunch and dinner daily with Sunday brunch. Major credit cards.* □ Housed in a restored stagecoach stop, featuring typical American and some classic continental dishes. Handsomely restored dining room with floral wallpaper, pressed tin ceilings and marble-topped candle-lit tables. Stately, clubby bar adjacent.

WINELAND LODGINGS
**PRICE KEY: A two-person room for $35 or less = $; $36 to $50 = $$;
$51 to $75 = $$$; $76 to $100 = $$$$; more than $100 = $$$$$.**

Mendocino County

Boonville Hotel ● ☆☆☆ $$$$ to $$$$$

□ *Highway 128 at Lambert Lane (P.O. Box 326), Boonville, CA 95415; (707) 895-2210. MC/VISA. Rates include continental breakfast.* □ Refurbished historic hotel with Early American style rooms featuring down comforters, fresh flowers and other amenities; all rooms are non-smoking. **Boonville Hotel Restaurant** listed above.

Days Inn ● ☆☆ $$$ to $$$$

□ *950 N. State Street (Low Gap Road), Ukiah, CA 95482; (707) 462-7584. Major credit cards.* □ Room phones, TV, pool. **Restaurant** serves dinners nightly; full bar service.

Fetzer Bed & Breakfast ● ☆☆☆☆ $$$$$

□ *13601 Eastside Rd. (P.O. Box 611), Hopland, CA 95449; (800) 846-8637. (www.fetzer.com) Major credit cards. Ten units, all with private baths; continental breakfast.* □ The carriage house, cottage and main house of the historic A.W. Foster ranch have been fashioned into a country style inn. Some rooms with patios, kitchenettes or sitting rooms; seasonal pool. Near the Fetzer Vineyards visitor center.

Super Eight Motel ● ☆☆ $$ to $$$

□ *1070 S. State St. (Talmage), Ukiah, CA 95482; (707) 462-6657. Major credit cards.* □ Thirty-one room motel with TV movies, room phones and pool; some in-room spa tubs. **Caffé** serves lunch and dinner Tuesday-Saturday and Sunday brunch; closed Monday. American-Greek; full bar service.

Vichy Springs Resort ● ☆☆☆☆ $$$$$

□ *2605 Vichy Springs Rd. (three miles east of U.S. 101), Ukiah, CA 95482; (707) 462-9515. (www.vichysprings.com) Major credit cards.* □ Historic 1854 hot springs resort with naturally warm carbonated mineral baths, Swedish massage, Olympic sized swimming pool, hot therapy pool and other amenities. Modern furnished rooms in a ranch style building, plus eight guest cottages with fireplaces. Rates include breakfast and the use of mineral baths and pools.

Bed & breakfast inns

Philo Pottery Inn ● ☆☆ $$$$$

□ *8550 Highway 128 (P.O. Box 166), Philo, CA 95466; (707) 895-3069. Five rooms, three with private baths; continental breakfast. MC/VISA.* □ Restored 1888 redwood farmhouse that once served as a stage stop. Rooms furnished with American antiques, old fashioned beds with patchwork quilts and down comforters. Wood stove and library in living room; airy front porch with English garden.

Thatcher Inn ● ☆☆☆☆ $$$$ to $$$$$

□ *13401 S. Highway 101 (Center Street), Hopland, CA 95449; (707) 744-1890. Twenty rooms with private baths; full breakfast and Sunday champagne brunch. MC/VISA, AMEX.* □ Impeccably restored inn, housed in an 1890 stage stop hotel. Victorian and American antiques, floral print wallpaper, brass beds and armoires. Comfortable library with easy chairs and fireplace. Lounge and **restaurant** (see listing above).

Lake County

Best Western El Grande Inn ● ☆☆ $$$$

□ *15135 Lakeside Dr. (P.O. Box 4598), Clear Lake, CA 95422; (800) 528-1234 or (707) 994-2000. Major credit cards.* □ A 68-unit motel; TV with fee movies; some suites with refrigerators; pool, hot tub. **Restaurant** serves American fare; breakfast through dinner daily; full bar service.

Konocti Harbor Resort & Spa ● ☆☆☆☆ $$$$ to $$$$$

□ *8727 Soda Bay Rd., Kelseyville, CA 95451; (800) 660-LAKE or (707) 279-4281. Major credit cards.* □ Large lakeside resort with extensive landscaped grounds; marina, rental boats, two pools, playground, miniature golf, health spa, tennis; planned activities in summer. Rooms have TV, radios and phones. Kitchen apartments available. **Restaurant** serves American fare; breakfast through dinner daily; full bar service.

Bed & breakfast inns

Forbestown Inn ● ☆☆☆ $$$$ to $$$$$

□ *825 Forbes St. (Ninth Street), Lakeport, CA 95453; (707) 263-7858. Four rooms, one with private bath; full country breakfast. MC/VISA, AMEX.* □ Attractive 1869 Victorian in downtown Lakeport. Rooms nicely furnished with American oak antiques, floral drapes, king and queen beds. Landscaped grounds; pool and spa.

Mendocino-Lake county information sources

The Greater Ukiah Chamber of Commerce, 200 S. School St., Ukiah, CA 95482; (707) 462-4705.

Mendocino County Alliance, 525 S. Main St., Suite E, Ukiah, CA 95482; (866) 446-3636. *(www.gomendo.com)*

Lake County Visitor Center, 875 Lakeport Blvd., Lakeport, CA 95453; (800) 525-3743 or (707) 263-9544. *(www.lakecounty.com)*

Give...wine unto those that be of heavy hearts.
Let them drink, and forget their poverty,
And remember their misery no more.
— Proverbs of Solomon 31:6-7

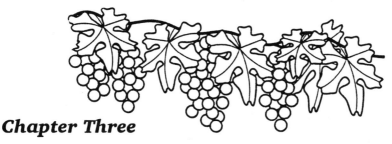

Chapter Three
NORTHERN SONOMA
From red wines to redwoods

Mention Sonoma and most wine enthusiasts think of the Sonoma Valley and winery pioneers General Vallejo and Count Haraszthy. That's chronologically correct, since the California wine industry's roots go deep into Sonoma Valley soil.

Today, however, northern Sonoma County has more wineries, more vineyard acres and produces more wine than its better known neighbor. In all of California, it's second only to the Napa Valley in total premium wine grape acreage, with more than 30,000 acres of vines.

A scenic southern extension of Mendocino County, northern Sonoma is a mix of tawny hills, redwood groves in hidden canyons and shady clusters of oaks bearded with Spanish moss. More than 1,400 miles of rural roads invite aimless wandering and spontaneous picnics beside trickling creeks. The Sonoma Coast, like the Mendocino Coast above, is a spectacular sweep of sea stacks, velvety green headlands and charming yesterday towns weathered—like old men of the sea—by ocean breezes.

Let's not forget the main reason we came here. The north county's gravelly, loamy soils along the flanks of the Russian River and Dry Creek produce some of America's premier wines. The region offers a further advantage for the winetasting crowd—uncrowded wineries ranging from tiny and rustic to historic and grandiloquently modern.

A few decades ago, this area was busy with hop yards and orchards. Some unused hop kilns survive, marked by their distinctive conical towers; a couple have been converted to wineries. Plums once were so profuse that the Healdsburg Chamber of Commerce sponsored annual tours to view the pretty pink-white blossoms. The area still blooms with springtime color, although it's wild mustard, California poppies and the tender green buds of awakening grapevines.

The first settlers in this area were not pious mission padres or grape stompers. They were Russian fur hunters, working down the coast from Alaska. Seeking the slippery sea otter, they established a colony called Romazov on the Sonoma Coast in 1809, followed three years later by the fortress of Rossiya—now Fort Ross State Historic Park. Concerned by this intrusion, Mexican officials began moving north from San Francisco in the 1820s. They granted huge tracts of land to favored soldiers and politicians who had helped in their recent war for independence from Spain.

The Russians eventually withdrew and northern Sonoma County became the domain of contented *rancheros* who ran their cattle over the grassy hills. The first American to settle here was Cyrus Alexander. Arriving in the 1840s, he managed one of the Mexican land grants for several years in exchange for 9,000 acres of land. He never produced wine but he did plant some of the area's first grapes. The valley enclosing his ranch now bears his name.

The first vintners of significance were the brothers Korbel. Francis, Joseph and Anton settled along the Russian River in 1882, logged off the redwoods and began planting vineyards. The Korbel winery survives to this day as one of the largest producers in the area. More European vintners followed and hundreds of acres were soon graced by vines. Unhappily, Sonoma County was one of the first areas in the country to be hit by phylloxera. Even Luther Burbank, recently settled in Santa Rosa, joined the fight against the deadly scourge. Several wineries closed before root grafting ended the crisis. Then many of the survivors were finished off by Prohibition.

The ultimate optimist

One, however, was started right in the middle of Prohibition by an Italian optimist. John Pedroncelli bought a defunct winery in Dry Creek Valley in 1927, gambling that the foolish law soon would be repealed. His gamble paid off and his sons John, Jr., and Jim still run the place.

Generally warmer than Mendocino and the Sonoma Valley, northern Sonoma County produces excellent reds, particularly Zinfandel; see box on page 70. It's also noted for its award winning Cabernet Sauvignon, Pinot Noir and Chardonnay.

We'll tour wineries in the area's three major viticultural regions. Alexander Valley lies alongside U.S. 101, extending from the Mendocino County border south to Geyserville, and east toward the Mayacamas Mountains. Dry Creek Valley lies to the southwest and the Russian River Valley is below that, extending southwest from Healdsburg.

Several towns along our routes offer restaurants and other respite. Burgeoning Santa Rosa, with more than 114,000 residents and growing, forms a suburban plug for the lower end of north county. Although it has ample cafés and motels and a good museum or two, we don't regard it as a wine country town. It is instead the northern outpost for San Francisco Bay Area sprawl. However, the area to the north becomes quickly rural.

Although you haven't quite hit the northern wine country as you approach Santa Rosa, you will encounter an excellent new visitor center with material about the wineries ahead. The **Sonoma County Wine & Visitors Center** is an attractive Spanish style complex just off U.S. 101 in Rohnert Park, south of Santa Rosa. To reach it, take the Country Club Drive exit and head toward the Red Lion Inn on a frontage road east of the freeway; the new facility is on the north end of the Red Lion complex. Inside, you'll

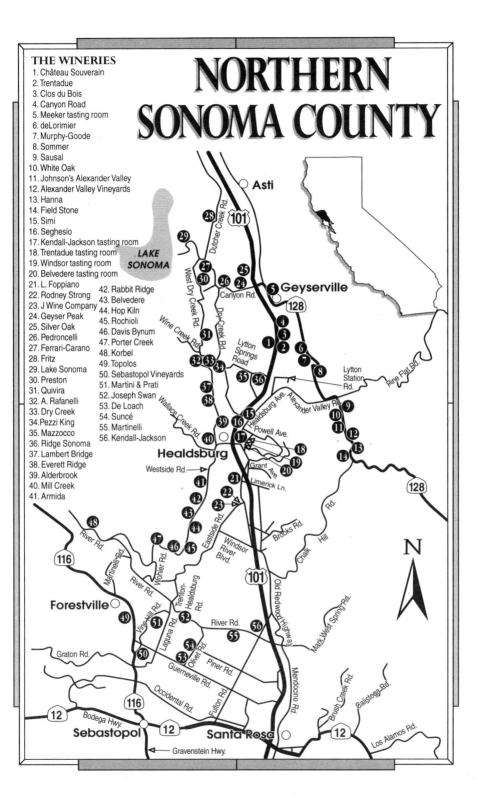

NORTHERN SONOMA COUNTY

THE WINERIES

1. Château Souverain
2. Trentadue
3. Clos du Bois
4. Canyon Road
5. Meeker tasting room
6. deLorimier
7. Murphy-Goode
8. Sommer
9. Sausal
10. White Oak
11. Johnson's Alexander Valley
12. Alexander Valley Vineyards
13. Hanna
14. Field Stone
15. Simi
16. Seghesio
17. Kendall-Jackson tasting room
18. Trentadue tasting room
19. Windsor tasting room
20. Belvedere tasting room
21. L. Foppiano
22. Rodney Strong
23. J Wine Company
24. Geyser Peak
25. Silver Oak
26. Pedroncelli
27. Ferrari-Carano
28. Fritz
29. Lake Sonoma
30. Preston
31. Quivira
32. A. Rafanelli
33. Dry Creek
34. Pezzi King
35. Mazzocco
36. Ridge Sonoma
37. Lambert Bridge
38. Everett Ridge
39. Alderbrook
40. Mill Creek
41. Armida
42. Rabbit Ridge
43. Belvedere
44. Hop Kiln
45. Rochioli
46. Davis Bynum
47. Porter Creek
48. Korbel
49. Topolos
50. Sebastopol Vineyards
51. Martini & Prati
52. Joseph Swan
53. De Loach
54. Suncé
55. Martinelli
56. Kendall-Jackson

LAKE SONOMA

Asti

Geyserville

Healdsburg

Forestville

Sebastopol

Santa Rosa

N

find displays concerning wineries of the northern county and Sonoma Valley, which we visit in the next chapter. Wines from two county vintners are tasted each day, on a rotating alphabetical basis. The center sells wine from most area wineries, plus wine related gift items. It also has wine country videos and computer access to 3,600 books and eighty magazines of the Sonoma County Wine Library. The center is open daily 10 to 5 with tasting from 11 to 4. For information call (707) 586-3795.

Continuing north from Rohnert Park through Santa Rosa, you'll shortly encounter Healdsburg, which *is* a wine country town. It's surrounded by vineyards and has a few downtown tasting rooms. Citizens of this town of 10,000 are doing a fine job facelifting their downtown area to preserve its vintage look. The tree-shaded, landscaped Healdsburg Plaza is rimmed by a bevy of boutiques, antique shops and a good restaurant or two. Several motels and inns permit wineland wanderers to bed down near the vineyards.

North of Healdsburg, Geyserville and Cloverdale also are amidst the vines, although they have fewer facilities. Tiny Geyserville offers two fine Victorian era B&Bs and a new inn (see below), while Cloverdale has a handful of small motels and cafés.

Alexander Valley

Old Cyrus would be pleased to learn that the valley bearing his name still is essentially agricultural. No city disturbs its bucolic tranquility. Geyserville sits between Alexander and Dry Creek valleys. The closest thing to a community within the valley is the grizzled **Alexander Valley Store,** a general mercantile in the classic sense.

Less hilly than Dry Creek or Russian River valleys, Alexander is a patchwork of vineyards and pasturelands, flanking the upper reaches of the Russian River. The land climbs gently eastward toward low hills, giving way to clusters of oaks and groves of madroñas.

ALEXANDER VALLEY WINERY TOUR ● If you drive to the top of Sonoma County on U.S. 101, you'll see hundreds of acres of vineyards but no tasting rooms. The Italian Swiss Colony in the tiny town of Asti—one of the area's earliest wineries—is no more, although an historic landmark sign survives. The facility was purchased by Wine World, Inc., and the tasting room is closed.

Your first opportunity to sample northern Sonoma wine comes just south of **Geyserville.** Take the Independence Lane exit and follow it west briefly to the architecturally striking **Château Souverain.** Cross back under the freeway, turn left on the frontage road (Geyserville Avenue) and head toward Geyserville. You'll encounter three wineries in rather rapid succession, all on the right: **Trentadue, Clos du Bois** and **Canyon Road Cellars.** Press northward, staying with Geyserville Avenue as it zigs and zags a couple of times under the freeway. When you reach the rustic downtown area of Geyserville, you'll see the tasting room for **Meeker Vineyard** on your left, housed in an old masonry bank building.

From here, head inland on Highway 128 into the Alexander Valley. You'll shortly encounter **deLorimier Vineyards and Winery** in a shingle sided barn on your right. A couple of miles beyond is **Murphy-Goode Estate Winery,** also on the right. Staying on 128 (which does a few rural 90-degree turns), you next reach **Sommer Vineyards** and **Sausal Winery,** both on the left. Between them is the earlier mentioned **Alexander Valley Store** at the junction of 128 and Alexander Valley Road. This century-old general store provides necessities and a small bar for locals, plus picnic fare and a selection of regional wines.

A bit farther on Highway 128 is the imposing **White Oak Winery** on the right. Just beyond is **Johnson's Alexander Valley Winery** down a long vineyard lane to the right, then **Alexander Valley Winery** uphill to the left. As the valley approaches Mount St. Helena and starts becoming attractively rumpled, you'll hit the impressive **Hanna Winery** uphill on your left, and just beyond, **Field Stone Winery** on the right. To reach the next winery tour, retrace your route briefly, turn left onto Alexander Valley Road and follow it past the general store to Healdsburg.

Château Souverain • T

Independence Lane at Highway 101 (P.O. Box 528), Geyserville, CA 95441; (707) 433-8281. (www.chateausouverain.com) Daily 10 to 5; all current releases and some older vintages available for tasting. Good selection of wine-related gift items and apparel. See listing under "Wine country dining" for Château Souverain Restaurant.

One of the county's more striking winery structures, Château Souverain is an architectural blend of hop kiln and French manor house. The tasting room is trimmed with bright splashes of color and hanging tapestries. The facility recently was named one of *Wine and Spirits* magazine's "wineries of the year."

Tasting notes: Tastings are conducted either at an attractive bar or at café tables. The list includes Sauvignon Blanc, Chardonnay, Pinot Noir, Zinfandel, Merlot and Cabernet Sauvignon. Each has strong varietal character and its Dry Creek Zinfandels and Russian River and Carneros Chardonnays have won three *Wine Spectator* "Top 100" awards. Prices: *$$ to $$$.*

Vintners choice: "My favorites include our Alexander Valley Cabernet Sauvignon and Sonoma County Chardonnay," says winemaker Tom Peterson.

Trentadue Winery • T ✕ 🍷

19170 Geyserville Ave., Geyserville, CA 95441; (707) 433-3104. Daily 11 to 4:30; MC/VISA, DISC. (www.trentadue.com) Four selections may be tasted from current list. Nice giftware selection and deli items; shaded picnic area.

You'll likely be greeted by a tail-wagging dog or two at this family-owned ranch complex amidst the vines. The combined tasting room and gift shop is upstairs in a masonry block winery building. A long list of wines and a good selection of glassware, wine related items and other giftwares will tempt the visitor. Leo Trentadue started the winery in 1969 and has expanded his operation considerably. The family built the main winery in 1972, and recently added a hospitality center to host special vineyard events.

WINERY CODES • *T* = tasting with no fee; *T$* = tasting for a fee; *GT* = guided tours; *GTA* = guided tours by appointment; *ST* = self-guiding or informal tours; ✕ = picnic area; 🍷 = gift shop or a good giftware selection.

WINE PRICES • *$* = average price under $10 per bottle; *$$* = $10 to $14; *$$$* = $15 to $19; *$$$$* = $20 or more

Tasting notes: Trentadue wines are uniformly excellent and the primary focus is reds. The list includes some mature Zins and Cabs ready for drinking, yet with enough body to be put down for a few more years. Among our favorites were a robust Zinfandel, a hearty Old Patch Red blend, full-flavored Petite Sirah and a full flavored and fruity Chardonnay. Trentadue also offers some fine Ports and sparkling wines. Prices: *$$ to $$$$*.

Vintners choice: "Merlot, Petit Sirah, Carignane and Old Patch Red," says Cindy Trentadue.

Clos du Bois • T ✕ 🏠

19410 Geyserville Ave. (P.O. Box 940), Geyserville, CA 95441; (800) 222-3189 or (707) 857-3100. (www.closdubois.com) Daily 10 to 4:30; major credit cards. Most varieties tasted. Good selection of gift and wine logo items.

Founded in 1974 by wine grower Frank Woods, Clos du Bois has grown rapidly to become one of the largest producers in northern Sonoma County. Its annual output is more than half a million cases. Started in Healdsburg, it now occupies an expansive industrial strength complex just below Geyserville. More attractive than the metal roofed winery is the tasting room, located behind the complex in a pleasing atrium-style structure. Among its select variety of giftwares are Saran-wrapped picnic baskets with a bottle of Clos du Bois wine and—something unique for a tasting room—a CD listening station for a selection of "wine tasting music." Covered picnic tables are just outside.

Tasting notes: The wines are uniformly excellent—with numerous medals to prove it. The rather lengthy list includes the typical Sauvignon Blanc, Chardonnay, Merlot, Cabernet Sauvignon, Shiraz, Merlot and Zinfandel, plus lesser known wines and proprietary blends, including Tempranillo, Malbec and several Meritage selections. Prices: *$$ to $$$$*

Canyon Road Cellars • T ✕ 🏠

19550 Geyserville Ave., Geyserville, CA 95441; (800) 793-WINE or (707) 857-3417. (www.canyonroadwinery.com) Daily 10 to 5; MC/VISA. Most varieties tasted. Good selection of gift and specialty items, plus a deli offering picnic fare. Landscaped picnic area.

A handsome mansard roof style winery is the new home of Canyon Road, which was started in one of the county's oldest wineries. The tasting room is tucked into an adjacent metal-sided cottage with a grape arbor over the porch. Owners of Geyser Peak Winery north of Geyserville bought the 1908 Nervo Winery across the freeway in 1974. Geyser Peak was then bought out by the Trione family of Santa Rosa, who changed the name of the old Nervo Winery to Canyon Road. It later was moved to this attractive facility just south of Geyserville.

Tasting notes: The current releases are quite good and very modestly priced. They include Sauvignon Blanc, Johannisberg Riesling, Chardonnay, Merlot and Cabernet Sauvignon. The lone survivor with a Nervo label is a blend called Winterchill White. Considerably more pricey than the current releases are reserve wines that include Merlot, Cab, Viognier and Shiraz. Overall price range: *$ to $$$$*.

The Meeker Vineyard tasting room • T

21035 Geyserville Ave., Geyserville, CA 95441; (707) 431-2148. Daily 10:30 to 5; MC/VISA. Most varieties tasted.

This appealing tasting room occupies the old Bank of Geyserville, and several of the original teller cages are still intact. Eventually, a new winery will be built in the Dry Creek Valley, so this "bank vault tasting room" may or may not be here when you pass through Geyserville.

Tasting notes: The list is brief and the wines are quite good. It features a two Zinfandels with nice hints of oak, a full-bodied Cabernet Sauvignon and an excellent Merlot that has won several awards. Most Meeker wines are issued under the Gold Leaf Cuvée label. Prices: *$$$ to $$$$.*

deLorimier Vineyards and Winery • T ST ✕

2001 Highway 128 (P.O. Box 487), Geyserville, CA 95441; (800) 546-7718 or (707) 857-2000. (www.delorimierwinery.com) Thursday-Sunday 10 to 4:30. Most varieties tasted. Picnic area and informal self guided tours.

Established in 1985, this attractive family-owned winery occupies a shingle-sided redwood structure nestled among the vineyards in the heart of the Alexander Valley. The small tasting room is upstairs above the winery and a single picnic table sits out front.

Tasting notes: Good fruit and full, clean taste are evident in deLorimier's select list. It consists of a red Meritage style called Mosaic and a white Spectrum blend of Sauvignon Blanc, Semillon and Viognier; plus Sauvignon Blanc, Chardonnay, Sangiovese and Merlot. For those with sweet teeth, try the nectar-like late harvest Semillon. Prices: *$$ to $$$$.*

Vintners choice: "Mosaic and Spectrum typify our dedication to quality and excellence," says a winery spokesperson.

Murphy-Goode Estate Winery • T

4001 Highway 128 (P.O. Box 158), Geyserville, CA 95441; (707) 431-7644. Daily 10:30 to 4:30; MC/VISA, AMEX. Select varieties tasted. A few wine related gift items.

Tim Murphy joined fellow Alexander Valley winegrower and marketing specialist Dave Ready to establish the winery in 1985. The modern, medium-sized no-frills winery is fronted by an appealing cathedral-ceiling tasting room and surrounded by 300 acres of prime vineyards. "It's not a lifestyle to us," Murphy said. "It's our life."

Tasting notes: Murphy-Goode is known for its crisp, fruity Fumé Blanc and award-winning Chardonnay, both in regular and reserve renditions. The list also features a large cast of full flavored reds, including Zinfandel, Cabernet Sauvignon and Merlot. *$$ to $$$$.*

Vintners choice: "The reserve Fumé Blanc is our signature wine; much of our effort goes into it," said our tasting room hostess.

Sommer Vineyards • T ✕ 🏠

5110 Highway 128, Geyserville, CA 95441; (800) 433-1944 or (707) 433-1944. (www.sommervineyards.com) New tasting room wasn't yet open at press time; call for hours.

The former Alexander Valley Fruit and Trading Company is undergoing extensive renovation. Steve and Candace Sommer founded AVF&TC in 1984, on land where Steve had planted vineyards in 1974. They sold both wines and locally grown fruit. Near the turn of the century, they decided to give the winery their family name, bring their children into the operation and focus on wines from their own vineyards.

Tasting notes: The new winery will specialize in Zinfandel, Cabernet, Sangiovese, Merlot and Syrah. Meanwhile, it has an AVF&TC inventory of

Zinfandel, Cabernet Sauvignon, Sangiovese, Syrah, Merlot and Old Vine Zinfandel Port, most of which is available for tasting.

Sausal Winery • T ✗

7370 Highway 128, Healdsburg, CA 95448; (800) 500-2285 or (707) 433-2285. (www.sausalwinery.com) Daily 10 to 4; MC/VISA. Selected wines tasted. A few wine related gift items; small picnic area.

Prim landscaping and an arbor-shaded picnic area accent this small complex, perched on an upslope, half a mile off Highway 128. The small, simple tasting room is fused into the end of the handsome redwood winery. The facility dates from 1973 although the Demostene family owners have been growing grapes in the Alexander Valley since 1925. Some of their vines are older still, dating back to 1877; these grapes go into their Century Vines Zinfandel. Four children of pioneer grape grower Leo Demostene operate the winery today. Since Zinfandels are a major focus, the winery recently started a ZinFanz Club with special prices and offerings for members.

Tasting notes: Sausal's repertoire is small—about six or eight wines and at least three are open for tasting on a given day. We sipped excellent Zinfandel and Cabernet which, typical of Sausal wines, were well-rounded with little hint of tannin or wood. Others on the list include Sangiovese, Private Reserve Zinfandel, Century Vines Zinfandel and a proprietary wine called *Sogno Della Famiglia*. The latter three are not available for tasting. Prices: **$ to $$$$**

Vintners choice: "We specialize in Zinfandels—all estate grown, some from vineyard more than a hundred years old," reports the winery's Peachie Dunlavy.

White Oak Vineyards & Winery • T & T$ ✗ 📷

7505 Highway 128, Healdsburg, CA 95448; (707) 433-8429. (www.whiteoakwines.com) Daily 10 to 5; MC/VISA. Most varieties tasted free; reserve wine tasted for a fee, which applies toward purchase.

White Oak has come a long way since its early days in a Healdsburg industrial area. Founded in 1981 by former fisherman and building contractor Bill Meyers, the winery now occupies a splendid tile-roofed Mediterranean-Italian villa in the Alexander Valley. It's surrounded by elaborately landscaped grounds and a cascading fountain. The tile-floor tasting room offers a tasteful selection of giftwares. Sippers at the polished counter can enjoy vineyard views through large Roman arch windows.

Tasting notes: The brief and tasty list features a pair of lush and delicious Chardonnays, Zinfandels from the Napa and Alexander valleys with great berry flavor and a full-flavored Napa Valley Merlot. Available for tasting for a small fee is Myers Reserve Red. Prices: **$$$ to $$$$**.

Johnson's Alexander Valley Winery • T ST ✗

8333 Highway 128, Healdsburg, CA 95448; (707) 433-2319. (www.johnsonwines.com) Daily 10 to 5; MC/VISA, AMEX. Most varieties tasted. Some wine related gift items; small picnic area.

A century-old barn on this weathered family ranch complex holds a couple of surprises—modern winemaking equipment and a grand theater organ. Ranks of pipes fill much of the winery, standing alongside stainless steel fermenters and aging casks. The tasting room itself is a rustic affair—a wooden counter in a corner. Johnson family members have been organ buffs for years and they've assembled an antique from Sacramento's old Capitol Theater. Which is all very strange, because no one in the family plays. However, they often host organ concerts with guest performers. The small, century-old winery is presently owned by Tom and Gail Johnson; their daughter Ellen is the enologist.

Tasting notes: Wines are available only at the winery and a few local outlets. The brief list consists of a fruity Chardonnay, a crisp Johannisberg Riesling, a powerful and nicely complex Zinfandel and a full-favored Pinot Noir. Prices: *$ to $$$*

Alexander Valley Vineyards • T ✗

8644 Highway 128 (P.O. Box 175), Healdsburg, CA 95448-0175; (800) 888-7209 or (707) 433-7209. (www.avvwine.com) Daily 10 to 5; MC/VISA, AMEX. Most varieties tasted. Some wine related gift items; picnic area.

This facility is as modern as neighboring Johnson's is rustic. The adobe brick and wood winery is set in rumpled foothills above Highway 128, rimmed by landscaped grounds and sheltered by moss-bearded oaks. With vineyards in the foreground and a meadow rising beyond, it's one of the valley's most pleasing spots. The warm wood tasting room is made even warmer—during chilly weather—by an inviting fireplace. Outside, picnic tables occupy a wooden deck; others reside in the shade of cedars and great gnarled oaks.

This also is an historic spot, occupying lands settled by Cyrus Alexander a century and a half ago. His grave site is on a hill above the winery. The Wetzel family purchased this land in 1963, planted vines and began producing premium varietals in 1975. All are estate produced.

Tasting notes: Hank Wetzel's reds are full-bodied yet light in tannin, with a touch of wood. We noted a pleasant spiciness in the Merlot, and the Gewürztraminer was complex and dry with a nippy finish. Cabernets were big wines, suitable for aging. Others on the list include Chenin Blanc and Chardonnay. Prices are rather modest for the quality: *$ to $$$.*

Vintners choice: "Cabernets," said Hank. "They're very stylistic, and older wines are available on request."

Hanna Winery • T & T$ ✗ 🏠

9280 Highway 128, Healdsburg, CA 95448-9022; (800) 854-3987 or (707) 431-4310. (www.hannawinery.com) Daily 10 to 4; MC/VISA. Most current releases tasted free; modest fee for some reserve wines. Tasteful gift and wine logo items. A second winery and tasting room are at 5353 Occidental Road in the Russian River Valley; (707) 575-3371. Same hours as the Alexander Valley facility; giftwares and picnic area; tours by appointment.

A landscaped, tree-lined lane leads through the vineyards to one of Sonoma County's most attractive wineries. One of two Hanna facilities in the county, it sits on a knoll above the vines. A handsome tasting room suggests—from the outside—a large and stylish Swiss chalet with a stone base, arched windows and a red tile roof. Within, it's even more imposing, with an atrium ceiling held up by massive angled beams. Art decorates the walls and views from those oversized arched windows are quite splendid.

Hanna Winery was established in 1987 by Dr. Elias Hanna, a noted San Francisco cardiac surgeon; he started with a twelve-acre vineyard in the Russian River Valley. Dr. Hanna now owns 600 acres in the Alexander and Russian River valleys and Mayacamas Mountains, with a second winery in the Russian River Valley.

Tasting notes: The select Hanna list features nicely crafted traditional varietals, such as Sauvignon Blanc, Chardonnay, Pinot Noir, Zinfandel, Merlot, Cabernet Sauvignon and Syrah. Hillside Blend is a busy stir of Sangiovese, Cabernet Franc, Malbec, Merlot, Nebbiolo, Syrah and Petite Verdot. Prices are on the high side here, ranging beyond $50 for some reserves: *$$$ to $$$$.*

Field Stone Winery ● T ST ✗

10075 Highway 128, Healdsburg, CA 95448; (800) 54-GRAPE or (707) 433-7266. (www.fieldstonewinery.com) Daily 10 to 5; MC/VISA. Most varieties tasted. A few wine related gift items; oak-shaded picnic area.

The tasting room of this earthy, oak-shaded winery seems to have sprung from that earth. It's bunkered into a hillside like a stylish root cellar, and faced with local stone. More conventional woodsided winery buildings are just beyond this appealing tasting bunker. Wine barrel picnic tables with stools fashioned from cable spools complete this curiously pleasing bucolic setting.

The winery is owned by former Presbyterian minister John C. Staten and his wife Katrina. It was built by Katrina's father, formerly Berkeley mayor Wallace Johnson in 1977. When he died unexpectedly, the minister and his wife decided to go into the wine business. Staten doesn't see this as a career contradiction. He points out that the first miracle of Jesus was to turn water into wine. Taken in moderation, wine can be "a vital element in the fellowship among human beings," he says.

Tasting notes: The minister turned vintner produces a tasty selection of wines. Among those we sampled were a lush and herbal Chardonnay, a light yet spicy Sangiovese, a full-bodied Cabernet Sauvignon with firm tannins and a deep flavored Petite Sirah. Others on the winery's list include Sauvignon Blanc, Gewürztraminer, Merlot and an excellent Vintage Port. Prices: *$$ to $$$$.*

Healdsburg & surrounds

Not only is Healdsburg in the heart of the wine country, some wine outlets are in the heart of Healdsburg. Several tasting rooms, orphaned from their wineries, are situated here.

As we mentioned earlier, this town of 10,000 is worth a stop for its landscaped plaza, boutiques, antique stores, restaurants and bed and breakfast inns. Neighborhood streets are shaded by mature trees, some sheltering century-old Victorian homes.

HEALDSBURG AREA WINERY TOUR ● Visitors to Healdsburg can do a fair amount of wine sampling afoot, since several wineries have their tasting rooms here, and a couple of wine shops offer bottles and/or drinks by the glass from dozens of California vintners. We much prefer tasting rooms linked to wineries, where we can absorb the charm of aging cellars, sniff the aromas of sleeping wines and perhaps enjoy a picnic beside the wines. However, these orphaned tasting rooms—which are becoming more common—do offer the opportunity of sampling before buying.

Coming into town from your Alexander Valley trek, you'll blend onto Healdsburg Avenue and encounter the nicely landscaped **Simi Winery** complex on your right. Continue several blocks toward town and turn right (west) onto Grant Street. Follow it to Grove Street, go right again and drive a few blocks north to **Seghesio Family Vineyards** on the right. Return to Healdsburg Avenue and continue south into downtown. Note the Spanish colonial **Swenson Building** shopping complex with its domed clock tower on your right, opposite Healdsburg Plaza. This is a good place to park and start walking.

Start with the **Kendall-Jackson Tasting Room** in the Swenson complex. From there, cross Healdsburg Avenue and follow Plaza Street two blocks alongside the Plaza to the **Trentadue Tasting Room** at the corner of Center Street. Continue another block to the **Russian River Wine Company** at 132 Plaza Street. It's not a winery but a fine wine shop featuring about 200 selections from eighty California wineries, including hard-to-find specialty items. "We taste over 2,000 premium wines to select those that we offer in our shop," says wine broker George Bato. The shop is open daily 9 to 5; (800) 477-0490 or (707) 433-0490.

Stroll back a block to Center Street, turn left past the Trentadue tasting room and you'll shortly encounter the **Windsor Vineyards** tasting room. Continue along Center to Matheson Street, where you might pause for a snack at **Oakville Grocery** (see below). Continue past the grocery-deli to **Tasting on the Plaza,** where you can sample **Belvedere** and several other wines.

Three wineries on the outer fringe of the Russian River Valley are near Healdsburg. Fetch your car and head south on Healdsburg Avenue, ducking under the freeway. The route becomes Old Redwood Highway and about a mile beyond town, you'll encounter **L. Foppiano Wine Company** on your right. A short distance beyond are **Rodney Strong Vineyards** and **J Wine Company,** also on the right. They sit side by side among the vines.

Simi Winery ● T$ GT ✕ ⋒

16275 Healdsburg Ave., Healdsburg, CA 95448; (707) 433-6981. (www.simiwinery.com) Daily 10 to 4:30; major credit cards. Most varieties tasted for a fee, which applies toward wine purchase. Good gift shop selection. Guided tours at 11, 1 and 3 daily March-November and 11 and 2 the rest of the year. Redwood- shaded picnic areas.

Venerable Simi is an island of yesterday, surrounded—but not altered—by the swelling city of Healdsburg. Its massive rough-cut stone winery with three-foot-thick walls was built by Chinese laborers in 1890. More practiced Italian stonemasons later added a smoother section. A modern octagonal tasting room stands nearby. The park-like complex—even the parking lot—is carefully landscaped and shaded by redwoods. (If we had a category for most attractive winery carpark, Simi would win.)

A one-hour tour provides a look at modern winemaking in an ancient, pleasantly musty yet spotlessly clean environment. Wine ferments in glossy stainless steel and sleeps in six thousand barrels in a time-worn loft. The sight would send a Dominican monk into ecstasy.

The Simi label was established in San Francisco in 1876 by Giuseppe and Pietro Simi, who purchased grapes from Sonoma County growers. In 1881, they moved to Healdsburg and planted vineyards in the adjacent Alexander Valley. The winery was inherited in 1904 by Giuseppe's daughter, Isobel Simi Haigh. In an era when women were expected to tend to the stove and their knitting, the remarkable lady took charge. She ran the operation for sixty-six years, surviving Prohibition, the Depression and male chauvinism before selling the winery in 1969. It went through several owners, and is now part of the Eckes family winery collection that includes Franciscan, Mount Veeder and Quintessa in the Napa Valley and Estancia Estates in Monterey County.

Tasting notes: Although it's one of northern Sonoma's largest wineries with an output of 140,000 cases, Simi focuses on a few select varietals. The current wines—uniformly tasty—include Sauvignon Blanc, Chardonnay, Zinfandel, Cabernet Sauvignon, a white Meritage, Shiraz and Merlot. Prices: *$$ to $$$$.*

Seghesio Family Vineyards • T ⚔ 🏠

14730 Grove St., Healdsburg, CA 95448; (707) 433-7764. (www.seghesio.com) Daily 10 to 5; MC/VISA, AMEX. Most varieties tasted. Fair selection of giftwares; picnic area.

One of California's oldest wine families, the Seghesio clan started crushing grapes in 1895. The present family winery has stood for several decades on the edge of Healdsburg, which is about to grow out and envelope it. The current generation recently opened a handsome tasting room with a vaguely Spanish look and lofty ceilings. A gracefully curved tasting counter with decorative-bordered windows look into the aging cellars. Outside, ancient gnarled oaks and towering evergreens shade picnic tables. A fountain and landscaped grounds enhance the industrial-strength winery buildings.

Tasting notes: The Seghesio list features some of the more recently-popular Italian wines. Among the varietals are a light and crisp Arnels, a fruity white Pinot Grigio, a Nebbiolo with a rich berry taste, a hearty Barbera and a spicy Sangiovese. The family also offers several versions of Zinfandel which—in fact—is a clonal twin to Italy's Primitivo. *Omaggio* is a full-flavored blend of Cabernet Sauvignon, Merlot, Sangiovese and Barbera. The winery also makes a slightly sweet Moscato Blanco and a Port blended from Cabernet Sauvignon, Petit Sirah and Pinot Saint George grapes. Prices: *$$ to $$$$.*

Kendall-Jackson tasting room • T$ 🏠

337 Healdsburg Ave., Healdsburg, CA 95448; (800) 769-3649 or (707) 433-7102. (www.kj.com) Daily 10 to 5; MC/VISA. Several varieties tasted for a moderate fee. A nice selection of giftwares and wine logo items.

Far from the Lake County vineyards that made Kendall-Jackson one of California's award-winning wineries, this downtown Healdsburg tasting room offers samples of many of those wines. Established in Lake County in 1983 by Jess Jackson, K-J has since blossomed into eight different "flavor domaines" from northern Sonora through the Napa Valley to Santa Barbara County.

Tasting notes: The Kendall-Jackson wines are uniformly excellent. From the white side, sippers can chose from a variety of Chardonnays, Sauvignon Blanc and Johannisberg Riesling. The reds are mostly classic French varietals—Cabernet Sauvignon, Merlot and Pinot Noir, along with the ubiquitous Zinfandel. They come in a variety of labels and price ranges: *$ to $$$$.*

Trentadue tasting room • T 🏠

Center and Plaza streets; Healdsburg, CA 95448; (707) 433-1082. (www.trentadue.com) Daily 10 to 5; major credit cards. A few wine logo and gift items.

The Trentadue family recently opened this satellite tasting room in addition to the one at the Geyserville winery. See page 49 for details.

Windsor Vineyards tasting room • T 📷

308-B Center Street, Healdsburg, CA 95448; (800) 204-9463 or (707) 433-7302. (www.windsorvineyards.com) Weekdays 10 to 5 and weekends 10 to 6. Major credit cards. Four samples offered free from an extensive list. Good selection of wine-related gift items.

Although Windsor has won its share of medals, it's noted mostly for its marketing gimmickry. The firm specializes in mail order catalog sales and personalized labeling. If you want to serve Fumé Blanc labeled "Bottoms up from Beverly and Bill" at your next party, this is the place.

Tasting notes: The long list includes the usual premium varietals such as Chardonnay, Johannisberg Reisling, Semillon, French Colombard, Fumé Blanc and Gewürztraminer—and that's just the whites. Among the reds are Merlot, Pinot Noir, Petit Sirah, Syrah, Sangiovese, Carignane and Zinfandel. The style is mostly drink-it-now fruity with light wood, and the wines have won a fair share of medals. They're available only at the tasting room or by mail order. Prices range rather widely: *$ to $$$$.*

Tasting on the Plaza • T ST ✗

250 Center St., Healdsburg, CA 95448; (800) 433-8296 or (707) 431-4430. (www.belvedere.com) Daily 10 to 5; MC/VISA. A a few gift items.

Belvedere winery's downtown tasting room also offers samples from a couple of other wineries—Gary Farrell Wines and Floodgate Vineyards. For more on Belvedere, see page 72.

L. Foppiano Wine Co. • T ST ✗

12707 Old Redwood Highway (P.O. Box 606), Healdsburg, CA 95448; (707) 433-7272. (www.foppiano.com) Daily 10 to 4:30; MC/VISA, AMEX, DISC. Most varieties tasted. Some wine related gift items. Casual tours by appointment. Shaded picnic areas.

One of the county's pioneer wineries, the Foppiano facility looks its age, although modern equipment lurks beneath its weathered exterior. It was established by John Foppiano in 1896 and the family made jug wines for decades. Leaders of the third and fourth generations, both named Louis, have shifted the focus to premium varieties. An unadorned, square-shouldered stucco building houses the century-old winery and a cottage-style hospitality center invites tasting. A few picnic tables are parked under shade trees behind the tasting room.

Tasting notes: Although the winery is unpretentious, the wines are excellent. We encountered two outstanding reds—a lush, spicy Cabernet Sauvignon and a near-perfect Zinfandel. Other varieties offered under the family label are moderately priced Sauvignon Blanc, Chardonnay and Petite Sirah. Older vintages are available at predictably higher prices. Foppiano also markets honest, drinkable varietals under the Riverside Vineyards label, priced well under $10. Overall prices: *$ to $$$$.*

Vintners choice: The Foppianos have been making red wines for a century, explained our tasting room hostess, and they're particularly proud of the Petit Sirah and Zinfandel. "We're mostly a red wine winery."

Rodney Strong Vineyards • T & T$ ST ✗

11455 Old Redwood Highway, Healdsburg, CA 95448; (800) 678-4763 or (707) 431-1533. (www.rodneystrong.com) Daily 10 to 5; major credit cards. Most varieties tasted free; a modest fee for others. Some wine related gift items.

Nice picnic area on "The Green," a lawn area near the vineyards; informal tours. The winery also hosts concerts during the summer; call for schedule and ticket information.

This is one of the area's more interesting architectural creations—an earth-hugging structure of laminated beams and textured concrete. Before entering the tasting room, take a left or right just inside the winery door and stroll around the suspended walkway. You'll get a bird's eye view of the operation, from fermentation tanks to huge oak aging casts. The tasting room is cantilevered above it all.

Rodney Strong started in the wine business thirty-five years ago, peddling mail-order wines out of a tasting room in Tiburon. The operation expanded to an old winery in Windsor and has gone through assorted ownerships. In 1889 it was purchased by the Kleins, a three-generation California agricultural family. Many of its wine grapes are drawn from the original vineyards selected by Strong decades ago.

Tasting notes: The list has been pared in recent years, offering a few select French varietals. The overall style is soft and fruity with low tannins. The current list includes Sauvignon Blanc, a couple of Chardonnays, a pair of Pinots Noir and Merlots, Zinfandel and three treatments of Cabernet sauvignon. Prices: *$$ to $$$$.*

J Wine Company ● *T$ GTA* ✕ 🏠

11447 Old Redwood Hwy. (P.O. Box 1919), Healdsburg, CA 95448; (707) 433-8843. (www.jwinecompany.com) Daily 11 to 5.; MC/VISA, AMEX. Sparkling and tables wines tasted for a fee. Choice selection of giftwares and specialty food items; picnic terrace. Conducted tours by appointment.

The former Piper Sonoma Cellars, opened here by Piper Heidsiek of France's Remy Martín, was purchased in the mid-1990s by the father-daughter team of Tom and Judy Jordan. It is currently owned by Judy, who pursued a career as a globe-trotting geophysicist before joining her family in the wine business. Her parents are owners Jordan Vineyard and Winery, and Judy served as their marketing and sales manager from 1987 until 1991.

The winery and high-style tasting room are in a textured concrete structure fronted by a terrace and formal gardens. To reach the tasting room, one crosses a moat over a bridge with floral planter boxes along its rails—a nice touch. Focal point of the ultramodern facility is a pair of copper colored panels embedded with crystals, rising above the long tasting counter. Tours of this modern facility take visitors along an elevated balcony for vistas of the fermentation room with its steel tank forest, barrel aging cellars, riddling racks and bottling line.

Tasting notes: Sparkling wines can be tasted for a modest fee per sample. For a slightly less modest fee, visitors can match a variety of appetizers with still wines. This stylish facility produces several versions of sparkling wine, plus Chardonnay and Pinot Noir, which—of course—are the ingredients of a fine sparkler. The bubbly and still wines are excellent, with prices to match: *$$$$.*

Dry Creek Valley

Dry Creek Valley is one of our favorite winetasting haunts. We challenge any wineland to match this pastorale. Vineyards carpet the narrow valley floor and ascend its benchlands. Live oak thickets crown rounded knolls and redwood groves are tucked into secret ravines. Ancient Zinfandel vines cover steep hillsides like knotted fists. Family farms with rusty pick-ups sitting out front share the valley with sleek new wineries built by urban millionaires who seek solace under a rural sun.

There's even a rustic Dry Creek country store to confirm the valley's rural heritage. Never mind that it sells *foi gras* and camembert in its deli.

The broad shoulders of Warm Springs Dam plug the upper end of the valley. Built in the eighties, the dam provides—ironically—a year-around trickle for the once seasonal Dry Creek. Since it's an earthen dam covered with grass, its dominance of the upper valley is subtle. The reservoir, Lake Sonoma, offers water sports, fishing, shoreside hiking, camping and picnicking.

The valley is noted for producing big, perfectly-balanced Zinfandels from vines predating Prohibition. Zin is the valley's most widely planted grape. The moderate coastal-tempered climate is ideal for Chardonnay, Pinot Noir and Cabernet Sauvignon as well.

DRY CREEK VALLEY WINERY TOUR • This tour is rather complex because of the valley's winding roads, a couple of dead ends and scattered locations of wineries. They aren't far apart, but they're not in orderly rows. Dry Creek and West Dry Creek roads run parallel through the valley, linked by ladder rungs of crossroads.

Start just north of **Geyserville**, taking the Canyon Road exit from U.S. 101. Go briefly west to long-established **Geyser Peak Winery,** within sight of the freeway. From Geyser Peak, follow the frontage road (Chianti Road) three miles to **Silver Oak Cellars**. Backtrack to the freeway interchange, turn right (west) onto Canyon Road and you soon encounter **Pedroncelli Winery** on the right. The route T-bones into Dry Creek Road just beyond; turn right, drive about half a mile and you'll see the impressive **Ferrari-Carano** facility, near the junction with Dutcher Creek Road.

Head up Dutcher Creek Road 1.5 miles to **Fritz Winery** at the end of a steep wooded lane. Return to Dry Creek Road and follow it north toward Warm Springs Dam to **Lake Sonoma Winery,** up a lane to your right. Backtrack on Dry Creek to Yoakim Bridge Road (just short of Canyon Road), turn right and cross over to West Dry Creek Road. Go right again and follow this scenically twisting road to **Preston Vineyards and Winery,** at the end of a long country lane. Return to the junction of West Dry Creek and Yoakim Bridge and you'll see a lane to your right, leading to Raymond Burr Vineyards, established in 1986 by the famed actor. However, tasting is by appointment only; (888) 900-0024. Continue about three miles south on West Dry Creek to **Quivira Vineyards** on the left and **A. Rafanelli** on the right. Turn left (east) onto Lambert Bridge Road, cross its ancient namesake bridge and you'll soon see **Dry Creek Vineyard** on the right and **Pezzi King** on the left.

Just beyond, at Lambert Bridge and Dry Creek Road, you'll encounter **Dry Creek General Store.** It comprises the total "town" of Dry Creek, claiming a population of four. The inviting old store offers a deli, local wine selections and essentials such as food, clothing and fishing worms. Local boys sip their Coors at a tiny bar in a corner of the store. Picnic tables out front encourage visitors to linger. Since most people ask, that palatial mansion on the hill behind the store is not the residence of a wine baron. It was built by an area doctor.

Continue south a short distance to Lytton Springs Road, turn left and climb rolling hills to **Mazzocco Vineyards** and **Ridge Vineyards-Sonoma**, both on the right. From here, you must backtrack a bit. Return to Dry Creek Road and the general store, then take Lambert Bridge Road back to West Dry Creek Road and turn left. Are we lost yet?

Head south on West Dry Creek over gently rumpled foothills to **Lambert Bridge Vineyards** and **Everett Ridge Vineyards & Winery,** both on the right. West Dry Creek is an exceptionally scenic route, lined with oak thickets, occasional redwoods, vineyards and small family farms. The winding lane up to Everett Ridge is particularly appealing.

Just below here, West Dry Creek bumps into Westside Road near the bold arched gateway to Madrona Manor. Once the home of wealthy pioneer John Alexander Paxton, it's now an opulent inn and restaurant; see page 83. Turn left onto Westside Road, heading east toward Healdsburg; fork to the right onto Mill Street as you approach town. Just short of the freeway, go right on Magnolia, following signs a short distance to **Alderbrook Winery.** From here, it's a quick hop back to Healdsburg.

Geyser Peak Winery • T & T$ ✗ 📦

22281 Chianti Rd., Geyserville, CA 95441; (800) 255-9463. (www.geyser-peak.com) Daily 10 to 5; MC/VISA, AMEX. Free tasting of most varieties; fee for reserve tasting. Extensive gift selection; covered picnic area.

The large Geyser Peak complex sits at the gateway to Dry Creek Valley. It's a comely facility with landscaped grounds, terraced patios and a stone-faced ivy-covered winery built against a wooded hillside. It's difficult to believe that freeway traffic is but an exhaust belch away.

Geyser Peak traces its heritage from 1880, when it was established by pioneer Sonoma County winemaker Augustus Quitzow. The winery has gone through a variety of proprietors through the decades, alternately producing bulk wine, jug wines, varietals and brandy. Major expansion came after Schlitz Brewery bought the facility in 1972. Under Schlitz, the Summit brand wine-in-a-box was born, although the label has since been sold to another winery. Schlitz was purchased by in 1982 by Stroh's Brewing, which had no interest in winemaking so Geyser Peak was sold to the Henry Trione family of Santa Rosa. It's now owned by Jim Beam, distillers of good Kentucky Whiskey.

Tasting comments: Geyser Peak's wine list is rather versatile, offering relatively modest priced Sauvignon Blanc, Chardonnay, Johannisberg Riesling, Gewürztraminer, Cabernet Sauvignon, Merlot, Zinfandel and Shiraz. All are perfectly decent, well-made wines. Older, full flavored and pricier versions of these varietals are available in the Reserve Wines, Block Collection and Bin Series. And if you're really feeling spendy, inquire about the Cellar Collectibles. Prices: *$$ to $$$$.*

Silver Oak Cellars • T$ GTA

24625 Chianti Rd., Geyserville, CA 95448; (800) 273-8809. Monday-Friday 9 to 4, Saturday 10 to 4, closed Sundays and holiday weekends; MC/VISA. Tasting for a fee (which buys the glass). Guided tours by appointment; tasting appointments recommended on Saturdays.

Napa Valley's masters of Cabernet, Justin Meyer and Ray Duncan, expanded to northern Sonoma County with the purchase of the former Lyeth Winery in 1992. This new acquisition, a Normandy style gray and white

A ROSÉ BY ANY OTHER NAME?

Rosé is no longer the Rodney Dangerfield of American wines. For years, many wine enthusiasts—including this one—regarded pink wine as a poor compromise between red and white. Marketing strategies by some firms suggested that rosé "goes with anything," which didn't help its status. Diners intimidated by long wine lists would seek refuge in rosé.

Traditionally, most pink wine was made from Grenache, a sweet, high-yield grape from southern France. Rosé originated there and the word is French for "pink." You probably know that it's made from red grapes by withdrawing the skins early during fermentation. Since most of the color and body come from the skins, this produces a light, fruity wine. (On rare occasion, it's made by blending red and white wine.) France has made some great rosés, although most of that produced in California was considered rather ordinary.

Then in 1958, Sonoma County's Pedroncelli family bottled and marketed a rosé made from high-quality Zinfandel grapes, labeling it "Zin Rosé." The raspberry-like complexity of Zinfandel produced a much more pleasing pink wine, and it began winning awards. Others followed, with names like Rosé of Cabernet, Rouge Noir and the notorious "white Zinfandel" (which is actually pink). August Sebastiani produced a pink Gewürztraminer and called it Eye of the Swan.

In the 1970s, wine writer Jerry Mead coined the term "blush wine" to describe a premium rosé produced at northern Sonoma's Mill Creek Vineyards, and the floodgates were opened.

Soon, Zinfandel Blush, Cabernet Blush, Pinot Blush and white Zinfandel were among America's best-selling wines. White Zin led the pack, particularly after Sutter Home's Bob Trinchero got into the act. Buying up every loose grape he could find and mass producing white Zin, he practically cornered that market. By the early 1990s, he was selling 2.5 million cases of his white Zinfandel a year, catapulting Sutter Home from one of Napa Valley's smallest wineries to one of its largest. Pink wine comprises about thirty percent of America's wine sales, and at least half of that is white Zin.

Pedroncelli's Zin Rosé is still an excellent wine, and it's still winning awards. It and other "blush" wines continue to be leading sellers. Finally, California's rosés are getting some respect.

structure, sits elegantly behind wrought iron gates, and the classic look continues inside. The original Silver Oak was established in the Napa Valley in 1972 and that operation continues to thrive; see listing in Chapter Five, page 124. Incidentally, Meyer also is the author of one of the more sensible books written about the grape, *Plain Talk About Fine Wine*.

Tasting notes: Silver Oak produces only 100 percent varietal Cabernet Sauvignon, drawing grapes from the Alexander and Napa valleys. They're aged in American oak instead classic French wood, giving them a distinct spicy-soft finish. The Alexander Valley Cabernet, grown and produced here, is excellent—gently complex and piquant with a light tannic finish. None are released until they have matured for several years. Prepare for sticker shock: The array of accolades earned by Silver Oak suggests that the wines are worth the prices: **$$$$.**

Pedroncelli Winery ● T GTA ✕

1220 Canyon Road, Geyserville, CA 95441; (707) 857-3531. (www.pedroncelli.com) Daily 10 to 5; MC/VISA, AMEX. Most varieties tasted. A few wine logo gift items; small deck with picnic tables. Guided tours by reservation.

Founded during Prohibition by John Pedroncelli, the winery has grown considerably under the guidance of his two sons. It now turns out about 100,000 cases annually. Jim handles much of the business and John is the primary winemaker.

We've watched the Pedroncelli complex grow for a quarter of a century. The tasting room, once a counter in a cinderblock storage building, is now in an attractive, airy structure with high ceilings and a curving bar. Picnic tables near the vineyards encourage visitors to linger in this bucolic setting. It's all part of a pleasing, ranch-style complex of redwood buildings cradled among vine and oak-thatched hills between the Alexander and Dry Creek valleys.

Tasting notes: The Pedroncellis like their whites crisp and lean, and it was evident in their spicy Chardonnay and fruity Chenin Blanc. The Pinot Noir was soft and berry-like and a Cabernet Reserve was outstanding—big, powerful and complex. The Zinfandel—one of the Pedroncellis' best wines— was predictably excellent. *The Wine Spectator* has rated it a best buy for an inexpensive Zin. Prices: **$ to $$$.**

Vintners Choice: "Zinfandel, which we've been making for forty years," says third-generation Julie Pedroncelli. "We can draw from excellent Dry Creek Valley grapes."

Ferrari-Carano Vineyards and Winery ● T$ GTA 🏵

8761 Dry Creek Rd., Healdsburg, CA 95448; (707) 433-6700. (www.ferrari-carano.com) Daily 10 to 5; major credit cards. Selected wines tasted. Tasteful line of giftwares and clothing. Tours by appointment.

Ferrari-Carano is a striking blend of manor house, castle and leading edge winery. Its centerpiece is Villa Fiore, *House of Flowers*, an opulent 20,000-square-foot Italianate style hospitality center. It's surrounded by five acres of theme gardens with more than 2,000 species of flowers, shrubs and trees, plus winding walks and waterfalls. Fronted by a formal entryway and rimmed by billiard-green lawns, this is northern Sonoma County's most palatial winery complex.

All this largess comes from Don and Rhonda Carano, owners of the El Dorado and Silver Legacy casino hotels in Reno. The double-jointed winery name pays homage to Rhonda's grandmother, who inspired her interest in wine and food.

Tasting notes: The Ferrari-Carano roster is brief but first rate—Fumé Blanc, Chardonnay, Merlot, Siena (a Sangiovese-Cabernet Sauvignon blend) and Trésor, a fine red Bordeaux blend. Prices: **$$ to $$$$.**

Fritz Winery ● T GTA ✕

24691 Dutcher Creek Rd., Cloverdale, CA 95425; (800) 418-9463 or (707) 894-3389. (www.fritzwnery.com) Daily 10:30 to 4:30 (hours may be shorter in winter); MC/VISA. Most varieties tasted. Nice selection of giftwares; picnic area; tours by appointment.

Bunkered dramatically into a wooded hillside, this is one of the area's more appealing wineries. Terraced landscaping leads to a white stucco building with tall Spanish arch windows. Most of the three-tiered winery is built into the earth and it's surrounded by redwoods instead of vines. The tasting room is dramatically simple, with a high curved ceiling and warmed—when needed—by a friendly Franklin stove. When you enter, say hello to Fritzie the cat, who'll likely be playing with a wine cork.

Barbara and Jay Fritz started their winery in 1979, with a focus on conservation, winemaking technology and informality. In 1996, they decided to concentrate on a few single-vineyard wines. They reduced their production by two-thirds, built underground aging caves and began using native yeast to ferment most of their wines. The result? The wines are winning many medals and are sold only by allocation.

Tasting notes: An outstanding Rogers' Reserve Zinfandel caught our attention—peppery with a great raspberry taste. Other worthies were a lush and fruity Dutton Ranch Chardonnay, a crisp and fruity Pinot Blanc wine called *Melòn*, and a soft and dry Sauvignon Blanc. The list features several versions of Chardonnay and Zinfandel, a late harvest Zin and a Merlot. Prices: *$$ to $$$$*.

Lake Sonoma Winery • T ST ✕ 🏠

9990 Dry Creek Rd., Geyserville, CA 95441; (707) 473-2999. Daily 10 to 5. Most varieties tasted; MC/VISA. Wine oriented collectibles and deli with picnic fare and specialty food items. Shaded picnic areas; informal winery tours.

This handsome hillside winery features modern pavilion style architecture with a covered colonnade. The airy tasting room and a large observation deck offer fine views of Dry Creek Valley and nearby Lake Sonoma. A shaded picnic area is tucked into a shady grove. Located on a twenty-acre hillside estate, the winery was founded in 1977 and named for the reservoir that it overlooks. It was operated by the Don Polson family in the 1990s and is now owned by the Korbel family. It produces about 10,000 cases of wine a year, heading for an ultimate capacity of 20,000 cases.

As an added attraction, the firm has established a branch of its Russian River Brewing Company adjacent to the wine tasting pavilion. Visitors thus have a choice of tasting wine or sipping suds—or both.

Tasting notes: The winery focuses on Zinfandel, Chardonnay and Cabernet Sauvignon, drawing from Dry Creek Valley vineyards and from the neighboring Russian River and Alexander valleys. Prices: *$$ to $$$*.

Preston Vineyards • T ✕ 🏠

9282 West Dry Creek Rd., Healdsburg, CA 95448; (707) 433-3372. (www.prestonvineyards.com) Daily 11 to 4:30; MC/VISA. Most varieties tasted. Wine logo items and books; picnic area under an arbor.

How could one not like a winery that greets you with a neon "Drink Zin" sign. The winery is simple and its setting is pleasingly woodsy—in a multi-gabled barn beside a creek. Although it's built into the main winery building, the tasting room has a pleasant cottage effect, with polished wooden floors, drop lamps and an adjacent brick floor porch. Check about the grounds and you'll see a Spanish style *forno* outdoor oven and a bocce ball court. This small and informal winery, established by Lou and Susan Preston, is that kind of place. The Prestons also produce wine vinegar, olive oil and breads baked in a wood-burning oven, which are available at the winery.

Tasting notes: The list contains some of the newly popular wines such as Mourvèdre, Marsanne and Sangiovese, plus tasty versions of the more familiar Sauvignon Blanc, Barbera, Zinfandel, Syrah and a red Rhône blend called Faux. On the dessert side resides Muscat Brûlé and Moscato Curioso. The Sauvignon Blanc and was dry and fruity with a crisp edge. Most of the reds were rather herbal, a pleasant effect. The Barbera had a nice berry taste and the Zinfandel had a pleasant raspberry flavor. *$$ to $$$$.*

Quivira Vineyards • T ✕ 📷

4900 W. Dry Creek Rd., Healdsburg, CA 95448; (800) 292-8339 or (707) 431-8333. (www.quivirawine.com) Daily 11 to 5; MC/VISA. Most varieties tasted. Wine-related gift items; picnic arbor.

Housed in an appealing ivy-entwined modern barn, Quivira presents a pleasantly bucolic picture, with picnic tables under olive trees and a wisteria-entwined arbor out front. Window walls in the attractive tasting room allow sippers to peer at sleeping casks in the winery. Quivira was established in 1987 by Holly and Henry Wendt, specializing in a small list of estate grown wines. There's an interesting legend behind the winery's name. In 1540, thirty-year-old Francisco Vásquez de Coronado was sent from Mexico City into the American southwest in search of the seven golden cities of Cíbola. He found no gold and he was further led astray by a clever Indian who told him of a fabulous city of Quivira, far to the north. It was a ploy to divert Coronado from raiding his village. Returning to Mexico frustrated and with no riches, he nevertheless named the new country he'd explored Quivira. He did not, however, reach the Dry Creek Valley. The Wendts just like the legend.

Tasting notes: The brief list won't lead wine tasters astray. Sauvignon Blanc is nicely complex with lots of fruit. The Zinfandel, a frequent medal winner, is excellent, with plenty of raspberry taste and a nip of tannin. The Wendts also offer an interesting proprietary wine—Dry Creek Cuvée, a blend of Mourvèdre, Syrah, Zin and Grenache. Prices: *$$ to $$$$.*

"We are known for Zinfandel, Sauvignon Blanc and other red wines," reports a winery spokesperson.

A. Rafanelli Winery • T

4685 West Dry Creek Rd., Healdsburg, CA 95448; (707) 433-1385. Daily 10 to 4. No credit cards. Most varieties tasted. Guided tours by appointment.

This small, attractive barnboard style winery is tucked into a wooded grove, reached by a narrow lane framed in a split-rail fence. Trees and landscaping accent the setting. The winery was established three generations ago by the Rafanelli family and is currently owned operated by David and his wife Patty.

Tasting notes: The tasting ritual is simple and brief, since this 12,000-case winery produces only two varietals—Zinfandel and Cabernet. Both are palate pleasers, exhibiting strong varietal character. Prices: *$$$$.*

Dry Creek Vineyard • T ✕

3770 Lambert Bridge Rd. (P.O. Box T), Healdsburg, CA 95448; (707) 433-1000. (www.drycreekvineyard.com) Daily 10:30 to 4:30; MC/VISA. Most varieties tasted. A few wine related gift items; picnic area on a lawn near the tasting room.

David Stare is one of Dry Creek's first new generation vintners, arriving in 1972. For some reason, my clearest recollection of Dave—from an early interview—was that he was California's first vintner to get a personalized license plate. Naturally, it read: WINERY. It's still on one of the winery's pickups.

He's better known as a producer of consistent award-winning wines, notably Fumé Blanc and Zinfandel. Through the years, he has built his winery's capacity to 100,000 cases. The tasting room is in a nice setting—a sturdy structure suggestive of a manor house, climbing with ivy and rimmed by old trees and new lawns.

Tasting notes: Although we're red wine fans and this is red wine country, we were impressed with Dry Creek's crisp, fruity and perfectly balanced Chenin Blanc and Fumé Blanc. A nutty flavored reserve Chardonnay was excellent as well; one of the valley's best. A classic Cabernet Sauvignon with a proper chili pepper nose, Merlot, Fumé Blanc, Zinfandel, Pinot Noir and red Meritage round out Dave's list. Prices: *$ to $$$$.*

Vintners choice: "Our Fumé Blanc is considered the benchmark of this variety," says winemaker Jeff McBride. "We've developed a reputation for Dry Creek Valley appellation Zinfandel, reserve Chardonnay and Meritage, as well."

Pezzi King Vineyards ● T ✗ 🏠

3805 Lambert Bridge Rd., Healdsburg, CA 95448; (800) 411-4758 or (707) 431-9388. (www.pezziking.com) Daily 10 to 4:30. Most varieties tasted. Good selection of giftwares; picnic tables.

Pezzi King is one of the Dry Creek Valley's more attractive wineries and tasting rooms. A trellis supported by stone columns rims the winery, creating an inviting colonnade from the parking area to the tasting room. Picnic tables sit beneath the trellis; others are on a deck in front of the tasting room, offering views of vineyards and wooded hills. Still more tables are terraced down a sloping lawn toward the vineyards. Exposed trusses support the tasting room ceiling and a crackling fireplace invites one to linger and sip.

The winery was established by Robert Stemmler in 1977, then it was purchased by the Pezzi and King group in 1993.

Tasting notes: The list was brief and the wines were tasty when we last passed. Our favored whites were a fruity and crisp Fumé Blanc, a lush Chardonnay with a hint of oak and a rich late harvest Sauvignon Blanc. The reds were a spicy Merlot and a peppery Cabernet Sauvignon with nice oak underpinnings. Prices: *$$ to $$$$.*

Mazzocco Vineyards ● T ✗

1400 Lytton Springs Road, Healdsburg, CA 95448; (707) 431-8159. (www.mazzocco.com) Daily 10 to 4:30; MC/VISA. Most varieties tasted. Small number of wine related items. Picnic tables on balcony overlooking an airport.

Mazzocco's location on a vineyard slope overlooking the Healdsburg Airport is no accident. Its founder, Dr. Thomas Mazzocco, is a private pilot. He selected this spot for a quick commute when he built the winery in 1985. Visitors to the small facility can enjoy the view of vines and planes from a picnic deck outside a new hospitality center and gift shop.

Tasting notes: The hilly slopes along Lytton Springs Road are Zinfandel country. Thousands of vines—some a century old—line this pleasantly winding route. So it's no surprise that Mazzocco produces excellent full-bodied Zins. Two to three varieties are generally available, although the supply is sometimes exhausted. Mazzocco's Cabernet Sauvignon is done Bordeaux

Ancient vines and an old farm house create a pastoral scene along Westside Road in the Russian River Valley

style, blended with Merlot and Cabernet Franc. We found it to be soft and lush yet full flavored. Other choices include Merlot, Chardonnay and Matrix, a Meritage blend of Cabernets Sauvignon and Franc, Merlot, Petit Verdot and Malbec. Prices: **$$$ to $$$$.**

Vintners choice: "We're famous for the big, hearty style of our Zinfandel," said a voice from the winery.

Ridge Vineyards-Sonoma ● T ✕

650 Lytton Springs Rd., Healdsburg, CA 95448; (707) 433-7721. Daily 10 to 4; MC/VISA. A few wine related items; some picnic tables near the winery.

This one of the more appealing of northern Sonoma County's small wineries. The hillside setting is impressive, amidst ancient Zinfandels with trunks the size of young oaks. The tasting room, a counter at the rear of the winery, is both funky and classy. It's set amidst barrels and tanks, with a Persian rug on the floor. There is an implied invitation to relax and linger here.

Established in 1977 as Lytton Springs Winery, the facility in 1991 became part of Ridge Vineyards of Santa Clara County's Montebello Ridge, another winery famous for its Zins. This northern extension of Ridge draws from the surrounding ancient vines to produce some of the finest Zinfandels in California.

Tasting notes: These are *big* Zins—lush, complex, full of berries, with a good tannin finish. Reach for your checkbook or VISA if you're a Zin lover, for prices are in the upper ranges. Bear in mind that the yield from ancient vines is very low. Also on the list are a private reserve Cabernet and a Cab-Merlot-Zin blend. Many Ridge Vineyards wines also are available here; see tasting notes in Chapter Seven, page 187. Prices: *$$ to $$$$.*

Lambert Bridge Vineyards • T GTA ✕

4085 W. Dry Creek Rd., Healdsburg, CA 95448; (800) 975-0555 or (707) 431-9600. (www.lambertbridge.com) Daily 11:30 to 4:30; major credit cards. Select wines tasted. Gazebo and picnic area overlooking Dry Creek Valley. A few wine related items; tours by appointment.

Perched in a wooden glen above scenic Dry Creek Valley, Lambert Bridge is particularly appealing. It's in a redwood structure accented by a wisteria trellis, and the tasting room is within the working winery, surrounded by tiered barrels. A fireplace occupies one end of the structure. The sloping grounds are elaborately landscaped, terraced by stone retaining walls.

Tasting notes: Lambert's list is short and first rate. Chardonnay was excellent, full and spicy with oak accents from extended barrel aging. The Merlot, Cabernet Sauvignon, Petite Sirah and Crane Creek Cuvée Meritage are soft and full flavored, with a tannin finish that will stand up to aging. Other full flavored wines on the list are Zinfandel, Sauvignon Blanc and Viognier. Prices: *$$$ to $$$$.*

Vintners choice: "Merlot is what we're best known for," said a winery voice.

Everett Ridge Vineyards & Winery • T ✕ 🏠

435 W. Dry Creek Rd., Healdsburg, CA 95448; (707) 433-1637. (www.everettridge.com) Daily 11 to 4:30 May through October and Tuesday-Sunday 11 to 4 the rest of the year; MC/VISA, DISC. Most varieties tasted. Wine oriented gifts and picnic area. Group tours only, by appointment.

If you visited this winery when it was pleasantly scruffy Bellerose, you'll be startled by its new look. Weathered farm buildings have been renovated and given a good coat of redwood stain. Grounds are elaborately landscaped and a picnic area with umbrella tables offers vistas of vineyards and wooded hills. All of this painting, patching and renovating is the work of Jack and Anne Air, who purchased Bellerose in 1996. They named it in honor of the Everett Wise, who started a winery here way back in 1878. Bellarose had been established exactly a century later 1978 by Charles and Nancy Richard.

Like the Richards, Jack and Anne follow organic and biodynamic farming methods to produce full flavored wines that have won an impressive number of awards. Tastings are conducted in a cozy space that offers a small collection of giftwares, including some wonderfully ostentatious wine-theme neckties.

Tasting notes: The short but tasty list consists of a crisp Mendocino County Sauvignon Blanc; a fruity yet dry Russian River Valley Chardonnay; an award winning peppery Dry Creek Valley Zinfandel with a hint of oak; a

Sonoma Valley Syrah with intense fruit flavor; and a soft, full-flavored Dry Creek Valley Cabernet Sauvignon. Available for purchase although not tasted is an intense, peppery Nuns Canyon Vineyard Syrah. *$$$ to $$$$.*

Alderbrook Winery • T GTA ✕ 🐚

2306 Magnolia Dr., Healdsburg, CA 95448; (800) 655-3838 or (707) 433-5987. (www.alderbrook.com) Daily 10 to 5; major credit cards. Most varieties tasted. Nice selection of giftwares; picnic tables overlooking the vineyards.

Although close to the freeway, Alderbrook is sheltered by vineyards and it's attractive within. Lots of windows and white painted knotty pine accent the cheerful, open tasting room, which is housed in a primly attractive gray and white-trimmed bungalow. The nicely landscaped grounds are popular for picnicking. The winery itself is housed in a refurbished 85-year-old redwood barn nearby. The facility was started in 1981 by a partnership of Mark Rafanelli, John Clark and Philip Staley. It was purchased recently by seven partners based in Colusa, California.

Tasting notes: Alderbrook focuses on vines that do well in the southern tip of Dry Creek Valley. Their core wines—Zinfandel, Chardonnay, Sauvignon Blanc and Russian River Pinot Noir—exhibit strong varietal character. Other tasty items on the list are Gewürztraminer, Viognier, Cabernet Sauvignon, late harvest Sauvignon Blanc and Port. Prices: *$ to $$$.*

Vintners choice: "Our OVOC (old vine, old clone) Zinfandel is a wonderful choice. It's full bodied and succulent with a smooth finish," says the winery hospitality director.

Russian River Valley

The Russian River flows the length of northern Sonoma County, passing through the Alexander Valley before reaching the Russian River Valley. However, the Russian River appellation refers specifically to the lower part of the stream, from the point where it's joined by Dry Creek.

Initially, the terrain differences are subtle, and the lower Russian River Valley rivals Dry Creek in natural beauty. Farther west, the river swings away from the vineyards. It flows through an old fashioned riverbank resort area that has been popular since the 1920s.

Russian River vineyards occur in two distinct areas. The first group is clustered in rolling hills along Westside Road between Healdsburg and Rio Nido. The second gathering is south of the river, in a mix of farmlands and evergreen clusters. Both areas are accented here and there by redwoods. As in Dry Creek Valley, gentle and forest-clad mountains are never far away and side roads invite wandering into concealed canyons.

One side trip in this area is particularly inviting. From Westside Road near Hop Kiln Winery, turn right onto Sweetwater Springs Road. Follow its winding course uphill, past a cheerful creek, into darkened redwood groves, through the tiny old town of Sweetwater Springs and up to a high point offering views of half the county. Staying on its corkscrew course, you'll emerge below the redwood groves and hiking trails of Austin Creek State Recreation Area.

RUSSIAN RIVER WINERY TOUR • From Alderbrook Winery, where you've just finished a final sip of Sauvignon Blanc, retrace your route southwest on Mill Street to Westside Road. Or retire for the night in next-door **Healdsburg** and start afresh tomorrow.

Your first winery encounter will be **Mill Creek** on the right. It's techni-cally in the Dry Creek Valley, but for tour purposes, we're including it with other Westside Road vintners. From there, you'll hit a string of wineries, be-ginning with **Armida,** a short distance beyond Mill Creek and up a hill to your right. Continuing on Westside Road, you'll encounter **Rabbit Ridge** and **Belvedere,** both on the right, then **Hop Kiln** and next-door **Rochioli,** both on the left, **Davis Bynum** on the right and finally, tiny **Porter Creek,** is a short distance up a side road on the right.

As Westside Road blends into River Road, continue west to the baronial wine estate of **Korbel.** Then backtrack on River Road for about three miles—crossing the Russian River—and turn right onto Martinelli Road. It winds through a mix of thick woods and vineyards for a couple of miles until it hits the Gravenstein Highway (Route 116). Turn left and follow it briefly to **Forestville.** About a mile beyond the tiny town, you'll see **Topolos at Russian River** on the right.

Immediately beyond Topolos, also on the right, is **Kozlowski Farms** at 5566 Gravenstein Highway. It's not a winery but a farm foods outlet special-izing in organically produced jams, sauces, chutneys, relishes, homemade pies and other goodies. Dozens of items are available for tasting, and the place has a picnic area. The stuff isn't cheap, but it's excellent. Hours are 9 to 5 daily.

Stay alert from this point, because the route gets complicated. Interesting wineries are scattered along a webwork of farm roads in this flatter part of the valley. About a mile from Kozlowski, watch for Green Valley Road; it's just beyond the larger Guerneville Road intersection. Turn left onto Green Valley and you'll see **Sebastopol Vineyards** immediately on your right. (**NAVIGATIONAL NOTE**: This winery is open only Friday through Sunday, so if you're here on another day, bypass it by making your left turn onto Guerneville Road instead of Green Valley.)

From Sebastopol Vineyards, continue about half a mile on Green Valley Road, turn left onto Vine Hill Road and then right on Guerneville Road. Fol-low Guerneville about a mile to Laguna Road, turn left and drive another mile to **Martini & Prati** on your left, marked by a tall water tower. If it's a weekend, continue a couple of miles on Laguna Road, take a hard right onto Trenton Road and drive a short distance to **Joseph Swan Vineyards** on your right. It's open Saturday and Sunday only. Whether or not you visit Swan, take Laguna Road back to Guerneville Road and turn left (west). Drive about three miles to Olivet Road and go left again. You'll soon see **De Loach Vineyards** and just beyond, **Suncé Winery**; both are on your left.

Still on course? It gets easier from this point. Continue north about a mile on Olivet Road, turn right onto River Road and you'll shortly encounter **Martinelli Winery** on your right. Press west about two miles on River Road, turn left onto Fulton Road at a traffic light and follow it briefly north toward the opulent **Kendall-Jackson Wine Center.**

Mill Creek Vineyards ● T ✕

1401 Westside Rd. (P.O. Box 758), Healdsburg, CA 95448; (707) 431-2121. (www.mcvonline.com) Daily 10 to 5; MC/VISA, AMEX. All current re-leases tasted. A few wine related items; picnic area.

An old fashioned water wheel is a focal point of this small, rustically handsome winery tasting room, which sits among hillside vineyards. The winery is operated by the third and fourth generations of the Kreck family.

ZAPPING ZIN AS AMERICA'S WINE

Should Congress designate Zinfandel as America's wine? Getting federal recognition for Zin is one of the aims of a group called Zinfandel Advocates & Producers, or ZAP for short. Formed in 1992 by Zinfandel makers and enthusiasts, it's a non-profit organization devoted to furthering the stature of what has been called the "Mystery Grape."

And what's the mystery? No one knows exactly where Zinfandel came from, even though it's the most commonly planted premium varietal in California. The roots of virtually all other popular wines have been traced to specific European countries. But not Zin.

A popular belief is that Hungarian entrepreneur Agoston Haraszthy included Zinfandel in grape cuttings he imported from Europe in the 1860s. However, research has defrocked that theory. Author David Darlington devoted an entire book, *Angels' Visits*, to Zinfandel and its origins. He points out that it was being grown as a table grape in New England in the 1830s, long before Haraszthy ever reached America.

What, then, is the source of the Mystery Grape? Like the best of mysteries, this one may never be solved. Researchers find no reference to the word "Zinfandel" in European documents. However, an exact DNA match, Primitivo, was discovered in southern Italy in 1967. Lab tests proved that it is indeed a clonal twin to our Zin. And where did Primitivo come from? Possibly from the Mideast, according to wine historian Charles Sullivan. Italy was a crossroads of early civilizations, and Greeks or Albanians being pushed westard by the Ottoman Turks might have brought the vine. However, with 2,000 grape varieties growing in Italy today, it's impossible to trace most of their origins.

American Zinfandel *has* been traced—to mid-nineteenth century New England nurserymen. Long Island's Robert Prince listed a black "Zinfardel" in his 1850 botanical catalog. Captain F.W. Macondray of Massachusetts may have introduced Zinfandel to California when he traveled to San Francisco in 1848.

Unlike its more genteel European ancestors, Zinfandel has a typically audacious American attitude. It's sassy and lively on the palate, and it's versatile, suitable for everything from light, fruity blush wines to rich, heavy ports. Young plants produce soft Beaujolais-style reds; old vines yield huge, complex wines rivaling venerable Cabernets.

As author Darlington suggests, Zin is a slightly flawed beauty, like Meryl Streep. It's more intriguing and approachable than some paragon of perfection. Those who venerate Cabernet and Chardonnay are considered aficionados. We Zinfandel enthusiasts are more of a cult.

Speaking of cults, ZAP members work tirelessly—between sips of Zin—to further the wine's popularity. The group's major function is a Zinfandel tasting held early each year in San Francisco. It attracts scores of participating wineries and thousands of happy sippers. The *Guinness Book of Records* says it's the world's largest single-varietal wine tasting. If you'd like to join this Zin-loving cult and learn about its annual tasting and other activities, contact: Zinfandel Advocates & Producers, P.O. Box 1487, Rough & Ready, CA 95975; (530) 274-4900. WEB SITE: *www.zinfandel.org*; E-MAIL: *info@zinfandel.org*.

The founders and their children built much of the tasting room and winery by hand, using logs from their property.

Although the water wheel is useful only as an ornament, it has earned landmark status, having appeared several years ago on the cover of *The Californias,* the state's tourist promotion magazine. The simple tasting room—with water wheel attached—looks convincingly rustic, although it was built in the 1970s.

Tasting notes: If you're attracted by the ornamental water wheel, you may stay for the wines, which we found to be very good and fair priced. The Chardonnay was complex and spicy with gentle acid. A Cabernet Sauvignon was soft and ready to drink, with a nice chili pepper nose and herbal flavor. Zinfandel, Merlot and Sauvignon Blanc also appear on their list. Prices: *$$ to $$$$.*

Vintners Choice: "Our Merlot was served in the White House and we've been famous for it ever since," Vera Kreck reported proudly. "Our Sauvignon Blanc also has done very well, winning several gold medals and a best of show award, and our Gewürztraminer was the top winner at a recent California State Fair judging."

Armida Winery ● T ST GTA ✕

2201 Westside Rd., Healdsburg, CA 95448-9342; (707) 433-2222. (www.armida.com) Daily 11 to 5; MC/VISA. Most varieties tasted. Good giftware selection; picnic deck.

Three eye-catching geodesic domes on the wooded brow of a hill mark this winery. It was founded in 1989 by Bob Armida, an executive with E.F Hutton. After purchasing a defunct winery and sprucing up those curious geodesic domes, he and his wife Rita opened their tasting room in 1994. They had purchased some Russian River vineyards ten years earlier, with an eye on early retirement and a second career as vintners. Going back further, Bob had spent summers in this area with his Italian grandparents, who settled here in 1906.

A focal point of the winery's nicely landscaped grounds is a duck pond with a picnic deck at its edge, which has a great view of the pool, with vineyards and mountains beyond. Even the parking lot has this nice view, as does the attractive tasting room—through a large picture window behind the tasting counter.

Tasting notes: Since all wines are estate bottled, the Armidas can control their product from start to finish. They have won an impressive array of awards. The Chardonnays we tasted were excellent—full-mouthed, nutty and lush. A Pinot Noir was light and yet full flavored with a hint of tannin, and a Merlot was richly mellow, with good berry flavor. The Cabernet was excellent with lots of berries and a chili pepper accent. Prices: *$$$ to $$$$.*

Vintners choice: "My favorite wine?" Bob grins. "It depends on what I'm eating. Chardonnay is our most popular."

Rabbit Ridge Winery & Vineyards ● T$ ✕

3291 Westside Rd., Healdsburg, CA 95448; (707) 431-7128. (www.rabbitridgewinery.com) Daily 11 to 5; MC/VISA. Most varieties tasted for a small fee, which is applied toward wine purchase. A few wine logo items; picnic area.

There was no ridge called Rabbit when Eric Russell established his winery and vineyards here. "Rabbit" was and possibly still is his nickname. As a track star at San Jose State University, he competed barefoot and—according to his friends—ran like a rabbit. His pace is considerably slower now, as he crafts wines in a simple barn-style winery. He began this operation in 1989 and opened a tasting room ten years later.

Fused into the main winery building, the curved barnboard tasting room offers windowed views of vineyards and wooded hills. Inside, it's counterbalanced by a curved tasting counter set on glass bricks. A few picnic tables linger outside.

Tasting notes: Russell's list—mostly red—offers an interesting mix of typical French varietals, several Italian varieties and numerous versions of Zinfandel. A dozen of the more than thirty wines on his list generally are open for tasting. Our favorites were an herbal Chardonnay, a lush and smooth Sangiovese and a typically spicy Zinfandel from Amador County. Others on the list are Viognier, Pinot Noir, Barbera, Merlot, Syrah and Cabernet Sauvignon. Many of the varietals are moderately priced, with costs going higher for a few reserves: *$ to $$$$.*

Belvedere Winery • T ✕ 📷

4035 Westside Rd., Healdsburg, CA 95448; (800) 433-8296 or (707) 433-8236. (www.belvederewinery.com) Daily 10 to 4:30; MC/VISA. Most varieties available for tasting (limit of four samples). Nice selection of wine related gift items and works by local artists; picnic deck adjacent to the tasting room.

Belvedere is a comely redwood-sided winery in a pleasing locale amongst hillside vineyards. A short drive takes you to this neat complex, carefully set into the sloping landscape and shaded by young redwoods. Honeysuckle droops from a porch overhanging the tasting room. Lawns and blooming flowers on series of terraces give the place a park-like quality. It is in fact a virtual botanical garden.

Winery founder Peter Friedman selects grapes from a variety of county vineyards to produce his reserve wines, which are sometimes issued with thematic labels. For instance, proceeds from his "Gifts of the Land Series," bearing wildlife labels done by noted artist Rod Frederick, went to conservation causes. Despite its prim, compact look, this is not a small operation. Belvedere produces about half a million cases a year.

Tasting notes: The wines on Belvedere's brief list have won more than their share of medals. They include a lush Alexander Valley Chardonnay, a lighter fruity Sonoma County Chardonnay, an excellent Sonoma County Merlot, plus big-flavored Dry Creek Valley Zinfandel and Cabernet Sauvignon. The winery also issues reserve versions of Chardonnay, Merlot and Cabernet. Prices: *$$ to $$$$.*

Hop Kiln Winery • T ST ✕

6050 Westside Rd., Healdsburg, CA 95448; (707) 433-6491. Daily 10 to 5; MC/VISA, AMEX. Most varieties tasted. Some wine related gift items; art exhibits. Picnic tables under sheltering fig tree, others near a pond.

After visiting a pretend water wheel, we go to a real hop kiln—at least a former one. Dr. L. Martin Griffin succeeded in preserving the esthetics of a century-old hop dryer when he converted it into a winery in the 1970s. Some of the original equipment is intact and the tasting room is fashioned of aged wood, in keeping with the antiquity of the place. Adorned with the works of local artists, it occupies a mezzanine above the winery. A tour thus consists of walking to a railing and peering down at stainless steel vats and wooden barrels. The triple towered Hop Kiln is a registered historical landmark. The grounds are casual, pleasant and bucolic, with trellised gates, informal landscaping and a pond where waterfowl like to hang out.

Tasting notes: The list is surprisingly long for a winery that issues only 10,000 cases a year, but Marty Griffin likes to work with small lots. The Zinfandel was full, complex and acidic, yet comfortably soft, one of the better produced in this region. Others on the list are white Zinfandel, Chardonnay, Johannisberg Riesling, a fruity white called A Thousand Flowers, Cabernet Sauvignon and a good jug red. Prices are moderate: *$$ to $$$$.*

Vintners Choice: "Zinfandel and Marty Griffin's Big Red," said a winery spokesperson. "Our wines are known for being robust and fruity."

Rochioli Vineyard and Winery • T ⤬

6192 Westside Rd., Healdsburg, CA 95448; (707) 433-2305. (www.rochioliwinery.com) Daily 10 to 5 February-November and 11 to 4 December-January; MC/VISA, AMEX. Shaded picnic area overlooking the vineyards.

Next door to Hop Kiln, Rochioli has the look of comfortable rural prosperity. Passing through a stone gate, you enter a tidy farm complex shaded by ancient trees and accented with landscaped grounds. Picnic tables occupy a vineyard-view patio. A trim little tasting room overlooking the vines is brightened by art and photo exhibits. The Rochioli family has been producing wine in northern Sonoma County since the end of Prohibition, planting some of the area's first varietals. The present winery, producing about 9,000 case a year, was established in 1982 to craft small lots of wines by merging traditional methods with modern technology.

Tasting notes: The Rochioli list is brief and excellent, featuring Sauvignon Blanc, Chardonnay, Pinot Noir and Zinfandel, all full-flavored and exhibiting fine varietal character. Prices: *$$ to $$$$.*

Vintners choice: "We're known for our Chardonnay and Pinot Noir," said Theresa Rochioli.

Davis Bynum Winery • T ⤬

8075 Westside Rd., Healdsburg, CA 95448; (800) 826-1073 or (707) 433-5852. (www.davisbynum.com) Daily 10 to 5; MC/VISA. Most varieties tasted free; small fee for some limited release wines. A few wine related gift items; picnic patio beside winery.

Sitting just above a prim farm complex, the straightforward masonry block structures of the Davis Bynum Winery are dressed in attractive landscaping. Young redwoods shade picnic tables. The tasting room, off the main winery, is small, neat and inviting; its walls are adorned with local artworks. On cool days, a fire crackles in a Franklin stove. Former newspaperman Davis Bynum started his winery in 1965 in a warehouse and store front in Albany, a town near Oakland and far from the nearest serious grapevine. He moved to this former hop ranch in 1973. Wine grapes are drawn from several premium vineyard areas.

Tasting notes: Bynum's list is weighted toward reds with just a pair of pale wines—a fruity Fumé Blanc and a lush, full-flavored Chardonnay. Among the reds, all full-bodied, are Pinot Noir, Zinfandel, Merlot and a couple of Cabernets, plus a Westside Road Meritage. Prices: *$$ to $$$$.*

Porter Creek Vineyards • T

8735 Westside Rd., Healdsburg, CA 95448; (707) 433-6321. Daily 10:30 to 4:30 in summer, weekends only the rest of the year; MC/VISA. Selected wines tasted.

You've heard of home winemakers operating out of their garage. Soft-spoken George R. Davis is a *professional* winemaker doing that. Actually, only the tasting room is garaged, and it's a rustic classic: a plank laid over wine barrels. The small winery is up a dusty lane in Porter Creek Valley, just beyond a 1920s-style cottage. The setting hearkens back to the wine country's earlier days, when one stopped by the local vintner with an empty jar to have it filled. George's operation is hardly archaic, however, and his wines have won several awards. He's been doing business here since 1978, drawing grapes mostly from his hillside vineyards of Pinot Noir and Chardonnay.

Tasting notes: From George's small list, we discovered an excellent Chardonnay, full and complex, crisp and perfectly balanced; a light yet full-flavored Estate Pinot Noir and a lush, berry-like Hillside Pinot. A tasty Pinot Blanc is quite inexpensive. Prices: *$ to $$$.*

Vintners choice: "Pinot Noir from our own hillside vines produces a flavorful, nicely concentrated wine," said George.

Korbel Champagne Cellars ● T GT 🏠

13250 River Rd., Guerneville, CA 95446; (707) 824-7000. (www.korbel.com) Daily 9 to 5; MC/VISA. Most varieties except brandy tasted. Extensive gift selection, deli and market; microbrewery. Winery tours daily at various times; garden tours at 11, 1 and 4.

This isn't just a winery; it's an institution. From a visitor standpoint, it's one of the most interesting such institutions in California. Started in 1882, it evolved into a baronial estate with great stone, vine-covered buildings, a tower right out of medieval Germany and old style European gardens. The setting is equally impressive, in a narrowing of the Russian River Valley, rimmed by wooded hills on one side and a vineyard tilting toward the redwood-bordered river on the other.

The setting so resembles central Europe that television's old *Combat* series was filmed here for two years. During the shooting, the obliging special effects people blew up old redwood stumps that had been cluttering up the vineyards for decades.

The Korbel tour is one of the most comprehensive in the business. Guests gather at a tiny railway station that once served the valley, visit a formal garden, then stroll into the ancient, wonderfully musty stone cellar. There, a well-done mini-museum recalls the Korbel story with old photos, documents and artifacts. Visitors move from the museum to a theater for a nicely photographed slide show, then they're led through the champagne cellars where the complex process is explained. Finally, eager to sample what they've been studying, they're escorted to the plush, carpeted hospitality center for a tasting conducted by their guide. One learns a remarkable statistic on this tour: Korbel produces seventy percent of all the *méthode champenoise* made in this country—more than one million cases annually.

Assorted Korbels operated the winery until 1954, when it was purchased by the Heck family, with Gary B. Heck presently at the helm.

Tasting notes: The sparkling wines, ranging from semi-dry to dry, are clean, crisp and good buys. Although it has been making mostly sparkling wine and brandy for more than a century, the firm also produces tasty Chardonnay and Cabernet Sauvignon. *$$ to $$$.* A recent addition is a microbrewery, whose brews can be sampled.

Topolos at Russian River Vineyard • T GTA 🛍

5700 Gravenstein Highway N., Forestville, CA 95436; (800) TOPOLOS or (707) 887-1575. (www.topolos.com) Daily 11 to 5:30; major credit cards. Most varieties tasted. Good giftware selection; guided tours by appointment. Restaurant; see listing under "Wine country dining" below.

This pleasantly rural winery complex looks like it was designed by 1960s flower children. The tasting room is small and cozy, fashioned of old wood. Weather-darkened buildings hold assorted winemaking gear. A nearby garden is planted with native flowers and grasses. Above all this, the soft clink of glassware announces the presence of a restaurant, which features a Greek-accented menu.

This earthy operation—started in 1963—is the work of Michael, Jerry and Christine Topolos. They produce tasty wines in small, carefully nurtured lots. Not surprisingly, the grape picking, winemaking and even labeling are done by hand. They use, whenever possible, pesticide-free grapes.

Tasting notes: This is serious Zin country. From this bucolic setting emerge some excellent wine buys—particularly if you like big, assertive Zinfandels. You'll generally find four or five on the tasting list, with full, berry-like and peppery flavors. Also on the list is a soft and herbal Sauvignon Blanc and a full-flavored Alicante Bouschet. Rarely bottled in California, Alicante is a French cross breed of Grenache, Tenturier du Cher and Aramond grapes, producing an inky dark, full-bodied red. Prices: *$ to $$$.*

Vintners choice: "Our Zinfandel from old vines, Bat Flight White and Zinfandel Port," reports a voice from Topolos.

Sebastopol Vineyards • T ✗

8757 Green Valley Rd., Sebastopol, CA 95472; (707) 829-WINE. (www.sebastopolvineyards.com) Friday-Sunday 11 to 4. Most varieties tasted; picnic area.

This small winery and tasting room occupy Spanish style structures in an old-fashioned and prosperous farm complex. It was established in 1995 by Joe and Tracy Dutton, whose farming families go back five generations in this area. The 900-acre Dutton Ranch was founded in 1963 by Warren and Gail Dutton, who produce grapes, apples and assorted other produce. Their son Joe continues as the ranch's vineyard manager while running the winery with his wife Tracy. She is the daughter of Paul Every and Carol Kozlowski Every, co-owners of Kozlowski Farms.

Tasting notes: From their own Dutton Ranch vineyards, the family produces Estate Chardonnay, Pinot Noir and Syrah. Prices: *$$ to $$$.*

Martini & Prati Winery • T ✗ 🛍

2191 Laguna Rd., Santa Rosa, CA 95401; (707) 823-2404 or (707) 829-6150. (www.martiniprati.com) Daily 11 to 4; MC/VISA. Four samples offered from a list of several current releases. Giftwares and specialty foods. Picnic area near the tasting room.

Amidst operations ranging from upscale to deliberately funky, we've found an old fashion winery making old fashioned wines. And it has been doing so for a century. Founded in 1902, Martini and Prati is one of the oldest wineries in Sonoma County. A water tower crowns this busy complex, which looks more like an industrialized farmyard than a winery, with its cluster of pitched-roof warehouses and scatter of equipment. It's obviously been "added-to" as the winery grew since its founding.

Members of the Martini and Prati families have run the place since 1951, although assorted Martinis go back to 1902. This is a big operation, producing two million gallons of wine sold in bulk, plus 15,000 or so cases for Martini & Prati labels. Did we say this place was old fashioned? If you bring your own container, you can get wine directly from a tank.

Tasting notes: The Martinis and Pratis have trimmed their list somewhat in recent years, focusing on a few traditional varietals. Their wines tend to be light and dry in typical Italian fashion. Offerings when we last visited were Sauvignon Blanc, Vino Grigio, Chardonnay and Colombard among the whites. Reds were Pinot Noir, Merlot, Zinfandel, and a blend called Tesoro Di Elmo, in honor of founder Elmo Prati. Also available are a really inexpensive Vino Rosso jug wine and sweet Muscat. Prices are among the least expensive in Sonoma County: *$ to $$$.*

Joseph Swan Vineyards • T

2916 Laguna Rd. (at Trenton Road), Forestville, CA 95436; (707) 573-3747. Weekends 11 to 4:30; closed during January. Most varieties tasted.

This small, intimate facility founded in 1969 by the late veteran winemaker Joseph Swan occupies a pleasantly scruffy metal sided barn, shaded by gnarled oaks. The simple tasting room shares space with barrels and vats in the winery. A single picnic table occupies a nearby lawn.

Tasting notes: The winery produces small lots of Chardonnay, Cabernet Sauvignon, Pinot Noir and Zinfandel. Prices: *$$ to $$$.*

De Loach Vineyards • T GT ✕

1791 Olivet Rd., Santa Rosa, CA 95401; (707) 526-9111. (www.deloach-vineyards.com) Daily 10 to 4:30; major credit cards. Most current releases tasted. Lawn picnic area; guided tours conducted weekdays at 2 and weekends at 11 and 2.

A Japanese courtyard marks the entry to this modern redwood ranch-style winery, offering an interesting architectural mix. Art decorates the walls of the tasting room and glossy ceramic tile covers the floor and tasting bar. After sipping, visitors can adjourn to a lawn picnic area near the vineyards and—something unique for wineries—pitch a game of horseshoes. Located on a plain between the Russian River Valley and Santa Rosa, the winery was established by the De Loach family in 1975. Many of its varietal wines are estate bottled.

Tasting notes: The rather long De Loach list focuses mostly on reds, yet we felt that whites were some of their best wines. The Chardonnay was fruity and well balanced and the Fumé Blanc soft and rich. Of the reds, the Zinfandel was full-flavored and spicy and the Cabernet Sauvignon was hearty and lush with hints of wood. We even liked the surprisingly assertive white Zinfandel. French Colombard, Gewürztraminer, Pinot Noir, Merlot, Sangiovese, Pinot Gris, Petite Sirah and Port complete the list. Prices: *$ to $$$$.*

Vintners choice: "We're especially proud of our Chardonnays and Zinfandels," says a winery voice.

Suncé Winery • T ✕

1839 Olivet Rd., Santa Rosa, A 95401; (707) 526-9463. (www.suncewinery.com) Daily 10 to 5; major credit cards. Most varieties tasted. A few wine logo items.

The radiant sun on the label, the equally warm smile on the face of pretty co-owner Janae Franicevic and the neat yellow and white buildings tell you that this is a cheerful, upbeat place. Janae and winemaker husband Frané bought a small stock farm in late 1998 and have fashioned it into an inviting little winery, producing about 2,000 cases a year. The stock barn has become the winery and the tasting room is housed in a former storage shed. No longer shed-like, it has been renovated and made remarkably cheerful with a skylight, tile tasting counter and light walls adorned with local art. The family lives in a matching yellow and white cottage up front.

Suncé, which means "sun" in Croatian, is a three-person operation: Frané makes the wine, Janae handles the business and marketing end and her longtime friend Kimberly Harbaugh is tasting room and sales manager. A native of Croatia, Frané is a third-generation vintner. His father grew grapes and his grandfather had a small winery in the old country. Frané made wine in America for ten years before opening his own winery. Appropriately he met Janae in another winery's tasting room.

Tasting notes: Frané's wines are excellent—straightforward and with lots of fruit. Although production is small, he has a remarkably long list of wines, both white and red. Our favorite whites were a wonderfully crisp and fruity Sauvignon Blanc with a touch of Muscat, and a spicy North Coast *Mistral*, which is a field blend of Chenin Blanc and Chardonnay. (Both vines grow in the same field and they're picked and blended together.) Of the reds, a Gamay-style wine called Valdiguie was refreshingly light yet with lots of fruit; a Russian River Old Vine Zinfandel was excellent, with lots of berries and spice; the Cabernet Sauvignon had a great chili pepper taste with soft tannins; and a Syrah displayed the nice spice of a Zin and the body of a Cab. Prices: *$$ to $$$$*.

Vintner's Choice: Frané's current favorites are his Merlot and Mariage, a blend of Zinfandel and Valdiguie. As for Janae: "It changes with my moods. Right now I'm into Cabernet."

Martinelli Winery • T ✗ 🏠
3360 River Rd., Windsor, CA 95492; (800) 346-1627 or (707) 525-0570. Daily 10 to 5; MC/VISA. Most varieties tasted. Extensive gift and specialty foods selection and art gallery; picnic area.

This combined winery and farm products market is housed in a cheerful red century-old hop barn. For decades, this was the Martinelli Apple Barn, specializing in apples and farm fresh produce. A stable of wines was added a few years ago. The tasting counter is surrounded by a virtual country store of giftwares, wine logo items, specialty clothing and foods, with an emphasis on Sonoma County products, including fresh produce. Artwork—most of it for sale—adorns the weathered walls. An inviting picnic arbor is out front.

Tasting notes: Martinelli wines are unfined and unfiltered, exhibiting strong, complex character. The list includes a crisp Sauvignon Blanc, several versions of lush and fruity Chardonnay, spicy Gewürztraminers in three versions, and an herbal and very berry Pinot Noir. For dessert, sip a rich wine with a great name: Jackass Hill Muscat Alexandria. Prices: *$$$ to $$$$*.

Kendall-Jackson Wine Center • T$ ✗ 🏠
5007 Fulton Rd., Fulton, CA 95439; (707) 433-7102. (www.kj.com) Daily 10 to 5; major credit cards. Selected wines tasted for a modest fee, which includes the glass. Extensive giftware selection and attractive picnic area.

This opulent French style estate, which begs to be nestled along a meandering stream in Bordeaux instead of Highway 101, once was the home of Château De Baun, which featured wines from the Symphony grape. Symphony didn't get enough sympathy from wine drinkers, so it was sold in 1996 to the expanding Kendall-Jackson empire.

Inside, sheltered from the freeway noise, the tasting room oozes old world ambiance of brass chandeliers, etched glass and carefully-select artworks. We're tempted to call this a tasting *salon*, with its curved brass-trimmed counter and other posh touches. Here, the many different wines of the Kendall-Jackson combine may be sampled. K-J has retained De Baun's almost excessively opulent interior, while taking up some of this great open space with a choice selection of giftwares and wine logo items. The grounds, appropriate to a château, has formal gardens, a fountain and gazebo. Particularly interesting is the California Viticultural Exhibit, a demonstration vineyard featuring thirty-two grape varietals and sixteen trellis systems. It was created by Santa Rosa Junior College and Kendall-Jackson.

Tasting notes: See the Kendall-Jackson Tasting Room listing above on page 56.

THE BEST OF THE BUNCH

The best wine buys ● Canyon Road Cellars in Alexander Valley; Pedroncelli Winery in Dry Creek Valley; Simi Winery and Foppiano Wine Company in Healdsburg; Alexander Valley Vineyards in the Alexander Valley; Rabbit Ridge, Topolos and Martini & Prati in the Russian River Valley.

The most attractive wineries ● Simi Winery and J Wine Company near Healdsburg; Ferrari-Carano Winery and Lambert Bridge Vineyards in Dry Creek Valley; Château Souverain, White Oak Winery and Hanna Winery in Alexander Valley; Hop Kiln Winery, Korbel Champagne Cellars and De Loach Vineyards, all in the Russian River Valley.

The most interesting tasting rooms ● Clos du Bois, White Oak Winery, Alexander Valley Vineyards and Field Stone Winery in the Alexander Valley; Ferrari-Carano Winery and Fritz Winery in Dry Creek Valley; Seghesio and J Wine Company in the Healdsburg area; Mill Creek Vineyards, Hop Kiln Winery, Korbel Champagne Cellars and the Kendall-Jackson Wine Center in the Russian River Valley.

The funkiest tasting rooms ● Johnson's Alexander Valley Winery in the Alexander Valley; Ridge-Sonoma Vineyards in Dry Creek Valley, and Porter Creek Vineyards and Topolos in the Russian River Valley.

The best gift shops ● Canyon Road Cellars in Alexander Valley; Kendall-Jackson and Windsor tasting rooms in Healdsburg; Ferrari-Carano Winery and Lake Sonoma Winery in Dry Creek Valley; Korbel and Kendall-Jackson Wine Center in the Russian River Valley.

The best picnic areas ● Field Stone Winery in Alexander Valley; Simi Winery, Rodney Strong Vineyards and Piper Sonoma Cellars in the Healdsburg area; Lake Sonoma Winery and Lambert Bridge Vineyards in Dry Creek Valley; Armida Winery, Hop Kiln Winery and Korbel Champagne Cellars in the Russian River Valley.

The best tour ● Korbel Champagne Cellars in the Russian River Valley.

Wine country maps and events

Winery maps and guides • Free **Russian River Wine Road** map of wineries, restaurants and lodgings, available throughout the area, or contact Russian River Wine Road, P.O. Box 46, Healdsburg, CA 95448; (800) 723-6336 or (707) 433-6782. *(www.wineroad.com)*

Wineland events • Sonoma County Wine & Visitors Center sponsors a series of culinary and wine events throughout the year; call (707) 586-3795 or write to 5000 Roberts Lake Rd., Rohnert Park, CA 94928. OTHER EVENTS: Winter Wineland, with two days of tasting and tours in mid-January, (800) 723-6336; barrel tasting at more than seventy participating wineries in early March, (800) 723-6336; A Wine & Food Affair in November, (800) 723-6336; Sonoma County Showcase and Wine Auction in July, (707) 586-3795; and Sonoma County Harvest Fair in October, (707) 545-4203.

BEYOND THE VINEYARDS

Lake Sonoma, created by the construction of Warm Springs Dam in the mid-1980s, out-draws the wineries. Hundreds of thousands of the beer and boating set flock here each summer. Facilities include a visitor center, fish hatchery, boat launches, marina, hiking trails, picnicking and camping.

In Healdsburg, you can visit the **Healdsburg Historical Museum** in the 1911 Andrew Carnegie Library building at 221 Matheson Street. Books and documents relating to the California wine industry and early-day wine artifacts are featured in the **Sonoma County Wine Library Collection** in the Healdsburg library at 139 Piper Street; (707) 433-3772.

Earlier in this century, the lower **Russian River Valley** was home to posh and glitzy riverside resorts. At lantern-lit dance pavilions, revelers swayed under the stars to the swinging sounds of Harry James and Jimmy Dorsey. Those days are gone, but many resorts survive in a scaled down and sometimes funky fashion. Canoeing and swimming are popular; be advised that you're likely to encounter a nudie beach or two.

A winding drive north from Guerneville on Armstrong Woods Road takes you to the hushed redwood groves of **Armstrong Redwoods State Reserve** and **Austin Creek State Recreation Area**, with hiking, picnicking and such. If you head downstream on State Highway 116, you can explore the stunning sea stack vistas of the **Sonoma Coast**. Prowl about New England-style **Jenner**, then go south to **Bodega** and **Bodega Bay**, forever marked as the bucolic setting for Alfred Hitchcock's *The Birds*. Much of the ocean front is part of **Sonoma Coast State Beach** with hiking, picnicking, camping, swimming (on rare warm days) and beach-bundling.

If you head north from Jenner, your route will twist along the splendid coastline to **Fort Ross State Historic Park,** a faithful reconstruction of an early Russian fortress and fur trading post. Beyond is **Salt Point State Park,** a classic ecological wedge of coastal environment, stair-stepping from rough-hewn surf to evergreen highlands. **Kruse Rhododendron State Reserve** with its stunning spring blooms is just above that.

Northern Sonoma County attractions

The Healdsburg Museum • *221 Matheson Street, Healdsburg; (707) 431-3325. Tuesday-Sunday noon to 5; free admission.* □ Local history exhibits in a classic Carnegie library building.

Sonoma County Wine Library Collection ● *City Library, 139 Piper St., Healdsburg; (707) 433-3772.* □ Early winery artifacts and extensive collection of wine oriented books and documents; hours vary.

WINE COUNTRY DINING

PRICE KEY: Dinner entrée with soup or salad, without drinks or dessert for under $10 = $; $10 to $14 = $$; $15 to $25 = $$$; over $25 = $$$$.

Bear Republic Brewing Company ● ☆☆ $ to $$

□ *345 Healdsburg Ave., Healdsburg; 433-2337. Italian; full bar service. Lunch through late evening daily. MC/VISA.* □ Stylish contemporary brewpub in the rear of the Swenson Building shopping complex. Brewpub fare, plus several pastas, garlic chicken and British favorites such as Cornish pub pie and Ploughman's supper. The look is typical microbrewery, with brewing kettles and open beam ceilings.

Bistro Ralph ● ☆☆☆ $$$ to $$$$

□ *109 Plaza St., Healdsburg; (707) 433-1380. Contemporary American; full bar service. Lunch weekdays and dinner nightly. MC/VISA.* □ Attractive storefront restaurant on Healdsburg Plaza, featuring regional American fare such as roast duck breast, beef filet and salmon. Pleasing décor with exposed heating ducts, pressed tin ceilings and drop lamps over white nappery tables.

Catelli's The Rex ● ☆☆☆ $$ to $$$

□ *241 Healdsburg Ave., Healdsburg; (707) 433-6000. Italian-American; full bar service. Lunch weekdays and dinner nightly. MC/VISA.* □ Longtime Geyserville favorite recently moved to fancier digs in Healdsburg, just south of the plaza. The menu, heavily Italian, is busy with pastas, parmigiana, steaks, seafoods and chops.

Château Souverain Café ● ☆☆☆ $$$$

□ *400 Souverain Rd. (Highway 101 at Independence Lane), Geyserville; (707) 433-3141. (www.chateausouverain.com) "Wine country cuisine"; wine and beer. Lunch daily and dinner Friday-Sunday. Reservations recommended. MC/VISA, AMEX.* □ Elegant French bistro style café with a dining room and patio, offering impressive views of the Alexander Valley. The café is done in pink and beige, accented by chandeliers and embroidered panels.

El Farolito Mexican Restaurant ● ☆☆ $ to $$

□ *128 Plaza St., Healdsburg; (707) 433-2807. Mexican; wine, beer and margaritas. Lunch through dinner daily. Major credit cards.* □ Simply attired Latino café near the plaza with typical smashed beans and rice fare. Sauces are homemade and chili rellenos are a specialty.

Healdsburg Coffee Company ● ☆ $ to $$

□ *312 Center St., Healdsburg; (707) 431-7941. American; light fare; wine and beer. Breakfast through late afternoon daily. MC/VISA.* □ A cheerful place offering soup, salad, sandwiches, quiche, espresso and local wine; specialty coffees and thirty varieties of coffee beans. On Healdsburg Plaza, with homey oak-antique décor.

John Ash & Co. ● ☆☆☆☆ $$$

□ *4330 Barnes Road (River Road), Santa Rosa; (707) 527-7687. "Regional wine country cuisine"; full bar service. Lunch and dinner daily except Monday. MC/VISA.* □ Award-winning restaurant with creative fare assembled by chef-owner John Ash, with a focus on local ingredients. Extensive wine list. Located on the edge of the northern Sonoma wine country with a vineyard view, near River Road and U.S. 101.

Oakville Grocery Co. • ☆☆ $ to $$

124 Matheson St., Healdsburg, CA 95448; (707) 433-3200. (www.oakvillegrocery.com) International deli; wine and beer. Late morning to early evening. MC/VISA. ☐ Not a restaurant, this is a combined deli, specialty foods store and wine shop with an extensive selection of each. Build lunch or a snack at the deli and adjourn to a patio dining area out front.

Russian River Vineyards Restaurant • ☆☆ $$$

☐ *Topolos Winery at 5700 Gravenstein Highway N., Forestville; (707) 887-1562. Continental with a Greek tilt; wine only. Lunch and dinner daily with Sunday brunch. Major credit cards.* ☐ Cheerful place with eclectic décor and menu, perched atop the Topolos Winery tasting room. Fare includes Mediterranean dishes such as *Souvlaki* (spicy lamb brochette), prawns Santorini and essential American New York peppercorn steak. Patio dining.

WINELAND LODGINGS
**PRICE KEY: A two-person room for $35 or less = $; $36 to $50 = $$;
$51 to $75 = $$$; $76 to $100 = $$$$; more than $100 = $$$$$.**

The list below represents lodgings near northern Sonoma County's vinelands. There's a considerably larger selection of motels, bed and breakfast inns and a few hotels in Santa Rosa. Small resorts line the Russian River and more are in communities along the Sonoma Coast. For information on these places, contact chambers of commerce listed at the end of this chapter.

Best Western Dry Creek Inn • ☆☆ $$$ to $$$$$

☐ ☐ *198 Dry Creek Rd. (at U.S. 101), Healdsburg, CA 95448; (800) 222-5784 or (707) 433-0300. Major credit cards.* ☐ A 102-room motel with TV movies, room phones and in-room coffee service. Pool, spa and fitness room; gift bottle of wine and free continental breakfast. Near Lake Sonoma and the Russian River.

Fairview Motel • ☆ $$ to $$$

☐ *74 Healdsburg Ave. (at U.S. 101), Healdsburg, CA 95448; (707) 433-5548. Major credit cards.* ☐ Eighteen rooms with TV movies and phones; pool, spa and playground.

Geyserville Inn • ☆☆☆ $$$$ to $$$$$

☐ *21714 Geyserville Ave., Geyserville, CA 95441; (877) 857-4343 or (707) 857-4343. (www.geyservilleinn.com) Major credit cards.* ☐ Attractive 38-room inn near Canyon Road, convenient to northern Sonoma wineries. Some rooms with fireplaces, balconies or patios; pool and spa. All non-smoking.

Hotel La Rose • ☆☆ $$$

☐ *308 Wilson St. (Highway 101 downtown exit), Santa Rosa, CA 95401; (800) 527-6738. Major credit cards.* ☐ National historic landmark hotel built in 1907; renovated in 1999 and featuring American turn-of-the-last-century décor. Forty-nine individually decorated rooms in the hotel and carriage house. On the northern edge of Santa Rosa in historic Railroad Square; not far from the wine country. **Joseph's Restaurant & Bar** serves lunch Tuesday-Friday and dinner nightly. French-continental fare; full bar service.

Huckleberry Springs • ☆☆☆ $$$$$

☐ *8105 Old Beedle Rd. (end of Tyrone Road; P.O. Box 400), Monte Rio, CA 95462; (800) 822-2683 or (707) 865-2683. Prices include full breakfast. Four units with private baths. MC/VISA, DISC.* □ Modern, luxurious country lodge on fifty-six acres. Contemporary furnishings in cottages; old style lodge with antiques, folk art and graphics collection. Landscaped Japanese-style spa and private massage cottage. **Dinners** offered Wednesday and Saturday nights.

Bed & breakfast inns

Applewood ● ☆☆☆☆ $$$$$

□ *13555 Highway 116 (Mayes Canyon Road), Guerneville, CA 95446; (707) 869-9093. Sixteen units, all with TV, room phones and private baths; full breakfast. major credit cards.* □ Opulent Mission revival mansion surrounded by lush landscaping, built in 1922 during the salad days of Russian River resorts. Furnished with European and American antiques and original artwork. Several rooms have fireplaces and spa tubs or showers for two. Pool, spa, formal gardens. **Restaurant** offers wine country dinners for guests and the general public.

Belle de Jour Inn ● ☆☆☆ $$$$$

□ *16276 Healdsburg Ave. (opposite Simi Winery), Healdsburg, CA 95448; (707) 431-9777. (www.belledejourinn.com) MC/VISA.* □ Posh accommodations in a ranch style complex near downtown Healdsburg. Antique and contemporary furnishings; fireplaces, spas and refrigerators in rooms. Breakfast served in the dining room of an 1869 ranch home.

Camellia Inn ● ☆☆ $$$$ to $$$$

□ *211 North St., Healdsburg, CA 95448; (800) 727-8182 or (707) 433-8182. (www.camelliainn.com) Nine rooms, seven with private baths; breakfast buffet. MC/VISA, DISC.* □ Nicely appointed rooms in an 1869 Italianate Victorian two blocks from Healdsburg Plaza. Furnished with Victorian and American antiques. Spa tubs and gas fireplaces in some rooms. Pool open in summer; landscaped gardens.

Grape Leaf Inn ● ☆☆☆ $$$$ to $$$$$

□ *539 Johnson St. (Grant Street), Healdsburg, CA 95448; (707) 433-8140. (www.grapeleaf.com) Seven rooms with private baths; full breakfast. MC/VISA.* □ Beautifully restored 1900 Queen Anne Victorian. Nicely appointed rooms with whirlpool tubs and showers for two, skylight roofs, air conditioning. Wraparound porch and landscaped, tree-shaded yard. Within walking distance of restaurants and shops.

Healdsburg Inn on the Plaza ● ☆☆☆ $$$$$

□ *110 Matheson St. (Healdsburg Avenue), Healdsburg, CA 95448; (707) 433-6991. (www.healdsburginn.com) Ten rooms, all with TV and VCRs, phones and private baths; full breakfast; free champagne brunch on weekends. MC/VISA.* □ Stylish old inn with Victorian furnishings and original art works. Bright, cheerful rooms, all with fireplaces and balconies; some overlooking Healdsburg Plaza. Solarium and roof garden, gift shop and gallery with works of California artists.

Hope-Bosworth & Hope-Merrill houses ● ☆☆☆ $$$$$

□ *21238 and 21253 Geyserville Ave. (P.O. Box 42), Geyserville, CA 95441; (707) 857-3356. Twelve rooms with private baths; full breakfast. MC/VISA.* □ Two elegant Victorians across the street from one another near downtown Geyserville. The early American 1904 Hope-Bosworth and Victorian-style Hope-Merrill house are furnished with antiques and silk-screened wallpapers. Some rooms with fireplaces and spas. Library, Victorian gardens, heated pool and vineyard gazebo.

Madrona Manor Wine Country Inn ● ☆☆☆☆ $$$$$

☐ *1001 Westside Rd. (P.O. Box 818), Healdsburg, CA 95448; (707) 433-4231. Twenty-two rooms and suites with private baths, phones and data ports; full breakfast. Major credit cards.* ☐ Beautifully restored 1881 Victorian mansion in a complex that also includes a carriage house, "Schoolhouse Suites" and garden cottage. Furnished with antiques; fireplaces in many units. Located on eight wooded, landscaped acres with a heated summer pool. Elegantly styled **Madrona Manor Restaurant** serves dinner and Sunday brunch.

Ridenhour Ranch House Inn ● ☆☆ $$$$$

☐ *12850 River Rd. (next to Korbel), Guerneville, CA 95446; (707) 887-1033. Eight rooms with private baths, full breakfast. MC/VISA, AMEX.* ☐ Ranch style redwood home furnished with American and English antiques and Oriental rugs. Six rooms in ranch house and two cottages; some units with TV. Hot tubs, gardens and meadows on more than two acres; near wineries and redwood groves.

Santa Nella House ● ☆☆ $$$$$

☐ *12130 Highway 116 (at Odd Fellows Park Road), Guerneville, CA 95446; (707) 869-9488. Four rooms with private baths; full breakfast. MC/VISA.* ☐ An attractively refurbished Victorian with a wrap-around veranda on two acres in a redwood grove. Rooms furnished with English antiques, fireplaces and fresh-cut flowers. Near Korbel Winery, Russian River beaches and Armstrong Redwood Grove.

Vintners Inn ● ☆☆☆☆ $$$$$

☐ *4350 Barnes Rd., Santa Rosa, CA 95403; (800) 421-2584 or (707) 575-7350. Forty-four rooms with private baths; full breakfast. Major credit cards.* ☐ Opulently modern country inn with full resort amenities. Rooms have balconies or patios; some have fireplaces. Spa and sun decks. **John Ash & Co.** restaurant adjacent; see above.

Northern Sonoma County information sources

Geyserville Chamber of Commerce, P.O. Box 276, Geyserville, CA 95441; (707) 857-3745. *(www.geyservillecc.com)*

Healdsburg Chamber of Commerce, 217 Healdsburg Ave., Healdsburg, CA 95448; (707) 433-6935. *(www.healdsburg.org)*

Lake Sonoma Recreation Area, 3333 Skaggs Springs Rd., Geyserville, CA 95441-9644; (707) 433-2200.

Russian River Chamber of Commerce, 16209 First St. (P.O. Box 331), Guerneville, CA 95446; (800) 253-8800 or (707) 869-9000. *(www.russianriver.com)*

Santa Rosa Conference & Visitors Bureau, 9 Fourth St., Santa Rosa, CA 95404; (800) 404-ROSE. *(www.visitsantarosa.com)*

Sonoma County Wine Library, Healdsburg City Library, 139 Piper St., Healdsburg, CA 95448; (707) 433-3772.

Sonoma County Wine & Visitors Center, 5000 Roberts Lake Rd., Rohnert Park, CA 94928; (707) 586-3795. *(www.sonomawine.com)*

Windsor Chamber of Commerce, 8499 Old Redwood Highway, Windsor, CA 95492; (707) 838-7285. *(www.windsorchamber.com)*

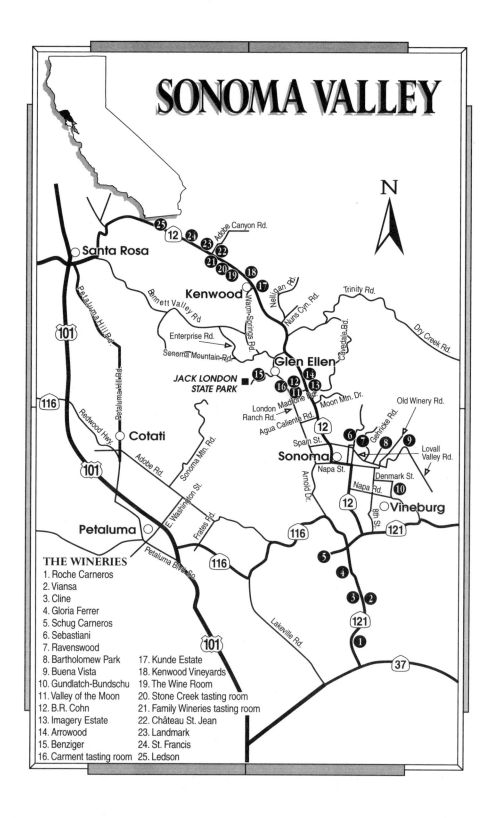

SONOMA VALLEY

N

Santa Rosa

Adobe Canyon Rd.

Kenwood

Trinity Rd.

Bennett Valley Rd

Nelligan Rd.

Nuns Cyn. Rd.

Dry Creek Rd.

Petaluma Hill Rd.

Enterprise Rd.

Warm Springs Rd.

Sonoma Mountain Rd.

Cavedale Rd.

GLEN ELLEN
Glen Ellen

JACK LONDON
STATE PARK

Old Winery Rd.

Moon Mtn. Dr.

Gehricke Rd.

London
Ranch Rd.

Madrone Rd.

Lovall
Valley Rd.

Agua Caliente Rd.

Spain St.

Cotati

Sonoma Mtn. Rd.

Sonoma

Napa St.

Denmark St.

Redwood Hwy.

Adobe Rd.

Napa Rd.

Vineburg

Arnold Dr.

8th St.

Petaluma

E. Washington St.

Frates Rd.

Petaluma Blvd. So.

THE WINERIES

1. Roche Carneros
2. Viansa
3. Cline
4. Gloria Ferrer
5. Schug Carneros
6. Sebastiani
7. Ravenswood
8. Bartholomew Park
9. Buena Vista
10. Gundlatch-Bundschu
11. Valley of the Moon
12. B.R. Cohn
13. Imagery Estate
14. Arrowood
15. Benziger
16. Carment tasting room

17. Kunde Estate
18. Kenwood Vineyards
19. The Wine Room
20. Stone Creek tasting room
21. Family Wineries tasting room
22. Château St. Jean
23. Landmark
24. St. Francis
25. Ledson

Lakeville Rd.

Fill the bowl with rosy wine,
Around our temples roses twine,
And let us cheerfully awhile,
Like the wine and roses, smile.
— Abraham Cowley

Chapter Four

SONOMA VALLEY
A cuvée of California wine and history

About thirty years ago, as I was wrapping up an interview with vintner Sam Sebastiani, his father August poked his head through the doorway.

"You got any plans tonight?" he asked.

I shook my head.

"The hell you don't. You and I are going to dinner."

"Sure." I welcomed the prospect of an evening with this Sonoma Valley wine legend. "But, why the sudden invitation?"

August frowned. "I've got one of those fancy New York wine writers in my office and I need an excuse to get rid of him."

Later, we adjourned to the Sonoma Grove Restaurant, where "Gus addressed the waitress with his usual gentle gruffness: "Bring my friend here the second best steak in the house. I'll take the best one and bring us a bottle of Zinfandel."

"Of course, Mister Sebastiani." The waitress grinned wickedly. "What brand?"

August's death in 1980 closed a significant chapter in the Sonoma Valley wine history book. Friendly but incisive, folksy yet astute, he turned a bulk winery into the Sonoma Valley's largest producer of varietals. When a wine glut hit in the 1970s, he introduced "jug varietals," marketing premium wines in 1.5-liter bottles at affordable prices. He was the first American winemaker to produce *nouveau* style Gamay Beaujolais and release it within weeks of bottling, in the French tradition.

At home in bib overalls, ill at ease in suit and tie, he hosted elegant harvest dinners in San Francisco to exhibit Sonoma Valley wines to the press and to the world. Not to be overshadowed, his wife Sylvia earned a reputation as a fine cook and authored a best-selling cookbook, *Mangiamo*.

Although Sonoma Valley is famous for its wine legends of Haraszthy and Vallejo, the Sebastiani family has written much of its current history. The saga began in 1904 when Italian immigrant Samuele Sebastiani began producing bulk wines. His son August joined him in the business in 1934. When Samuele died in 1946, August changed the focus to varietals and built the winery into one of the largest in America. Sebastiani and Sonoma are almost synonymous. The name reaches beyond the winery to appear on a theater, a depot and on street signs.

The family remains the valley's largest wine producer, shipping four million cases a year. Sylvia, her youngest son Don, daughter Maryanne and her husband Dick Cuneo run the operation today. After a 1986 family feud resembling a script from the old *Falcon Crest* TV series, eldest son Sam left to form his own winery, Viansa, which continues to thrive in the Carneros district. This is a gently hilly appellation just north of the San Pablo arm of San Francisco Bay, shared by the Napa and Sonoma valleys.

If that family spat resembles a TV script, the rest of Sonoma's history reads like a Gothic novel. In 1823, a year after Mexico freed itself from Spain, maverick priest José Altimira bolted from San Francisco's cold and damp Mission Dolores to form a new branch north of the bay. Although the church condemned his action, he was supported by the Mexican California governor and his mission survived. It was the only one in California established under Mexican rule. Altimira named it San Francisco Solano, in honor of a missionary to the Peruvian Indians.

In the 1830s, when the Mexican government stripped the missions of their vast landholdings, young Army official Mariano Guadalupe Vallejo was given the task of dissolving Mission Solano. In doing so, he laid out a town with a classic plaza as its focal point. He called it Sonoma, a name local Indians had given the valley. The plaza remains as its historic centerpiece.

As more Americans arrived, Mexico began losing its grip on its northern outpost of California. On June 14, 1846, a rag-tag bunch of Sacramento Valley gringos marched on Sonoma, imprisoned an angry, sputtering Vallejo in his own barracks and proclaimed California as an independent republic. The group fashioned a crude flag with the outline of a bear (which looked more like a pig), and raised it over the plaza. These "Bear-Flaggers" were later described by Vallejo's sister as a "group of rough-looking desperados."

It was the shortest republic on record. Less than a month later, on July 9, a U.S. Naval force led by Commodore John Sloat captured Monterey and annexed California to the United States.

From that point forward, Sonoma's history is concerned mostly with wine. Vallejo, an American supporter even before his imprisonment, became the town's leading citizen and its first major grape grower. Wayfaring Hungarian "Count" Agoston Haraszthy arrived in 1856; See page 17. A year later, he established Buena Vista, which ultimately became the largest winery in

---

WINERY CODES ● *T* = tasting with no fee; ***T$*** = tasting for a fee; ***GT*** = guided tours; ***GTA*** = guided tours by appointment; ***ST*** = self-guiding or informal tours; ✕ = picnic area; 🎁 = gift shop or a good giftware selection.

WINE PRICES ● *$* = average price under $10 per bottle; ***$$*** = $10 to $14; ***$$$*** = $15 to $19; ***$$$$*** = $20 or more

America. Traveling to Europe under state legislative sanction in the early 1860s, he imported hundreds of thousands of varietal grape cuttings. They formed the foundation for today's premium California wines. It's not an exaggeration to call Haraszthy the father of California viniculture and Sonoma the cradle of the state's premium wine industry.

Like other California winelands, the valley suffered from a late nineteenth century wine glut, then phylloxera and finally Prohibition. Haraszthy's failing Buena Vista Winery was shut down when the 1906 earthquake caved in its cellars.

Three wineries preserve the shards of Sonoma Valley's vineland history. Buena Vista was re-opened in 1943 by news executive Frank Bartholomew and it continues to thrive under its current owners, the Moller-Racke family of Germany. The Sebastiani family owns many of the original mission and Vallejo vineyards. Bartholomew Park Winery (formerly Hacienda Wine Cellars) has some of Haraszthy's old vineyards and a replica of his Pompeiian style villa.

Another historical figure left his mark on the Sonoma Valley, although he blended words, not wine. Jack London, fresh from his literary triumphs, bought land above Glen Ellen in 1905 and devoted the last eleven years of his life to building his "Beauty Ranch." The Valley of the Moon, an Indian description of this scenic land, was popularized in London's book by that name.

Sonoma Valley's wineries are grouped in two areas—from the town of Sonoma south through the Carneros district to San Pablo Bay, and northward up the valley to Glen Ellen and Kenwood.

SONOMA-CARNEROS WINERY TOUR ● To approach Sonoma

from the San Francisco Bay Area, go east on State Highway 37 from U.S. 101 above San Rafael, then turn north onto State Highway 121 at **Sears Point Raceway.** You've entered the Carneros appellation, and this route is appropriately called the Carneros Highway. You'll soon encounter two modern wineries perched on upslopes and surrounded by vineyards: **Roche Carneros Estate Winery** and **Viansa**, both on the right.

Just beyond Viansa, **Cline Cellars** sits back among the vineyards on the highway's left side and beyond that, a narrow lane leads to the left and uphill through vineyards to **Gloria Ferrer Champagne Caves**. At a three-way stop where highways 121, 12 and 116 all collide, continue briefly through a stop sign on Highway 121, then turn left and follow a long lane through upsloping vineyards to **Schug Carneros Estate Winery.** Return to that junction and continue straight ahead onto Highway 121, which now has merged with Highway 12. After a short distance, swing left onto Highway 12 at a "Y" intersection, following a Sonoma sign.

This route becomes Broadway and bumps into **Sonoma Plaza.** Take a right at the stop sign, drive to Fourth Street, turn left and follow it to **Sebastiani Sonoma Cask Cellars.** Its extensive facilities border the corner of Fourth and Spain streets. Go east on Spain a few blocks, then turn north (left) onto Gehricke Road and follow it uphill to **Ravenswood,** tucked among the trees.

Return to Spain Street and continue east until it becomes Lovall Valley Road. At a kink in Lovall Valley, head northeast on Castle Road to **Bartholomew Park Winery**. Note the reconstructed Haraszthy villa crowning a low hill as you approach. Retreat to Lovall Valley Road, stay with it briefly and turn left onto Old Winery Road, lined with giant eucalyptus trees. This takes you to historic **Buena Vista Carneros Winery** at road's end.

Your final Sonoma area stop is **Gundlach-Bundschu Winery,** which is a bit tricky to reach, so stay alert. Follow Old Winery Road south from Buena Vista, turn right onto Napa Street then quickly left onto Eighth Street and follow it two-thirds of a mile to Denmark Street. Go left and travel about three-fourths of a mile, then turn left onto a lane marked by ornamental stone walls.

Roche Carneros Estate Winery ● T & T$ GTA ✕

28700 Arnold Drive (1 Carneros Highway), Sonoma, CA 95476; (800) 825-9475 or (707) 935-7115. (www.rochewinery.com) Daily 10 to 5 (until 6 in summer); major credit cards. Most wines tasted free, fee for some reserves. Gifts and specialty food selection. Picnic area; tours by appointment.

Perched on a hilltop and housed in a double-pitched roof structure suggestive of an urban barn, Roche offers a pleasing view of the Carneros region, San Pablo Bay and Sonoma Valley. Picnickers can enjoy the view from tables near the winery. The tasting room is spacious and inviting, like an oversized living room. Samples of Sonoma Valley specialty foods are offered in the gift area.

Joseph and Genevieve Roche purchased a cattle ranch in 1977 then, realizing they had fine vineyard lands, began planting vines in 1982. They chose to concentrate on Chardonnay and Pinot Noir, which do well in the Carneros appellation. They're still the best of Roche's wines. The small, stylish family winery produces about 6,500 cases a year.

Tasting notes: Roche wines come in two price ranges. A pair of Chardonnays and Pinot Noir Blanc are in the low teens. Both Chards exhibited good varietal character, rich and long on fruit. The higher end Pinot Noir and Merlot also were outstanding, complex and full flavored. The unfiltered Pinot Noir was excellent. Prices: *$$ to $$$$.*

Viansa Winery ● T & T$ ST & GTA ✕ 🏠

25200 Arnold Dr. (Highway 121), Sonoma, CA 95476; (707) 935-4700. (www.viansa.com) Daily 10 to 5; MC/VISA. Choice of four wines tasted free; reserve wines by the glass for a fee. Extensive giftware selection and large deli with picnic fare and gourmet food items. Valley-view picnic area; informal tours through the oak aging cellar, or guided tours by appointment.

When Sam J. Sebastiani left the family business in 1986, he and his wife Vicki combined their names and came up with "Viansa." Their opulent Tuscan style winery reflects Sam's touch of elegance and Vicki's flair for wine and food. Tucked high into the brow of a hill above the Carneros, it's now old enough to begin weathering a bit, appropriate to its appearance as a tile-roofed villa in old Tuscany. A nearby picnic area offers a 360-degree view.

The tasting room, aptly described by Sam and Vicki as their "Italian Marketplace," is one of the valley's most appealing, offering an extensive giftware, cook book, wine book and specialty food shop. More than two dozen sauces, dips, pestos and toppings can be sampled. The Viansa kitchen issues pastas, *foccacia* bread sandwiches, salads, deli items, desserts and other "California-Italian" fare.

It may be our imagination, but a figure in a mural behind the deli counter—a reclining Roman aristocrat immersed in the good life—bears a passing resemblance to Sam.

Appropriate to the memory of his father, Sonoma Valley wine pioneer August Sebastiani, Sam has created a ninety-acre wetland on the property for migrating waterfowl. More than thirty species of birds hang out there, and tours are conducted periodically. ("Gus" was an accomplished amateur ornithologist and had his own duck pond among his vineyards.)

Tasting notes: Sam has added several Italian varietals to his list, including Pinot Grigio, Arneis and Vernaccia among the whites and Aleatico, Dolcetto, Anatra Rosso and Sangiovese on the red side. Among the more traditional wines are a lush and silky Chardonnay, a fruity and nicely acidic Sauvignon Blanc, big bodied and deep flavored Merlot and a classic peppery Cabernet Sauvignon with a touch of oak. Prindelo is a blend of Primitivo, Zinfandel and Teroldego, with a great berry flavor. Prices: *$ to $$$$*.

Vintners choice: "Our Cabernet Sauvignon is currently the highlight because of the blend of vineyards from Napa and Sonoma," according to Sam.

Cline Cellars ● T & T$ GTA ✕

24737 Arnold Drive, Sonoma, CA 95476; (707) 935-4310. (www.clinecellars.com) Daily 10 to 6. Choice of four wines tasted free, plus reserve and limited bottling tasting for a fee. A few wine logo and deli items; picnic area. Guided tours by appointment.

Fred Cline got into the wine business in 1982 by using a small inheritance from his grandfather Jacuzzi—that's right; the inventor of the whirlpool bath—to buy the old Firpo Winery on the California delta east of San Francisco. He parlayed that $12,000 into a $3 million debt, but his wines won awards and sold well, and he was able to buy an historic Carneros region ranch in 1991. Younger brother Matt joined the operation in 1986 while it was still on the delta. Both are graduates of the University of California at Davis. Their Carneros tasting room occupies a handsome nineteenth century white clapboard farmhouse with a wrap-around porch. Low stone walls, a grassy picnic area and landscaping complete a pleasantly bucolic setting.

Tasting notes: The Clines have excelled with newly popular Rhône wines such as Mourvèdre, Syrah, Carignane and Alicante Bouschet. Matt earned a "winemaker of the year" title a few years back and the Clines have won a considerable collection of awards. Their *Côtes D'Oakley*—a blend of Mourvèdre, Carignane, Zinfandel and Alicante Bouschet—is soft and light yet full-flavored. The Carignane varietal also had a pleasant tannic finish, with a rich berry flavor and the Mourvèdre varietal offered a pleasant herbal taste. Others on the Cline list include a varietal Syrah, Zinfandel and white Rhônes such as Marsanne, Roussanne and Viognier. Prices: *$ to $$$$*.

Vintners choice: "Our Zinfandel and Mourvèdre varietals and Oakley Cuvée are particularly appealing," said a Cline team member.

Gloria Ferrer Champagne Caves ● T$ GT

23555 Highway 121 (P.O. Box 1427), Sonoma, CA 95476; (707) 996-7256. (www.gloriaferrar.com) Daily 10:30 to 5:15; major credit cards. Sparkling wines and table by the glass or sampled at moderate prices. Some wine related gift items. Guided tours daily; call for times.

From Viansa's Tuscany, we are ferried to the hills of Spain, where the Ferrer family has produced sparkling wine for five centuries. In 1986, they transported the essence of rural Barcelona to this hillside niche in the

Carneros. The tile-roofed winery with its graceful Spanish arches shields an underground *cava*, where sparkling wines are coaxed into graceful maturity.

Plan to arrive at tour time to take the full measure of this elegant facility. You'll view fermenting tanks and a bottling line from a gallery, then descend into gunnited caves under twenty feet of earth. Here, great tiers of sparkling wine glisten dully in the subdued light. Along the way, you absorb a quick course in *méthode champenoise* as practiced by the Ferrer family. The tour adjourns to the stylish *Sala de Catadores* (Hall of the Tasters) for a bit of the bubbly.

Tasting notes: Three sparkling wines are sold by the glass—Gloria Ferrer Brut, Royal Cuvée and Carneros Cuvée. Our Ferrer Brut was crisp and faultlessly clean, with subtle aromas and tastes of the fruit. The wines have won numerous awards, including a best of show at a San Francisco Wine Expo. Pinot Noir and Chardonnay table wines have been added to the Ferrer list; they are, of course, the classic ingredients for sparkling wines. Prices: *$$$ to $$$$.*

Schug Carneros Estate Winery • T ✕

602 Bonneau Rd., Sonoma, CA 95476-9749; (800) 966-9365 or (707) 939-9363. (www.schugwinery.com) Daily 10 to 5; MC/VISA. Select varietals tasted. A few giftware items; picnic deck.

After spending ten years as winemaker for Joseph Phelps Vineyards, German immigrant Walter Schug established his own winery in the Carneros region in 1980. His vineyard roots go back considerably further. A third generation vintner, he has been making wine for half a century, beginning at the family estate of Staatsweingut Assmannshausen in Germany. His small winery, in a kind of Bavarian-looking structure, sits above tilted vineyards with a dramatic backdrop of grassy bread loaf shaped hills. The winery offers an imposing view of the valley, which is even better if you adjourn to a picnic deck on a second level.

Tasting notes: The Schug list is limited and excellent; he produces a silky Chardonnay with a touch of oak, a crisply dry Sauvignon Blanc, softly complex and mouth-filling Pinot Noir, deep-flavored Merlot and a classic peppery Cabernet Sauvignon. Prices: *$$ to $$$$.*

Vintner's choice: Schug's first love is Pinot Noir, according to a winery spokesperson. He launched his own winery to pursue his quest for a perfect Pinot.

Sebastiani Sonoma Cask Cellars • T GT ✕ 🏮

389 E. Fourth St., Sonoma, CA 95476; (707) 938-5532. Daily 10 to 5. Most varieties tasted. Good giftware selection. Picnic areas near the winery and along the vineyards on Spain Street. Frequent tours; call for hours.

Sebastiani Sonoma Cask Cellars, whose history we've already covered, forms a transition between town and country. The ancient cut-stone winery is on the edge of a tidy old residential area, while vineyards stretch toward low hills. Nearly 150,000 people a year throng through the winery. The tours are quick and efficient, spilling their happy cargo into the large tasting room.

The handsome old tasting room was being rehabilitated as part of an earthquake retro-fit as we went to press. When it's reopened, expect to see a grand space sheltered by ancient cut stone walls, and family history items such as old photos, Samuele's original basket press and vintage winemaking equipment. A stained glass window depicts the winery logo, and a portion of it glitters from this book's cover. The tasting room also is adorned with one of the largest wood carving exhibits in America. A remarkable gentleman named Earle Brown took up woodcarving when most men retire, and spent the next decade or so inscribing images on every door, barrel top, cask and other exposed wood surface he could find in the winery.

Tasting notes: If the tasting room is still being renovated when you arrive, you can sample wines at Sebastiani on the Square at 103 W. Napa Street, corner of First. Four wines were available from a list that included Chardonnay, Pinot Noir Blanc, Merlot, Syrah, Sangiovese, Mourvèdre, Zinfandel, Cabernet Sauvignon and a Symphony dessert wine. These wines are fruity and crisp and not overly filtered or fined, which is a tendency of many high volume wineries. The complete Sebastiani list is very broad-based, ranging from premium varietals to jug wines, including varietal jugs introduced by August. Prices: *$ to $$$$.*

Ravenswood ● T GTA ✗ 📷

18701 Gehricke Rd., Sonoma, CA 95476; (707) 938-1960. (www.ravenswood-wine.com) Daily 10 to 4:30; MC/VISA, DISC. Selected wines tasted. Good selection of giftwares and wine logo items. Picnic area with hillside and vineyard views. Guided tours at 10:30 by reservation.

This is where you go for a little Zin. Or perhaps a lot, if you love the "mystery grape" as we do. This winery, tucked into a wooded slope and besieged by vineyards, specializes in Zinfandel. And most are BIG Zins. We came away with a mixed case. The rustic, stone fronted tasting room looks properly ancient, yet it was opened in early 1991. A picnic terrace offers fine views of vines, pines, giant eucalyptus, wooded slopes and the edges of Sonoma below.

Ravenswood began life in the mid-70s in a prefab warehouse in Sonoma, then moved to this more enticing spot. Winemaker Joel E. Peterson is obsessed with the notion of bringing out all the earthy, powerful character of Zinfandel, and he usually succeeds. Tasters who like big red wines give his Zin high marks.

"No wimpy wines allowed," reads a sign in the small tasting room.

Tasting notes: Although Zinfandel still rules, the proprietors have shifted toward some interesting Bordeaux style blends of Cabernet Sauvignon, Cabernet Franc and Merlot. Most are lush and mellow, with enough tannin to encourage aging. A Vintners Blend Merlot is soft and ready to drink, and a couple of Cabs exhibit lots of berries, hints of spice and wood. Still, we go for the Zin; the Dickerson and Old Vine are among the best of the lot, with big berries and concentrated tannin—suitable for a long sleep. Prices: *$$ to $$$$.*

Bartholomew Park Winery ● T GTA ✗

1000 Vineyard Lane, Sonoma, CA 95476; (707) 935-9511. (www.bartholomewparkwinery.com) Daily 10 to 4:30; MC/VISA. Most varieties tasted. Wine history museum. Haraszthy villa open Wednesday, Saturday and Sunday noon to 4; shorter hours in winter. Some gift items in the tasting room. Oak-shaded picnic area overlooking the vineyards; guided tours by appointment.

The "villa" catches your eye before you see the winery. It's a reconstruction of the Pompeiian mansion built in 1864 by Count Haraszthy. It has been furnished to the period and is staffed by a docent on Wednesdays, Saturdays

Decades of ivy lace the rough stone walls of Buena Vista Carneros Winery, established in 1857 by Agoston Haraszthy.

and Sundays. Visitors are free to look around and admire the splendid old European furnishings, grand piano and crystal and brass chandeliers.

The winery and tasting room are just up the road—housed in a century-old Spanish-California structure that once served as an annex for the "Home for the Feeble Minded," predecessor to Glen Ellen's Sonoma State Hospital. A tasting room occupies one end of this grand old brick, stone and wooden structure. A fine museum fills the rest of the old winery building. Your eye first catches an outstanding black and white photo display of contemporary Sonoma County grape growers. Exhibits then travel back through to the 1850s when Haraszthy planted vines here and establish the nearby Buena Vista Winery. Other displays trace the growth of the local wine industry. An appealing focal point is an 1800s wine picnic scene with a surrey and wicker picnic basket.

News executive and wine connoisseur Frank Bartholomew and his wife Antonia, who reopened Buena Vista in 1943, established a winery here as well—three decades later. It then functioned for several years as Hacienda Winery under A. Crawford Cooley and his son Robert. In 1994, it was purchased by the Bundschu family of Gundlach-Bundschu Winery and named in honor of Bartholomew. It has been converted into something of an historic shrine to both Haraszthy and Bartholomew. A Bartholomew foundation has been established to operate the historic facility, where about 4,000 cases of wine a produced each year.

Tasting notes: Bartholomew Park labels offer glimpses of Sonoma Valley wine history, although one doesn't buy these wines just for the1 labels.

Those we tasted were quite good and fair priced. A pair of Chardonnays displayed strong variety character with lots of fruit and a bit of spice; an aged Zinfandel had a great raspberry nose that galloped into the taste; a Merlot offered herbs and raspberries in the aroma and taste, and a properly aged Cabernet Sauvignon was classic—full-flavored and mellow with a light chili-pepper tang. Prices: *$$ to $$$$.*

Buena Vista Carneros Winery ● T & T$ GT & ST ✕ 📷

18000 Old Winery Rd. (P.O. Box 1842), Sonoma, CA 95476; (707) 938-1266. (www.buenavistawinery.com) Daily 10 to 5; major credit cards. Most varieties tasted; some free, others for a fee. Extensive gift selection and specialty foods; art gallery. Self-guided tours plus historical presentations at 11 and 2 in summer, and at 2 p.m. only the rest of the year. Picnic areas.

If any winery in America is steeped in antiquity, it is Buena Vista, started by Haraszthy in 1857. It was restored by Bartholomew in 1943 and was owned by Youngs Market Company of Los Angeles until the Moller-Racke family of Germany purchased it in the 1980s. The word "Carneros" was added to the winery name to reflect the source of most of its grapes. The original winery is shaped of rough blocks quarried from its own tunnels. Bunkered into a steep slope, shaded by giant eucalyptus, it exudes the mystique of a viticultural Mayan ruin. Peeking into the grottoes of the ancient winery or its next-door Press House, you can see the pick marks where Chinese laborers dug the tunnels.

Self-guiding tours take you through the fountain courtyard and into the ancient recesses of the original wine cellars. Historical tours trace the trail of Agoston Haraszthy, which began in strife-torn Hungary and ended at this place. The tasting room, in the Press House, is rimmed by a balconied art gallery, where works of San Francisco Bay Area artists are on display. The culturally conscious Moller-Racke family sponsors a fall Shakespeare Festival in the courtyard.

Tasting notes: Four gratis tastings are offered from a list that covers most varietals. Older reserve wines can be sampled for a fee. We liked the complex, buttery spiciness of the Carneros Chardonnay and the herbal flavor of a Sauvignon Blanc. The Carneros Cabernet Sauvignon also was herbal, with a soft finish. Buena Vista makes one of society's better cream sherries—velvety, nutty and lush. Prices: *$$ to $$$$.*

Vintners choice: "We're known for our Chardonnay, Pinot Noir and Cabernet," said the tasting room manager.

Gundlach-Bundschu Winery ● T ✕

2000 Denmark St., Sonoma, CA 95476; (707) 938-5277. (www.gunbun.com) Daily 11 to 4:30; MC/VISA. Most wines tasted. Some wine related gift items. Picnic pavilion with a valley view.

Gundlach-Bundschu combines antiquity, a modern wine facility and hearty humor. There's a festive, laid-back collegiate atmosphere to this ancient place; it's one of our favorite stops on the California wine tour. Lively contemporary music fed by an unseen CD fills the ancient cellars and the place is decorated with off-beat Gundlach-Bundschu posters, which can be purchased. One shows a highway patrolman telling a motorist in an old Kaiser: "If you can't say *Gundlach-Bundschu Gewürztraminer,* you shouldn't be driving!" A sign invites wine enthusiasts to join the "Wine of the Moment Club."

This upbeat facility indeed is ancient. Jacob Gundlach started the winery in 1858 and was joined by Charles Bundschu, who married his daughter, in 1862. The 1906 earthquake destroyed their San Francisco warehouse and Prohibition closed the winery. However, the Bundschus continued growing grapes in the Sonoma Valley. Jim, great-great-great grandson of Charles, decided to re-open the ancient winery in the early 1970s.

Tasting notes: Jim Bundschu's winery produces the best Gewürztraminer in the valley, with a great crushed flower petal nose and taste. Yet the reds are the best product. Try the berry-rich, slightly spicy Bearitage, a blend of Cabernet Sauvignon, Merlot and Zinfandel; the label's great, too. The Pinot Noir was remarkably spicy for this variety, with a typical big berry taste. The Cabernet Sauvignon was outstanding—inky black, rich and capable of hanging around for a decade or so. Others on the list are Gamay Noir, Cabernet Franc, Riesling and Polar Bearitage (a white version of Bearitage with Chardonnay, Sauvignon Blanc and Semillon). Prices: *$$ to $$$$.*

Vintners choice: "Reds, because," Jim said, flatly.

GLEN ELLEN-KENWOOD WINERY TOUR ● From Sonoma Plaza,
take Spain street west several blocks and go right onto State Highway 12 (the Sonoma Highway), headed northwest toward Santa Rosa. You'll pass the strung out, unplanned scatter of three communities—Boyes Hot Springs, Fetters Hot Springs and Agua Caliente. This is the least appealing part of the Sonoma Valley. As the town names suggest, it was once a hot springs resort area. Boyes was spring training grounds for the old San Francisco Seals and Oakland Oaks. Today however, with the lone exception of the beautifully refurbished Sonoma Mission Inn, this once glossy tourist area is a rather mundane string of storefronts, strip malls and houses.

Once you clear Fetters, you enter open countryside and—by contrast—the prettiest part of the Sonoma Valley. Vineyards climb gentle slopes, nudging foothills of the Mayacamas Mountains to the east. Looking west, you see more vines scattered across the level valley floor; the Sonoma Mountains fill that horizon. Continue on Highway 12 to Madrone Road, turn left and you'll shortly encounter **Valley of the Moon Winery** on your right. Return to Highway 12, continue north briefly and you'll see the entrance to **B.R. Cohn Winery** on your left. From there, drive a brief distance to the new **Imagery Estate Winery & Art Gallery** and **Arrowood Winery**, both reached by a short drive up a vineyard slope to your right.

Press northward on Highway 12 for about two miles, turn left onto Arnold Drive and pass through the vintage hamlet of **Glen Ellen,** with its picturesque brick and wooden stores. Veer to the right onto London Ranch Road, which takes you to **Benziger Family Winery,** up the hill about half a mile on your right. You'll likely want to continue to **Jack London State Historic Park** up the road a bit. It preserves London's ranch, the ruins of his Wolf House stone mansion and the home of his wife, Charmian.

Return to Glen Ellen and take Arnold Drive south less than a mile to **Carmenet Marketplace**, a tasting room in the Jack London Village shopping complex. Then take Arnold Drive back through town to Highway 12 and continue northward, headed for **Kenwood,** where many of the valley's wineries and tasting rooms are clustered. You'll first see **Kunde Estate Winery** and—in less than half a mile—**Kenwood Vineyards**; both are uphill on your right. Entering the small town of Kenwood, you'll encounter three tast-

MEDAL, MEDAL, WHO'S GOTTA MEDAL?

As you visit assorted wineries, you'll note that many have walls full of ribbons. Does this mean that all their wines are wonderful? How can so many wineries win so many prizes? Doesn't anyone ever lose?

A gold medal doesn't mean that a wine won first place. It means that it scored high in a blind tasting, meeting the criteria for that particular varietal. A gold medal is a *rating*, like getting an "A" in algebra. Several wines entered in a particular competition may be worthy of a gold or silver or bronze—or none, for that matter.

To further cloud the issue of who won how many medals, some smaller wineries don't enter many competitions because they can't afford the gratis bottles that they're expected to provide. They may make wonderful wines, but have few medals to show for them.

Are we suggesting that medals aren't important; that just about any wine can win? What does all this medal business mean?

It means that California produces a lot of remarkably good wines, and that awards are *one* measure of their excellence, at least in the minds and taste buds of a particular tasting panel.

If you want to take this awards business seriously, look for wines with sweepstake or best of show awards, which *are* one of a kind.

What we seek, when we snatch up our MasterCard and go afield to replenish our wine cellar, are award-winning wines at modest prices. Yes, you can find them. A surprising number of inexpensive wines are bedecked with gold and silver tasting awards.

The best buys often are those from long established vintners such as Sebastiani, Pedroncelli, Fortino and Fetzer—family-owned wineries whose mortgages have long since been paid off. The newer wineries with smart young U.C. Davis grads as winemakers certainly are capable of producing great wines, but they may have large debts to pay off, which is reflected in the price per bottle.

When all else fails, fall back on your most trusted authority—your taste buds.

---

ing rooms detached from their wineries. They are in order of appearance—all on your left—**The Wine Room** across from Kenwood Vineyards, **Stone Creek Winery tasting room** and then **Family Wineries** tasting room. You'll next see **Château St. Jean Winery**, up a vineyard lane to the right. A bit north of Kenwood, at Highway 12 and Adobe Canyon Road, is **Landmark Vineyards**. Just over a mile beyond, at the corner of Highway 12 and Pythian Road, is the Tuscan style **St. Francis Winery**. A bit farther along is a virtual castle of a winery, **Ledson,** set against a wooded bluff above gently tilted vineyards. Highway 12 continues into the heart of Santa Rosa and eventually links with U.S. 101 freeway.

Valley of the Moon Winery • T GT ✕

777 Madrone Rd. (P.O. Box 1950), Glen Ellen, CA 95442; (707) 996-6941. (www.valleyofthemoonwinery.com) Daily 10 to 4:30; major credit cards. Selected wines tasted. Good selection of wine logo items and giftwares. Tree-shaded picnic area. Guided tours daily at 10:30 and 2.

One of Sonoma County's oldest wineries, Valley of the Moon was established in the 1860s and was operated at one time by Senator George Hearst. Closed by Prohibition, it came back to life in 1942 when Enrico Parducci, founder of the San Francisco Sausage Company, purchased the site. His son Harry, grandson Harry Jr., and assorted other family members operated the facility until it was purchased by the Heck family of the Russian River Valley's Korbel Champagne Cellars.

The once weathered old winery has been extensively renovated by the Hecks, although it still retains much of its yesterday charm. Note the giant four-century-old bay laurel out front, casting shade on the ruggedly handsome stone tasting room.

Tasting notes: Once home to substantial everyday wines, Valley of the Moon now focuses more on premium varietals such as Pinot Blanc, Chardonnay, Syrah, Sangiovese and Zinfandel. A specialty is a smooth, full-flavored Cabernet-Merlot blend called *Cuvée de la Luna*. Prices: *$$ to $$$.*

B.R. Cohn Winery • T & T$ ✕

15140 Sonoma Highway, Glen Ellen, CA 95442; (800) 330-4064 or 938-4064. (www.brcohn.com) Daily 10 to 5. Select varieties tasted free; fees for reserve wines; MC/VISA. Some wine logo gift items. Picnic area; guided tours by appointment.

Housed in neatly kept old farm buildings, the Cohn Winery complex crowns a hill shaded with olive trees, which is logical, since this originally was an olive ranch. The primly attractive tasting room occupies a cute little cottage. Winery founder Bruce Cohn comes from a curious background for a vintner—TV and radio broadcasting and talent management. He discovered the Doobie Brothers in San Francisco and helped guide them to fame. However, he's not an entrepreneur who dabbles in wine as a second profession. He grew up in the Forestville area and has long been interested in wine. He bought his appropriately named Olive Hill Vineyard in 1974 and opened his winery a year later—while still keeping at least one finger on the pulse of the entertainment industry.

Tasting notes: Cohn's brief list consists of several renditions of Chardonnay, Cabernet Sauvignon and Merlot. The Cabs are excellent, often with firm tannins that encourage aging. However, we felt that his reserve Chardonnay was one of his best wines, with outstanding lush flavors and a soft touch of wood. Merlot, the only other wine available when we visited, was soft and drinkable with a slight hint of wood. Prices: *$$$ to $$$$.*

Imagery Estate Winery & Art Gallery • T$ ST 📷

14335 Highway 12, Glen Ellen, CA 95442; (877) 550-4278. (www.imagerywinery.com) Friday-Sunday 10 to 4:30; major credit cards. Most varieties sampled for a fee. Art gallery of wine label originals, good giftware selection, bocce ball court. Self-guiding tour and "winery trail."

Opened in 2000, this striking facility houses the distinct wine label art collection of the Benziger family. It also samples and sells Benziger's high end Imagery Wines. Several years ago, the family started seeking artists to create distinctive labels for their Imagery series. Each vintage of each varietal is assigned its own label and—according to winery sources—artists now clamor for the privilege of creating an Imagery label. Many of the originals are on display in this new facility. The elegant complex also has formal gardens and an Appellation Trail, which takes people on an abbreviated walking tour of Sonoma Valley wine regions.

Arrowood Vineyards and Winery ● GT

14347 Sonoma Hwy. (P.O. Box 1240), Glen Ellen, CA 95442; (707) 938-5170. (www.arrowoodvineyards.com) Daily 10 to 4:30; MC/VISA. Tasting sometimes available. A few wine related items; guided tours.

Housed in an appealing rural New England style structure, Arrowood is tucked into a hillside vineyard. It doesn't always offer tasting, but if a bottle happens to be open, visitors are welcome to sample some of the valley's finest wines. They can be purchased in the bright and airy Hospitality House, with a wrap-around veranda overlooking the vineyards. Wicker chairs invite visitors to linger over the view.

San Francisco native Richard Arrowood made wine—and won medals—for several other vintners before he and his wife, Canadian-born Alis Demers Arrowood, opened this facility in 1987. For the first three years, she practically ran the winery while he fulfilled his obligations as winemaker at Château St. Jean. With Richard now full time at Arrowood, his wife and business partner focuses on sales and marketing.

Tasting notes: Richard's initial plan was to produce exceptional Chardonnay and Cabernet Sauvignon, buying select grapes from different vineyards. He has since added white Riesling, Merlot, Syrah, Pinot Blanc and Malbec to his list. For a particularly rich experience, try the Hoot Owl Creek Late Harvest Riesling. Arrowood's hand-crafted wines from select vineyards are predictably pricey: **$$$$.**

Benziger Family Winery ● T & T$ GT & ST ✗ 📷

1883 London Ranch Rd., Glen Ellen, CA 95442; (888) 490-2739 or (707) 935-4046. (www.benzinger.com) Daily 10 to 5; major credit cards. Most varieties tasted free; modest fee for reserve tasting. Good selection of wine logo and gift items. Informal self-guiding tours and Sonoma Mountain Tram car tours at frequent intervals; call for hours. Vineyard Discovery Center.

This is one of the wine industry's more startling success stories. In 1981 at the urging of his son Mike who had come to California to ski and surf, New York wine merchant Bruno Benziger started Glen Ellen Winery. He began buying grapes from more than 250 growers, and soon was shipping 3.7 million cases of wine worldwide. The family then sold Heublein its Glen Ellen line of wines—which accounted for more than ninety percent of production—while retaining the winery to focus on its Benziger label.

The facilities are located in a wooded vale surrounded by vineyards. It appears to be a sprawling yet well-maintained farmyard with its random scatter of neat white clapboard buildings, shaded by mature oaks. However, all except the original house are of recent vintage. Visitors can make a quick study of viticulture in the Vineyard Discovery Center, and take a tractor-drawn open air tram car around the large Benziger wine estate. The attractive knotty pine visitor center has a nice selection of giftwares and two tasting counters—one for current releases and one for reserves.

Tasting notes: Fumé Blanc, Chardonnay, Pinot Noir, Merlot, Zinfandel, Syrah, Cabernet Sauvignon and a Muscat Canelli dessert wine make up the Benziger list. Our favorite were a silky, spicy Chardonnay, a soft and mouth-filling Pinot Noir and a light and crisp Zinfandel. A second label called Benziger Imagery features small lots of varietals such as Viognier, Aleatico,

Cabernet Franc and Syrah. They can be tasted here for a fee, along with Benziger label reserves, and at the new Imagery Estate Winery and Art Gallery on Highway 12; see above. Prices: *$$ to $$$$*.

Vintners Choice: "The most popular Benziger wines are the Sonoma County Chardonnay, Cabernet Sauvignon and Merlot, but smaller production Zinfandel and Pinot also are enjoyable," said a winery source.

Carmenet Marketplace and History Center • T & T$

In Jack London Village at 14301 Arnold Dr., Glen Ellen, CA 95443; (707) 996-5870. Daily 10 to 5; major credit cards. Select varietals tasted free; small fee for reserves. Good selection of giftwares.

Carmenet Winery is located on Moon Mountain Drive in the Sonoma Valley, although it tasting room occupies a part of the Jack London Village shopping complex. More interesting than its tasting room is the History Center, an adjacent corridor lined with old photos and artifacts of the early days of Glen Ellen and the Sonoma Valley. Jack London is represented, of course, since he spent the last years of his life in Glen Ellen. Two other famous personalities also lived here and are represented in the museum—General H.H. "Hap" Arnold (for whom Arnold Drive is named), the last World War II commander of the U.S. Army Air Force; and author and gourmet cook Mary Francis Kennedy Fisher, better known as M.F.K. Fisher. Next door to Carmenet Marketplace is the Olive Press, where one can buy olive oil and related products, and watch olives being squished.

Tasting notes: The Carmenet wine list includes Chardonnay, Sauvignon Blanc, French Colombard, Cabernets Sauvignon and Franc, Zinfandel and three versions of Merlot, plus *Copa de Moscato* and Port Zinfandel for dessert. Prices: *$$ to $$$$*.

Kunde Estate Winery • T GTA ✕

10155 Sonoma Hwy. (Box 639), Kenwood, CA 95452; (707) 833-5501. (www.kunde.com) Daily 10 to 4:30; MC/VISA, AMEX. Most wines tasted. A few wine logo items; shaded picnic area. Cave tours by appointment Friday through Sunday.

This "estate" is a dramatic multi-gabled winery rising from the vineyards on an upslope from the highway. It was completed in the early 1990s by Bob Kunde, the fourth generation of a German immigrant family that has been growing grapes here since 1904. Grapes from Kunde's 2,000-acre ranch kept winning awards for other vintners, so he decided to garner a few medals for himself, which he certainly has—particularly for his Chardonnays. This is a family operation, with Bob's two sons, daughter and two nephews active in the winery. The tasting room occupies a large swatch of the impressive winery building. Even more impressive—and often open for special events—are aging cellars burrowed into an adjacent hill, with vines planted atop them.

Tasting notes: Kunde's list includes Sauvignon Blanc, Merlot, Zinfandel, Cabernet Sauvignon and some interesting proprietary blends. Although we're red wine fans, we liked the fruity, flowery-nosed Magnolia Lane Sauvignon Blanc and lush, spicy reserve Chardonnay. Most of Kunde's reds are *big*, with tannins that want more sleep. An unfined and unfiltered Cabernet Sauvignon was one of the best we've tasted in the valley. A rich and spicy Rhône style blend, *Vallee de la Lune,* also exhibited a nice tannic finish. Others on the busy list are Viognier, Syrah, Gewürztraminer and Cabernet Franc. Prices: *$$ to $$$$*.

Kenwood Vineyards • T [icon]

9592 Sonoma Hwy., Kenwood, CA 95452; (707) 833-5891. (www.ken-woodvineyards.com) Daily 10 to 4:30; MC/VISA. Most varieties tasted. Good selection of wine related items and giftwares.

The winery occupies a wood-sided ranch style structure amidst the vineyards, upslope from the highway. The grounds are carefully kept, with terraced gardens and fieldstone borders. The large, airy tasting room suggests an oversized chalet, with wood paneled walls and open beams. It's a nice example of rustic taste and style.

The facility came to being in 1970 when the Martin Lee family bought the old Pagani Brothers Winery, with an eye toward premium varietals. They kept their focus, and Kenwood wines win a generous share of medals. The Lee family also exhibited an artistic bend. Each year their Cabernet Sauvignon "Artist Series" featured a label done by a noted artist, ranging from Pablo Picasso to realist Alan Wolton. The winery is now owned by Gary Heck of Korbel Champagne Cellars. The award winning wines and artistic labels continue under his hand.

Tasting notes: Wines available for tasting are posted daily, and they represent a liberal portion of the list. Our favorite was a Beltane Ranch Chardonnay, barrel fermented with good fruit, spiciness and crisp acid. Jack London Pinot Noir was full flavored and berry-like with a soft drink-it-now finish. The Sonoma Valley Zinfandel had an herbal nose and taste and a crisp nip of tannin. Prices: *$ to $$$$.*

Vintners choice: "Sauvignon Blanc and Jack London Cabernet Sauvignon," spoke a voice from the winery.

The Wine Room • T ✕ [icon]

9575 Sonoma Hwy., Kenwood, CA 95452; (707) 833-6131. (www.the-wine-room.com) Daily 11 to 5; major credit cards. Various wines tasted. Extensive wine logo, giftware and curio selection. Small picnic area.

Some will remember this downtown Kenwood building as the tasting room for the Smothers Brothers Winery. Their wines are still featured here, now under the Smothers/Remick Ridge Vineyards label. The facility also offers sips from several other vintners—Tantalus Winery, Kaz Vineyard & Winery, Moondance Cellars, Adler Fels and Cale Cellars. The storefront tasting room has a good selection of gift items, including some Smothers Brothers curios.

Stone Creek Winery tasting room • T & T$ ✕

9380 Sonoma Hwy., Kenwood, CA 95452; (707) 833-5070. (www.stone-creekwines.com) Daily 10:30 to 5; MC/VISA. Most varieties tasted free; small fee for reserve wines. Nice selection of giftwares. Lawn picnic area.

Stone Creek Winery is based in the Napa Valley, the source of most of its wines. This facility was opened to catch the growing wine tasting traffic through Kenwood. It's an appealing sipping stop, housed in a carefully restored 1890 schoolhouse, complete with front porch swings and a white picket fence. Stone Creek is owned by the Jacobs family, which has been in the wine and spirits business in California for more than 120 years.

Tasting notes: Stone Creek's list runs the classic varietal gamut—Fumé Blanc, Chardonnay, Gewürztraminer, Viognier, Merlot, Pinot Noir, Zinfandel and Cabernet Sauvignon. The style is soft and fruity for the whites; smooth and berry-like for the reds. Even the Gewürztraminer was crisply dry without the typical pronounced floral favor. The Chard, with lively fruity notes, was our favorite white. Of the reds, we liked a light fruity Merlot. The Cabernet and Zin were soft and lush, ready to drink. *$$ to $$$.*

Family Wineries of Sonoma Valley • T

9200 Sonoma Hwy., Kenwood, CA 95452; (707) 833-5504. (www.family-wineries.com) Daily 11 to 6; major credit cards. Variety of wines tasted; a few wine-oriented gifts and specialty food items.

Located on the ground floor of a two-story house, Family Wineries offers about thirty wines from seven different wineries. The participants are Deerfield Ranch Winery, Sable Ridge Vineyards, Mayo Family Winery, Noel Wine Cellars, Nelson Estate Winery, Suncé Winery and Meredith Wine Cellars.

Château St. Jean • T$ ST ✕ 📷

8555 Sonoma Hwy., Kenwood, CA 95452; (800) 543-7572 or (707) 833-4134. (www.chateaustjean.com) Daily 10 to 4:30; MC/VISA, AMEX. Most wines tasted for a fee. Some wine logo and giftware items; shaded picnic areas. Self-guided tours daily from 10:30 to 4.

St. Jean (as in denims) is a château in every sense of the word. The tasting room and offices are in the Mediterranean style manor house of a former country estate. The winery occupies a beige stucco creation with a distinctive witch's hat tower, which provides no useful function except to offer fine views of the countryside. A formal courtyard with rose gardens, fountains and statuary forms a pleasing link between the winery and tasting room. It's a handsome facility with a dormer ceiling held up by wood laminated trusses.

Guided tours take you through the towered structure too comely to be called a winery. From carpeted hallways, you look down upon rows of stainless steel and tiers of French oak. Graphics along the wall offer a flash course in winemaking. A winding stairway leads to the medieval-style tower for a view of russet tile rooftops and the greater Sonoma Valley. Established in 1979, the winery was purchased in 1984 by Suntory International of Japan.

Tasting notes: The list is small yet versatile and the wines are quite fine. This is particularly true of the several Chardonnays, which are a house specialty. Others on the list are Pinot Noir, Merlot, Cabernet Sauvignon, Cabernet Franc, a sweet late harvest Gewürztraminer and a sparkling wine called Grand Cuvée. Prices: *$$ to $$$$.*

Landmark Vineyards • T & T$ GTA ✕ 📷

101 Adobe Canyon Rd., Kenwood, CA 95452; (800) 452-6365 or (707) 833-0053. (www.landmarkwine.com) Daily 10 to 4:30; major credit cards. Selected wines tasted free; moderate fee for reserves. Good selection of wine related items and specialty foods. Picnic tables and bocce ball court; guided tours by appointment.

This pleasing Mediterranean style facility of beige stucco with shake roofs wraps around a large courtyard. A tile-floored, vaulted-ceiling tasting room and a stylish gift and gourmet food shop occupy one wing of this complex. An imposing mural of the winery's premiere product, Chardonnay, dominates the wall behind the tasting counter. Established in 1974, Landmark began operations northern Sonoma County near Windsor, then moved to this site in mid-1990. The winery's proprietor, Damaris Deere Ethridge, is a great granddaughter of farm implement pioneer John Deere.

Tasting notes: Chardonnays dominate the short list and they're excellent. A Courtyard Cuvée was rich and complex, and an Overlook Chard had a wonderfully nutty taste with a crisp yet silky finish. Landmark also produces a medium body Zinfandel, full-flavored Pinot Noir and a light and fruity Sauvignon Blanc. Prices: *$$ to $$$$.*

Vintners choice: "Our award-winning premium Chardonnays," says winery president Michael D. Colhoun, Damaris' son. "They will cellar and age for a good amount of time."

St. Francis Winery • T & T$ GTA ✕ ⑩

500 Pythian Rd., Santa Rosa, CA 95409; (800) 543-7713 or (707) 833-4666. (www.stfranciswine.com) Daily 10 to 4:30. Most varieties tasted free; fee for reserve tasting. Good giftware selection; picnic garden; guided tours by appointment.

Once the close neighbor of Château St. Jean, St. Francis moved to an opulent Tuscan style visitor center in the spring of 2001. It's a handsome complex with a stylish tasting room, landscaped grounds and facilities for special events. While not quite the rival of castle-like Ledson just to the north, it's one of the Valley of the Moon's more appealing wine facilities.

St. Francis was started in 1972 by Joseph and Emma Martin. They have built a following for their Merlot and other ribbon-winning varietals, as they gradually built up their winery and visitor facility to its present attractive state.

Tasting notes: The Sonoma County Cabernet Sauvignon was our favorite, big and peppery, with nice oak tones. A Zinfandel from old vines and aged in American oak was excellent as well, lushly berry-like and gently spicy. A Sonoma County Chenin Blanc had the proper flower petal aroma and flavor, and the Chardonnay was buttery and spicy. Prices: *$$ to $$$.*

Ledson Winery & Vineyards • T$ ✕ ⑩

7335 Highway 12, Santa Rosa; mailing address: P.O. Box 653, Kenwood, CA 95452; (707) 833-2330. (www.ledson.com). Daily 10 to 5; major credit cards. Extensive giftware selection and country store with specialty food items and a deli; attractive picnic grounds.

It's simply called "The Castle" and nothing about it is simple. This gorgeously ostentatious multi-gabled brick structure, surrounded by landscaped grounds, is the most opulent wine estate in California. Nothing is understated; every aspect of this places pushes elegance close to the tacky point. Step inside and admire the gift shops with marble fireplaces, the twin tasting rooms sharing a see-through hearth, the cathedral-arch beveled glass windows, the hardwood floors with their laminated borders, the coffered ceilings. The marketplace-deli rivals any gourmet shop and it offers samples of its tasty fare, from cheeses to dipping oils.

All of this is the creation of one of Sonoma County's oldest families. Specifically, it's the conception of Steve Ledson and his wife Michele. His English ancestors came to this area more than a century ago, homesteaded great chunks of land and—through the decades—became one of Sonoma County's most successful growers and ranchers. Ledsons have grown grapes here since 1862 but had never operated a winery, so Steve decided it was about time to press some of the family grapes. He began creating his winery in 1993, released his first wines in 1997 and finally opened "The Castle" in 1999.

Tasting notes: The Ledson wines are excellent and for their prices, they should be. Some reserves approach $100 a bottle; current releases start in the high teens and go higher. We tasted a wonderful *sur lie* Russian River Chardonnay, a rich and fruity Johannisberg Riesling with a hint of sweet; and a spicy and full-flavored Merlot. Others on the brief list are Zinfandel and a rich Orange Muscat. More varietals may be added later. Prices: *$$$ to $$$$*.

THE BEST OF THE BUNCH

The best wine buys ● Sebastiani Sonoma Cask Cellars, Benziger Family Winery and Valley of the Moon Winery.

The most attractive wineries ● Viansa, Gloria Ferrer Champagne Cellars, Buena Vista Carneros, Kunde Estate Winery, Kenwood Vineyards, Château St. Jean, Landmark Vineyards, St. Francis Winery and Ledson Winery.

The most interesting tasting rooms ● Viansa, Sebastiani, Buena Vista Carneros, Landmark Vineyards, St. Francis Winery and Ledson Winery.

The funkiest tasting room ● Gundlach-Bundschu Winery.

The best gift shops ● Viansa, Sebastiani, Buena Vista Winery, Landmark Vineyards, St. Francis Winery and Ledson Winery.

The nicest picnic areas ● Viansa, Schug Carneros Estate, Ravenswood, Bartholomew Park Winery, Buena Vista Winery, Gundlach-Bundschu Winery, Benziger Family Winery and Château St. Jean.

The best tours ● Gloria Ferrer Champagne Cellars (guided), Sebastiani (guided), Buena Vista (historic; also self-guiding), Château St. Jean (self-guiding).

Wine country maps and events

Winery maps and guides ● *Sonoma Valley Visitors Guide* that lists area wineries is available free from the Sonoma Valley Visitors Bureau at 453 First Street on the Sonoma Plaza, or call (707) 996-1090. *(www.sonoma-valley.com) Sonoma Valley Guide* published by the *Sonoma Index-Tribune* also lists area wineries; available free at the visitor center or at many wineries. *Heart of the Valley* guide listing Valley of the Moon wineries available from participating vintners.

Wineland events ● Heart of the Valley barrel tasting at several Valley of the Moon area wineries, mid-March; (707) 833-5891. Sonoma Valley Wine Festival, early July; (707) 938-6805. Sonoma Valley Harvest Wine Auction, early September; (707) 935-0803. Valley of the Moon Vintage Festival, oldest in California with parade, grape stomps, wine tasting, late September; (707) 996-2109. Throughout the year, individual wineries also sponsor various events.

BEYOND THE VINEYARDS

Sonoma is the historic focal point of the valley and you may want to spend considerable time here. Start at the eight-acre **Sonoma Plaza** with its 1906 mission revival **City Hall.** It was built with four matching "front doors" so none of the surrounding merchants would feel slighted. The **Bear Flag Monument** honoring California's brief tenure as a republic stands at the plaza's northeast corner.

The **Sonoma Valley Visitors Bureau** occupies a 1913 Carnegie library building on the Plaza's east side; open daily 9 to 5. It faces the Italianate **Sebastiani Theatre,** a classic old movie house with a 72-foot tower. Boutiques, antique shops, restaurants and bakery-cafés rim the plaza; more are tucked into cozy pedestrian malls. Various elements of **Sonoma State Historic Park** line Spain Street on the top side of the plaza—Mission San Francisco Solano, Sonoma Barracks, Toscano Hotel and the site of Casa Grande, once General Vallejo's home and headquarters.

A few blocks south on Spain Street, you'll encounter Vallejo's final home, a striking gingerbread Victorian called **Lachryma Montis,** Latin for "mountain tear." Dozens of other yesteryear buildings occupy the streets of old Sonoma. To spot them, you can purchase a copy of the Sonoma League for Historic Preservation's *Sonoma Walking Tour* at the visitor's center.

In addition to wine, history and shopping, a fourth element helps draw Sonoma's nearly one million annual visitors—food. Since wining and dining are closely allied, the town has a reputation as a specialty food center. These places, most of them on or near the plaza, are worthy of your attention:

Sonoma Cheese Factory, on the north side of the plaza at Two Spain St., is a large deli and café specializing in local and international cheeses. Through a window, you can watch "jack" style cheese being made. Tables are inside and under an outdoor vine-covered awning. Daily 9 to 6; (800) 535-2855 or (707) 996-1931. *(www.sonomajack.com)*

Vella Cheese Company, a block east of the mission, then a block north at 315 Second St., is Sonoma's other pioneer cheese-making firm, offering specialty foods and picnic fare. Housed in a 1905 rough-cut stone brewery building, it's open Monday-Saturday 9 to 6 and Sunday 10 to 5; (800) 848-0505 or (707) 938-3232. *(www.vellacheese.com)*

The Cherry Tree specializes in cherry juice, cider and other fruit juices and food items. Its main store is at 1901 Fremont Drive (Highways 12-121), just east of Broadway on the route to Napa. The smaller, original cherry tree stand is south on Highway 121 as you come in from the Bay Area. Hours are 6:30 a.m. to 8 p.m. at the Fremont Drive store and 9 to dusk at the stand; (707) 938-3480.

Wine Exchange of Sonoma at 452 First Street East compliments the specialty food outlets, offering dozens of wines local and from afar, 251 beers, plus assorted wine and beer publications. Fee tastings of wines and beers are available daily; (707) 938-1794.

Sonoma Valley attractions

Jack London State Historic Park ● *London Ranch Road, Glen Ellen; 938-5216. Daily 10 to 5; modest admission charge.* □ Famous author's ranch, Wolf House ruins and the restored home of his wife, Charmian.

Sonoma State Historic Park ● *Downtown Sonoma; (707) 938-1578. Daily 10 to 5; modest admission charge (one ticket good for all park elements).* □ The historic park includes Mission San Francisco Solano, Sonoma Barracks, La Casa Grande and Toscano Hotel all on Sonoma Plaza, and General Vallejo's Home, south of the plaza off Spain Street.

Train Town ● *On Broadway a mile south of the square; (707) 938-3912. Open 10 to 5, daily in summer and Friday-Sunday the rest of the year.* □ Miniature train rides through a busily landscaped park; also a carousel and kiddie play area.

Other southern Sonoma County lures

We've fashioned a loop tour that touches other points of interest in the county's southern half. From Sonoma Plaza, drive south on Broadway, perhaps stopping for a choo-choo ride at **Train Town** on your left (see above). About a mile beyond, turn right onto Watmaugh Road, which crosses Arnold Drive, then swings left and blends onto Stage Gulch Road (Highway 116). This takes you into rolling hill country, thatched here and there with oak clusters and madroña groves.

Follow Stage Gulch two and a half miles, turn left onto Adobe Road and follow it to **Petaluma Adobe State Historic Park,** a reconstruction of Vallejo's ranch headquarters. Continue on Adobe Road about a mile and a half, turn left onto Washington Street and take it into **Petaluma.** You'll cross U.S. 101 freeway and wind up in the heart of this old town with the funny name. It's noted for false front and rare iron front stores downtown, and for some attractive Victorian homes on its tree-lined residential streets.

Once you've explored the town, follow D Street (lined with some fine old homes) until it becomes Red Hill Road. Drive nine miles to **Marin French Cheese Factory.** You can watch camembert and other smelly cheeses being made, then buy some cheese and wine and picnic beside a duck pond. You're now in Marin County, but never mind that. This route takes through some of the prettiest hilly landscape in all of northern California. Stay on Red Hill (which becomes Petaluma-Point Reyes Road) until it intersects Highway 1 at **Tomales Bay,** about ten miles from the cheese place. Tomales is a narrow inlet formed by the famous San Andreas Fault—infamous if you're a fidgety California resident who fears earthquakes.

From here, you could stray completely off course by heading south to **Point Reyes National Seashore** on the Point Reyes Peninsula. Or bear with us and bear north on State Route 1 along the skinny bay's eastern shore, passing funky little **Marshall,** a town that seems transported from the New England seacoast. Continue to the equally rustic town of **Tomales,** seven miles north, then turn seaward and prowl the hideaway coastal hamlet of **Dillon Beach.** Press on north to **Bodega Bay,** a bucolic harbor town made famous by Alfred Hitchcock's film, *The Birds.* From here, you can head inland on the Bodega Highway to **Sebastopol,** then follow Highway 12 through **Santa Rosa** and back into the Valley of the Moon at Kenwood.

If you plan to travel from the Sonoma Valley to the Napa Valley, a dramatic and rarely used approach is over Trinity Grade, which branches eastward from Route 12 between Kenwood and Glen Ellen. It twists high into the evergreen reaches of the Mayacamus Mountains, offering views of the Valley of the Moon to the west and—once you start down the other side—the Napa Valley's green patchwork of vineyards. The road hits the Napa Valley's Highway 29 in Oakville; the route is known on this side as the Oakville Grade.

WINE COUNTRY DINING

PRICE KEY: Dinner entrée with soup or salad, without drinks or dessert for under $10 = $; $10 to $14 = $$; $15 to $25 = $$$; over $25 = $$$$.

It will come as no gastronomic surprise that many of Sonoma Valley's restaurants are of the Italian persuasion, although a good mix of *nouveau,* essential American, continental and Mexican fare can be found as well.

Café Citti ● ☆☆☆ $$

☐ *9049 Sonoma Highway, Kenwood; (707) 833-2690. Italian; wine and beer. Lunch through dinner daily. MC/VISA.* ☐ Attractive, cozy Italian *trattoria* in a cottage near the vineyards on the edge of Kenwood. Fresh pasta with a variety of sauces, plus classic cacciatoris, parmigianas and such; patio dining. Local and Italian wines by the glass; specialty foods for sale.

Coffee Garden and Gift Shop ● ☆ $

☐ *415 First Street West, Sonoma; (707) 996-6645. Bakery-café. Breakfast through late evening daily.* ☐ Handy stop for a quite bite, housed in an 1836 adobe. It offers assorted coffees, espressos and such, pastries and muffins for breakfast, plus soups, salads and sandwiches. Sidewalk tables and dining patio; gift shop adjacent.

Cucina Viansa ● ☆☆ $ to $$

400 First Street East (Spain), Sonoma; (707) 935-5656. (www.viansa.com) Italian-American deli. Lunch through dinner daily. MC/VISA. ☐ Very appealing deli and bistro, featuring daily rotisserie fare, panini, pastas and deli items, plus many specialty foods. Also functions as a tasting room for Sam and Vickie Sebastiani's Viansa winery; see above on page 88.

Della Santina Trattoria ● ☆☆☆ $$

☐ *133 E. Napa St. (opposite the plaza), Sonoma; (707) 935-0576. Northern Italian; wine and beer. Lunch through dinner daily. MC/VISA.* ☐ Cute and prim Italian restaurant tucked comfortably behind old cut stone walls, with white nappery and ceiling fans. The usual range of pastas, plus *rosticceria* (spit roasted) specialties. Extensive wine list with fifty-three varieties, including many by the glass.

Depot Hotel Cucina Rustica Restaurant ● ☆☆☆ $$

☐ *241 First Street West (Spain Street), Sonoma; (707) 938-2980. Northern Italian; wine and beer. Lunch Wednesday-Friday and dinner Wednesday-Sunday. Major credit cards.* ☐ Chef-owned restaurant with dining at poolside in a landscaped garden, or in a country inn setting indoors. Fresh seafood and homemade pastas are a specialty, plus Northern Italian dishes.

Eastside Oyster Bar & Grill ● ☆☆☆ $$

☐ *133 E. Napa St. (just off the plaza), Sonoma; (707) 939-1266. California nouveau and oyster bar; wine and beer. Lunch and dinner daily with Sunday brunch. Major credit cards.* ☐ Another trendy café residing in an old Victorian, with lofty ceilings, tile floors and white nappery, featuring oysters, shellfish, fresh fish and other *nouveau* entrées. Patio garden.

Glen Ellen Inn ● ☆☆☆ $$

☐ *13670 Arnold Dr., Glen Ellen; (707) 996-6409. California cuisine; wine and beer. Dinner nightly except Wednesday. MC/VISA.* ☐ Cute and cozy café in a Cape Cod cottage with an open kitchen. Offerings from the changing menu emphasize fresh, locally produced ingredients. Sonoma Valley wines featured; outdoor dining near an herb garden.

Kenwood Restaurant ● ☆☆☆☆ $$$

☐ *9900 Sonoma Highway, Kenwood; (707) 833-6326. French country cuisine; full bar service. Lunch through dinner daily except Monday and Tuesday. MC/VISA.* ☐ An open, cheerful place among the vineyards, with an outdoor dining patio if you want to get closer to the grapes. Changing menu with a strong *nouveau* tilt offers a mix of French and American regional dishes.

La Casa ● ☆☆ *$*

☐ *121 E. Spain St. (opposite the mission), Sonoma; (707) 996-3406. Mexican; full bar service. Lunch through dinner daily. Major credit cards.* ☐ Cheery little Latin place across from the mission, locally popular. Extensive menu features the usual Mexican specialties, singly or in *combinaciòns*. If you're feeling some south of the border patriotism, order the "Mexican flag"—three enchiladas draped with white sour cream, red ground beef and cheese, and green verde sauces.

Murphy's Irish Pub ● ☆☆ *$$*

☐ *464 First Street East (in an alley arcade), Sonoma; (707) 935-0660. Irish-American; full bar service. Lunch through late dinner daily. MC/VISA.* ☐ Guinness stout in the wine country? Sure, and why not? This lively pub, dressed up in Irish regalia, offers pub grub such as fish & chips, meat pies and Irish stew, served with an assortment of ales, pilsners and stouts. Oh, yes—Sonoma Valley wines are featured, if you prefer. Live entertainment—often Irish—is featured frequently; an Irish gift shop is adjacent.

Piatti Restaurant & Bar ● ☆☆☆ *$$$*

☐ *405 First Street West (in the El Dorado Hotel), Sonoma; (707) 996-2351. Regional Italian; full bar service. Lunch through dinner daily. MC/VISA.* ☐ Lively *trattoria*, popular as a business lunch hangout. Open kitchen with wood-burning rotissiere; assorted pastas and other Italian fare. Tree-shaded dining patio.

Vineyards Inn ● ☆☆ *$$*

☐ *8445 Sonoma Highway (Adobe Canyon Road), Kenwood; (707) 833-4500. Spanish, Mexican, American; full bar service. Lunch and dinner daily except Tuesday. MC/VISA.* ☐ Mexican fare served in an early American-style inn. Large menu also strays north of the border, offering gringo fare such as filet mignon and even lamb chops.

Zeno's on the Plaza ● ☆☆ *$$*

☐ *420 First Street East, Sonoma; (707) 996-4466. Traditional Italian; full bar service. Lunch through dinner daily. Major credit cards.* ☐ Not at all trendy, Zeno's is an old fashion Italian restaurant with red checkered tablecloths, dark woods, bentwood chairs and tables topped with *raffia* bottles. A variety of sauces can be poured over spaghetti, linguine, angel hair or penna pastas cooked to order. Other *Italiano* standards are offered as well.

WINELAND LODGINGS

**PRICE KEY: A two-person room for $35 or less = $; $36 to $50 = $$;
$51 to $75 = $$$; $76 to $100 = $$$$; more than $100 = $$$$$.**

Even with the Sonoma Valley's popularity, motels are rather scarce. The area offers an assortment of bed & breakfast inns, historic hotels and—for those with a taste and budget for luxury—the Sonoma Mission Inn and Spa. Nearby Santa Rosa and Petaluma have several motels.

Best Western Sonoma Valley Inn ● ☆☆☆ *$$$$$*

☐ *550 Second Street West (a block west of plaza), Sonoma, CA 95476; (800) 334-5784 or (707) 938-9200. Rates include complimentary breakfast and gift bottle of wine. Major credit cards.* ☐ Nicely appointed 82-unit motel with pool and spa. Rooms have TV movies, phones, refrigerators; most have fireplaces.

El Dorado Hotel ● ☆☆☆ $$$$

□ *405 First Street West (on the plaza), Sonoma, CA 95476; (800) 289-3031 or (707) 996-3030. Rates include bottle of wine on arrival and continental breakfast. MC/VISA, AMEX.* □ Refurbished 26-room mission-style hotel. Attractive rooms with terraces overlooking courtyard or plaza; continental furnishings with Spanish accents; swimming pool. **Ristorante Piatti** listed above.

Kenwood Inn & Spa ● ☆☆☆ $$$$$

□ *10400 Sonoma Hwy. (downtown), Kenwood, CA 95452; (800) 353-6966 or (707) 833-1293. Rates include full breakfast. MC/VISA, AMEX.* □ An opulent Italian style villa with twelve rooms, all with private baths, Mediterranean furnishings, feather beds and other resort amenities; complimentary wine. Extensive landscaped grounds among the vineyards. Separate spa building offers massage, facial and body treatments; fitness workouts.

Sonoma Hotel ● ☆☆ $$$$ to $$$$$

□ *110 W. Spain St. (northwest corner of plaza), Sonoma, CA 95476; (800) 468-6016 or (707) 996-2996. (www.sonomahotel.com) Rates include continental breakfast and evening wine tasting. MC/VISA, AMEX.* □ Newly renovated 1874 hotel; sixteen rooms with private baths, featuring antiques and wine country décor. **Restaurant** serves lunch and dinner daily; full bar service.

Sonoma Mission Inn and Spa ● ☆☆☆☆ $$$$$

□ *100 Boyes Blvd., Boyes Hot Springs; mailing address P.O. Box 1447, Sonoma, CA 95476; (800) 862-4945 or (707) 938-9000. Major credit cards.* □ Elegant Mediterranean style resort on seven acres with a health spa, natural hot artesian mineral water pools, golf, swimming pool and other facilities. The 228 beautifully appointed rooms have full resort amenities. **Poolside Restaurant** serves wine country cuisine with international accents; **Big Three Diner** offers an eclectic American menu; breakfast through dinner daily; full bar service.

Bed & breakfast inns

Beltane Ranch Bed & Breakfast ● ☆☆☆ $$$$$

□ *11775 Sonoma Highway (P.O. Box 395), Glen Ellen, CA 95442; (707) 996-6501. Four rooms, all with private baths and private entrances; full breakfast. No credit cards.* □ An 1892 Colonial style ranch house in a pleasant country setting with a vineyard and valley view. Tennis court, tree-shaded gardens, hammocks and hiking trails. Attractive rooms are furnished with American and European antiques.

Gaige House ● ☆☆☆☆ $$$$$

□ *13540 Arnold Dr. (half mile off Highway 12), Glen Ellen, CA 95442; (707) 935-0237. Fifteen rooms and two cottages with private baths, phones and TV; full breakfast. Major credit cards.* □ Elegantly restored 1890 Italianate mansion in a creekside setting, furnished with American and Asian antiques. Eight units have fireplaces. Pool and hot tub; short walk to town.

Glenelly Inn & Properties ● ☆☆☆ $$$$$

□ *5131 Warm Springs Rd. (off Arnold Drive), Glen Ellen, CA 95442; (707) 996-6720. Eight rooms, all with private baths; full breakfast. MC/VISA.* □ A refurbished 1916 country resort in the French colonial style. Rooms done in

American and European antiques. One-acre landscaped grounds with spa and rose garden. Off-site vacation rentals also available.

Sonoma Chalet ● ☆☆ $$$$$

☐ *18935 Fifth Street West (Verano Avenue), Sonoma, CA 95476; (707) 938-3129. Seven units, four with private baths; continental breakfast. MC/VISA, AMEX.* ☐ Nicely restored country-style complex with rooms in a farmhouse, plus private cottages. Furnished with early American antiques; fireplaces, wood-burning stoves. Spa, bicycles, complimentary Sherry.

Thistle Dew Inn ● ☆☆☆ $$$$$

☐ *171 W. Spain St. (a block west of plaza), Sonoma, CA 95476; (707) 938-2909. Six rooms, all with private baths; full breakfast. MC/VISA, AMEX.* ☐ Lodgings in an 1869 Victorian and a 1905 early American home, furnished with turn-of-the-century antiques, arts and crafts. Spa, bicycles, afternoon *hors d'oeuvres.*

Trojan Horse Inn ● ☆☆☆ $$$$$

☐ *19455 Sonoma Hwy. (between West Napa and Spain), Sonoma, CA 95476; (707) 996-2430. Six rooms, all with private baths; full breakfast. MC/VISA, AMEX.* ☐ Victorian style farmhouse with extensive landscaped grounds on the banks of Sonoma Creek. Rooms furnished with English and American antiques; armoires and brass beds. Complimentary bicycles and evening cocktails.

Victorian Garden Inn ● ☆☆☆ $$$$$

☐ *316 E. Napa St. (a block and a half east of the plaza), Sonoma, CA 95476; (800) 543-5339 or (707) 996-5339. (victoriangardeninn.com) Four rooms, three with private baths, one cottage with fireplace; full breakfast. MC/VISA, AMEX.* ☐ An 1880 Greek Revival style home furnished with country antiques. Pool, therapeutic spa, landscaped grounds and patio; complimentary evening coffee, tea and snacks.

Sonoma Valley information sources

Sonoma County Wine & Visitors Center, 5000 Roberts Lake Rd., Rohnert Park, CA 94928; (707) 586-3795. *(www.sonomawine.com)*

Sonoma State Historic Park, P.O. Box 167, Sonoma, CA 95476; (707) 938-1519.

Sonoma Valley Visitors Bureau, 453 First Street East, Sonoma, CA 95476; (707) 996-1090. *(www.sonomavalley.com)*

Those lodes and pockets of earth, more precious than the precious ores, that yield inimitable fragrance and soft fire; those virtuous Bonanzas, where the soil has sublimated under sun and stars to discover something finer, and the wine is bottled poetry... — **The Silverado Squatters by Robert Louis Stevenson**

Chapter Five

NAPA: DOWN VALLEY

The south end: Napa to Rutherford

Approached from the south, America's most famous wine valley appears to be more of a plain. The landscape, too gentle here to be called hilly, cradles the Napa River as it wanders aimlessly through a delta toward the San Pablo arm of San Francisco Bay.

From its outskirts, Napa—the valley's foundation city—seems little different from any other mid-sized American community. It could as well be Cedar Rapids, Iowa, or Boise, Idaho. Driving along the freeway portion of Highway 29, you see few clues to a fabled wineland.

Yet vineyards are all about you, crouching behind the subtly rolling terrain. The Carneros region is just to the southwest, where the Napa and Sonoma valley flood plains merge at the edge of the bay. More vines garnish foothills of the Vaca Range to the northeast, shielded from view by spreading Napa suburbs. Other vineyards stride up the flanks of the Mayacamas Mountains to the northwest. None of these are apparent as you skirt the western edge of Napa. Then as clear the northern edge of town, grape vines begin to appear, eventually covering the valley floor like shag carpeting.

As you continue north on Highway 29, the two low mountain ranges draw near to create the vision of the Napa Valley so familiar to Americans. Ranks of vines march away from the highway like a retreating army in green camouflage. Ivy-walled wineries stand at roadside; mansions built by yesterday's wine barons sulk behind protective cloaks of trees. As you travel further into the valley toward Oakville, the great bulk of Mount St. Helena commands the northern horizon.

Two main routes, Highway 29 and the Silverado Trail, run roughly parallel along the valley's edges, linked by crossroads to form a crooked ladder. Vineyards line both main highways as well as the ladder-rung crossroads.

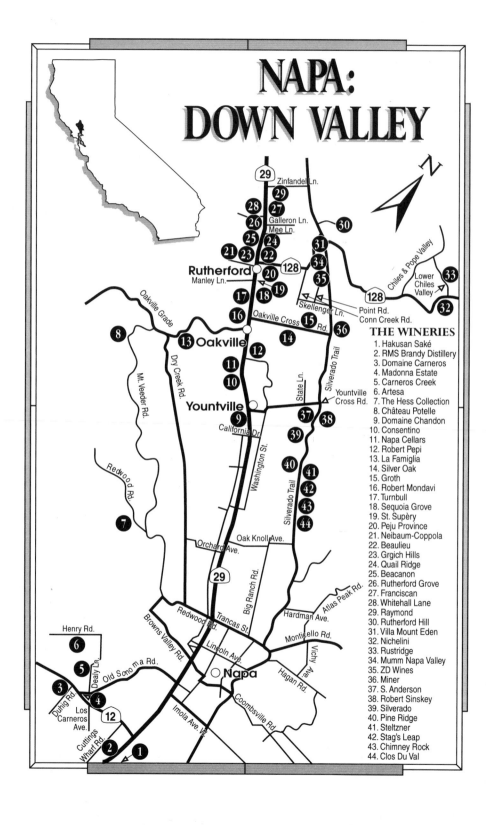

NAPA: DOWN VALLEY

Zinfandel Ln.

Galleron Ln.
Mee Ln.

Rutherford
Manley Ln.

Chiles & Pope Valley

Lower
Chiles
Valley

Point Rd.
Conn Creek Rd.

Skellenger Ln.

Oakville Grade

Oakville Cross Rd.

Oakville

Dry Creek Rd.

Mt. Veeder Rd.

Yountville
Cross Rd.

State Ln.

Silverado Trail

Yountville

California Dr.

Redwood Rd.

Washington St.

Oak Knoll Ave.

Orchard Ave.

Silverado Trail

Big Ranch Rd.

Atlas Peak Rd.

Henry Rd.

Browns Valley Rd.

Old Sonoma Rd.

Redwood Rd.

Trancas St.

Lincoln Ave.

Hardman Ave.

Montigello Rd.

Vichy Ave.

Hagan Rd.

Napa

Dealy Ln.

During Rd.

Los
Carneros
Ave.

Cuttings
Wharf Rd.

Imola Ave. W.

Coombsville Rd.

THE WINERIES

1. Hakusan Saké
2. RMS Brandy Distillery
3. Domaine Carneros
4. Madonna Estate
5. Carneros Creek
6. Artesa
7. The Hess Collection
8. Château Potelle
9. Domaine Chandon
10. Consentino
11. Napa Cellars
12. Robert Pepi
13. La Famiglia
14. Silver Oak
15. Groth
16. Robert Mondavi
17. Turnbull
18. Sequoia Grove
19. St. Supèry
20. Peju Province
21. Neibaum-Coppola
22. Beaulieu
23. Grgich Hills
24. Quail Ridge
25. Beacanon
26. Rutherford Grove
27. Franciscan
28. Whitehall Lane
29. Raymond
30. Rutherford Hill
31. Villa Mount Eden
32. Nichelini
33. Rustridge
34. Mumm Napa Valley
35. ZD Wines
36. Miner
37. S. Anderson
38. Robert Sinskey
39. Silverado
40. Pine Ridge
41. Steltzner
42. Stag's Leap
43. Chimney Rock
44. Clos Du Val

The Napa Valley is everything one would expect—only busier. Nearly 250 wineries dot the landscape; some of the larger ones draw more than 300,000 visitors a year. Tour buses may inundate tasting rooms without warning; insurance widows from Indiana will giggle nervously and ask for a sip of something sweet. Highway 29 can become traffic-tangled on summer weekends. Gimmicks such as the Napa Valley Wine Train and theme shopping centers lure visitor hoards.

Yet you can find picturesque, tucked-away wineries with tasting rooms that are rarely crowded, winding country lanes bereft of cars, and lonely ramparts with valley vistas to draw your breath away.

To avoid crowds, visit the Napa Valley on a weekday, when even the major wineries are uncrowded. If that's not practical (most of us work for a living), focus on wineries off Highway 29. The Silverado Trail, running through more attractive terrain in the Vaca foothills, entices only a fraction of the valley's visitors. Finally, get an early start. Yes, it may seem odd to drink before lunch, but you're here to taste and learn about wine. Most tasting rooms open at 10 a.m., yet crowds rarely peak until after noon. Consider retreating to your hotel pool in the late afternoon—the busiest time of day for winery tasting rooms.

Sipping fees

Many valley wineries charge for tasting, a practice which we approve, since it discourages those out for a free drinking spree. Tasting room folks scornfully refer to them as "recreational drinkers." Fees are nominal—a few dollars to sample a variety of wines. Often, you can keep the glass, which bears the winery's logo, or you can apply the charge toward a purchase. Glasses come in assorted sizes, so one winds up with a rather eclectic collection. (When we mentioned this to a tasting room host, he grinned and quipped: "Just come back eight times and you'll have a matched set.")

We were impressed by the overall excellence of the wines as we visited the valley's tasting rooms. Despite its touristy reputation, the Napa Valley is home to serious vintners who produce some of America's finest wines. Not surprisingly, they're generally more expensive that similar varieties from other areas. Even unprocessed grapes command a higher price. They may be no better than comparable Sonoma or Mendocino fruit, but these are *Napa* grapes, thank you!

Incidentally, if you're biking through the Napa Valley, both Highway 29 and the Silverado Trail have bike lanes. The Silverado is more scenic and less congested.

Even though the valley has two hundred-plus wineries, most are small. The ten largest control a third of the grape crop and produce forty percent of the wine. Among them are Charles Krug, Louis Martini, Robert Mondavi, Beringer and Beaulieu—all familiar names to wine fans. Yet with all of the Napa Valley's viticultural largess, this fabled Eden produces only two percent of California's wines. Most, about eighty percent, comes from the San Joaquin Valley.

California's most famous wine valley isn't its first. By the time Napa wine production began in earnest in the 1860s, vineyards around Los Angeles had passed their peak and Sonoma was regarded as the cradle of commercial viniculture. However, it now surpasses every wine producing area in America, not in overall wine production or vineyard acreage, but in the total number of wineries.

A hunter-gatherer Native American tribe variously called Wappo or Nappa inhabited the valley for nearly 4,000 years. "Nappa" may mean "bountiful place" or salmon or spear point or grizzly bear. We will never know, for the gentle Stone Age Wappo—victims of servitude, disease and bullets dealt by the Spanish and later American settlers—exist no more.

When Mission San Francisco Solano was established in Sonoma in 1823, the Napa Valley was seen as suitable only for grazing land. Huge chunks of it were granted to citizens of the newly-freed Mexico who had helped in its fight for independence from Spain. But for the most part it remained undeveloped—the domain of deer, grizzlies and wild oats.

The first outside settler was American frontiersman George Calvert Yount. After working for Sonoma's Mariano Vallejo, he was granted Rancho Caymus in the Napa Valley in the 1830s. The first American citizen to obtain a Mexican land grant, he planted vineyards and orchards near the town named in his honor. It's likely that he made a bit of wine from Mission grapes for his table and thus became one of the valley's earliest vintners.

Legendary families

Napa's first commercial wine production is attributed to John Patchett in 1858. Then came families whose names still ring in Napa Valley history books—Charles Krug in 1860, Jacob Schram of Schramsberg in 1862, the Beringer brothers in the 1870s, Gustave Niebaum of the former Inglenook in 1899 and Georges de Latour, who established Beaulieu in 1900.

Others left their marks on the valley, as well. Flamboyant Mormon Sam Brannan, who had shouted out California's 1848 gold discovery in the streets of San Francisco, built the valley's first mineral springs resort in 1868. Styled after the grand Saratoga spa of New York, it was called by Brannan—perhaps in drunken jest—"the Calistoga of Sarifornia." During the summer of 1880, impoverished, ailing Scottish writer Robert Louis Stevenson and his bride Fanny spent their honeymoon in an old mining shack high in the flanks of Mount St. Helena. (See box in Chapter Six.)

Napa Valley's history pursued the typical pattern—the 1870s wine price crash, phylloxera, Prohibition, Repeal and a gradual rebuilding during last century's first half. The Christian Brothers came to the valley in 1930, Louis M. Martini established his winery in 1933 and Cesare Mondavi bought the Charles Krug facility ten years later. When Cesare died in 1959, it was passed to sons Peter and Robert. World War II slowed vineyard and winery growth. Life moved slowly in the idyllic valley for many quiet years.

Then, after a family spat said to be one of the seeds for TV's old *Falcon Crest* series, Robert Mondavi left Krug. In 1966, he opened the first "new" winery in the valley in several years. Indeed, it was a new concept—one of the first wineries designed for public tours, vineyard concerts and other special events. The energetic, outspoken Mondavi has become a leading de-

---

WINERY CODES ● *T* = tasting with no fee; *T$* = tasting for a fee; *GT* = guided tours; *GTA* = guided tours by appointment; *ST* = self-guiding or informal tours; ✕ = picnic area; 📷 = gift shop or a good giftware selection.

WINE PRICES ● *$* = average price under $10 per bottle; *$$* = $10 to $14; *$$$* = $15 to $19; *$$$$* = $20 or more

fender of wine's public image and a foe of what he calls "neo-prohibitionists." Not surprisingly, he is one of the chief subjects in James Conaway's rather revealing book, *Napa: The Story of an American Eden*. Now something of a legend, he has expanded his empire to include several other wineries around the state, along with a very successful jug wine operation in Woodbridge.

America's sudden "discovery" of wines in the late 1960s was both a boon and a menace to the Napa Valley. Vineyard acreage tripled and wineries multiplied; the valley became the target of every tour bus route. Many visitors put down roots and Napa's suburbs swelled northward, threatening prime vine land. A four-lane expressway bullied its way through the vineyards, seeking to alleviate Highway 29 congestion.

Vintners and other concerned citizens rushed to rescue their enchanted land. An agricultural preserve was established in 1968 to protect prime vineyards. The new highway was stopped at Yountville, so the rest of Highway 29 remains congested, particularly on weekends. Residents wisely decided that the cure would have been more painful than the illness.

Despite its growing popularity, the area still has its quiet moments and quiet places. Early on a weekday morning, you can discover a Napa Valley much like that observed by Robert Louis Stevenson in 1880:

The stirring sunlight and the growing vines, and the vats and bottles in the caverns, made a pleasant music for the mind.

Since the valley has more wineries than any other area in America, we've divided it into two chapters. We use the local reference, "down valley" for the southern end and "up valley" for the north. In touring down valley, we'll divide it again, first visiting the Carneros and Mount Veeder areas near Napa, then the heart of the valley along Highway 29 and the Silverado Trail.

CARNEROS-MOUNT VEEDER WINERY TOUR ●

As we mentioned earlier, the Sonoma and Napa valleys share the Carneros. Cooled by bay breezes, this gentle terrain is ideal for Chardonnay and Pinot Noir. Much of it goes into sparkling wines and three champagneries are located here. The tilted, rocky soils of nearby Mount Veeder in the Mayacamus range nurture exceptional Cabernets.

Napa's Carneros can be reached by two approaches from the Bay Area. From U.S. 101, turn east onto State Highway 37 north of Novato, then swing north onto Highway 29 in Vallejo. If you're following Interstate 80 north, take Highway 37 west through Vallejo, and then turn north onto Route 29. The first two wineries you will encounter are not wineries in the conventional sense. The first makes Japanese saké and the second produces French style pot still brandy.

Head north from Vallejo on Route 29 and, after about six miles, turn right onto Highway 12 at the Fairfield-Sacramento sign, and then go left at the first signal onto Kelley Road. You'll see the entrance to **Hakusan Saké Gardens** on the left. After visiting Hakusan, continue north on Kelly Road, since it merges back into Route 29/12. After a short distance, fork left to stay with this twin route, then after two miles go west on Highway 121/12 (following a Sonoma sign) into the Carneros region. After a bit over a mile, turn left onto Cuttings Wharf Road and follow it a mile to **RMS Brandy Distillery,** on your left.

Return to Highway 121/12, turn left and continue into the Carneros region. This is subtly rolling terrain, as softly contoured as a slender woman.

Many vineyards but few winery tasting rooms occupy this area. You'll shortly encounter the palatial **Domaine Carneros** on the left at the Duhig Road junction. From here, you may want to follow Duhig into the Carneros terrain, enjoying vineyard vistas and distant blue slices of San Pablo Bay.

Return to Highway 121 from Domaine Carneros, go east briefly, fork left onto Old Sonoma Road and you'll shortly see **Madonna Estate/Mont St. John Cellars** on your right. Now, continue on Old Sonoma a short distance to Dealy Lane, go left and follow it just under a mile to **Carneros Creek Winery.** Continue past Carneros Creek for about a mile as the road takes a couple of ninety-degree turns, which puts you on Henry Road. A curving lane to your left leads to the top of a low hill to the dramatic **Artesa Winery**, bunkered into that hilltop.

Return to Old Sonoma Road and follow it into the city of **Napa**. Just short of the freeway, turn left at the Calistoga-San Rafael sign and drive a mile along a frontage road, past Napa Valley Center and a large Napa Factory Stores outlet center. Make a sharp right onto First Street, cross over the freeway and take a right-hand cloverleaf down to it. You're now headed north into the Napa Valley.

The freeway ends at a stoplight at the intersection of Redwood Road; go left onto Redwood and follow it west into the foothills of wooded Mount Veeder. After more than four winding and scenic miles, turn left at the junc-

WINE TASTING

tion of Redwood and Mount Veeder roads (staying on Redwood). The impressive **Hess Collection** winery is about a mile beyond, on your left.

Return to the junction and turn left onto Mount Veeder Road, following its route west along an attractive creek valley. It winds steeply into the Mayacamas, passing bearded oaks, pines and occasional redwoods. After seven miles, you'll see a small sign to **Château Potelle,** reached by a steep and winding one-mile asphalt road. Stay alert, since it's easy to overshoot the turnoff. (**NOTE:** The winery has limited hours, so call ahead before making this climb into the hills.)

From Château Potelle, continue a bit over a mile downhill on Mount Veeder until it ends at Dry Creek Road. Go right, then right again after less than half a mile, staying on Dry Creek. After about ten miles, Dry Creek T-bones into Redwood Road; turn left and you're in Napa suburbs.

This route is more scenery than winery and we feel that the drive into the thickly wooded Mayacamas Mountains is worth the effort. If you don't care for excessive twisting and turning, you could skip Château Potelle and follow Redwood Road from the Hess Collection back to Napa.

Hakusan Saké Gardens ● T$ ST

Highway 12 at Highway 29 (One Executive Way), Napa, CA 94558; (707) 258-6160. Daily 10 to 5; MC/VISA. Saké samples tasted for a very modest fee. Some gift items. Self-guiding tours; formal Japanese garden adjacent to tasting room.

Why not start your tour with the wine of another nation? Hakusan is the only *sakery* in the Napa Valley, producing Japanese rice wine from rice grown in California's Sacramento Valley. Sips of cold and warm saké and a sweet dessert wine are served in a large, airy tasting room done in Tokyo-modern style, furnished like a spacious Japanese restaurant. From here, you can walk past windows of the modern, warehouse-like brewery. Signs tell you what you're seeing. Your path then leads you through a tranquil (except for adjacent Highway 29 traffic) Japanese garden, back to the hospitality center. *Hakusan,* incidentally, means "white mountain."

Saké has been traced to 700 B.C., when it was called *kuchikami no saké,* which describes how it was made. Rice and chestnuts or millet were chewed into a wad, then spat into a wooden tub to ferment. Fortunately, today's production methods are a bit more clinical.

Tasting notes: Saké has a crisp pleasantly pungent apple or tropical fruit taste, a bit like a dry Sauvignon Blanc. The dessert saké is sweet yet crisp; think of a *very* light bodied Muscat dessert wine. Prices: *$ to S$$.*

RMS Brandy Distillery ● GT 📷

1250 Cuttings Wharf Rd., Napa, CA 94559; (707) 253-9055. Daily 10 to 5 in summer and 10:30 to 4:30 the rest of the year; MC/VISA, AMEX. Tour of brandy distillery, with "sensory evaluation," No tasting, since it's forbidden by federal law. Retail shop offering brandies and an extensive selection of logo items and giftwares.

RMS Distillery makes brandy the old fashioned way—by burbling especially prepared wine in copper kettles, capturing and condensing the alcohol and essence much the same way as Cognac is made in France. No surprise, since it is owned by *La Belle Françoise'* Remy Martin. Most American brandies are made in a "continuous column" device in which the vapors are collected at various levels. Brandy aficionados say the French method, called *alambic,* produces a more full-flavored and complex brandy, while the American version is lighter and smoother.

A thirty-minute tour of this sleek tile roof facility reveals the simple yet technically sophisticated method of producing Cognac style brandy. The tour begins with an audio-visual demonstration employing a cleverly mechanized one-quarter scale model of an alambic distillery. Visitors adjourn to the still house to admire the full-scale handcrafted copper stills, then they inhale the heady aroma of aging brandies in the barrel room.

Sniffing notes: The tour ends in the library for a "sensory evaluation of RMS Distillery's various products"—which means that you can only sniff. Several types of brandy and brandies in various stages of production can be swirled and inhaled from—well, snifters. These brandies are not inexpensive products, beginning at more than $20 for a 350 milliliter pear liqueur and ascending from there. After inhaling this heady ambrosia and taking home a bottle of the *pear de pear*, we think it's worth it.

Distillers choice: "Our fourteen-year-old "QE" Quality Extraordinaire brandy," says the distillery's Barbara Secor.

Domaine Carneros ● T$ GT

1240 Duhig Rd. (P.O. Box 5420), Napa, CA 94558; (707) 257-0101. (www.domainecarneros.com) Daily 10:30 to 6; MC/VISA, AMEX. Sparkling wines sold by the glass. Some wine related gift items. Guided tours hourly from 11 to 4 from April through November, and at 11, 1 and 3 the rest of the year.

This sparkling wine facility, an offspring of France's Champagne Tattinger, is among the valley's more elegant wine properties. Completed in 1987 and styled after the Tattinger family's Château de la Marquetterie in the French Champagne district, it is an imposing presence, crowning a low hill in the heart of the Carneros.

After admiring a portrait of Madame Pompadour, the beaded glass chandeliers, high coffered ceilings and the view, you can seat yourself in a cane-backed chair at a brass and glass table. There, you are served a sparkling wine for a fee, with *hors d'oeuvres*, of course. On warm days, you can adjourn to a view deck. Tours are thorough and informative, amounting to a cram course in sparkling wine production. It begins with a nicely done multimedia show, presented in a fashionable little drawing room with a window into the winery. The tour then proceeds to a windowed gallery above the aging cellar and production floor.

Tasting notes: The Sparkling Brut, Domaine Carneros' primary product, was pleasantly complex and mouth-filling, with a nice crisp Chardonnay finish. Others on the list are Brut Rosé, Blanc de Blanc and a table wine, Famous Gate Pinot Noir. Prices: *$$$$.*

Madonna Estate/Mont St. John Cellars ● T GTA ✗

5400 Old Sonoma Rd., Napa, CA 94558; (707) 255-8864. (www.madronaestate.com) Daily 10 to 5; MC/VISA, AMEX. Most varieties tasted. Some wine logo gift items. Shaded picnic area, plus a barbecue area available by reservation. Tours by prior arrangement.

The Louis Bartolucci family has been making Napa Valley wines since the 1920s. Founder Andrea Bartolucci came to America from Italy in 1913 and started his first winery in 1922 in Oakville. Succeeding generations moved the operation to this small, attractive California mission style facility in the 1971, where they produce about 15,000 cases a year. In a separate "entertainment room," visitors can watch a film tracing the winery's production techniques from vineyard to bottle.

Tasting notes: Chardonnay, Pinot Grigio Blanc, Johannisberg Riesling, Gewürztraminer and *Muscat di Canelli* occupy the white list; Cabernet Sauvignon, Merlot and Pinot Noir are the reds. A Chardonnay was exceptional and the Gewürztraminer was lush and rich without being sweet. Of the reds, we were impressed by the spicy-berry nose and complex flavor of the Pinot Noir. The wines were uniformly good, with moderate prices: *$$ to $$$$.*

Vintners choice: "Carneros is the ideal region for Chardonnay and Pinot Noir, and I would select those as our best wines," says Sue Bartolucci. "Our Pinot has won an international gold medal."

Carneros Creek Winery ● T$ ST ✕

1285 Dealy Lane, Napa, CA 94558; (707) 253-WINE. Daily 10 to 5; major credit cards. Most varieties tasted for a fee. A few wine logo items. Picnic area under an arbor.

"We like to enter into a dialog with visitors," says Carneros Creek's hospitality and retail manager Stacy Manley. This small winery is serious about Pinot Noir and folks here like to talk with serious minded wine enthusiasts, even offering tastes of rare library selections. Established in this region in 1972 specifically to pursue the Pinot, the winery is a leader in clonal research and has won numerous awards for its noble Burgundian-style wines. The appearance of the place belies its serious intent. It resembles a suburban home with an oversized garage. However, it is growing; a modern new production facility and visitor center opened recently.

Tasting notes: The list, not surprisingly, is mostly Pinot Noir, offered in several different styles. Also available are Chardonnay, Cabernet Sauvignon and Merlot. We particularly liked the Fleur de Carneros Pinot, light yet complex with a powerful berry focus brought about by cloning. A Signature Reserve Pinot was spicy, peppery and awesome. The barrel fermented Chardonnay was properly buttery and spicy, with a light finish. Prices: *$$ to $$$$.*

Artesa Vineyards & Winery ● T$ GT & GTA 🏮

1345 Henry Rd., Napa, CA 94559; (707) 224-1668. (www.artesawinery.com) Daily 10 to 5; MC/VISA. One fee for tasting six wines from the current release list, and another for sampling three reserve wines. Sparkling wines available for purchase by the glass. Tasteful selection of giftwares. Tours of winery and wine museum at 11 and 2, or by reservation.

One the most impressive wineries and tasting rooms in America isn't just another elaborate estate, *faux* French château or pretend castle. Artesa is an imposing $40 million two-tiered pyramid bunkered into a hilltop. Rimmed by reflection ponds and boldly gushing fountains, it appears from afar to be a well-groomed grass-covered Mayan temple. Step inside and you're in a starkly modern space decorated with choice *objets de art*; inverted triangle windows offer grand views of the Carneros region. Curving twin tasting counters invite visitors to sample Artesa's fine wines; dainty little tables invite them to linger. A select ensemble of giftwares completes this picture of ultra-modern opulence.

This striking facility is the creation of the Codornui family of Barcelona. They bought several hundred acres of Carneros land then hired a bright young Spanish architect, Domingo Triay, to design a winery. After walking every acre of the land, he chose to put the winery in—not on—the area's highest hill. Workers removed the top of the hill, installed the two-tiered winery and hospitality center and then more or less replaced the hilltop by creating a twin-level pyramid. Initially called Codornui Napa, it was completed in 1991 to produce sparkling wines. A line of still wines was added in late 1999 and the name was changed to Artesa, or "artistic" in Spanish.

Tasting notes: We only wish we could afford these wines! Crafted by winemaker Don Van Staaveren, these are some of the best we've ever tasted. A Chardonnay was gorgeously lush and tasty with hints of oak. Each of three Pinot Noirs was progressively richer and spicier. One Merlot was full of berries; the other full of spice. Two Cabernets were lush and mouth-filling with classic chili pepper flavors. Artesa still produces sparking wines, including a Napa Valley Brut and Reserve Cuvée. Prices begin in the high teens and travel well beyond: *$$$ to $$$$.*

The Hess Collection ● T$ ST 🏛

4411 Redwood Rd. (P.O. Box 4140), Napa, CA 94558; (707) 255-1144. Daily 10 to 4; MC/VISA. Several wines tasted for a modest fee. Good selection of gift and art items. Self-guiding tour of the art museum, with views into the winery. Periodic slide shows about the winery and vineyards.

In a word or two, the Hess Collection is one of the most impressive inner spaces in California's wine country. It's a Château-like structure with an attractive island-counter tasting salon, windows peeking into the winery and an art gallery with dazzling white walls set against old stone. Despite the look of old world formality, staff members are friendly and helpful as they guide folks through tastings. Visitors may wander about the gallery on their own. The art? It's on the leading edge of the modern movement which, like a dry martini, is an acquired taste.

The ninth generation member of a Swiss brewing family, Donald Hess inherited a small fortune and soon turned it into a large one. He diversified into mineral water, restaurants and vineyards. He established this elegant combined winery and art gallery in 1989. The original winery was built at the turn of the century by Oakland businessman Theodore Gier. Then the Christian Brothers, a Catholic teaching order, purchased it in 1932 and established an adjacent novitiate. It functioned as Mont La Salle Vineyards until Hess acquired the property in 1986 and began an extensive renovation.

Tasting notes: The winery bottles Cabernet Sauvignon, Chardonnay, Merlot and Zinfandel. Many are offered in two versions—the upscale Hess Collection, and the moderately priced Hess Select. A Hess Collection Chardonnay was lush, nutty and silky, while a Hess Select was fruitier and less complex yet quite tasty. The Hess Collection Cabernet, peppery and spicy with a nippy tannic finish, was exceptional. Prices: *$$ to $$$$.*

Château Potelle ● T ✗

3875 Mount Veeder Rd., Napa, CA 94558; (707) 255-9440. Thursday-Monday 10 to 5 in summer; shorter hours the rest of the year. Select varieties tasted. Picnic tables in a grove with a vineyard view.

Potelle is a château in name only; the title comes from a family manor house in France. Founders Jean Noel and Marketta Fourmeaux arrived from the French wine country in the early 1980s and began this winery in 1985. Scattered over wooded slopes, the small facility more resembles an American hill country farmyard than a French manor. It's an appealing place in a woodsy sort of way, with a barn of a winery and small tasting room in a clapboard cottage. A deck offers impressive views of tilted vineyards and the surrounding hills. One of the winery's most pleasing aspects is its far removal from the madding crowds of the Napa Valley.

Tasting notes: Château Potelle produces limited quantities of three varietals, hand-crafting them in the European style—Sauvignon Blanc, Cabernet Sauvignon and Zinfandel. They're generally excellent and have won numerous awards. Prices: *$$$ to $$$$.*

DOWN VALLEY WINERY TOUR ● Finding wineries in this end of the valley requires no great navigational feat. They stand in obedient ranks along Highway 29 and the paralleling Silverado Trail, or on the crossroads that connect the two.

We left you at the intersection of Redwood Road and Highway 29 in the last tour. Turn left (north) onto the highway, which is mostly a limited access expressway between here and **Yountville**. Shortly after it temporarily resumes full freeway status, take the Yountville exit and turn left onto Washington Street.

Within a couple of blocks, you'll see the **Napa Valley Tourist Bureau** on your right, at 6488 Washington. It's not an official visitor center but a no-fee booking agency for Napa Valley lodgings, tours, balloon flights and other activities, and it sells maps and guides to the area. It's open weekdays 10 to 4 plus weekends in summer; (707) 944-1558. The **Yountville Chamber of Commerce** is a bit beyond, on the right at a Y-intersection where Young Street splits off from Washington; it shares a shingle-sided building with the Yountville Community Center at 6516 Yount Street; open Monday-Saturday 10 to 3; closed Sundays; (707) 944-0904.

You may want to explore the assortment of shops, boutiques and galleries in this tourist-oriented town. Many are in **Vintage 1870,** a former winery turned theme shopping center across Washington Street from the chamber. Nicely done in old brick, the center has a wine-tasting facility offering sips for a modest fee, plus several restaurants. Most Vintage 1870 shops are open 10 to 5:30; some restaurants remain open longer.

Having done with Yountville, go west under the freeway on California Drive, then follow signs to the right to **Domaine Chandon.** Return to Highway 29 and continue north; it ceases being a freeway and the wineries present themselves in quick order, so keep a wary eye. **Cosentino Winery** is on the left, just beyond the popular Mustard's Café, then **Napa Cellars** also on the left a few yards beyond; and **Robert Pepi Winery,** about a quarter of a mile farther, up a vineyard lane to the right.

Now, turn left onto Oakville Grade in the hamlet of **Oakville** and drive about a mile up to **La Famiglia** in the Mayacamas foothills. Along the way, you might stop at the **Carmelite Monastery** and browse through its gift shop, which occupies a clapboard building below the monastery; open Tuesday-Sunday 11 to 3:30. The chapel above generally is open to the public only during mass, at 8 a.m. weekdays and 9 a.m. Sunday; (707) 944-9408.

Return to Highway 29 and stop for a browse through **Oakville Grocery** on the corner of Oakville Cross Road. It's a country grocery store turned designer deli, with cheeses, meats, assorted olives, fresh pastas, breads, patés, prepared salads, a small produce section and a huge local wine selection. It's a one-stop picnic builder, although most items are a bit pricey.

From the grocery, follow Oakville Cross Road a mile east to **Silver Oak Cellars**, up a lane to your right. Continue briefly east on Oakville Cross to **Groth Vineyards and Winery,** on your left. Then retreat to Route 29, continue north and you'll soon encounter the Spanish mission style **Robert Mondavi Winery** on the left. Just beyond, also on the left, is **Turnbull Wine Cellars** and briefly past that is **Sequoia Grove Vineyards** on the right. Next in order are **St. Supéry Winery** and next-door **Peju Province.** As you approach the small town of **Rutherford,** turn left just past Niebaum Lane for **Niebaum-Coppola Estate Winery.** Immediately beyond on the right is **Beaulieu Vineyard,** followed by **Grgich Hills Cellar** on the left.

A bit farther along, **Quail Ridge** and **Beaucanon** are across the highway from one another. To reach Quail Ridge, turn right onto a small lane, drive past a ranch complex and then turn right into the winery. Return to the highway and—when the busy traffic clears—shoot straight across to Beaucanon. Just up the highway, small **Rutherford Grove** and large **Franciscan Estates** are across from one another—Rutherford on the left; Franciscan on the right. Briefly beyond is **Whitehall Lane,** on the left.

A few hundred feet from Whitehall, turn right onto Zinfandel Lane, stop at **Raymond Cellars** up a gravel lane on your right, then continue on to the Silverado Trail. Swing south on Silverado and watch for Rutherford Hill Road, leading to the left through the posh **Auberge du Soliel** resort to **Rutherford Hill Winery.** Continue a bit farther south on to **Conn Creek Winery,** on your right.

If you'd like to venture into the mountains and discover a couple of tucked-away wineries, go north briefly on Silverado, then follow 128 east; the route here is called Sage Canyon Road. (**NOTE:** One of the wineries—Nichelini—has limited hours, so this route is best run on weekends; see the listing below.) You'll pass **Lake Hennessey,** Napa's water supply, then wind steeply into the flanks of the Vaca Range to **Nichelini Winery,** perched precariously on the right edge of the highway. Drive a short distance beyond, turn left onto Lower Chiles Valley Road and follow it into the bucolic Chiles Valley. After about two and a half miles, you'll see **Rustridge Winery,** part of a ranch yard on your right.

Return to Silverado and continue south; you'll soon encounter **Mumm Napa Valley** on the right, with **ZD Wines** practically next door. About a mile below is **Miner Family Winery** on the left. After another mile, turn right onto Yountville Cross and drive a short distance to **S. Anderson Vineyard** on the left. Back on Silverado, **Robert Sinskey Vineyards** occupies a ridge just across the highway.

Pressing south, you enter the Stags Leap district in the Vaca foothills, whose sloping, rocky soils produce some of Napa's finest wines. The name didn't come from a suicidal deer; it was inspired by a rocky deer-shaped promontory. You'll shortly see **Silverado Vineyards** crowning a hill rising from the valley floor, and then **Pine Ridge Winery;** both are on the right. Just beyond is **Steltzner Vineyards** on the left. Coming up are **Stag's Leap Wine Cellars, Chimney Rock Winery** and finally, **Clos Du Val,** all on the left.

Probably having grown weary of all this, you can follow Silverado Trail back to Napa. It bumps into Trancas Street and a right turn will take you to Highway 29.

Domaine Chandon ● T$ GT 📦

One California Dr., Yountville, CA 94599; (707) 944-2280. Daily 10 to 6; MC/VISA, AMEX. Sparkling wine sold by the glass. Extensive gift selection; champagne museum exhibits. Tours every hour from 11 to 5; salon open until 6. Domaine Chandon Restaurant listed below, under "Wine country dining."

Occupying a garden-like setting just below the Yountville Veterans Home, Domaine Chandon is the first of the Napa Valley's several sparkling wine houses. Like the others, it uses the classic *méthode champenoise* system. The chamagnery more resembles a country club than a winery, bunkered into the landscaped terrain, with barrel arched roofs and rimmed by moats, fountains, and patios. All it lacks is a golf course.

Tours assemble in the entry corridor, where graphics and exhibits trace the process of sparkling wine from Dom Pérignon's accidental discovery three centuries ago. Tour groups stroll past giant bullet-nosed horizontal fermenting tanks, watch a gyro-riddler in action and follow the seventeen steps required to conduct sparkling wine's disgorging and bottling process. You can get a glass of bubbly for a fee in the tasting salon or on a sunny patio. Thirsty souls can bypass the tour and go directly to the gift shop and salon.

Tasting notes: Our glass of Vintage Brut was excellent; we like its exploding effervescence and crisp, lingering finish. Domaine Chandon also produces Blanc de Blancs, a classic Chardonnay and Pinot Noir blend called *Étoile*, plus *Étoile Rosé*, Reserve Cuvée, Blanc de Noirs, Brut Classic and *Fleur de Vigne* which is a Chardonnay, Malvasia Bianca and Muscat Canelli blend. Prices: *$$$ to $$$$.*

Cosentino Winery ● T$

7415 South St. Helena Hwy. (P.O. Box 2818), Yountville, CA 94599. Daily 10 to 5:30; MC/VISA. Most varieties tasted for a modest fee, which includes the glass. A few wine related gift items.

Built in 1990, Cosentino Winery suggests a cross between a château and a French military barracks, with its flat, rather austere façade with dormer windows. There's nothing austere about the wines, however. Founder Mitch Cosentino won 400 awards in just ten vintages, including many best of show and sweepstake medals. He was America's first vintner to produce a red Meritage, the Bordeaux-inspired blend of Cabernet Sauvignon, Cabernet Franc and Merlot. It earned the sweepstakes award over 1,900 National Wine Competition entries in 1990. Cosentino started out in Modesto in 1981, then moved to the Napa Valley to get closer to the grapes which had been gathering all those medals.

Tasting notes: "The Sculptor" Chardonnay was exceptional—spicy, nutty and silky with a hint of wood and gentle acid finish. Cosentino's Pinot Noir was light and fruity—suggestive of a young Zinfandel, while the Cabernet Franc was peppery yet soft, with delicate tannin. Cabernet Sauvignon displayed classic chili pepper and berry attributes, with hints of oak. "The Poet" red Meritage was soft and spicy, deserving of its sweepstakes award. Other wines on Cosentino's long list include Sauvignon Blanc, white Meritage, Viognier, Gewürztraminer, Merlot and a few Italian blends. Prices: *$$ to $$$$.*

Vintners choice: "We're noted for our full bodied reds, such as Meritage, Cabernet Sauvignon, Cabernet Franc and Merlot," said a winery voice.

Napa Cellars ● T$ ✗

7481 South St. Helena Hwy., Oakville, CA 94562; (800) 535-6400 or (707) 944-2565. Daily 10 to 5; MC/VISA, AMEX. Most varieties tasted for a modest fee, which includes the glass. A few giftwares. Shaded picnic area amongst the vines.

A tasting room in a yurt? Or is it a geodesic dome? Whatever its architectural pedigree, this is a pleasant, comfortable venue for sampling the fine Napa Cellars' wines. The winery itself—visible from the tasting room—is more business-like, a large square structure just beyond the geodesic yurt. It was opened in 1976 and the first wines were produced five years later under the Napa Cellars label. It became DeMoor Winery in 1983, then returned to the Napa Cellars label when the Frank and Rombauer families purchased it in the mid-1990s.

Tasting notes: Only four wines were on the list when we last passed and they were quite good—a "she's got legs" Chardonnay with great fruit and hints of oak; a Cabernet Sauvignon with big berry flavor and a soft finish, a tasty-spicy versions of Syrah and Sangiovese. Prices: *$$$ to $$$$.*

Robert Pepi Winery ● T$

7585 South St. Helena Hwy. (P.O. Box 328), Oakville, CA 94562; (707) 944-2807. (www.robertpepi.com) Daily 10:30 to 4:30; MC/VISA. Current releases available for tasting for a modest fee, which includes the glass.

The Pepi Winery is a handsome Italianate stone and wood affair crowning a low hill above the vineyards. Carved doors beneath a stone arch lead into the tasting room and windows offer peeks into the winery. It's a pleasant spot—a welcome retreat from the din of Highway 29, and it offers nice valley views. Robert and Ora Pepi, wanting to recapture the longtime winemaking traditions of their families in Lucca, Italy, purchased vineyards here in 1966. They built their winery in 1981, reflecting their Italian heritage to its Mediterranean architecture. The small facility produces about 25,000 cases of wine a year.

Tasting notes: Sauvignon Blanc dominates production in this family-owned winery. Others on the brief and excellent list are Cabernet Sauvignon, Chardonnay and Sangiovese Grosso, the traditional grape of Tuscany, a light yet full-flavored red. Prices: *$$ to $$$$.*

La Famiglia di Robert Mondavi ● T$ GTA ✗ ▥

1595 Oakville Grade (P.O. Box 363), Oakville, CA 94562; (888) 453-9493 or (707) 944-2811. (www.lafamiglia.com) Daily 10 to 4:30; MC/VISA, AMEX. Two-tiered tasting fees, waived for wine purchases. A few wine logo items. Picnic area with an impressive valley view. Guided tours by appointment, daily at 10:30 and 2.

Robert Mondavi's offspring—Mike, Tim and Marica—purchased the small, ten-year-old Vichon Winery in the middle 1980s. In 1998, the name was changed to La Famiglia. Despite the winery's relative youth, its pink stucco Spanish colonial architecture and ivy-covered façade give it a venerable look. Barrel-potted flowers add a touch of color. The site is impressive; it's notched into a steep slope off Oakville Grade in the Mayacamas foothills. Views from the winery and from a laurel and oak-shaded picnic area are elegant. And a nice touch: Soft music from the tasting room is piped into the picnic grounds. Tasting happens in an attractive room embellished with a

WARNING: WINE IS GOOD FOR YOU

"Prohibitionists say that drinking is bad for you, but the Bible says that Noah made wine and drank it, and he only lived to be 950 years old. Show me an abstainer who ever lived that long." — Will Rogers

Medical studies have confirmed what Noah and Will knew all along, that moderate wine consumption is good for you. Not just harmless, but *beneficial*. This comes as bad news to neo-prohibitionists who have succeeded in having every winery tasting room, wine price list and bottle tattooed with federal warning labels.

A couple of decades ago, a major statistical survey revealed that moderate users of alcohol live longer than teetotalers. Subsequent studies have shown that wine consumption, particularly red wine, helps prevent heart disease.

Studies have shown that wine consumption increases high density lipoprotein (HDL) in the blood. That's the so-called "good cholesterol" which helps clear low density cholesterol (LDL) from arterial walls. Since red wine appears to be more effective than white, researchers think fruit-rich polyphenols—tannins—may play a major role.

A Canadian study suggests that red wine may help counteract cancer. In laboratory tests, doses of gallic acid (a tannin component) prevented carcinogenic agents from mutating chromosomes. Such mutations are precursors to cancer. Although this hasn't yet been proven, most experts agree that wine doesn't *cause* cancer. No study has found a positive link between moderate wine use and increased cancer rates. Laboratory rats kept constantly crocked have refused to become malignant. Despite this, wine's enemies want it labeled as a carcinogen, right up there with tobacco and burnt barbecued ribs.

Red wine plays another role, as an effective although short-lived disinfectant. In numerous tests, it has destroyed a variety of bacteria and viruses, including cholera and typhoid germs. It's not the alcohol, but the polyphenols, that kill the little critters. Ancient Greeks used wine as a disinfectant on combat wounds. Modern travelers add it to water in sanitation-poor countries to kill bacteria. Tests have shown that red wine concentrate can be effective against cold sores.

Louis Pasteur, noting that wine destroyed infection, called it "the most healthful and hygienic of beverages."

Statistics confirm wine's role as a health aid. French and Italians, who drink nearly ten times as much wine as Americans, outlive us. Even poverty-level Italians live longer than the average American, despite poor medical care and sanitation.

Other surveys indicate that people who get most of their spirits from wine have fewer heart attacks than those who drink mostly beer or hard liquor. However, some studies suggest that *all* types of alcoholic beverages are benificial. Surveys also have found a positive link between exercise, moderate drinking and lowered cholesterol rates.

Writer Michael Brody speculated in an article in *Barons Weekly* several years ago: "This suggests that the best medicine for one's heart may be jogging from bar to bar—finally answering the question of how journalists manage to live so long."

vineyard mural; it's off the main winery and visitors can peak into the aging cellars through windowed doors.

Tasting notes: The winery focuses primarily on some of the newly popular Italian varieties—Pinot Grigio, Barbera, Sangiovese, Muscato Bianco and Nebbiolo. One of the better wines is a rich and fruity Muscato Bianco. Prices: *$$ to $$$$*.

Silver Oak Cellars ● T$ GTA

915 Oakville Cross Rd. (P.O. Box 414), Oakville, CA 94562; (800) 273-8809. Monday-Friday 9 to 4, Saturday 10 to 4, closed Sundays and holiday weekends; MC/VISA. Tasting for a fee, which buys the glass. Guided tours by appointment; tasting appointments recommended on Saturdays.

Justin Meyer and Ray Duncan established Silver Oak in 1972 and the present facility was completed in 1987. Their intent was to produce a single and exceptional wine—Cabernet Sauvignon. Meyer, who guides the winemaking, obviously has exceeded, winning many awards. The partners expanded to a second winery near Geyserville in 1992; see Chapter Three, page 60. With the opening of that facility, Silver Oaks became the only American winery with two totally integrated estates—one in the Napa Valley and another in the Alexander Valley.

A slender tree-lined lane leads through the vineyards to this comely Mediterranean style cut-stone facility, with a brown tile roof and dormer windows. The pleasant hospitality room is paneled with redwood from old wine tanks. An adjacent wine library contains every vintage produced by Silver Oak. Surprisingly, this fashionable facility is part of a made-over dairy barn.

Tasting notes: Silver Oak produces only 100 percent varietal Cab, drawing its grapes from Napa Valley and Sonoma's Alexander Valley. They're aged in American oak instead of the classic French, giving them a distinct spicy-soft finish with only subtle touches of wood. Wines are aged three years on wood then another year in the bottle before their release. The glass—which you get to keep—is an impressively large thing, ideal for sloshing, sniffing and sipping. Prepare for sticker shock: Silver Oak's Cabernets are *very* pricey; *$$$$*.

Groth Vineyards and Winery ● T$ GTA

750 Oakville Cross Rd. (P.O. Box 390), Oakville, CA 94562; (707) 944-0290. Monday-Saturday 10 to 4, closed Sunday; MC/VISA, AMEX. Guided tours by appointment at 11 and 2. Modest tasting fee.

Dennis and Judy Groth have reversed their roles, both professionally and geographically. In past years, many wineries left Santa Clara County, crowded out by the growing Silicone Valley computer industries. Dennis did the reverse, leaving his Santa Clara valley post as CEO of Atari to establish vineyards in the Napa Valley. He crushed his first wine in 1982 and opened a handsome salmon colored California mission style winery and tasting room in 1990. Even though he now prefers planting grapes to planning computer games, he wanted to retain something of the Santa Clara Valley's Spanish architectural heritage. The attractive tasting room and adjacent patio overlook the family vines, and visitors can peek through Spanish arch windows into the main winery's barrel storage facility.

Tasting notes: The Groths produce select lots of Sauvignon Blanc, Chardonnay, Cabernet Sauvignon and Merlot. The Cabernet reserve exhibits full body, a deep color, with a rich and earthy taste. The Merlot is unusually complex, with layered flavors and a silky texture. The Chardonnay displays those nutty undertones typical of this classic white. Prices: *$$ to $$$$*.

Robert Mondavi Winery • T & T$ GT & GTA 📷

7801 South St. Helena Hwy. (P.O. Box 106), Oakville, CA 94562; (800) 228-1395 or (707) 226-1335. Daily 9 to 5; major credit cards. Periodic guided tours followed by a three-wine tasting; other wines tasted for a fee. Tours don't require reservations, although they're recommended, particularly in the summer and on weekends. Good giftware selection.

The Mondavi winery has a mission-like quality, perhaps appropriate to the owner's crusade to elevate wine's status and defend it from his "neo-prohibitionists." When Robert Mondavi broke away from the family fold in the 1960s, he had three goals—to produce exceptional wines, to build the first winery designed for cultural offerings, and to enhance wine's public image. Along the way, he has propelled his facility into one of the largest producers in the Napa Valley.

Your visit can begin with a tour, first to the adjacent vineyards, then inside the winery, housed in a wing of this Spanish style facility. It's designed as a shallow "V" that encloses a lawn area used for Mondavi's popular summer concerts and other functions. The arched central entrance, not accidentally, forms a natural podium for performers. Visitors choosing to bypass the tour can go straight to one of two tasting rooms to sample wines for a fee.

Tasting notes: Mondavi was one of the first producers of Fumé Blanc, a Sauvignon Blanc with a distinctive but subtle smoky flavor. Indeed, the name translates as "white smoke." It's still one of our favorite Mondavi wines, crisp and clean with that dusky finish. The Cabernet Sauvignon also was excellent, peppery with soft spices, good berries and a medium tannic finish. An Old Vine Zinfandel had great spice and classic raspberry flavor. The *Muscato D'Oro* dessert wine had a rich honey nose and a focused yet curiously light taste. Other Mondavi wines include Merlot, Pinot Noir, Chardonnay and a rich—and expensive—botrytis Sauvignon Blanc. Prices: *$$$ to $$$$*.

Turnbull Wine Cellars • T$ GTA ✕

8210 South St. Helena Hwy.(P.O. Box 29), Oakville, CA 94562; (800) 887-6285 or (707) 963-839. (www.turnbullwines.com) Daily 9 to 4; major credit cards. Select wines tasted for a fee, which can apply to purchase. A few wine logo items.

This small family winery is housed in a modern barnboard structure sitting among the vineyards. A grape arbor on an attractive patio signals the way to a cozy tasting room tucked into a corner of the winery. Changing art exhibits dress up the walls. The Johnson and Turnbull families established the winery in 1979 as Johnson Turnbull Vineyards. It was purchased by Patrick O'Dell in 1993 and renamed Turnbull Vineyards. The name and bull's head label honors the origin of the family name. In the fourteenth century, Britain's Robert of Bruce gave the name to one of his retainers after he had diverted a bull that was charging the king.

Tasting notes: Turnbull wines are mostly red, although a crisp and lemony Sauvignon Blanc and buttery Chardonnay are on the list. Among the reds, we liked a peppery Merlot with a touch of oak (and a touch of Cabernet Sauvignon), an earthy Sangiovese and a smooth Cabernet with hints of spice.

Others on the list are Merlot, Syrah, Zinfandel and a Carignan-Mourvèdre blend called Old Bull Red. Prices: *$$$ to $$$$.*

Sequoia Grove Vineyards • T$ GT & ST ✕
8338 South St. Helena Hwy., Rutherford, CA 94573; (707) 944-2945. (www.sequoiagrove.com) Daily 10:30 to 5; MC/VISA, AMEX. Various fees for sampling current release, reserve and "Collector's Cellar" wines. A few wine related gift items. Small picnic area in front of the winery and another near a stream below the tasting room. Tours at 2 and 4 p.m.

This small facility indeed sits in its own personal sequoia grove, a rustic island in time and space among its larger, sleeker winery neighbors. However, it is big in reputation, having been picked a few years ago as winery of the year by the *International Wine Review.* Obviously, it wins a sizable share of medals. The cozy tasting room is located in an 1860 weathered wood and stone barn. From there you can stroll into the adjacent winery, of a much more recent vintage. The operation was established in 1978 by James Allen.

Tasting notes: We were impressed by the low prices of the Allen Family label Chardonnay, Gewürztraminer and a Napa Valley Cabernet Sauvignon. All three were exceptional wines. A Carneros Chardonnay had a nice mix of fruit, soft acid and spice, and a rather pricey reserve Cabernet was exceptional with a great herbal nose, berry-like taste and a soft touch of wood. Prices: *$$ to $$$$.*

Vintner's Choice: "Our Cabs are friendly, mellow and drinkable, yet with a big body that will improve with age," says assistant winemaker Michael Trujillo.

St. Supèry Vineyards and Winery • T$ GT & ST 🐾
8440 South St. Helena Hwy. (P.O. Box 38), Rutherford, CA 94573; (707) 963-4507. (www.stsupery.com) Daily 9:30 to 5; MC/VISA. Selected wines tasted for a small fee. Good assortment of wine logo items, giftwares and clothing. Guided tours and self-guiding walks through the winery.

Don't be put off by the exterior look of this low-slung winery, which has all the charm of a government office building. Inside you'll find bright, carpeted corridors lined with art, photos and wine displays. St. Supéry offers the most informative self-guiding tour in the Napa Valley and the winery properly calls itself a "wine discovery center." Walkways are suspended above the working winery and graphics explain in detail what you're seeing. Charts and maps discuss wine production in the Napa Valley, America and the rest of the world. A unique "essence" station gives visitors exaggerated whiffs of the aromas they should seek in a good Cabernet Sauvignon and Sauvignon Blanc.

And who's Supéry? No saint, he was Edward St. Supéry, who owned a winery on this site in the last century. The present facility was launched by longtime valley winemaker Robert Broman in 1989. Despite its relative youth, it's one of the valley's larger producers. A comely gingerbread Victorian home adjacent to the winery is now a museum, which can be toured by appointment. Special reserve tastings are also held there.

Tasting notes: The overall character of the wines is light, fruity and crisp. Among the whites are Sauvignon Blanc, Chardonnay, Semillon and white Meritage. Reds on the list include red Meritage, several versions of Cabernet Sauvignon and Merlot. Prices: *$$ to $$$$.*

Peju Province ● T$ ✕

8466 South St. Helena Hwy. (P.O. Box 478), Rutherford, CA 94573; (800) 446-7358 or (707) 963-3600. (www.peju.com) Daily 10 to 6; MC/VISA. Conducted tasting of select varieties for a small fee, which applies toward wine purchase. Limited but nice choice of gift items and good selection of wine and cook books. Arbor-shaded picnic area.

This handsome Normandy style winery—stucco with stone corner accents—is one of the valley's newer additions, completed in the early 1990s. Owners Anthony and Herta Peju have been around longer than that, however, operating a smaller facility in this area since the 1980s. Their 15,000-case-a-year facility has made quite an impression, earning a winery of the year title from *Wine and Spirits* magazine in 1994 and winning numerous medals.

The Pejus have created an appealing showplace for their award-winning wines. As visitors approach the winery, they pass through formal gardens with modernistic sculptures, fountains, plazas and a picnic arbor. The tasting room, in the main winery building, has a high atrium ceiling with skylights to let the Napa Valley sun spill through. Potted plants, polished woods, works of art and twin tasting bars complete the pleasing interior picture.

Tasting notes: The two varietals we were offered in the conducted tasting—Chardonnay and Cabernet Sauvignon—were outstanding. The Chard was lush and spicy with a hint of wood and the Cab had a nice peppery nose and flavor and light tannin. Two proprietary wines also are tasty. The Provence blend of Cabernet Franc, Chardonnay and French Colombard tasted like a good French rosé. The Carnival was nice if you like slightly sweet wines; it's mostly French Colombard, soft and flowery. Peju also produces a Merlot, Cabernet Franc and Petit Verdot. Prices: **$$ to $$$$.**

Vintner's choice: "Our flagship wines are the Cabernets," said a winery spokesperson.

Niebaum-Coppola Estate Winery ● T$ GTA$ 🎦

1991 South St. Helena Hwy. (P.O. Box 208), Rutherford, CA 94573; (707) 968-1177. (www.niebaum–coppola.com) Daily 10 to 5. Four wines tasted for a fee, which includes the glass. Ninety-minute historic winery tours with a private tasting; tour size is limited so call for reservations and times. Wines available by the glass or by the bottle in the Wine Bar.

Francis Ford Coppola made a fortune with films such as *Apocalypse Now* and *The Godfather* series, then he spent most of it purchasing and renovating the famed Inglenook Winery. Showing proper respect for this historic institution, he even resurrected the name of its founder, naming it Niebaum-Coppola. Finnish sea captain and fur trader Gustave Nybom (later spelled Niebaum) put down roots here in the 1880s and eventually built an impressive stone winery and elaborate Victorian mansion. Both survive today as keystones on the extensive grounds. One early-day writer described the courtyard as "large enough to accommodate several locomotives."

Inglenook was part of the Heublein corporation before its purchase by Coppola. The veteran filmmaker is hardly a newcomer to the valley, or to winemaking. He bought some of Niebaum's old vineyards in 1975, then purchased more acreage and the historic winery in 1995, thus reuniting two elements of Gustave's original estate. Extensive renovation in the barrel arched wine cellars has created a handsome showplace for visitors. A major attraction is the Centennial Museum, which traces the successful careers of two immigrant families—the Niebaums and Coppolas. Exhibits occupy two floors of the great stone winery building. Among them are historic photos and winery relics of the Niebaum era, plus displays concerning the development of motion pictures. The museum features a detailed retrospective of Coppola's family and career, including several of his Oscars and film memorabilia such as costuming for *Bram Stoker's Dracula*, a Tucker automobile from *Tucker: A Man and His Dream* and Don Corleone's desk and chair from *The Godfather*.

Tasting notes: Although Coppola has invested millions in the winery, he offers some surprisingly inexpensive wines, starting in the low teens. The Francis Coppola series includes Talia Rosé, Bianco and Rosso, perfectly decent everyday wines. His Diamond Series, from the mid to high teens, include traditional varietals such as Chardonnay, Merlot, Zinfandel and Syrah. Niebaum-Coppola Estate Wines go considerably higher. Prices: *$$ to $$$$.*

Beaulieu Vineyard • T & T$ GT 🏶

1960 South St. Helena Hwy., Rutherford, CA 94573; (707) 963-2411. (www.bv-wine.com) Daily 10 to 5; MC/VISA, AMEX. Select wines tasted free; older wines tasted in the Georges de Latour Private Reserve Room for a fee. Attractive gift shop with good selection; periodic guided tours; audio-visual show.

Beaulieu's corporate ownership hasn't dimmed its historic reputation for wines, which was established by legendary winemaker Andre Tchelistcheff. He guided Beaulieu's wine production for more than four decades until his recent death. The winery's Cabernets are among the most honored in the country, and are consistent medal winners. Beaulieu dates back to the turn of the last century, founded by Georges de Latour. The original structure survives, a great stone fortress-like affair covered with decades of ivy.

The adjacent hexagonal wood-paneled tasting room is one of the valley's more stylish. And it's wonderfully civilized. A smiling attendant hands you a sample of Sauvignon Blanc the moment you enter. You can seek more sips at a small tasting bar. An extensive gift and wine shop occupies a lower floor reached by a spiral stairway. An historical display tells the story of Beaulieu and its position in Napa Valley history. Twenty-minute tours are given periodically.

Tasting notes: Beaulieu's list is large, accommodating most of the classic wines plus some of the newly popular French and Italian varietals. We particularly savored a Sonoma Chardonnay with a nutty, rich and buttery flavor. The Napa Valley Cabernet Sauvignon had a spicy nose, fine berry-cinnamon taste and softly acidic finish. Equally appealing was a reserve Carneros Pinot Noir with nice berries in the bouquet and pleasing raspberry flavor. The *Muscat de Frontignan* dessert wine was cherry like, spicy and nutty—so intense it could pose as a liqueur. Prices: *$$ to $$$$.*

Grgich Hills Cellar • T & T$ GT

1829 South St. Helena Hwy. (P.O. Box 450), Rutherford, CA; (707) 963-2784. Daily 9:30 to 4:30; MC/VISA, AMEX. Current releases tasted for no fee on weekdays; modest tasting fee on weekends. Small selection of gift items. Tours at 11 and 2 weekdays and 11 and 1:30 weekends.

Croatian Miljenko Grgich's name may be unpronounceable, but it's on the tongue of every serious wine aficionado. His medium-sized winery is a consistent award winner; a Grgich Chardonnay once beat out serious French competition to be declared the world's best of its kind. Winemaker Grgich, who looks more like poet with a soft, round face topped by a beret, says simply: "I baby my wines."

Grgich Hills wasn't named for adjacent mountains. Mike Grgich and Austin Hills are its founders, establishing the facility on the Fourth of July, 1977. The vaguely Spanish-style structure, trimmed with ivy, houses a small, wood-paneled tasting room decorated mostly with press notices and awards. It's easy to tour the winery visually, standing at the tasting counter, glass in hand. Or you can join a walking one, twice a day.

Tasting notes: We discovered one of our favorite Zinfandels here, from a Sonoma vineyard with a luxuriously peppery aroma and wonderful berry flavor. The Napa Valley Cabernet had a great nose—a mixed banquet of spice, pepper, berries and soft wood, with a flavor to match. A Napa Valley Fumé Blanc was more flowery than smoky, with a buttery, almost Chardonnay-like taste. And the Chardonnay itself? Crisp, spicy, soft and silky. Prices: *$$ to $$$$.*

Vintners choice: Marketing manager Bob Hattaway was reluctant to choose: "Each wine is treated as a special child—none better or less than the other."

Quail Ridge ● T$ ✕

1155 Mee Lane, St. Helena; mailing address: Rutherford Benchmarks, Inc., P.O. Box 460, Rutherford, CA 94573; (800) 706-9463 or (707) 963-9738. (www.quailridgewines.com) Daily 10 to 5; MC/VISA. Most wines tasted for a moderate fee.

This small 5,000-case winery and its appealing little tasting room occupy a vine covered stucco building among the grapes. A pair of picnic tables shaded by an arbor overlook a small pond. Previously called Domaine Napa and owned by Michel Perret of Côtes de Provençe in France, it was purchased in 1995 by Rutherford Benchmarks, which owns several other small wineries. The firm is comprised of Richard Connaughton, who left a career as a high tech executive to enter the wine business; Anthony Bell, former general manager and winemaker at Beaulieu and Brent Simpson, a veteran wine marketer.

Tasting notes: Lots of fruit and spice are the benchmarks of this Rutherford Benchmarks winery. The small lists consists of a rich and spicy Sauvignon Blanc, a lush and piquant Chardonnay, a soft Merlot with lots of spice, and a peppery Cabernet Sauvignon. Prices: *$$ to $$$$.*

Vintner's choice: "I like very much our Sauvignon Blanc and Cabernet. The Sauvignon Blanc stands up nicely to foods." boasted a winery voice.

Beaucanon ● T & T$ GTA

1695 South St. Helena Hwy., St. Helena, CA 94574; (800) 660-3520 or (707) 967-3520. Daily 10 to 5; major credit cards. Selected wines tasted free; limited selections tasted for a fee, which can apply to a wine purchase. A few wine related gift items. Guided tours by appointment.

After two and a half centuries of practice, it's a safe bet that the de Coninck family of France's Bordeaux region knows how to make wines. Jacques de Coninck, who owns a large negociant in St. Emilion, established Beaucanon in 1986. It's operated by two of his children—Louis, the winemaker; and Chantal, who manages vineyard and winery operations. The winery is a simple, attractive Bordeaux style structure with a vaulted ceiling and simplicity of décor, which carries into the spacious, well groomed tasting room. The tasting counter is set atop a row of old wine presses; beyond is a window into the main winery.

Tasting notes: Beaucanon has pared its list to feature a few carefully crafted wines. When we last sipped, we enjoyed a crisp Chardonnay with hints of spice, a full-flavored Merlot with a subtle oak undertone, and a classic French oak aged Cabernet Sauvignon with a great spicy chili pepper taste. Prices: *$$$ to $$$$.*

Rutherford Grove ● T$ ☒

1673 South St. Helena Hwy., (P.O. Box 552), Rutherford, CA 94573; (707) 963-0544. (www.rutherfordgrove.com) Daily 10 to 4:30; MC/VISA. Selected wines tasted for a modest fee. A few wine related gift items; picnic area.

The Pestoni family's small facility, reached by a long lane lined with olive trees, is a folksy island of intimacy afloat in a sea of much larger wineries. Winegrowers and winemakers in the Napa Valley for five generations, the Pestonis purchased Rutherford Vintners from Bernard and Evelyn Skoda in the 1994 and renamed it Rutherford Grove. The stone cottage tasting room is tucked into a eucalyptus grove, with a couple of picnic tables nearby. The winery facility also includes the Pestoni's Napa Valley Grapeseed Oil Company. This cooking oil derived—obviously—from grapeseeds, is available at the tasting room.

Tasting notes: The Pestonis' produce full-flavored versions of the popular varietals. Among them are a complex and silky Chardonnay, a very berry Merlot, a spicy Cabernet Sauvignon, a smooth and full-flavored Petite Sirah and a medium body Sangiovese. They also offer an inexpensive *Monte*

MUSIC IN THE VINEYARDS

Carasso red table wine that's mostly Cabernet Franc, and a rich Rosé of Cabernet Franc: **$$ to $$$.**

Franciscan Estates • T$ 🏛

1178 Galleron Rd. (P.O. Box 407), Rutherford, CA 94573; (707) 963-7111. (www.franciscan.com) Daily 10 to 5; MC/VISA. Select varieties tasted for a small fee, applied toward wine purchase. "Education Center" and visitor center with an extensive gift selection.

This appealing redwood-sided winery sits on nicely landscaped grounds alongside Highway 29 (despite the Galleron Road address). Established in 1972, it passed through an assortment of owners including Silver Oak's Justin Meyer, then it was purchased in 1979 by the Eckes family of Germany. Under the leadership of president Agustin Huneeus, Franciscan produces only estate wines, using traditional techniques, with natural yeast fermentation. Coupling this with modern pruning and trellising techniques, it has earned considerable praise among wine aficionados.

Educational seminars and conducted tastings are offered daily at the newly renovated Education Center. This should be a required stop for folks who are serious about wine.

Tasting notes: Franciscan's wines are uniformly excellent and priced accordingly, starting in the high teens. The winery specializes in classic Bordeaux varietals such as Cabernet Sauvignon, Merlot and Chardonnay. Particularly noteworthy are the *Magnificat* red Meritage blend and *Cuvée Sauvage* Chardonnay, the Napa Valley's first wild yeast fermented wine of this type. Stepping beyond Bordeaux, Franciscan produces a fine full-bodied yet smooth Zinfandel. Prices: **$$$ to $$$$.**

Whitehall Lane Winery • T$

1563 South St. Helena Hwy., St. Helena, CA 94574; (800) 963-9454 or (707) 963-9454. (www.whitehalllane.com) Daily 11 to 6; major credit cards. Most varieties tasted for fee. A few gift items.

Originally opened in 1979 by architect-winemaker Art Finkelstein and his brother Allen Steen, Whitehall was purchased by an international wine conglomerate in 1988. Then the Leonardini family of San Francisco bought it in 1993, bringing it back into American ownership. With that has come an "Americanization" of wine style, producing fruitier and less woody wines aged in American oak. Architect Finkelstein designed the simple convergence of lines, angles and geometric shapes that comprise this gray and beige winery. The tasting room is a cozy space, decorated mostly with bottles, medals and a few wine logo items.

Tasting notes: Whitehall has won several awards with its relatively short list of wines. We liked the pronounced fruity and spicy taste of its Chardonnay, the crispness of the Sauvignon Blanc, the spicy and rich berry taste of the Merlot and the big flavor and soft oak in the Cabernet Sauvignon. For dessert, we sipped *Belmuscato*, a sweet yet crisp *pretty Muscat.* Prices: **$$ to $$$$.**

Raymond Vineyard and Cellars • T & T$ GTA

849 Zinfandel Lane, St. Helena, CA 94574; (800) 525-2659 or (707) 963-3141. Daily 10 to 4; MC/VISA. Selected wines tasted free; fee for some reserves. Small giftware selection. Tours by appointment, usually at 11 a.m.

The Raymond family goes far back in Napa's winemaking history, although their modern winery dates from 1974. Shortly after Repeal, Roy Raymond started working at Beringer, where he met and married Martha Jane. Their sons operate things now, with Walter making wine and Roy, Jr., marketing it. Raymond produces about 300,000 cases a year, with grapes drawn from vineyards surrounding their winery, which is near the valley's geographic center. The winery is a comely low-rise structure—a modern oversized bungalow, painted green to blend in with the surrounding vineyards. An airy, open tasting room occupies one corner.

Tasting notes: Wines are presented in three different labels—Amberhill, Napa Valley Reserve and Generations. Varietals are Chardonnay, Sauvignon Blanc, Cabernet Sauvignon, Merlot and Pinot Noir. The Sauvignon Blanc was herbal and crisp with a nice tart finish and a three-year-old Chard was properly buttery and spicy, with a touch of oak. A Cabernet, two years in oak and two in the bottle, was smooth and complex with good berries and a touch of oak and tannin. Prices: *$$ to $$$$.*

Vintners choice: "Our Generation Chardonnay and Cabernet; limited production; the best of each vintage," quoth the winery's Kas McGregor.

Rutherford Hill Winery • T$ GT ✕ 📷

200 Rutherford Hill Rd. (P.O. Box 427), Rutherford, CA 94573; (800) 726-5226 or (707)963-1871. (www.rutherfordhill.com) Daily 10 to 5; MC/VISA, AMEX. Most varieties tasted for a fee, which includes the glass. Cave tours several times daily; call for schedules. Good choice of giftwares and wine logo items. Two picnic areas.

Rutherford Hill is a particularly striking facility, a monumental weathered wooden structure with flying buttresses, set in a wooded notch high above the valley. Tours take visitors through aging caves tunneled into the hillside, then into the state-of-the-art winery. One picnic area is tucked into an oak grove; another is shaded by olive trees and provides nice valley views.

The weathered winery and aging caves suggest antiquity, yet the facility dates from 1976, when it was founded as a limited partnership. Tunneled by modern machinery and coated with gunnite, the cave network covers nearly a mile; it's claimed to be the longest set of wine burrows in America. The tasting room is reached through tall cathedral-like doors at one end of the main winery. Heavy beams support the lofty ceiling. The atmosphere is that of a grand mountain ski chalet.

Tasting notes: The lists consists of Chardonnay, Sauvignon Blanc, Gewürztraminer, Merlot and Cabernet Sauvignon.

Several versions of Chard and Cab are available. We particularly liked the fruity, toasty current release Chardonnay and a nicely balanced, berry-flavored Cabernet. The Merlot had a spicy, herbal nose and good berries in the taste, with an acid nip at the end. The Zinfandel Port was nutty and fruity—an exceptionally rich sipping wine. Prices: *$$ to $$$$.*

Vintners choice: A voice from within said: "We call ourselves the Merlot winery."

Villa Mount Eden on Conn Creek • T GTA 📷

8711 Silverado Trail, St. Helena, CA 94574; (707) 963-9100. (www.silveradotrail.com) Daily 10 to 4; MC/VISA, AMEX. Most varieties tasted. Good gift and wine logo selection. Guided tours by appointment.

This prim little winery would look at home in Madrid, with its white stucco and Spanish arches. The Mediterranean theme carries into the tasting room, accented with iron chandeliers, carved wooden furniture and a rough tile floor. Slices of the modern, efficient winery are visible through large windows. The facility was founded in 1974 as Conn Creek Winery. Winemaker Mike McGrath took over the operation in the 1990s and renamed it in honor of the original Villa Mount Eden Winery, established in this area in 1881.

Tasting notes: Meritage, Zinfandel, Merlot, Cabernet Sauvignon and a late harvest Sauvignon Blanc comprise the brief list. Our favorites were a rich, raspberry accented Zinfandel and a fine Cabernet that was peppery, berry-like and velvety. Prices: *$$ to $$$$.*

Nichelini Winery ● T ST ✕

2950 Sage Canyon Rd., St. Helena, CA 94574; (800) WE-TASTE or (707) 963-0717. (www.nicholiniwinery.com) Weekends only, 9 to 6 April-October; and by appointment on weekdays the rest of the year; MC/VISA. Most varieties tasted. Some wine logo gift items. Informal peeks into the winery; wooded picnic areas.

This delightfully rustic winery seems to cling precariously to the edge of the highway, threatening to topple into a wooded canyon. However, it has managed to hold on since 1890, when it was founded by Italian-Swiss immigrant Anton Nichelini. His descendants still run the place, using a mix of ancient and modern equipment to produce notable wines—mostly reds. There's nary a vine in sight, however; the winery is surrounded by ancient walnut trees planted by Anton. The grapes flourish in nearby Chiles Valley.

Tasting is conducted in the original hand-hewn stone wine cellars. On nice days, it's moved outdoors; you can settle onto a nearby bench to sip your wine and listen to the soft sounds of the forest. Picnic tables are terraced about this charmingly weathered winery complex.

Tasting notes: We particularly liked Nichelini's full-bodied, old vine Zinfandel, with a proper tannic nip at the end. The winery also does a Sauvignon Vert, a white Bordeaux noted for its dry zesty flavor, plus full-flavored Chenin Blanc, Sauvignon Blanc, Chardonnay and Johannisberg Riesling. Prices are modest: *$ to $$.*

Vintners choice: "We pride ourselves in Zinfandel because our mountain-located vineyards produce excellent grapes," says Toni Nichelini Irwin.

Rustridge Winery ● T ✕

2910 Lower Chiles Valley Rd., St. Helena, CA 94574; (800) 788-0263, (707) 965-2871 or (707) 965-9353. (www.rustridge.com) Daily 10 to 4; major credit cards. Most varieties tasted. Shaded picnic area.

You first pass a ranch style bed and breakfast, a race horse paddock and a scattering of farm equipment and tired trucks before you find the Rustridge winery and tasting room. Both occupy a converted cinderblock hay barn, with stainless steel fermenting tanks out front. The tasting room is a wide spot in the middle of the small winery, which produces only a few thousand cases a year.

This remote winery, part of a working ranch and horse farm, was established in 1985 by brothers Grant and Stan Meyer. Their sister Susan now runs the operation with her husband Jim Fresquez. They also operate a bed and breakfast in their southwest ranch style home; see listing below, on page 145. You won't always find the tasting room staffed, but yell or honk your horn and someone will come. A friendly farm hand climbed off a tractor to serve us.

Tasting notes: Chiles Valley's warm, breezy climate produces *big* reds. We liked a full-flavored Cabernet, nearly black in color and with tannin suitable for aging; and an equally assertive Zinfandel with nice berries and a tannic nip. Others on the list included a rich, full-bodied Sauvignon Blanc; a soft and silky Chardonnay with tropical fruit flavors and vanilla oak; and a smooth late harvest Riesling, rich with fruit yet with a surprisingly dry finish. Rustridge wines are produced from organically grown, pesticide free grapes. Prices: *$$$ to $$$$*.

Vintners choice: "Our Cabernet Sauvignon and Zinfandel," said Susan.

Mumm Napa Valley ● *T$ GT* 🏚

8445 Silverado Trail (P.O. Drawer 500), Rutherford, CA 94573; (800) 686-6272 or (707) 942-3434. Daily 10:30 to 6 in summer and 10 to 5 the rest of the year; major credit cards. Sparkling wine by the glass for a fee. Separate gift shop with good wine logo and book selection. Tours hourly from 10:30 to 6 in summer and from 11 to 3 in winter.

France's legendary Mumm set up shop in the Napa Valley in the mid-1980s. The personnel adhere to the French custom of avoiding the term champagne, unless it's from that particular district in France. The Napa Valley Mumm product is sparkling wine, if you please. Advance scouting for a Napa Valley site, cleverly called "Operation Lafayette," began in 1979, and the champagnery has grown in stages. The hospitality facility, with a fashionable gift shop and airy tasting salon, was completed in 1990.

The structure is architecturally curious—a wood-sided creation suggestive of a king-sized California barn. It hovers low to the ground, and the guided tour reveals that much of it is underground, in true French champagnery fashion. The tour begins with an examination of a demonstration vineyard of Pinot Noir, Chardonnay and Meunier grapevines that are the basis for most premium sparkling wines. It then adjourns to the huge partly submerged facility, where 200,000 cases are produced each year.

Tasting notes: We sampled three sparkling wines and agreed with a recent edition of *The Wine Spectator,* which rated Mumm as America's best bubbly. The Vintage Reserve was crisply perfect with a splendid finish; the Winery Lake was explosively fruity and the Blanc de Noirs was soft with a strong hint of the parent Pinot Noir grape. Prices: *$$$ to $$$$*.

ZD Wines ● *T$ GTA*

8383 Silverado Trail, Napa, CA 94558; (707) 963-5188. (www.zd-wines.com) Daily 10 to 4:30. Current releases tasted for a fee. Tours by appointment, or informal ones can be arranged if staff members are available.

Originally housed in a modest structure, ZD has expanded into a modern winery with a spacious tasting room brightened by oversized windows. A fireplace sometimes crackles in a corner, inviting visitors to linger, sip wines and ask consequential questions such as: "What does ZD stand for?"

Winemaking started out as a hobby for aerospace engineers Gino Zepponi and Norman de Leuze. When wine critics began taking them seriously, they opened a full-time winery in 1969. And now you know what ZD stands for.

The operation was started in Sonoma County, then shifted to the Napa Valley in 1979. It's now run by the de Leuze family and it is indeed a family affair. Norman is CEO, his wife Rosa Lee and their son Brett handle marketing, eldest son Robert is the winemaker and daughter Julie is administrative director.

Tasting notes: It's a quick list: Chardonnay, Cabernet Sauvignon, Merlot and Pinot Noir. After tasting the wonderfully nutty-spicy Chard, the peppery berries of the Cab and the lushly herbal Pinot, we decided that they're definitely worth the rather high prices: *$$$ to $$$$.*

Miner Family Winery ● T$ GTA ✗ 📷

7850 Silverado Trail (P.O. Box 367), Oakville, CA 94562; (800) 366-WINE or (707) 944-9500. (www.minerwines.com) Daily 11 to 5; MC/VISA, AMEX. Most wines tasted for a fee. Good selection of gift wares; view picnic deck. Guided tours by appointment.

This strikingly modern three-tired stucco winery on a slope above vineyards will catch your eye as you cruise along the Silverado Trail. It was completed in 1998 by longtime Napa Valley vintners Dave and Emily Miner and his parents, Ed and Norma Miner. Dave is president of Oakville Ranch Vineyards, from where they draw many of their grapes. The impressive tasting room is accented by a polished tasting bar with drop lamps. Note the wood laminated grape theme border at the base of an elaborately carved table, which is laden with gift and wine logo items. A balcony with picnic tables offers pleasant views of the countryside.

Tasting notes: While not inexpensive, the Miner wines are excellent and have won a good share of medals. Selections include most of the classic varietals—several versions of Chardonnay, Merlot and Cabernet Sauvignon and a spicy Sangiovese. Most of the wine are available in magnums. Prices: *$$$$.*

S. Anderson Vineyard ● T$ GT$

1473 Yountville Cross Rd., Yountville, CA 94599; (707) 944-8642. Daily 10 to 5. Three to five wines tasted for a modest fee. Some wine logo items. Tours of wine caves daily at 10:30 and 2:30 for a small charge per person; appointments requested for groups of six or more.

Stanley and Carol Anderson started their vineyards in 1971, but didn't open their tasting room until 1990. It occupies a sort of glorified stone shed that once served as a pump house. More impressive are aging caves tunneled into a hill on the family estate. These stone rooms with lofty ceilings and cobbled floors are haven to nearly half a million bottles of sparkling wine and Chardonnay. The caves and adjacent winery can be visited on twice-daily tours. Visitors to the tiny tasting room can adjourn to tables on a landscaped terrace for more elbow room.

Tasting notes: Sparkling wine (which the Andersons dare to call Champagne) and Chardonnay, Cabernet Sauvignon and Merlot make up the list. Our flight of five wines went thus—A Stags Leap Chardonnay was spicy and balanced with enough acid for aging; Proprietor's Reserve Chardonnay was softer, more subtle and fruity with hints of oak; the Blanc de Noirs was surprisingly fruity and complex for a sparkling wine; the Brut Champagne had a nice grapey nose with a fruity flavor and gentle acid finish; the Rosé Champagne was a sparkling mouthful, accenting its Pinot Noir grapes. Prices: *$$$ to $$$$.*

Robert Sinskey Vineyards ● T$ GTA

6320 Silverado Trail, Napa, CA 94558; 944-9090. Daily 10 to 4:30; MC/VISA. Most varieties tasted for a fee. Some wine related gift items. Guided tours by appointment.

Like many Silverado wineries, Sinskey occupies an impressive vantage point in the flanks of the Vaca Range. It's architecturally intriguing, with a high, ridge-like wooden center flanked by low stone walled wings. A deck off the winery invites one to lounge and enjoy a stellar view of the Napa Valley. The winery interior is a nice mix of wood and stone. The tasting room's high ceiling is held aloft by a web-work of stained wooden struts; French doors offer a view of vats, barrels and stainless steel. Tours take visitors to a grapevine "petting zoo," through the winery and into caves tunneled into a slope.

Opthamologist Robert Sinskey established the winery in the 1980s and completed the present facility in 1988. His son Rob is manager and marketing director. Tiny as Napa wineries go, with an output of 10,000 cases, it's nonetheless an attention-getter, having won numerous awards.

Tasting notes: Chardonnay, Pinot Noir, Merlot and a Bordeaux style Claret complete the brief Sinskey list. All are well-crafted wines. Prices: *$$ to $$$$.*

Silverado Vineyards • T GTA

6121 Silverado Trail, Napa, CA 94558; (707) 257-1770. Daily 10:30 to 5; MC/VISA. (www.silveradovineyards.com) Most varieties tasted. Some wine related gift items. Guided tours by appointment.

Lillian Disney, widow of Mickey Mouse's creator, purchased several acres of Stags Leap vineyards in the 1970s with her son-in-law and daughter, Ron and Diane Disney Miller. Construction of their winery began in 1981. Its name honors the memory of Robert Louis Stevenson, whose *Silverado Squatters* was penned on the slopes of nearby Mount St. Helena. Crowning a vineyard hill, Silverado is among the valley's more attractive wineries. Its fieldstone walls, ivy covered Spanish colonnade, arched windows and lofty ceilings give it the feel of an ancient abbey. The tasting room, occupying a portion of the main winery, is a study in old world refinement with a Spanish tile floor and wood panels.

Tasting notes: The Silverado list includes Sauvignon Blanc, Chardonnay, Sangiovese, Cabernet Sauvignon and Merlot. We were impressed with the barrel-fermented Chardonnay, full and complex with a crisp acid finish, and a classic Cabernet Sauvignon with a wonderful spicy bouquet and lush, complex flavor, tannic and suitable for aging. Prices: *$$ to $$$$.*

Pine Ridge Winery • T$ GTA ✗ ⭑

5901 Silverado Trail, Napa, CA 94558; (800) 486-0503 or (707) 253-7500. (www.pineridgewinery.com) Daily 11 to 5; MC/VISA. Fees for current release and reserve tastings. Extensive selection of wine theme clothing and related items. Picnic area with barbecues and a swing set. Tours of the winery and caves daily at 10:15, 1 and 3 by appointment.

Pine Ridge presents a pleasing picture, tucked into the pine-shaded hollow of a hill on the valley side of the highway. A flower-lined walkway leads to a spacious tasting room. From there, visitors can peek into the cellar, where long rows of sleeping wines reside. Gary Andrus, one of the valley's most respected winemakers, and his wife Nancy, bought a vineyard in the Stags Leap district in 1978, purchased other vineyards, then released their first wines in 1981. During their first decade, they won 114 medals, particularly for their Cabernet Sauvignon. Production began modestly, then had increased to 65,000 cases by the Millennium.

Tasting notes: Current releases when we last paused were a citrusy-spicy Chenin Blanc-Viognier blend; a silky Carneros Chardonnay with hints of oak; plus Crimson Creek and Carneros Merlots, both full flavored and excellent. Limited release wines include Stags Leap Chardonnay, Howell Mountain Cabernet Sauvignon, Archery Summit Pinot Noir and Archery Summit Vireton. The latter is a blend of Pinot Gris, Chardonnay and Pinot Blanc, with grapes brought all the way from the Willamette Valley in Oregon. Prices: **$$ to $$$$.**

Vintners choice: "We're well known for our vineyard designated Cabernet," said Nancy Andrus.

Steltzner Vineyards ● *T$ GTA* 🏮

5998 Silverado Trail, Napa, CA 94558; (707) 252-7272. (www.steltzner.com) Monday-Saturday 10 to 4:30 and Sunday noon to 4:30; major credit cards. Most current releases tasted for a modest fee. A few giftwares and wine logo items. Guided tours by appointment.

The Steltzner winery occupies a pink stucco "modern mission style" building with a clock tower, and the cozy tasting room is tunneled into an adjacent hillside. Wine sampling is conducted at a counter suggestive of a kitchen sink, although the rather basic tasting room is made charming by its presence in a cave. Third-generation Californian Dick Steltzner and his family began purchasing vineyards in 1965 and opened this winery in 1983. The Mediterranean style winery building, topped by a third-story observation tower, was completed in 1995.

Tasting notes: The brief list focuses on the basic French varietals, all nicely crafted by owner-winemaker Steltzner. The list includes Sauvignon Blanc, Chardonnay, Merlot, Cabernet Sauvignon and a Claret blend of several French reds. Steltzner's primary focus is Cabernet, which he produces in several versions. Prices: **$$ to $$$$.**

Stag's Leap Wine Cellars ● *T$ GTA* ✕

5766 Silverado Trail, Napa, CA 94558; (707) 944-2020. Daily 10 to 4; MC/VISA. A choice of five wines tasted for a modest fee, which includes the glass. Wine oriented gift selection. Oak-shaded picnic area; guided tours by appointment.

Started in 1972 by Warren and Barbara Winiaraski, Stag's Leap has been growing by—forgive us—leaps and bounds. (They added an apostrophe to "Stag's" to separate the winery name from the appelation.) Starting with one small building, the Winiaraskis now have an extensive complex with an attractive ivy-entwined Spanish style main winery and separate white wine facility. Gnarled oaks and appealingly casual landsscaping enhance the setting. The tasting room is a simple counter in one end of the main winery building. A second counter is added when things get busy in summer. From here, one can watch the business of winemaking. Tours are available by advance request.

Tasting notes: Stag's Leap has trimmed its list in recent years, concentrating on Chardonnay, white Riesling, Sauvignon Blanc, Cabernet Sauvignon, Merlot and Petit Sirah. Most carry the Hawk Crest label. We tasted a bright, light and fruity Sauvignon Blanc; a couple of impressive Chardonnays, both spicy and silky with crisp finishes and hints of wood; and an outstanding Cabernet, big and complex with a brisk tannic finish. Prices: **$ to $$$.**

Chimney Rock is one of the Napa Valley's most attractive small wineries, with the elaborate facade of its distinctive South African Dutch architecture.

Chimney Rock Winery • T$ GTA

5350 Silverado Trail, Napa, CA 94558; (707) 257-2461. Daily 10 to 5; MC/VISA, AMEX. Four wines tasted for a fee, which includes the glass. Three vintage wines tasted for a higher fee. Small selection of gift items; guided tours by appointment.

With its ornate Dutch Colonial architecture, Chimney Rock is one of the valley's most striking small wineries. The two-building complex was fashioned after a winery in the Cape Colony of South Africa. Note the elaborate frieze on the main building, portraying Ganymede, cup bearer to Zeus and other Mount Olympus celestials. The tasting room-hospitality center is a study in old world elegance, with gleaming white walls, polished wood trim, a brass chandelier and nineteenth century furnishings. It's surrounded by manicured lawns and a protective ring of slender poplars which present a dazzling display of yellow in the fall.

All of this is the creation of Sheldon and Stella Wilson, who purchased the eighteen-hole Chimney Rock Golf Course in 1980, planted half of it in vineyards and converted the remaining half into a nine-holer. They opened their winery ten years later.

Tasting notes: We tasted an herbal, complex and nicely balanced Cabernet Sauvignon and a bright, crisp Fumé Blanc with a great floral nose and just a hint of duskiness. Others on the short list are a surprisingly assertive Rosé of Cabernet and Elevage, a full-flavored Bordeaux stye blend of Merlot, Cabernet Sauvignon and Cabernet Franc. Prices: *$$$ to $$$$.*

Clos Du Val • T$ GT & GTA ✗

5330 Silverado Trail (P.O. Box 4350), Napa, CA 94558; (707) 252-6711. Daily 10 to 5; MC/VISA. Four wines tasted from the list of current releases for a modest fee, which applies toward wine purchases. Selected gift items including whimsical Ronald Searle posters and T-shirts. Oak-shaded picnic tables. Guided tours daily at 10:30, or by appointment.

Sitting upslope in a wooded grove, Clos Du Val was established in 1972 by John Goelet and French winemaker Bernard Portet. They had in mind a noble yet rather simple château, although it has grown to rather cathedral-like proportions. Both are still principals in the operation. The tasting room is an imposing space with towering ceilings accented by ornate woods, conglomerate walls and tile floors. Lofty windows offer views into the working winery. In recent years, the ivy-entwined winery has been dressed up with expanded landscaping and a bike path leading to the highway.

Tasting notes: A number of Cabernet vintages top the list. We tasted a complex and spicy aged Cab and one of Napa's better Zinfandels—herbal, peppery and tasty, with enough tannin to encourage aging. A Chardonnay was crisp, clean and pleasantly light. Vin Gris, Pinot Noir, Sangiovese and Merlot complete the list. Buyers can select from a range of several vintages of some wines, particularly the Cabs. Prices: *$$ to $$$$.*

THE BEST OF THE BUNCH

The best wine buys ● Madonna Estate/Mont St. John Cellars in the Carneros; Sequoia Grove Vineyards and Franciscan Vineyards along Highway 29, Nichelini Winery in the Chiles Valley and Stag's Leap on the Silverado Trail (Hawk Crest line).

The most attractive wineries ● RMS Brandy Distillery and Domaine Carneros in the Carneros; The Hess Collection on Mount Veeder; Domaine Chandon, Robert Mondavi Winery and Peju Province on Highway 29; Rutherford Hill Winery, Silverado Vineyards, Miner Family Winery, Chimney Rock Winery and Clos Du Val on the Silverado Trail.

The most interesting tasting rooms ● Domaine Carneros in the Carneros; Domaine Chandon and Beaulieu Vineyard on Highway 29; Conn Creek Winery, Rutherford Hill Winery, Silver Oak Cellars, Silverado Vineyards, Miner Family Winery, Chimney Rock Winery and Clos Du Val on the Silverado Trail.

The funkiest tasting rooms ● Nichelini Winery and Rustridge Winery in the Chiles Valley, and Steltzner Vineyards on the Silverado Trail.

The best gift shops ● The Hess Collection on Mount Veeder; Domaine Chandon, Robert Mondavi Winery, Beaulieu Vineyard and Franciscan Vineyards on Highway 29; and Mumm Napa Valley and Clos du Val on the Silverado Trail.

The nicest picnic areas ● Château Potelle on Mount Veeder; La Famiglia Winery on Oakville Grade; Rutherford Hill Winery, Pine Ridge Winery, Stag's Leap Cellars and Clos Du Val on the Silverado Trail; Nichelini Winery in the Chiles Valley.

The best tours ● RMS Brandy Distillery (guided) and Domaine Carneros (guided or self-guiding) in the Carneros; Hess Collection (self-guiding) on Mount Veeder; Domaine Chandon (guided), St. Supéry Winery (self-guiding) and Beaulieu (guided) on Highway 29; Rutherford Hill Winery (guided cave and winery tour) and Mumm Napa Valley (guided) on the Silverado Trail.

Wine country maps and events

Winery maps and guides ● Curiously, in America's most famous wineland, there is no overall Napa Valley map produced by a vintners' association, although you can get maps and other material from the **Napa Val-**

ley Conference and Visitors Bureau at 1310 Napa Town Center, Napa, CA 94559; (707) 226-7459. A simple map-flyer, *Napa Valley's Historic Silverado Trail,* lists wineries on or near that route and it's available free at most member wineries; or contact Silverado Trail Winery Association, 3212 Jefferson St., Suite 143, Napa, CA 94558. *(www.silveradotrail.com)*

A plethora of commercial Napa Valley publications exists. You'll find them in wineries, gift shops and lodgings through the Napa Valley. The slick magazine **Destination Napa Valley**, free throughout the valley, has a handy pull-out winery map with details on hours, prices and winetasting. *Spotlight's Wine Country Guide,* pocket-sized and also free, covers Napa, Sonoma, Mendocino and Lake Counties, with winery maps and listings, plus advertisements for lodgings, restaurants, attractions and activities.

Wineland events ● Napa Valley Mustard Festival with wine tasting, food and activities, mid-March; (707) 226-7459. Taste of Yountville wine and food tasting, mid-March; (707) 944-0904. Art in the Carneros with art exhibits and wine tastings at Carneros district wineries, mid-April; (707) 226-7459. Napa Valley Wine Auction, first week of June; (707) 226-7459. Mondavi Summer Music Festival, June-August; (707) 226-1395. Napa Town & Country Fair in Napa, featuring local winery exhibits, early August; (707) 253-4900. Harvest Crush celebration at Vintage 1870 featuring area winemakers, plus food and entertainment, September; (707) 944-2451.

BEYOND THE VINEYARDS

Wine's the thing in the southern end of the valley, although the area has a few other lures as well. The city of **Napa**, which we bypassed in our eagerness to reach the vineyards, offers several attractions. It's the valley's commercial center and home to 56,000 souls—half the county's population.

Although its suburbs are typical shopping center-service station Americana, the old fashioned downtown area shouldn't be overlooked. The small business district is well kept and attractive, with tree-lined streets, brick accented sidewalks and shops tucked into revitalized false front stores.

First and Main streets are the heart of old Napa; to reach it take the First Street exit east from Freeway 29. Carefully restored Victorian homes rim the downtown area. Many are concentrated along Jefferson, Clay and Polk streets, northeast of downtown. Also, visit the **Napa County Historical Society Museum** in the Goodman Library building at 1219 First Street.

Mountains cradling the Napa Valley lure lovers of winding roads and solitude. Pick any east-west route and you'll soon be surrounded by silence, whispered through pine and redwood forests and oak groves clustered on tawny hillsides.

Oakville Grade offers a good excuse to wind among the heights on your way to neighboring Sonoma Valley, with splendid views back down to the Napa Valley as you climb. It starts in Oakville, crests the Mayacamus Mountains and becomes Trinity Road as it twists and winds downhill to Highway 12 near Glen Ellen. Highway 121 winding northeast of Napa takes you to **Lake Berryessa,** a large reservoir offering the usual boating, waterskiing, camping, swimming and fishing lures. You can check into one of several resorts, get provisions at lakeside marinas and rent houseboats, fishing boats and other water toys. Call (707) 966-2111 for details.

If you follow Highway 128 west from Berryessa, then turn right onto Lower Chiles Valley Road, you'll pass high meadows, forests and vineyards of the secluded **Chiles Valley.** Beyond that, you encounter **Pope Valley,** another prime vineyard area. The tiny, prim Seventh-Day Adventist village of **Angwin** is home to **Pacific Union College** and a lot of good Christians. Interestingly, in this little hamlet in the hills above California's most famous wine country, one can't get a drink. Adventists forswear alcohol, tobacco and caffeine. Most are vegetarians and you'll find no meat or fish in the **College Market.** Its bulk food section, brimming with legumes, spices, whole-grain flour, dried fruits and candies is impressively extensive, however.

Down valley attractions

Napa County Historical Society Museum ● *In the 1901 Goodman Library Building at 1219 First St., Napa; (707) 224-1739. Tuesday and Thursday, noon to 4.* ☐ Nice collection of local history exhibits, including Napa Valley winery development.

Napa Valley Museum ● *55 Presidents Circle (between Domaine Chandon and the Yountville Veterans Home); (707) 944-0500. (www.napavalleymuseum.org) Wednesday-Monday 10 to 5.* ☐ Excellent regional historical museum with a distinctive ineractive wine exhibit and other state-of-the-museum-art displays.

Napa Valley Wine Train ● *1275 McKinstry St., Napa; (800) 427-4124 or (707) 253-2111.* ☐ Thirty-six-mile lunch, dinner and brunch train rides between the historic Napa railway depot and St. Helena, in beautifully refurbished vintage rail cars.

DOWN VALLEY DINING

PRICE KEY: Dinner entrée with soup or salad, without drinks or dessert for under $10 = $; $10 to $14 = $$; $15 to $25 = $$$; over $25 = $$$$.

Since it draws hundreds of thousands of visitors including many San Francisco Bay Area regulars, the Napa Valley supports some of northern California's better restaurants, as well as the usual casual tourist diners.

Bocconcini Cantinetta ● ☆☆ $$ to $$$

☐ *6525 Washington Street in Vintage 1870, Yountville; (707) 944-9780. Italian; wine and beer. Lunch through dinner daily. Major credit cards.* ☐ Cheerfully informal Italian café and deli in one of Vintage 1870's old brick buildings; dining indoors and out. Interesting pizzas and pastas, plus entrées such as veal scaloppini, grilled pork chops and rotisserie chicken.

Compadres Bar & Grill ● ☆☆ $$

☐ *6539 Washington St. (in Vintage Estate), Yountville; (707) 944-2406. Mexican; full bar service. Breakfast through dinner daily. Major credit cards.* ☐ Lively cantina serving an interesting mix of Mexican fare ranging from fajitas, *Latino* spiced fresh fish and chicken *pollo borracho.* The look is bright, cheery upscale California-Mexican; patio dining.

Domaine Chandon Restaurant ● ☆☆☆☆ $$$$

☐ *One California Drive, Yountville; (707) 944-2892. California-French; wine and beer. Lunch and dinner daily. Reservations essential; major credit cards.* ☐ At Domaine Chandon winery; one of the valley's more striking restaurants, with glass walls offering vineyard views. *Nouveau* menu features tasty American regional fare, often with French accents. Extensive California wine list.

Frankie, Johnnie & Luigi Too! ● ☆☆ $$

□ *6772 Washington St., Yountville; (707) 944-0177. Italian; full bar service. Lunch through dinner daily. Major credit cards.* □ More appealing than the silly name, it's a cheerful family pasta and pizza parlor with blonde woods, ceramic tile floors and red checkered tables. Large menu features assorted pastas, pizzas and typical Italian dinners such as chicken cacciatore, veal scaloppini and osso bucco. Large outdoor dining deck.

The French Laundry ● ☆☆☆☆ $$$$

□ *6640 Washington St. (Creek Street), Yountville; (707) 944-2380. Nouveau/French; four-course and five-course prix fixe dinners, plus lighter lunch fare. Lunch Friday-Sunday and dinner nightly; reservations essential.* □ Fashionable French Country café in a century-old cut stone former laundry building. The look is starkly simple, although the fare is legendary. The constantly changing menu features tasty French fare with American regional *nouveau* accents.

Mustards ● ☆☆☆ $$$

□ *7399 South St. Helena Hwy. (just north of Yountville), Napa; (707) 944-2424. Regional American; full bar service. Lunch through dinner daily. Major credit cards.* □ Trendy *nouveau* café with a designer American bistro look. Innovative and changing menu features offers creative American regional fare with Mediterranean and Asian accents, plus some interesting sandwiches. Outdoor patio.

Napa Valley Grille ● ☆☆☆ $$$

□ *6795 Washington St. (Washington Square), Yountville; 944-8686. California-Mediterranean; full bar service. Lunch and dinner daily. Major credit cards.* □ Contemporary café with a "wine country look" of jewel tone grape motif tapestry, wine rack room dividers and Napa Valley art. The frequently changing menu features *nouveau* fare, often with Mediterranean and Asian spicing. Extensive wine list; outdoor patio.

Pacific Blues Café ● ☆ $ to $$

□ *At Vintage 1870, Yountville; (707) 944-4455. American; wine and beer. Lunch through dinner daily. MC/VISA, AMEX.* □ Rustic and casual café in a 120-year-old brick railroad depot; indoor dining and outdoor deck. The fare is relatively inexpensive and often spicy, such as ribeye steak, smoked ribs, chili and vegetarian black beans.

Ristorante Piatti ● ☆☆☆ $$$

□ *6480 Washington St., Yountville; (707) 944-2070. Regional Italian; full bar service. Lunch and dinner daily. MC/VISA, AMEX.* □ A branch of the Sonoma *trattoria* with bright, airy California décor and a versatile Italian menu. Specialties include linguine seafood, marinated chicken breast and fresh pastas. Outdoor tables.

Rutherford Grill ● ☆☆☆ $$$

□ *1180 Rutherford Crossroad, Rutherford; (707) 963-1792; American; full bar service. Lunch and dinner daily. MC/VISA, AMEX.* □ Appealing restaurant in a modern fieldstone, shingle-roofed cottage rimmed by landscaping and vines, adjacent to Beaulieu Winery. Creative American *nouveau* fare featuring locally fresh meats and produce. Extensive local wine list; wine tasting bar; outdoor patio.

DOWN VALLEY LODGINGS

**PRICE KEY: A two-person room for $35 or less = $; $36 to $50 = $$;
$51 to $75 = $$$; $76 to $100 = $$$$; more than $100 = $$$$$.**

Although Napa has numerous motels and hotels, we focus primarily on
those near the vineyards.

Auberge du Soleil ● ☆☆☆☆ $$$$$

□ *180 Rutherford Hill Rd, Rutherford, CA 94573; (707) 963-1211). Rates
include continental breakfast. MC/VISA, AMEX.* □ Opulent fifty-unit Mediter-
ranean style resort in an olive grove; valley view suites in cottages with TV
movies, room phones, wet bars, fireplaces and other amenities. Pools, health
spa with masseuse and steam rooms, whirlpools and tennis. **Auberge du
Soleil Restaurant** serves "California wine country cuisine"; breakfast,
lunch and dinner daily; full bar service.

Best Western Inn ● ☆☆☆ $$$$$

□ *100 Soscal Ave. (Imola Street), Napa, CA 94558; (800) 528-1234 or
(707) 257-1930. Major credit cards.* □ Attractive 68-unit motel with TV mov-
ies, phones andin-room coffee; balconies; some rooms have refrigerators.
Pool and spa.

Chablis Inn ● ☆☆☆ $$$$ to $$$$$

□ *3360 Solano Ave. (Highway 29 at Redwood Road), Napa, CA 94558;
(800) 443-3490 or (707) 257-1944. (www.chablisinn.com) Major credit
cards.* □ Appealing 34-unit lodge at the edge of the wine country. Rooms
have satellite TV, phones, wet bars, refrigerators and coffee makers. Swim-
ming pool and spa; kitchenettes and spa tub units available.

The Château ● ☆☆☆ $$$$$

□ *4195 Solano Ave. (Highway 29 at Wine Country Avenue), Napa, CA
94558; (800) 253-NAPA or (707) 253-9300. (www.napavalleychateauho-
tel.com) Major credit cards.* □ A well-situated 115-unit motel on the edge of
the wine country. Rooms with TV movies and phones, some with refrigera-
tors. Pool and spa.

John Muir Inn ● ☆☆☆ $$$$$

□ *1998 Trower Ave. (Highway 29, near vineyards), Napa, CA 94558;
(800) 522-8999 or (707) 257-7220. Major credit cards.* □ Attractively land-
scaped 59-unit inn with TV movies, room phones, in-room coffee; some units
with kitchenettes, refrigerators and wet bars. Pool and spa.

Marriott Napa Valley ☆☆☆ $$$$$

□ *3425 Solano Ave. (Highway 29 at Redwood Road), Napa, CA 94558;
(800) MARRIOTT or (707) 253-8600. Major credit cards. Rates include conti-
nental breakfast.* □ A 191-room courtyard inn on the edge of the wineland.
Rooms have TV movies and phones and the usual 0amenities; lighted tennis
courts, spa and swimming pool. **Harvest Café** serves breakfast through din-
ner; **Characters Sports Bar** features light fare from lunch through dinner

Napa Valley Railway Inn ● ☆☆ $$$$ to $$$$$

□ *6503 Washington St. (adjacent to Vintage 1870), Yountville, CA 94599;
(707) 944-2000. Major credit cards.* □ Nine mini-suites cleverly built into
several railroad cars. Units have TV, with bay window alcoves to make them
roomier.

Silverado ● ☆☆☆☆ $$$$$

❑ *1600 Atlas Peak Rd. (Monticello, above the vineyards), Napa, CA 94558; (800) 532-0500 or (707) 257-0200. Major credit cards.* ❑ Long-established luxury resort with two eighteen-hole PGA golf courses, seventeen tennis courts, volleyball, cycling, jogging paths, spa and extensive conference facilities. Suites and cottages have kitchens, TV movies, phones and typical resort amenities. Breakfast through dinner service with three restaurants—**Vintners Court, Royal Oak** and **Bar and Grill**; full bar service.

Vintage Inn Napa Valley ● ☆☆☆☆ $$$$$

❑ *6541 Washington St., Yountville, CA 94599; (800) 351-1133 or (707) 944-1112. Rates include continental breakfast. Major credit cards.* ❑ American country style resort with eighty rooms; wet bars, TV with VCR rentals, phones, in-room coffee and wine, spa tubs. Adjacent to Vintage 1870.

Bed & Breakfast Inns

Beazley House ● ☆☆☆ $$$$$

❑ *1910 First St. (Warren), Napa, CA 94559; (800) 559-1649 or (707) 257-1649. Eleven rooms, all with private baths; full breakfast. MC/VISA, AMEX.* ❑ Napa's first B&B, opened in 1981, occupying an historic landmark Edwardian mansion. Rooms furnished with American and Victorian antiques; some have fireplaces and spas; phones available. Half an acre of lawns and landscaped gardens.

Blue Violet Mansion ● ☆☆☆☆ $$$$$

❑ *443 Brown St. (Oak and Laurel), Napa, CA 94559; (800) 959-2583 or (707) 253-BLUE. (www.bluevioletmansion.com) Seventeen rooms, all with private baths; full breakfast. MC/VISA.* ❑ Beautifully refurbished 1886 Queen Anne Victorian mansion listed on the National Register of Historic Places. Gorgeously furnished rooms with Victorian antiques and Oriental carpets; many have gas fireplaces and spa tubs or showers-for-two. Rose gardens, swimming pool and spa. Private candlelight champagne dinners can be arranged in rooms. **Violette's at the Mansion** restaurant serves *prix fixe* candlelight dinners to guests and the public.

Bordeaux House ● ☆☆☆ $$$$

❑ *6000 Washington St., Yountville, CA 94599; (707) 944-2855. Six rooms, all with private baths; continental breakfast. MC/VISA.* ❑ Attractive brick complex built around extensive gardens. Italian contemporary décor; rooms have private patios, air conditioning and fireplaces; complimentary wine.

Burgundy House ● ☆☆☆ $$$$$

❑ *P.O. Box 3156 (6711 Washington St.), Yountville, CA 94599; (707) 944-0889. Five units with private baths; full breakfast. MC/VISA.* ❑ Two-story 1874 fieldstone and river rock brandy former distillery fashioned into a country inn. Antique country furnishings; landscaped garden. Complimentary Port and Sherry.

Hennessey House Bed & Breakfast ● ☆☆☆ $$$$$

❑ *1727 Main St. (downtown), Napa, CA 94559; (707) 226-3774. (www.hennesseyhouse.com) Ten rooms, all with private baths; full breakfast. MC/VISA, AMEX.* ❑ A Queen Anne Victorian with extensive grounds, built by physician and former Napa mayor Dr. Edwin Hennessey. Rooms in main house and carriage house; each with different decorator theme, featuring European antiques. Two rooms with fireplaces, four with whirlpool tubs. Sun porch and sauna; gardens and trellis.

La Residence Country Inn ● ☆☆☆☆ $$$$$

□ *4066 South St. Helena Hwy. (north of town, beyond Salvador Avenue), Napa, CA 94558; (707) 253-0337. Twenty rooms, all with phones and private baths, fifteen with fireplaces; full breakfast. Major credit cards.* □ Opulent 1870 French-style mansion with adjacent "barn." Guest rooms in both buildings; American and European antiques. All rooms have CD players; some have TV. Two-acre landscaped grounds with a small vineyard, pool, spa, gazebo and brick patios.

Napa Inn ● ☆☆☆ $$$$$

□ *1137 Warren St. (a block west of Jefferson), Napa, CA 94559; (800) 435-1144, Eight rooms and suites, all with private baths; full breakfast. MC/VISA.* □ Renovated 1899 Queen Anne furnished with turn-of-the-century antiques and collectibles. Fireplaces and spa tubs in some units. Formal dining room, parlor with fireplace. Landscaped grounds on a quiet tree-lined street near shops and restaurants.

Oleander House ● ☆☆☆ $$$$$

□ *7433 South St. Helena Hwy. (near Mustards Grill), Yountville, CA 94599; (800) 788-0357 or (707) 944-8315. (www.oleander.com) Four rooms, all with private baths; full breakfast. MC/VISA, AMEX.* □ Contemporary country French style home with designer furnishings; high ceiling rooms with fireplaces and private patios or balconies. Spa in landscaped patio garden; complimentary beverages.

RustRidge Bed & Breakfast ● ☆☆☆ $$$$$

□ *2910 Lower Chiles Valley Road, St. Helena, CA 94574; (800) 788-0263 or (707) 965-9353. (www.rustridge.com) Three units with private baths; full breakfast. Major credit cards.* □ Tucked-away retreat with a winery and horse ranch, in the mountain-rimmed Chiles Valley, off eastbound Highway 128. The renovated 1940s ranch house, with Southwest décor and antiques, has fireplaces in the master bedroom and living room. Facilities include a spa, sauna, tennis courts, hiking and biking trails and—of course—the adjacent winery with its tasting room.

Down Valley information sources

Napa Valley Conference and Visitors Bureau, 1310 Napa Town Center, Napa, CA 94559; (707) 226-7459. *(www.napavalley.com)*

Napa Valley Tourist Bureau, 6488 Washington St., Yountville, CA 94599; (707) 944-1558. (A firm offering maps for sale, plus free reservation service for lodging and wine country tours).

Napa Valley Wine Library Association, P.O. Box 328, St. Helena, CA 94574; (707) 963-5145. *(www.napawinelibrary.org)*

Yountville Chamber of Commerce, P.O. Box 2064 (6516 Yount St.), Yountville, CA 94599; (707) 944-0904.

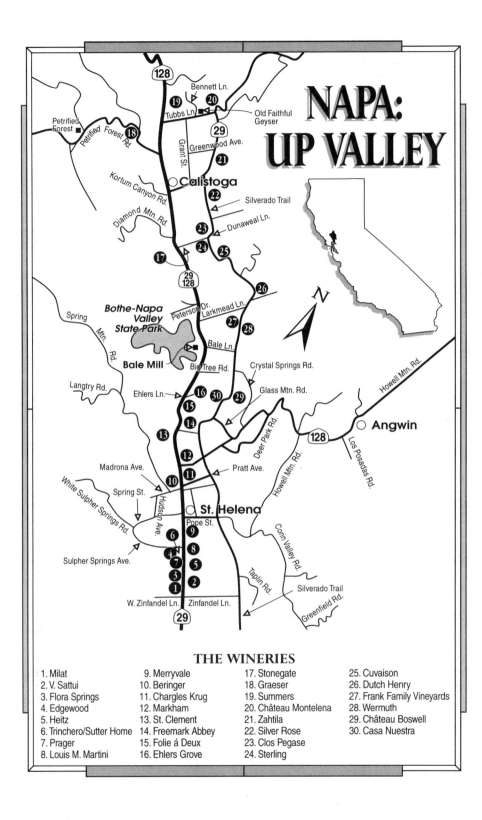

NAPA: UP VALLEY

THE WINERIES

1. Milat
2. V. Sattui
3. Flora Springs
4. Edgewood
5. Heitz
6. Trinchero/Sutter Home
7. Prager
8. Louis M. Martini
9. Merryvale
10. Beringer
11. Chargles Krug
12. Markham
13. St. Clement
14. Freemark Abbey
15. Folie á Deux
16. Ehlers Grove
17. Stonegate
18. Graeser
19. Summers
20. Château Montelena
21. Zahtila
22. Silver Rose
23. Clos Pegase
24. Sterling
25. Cuvaison
26. Dutch Henry
27. Frank Family Vineyards
28. Wermuth
29. Château Boswell
30. Casa Nuestra

An abstainer is a weak person who yields to the temptation of denying himself a pleasure.   **— Ambrose Bierce**

Chapter Six

NAPA: UP VALLEY
The north end: St. Helena to Calistoga

St. Helena is the maternity ward of the Napa Valley wine industry. The region's oldest wineries were born hereabouts and many still function. Among its nineteenth century dowagers are Charles Krug, Schramsberg, Inglenook and Beaulieu. However, not one is in the hands of a founding family, and some endured long periods of Prohibition-inspired dormancy. St. Helena's wine story, then, is one of history with hiccups.

Although several valley grape growing families go back many generations and some of their offspring have become vintners, the oldest facility still run by the founding family is Louis M. Martini Winery. It dates back—appropriately—to 1933, the year of Repeal. Second and third-generation family members now operate it. The senior Martini was a giant among vintners, one of the movers and shapers of the valley's modern wine industry and a founder of the Wine Institute, the wine trade's leading watchdog organization.

Many of St. Helena's wineries are monumental structures, built when labor was cheap and owners had a sense of Victorian grandeur. Today, they are the state's most-visited wineries. As many as 300,000 tourists a year are processed by efficient and friendly guides, given quick doses of history and quick sips of wine at the end of the tour. Indeed, some of these are called "history tours," for they take visitors through outmoded stone wineries and grandiloquent mansions used now only for aging cellars and for show.

Sadly, the grandest of these, the former Christian Brothers Greystone Cellars, built in 1888 by California gold rush millionaire William Bowers Bourn, has closed. It's now occupied by the Culinary Institute of America, with a Wine Spectator Greystone Restaurant open to the public; see "Where to dine" on page 169. Another popular St. Helena winery, whose history comes mostly from television, closed its tasting room several years ago. Spring Mountain Vineyards, portrayed as Falcon Crest on the TV series of that name, no longer hosts the public, although it remains a winery.

St. Helena is a picturesque country town that has become gentrified of late, with several tourist-inspired boutiques, galleries, upscale bakeries and of course, wine shops. The Napa Valley Wine Library is based here (see box on page 157) and shops and cafés are plentiful. However, this town of 5,100 residents tends to pull in its sidewalks early. When the last nearby tasting room has closed, most of the town's boutiques and galleries have closed as well. Restaurants remain open, of course, along with the ubiquitous Safeway and a good-ole-boy saloon called The Wine Cellar, smelling of yesterday's spilled beer.

The town's shops are worth a browse. We'd recommend breaking off from your winery touring with sufficient time to stroll its spotless sidewalks and nod pleasantly at the locals, who don't seem to mind all the hubbub. And certainly take time to visit the **Silverado Museum** which honors Robert Louis Stevenson's 1880 honeymoon stay. It contains one of the world's largest collections of Stevenson lore; see below under "Attractions."

After the shops have closed, use the last of the daylight to drive St. Helena's tree-lined residential streets. Admire handsome Victorian homes that speak of the days when adventuring Finnish sea captains, hard-working Italians and no-nonsense German immigrants built some of America's grandest mansions and wineries.

Calistoga, the other Up Valley community, is known more for mineral water and mud baths than for Merlot. The wineries are not far away, however, as new vineyards march ever northward. Founded as a resort by that capitalistic Mormon Sam Brannan, it wears its touristic mantle comfortably, quite pleased to be the Napa Valley's final visitor stop.

The town basks contentedly in the shadow of Mount St. Helena which, unlike its Washington state name-twin, isn't volcanic. Its conical shape with a dip in the top has fooled many a brochure writer and author, including Stevenson. The mountain is composed of faulted igneous rock, including silver-bearing cinnabar.

Like St. Helena, Calistoga is a comely little community, kept prim and prosperous by its place in tourism's limelight. It has the predictable assortment of boutiques, antique shops, restaurants and bed and breakfast inns. One can sink into a sensuously gooey mud bath burble in a mineral springs hot tub. Several attractions draw visitors to the area—a restored Sam Brannan resort cottage at **Sharpsteen Museum, Old Faithful Geyser** on Tubbs Lane, the **Petrified Forest** and **Robert Louis Stevenson State Historic Park**, a few miles up the mountain.

WINERY CODES ● *T* = tasting with no fee; *T$* = tasting for a fee; *GT* = guided tours; *GTA* = guided tours by appointment; *ST* = self-guiding or informal tours; ✕ = picnic area; 🎁 = gift shop or a good giftware selection.

WINE PRICES ● *$* = average price under $10 per bottle; *$$* = $10 to $14; *$$$* = $15 to $19; *$$$$* = $20 or more

The Up Valley winery tour is simple, since most of the tasting rooms stand alongside either Highway 29 or the Silverado Trail. A few are on crossroads between the two. We'll first send you up Highway 29 from St. Helena, and then down the Silverado from Calistoga.

HIGHWAY 29 WINERY TOUR ● We stopped at Zinfandel Lane just south of St. Helena in the last chapter. Your first tasting room encounter north of Zinfandel is **Milat Vineyards** housed on a small cottage style winery on your left. Big and bustling **V. Sattui Winery** is just beyond, on the right, with **Flora Springs tasting room** in a small storefront across the street. Then come **Edgewood Estate Winery** on the left, followed by **Heitz Cellars** on the right.

Venerable Sutter Home Winery, now called **Trinchero Family Estates**, arrives quickly on the left. **Prager Winery and Port Works** is just beyond and behind Sutter Home, up tree-lined Lewelling Lane. Back on Highway 29, **Louis M. Martini Winery** is across the street. Then, after about a quarter of a mile, you'll reach **Merryvale Vineyards** on the right, on the outer rim of St. Helena. Next door is the visitor center of the **St. Helena Chamber of Commerce** at 1010 Main Street, open weekdays 10 to 5 and Saturday 11 to 4:30.

Highway 29 becomes Main Street in St. Helena. To reach the **Silverado Museum,** turn right at Adams, drive two blocks to the end, then go left on Library Lane. Return to Main and follow it through town and beyond. It passes under a sheltering canopy of Dutch elms as three of the valley's most historic wine châteaux—two active and one not—appear in quick succession. **Beringer Vineyards** with its fabled Rhine House and castle-like **Greystone Cellars** (now home to the Culinary Institute of America) are on the left, and **Charles Krug Winery** is on the right. Just beyond Krug is **Markham Winery** also on the right and **St. Clement Vineyards** in an attractive Victorian just uphill on the left. **Freemark Abbey** comes next, a mile or so beyond on the right. It's in a busy complex with a winery, restaurants and several shops. Beyond, up a narrow lane to the right, is **Folie à Deux Winery**.

Just beyond Folie à Deux, turn right onto Ehlers Lane and follow it about a quarter of a mile to **Ehlers Grove** winery in a splendid old fieldstone building on your left. Then return to Highway 29 and continue north. You'll soon encounter **Bale Grist Mill State Historic Park** and a couple of miles beyond, the entrance to **Bothe-Napa Valley State Park,** both on the left. Continue north and then dip briefly to the right onto Dunaweal Lane for **Stonegate Winery**. From Stonegate, you can see Sterling Vineyards, perched on a distant hilltop like a whitewashed Moorish monastery. We're saving it for the back nine, since it's closer to the Silverado Trail. From here north, the valley narrows and becomes even more beautiful as Highway 29 takes you into Calistoga.

Milat Vineyards ● T$
1091 South St. Helena Hwy., St. Helena, CA 94574; (800) 963-0168 or (707) 963-0758. Daily 10 to 6; major credit cards. All current releases tasted for small fee, which buys the glass or can go toward wine purchase. A few wine logo items.

Housed in a cute little cottage style winery, Milat is a welcome haven from the bustle of its larger and more crowded neighbors. (However, it can get busy on weekends, since it sits on the main highway.) The hospitality room is a simple affair with tile floors and a small tasting counter. Two brothers, whose parents Richard and Izetta had been growing grapes since 1949, established their winery in late 1986. Bob and Mike Milat and their wives Joyce and Carolyn have a few acres of classic varietals surrounding their small facility, which they can nurture and monitor carefully to produce the proper results in the bottle.

Tasting notes: What the Milats seek, as they baby their grapes and control every step of production, is a few wines with strong varietal character. They certainly have succeeded. Their Chardonnay was buttery yet crisp and clean, with a touch of wood from French oak aging. The Chenin Blanc had a light flowery nose and taste with a slight hint of sweetness, and a proprietary blush wine called Zivio—a blend of Zinfandel and Cabernet—was light with a pleasant herbal nose and more character than a typical rosé. The Zinfandel had a nice dusky aroma and lush flavor—a really fine wine. The Cabernet was herbal and berry-like, with medium body, ready to drink. Prices: **$ to $$$$.**

Vintners choice: The Milats like them all, "because we make them from our own estate vineyards," says Joyce. They're available only at the winery.

V. Sattui Winery ● T ST ✕ ▥

1111 White Lane (Highway 29), St. Helena, CA 94574; (800) 799-2337 or (707) 963-7774. Daily 9 to 6 (closes at 5 November through February); MC/VISA, AMEX. Most varieties tasted. Extensive gift, wine logo, deli and specialty foods selection; picnic grounds surrounding winery. Self-guiding tour of the stone wine cellars.

In startling contrast to Milat, Sattui is a virtual supermarket of a winery and deli, with crowds thronging the tasting room and gift shop, and scattering about an extensive picnic area shaded by ancient oaks. On weekends, the winery even has parking lot attendants to help steer you to a vacant spot. This "marketing outreach" obviously is working. Sixty percent of Sattui's wines are sold here and the rest go by mail order.

One gets two quick impressions of Sattui, and they're both wrong. 1: The rugged stone castle-like tasting room and winery don't date back to King Arthur's day. Construction of the winery didn't begin until 1976. It took $3 million and a lot of stone to make them look ancient. 2: This isn't a big corporate operation, but a family winery. The original V. Sattui Wine Company was founded in San Francisco in 1885 by Genoan immigrant Vittorio Sattui. It was closed by Prohibition and never reopened, although Vittorio lived upstairs in the winery building until his death at age 94. Then his great-grandson Daryl decided he wanted to reestablish the family winery name. He worked for several Napa Valley vintners, found a plot of land and signed a $500 a month lease option. Funds were so limited that he and his wife lived in their VW bus for the first month while fixing up the property's ramshackle house and looking for investors. After nearly running out of money, they finally got their operation going in the early 1970s.

The winery named in honor of Daryl's great grandfather has since become one of the valley's largest. With its extensive deli, large gift selection and unabashed self-promotion, the winery gets about a quarter of a million visitors a year. Perhaps it's the sight of all those happy picnickers that keeps drawing them in.

Tasting notes: A winery designed with tourists in mind doesn't necessarily make ordinary wine; Sattui has its share of medal winners. The list includes most of the white and red standard-bearers. We liked a soft yet crisp Chardonnay and an estate Zinfandel with a nice spicy nose and crisp medium flavor. The Cabernet Sauvignon also had medium body and a good berry nose and taste. Both were four years old and ready to drink. Prices start below $10 and travel well beyond for the winery's extensive selection of older wines: *$ to $$$$.*

Flora Springs tasting room ● T$ GTA 🏠

677 South St. Helena Hwy., St. Helena, CA 94574; (707) 967-8032. (WEB: www.florasprings.com) Daily 10 to 5. Current releases and reserves tasted for modest fees. Fair giftware selection. Tours of nearby winery by reservation.

Leaded glass windows accent this attractive storefront tasting room. Sippers can sample current release and reserve wines at a tile-topped counter that occupies the center of the spacious facility. The winery is elsewhere, on Zinfandel Lane. Jerry and Flora Komes bought a vineyard with some tumbling down century-old stone buildings there two decades ago. This was supposed to be a retirement project, although the family eventually built a winery and then recently opened their tasting room on St. Helena Highway. The winery is a family project that also includes sons John and Mike Komes, Julie Komes Garvey and her husband Pat Garvey.

Tasting notes: Offerings include typical varietals, such as Sauvignon Blanc, Estate Chardonnay, barrel fermented reserve Chardonnay, Pinot Grigio and Sangiovese, plus several renditions of Merlot and Cabernet Sauvignon. Prices: *$$ to $$$$.*

Edgewood Estate Winery ● T ✗ 🏠

401 South St. Helena Hwy., St. Helena, CA 94574; (800) 755-2374 or (707) 963-7293. (www.edgewoodwines.com) Daily 11 to 5:30; MC/VISA. Most varieties tasted free. Nice giftware selection. Picnic tables with mountain and vineyard views.

This appealing stone winery has been through many manifestations since it was built in 1885 by English sea captain William Peterson. It was purchased by San Franciscan Robert Bergfield in 1891, shut its doors during Prohibition and then became the Napa Valley Wine Co-op in 1935. It functioned as Golden State Vintners before becoming Edgewood Estate Winery in 1996. The large industrial-looking Golden State facility is next door. Edgewood's venerable stone tasting room is rather striking—rustic on the outside and modern within, accented by high wood-paneled vaulted ceilings. A towering wall of wine bottles in repose rises toward that ceiling from behind the tasting bar. Picnic tables occupy a lawn on the park-like grounds; others are on a back patio.

Tasting notes: Offerings include a fruity and silky Chardonnay (the lone white on the list), A full-flavored Cabernet Franc, soft and smooth Malbec, medium-body and spicy Zinfandel, peppery Cabernet Sauvignon with soft touches of wood, and a subtly tannic and spicy Petite Sirah. All are 100 percent varietal. Prices: *$$$ to $$$$.*

Heitz Wine Cellars ● T GTA

436 South St. Helena Hwy., St. Helena, CA 94574; (707) 963-3542. Daily 11 to 4:30; MC/VISA. Selected wines tasted. Small wine logo selection; tours by appointment on weekdays.

Joe and Alice Heitz purchased a few acres of vineyards and started their winery in 1961. However, Joe didn't arrive in the Napa Valley as a novice to the business, nor was this a "change of career" move. He earned his masters degree at the highly regarded U.C. Davis, worked under the legendary Andrew Tchelistcheff at Beaulieu, then taught enology at Fresno State University for several years. The no-nonsense winemaker has made a name for himself as one of the area's premier producers of Cabernet Sauvignon, as well as award-grabbing Chardonnay and Zinfandel. The Heitz family has acquired a much larger facility elsewhere, although the original winery still stands beside St. Helena Highway, along with a small cottage tasting room. Here, visitors gather around a handsome carved walnut table to sip Joe's latest offerings.

Tasting notes: After forty years, this senior Napa Valley winemaker still focuses primarily on Cabernet Sauvignon, produced from several vineyards. The cabs we tasted from Martha's Vineyard and Bella Oaks Vineyard were outstanding. Other varietals on Joe's brief list are a lush and buttery Chardonnay, a smooth medium-bodied Zinfandel with hints of spice and a rich Grignolino. Heitz also produces a couple of Ports. Prices: *$$ to $$$$*.

Trinchero Family Estates/Sutter Home Winery • T & T$ 🏠

277 South St. Helena Hwy. (P.O. Box 248), St. Helena, CA 94574; (800) 967-4663 or (707) 963-3104. (www.sutterhome.com) Daily 10 to 4:30; major credit cards. A choice of three wines tasted free; small fee for reserve wines. Extensive giftwares selection.

You read the Bob Trinchero story in the rosé box in Chapter Three. He developed a blush version of Zin, called it white Zinfandel and catapulted Sutter Home from one of the valley's smallest to one of its largest wineries. It still dominates the white Zin market. The winery gets its name from Lina Sutter Leuenberger, daughter of an early Napa Valley vintner. She and her husband Emil established a winery here in 1874, then it was closed by Prohibition. In 1947, Italian immigrant brothers John and Mario (Bob's father) Trinchero bought the long-abandoned facility.

Wine tasting occurs in two different areas. Sutter Home wines are sampled in a country style tasting room and gift and gourmet food shop. A new luxury line of M. Trinchero wines are tasted in the adjacent Reserve Room. The elaborate Victorian home of the original owners, purchased by the Trincheros in 1986, stands nearby. It isn't open to the public, although visitor may stroll through the elaborately landscaped grounds.

Tasting notes: The fabled white Zinfandel *is* nearly white, unlike its pinker counterparts; it's crisp and light and we'd regard it as a good picnic wine. Hearty, full-bodied and serious Zinfandels emerged from here as well, produced mostly from Amador County grapes. We tasted a particularly berry-like and softly tannic four-year-old Amador County Reserve. A lighter Zin, available in 1.5 liter jugs and one of our everyday dinner wines, is a good buy. Chardonnay, Chenin Blanc, Cabernet Sauvignon, Merlot and white Merlot, Sauvignon Blanc, Gewürztraminer, Pinot Noir, Shiraz, Triple Cream Sherry and a sweet but light Muscato complete the list. M. Trinchero reserve wines are Chardonnay, Merlot and Cabernet Sauvignon. The winery also produces Fré, the country's largest selling alcohol-free wine. Sutter Home wines are very modestly priced, starting well under $10; M. Trinchero reserves begin in the mid-teens. Overall price range: *$ to $$$$*.

Vintners choice: "Reserve Zinfandel and white Zinfandel," said the winery's Diana Panigazzi—not surprisingly.

Prager Winery and Port Works • T$ ST ✕

1281 Lewelling Lane, St. Helena, CA 94574; (800) 969-PORT or (707) 963-PORT. (www.pragerport.com) Daily 10:30 to 4:30; MC/VISA. Most varieties tasted for a modest fee that applies toward purchase. Some wine logo gift items. Informal tours, consisting of a "3.5 minute glance around the winery."

Bewhiskered Jim Prager, who needs only a bourbon complexion to resemble Ernest Hemingway or perhaps Santa Claus, may greet you halfway up the walk as0 you approach his little country style winery. If the tasting room isn't crowded—meaning there aren't more than a few other people—he'll sit you down in one of four available chairs (unless it's occupied by a cat) and ply you with his Cabernets and Ports. Between sips, you can admire a corkscrew collection and old currency tacked on the walls and ceiling.

A former insurance broker from Orange County, Prager began the winery in 1979, squeezing his wife Imogene and their seven children into a small house on Lewelling Lane. He started his port works in the adjacent garage. Most of the seven kids are now involved in the operation, with Fresno State enology grad Peter as the winemaker, artistically inclined Jeff as the label designer and landscaper, John as vice president of winery operations, Katie as controller and Mary as marketing manager. With the winery in good family hands, Jim has gone into semi-retirement, although he still may be there to meet you halfway up the walk.

Tasting notes: The Pragers employ "native winemaking," using natural yeasts. The wines and ports are excellent and their prices—like their maker—are not modest. Prager's not bashful about selling you his wines: "How about two? One to kill and one to look forward to." Are the wines worth their lofty prices? Only your palate knows, and you can try before you buy. A five-year-old Cabernet Sauvignon was full flavored and spicy, fully capable of additional aging. The Royal Escort Port, made from Petit Sirah grapes, was lush, nutty and mouth-filling; and the Tawny Summer Port was light yet full flavored, with lots of fruit. It was a gold medal winner in a recent international wine competition. Prices: *$$$$*.

Vintners choice: "Our specialty is port," Prager said simply.

Louis M. Martini Winery • T & T$ GT ✕ 🏠

254 South St. Helena Hwy., St. Helena, CA 94574; (707) 963-2736. Daily 10 to 4:30; MC/VISA, AMEX. Most varieties tasted free; a modest fee for reserve wines (includes glass). Good selection of wine logo items; picnic area; daily guided tours.

As a teenager, immigrant Louis Martini peddled wines along with clams and mussels on the streets of San Francisco shortly after the 1906 earthquake. He and his parents rented a winery in Pleasanton in 1911, then he established a grape products company in the San Joaquin Valley in the middle of Prohibition. After Repeal in 1933, he opened his Napa Valley winery. A founder of the Wine Institute, the "grand old man" was a leading figure in California's wine industry until his death in 1974 at the age of eighty-seven.

Still family-owned, the winery does about a quarter million cases a year. Louis' original ivy-covered red brick winery still stands alongside Highway 29. It shelters aging cellars and a simple wood-paneled tasting room,

Frederick Beringer's Rhine House is a splendid example of the early mansions built by Napa Valley wine pioneers. Completed in 1883, it now houses the Beringer Vineyards tasting room and gift shop.

trimmed with family history exhibits. Picnic tables rest beneath ancient sycamores outside.

Tasting Notes: Several wines can be tasted free, although we recommend buying the logo glass and doing a side-by-side sampling to compare regular releases with reserve wines. It's interesting to check the fruity, soft flavor of an inexpensive Louis M. Martini Chardonnay with the spicier, more complex and expensive Napa Valley Reserve Chardonnay. A smooth, berry-flavored Louis M. Martini Cabernet Sauvignon under $10 held up well beside a peppery, powerful Monte Rosso Vineyard Cabernet selling in the high teens. Although the winery has long been known for its reds, third-generation winemaker Michael Martini also earns recognition and medals for his whites. The list covers most popular varietals including a rarely-produced California Barbera, plus several sherries. Prices are modest for the quality: **$ to $$$.** Older vintages are available at higher cost.

Vintners choice "Our vineyard-designated selections: Monte Rosso Zinfandel and Del Rio Chardonnay and Merlot," says Michael.

Merryvale Vineyards • T$ 🏺

1000 Main St., St. Helena, CA 94574; (707) 963-9777. (www.merryvale.com) Daily 10 to 5:30; major credit cards. Select varieties tasted for a modest fee. Nice selection of gift items.

Old timers will remember this vine-entwined masonry building as Sunny St. Helena, the winery where Cesare Mondavi got his start shortly after Repeal. It has closed and then reopened several times since then, under various tenants. The "modern" Merryvale was established in 1983 by Jack W. Schlatter of Switzerland and his son René.

The large tasting room, in the heart of the old winery, is one of the most esthetically pleasing in the wine country. It's a cavernous place held up by beam ceilings, with the look, aroma and feel of an ancient wine cellar. NOice displays of giftwares add pleasant splashes of color. A glimpse down long corridors extending from the tasting room reveals ranks of wine barrels.

Tasting notes: Merryvale wines come in three labels. The Classic Series includes moderately priced and highly drinkable Sauvignon Blanc, Chardonnay and Cabernet Sauvignon. Reserves are even better tasting versions of the same wines, plus a lush and full-flavored Merlot. An outstanding Chardonnay and proprietary blend called Profile occupy the high end Prestige series. Prices: *$$ to $$$.*

Beringer Vineyards ● T$ GT 📷

2000 Main St., St. Helena, CA 94574; (707) 963-7115. (www.beringer.com) Daily 9:30 to 5; major credit cards. Select tastings of current releases for a modest fee, which applies toward wine purchase. Extensive giftware selection. Tours every half hour.

One of the valley's vintage landmarks, the winery was founded in the 1870s by immigrant brothers Frederick and Jacob Beringer. It remained in the family until Nestlé Chocolate (Wine World Estates) bought it in 1971. Its centerpiece is the stunning half-timbered Rhine House, an elaborate mansion styled after the brothers' German home. It now accommodates the gift shop and tasting rooms and is easily one of the most gorgeous hospitality centers in all of California's wine country. It's also one of the most popular, attracting more than 200,000 visitors a year.

Tours begin near the original winery, which is an elaborate stone façade over caves dug by Chinese laborers into the steep slopes of Spring Mountain. They fill up quickly in the summer so get a free pass from the visitor center (not the Rhine House) as soon as you get there. Although most wine production occurs across the highway, an intelligent commentary provides a good understanding of the process as you tour the ancient cellars. Most of the caves have been shored up and gunnited; however, one has been left undisturbed since 1937. With lichen-stained ceilings and tiers of bottles covered with decades of dust and cobwebs, it suggests a wonderfully spooky Edgar Allan Poe scene.

Tasting notes: The Beringer repertoire covers most varietals, with a wide range of prices. Select wines are chosen each day for tasting. When we last passed, the list consisted of a sprightly Gamay Nouveau, rosé style white Merlot and a full-flavored Alluvium, which is a blend of Sauvignon Blanc, Chardonnay, Semillon and Viognier. Other wines on Beringer's long list include Johannisberg Riesling, Chenin Blanc, Gewürztraminer, Sauvignon Blanc, Chardonnay, Pinot Noir, Merlot, Cabernet Sauvignon, Viognier, Zinfandel, Cabernet Franc, Sangiovese and Petite Syrah. Prices: *$ to $$$$.*

Charles Krug Winery ● T$ ✕ 📷

2800 North St. Helena Hwy., St. Helena, CA 94574; (888) SIP-KRUG or (707) 963-5057. (www.charleskrug.com) Daily 10:30 to 5:30; MC/VISA, AMEX. Good giftware and picnic foods selection in Visitor Center; shaded picnic area adjacent.

Although the Krug name is legendary in the Napa Valley, the winery has been the bastion of the Mondavi family for decades. Established by Charles Krug in 1861 as the valley's first commercial winery, it was operated by family members until it was closed by Prohibition. Cesare Mondavi bought the empty facility in 1946 and ran it with his sons Peter and Robert until his death in 1959. After a family spat in the 1960s, Robert went his own way to start his down valley winery. Peter now runs Krug, with his sons Marc as winemaker and Peter, Jr., in charge of sales and finance.

Tasting notes: The Mondavis pioneered cold fermentation and used the valley's first bladder press to produce crisp, fruity whites. This style is evident today with the Sauvignon Blanc and Chardonnay. Krug also offers Pinot Noir, Zinfandel, Cabernet Sauvignon, Sangiovese and a proprietary Bordeaux style blend called Generations. Prices: *$$ to $$$$.*

Vintners choice: "The Vintage Selection Cabernets are the benchmark of Charles Krug winemaking," says a winery spokesperson.

Markham Vineyards ● *T ST* 🏠

2812 North St. Helena Hwy. (P.O. Box 636), St. Helena, CA 94574; (707) 963-5292. (www.markhamvineyards.com) Daily 10 to 5; major credit cards. Selected wines tasted for modest fees in white or red "flights." Good assortment of wine theme and other gift items; self-guiding tours in balconies above the winery.

The ancient stone winery at Markham now has a modern look—about $12 million worth. While preserving and restoring the winery's original lava rock, quarried from nearby Glass Mountain, current owners added two wings to create a handsome courtyard effect, with extensive landscaping, pools and trees. The attractive tasting room has an atrium ceiling and polished hardwood floors. Artworks grace the walls and a more extensive gallery of changing art exhibits occupies a second-floor balcony and adjacent corridors.

The winery dates from 1879 and is the valley's seventh oldest. French emigrant Jean Laurent came to California in search of gold, found none and began raising vegetables in the Napa Valley. He bought vineyard land in 1873 and started building the winery six years later. The operation later became a small co-op, then advertising executive Bruce Markham bought the crumbling old structure in 1978 and restored it. The facility is now owned by Mercian, Japan's largest wine company. Its president is Bryan Del Bondio, a Napa Valley native whose parents were longtime Inglenook employees.

Tasting notes: We went for the red flight, sipping two smooth and full flavored Merlots, a medium body Zinfandel and a nicely peppery Cabernet Sauvignon with a tannic nip. White choices consisted of Sauvignon Blanc, a pair of Chardonnays and a rich Muscat Blanc. Prices: *$$ to $$$$.*

St. Clement Vineyards ● *T$ GTA*

2867 North St. Helena Hwy. (P.O. Box 261), St. Helena, CA 94574; (707) 963-7221. Daily 10 to 4; MC/VISA, AMEX. Most varieties tasted for a fee. A few wine logo items. Guided tours by appointment and picnic area available by reservation.

An immaculately restored Victorian home with a witch's hat tower houses the tasting room of this old and new winery. Old because it was the eighth in the valley, bonded in 1879; new because it was re-opened by Dr. William Casey in the mid-1970s after a long period of dormancy. In the interim, the house served as a physicians' home and office.

LEARNING THE WINE GAME

You say you can't tell a Chardonnay from a Charbono? Are you taunted by vintage verbosity? Do you yearn to get comfortable with a wine list?

A series of field and sit-down seminars sponsored by the Napa Valley Wine Library Association can help take the mystery out of the grape. The association also conducts a yearly wine tasting, held each fall at the Silverado Country Club.

Anyone with a serious interest in wine can join the association for a modest annual membership fee, which provides access to seminars (although there are additional fees for those), the annual wine tasting and other activities. Members receive a periodic wine information newsletter and they have access to the 5,000-volume Napa Valley Wine Library collection, housed in the St. Helena Public Library. Contact the Napa Valley Wine Library Association, P.O. Box 328, St. Helena, CA 94574; (707) 963-5145. *(www.napawinelibrary.org)*

Called the Rosenbaum House, the splendid structure originally had the winery in its basement. It's still used to age St. Clement wines, and the parlor—flawlessly restored—serves as the tasting room. The main winery, a rugged stone-faced affair, is tucked against the hill behind the house, reached by appointment-only tours.

Tasting notes: We tasted St. Clement's short list of wine and they were fine: Sauvignon Blanc—nice fruity-veggie nose, spicy flavor and light acid; Chardonnay—very buttery, spicy-nutty, crisp finish; Merlot—lush, spicy nose, big berry flavor and tannic finish; Cabernet Sauvignon—wonderful nose, spicy and berry-like, soft tannins, to drink now or age. *$$ to $$$$.*

Freemark Abbey Winery • T$ GT ✕ 🍴

3022 North St. Helena Hwy. (P.O. Box 410), St. Helena, CA 94574; (800) 963-9898 or (707) 963-9694. (www.freemarkabbey.com) Daily 10 to 5 March through October and Thursday-Sunday 10 to 4 the rest of the year; major credit cards. Most current releases tasted for a modest fee (includes glass). Gift and specialty foods selection in tasting room; also gift shops nearby. Picnic area for winery patrons. Tours daily at 2.

One of the first tourist-oriented wineries in the valley, Freemark Abbey dates from the mid-1960s. The complex includes a gift shop, candle shop and two restaurants, the Abbey and Bravo Terrace (listed below under "Wine country dining"). This doesn't detract from the wine quality, or from its history. The original winery was built in 1886 by Josephine Tychson, California's first woman vintner. A seven-man partnership re-established the winery in the 1960s.

The tasting room is rather attractive, with a truss beam ceiling and stone fireplace with a comfortable couch. The restaurants and gift shops in this attractive, wooded complex are leased out to others.

Tasting notes: We tasted a pair of rich and buttery Chardonnays, several versions of Cabernet Sauvignon, a spicy Sangiovese with soft tannins, full-flavored and nutty Merlot, and a crisp and spicy Petit Sirah. Others on the list are Johannisberg Riesling, Viognier, Cabernet Franc and a dessert wine called Edelwein Gold. Prices: *$$ to $$$$.*

Folie à Deux Winery ● T GTA ⚔ ⓘ

3070 North St. Helena Hwy., St Helena, CA 94574; (800) 473-4454 or (707) 963-1160. (www.folieadeux.com) Daily 10 to 5; MC/VISA, AMEX. Most varieties tasted for a modest fee that includes the glass. Wine logo, clothing and specialty food items. Picnic tables near the tasting room; guided tours by appointment.

Is it shared fantasy or contented reality? You're sitting in a comfortable chair, sipping good wine in a pleasantly prim tasting room, being watched by a window-sitting cat with a Cheshire grin. You pick up the bottle and rotate it slowly in your hand. The label is an ink-blot test, suggesting dancing maidens in a scene from the fourth act of Shakespeare's *The Winter's Tale.* "I'll have another flagon of wine, please. Why is that cat staring at me? Am I in his chair?"

Folie à Deux was founded in 1981 by mental health professional Dr. Larry Dizmang. He bought an old sheep ranch with the intention of making wine, and two thoughts struck him at the time: **1.** A person has to be crazy to go into the wine business. **2.** Wine brings out the celebrative spirit in people. Folie à Deux is not a name borrowed from a Bordeaux château; it translates as "a shared fantasy or delusion by two closely-linked people."

The tasting room in an old yellow cottage provides quiet escape from the busy Napa Valley, if not from reality. The grounds, shaded by oaks and poplars, still has that bucolic ranch feel. Fortunately, the sheep are gone.

Tasting notes: The Dizmangs' winemaker crafts small, tasty lots of Chardonnay, Sangiovese, several versions of Zinfandel, Merlot, Cabernet Sauvignon and a sparking Napa Valley Brut. Prices: *$$$ to $$$$.*

Ehlers Grove ● T ⚔

3222 Ehlers Lane (P.O. Box 545), St. Helena, CA 94575; (800) 946-3635 or (707) 963-3200. Daily 10 to 5; MC/VISA. Most varieties tasted. Picnic tables under olive trees, available by reservation.

A splendid square-shouldered fieldstone building dating from 1886 houses one of the valley's more rustically handsome wineries. The structure was built by early winemaker Bernard Ehlers, an immigrant from Hanover, Germany. It went through assorted owners until it was purchased in 1968 by Mike and Lucy Casey. They still own the property, although they've leased the facility to others. Both Conn Creek and Vichon wineries got their start here. The newest manifestation began in 1993 when the Greenfield Wine Company moved in, completely restored the old building and began wine production.

This is a grand space. The tasting room consists of an L-shaped counter in a corner of the building, surrounded by aging barrels and ancient stone. Further, it's a peaceful retreat, just far enough from busy Highway 29 to be out of reach of most valley visitors and their noisy vehicles. It was uncrowded when we visited and the tasting session was unhurried and intelligently conducted by our winery host.

Tasting notes: The wines are bottled under two labels—Ehlers Grove and Cartlidge & Browne. A two-year-old Ehlers Grove Chardonnay was a classic of its type, lush and nutty with a slight hint of oak. The Ehlers Grove Sauvignon Blanc was so rich and silky that it *felt* like another Chardonnay, although the taste was Sauvignon-fruity. Two reds we tried, an Ehlers Grove Cabernet and Cartlidge & Browne Merlot, were full of berries and herbal.

The wines are excellent overall and quite modestly priced for their quality: **$$ to $$$.**
Vintners choice: "Chardonnay and Cabernet," says a winery spokesperson. "We feel they offer good value and consistent quality."

Stonegate Winery • T$ GTA ✕

1183 Dunaweal Lane, Calistoga, CA 94515; (877) 343-9463 or (707) 942-6500. Daily 10:30 to 4:30; MC/VISA, AMEX. Most varieties tasted for a modest fee. A few wine related giftwares. Small picnic area; guided tours by appointment.

Jim and Barbara Spaulding started this small family winery in 1973 and built it up to a 14,000-case production, with son David as vice president and winemaker. Jim retired in 1996 and sold the winery to a group of investors, although he continues to grow grapes for Stonegate. Stainless steel tanks sit outdoors beside a vineyard; casks and other winemaking gear are tucked inside a modest winery structure. The tasting room is reached via a small stone arch, which also appears on the label. It's friendly and cozy inside and not crowded—by design.

Tasting notes: Fumé Blanc, Sauvignon Blanc, Chardonnay, Cabernet Franc, Merlot and Cabernet Sauvignon comprise the list. The Cabernet had a spicy nose and subtly peppery taste, rich in berries with soft tannins. The Merlot was full-flavored, dusky and mellow—the pleasant taste of an old wine cellar. Prices: **$$$ to $$$$.**

CALISTOGA-SILVERADO TRAIL WINERY TOUR • Assuming you returned to Highway 29 from Stonegate and continued north, you're now in **Calistoga**, trying to choose between a mud bath and yet another tasting room. Set aside time to explore this neat old community at the foot of St. Helena, since it offers many diversions. We cover most of them in "Beyond the vineyards" below. Although most of the rest of the Napa Valley's wine scene has remained relatively static in recent years, several new wineries have cropped up in the Calistoga area.

When you reach the edge of town, continue straight ahead through a traffic signal on Foothill Boulevard (Highway 128) as if you're Geyserville-bound. After a mile, turn left at a stop sign onto Petrified Forest Road. Follow its twisting course another mile and turn left at the sign for **Graeser Winery**. A few twists and turns up a narrow lane will get you there. You can take Petrified Forest Road about three more miles to its namesake **Petrified Forest** attraction. Then return to Foothill Boulevard, continue north briefly and turn right onto Tubbs Lane. You'll soon see **Summers Winery** on your left. Continue on Tubbs Lane to **Old Faithful Geyser** (the signs won't let you miss it) and thence to **Château Montelena**, also on the left. It's reached by a short, twisting drive that takes you quickly into a wooded thicket.

Continue a brief distance on Tubbs Lane to Highway 29 and head south toward Calistoga. Just before you reach a left fork onto Silverado Trail, watch for **Zahtila Vineyards** in a small rural home complex on your left. Continue south, picking up Silverado Trail and you'll shortly see the elegant **Silver Rose Inn** complex and immediately beyond, the imposing **Silver Rose Cellars.** Less than a mile from Silver Rose, turn right onto Dunaweal Lane, then right again into the temple-like **Clos Pegase.** Just below, on the left, is **Sterling Vineyards,** crowning a hill and reached by a sky tram.

Return with us now to Silverado, continue southward and you'll see Spanish-style **Cuvaison Winery** on the left. In less than a mile, you reach **Dutch Henry Winery,** up a rise to your left. A short distance below, turn right onto Larkmead Lane for **Frank Family Vineyards** (Signs may still refer to the old name, Kornell-Larkmead.) Back on the Silverado Trail, you'll soon reach tiny **Wermuth Winery**; look for the small sign on the left. Another mile or so takes you to past the castle-like Château Boswell on the left, open by appointment only, and then to **Casa Nuestra,** a bit off the highway on your right, tucked into a farm complex. Continuing south to Zinfandel lane to complete your loop, you'll pass through beautiful rolling vineyards and wooded meadowlands. A few more wineries stand alongside the Silverado Trail, but none with tasting rooms that keep regular hours.

Graeser Winery • T$ ✗

255 Petrified Forest Rd., Calistoga, CA 94515; (707) 942-4437. (www.graeserwinery.com) Daily 10 to 5; MC/VISA. Most wines tasted for a modest fee. A few winery logo items.

A cute one-room schoolhouse building complete with a bell tower serves as the tasting room for this small winery, in a tree-shaded ranch yard west of Calistoga. The winery and vineyards occupy the Cole Ranch, purchased by Comstock mining millionaire Dr. D. Beverly Cole. More than a century later, former Marine officer Richard Graeser inherited the old ranch from his parents, who had owned it for several years. He had been farming in the Imperial Valley for twenty-five years and decided to turn his parents' ranch in to a vineyard. He began planting vines and building a small winery, with his first harvest coming in 1987. He produces about 2,000 cases a year.

Tasting notes: The list is brief and excellent. It includes a crisp and full flavored Chardonnay, a medium-body and subtly spicy Cabernet Franc, a full-bodied Merlot, and an excellent Cabernet Sauvignon which was blended with a bit of Cabernet Franc. Graeser also bottles a tasty—although not inexpensive—blend of Merlot, Cabernet Franc and Cabernet Sauvignon. Prices: **$$$ to $$$$.**

Summers Winery • T ✗

1171 Tubbs Lane (P.O. Box 496), Calistoga, CA 94515; (707) 942-5508. (www.sumwines.com or summerswinery.com) Daily 11 to 5; MC/VISA. Most varieties tasted free. A few wine-theme items; picnic area.

A vaguely Spanish style structure with a central arch passageway houses this small winery, which sits among its own vineyards. The simple tasting room occupies one end of the structure, and a couple of picnic tables sit on a deck. A "demonstration vineyard" of various grape varietals is adjacent to the winery. This operation started as a Merlot vineyard called Summers Ranch, planted in 1974 by Beth and Jim Summers, who were mortgage and investment bankers in San Francisco. In 1996, they bought the old San Pietro Vara Winery and began rehabilitating it. The tasting room was opened in 1997.

Tasting notes: The overall style of Summers wines was dry and crisp, with medium to full body. Among our samplings were Summers' hallmark Merlot with great fruit and a touch of oak, a full flavored Charbono with crisp tannins, a medium bodied Zinfandel and a crisp yet richly fruity Viognier that would make a great hot summer afternoon sippin' wine. Others on the list are Cabernet rosé, a *Rosso* table wine with a blend of Zinfandel and

Gamay, and a slightly sweet *Bianco* blend of Muscat Canelli and Chardonnay. Prices: **$$ to $$$$.**

Château Montelena Winery • T$ GTA

1429 Tubbs Lane, Calistoga, CA 94515; (707) 942-5105. (www.montelena.com) Daily 10 to 4; MC/VISA. Selected wines tasted for a fee. Some wine oriented gift items. Guided tours by appointment.

Sheltering trees, a mini-medieval castle and an Oriental lake provide one of the valley's more serene winery retreats. It's a place of discoveries, where visitors are invited to stroll the perimeter of Jade Lake, cross bright red arched bridges to tiny islands (when they're not occupied), converse with ducks, encounter stone knights guarding adjacent vineyard and pause under the quietude of Japanese maples.

Château Montelena's mixed heritage comes from two sources. In the 1880s, Alfred L. Tubbs, entrepreneur and state senator, hired a French architect to build a classic winery château, really more of a castle, with turrets and gun ports. Like many, it fell to ruin after Prohibition. The property was bought by a wealthy Chinese, Yort Frank, in the 1950s. He didn't revive the winery although he created an Asian showplace with a lake reminiscent of the old country. It was restored as a working winery in 1972 under the leadership of Jim Barrett and is thriving as a small family-run operation.

Tasting notes: Château Montelena's wines are excellent and they'd better be, since they carry some of the highest price tags in the area. The tasting fee also was rather high when we last stopped by, and one didn't get to carry away a souvenir glass. The brief list includes a lush, buttery and spicy Chardonnay, an outstanding Cabernet Sauvignon and a rich late harvest Riesling. Prices: **$$$$.**

Zahtila Vineyards • T$ GT

2250 Lake County Highway, Calistoga, CA 94515; (707) 942-9251. (www.zahtilavineyards.com) Daily 10 to 5; MC/VISA. Most varieties tasted for a modest fee, which applies toward wine purchase.

The small Zahtila winery occupies an attractively landscaped ranch yard just outside of Calistoga. Tasting happens over a green-checkered table cloth at a tiny tasting room in the front of the small wood-frame winery building. When the weather's warm, tasting adjourns outside, to a board laid over barrel tops. The winery was established in 1998 by Tony Zahtila, who "simply got tired" of his career as a regional manager for a national roofing company. He's learning the wine business as he goes and he has an expert teacher. His winemaker is the highly respected Corey Beck, a U.C. Davis grad who has made wine for some of the Napa Valley's most prestigious wineries.

Tasting notes: When we stopped by, Beck was making five different wines for Tony and they were all Zinfandels. Our tasting began with a light bodied estate Zin, then moved on to an excellent *Monte Rosso* Old Vines Zinfandel with lots of spice and fruit. Our favorite was a Dry Creek Old Vines Zin with wonderfully concentrated fruit and a spicy finish. Prices: **$$$$.**

Silver Rose Cellars • T$ GT ✕ ▥

400 Silverado Trail; mailing address: 351 Rosedale Rd., Calistoga, CA 94515; (800) 995-9381 or (707) 942-9581. (www.silverrose.com) Daily 10 to 5; major credit cards. Select wines tasted for a fee, which applies toward purchase. Extensive giftware, wine logo and specialty food items. Tours with barrel tasting daily at 11.

An ancient gnarled oak frames Silver Rose Cellars, one of the Napa Valley's most opulent wineries.

Elegance begets elegance. After operating the highly successful Silver Rose Inn for several years, investment banker J-Paul Dumont and his family opened their new Silver Rose Cellars in June, 2000. The facility is managed by his son Derrick. The multi-level complex is a pleasing study in stone and wood, rimmed by elaborate landscaping and a small lake. The octagonal tasting room features a lofty beam ceiling held up by bold peeled log columns. Tall windows look out upon the lake, gnarled oaks and new vineyards. Tables and chairs on a long deck just off the tasting room invite visitors to enjoy the view *al fresco*.

Tasting notes: The list is brief and the wines were excellent, starting with a silky smooth Chardonnay with hints of oak, and followed by *D'Argent*, an even more full-bodied Chard. The reds we tasted were a full-bodied yet soft Merlot, a spicy Cabernet Sauvignon with a classic chili pepper nose and taste, and Dentelle, a busy blend of Cabernets Sauvignon and Franc, Merlot, Zinfandel and Sangiovese. Prices: **$$$$.**

Clos Pegase ● T$ GT

1060 Dunaweal Lane, Calistoga, CA 94515; (707) 942-4901. Daily 10:30 to 5. Selected wines tasted for a modest fee. A few wine logo items. Guided tours daily at 11 and 3; wine and art lectures the third Saturday of each month, by appointment.

When multi-millionaire publisher Jan Shrem decided to build a shrine to wine and art in the 1980s, he sought logical sources. From Andre Tchelistcheff of Beaulieu fame he requested winemaking advice, and he asked the San Francisco Museum of Modern Art to sponsor an architectural competition. Tchelistcheff recommended Bill Pease as a winemaker and the museum selected Princeton architect Michael Graves to design a "temple of wine." The result: Clos Pegase wines consistently win awards and Graves' impressive salmon-colored post-modern Greek-Roman-Aztec wine temple is the darling of new-wave architects. (Bob Masyczek is the current winemaker.)

Clos Pegase is at once imposing and stark—a towering, columnar presence enclosing a simple courtyard. Modern art "constructions" are placed about extensive lawns. A giant mural of Bacchus rises behind the counter in the large tasting room, taunting you to another sip. Although the huge winery appears to stand alone above the vineyards, it's actually built against a small, steep hillside with caves cut into the cliff. They can be seen on reservation-only tours.

Tasting notes: Clos Pegase offerings range from a Sauvignon Blanc with a fruity melon flavor and hints of oak to Hommage, a proprietary blend of Cabernet Sauvignon, Cabernet Franc, Merlot and Petit Sirah. It's similar to a Meritage in blend, with a smooth full-bodied taste. Others on the list are a Chardonnay finished in French oak, a fruity and complex Merlot, and a full flavored and herbal Cabernet Sauvignon. Prices: *$$ to $$$$*.

Sterling Vineyards ● T$ ST 📷

1111 Dunaweal Lane (P.O. Box 365), Calistoga, CA 94515; (707) 942-4219. Daily 10:30 to 4:30; major credit cards. Moderate visitor fee includes tram ride, wine tasting and self-guided tour of the winery. Good selection of wine-oriented giftwares. Expect delays on the tram on summer weekends; the best bet is to arrive early in the day.

Sterling gleams from a hillock above the vineyards like a misplaced Moorish monastery. It's reached in rather novel fashion—one buys a sky tram ticket and rides above tawny, tilted meadows and oak clusters to this "winery in the sky." Once there, the Moorish impression continues. Sterling is a gleaming collection of white stucco walls, sunny patios, stainless steel tanks and dimly-lit wine cellars that seem older than they are. The self-guiding tour is among the best of the California wine country, adorned with explanatory graphics, historic wine art reproductions and wonderful quotes about the grape. Never mind the sky bucket gimmick. Once on top, the place exudes an aura of artistic class. The Napa Valley views are—sorry about this—sterling. After touring, one adjourns to a spacious tasting room or outside terrace, where current wines are served. An adjacent gift shop offers a good selection of wineware, books and such.

The winery was created in 1969 by four owners of a San Francisco-based paper company, then it became part of the Coca-Cola Company's wine venture in 1977. It was sold in 1983 to Seagram Classics Wine Company, the present owners.

Tasting notes: Sauvignon Blanc, Chardonnay, Merlot and Cabernet Sauvignon comprise the list. The Sauvignon Blanc was lush and herbal with soft fruit, almost a Chardonnay character; and Merlot exhibited a soft herbal nose with taste to match; and the Cab offered good berry flavor and a light tannic nip at the finish. Prices: *$$ to $$$$*.

Cuvaison Winery ● T$ GTA ✕ 📷

4550 Silverado Trail (P.O. Box 384), Calistoga, CA 94515; (707) 942-6266. Daily 10 to 5; MC/VISA, DISC. Most varieties tasted for a modest fee (includes glass). Good giftware selection. Shaded picnic area near the tasting room; guided tours by appointment.

We've always regarded Cuvaison as the little jewel of the Napa Valley. It's a pleasing, Spanish mission-style winery with a matching tasting room, sheltered by ancient oaks. The tasting parlor is a comfortable space, trimmed in oak, roomy yet busy with bottles, cases of wine and giftwares. A woodsy picnic area on a downslope offers views of vineyards and the distant Mayacamas Mountains. Cuvaison, which comes from the French term for fermenting red wines on their skins, was started in 1969 by two engineers. They sold it to New York publisher Oakleigh Thorne in 1974. Five years later, the Schmidheiny family of Switzerland purchased the winery along with 400 acres of Carneros vineyard land.

Tasting notes: Cuvaison currently features Chardonnay, Reserve Chardonnay, Cabernet Sauvignon, Merlot, Zinfandel and Pinot Noir. Winemaker John Thacher creates well balanced wines; they all exhibit full fruity flavor, with enough intensity to encourage aging. Drink them now or lay them away, suggests Thacher. Prices: *$$ to $$$.*

Dutch Henry Winery • T

4300 Silverado Trail, Calistoga, CA 94515; (707) 942-5771. (www.dutchhenry.com) Daily 10 to 5; MC/VISA. Most current releases tasted. A few wine logo items.

A modest stucco building on a terraced slope marks one of the valley's smaller operations, with an output of about 2,000 cases—and growing. Dutch Henry, named for a ravine in the hillside behind it, emerged when Kendall Phelps and Scott Chafen took over a defunct winery in 1991. Members of valley grape growing families, they're learning the winemaking craft as they go, calling in friends to help with the crush and using basket presses and hand labeling. The small winery is in a pleasant setting, shaded by gnarled madrones, oaks and eucalyptus, with vineyards tilted downhill to the Silverado Trail. The tasting room is a simple affair—a small counter occupying one end of the winery.

Tasting notes The current wines, which often sell out, include a buttery malolactic fermented Chardonnay, an intense Merlot suitable for aging, a huge Zinfandel with lots of berries and spice, a full-flavored Syrah, and a peppery Cabernet Sauvignon with a great berry taste and hints of wood. Prices: *$$$$.*

Frank Family Vineyards • T GT

1091 Larkmead Lane (P.O. Box 249), St. Helena, CA 95474; (707) 963-1237. Daily 10 to 5; major credit cards. Most wines tasted. A few wine logo items. Guided tours depart frequently between 10:30 and 3:45.

After a history-ridden journey spanning a century and numerous name and ownership changes, this classic old winery currently functions as Frank Family Vineyards. It was built in 1884 as Larkmead Winery and its main stone building was completed in 1906. After being closed by Prohibition, it was re-opened in 1952 by Hanns Kornell, one of the Napa Valley's most remarkable individuals. He had fled from a Nazi concentration camp in 1939, arrived flat broke in America and—after years of saving and winemaking—opened Hanns Kornell Champagne Cellars. He remained active in the business well into his 80s, then turned the operation over to his children. He died in 1994. Two veteran Napa Valley families, the Franks and Rombauers, purchased the winery in the 1990s. In 2001, it came under the management of Richard Frank.

The winery's frequently-departing tours teach you everything you ever wanted to know about making sparkling wine. You then return to a simple cottage style hospitality center to put to the taste what you've learned.

Tasting notes: We've long felt that the winery's sparklers were among the best in the valley, and they remain so under the Frank family tutelage. The Blanc de Noirs and Blanc de Blanc revealed good grape character and proper crispiness. Extra Dry (that wonderful winetalk antithesis) has a touch of sweetness while keeping its fruit flavor. The Franks have added a selection of red wines in addition to the sparklers, although they hadn't yet been bottled at press time. Prices: *$$$ to $$$$.*

Wermuth Winery ● *T ST* ✕

3942 Silverado Trail, Calistoga, CA 94515; (707) 942-5924. Daily 11 to 5; MC/VISA. Most varieties tasted. Casual tours; small picnic area.

This tiny operation is housed in a couple of pink corrugated sheds beside Ralph and Smitty Wermuth's home on the upside of the Silverado Trail. They started in 1981 and now produce about 4,000 cases a year, employing a classic Italian basket press and lots of personal attention. When Smitty isn't helping Ralph, she creates dainty little hand-painted note cards, which are for sale in the winery.

Wines are sampled in a small cottage tasting room and pipe-smoking, soft-spoken Ralph will autograph your purchase with a silver felt-tip pen. He'll also break into philosophical discussions at the slightest encouragement, so this is a good place to linger if you feel talkative. We wound up in a conversation about our company, and how the use of computers made small publishing enterprises possible.

Tasting notes: Ralph's list is rather short and inexpensive, particularly for the Napa Valley. The dry Colombard was herbal and fruity; a good picnic wine. His Zinfandel was light, yet with a pleasing and pronounced raspberry taste. The Gamay displayed surprisingly intense herbal flavor for a wine of this type, with a crisp, fruity finish. "It goes well with chocolates," Ralph said, offering a tin of chocolate bits. He was right. Then he pulled out a bottle of Zin, autographed it and presented it as a gift. (We never solicit, but we never turn down good Zin.) The inscription read: "Don't spill this on your computer." Prices: *$ to $$$.*

Casa Nuestra ● *T$ GTA* ✕

3451 Silverado Trail, St. Helena, CA 94574; (707) 963-3451. (www.casanuestra.com) Friday-Monday 11 to 5 or by appointment; MC/VISA. Several varieties tasted for a modest fee. A few wine related gift items. Picnic area; group tours by appointment.

Casa Nuestra's little yellow farmhouse is an inviting place to sip wine, with its fireplace, easy chairs, an old Naugahyde Mel's Diner booth and other properly curious furnishing. The name, appropriately, is Spanish for "our house." A tree-shaded picnic area reinforces the laid-back, down-home impression. The winery was bonded in 1980 by former civil rights attorney Gene Kirkham and his wife Cody. The San Francisco-born Kirkham became fed up with the pin-stripped city life, so he bought this small farm, grew a Mormon beard and started making wine. Learning the trade by trial and error, consulting county farm advisors and friendly neighbor vintners, he and his wife have become what the local paper once described as "happy farmers." These down home folks make excellent wines.

Tasting notes: No, *Tinto* isn't the Lone Ranger's wimpy Indian companion. It's Casa Nuestra's red blend, made from a polyglot of grapes that grow in the same vineyard and are harvested together—Zinfandel, Cabernet, Gamay, Pinot Noir, Mondeuse, Carignane, Alicante Bouschet and possibly Pfeffer. Our sample suggested a big Chianti, with lots of berries and spice yet curiously gentle. It has won a couple of gold medals and it's remarkably good for the price. Others we sipped were a spicy and lightly fruity Chenin Blanc; and *Quixote*, an impressively lush Meritage style wine with a big yet soft berry flavor. Why *Quixote*? "Because selling a Meritage style wine at this place is an impossible dream," says Kirkham. Others on the list are a spicy and very aromatic Cabernet Frank, a solid Cabernet Sauvignon, and a deeply fruity and rich late harvest Johannisberg Riesling. Prices: *$$ to $$$$.*

THE BEST OF THE BUNCH

The best wine buys ● Sutter Home Winery, Louis M. Martini, Beringer Vineyards, Charles Krug Winery, Freemark Abbey Winery and Casa Nuestra.

The most attractive wineries ● V. Sattui Winery, Beringer Vineyards, Château Montelena, Clos Pegase, Sterling Vineyards, Cuvaison Winery and Silver Rose Cellars.

The most interesting tasting rooms ● Edgewood Estate Winery, Sutter Home Winery, Merryvale Vineyards, Beringer Vineyards, Markham Vineyards, Clos Pegase and Silver Rose Cellars.

The funkiest tasting rooms ● Prager Winery, Graeser Winery and Casa Nuestra.

The best gift shops ● V. Sattui Winery, Sutter Home Winery, Beringer Vineyards, Charles Krug, Freemark Abbey Winery, Sterling Vineyards and Silver Rose Cellars.

The nicest picnic areas ● V. Sattui Winery, Cuvaison Winery, Freemark Abbey Winery and Casa Nuestra.

The best tours ● Beringer Vineyards (guided), Frank Family Vineyards (guided, sparkling wine) and Sterling Vineyards (self-guiding).

Wine country maps and events

Winery maps and guides ● The Calistoga and St. Helena chambers of commerce can provide maps and guides; see their listings at the end of this chapter. A simple map-flyer, ***Napa Valley's Historic Silverado Trail***, lists wineries on or near that route. It's available free at most member wineries; or contact Silverado Trail Winery Association, 3212 Jefferson St., Suite 143, Napa, CA 94558. *(www.silveradotrail.com)*

As we noted in the previous chapter, you'll find an abundance of commercial guides and magazines in tasting rooms, gift shops and visitor centers. The free slick magazine Destination Napa Valley has a handy pull-out winery map with details on hours, prices and winetasting. ***Spotlight's Wine Country Guide***, which is pocket-sized and also free, covers Napa, Sonoma, Mendocino and Lake Counties, with winery maps and listings, plus advertisements for lodgings, restaurants, attractions and activities.

Wineland events ● Napa Valley Wine Library Association courses (see box on page 163); (707) 963-5145. *(www.napawinelibrary.org)* Napa Valley Mustard Celebration in early February in Calistoga; (707) 259-9020. Napa

Valley Wine Auction, first weekend of June; (707) 226-7459 or (702) 942-6333. Napa County Fair in Calistoga, with local winery exhibits, early July; (707) 942-5111. Silverado Trail Winery Association open houses, mid-November; (707) 942-6333. Also see listings in Chapter Five.

BEYOND THE VINEYARDS

Napa's upper valley offers more non-winery attractions than the lower end. They're focused mostly around Calistoga, which was a spa before the valley became America's best known wine producing region. St. Helena has its share of lures as well, most notably the **Silverado Museum.**

If you like scenery with a twist (in the roads), turn west onto Madroña Avenue (the last stoplight on St. Helena's north side), follow it three blocks to Spring Mountain Road and turn right. It twists high into the thickly wooded **Mayacamus Mountains**, following a pretty little creek for much of the way. The route changes its name to St. Helena Road and, about twelve miles from town, it terminates at Calistoga Road. Turn right and follow that north; it blends into Petrified Forest Road and takes you into **Calistoga**.

Flamboyant Mormon entrepreneur Sam Brannan made Calistoga famous when he opened a spa, then he built a railroad from Napa to bring the tourists. Those rails still exist—traveled part of the way by the Napa Valley Wine Train—and the town continues to be a mecca for fans of mud baths and mineral water hot tubs. Resort operators tout the supposed therapeutic value of Calistoga's mineral water and they promote neck-deep mud baths and "European body wraps" to "purge your skin of toxins and restore its elasticin."

If you'd rather drink mineral water than sit in it, two major bottling companies are located here—Crystal Geyser at 501 Washington Street and Calistoga Mineral Water Company on the Silverado Trail at the edge of town. They have no public facilities although their products—straight and fruit flavored—are available all over town. If you prefer more kick to your fizz, **Napa Valley Brewing Company** operates a micro-brewery in the old water tower of the Calistoga Inn at 1250 Lincoln Avenue.

Calistoga is busy with shops and boutiques. Several are clustered in Sam Brannan's 1868 **Calistoga Depot**; some are housed in adjacent railroad cars. The Calistoga Chamber of Commerce is here, too, tucked into a cottage behind the depot. Other shops are strung along Lincoln Avenue, the main street. Also in town or nearby are the **Sharpsteen Museum and Sam Brannan cottage, Petrified Forest** and **Old Faithful Geyser.**

A seven-mile drive into the flanks of Mount St. Helena on Highway 29 takes you to **Robert Louis Stevenson State Park.** It's undeveloped and fun to explore (see box on page 169). If you press north on Route 29, you'll witness impressive mountain scenery and eventually wind up in Lake County. It's home to huge Clear Lake and several wineries described in Chapter Two. Another pretty route out of Calistoga is Highway 128 northwest, which delivers you to Mendocino County.

Up Valley attractions
St. Helena area

Bale Grist Mill State Historic Park and *Napa-Bothe State Park*
● *Highway 29, a few miles north of St. Helena; (707) 942-4575. Daily 10 to 5; admission fee.* □ Restored grist mill built by Dr. Edward T. Bale in 1846 and adjacent recreational park with hiking, picnicking and camping.

Silverado Museum • *1490 Library Lane, St. Helena; (707) 963-3757. Tuesday-Sunday noon to 4.* ☐ Excellent collection of objects concerning Robert Louis Stevenson and his 1880 honeymoon visit.

Calistoga

Old Faithful Geyser • *1299 Tubbs Lane, Calistoga; (707) 942-6463. Daily 10 to 6 May-September and 9 to 5 the rest of the year; admission fee.* ☐ Smaller than Yellowstone's but reasonably faithful, erupting about every 40 minutes; picnic area, gift and snack shop.

Petrified Forest • *Petrified Forest Rd. (five miles west), Calistoga; (707) 942-6667. Daily 10 to 6; admission fee.* ☐ A scattering of petrified trees, museum, gift shop and picnic area.

Robert Louis Stevenson State Historic Park • *Seven miles above Calistoga on Highway 29.* ☐ Site of the author's 1880 honeymoon; undeveloped, but with hiking trails and a monument at the honeymoon cabin site.

Sharpsteen Museum and Sam Brannan Cottage • *1311 Washington St., Calistoga; (707) 942-5911. Daily 10 to 4 April-October and noon to 4 the rest of the year; free.* ☐ Historic museum with a scale model of Sam Brannan's resort and a restoration of one of his cottages.

UP VALLEY DINING

PRICE KEY: Dinner entrée with soup or salad, without drinks or dessert for under $10 = $; $10 to $14 = $$; $15 to $25 = $$$; over $25 = $$$$.

St. Helena area

Brava Terrace • ☆☆ **$$$**

☐ *3010 North St. Helena Hwy. (Freemark Abbey complex), St. Helena; (707) 963-9300. French-American bistro; full bar service. Lunch and dinner daily; closed Wednesdays in winter. Major credit cards.* ☐ Charming bistro in an architecturally pleasing stone and wood A-frame, with an eclectic menu featuring local meats and produce and fresh pasta.

Gail's Café • ☆☆ **$**

☐ *1347 Main, St. Helena; (707) 963-3332. (www.napavalley.com/gails) American; wine and beer. Breakfast through lunch daily, plus dinner from April through October. MC/VISA.* ☐ Decidedly cute café with an American graffiti theme; walls covered with magazine covers, soft drink signs and autographed movie star black and white photos; 1950s style jukebox and other memorabilia. Fare includes old fashioned soda fountain items, pizzas and pastas, deli sandwiches, steak and daily specials, plus tasty breakfast fare.

Gillwoods Café • ☆☆ **$**

☐ *1313 Main St., St. Helena; (707) 963-1788. American; wine and beer. Breakfast through dinner daily in summer; breakfast through mid-afternoon the rest of the year. MC/VISA.* ☐ Old fashioned American storefront café in downtown St. Helena with wainscotting and ceiling fans. It dishes up roasted leg of lamb, Yankee pot roast and other basic fare; popular for breakfast.

Silverado Brewing Company Restaurant & Bar • ☆☆ **$$ to $$$**

☐ *3020 North St. Helena Hwy. (Freemark Abbey complex), St. Helena; (707) 967-9876. American; full bar service. Lunch and dinner daily except Wednesday. Major credit cards.* ☐ Handsome brewpub and dining room housed in one of the old Freemark Abbey stone buildings, with shiny new copper brewing vats at one end. It offers the usual hearty brewpub fare plus dinner entrées including prime rib, steak and braised lamb shank.

Wine Spectator Greystone Restaurant ● ☆☆☆ $$$

2555 Main St., St. Helena; (707) 967-1010. California cuisine; wine and beer. Lunch and dinner daily, plus tasting menus from mid-morning to late evening. Major credit cards. □ Visually striking wine-focused restaurant in the Culinary Institute of America complex. Master chefs and trainees prepare very creative fare for the frequently changing menu. Extensive wine list.

Calistoga

Bosko's Ristoranti ● ☆☆ $

□ *1364 Lincoln Ave., Calistoga; (707) 942-9088. Italian; full bar service. Lunch and dinner daily. MC/VISA.* □ Old fashion Italian restaurant with fieldstone walls, warm woods, walnut chairs, exposed ceilings and drop lamps. The fare is inexpensive and essential Italian—assorted fresh pastas and pizzas; a specialty is *varazze,* marinated chicken breast with bell peppers and broccoli in a tomato garlic sauce.

Café Sarafornia ● ☆☆ $$

□ *1413 Lincoln Ave., Calistoga; (707) 942-0555. American; wine and beer. Lunch through dinner daily. MC/VISA.* □ Pleasantly funky place with ceiling fans, wall murals and cozy booths, popular with locals and handy for quick, light bites. Pastas, salads, 'burgers and other sandwiches, along with a good variety of omelettes and other breakfast fare. The name comes from a legend that Calistoga founder Sam Brannan, in reference to New York's famous Saratoga mineral water spa, said after too many toasts: "I'll make this place the Sarafornia of Calistoga!"

Pacifico Restaurante Mexicano ● ☆☆ $$

1237 Lincoln Ave., Calistoga; (707) 942-4400. Mexican; full bar service. Lunch through dinner daily. Major credit cards. □ "Mexican modern" restaurant with a bright, airy interior, featuring creative and spicy Mexican entries, plus the usual tortilla-wrapped items. Extensive tequila list.

The Smokehouse ● ☆☆ $$

□ *1458 Lincoln Ave. (in the Calistoga Depot), Calistoga; (707) 942-6060. American; wine and beer. Breakfast through dinner daily. MC/VISA, DISC.* □ Informal café cleverly done up with waiting room benches for seats, slatwood walls, historic photos and a model train on a track above. "Full plate" dinners of pot pies, barbecued ribs or roasted fish come with vegetables, potatoes or slaw and cornbread. Lighter fare for lunch.

Soo Yuan ● ☆☆ $

□ *1354 Lincoln Ave., Calistoga; (707) 942-9404. Chinese; wine and beer. Lunch through dinner daily. MC/VISA, AMEX.* □ Cute little diner with cane drop lamps, hanging ivy and bits of bright Asian trim. The menu dances through most Chinese fare, from gentle Cantonese to spicy Szechuan.

Triple S Ranch Restaurant ● ☆☆ $$

□ *4600 Mt. Home Ranch Rd. (off Petrified Forest Road), Calistoga, CA 94515; (707) 942-6730. American; full bar service. Dinner nightly; closed Mondays in the winter. MC/VISA.* □ Down-home atmosphere in a Western style family restaurant in the hills west of Calistoga. Menu with rural Americana tilt, leaning toward steak, chicken and ham, with a couple of seafood items. At a family resort with wooded grounds, pool and hiking trails.

"...AND THE WINE IS BOTTLED POETRY"

A sign at the Napa Valley's southern entrance quotes a troubled, tubercular young Scottish writer who spent the summer of 1880 on the slopes of Mount St. Helena, seeking refuge from the damp fogs of San Francisco.

Robert Louis Stevenson had pursued Fanny Osbourne, a married American woman, from France to California, trying to convince her to leave her husband and marry him. She finally relented and they chose the Napa Valley for their honeymoon, accompanied by her son Samuel and their dog Chuchu. Still unpublished, the struggling writer was almost penniless, so they moved into an empty bunkhouse on the tailing dump of the old Calistoga Silver Mine on Mount St. Helena.

"The place was open like the proscenium of a theatre," he wrote, "and we looked forth into a great realm of air, and far and near on wild and varied country."

Ever the poet, Stevenson called their honeymoon haven Silverado. Traveling about the valley, they visited still-surviving landmarks such as Bale's Grist Mill, Schramsberg Winery and the Petrified Forest, where he found its owner, Charley Evans, to be a "far more delightful curiosity" than the stone trees.

Despite his illness, he hiked up Monitor Ledge to the top of the mine shaft to witness the stunning vista of the Napa Valley, often covered with a cottony fog blanket. "That vast fog-ocean lay in a trance of silence, nor did the sweet air of morning tremble with a sound."

Stevenson kept a diary called "Silverado Journal," and from this he compiled *The Silverado Squatters*, his first published work.

The honeymoon site is now part of Robert Louis Stevenson State Historic Park, reached by a seven-mile drive north from Calistoga on Highway 29. It's undeveloped, with no camping, water or other facilities. However, a few picnic tables sit near the concrete foundation of a former toll house below the mine. A one-mile hiking trail switchbacks up the mountain to the cabin site. The bunkhouse is gone; a monument erected by Napa Valley women's clubs marks the spot.

A difficult scramble over broken rock will deliver you to the mine, which is more of a slot cut into a silver-bearing ridge. A trail from the monument joins a forestry road that takes you to the top of the ridge. From there, you can enjoy Stevenson's dramatic Napa Valley view.

Memorabilia of Stevenson and his Napa Valley visit are preserved in the Silverado Museum at 1490 Library Lane, St. Helena, in the city library building. Hours are Tuesday through Sunday from noon to 4. Admission is free; phone (707) 963-3757.

Stevenson left his Silverado after two months. In renewed health and spirits, he became one of history's great authors. Sadly, he died just fourteen years later. An inscription on the women's club monument, taken from one of his poems, marks his passage:

Doomed to know not Winter, only Spring,
A being trod the flowery April blithely for a while,
Took his fill of music, joy of thought and seeing,
Came and stayed and went, nor ever ceased to smile.

UP VALLEY LODGINGS
**PRICE KEY: A two-person room for $35 or less = $; $36 to $50 = $$;
$51 to $75 = $$$; $76 to $100 = $$$$; more than $100 = $$$$$.**

St. Helena

El Bonita Motel ☆☆ $$$$$
❏ *195 Main St., St. Helena, CA 94574; (800) 541-3284 or (707) 963-3216. (www.elbonita.com) Major credit cards.* ❏ A 42-room remodeled art deco motel with nicely landscaped grounds on the edge of St. Helena, near the wineries. TV, room phones and some refrigerators. Pool, spa, volleyball court. Kitchenettes and suites available.

Harvest Inn ● ☆☆☆☆ $$$$$
❏ *One Main St., St. Helena, CA 94574; (800) 950-8466 or (707) 963-9463. Major credit cards.* ❏ Elegant brick Tudor style inn with elaborate landscaping, next to the vineyards on the edge of town. Fifty-four rooms, suites and cottages furnished with antiques; all with TV and phones; some fireplaces, wet bars and spa tubs. Two pools, wine bar, spa, rental bicycles.

Hotel St. Helena ● ☆☆☆ $$$$$
❏ *1390 Main St., St. Helena, CA 94574; (707) 963-4388. (www.hotelsthelena.com) Rates include continental breakfast. Major credit cards.* ❏ Cozily restored 1881 hotel in downtown St. Helena; some shared and some private baths; room phones; TVs available. All rooms have period décor. Lobby is a virtual museum of vintage dolls, toys and folk crafts. Wine and coffee bar open to the public; garden patio.

Meadowood Napa Valley ● ☆☆☆☆ $$$$$
❏ *900 Meadowood Lane, St. Helena, CA 94574; (800) 458-8080 or (707) 963-3646. Major credit cards.* ❏ Luxurious, secluded country resort with opulently furnished rooms. Extensive landscaped grounds; golf, tennis, croquet, pool, spa and hiking trails. **The Restaurant at Meadowood** features California cuisine; **The Grill** is a bistro-style café serving lunch through dinner daily; full bar service.

Bed & breakfast inns

Ambrose Bierce House ● ☆☆☆ $$$$$
❏ *1515 Main St., St. Helena, CA 94574; (707) 963-3003. (www.ambrosebiercehouse.com) Three suites with private baths; full breakfast.* ❏ Recently remodeled former home of noted author Ambrose Bierce, within walking distance of downtown St. Helena. Antique furnishings in common areas and suites. Sitting room, old style front porch; landscaped grounds with hot tub.

Cinnamon Bear Bed & Breakfast ● ☆☆ $$$$$
❏ *1407 Kearney St. (Adams), St. Helena, CA 94574; (707) 963-4653. (www.bbchannel.com/bbc/p213930.asp) Three rooms with private baths; full breakfast. MC/VISA, AMEX.* ❏ Early twentieth century redwood home with shady front porch; former mayor's residence. Furnished with antiques and early American arts and crafts, with a teddy bear theme. Comfy living room with fireplace. The owner is a pastry chef—reflected in the tasty breakfasts.

Erika's Hillside ● ☆☆☆ $$$$$
❏ *285 Fawn Park (off Silverado Trail), St. Helena, CA 94574; (707) 963-2887. Major credit cards. Two rooms and two suites with private baths; continental breakfast.* ❏ Remodeled century-old Swiss chalet on wooded,

landscaped three-acre estate; European furnishings with hand-painted *rose-maling*. Flower gardens between terraced rock walls, hot tub, valley views.

The Ink House ● ☆☆☆ $$$$$

☐ *1575 North St. Helena Hwy. (Whitehall Lane), St. Helena, CA 94574; (707) 963-3890. Seven rooms; five with private and two with shared baths; TV and phones; full breakfast. MC/VISA.* ☐ Elegant 1884 Italianate mansion listed on the National Register of Historic Places. Furnished with American, English, French and Italian antiques; twelve-foot ceilings; large guest rooms and common rooms. Roof observatory with 360-degree valley view.

Shady Oaks Country Inn ● ☆☆ $$$$$

☐ *399 Zinfandel Lane (Highway 29), St. Helena, CA 94574; (707) 963-1190. (www.shadyoaksinn.com) Five rooms with private baths; full "champagne breakfast."* ☐ Secluded inn on two acres with three units in a restored 1920s farmhouse and two in an 1887 fieldstone winery building. Rooms and common areas furnished with American antiques.

Wine Country Inn ● ☆☆☆ $$$$$

☐ *1152 Lodi Lane (Highway 29), St. Helena, CA 94574; (707) 963-7077. Twenty-four rooms with private baths; continental breakfast. MC/VISA.* ☐ A comfortable inn fashioned like an elegant early American country home, perched on a knoll overlooking hills and vineyards. Stylish rooms and common areas feature fireplaces, balconies, family-made quilts and antiques.

Calistoga

Calistoga Inn ● ☆☆ $$$ to $$$$

☐ *1250 Lincoln Ave. (Cedar), Calistoga, CA 94515; (707) 942-4101. Rates include continental breakfast. MC/VISA.* ☐ A renovated century-old inn with shared baths and "American comfortable" furnishings. **Napa Valley Brewing Company** microbrewery and restaurant are part of the complex; American fare, served from lunch through evening; full bar service including—of course—its own micro-brews.

Calistoga Village Inn & Spa ● ☆☆ $$$ to $$$$$

☐ *1880 Lincoln Ave. (Silverado Trail), Calistoga, CA 94515; (707) 942-0991. Major credit cards.* ☐ A 42-room inn with spa, featuring mud baths, mineral baths, massages and facials; swimming pool. Room have TV and phones.

Comfort Inn ● ☆☆ $$$$ to $$$$$

☐ *1865 Lincoln Ave., Calistoga, CA 94515; (800) 228-5150 or (707) 942-9400. Major credit cards.* ☐ A 55-unit motel with landscaped grounds, mineral water pool and spa, plus a sauna and steam room. Units have cable TV and phones, data ports, voice mail and in-room coffee.

Dr. Wilkinson's Hot Springs ● ☆☆☆ $$$$$

☐ *1507 Lincoln Ave. (Fairway), Calistoga, CA 94515; (707) 942-4102. (www.drwilkinson.com) MC/VISA, AMEX.* ☐ Historic 42-room resort that dates back half a century. TV and phones in rooms and bungalows; some with mini refrigerators. Full spa facilities with three mineral pools, massages, facials and mud baths. Two outdoor mineral water pools and indoor spa pool. Kitchenettes available.

Eurospa and Inn ● ☆☆ $$$$

☐ *1202 Pine St., Calistoga, CA 94515; (707) 942-6829. (www.eurospa.com) Rates include continental breakfast. MC/VISA, AMEX.* ☐ California ranch-style inn with thirteen attractive rooms; some with spa tubs and gas fireplaces. Spa facilities including whirlpool, mud baths and facials.

Golden Haven Spa & Resort ● ☆☆ $$$$ to $$$$$

□ 1713 Lake St., Calistoga, CA 94515; (707) 942-6793. (www.golden-haven.com) MC/VISA, AMEX. □ A 26-room motel and mineral spa. TV, no room phones; some rooms have spa tubs or saunas. Suites and kitchen units available. Spa facilities include mud baths, massages, hot water mineral pool and whirlpool spas; swimming pool.

Hideaway Cottages ● ☆ $$$$ to $$$$$

□ 1412 Fairway (Lincoln), Calistoga, CA 94515; (707) 942-4108. MC/VISA, AMEX. □ Seventeen cottages in a nicely landscaped setting with mature trees; most units have kitchens. Full spa facilities with mineral pool, mud baths and spa tubs; conference room.

Bed & breakfast inns

The Elms Bed & Breakfast ● ☆☆☆☆ $$$$$

□ 1300 Cedar St., Calistoga, CA 94515; (800) 235-4316 or (707) 942-9476. Seven rooms with private baths; five with fireplaces and TV; full breakfast. MC/VISA, AMEX. □ Elegant 1871 mansard-roofed Victorian, former judge's home, on the National Register of Historic Places. Nicely done rooms with European antiques; separate honeymoon cottage with kitchenette. Extensive landscaped grounds. Afternoon wine and cheese.

Larkmead Country Inn ● ☆☆☆ $$$$$

□ 1103 Larkmead Lane (between Highway 29 and Silverado), Calistoga, CA 94515; (707) 942-5360. Four rooms with private baths; full breakfast. No credit cards. □ Imposing 1918 early California winery estate furnished with English antiques, Persian carpets and artwork. Extensive landscaped grounds with mature hardwoods.

Silver Rose Inn ● ☆☆☆ $$$$$

□ 351 Rosedale Rd. (Silverado Trail), Calistoga, CA 94515; (707) 942-9581. (www.silverrose.com) Twenty rooms with private baths and TV; full breakfast. MC/VISA, DISC. □ Stylish modern-rustic country home on oak knoll with valley views from all guest rooms. Done in early American, Oriental and modern décor. Some rooms have spa tubs, fireplaces, porches or balconies. Landscaped grounds with pool, flagstone paths and rock garden. Hot spring spa with mud baths and massages; tennis courts, putting greens and spa tubs.

Up Valley information sources

Calistoga Chamber of Commerce, 1458 Lincoln Ave. (in the Calistoga Depot), Calistoga, CA 94515; (707) 942-6333. (www.calistogafun.com)

Napa Valley Conference and Visitors Bureau, 1310 Napa Town Center, Napa, CA 94559; (707) 226-7459. (www.napavalley.com)

Napa Valley Wine Library Association, P.O. Box 328, St. Helena, CA 94574; (707) 963-5145. (www.napawinelibrary.org)

St. Helena Chamber of Commerce, P.O. Box 124 (1010 Main Street, suite A), St. Helena, CA 94574; (800) 767-8528 or (707) 963-4456. (www.sthelena.com)

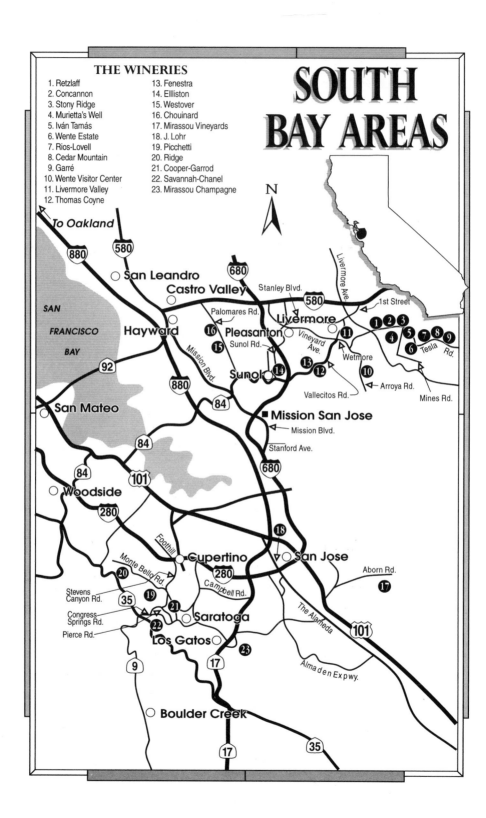

THE WINERIES

1. Retzlaff
2. Concannon
3. Stony Ridge
4. Murietta's Well
5. Iván Tamás
6. Wente Estate
7. Rios-Lovell
8. Cedar Mountain
9. Garré
10. Wente Visitor Center
11. Livermore Valley
12. Thomas Coyne
13. Fenestra
14. Ellliston
15. Westover
16. Chouinard
17. Mirassou Vineyards
18. J. Lohr
19. Picchetti
20. Ridge
21. Cooper-Garrod
22. Savannah-Chanel
23. Mirassou Champagne

SOUTH BAY AREAS

N

To Oakland

880 580

San Leandro

Castro Valley

Stanley Blvd.

680

580 1st Street

SAN Palomares Rd. Livermore

FRANCISCO Hayward Pleasanton Vineyard Ave.

BAY Sunol Rd. Wetmore

92 Mission Blvd. 880 Sunol Arroya Rd.

84 Vallecitos Rd. Mines Rd.

San Mateo

84

84 101 Mission San Jose

Mission Blvd.

Stanford Ave.

84 680

101

280 Woodside

Foothill

Cupertino San Jose

Monte Bello Rd. 280 Aborn Rd.

Stevens Campbell Rd.

Canyon Rd. 35

Congress Saratoga The Alameda

Springs Rd.

Pierce Rd.

Los Gatos 101

9 17 Almaden Expwy.

Boulder Creek

17 35

It's a naive, domestic Burgundy without much breeding, but I think you'll be amused by its presumption.
— caption on a *New Yorker* cartoon by James Thurber

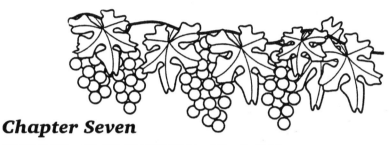

Chapter Seven

THE SOUTH BAY

Southern Alameda & northern Santa Clara counties

Silicon chips and suburbs have prevailed over Sauvignon Blanc and Semillon in much of southern Alameda and northern Santa Clara counties. 'Tis a pity, since these two wine producing areas southeast of San Francisco Bay appear on some of the earliest pages of California's history. Wineries such as Concannon, Wente and Mirassou date back more than a century. In fact, Mirassou is the oldest family-owned winery in California.

These venerable establishments and several newcomers are coping with the suburban spread in various ways. Some have set up shop in nearby foothills, or retreated even higher, particularly to Montebello Ridge of the Santa Cruz Mountains, southwest of San Jose. (However, Montebello Ridge has been invaded by luxury homes of Silicon Valley millionaires.) Other vintners such as Mirassou have remained firmly in place, with their wineries and tasting rooms surrounded by tract homes. They surrendered their vineyards to subdivisions and planted new vines elsewhere, mostly in Monterey County.

A glowing exception to this suburban vineyard invasion is the Livermore Valley of southern Santa Clara County. Agricultural preserves have been established to protect vineyards that have occupied these gentle hills for more than a hundred years. Suburbia does nibble at the edges and new housing tracts are within view of the Concannon and Wente wineries. However, urban sprawl has been reduced to a slow crawl, and completely stopped in some areas of the valley. Members of the Livermore Valley Winegrowers Association are promoting their area as an alternative to the Napa Valley, pointing out that it's less crowded, the wines are generally less expensive and it's closer to most of the San Francisco Bay Area's seven million residents.

The valley was settled by English sailor Robert Livermore, who picked up two Mexican land grants in 1830. He had grapes growing by the 1840s. Charles A. Wetmore, who served as California's chief viticultural officer, established Cresta Blanca Winery in 1882, followed by the arrival of Carl H. Wente and James Concannon the next year. At the start of the last century, the valley had 5,000 acres of vineyards and more than fifty wineries. Hit by phylloxera and Prohibition, the number had dwindled to six by the 1960s, although it's increasing again under the new agricultural zoning protection.

To the southwest, Santa Clara Valley's history also goes back more than two centuries. San Jose was born in 1777 as the state's first civil settlement and it served as California's first capitol from 1849 to 1851. By the mid-1850s, San Jose was a major wine producer and its surrounding Santa Clara Valley was called the "Garden Spot of the World." French vineyardist Pierre Pellier started a winery here in 1854. His daughter married Pierre Mirassou in 1881, beginning the Mirassou wine dynasty that persists to this day. At the beginning of the last century, the Santa Clara Valley had more than a hundred wineries and nearly 9,000 acres of vines.

The Santa Clara and Livermore valleys merge at the bottom of San Francisco Bay near present-day Fremont. Here, Mission San José de Guadalupe was established in 1797 (to the confusion of those who assume the mission is in the city of San Jose). In 1869, railroad baron and politician Leland Stanford and his brother Josiah started a winery just east of the mission. The Swiss-born Weibels took over in 1940 and operated a large facility here until recently, when spreading suburbia enveloped the vineyards and winery.

Santa Clara County's Montebello Ridge wineries came along much later, beginning with the establishment of Ridge Vineyards by three Stanford Research Institute couples in 1959. A few others have since settled in these steep, forested hills. Among them are Picchetti Winery, occupying the rustic site of the 1880s Picchetti Ranch.

Livermore and Santa Clara valleys, cooled by bay breezes, are known mostly for their whites; Cabernet Sauvignon and Petit Sirah are grown here as well. Montebello Ridge, higher but warmer, produces some excellent Zinfandels.

LIVERMORE VALLEY WINERY TOUR • We'll start this tour in downtown Livermore, and it's best to take it on a weekend since many of the smaller wineries have limited hours. Coming from the Bay Area, take the Livermore Avenue turnoff from Interstate 580 and go south into the downtown area. If you approach from the east on I-580, First Street (State Highway 84 exit) will get you there. From the south, take route 84 (Vallecitos Road) east from I-680. You'll be backtracking along some of the winery route but for the sake of order, we're starting everyone at the same place.

WINERY CODES • *T* = tasting with no fee; *T$* = tasting for a fee; *GT* = guided tours; *GTA* = guided tours by appointment; *ST* = self-guiding or informal tours; ✕ = picnic area; 🎁 = gift shop or a good giftware selection.

WINE PRICES • *$* = average price under $10 per bottle; *$$* = $10 to $14; *$$$* = $15 to $19; *$$$$* = $20 or more

From the old downtown area, follow Livermore Avenue south a bit over a mile until you see small **Retzlaff Vineyards** on your left. At this point you'll shed much of the town's suburbia—although it's spreading outward—and travel through a mix of vineyards and farm fields. Tawny rolling hills stand on the horizon. Continuing southeast, the route swings to the left and becomes Tesla Road. Just beyond is **Concannon Vineyard** and less than a mile away, **Stony Ridge Winery**; both are on the left. Immediately past Stony Ridge, turn right onto Mines Road for **Murietta's Well** winery; it comes up quickly on the right. Return to Tesla Road, turn eastward and you'll soon encounter **Iván Tamás Winery** on your right. Less than a mile beyond is the extensive complex of **Wente Vineyards Estate Winery,** also on the right. Continue out Tesla about half a mile for a trio of wineries, all on your left—**Rios-Lovell, Cedar Mountain** and **Garré**.

Now, retrace your path along Tesla Road and, just beyond Concannon, turn left onto Wente Street. It curves to the right into Marina Avenue, which bumps into Arroyo Road. Go left and you'll soon pass, on the right, **Ravenswood Historical Site,** an elaborate country estate and former winery. It's now administered by the Livermore Area Recreation and Park District.

Continuing along Arroyo Road, you'll encounter the attractively landscaped grounds of **Wente Vineyards Restaurant & Visitors Center** on the left. Reverse your route for about a mile, then take a left onto Wetmore Road and you'll soon see **Livermore Valley Cellars** on the right. Wetmore does a ninety-degree right turn and becomes Holmes Street. Within a few hundred yards, turn left at a stop sign onto East Vallecitos Road (State Highway 84). You're now well into the country, taking a gentle roller-coaster ride through undulating hills.

After less than a mile, you'll see **Thomas Coyne Winery** on an upslope to the left and just beyond, **Fenestra Winery,** housed in a wonderful old barn down on the right. Pressing on, you'll wind steeply over a set of low hills and then pass under Interstate 680. To avoid blending onto the freeway, fork to the right at the Sunol/Dumbarton Bridge sign just short of the interchange to stay with Highway 84; it becomes Niles Canyon Road.

After about a mile, veer to the right into the cute little community of **Sunol.** Just beyond its rustic false front business district, turn right onto Kilkare Road and follow it a short distance to the handsome cut stone **Elliston Vineyards** complex on the right. Return to Sunol, turn right to blend back onto Highway 84 and follow it through scenic, winding **Niles Canyon.** Its Alameda Creek is a popular weekend retreat for locals. After about four miles—immediately beyond a railroad bridge—take a sharp right up Palomares Road. Follow its steep, winding course uphill alongside a seasonal creek just under four miles to **Westover Vineyards.** Briefly beyond is **Chouinard Vineyards.** Both are on the left, tucked into the base of wooded hills.

From here, retrace your route to I-680, which you can follow south to the next winery tour. Worth a visit, if you're into California history, is **Mission San José.** To reach it, take the Mission Boulevard exit in Fremont and follow it east.

Retzlaff Vineyards ● *T* ✕

1356 S. Livermore Ave., Livermore, CA 94550; (925) 447-8941. (www.retzlaffwinery.com) Weekdays noon to 2 and weekends noon to 5; MC/VISA. Most varieties tasted. A few wine logo items; shaded picnic area.

A gravel lane flanked by vineyards and pepper trees takes you to this small winery in a weathered farm complex. Park beside a lawn picnic area and stroll to the tasting room, which occupies a corner of the winery. It was started in 1978 by home winemaker and chemist Bob Taylor and his wife Gloria Retzlaff Taylor. They began with the intention of selling grapes, then decided to produce their own wines, at the rate of about 3,000 cases a year.

Tasting notes: The Retzlaff lists consists of Sauvignon Blanc, Merlot, Gray Riesling, Chardonnay and Cabernet Sauvignon. The Riesling had a nice herbal nose and it was soft and buttery on the palate; Chardonnay was very fruity and silky, with only a hint of wood, and a two-year-old Cab offered a peppery nose, herbal flavor and soft finish. The Sauvignon Blanc was a crisply dry wine, bottled with a touch of Semillon. Prices start modestly and range upward: *$ to $$$$.*

Concannon Vineyard • T$ GT ✕ 👜

4590 Tesla Rd., Livermore, CA 94550; (925) 447-3760. (www.concannon-vineyard.com) Daily 10 to 4:30; sales until 5; MC/VISA. Five wines tasted from the current list. Good wine oriented gift selection. Nice picnic area; tours weekends at 1, 2 and 3 and weekdays on request.

The story goes that Irish immigrant Joseph Concannon, printer by trade, was asked by San Francisco Archbishop Joseph S. Alemany to make some good altar wine. Being a proper Catholic, Joe complied and thus started the first Gaelic winery in California. For generations, Concannons and Wentes were friendly rivals, making honest wines and sending their kids to the same schools. It remained thus until 1981, when Concannon was bought out by Deinhard and Partners, obviously non-Irish. Recently, the winery was purchased by the Livermore Valley Wine Association, a group of investors that includes members of the Wente family. One Concannon, great-grandson Jim, is still involved here, handling the winery's public relations.

The tasting room is housed in one of the century-old winery buildings. It's all done up in brick and wormwood paneling, decorated by quilts hanging like rural tapestries.

Tasting notes: Concannon wines are noted for their complexity, particularly for deep-flavored reds, which are unusual for the Livermore Valley. The Petite Sirah has long been a Concannon classic, richly flavored yet dry with medium body. Cabernet Sauvignon is soft and full, more like a Bordeaux. The Chardonnays range from medium to full bodied with nice fruit and hints of wood. Sauvignon Blanc is surprisingly fruity for this varietal. The Concannon list also includes Rhône style wines such as a dry and crisp Viognier and a big Syrah with full flavors yet gentle tannins. Prices: *$ to $$$$.*

Stony Ridge Winery • T

4948 Tesla Rd., Livermore, CA 94550; (925) 449-0458. (www.stonyridge-winery.com) Monday-Saturday 11 to 5 and Sunday noon to 5; major credit cards. Most varieties tasted; wine by the glass may be purchased. A few wine logo items. Deli-restaurant listed below.

At first glimpse, this attractive Spanish style facility more resembles a café than a winery, with an outdoor deck occupied by contented diners. It's both. A long tasting counter fills one side of the roomy, tile-floored hospitality center, and a busy deli-café thrives at the other. Despite the Spanish style look, both the restaurant and the wines have strong Italian accents.

One of the Livermore Valley's oldest "new" wineries, Stony Ridge was established in 1975 on the site of an even older facility, Ruby Hill Winery, which dates back to the nineteenth century.

Tasting notes: The list includes most of the classic varietals plus a couple of interesting Italian wines—Chardonnay, Johannisberg Riesling, Merlot, Cabernet Sauvignon, Orobianco and Nebbiolo, plus a white Zinfandel and Malvasia Bianca dessert wine. The Chardonnay had a flower petal nose, suggestive of a Sauvignon Blanc, yet with the crisp smokey character of a good Chard. Cabernets—several often are available—were soft, full flavored and ready to drink; some displayed enough tannin to encourage aging. Prices: *$ to $$$.*

Stony Ridge Deli Café ● ☆☆ $

□ *At Stony Ridge Winery; (925) 449-0660. Italian-American. Daily 11 to 5. (www.stonyridgewinery.com) Major credit cards.* □ This appealing little deli-café does a booming lunch business, with tables inside the tasting room and on a sunny deck with vineyard views. Offerings include Italian-American fare such as leg of lamb sandwiches, provolone terrine and an excellent Caesar salad served with a roasted garlic cluster.

Murietta's Well ● T ✕ 📷

3005 Mines Rd., Livermore, CA 94550; (925) 456-2390. (www.muriettaswell.com) Weekends 11 to 4:30. MC/VISA. Most varieties tasted. Nice giftware selection; picnic area.

Set back off the road, this winery occupies a cut stone building bunkered into a slope, rimmed by vineyards and pasturelands. The upper level tasting room is reached by steps accented with colorful Spanish tile. A picnic area occupies an adjacent concrete deck. Murietta's Well was established in 1989 on the site of an historic Livermore Valley ranch by Phil Wente and Sergio Traverso and produces about 8,000 cases of wine a year.

Iván Tamás Winery ● T & T$ ✕ 📷

5443 Tesla Rd., Livermore, CA 94550; (925) 456-2380. (www.ivantamas.com) Daily 11 to 4:30; MC/VISA. Most varieties tasted free; small fee for some reserves. Fair selection of giftware and specialty food items; picnic area.

The father and son team of Steve and Steven Mirassou established this winery in 1996 to produce "Cal-Italian" varietals, including varieties not made at the legendary family winery in San Jose. It occupies a large vaguely Mediterranean style stucco building; the tasting room resides in an adjacent cottage, graced by a vine-entwined arbor.

Tasting Notes: This Mirassou pair produces a mix of Italian and French varietals, along with the ubiquitous Zinfandel. On the list are Trebbiano, a light and fruity white; Pino Grigio, also light although richer; a couple of Chardonnays; a full-flavored Sangiovese accented with a bit of Cabernet and Merlot; a pair of Cabernets Sauvignon; a Zinfandel with a nice raspberry taste; and Brut sparkling wine. The lone proprietary wine is *Dopo Cena*, a lightly sweet Sauvignon Blanc. Prices: *$$ to $$$$.*

Wente Vineyards Estate Winery ● T GT ✕ 📷

5565 Tesla Rd., Livermore, CA 94550; (925) 456-2305. (www.wentevineyards.com) Daily 10 to 4:30; MC/VISA, AMEX. Most varieties tasted. Good selection of wine logo and specialty food items. Picnic area near tasting room. Tours daily; call for hours.

The Wentes and Concannons both started their wineries in 1883. After more than a century, fourth-generation Wentes are still at the helm. Only the Mirassou clan claims a longer uninterrupted California winery lineage. German emigrant Carl Heinrich Wente and his descendants have been and continue to be major forces in shaping the valley's wine industry. Carl began this California wine dynasty by purchasing Wetmore vineyards. In 1918 brothers Ernest and Herman Wente bought the facility from Carl's estate, starting Wente Brothers Winery, which remains in the family. The fourth generation of Eric, Phil and Carolyn manage the operation today. In 1981, the family purchased Wetmore's old Cresta Blanca facility, which functions as a winery, restaurant and hospitality center; see below.

Although many Wente vineyards have moved south to Monterey County and to the distant Livermore foothills, some vines still embrace the neat, business-like winery complex. The tasting room and adjoining gift shop are housed in an interesting adobe block and wood double octagon.

Tasting notes: Wente offers a very intelligent tasting form, useful in directing you and keeping track of your sips. The list covers most major varietals and side-by-side comparisons of similar varieties are possible. The wines are quite tasty and reasonably priced, with a balanced selection of reds and whites. The modestly priced Vineyard Selections include Sauvignon Blanc, Chardonnay, Merlot, Cabernet Sauvignon and Riesling, each exhibiting good varietal character. The Vineyard Reserve wines include Merlot and Cabernet Sauvignon from the Livermore Valley and a Chardonnay and Pinot Noir from Arroyo Seco in Monterey County, plus Brut Reserve sparkling wine. Prices: *$ to $$$.*

Vintners choice: "We were the first producers of Chardonnay here, with more than sixty consecutive vintages," said a Wente source. "We offer a lot of different styles and prices."

Rios-Lovell Winery • T GTA ✕ 📷

6550 Tesla Rd., Livermore, CA 94550; (925) 443-0434. (www.rios-lovell-winery.com) Tuesday-Friday 11 to 3 and weekends 11 to 5; MC/VISA. Most varieties tasted. Good selection of giftwares; picnic area.

A sturdy stucco building dressed up with stone corners houses this new winery, which sits above an elaborate park-like facility with gazebos and lawns. The large, airy tasting room has been dressed up with cheery murals of ancient winemaking scenes by artists Nicolai Larsen and Cynthia Kelly. A fun focal point here is a pair of human-sized stuffed bears, sitting at a table among the winery's extensive giftware selection. Out on the landscaped lawns, picnic tables occupy sheltering gazebos. Retired Oakland police officer Max Rios and his wife Katy Lovell started this winery in the mid-nineties.

Tasting notes: The Rios-Lovell list covers most of the typical varietals, such as Chardonnay, Gewürztraminer, Johannisberg Riesling, Sauvignon Blanc, Petit Sirah and several versions of Cabernet Sauvignon, Merlot and Zinfandel. Also available are a California sparkling wine and three dessert wines—*Muscat L'Orange*, Merlot *Dolce* and reserve Port. Prices: *$$ to $$$$.*

Cedar Mountain Winery • T GTA ✕

7000 Tesla Rd., Livermore, CA 94550; (925) 373-6636. (www.wines.com/cedarmountain) Weekends noon to 4; MC/VISA. Most wines tasted; several wine logo gift items. Large picnic area. Tours by appointment or when someone is available.

A large wine barrel out front, turned on end to make a sign, helps travelers find this winery. The facility itself is housed in a modern double-pitched roof barn style building, with the tasting room in an adjacent wood frame cottage. Cedar Mountain Winery was established in 1990 by Linda and Earl Ault, and it produces about 4,000 cases a year. Earl, a sculptor, painter and photographer, is the winemaker while Linda, an accomplished chef, shares the farming and management chores.

Tasting notes: Cabernet Sauvignon is Cedar Mountain's "flagship wine," winner of numerous medals. The winery also produces an excellent Port. Prices: **$$ to $$$$**

Vintners choice: "Our estate Cabernet Sauvignon has been getting ratings over ninety in *Wines and Spirits* and *The Wine Enthusiast magazine*," says Linda, then she adds immodestly: "We're now considered one of the top five Port producers in the U.S."

Garré Vineyards & Winery ● T$ ✕

7986 Tesla Rd., Livermore, CA 94550; (925) 371-8200. (WEB: www.garrewinery.com) Weekends 11 to 5; MC/VISA, AMEX. Select wines tasted for a modest fee. Garré Café serves lunch daily; see below.

A weathered ranch yard stands before the more attractive part of this winery complex, shielding it from the road. Beyond those old buildings is an attractive facility with an appealing cottage style café, a prim lean-to tasting room, a bocci ball court and a large winery building. Lawns and a few flowers accent this bucolic scene. The winery was established in 1999 by Steve Aracne and Bob Molinaro, two friends with different backgrounds but a common interest in wine. Steve is a retired Pleasanton police detective and Bob owns a local garbage company. So who's Garré? That was the maiden name of Bob's mother.

Tasting notes: The Garré list is brief and the wines are tasty. They include a spicy and dry Grenache, three renditions of Merlot and a full-flavored Cabernet Sauvignon with a classic peppery nip. Prices: **$$ to $$$$**.

Garré Café ● ☆☆ $

□ *At Garré Winery; (925) 371-8200. (www.garrewinery.com) American-Italian; wine and beer. Lunch to midafternoon daily. MC/VISA, AMEX.* □ Charming and homey café with a pitched knotty pine ceiling and country décor. Entrées include turkey, grilled lamb sausage, Italian pot roast, osso buco and assorted soups, salads, sandwiches, pastas and antipasto.

Wente Visitor Center ● T$ GT ✕ 🍴

5050 Arroyo Rd., Livermore, CA 94550; (925) 456-2405. (www.wentevineyards.com) Monday-Saturday 10 to 5, Sunday 11 to 5; MC/VISA, AMEX. Most wines tasted for a modest fee. Good selection of wine logo and specialty food items. Periodic tours; call for hours. Restaurant adjacent, listed below.

The Wentes have blended history, architectural beauty and hospitality at this Spanish-style facility. Started in 1882 as Charles Wetmore's Cresta Blanca Winery, it was purchased by the Wente family in 1981. After extensive rehabilitation, it was reborn as a modern champagnery called Wente Sparkling Wine Cellars. With the addition of more facilities, including a restaurant and golf course, it's now the Wente Vineyards Restaurant & Visitors Center. The attractive complex is accented by mature trees, lawns, gardens and an herb garden, where chefs from the adjacent restaurant pluck their seasonings.

The tasting room is housed in an enclosed former courtyard, with lofty coffered ceilings held up by imposing square columns. A small museum off the tasting room consists mostly of graphics tracing the history of the two founding families—the Wetmores and the Wentes. Tours take visitors through the modern winery and into 650 feet of aging caves tunneled into a hillside. Re-excavated and gunnited by the Wentes, they still have that wonderfully musty mushroom farm smell of ancient caverns.

Tasting notes: Both Wente's still and sparkling wines are available here; see tasting notes under Wente Vineyards Estate above.

The Restaurant ● ☆☆☆☆ $$$

☐ *At Wente Vineyards & Visitors Center; (925) 456-2460. Regional American; wine and beer. Lunch Monday-Saturday and dinner nightly plus Sunday brunch. Major credit cards.* ☐ Stylish dining room with warm woods, caneback chairs and linen nappery. Special events such as fixed price dinners with wine pairings are often scheduled. Entrees on the frequently changing menu focus on fresh—and when available—local ingredients, seasoned by the restaurant's own herb garden. Patio dining area.

Livermore Valley Cellars ● T ✕

1508 Wetmore Rd., Livermore, CA 94550; (925) 447-1751. Daily 11:30 to 5; MC/VISA. Most varieties tasted. A few wine logo items; small picnic area.

The smallest of the area wineries, Livermore Valley Cellars—often simply called LVC—occupies a weathered farmyard up a gravel lane. Charmingly funky are the best words to describe the farmyard and equally weathered tasting room. However, it is funk with humor. Wooden "stick-mannequins" lounge in a hammock and a lawn chair and hand-lettered signs incite visitors to ignore wine snobbery, relax and enjoy the wine. Winery production was cut back during the long California drought because owners Chris and Beverly Lagiss are dry farmers and felt there wasn't enough water to bring in a crop. However, the coming of rains in the past decade has seen a swelling of their wine list. Although they're getting along in years, it's apparent that the end of the drought ended any retirement plans.

Tasting notes: The LVC list offers an interest mix of varietals and blends, some with cleverly curious names. They include Hoopla, a multivineyard blend of reds; Semillion and the Lagiss "flagship wine" blend of Semillon and Chardonnay; a Semillon and Sauvignon Blanc blend; Alicante Bouschet in "Yin" (full-bodied) and "Yan" (lighter) versions; Whoopie, a young Zinfandel; Big Ass Zin, which requires no explanation; Syrah and Petit Sirah; and sweet versions of Chenin Blanc and Orange Muscat. Prices are modest for the most part: *$ to $$$*.

Thomas Coyne Winery ● T ST ✕

51 E. Vallecitos Rd.; mailing address: 2162 Broadmoor St., Livermore, CA 94550; (925) 373-6541. Weekends noon to 5; MC/VISA, DISC. Most wines tasted. Picnic area; informal tours.

Thomas Coyne started his small family winery in the 1989, and he has won an imposing number of awards. The tasting room is a simple, neat affair adjacent to the winery, where visitors can peek in for a view of vats, stainless steel and oak. A considerably better view is from the nearby picnic area, across the tawny hills of the Livermore Valley.

Tasting notes Coyne has quite a varied list for a small winery. His Pinot Blanc was light and fruity with a touch of oak; Viognier was a good sipping wine with a fruit bouquet; Syrah displayed good oak character from eighteen months on the wood; and El Dorado and Sonoma Merlots were herbal with nice berry flavors. The Bordeaux style red with sixty percent Cabernet Franc and forty percent Cabernet Sauvignon has won several major medals. Prices: **$$ to $$$.**

Vintners choice: "Merlot," Coyne says. "I get Merlot grapes from several appelations and they're all award winners."

Fenestra Winery • T ✕

83 E. Vallecitos Rd., Livermore, CA 94550; (925) 862-2292. (www.fenestrawinery.com) Weekends noon to 5; MC/VISA, AMEX. Most varieties tasted. A few wine logo items; shaded picnic area.

All it lacks is a Mail Pouch tobacco sign painted on the roof. Fenestra Winery occupies one of the most handsome old weathered barns in California. Bunkered into a hollow, surrounded by gnarled oaks and wild oats, this concrete and wooden structure is a classic of American country Gothic. It was built in 1889 by a pioneer farmer named George True. Inside, soft-spoken chemist Lanny Replogle makes wines while his wife Fran handles marketing. It's a weekend job, since Lanny teaches at San Jose State University; he started winemaking in 1976. On pleasant days, tastings are convened outside, beside the rustic oak-shaded picnic area.

Tasting notes: When it comes to winemaking, Lanny the chemist is no mad scientist. His wines are straightforward, full bodied and excellent, certainly not test tube products. They've won a good share of medals. He produces most of the popular whites and reds. Our choices were a nutty and spicy Semillon, a Chardonnay with deep and intense buttery flavor, a young Merlot with rich berry flavor and an aged Cabernet Sauvignon with a spicy nose and mellow berry-rich taste. Lanny's "user-friendly" everyday drinking wine has a great double *entendre* label to honor the barn-builder: True Red. Overall prices are modest: **$ to $$$.**

Elliston Vineyards • T 🍷

463 Kilkare Rd., Sunol, CA 94586; (925) 862-2377. (www.elliston.com) Weekends noon to 5 or by appointment on weekdays. Good selection of giftwares. Winetasters dinners conducted monthly; contact the winery for details.

Your eye is first drawn to a grand cut stone château that seems to have been transported here from the Rhine. It's surrounded by lush landscaping and mature trees, with a few vines out front. The attractive complex is owned by Donna and Keith Flavetta. The blue sandstone Victorian was built in 1890 by Henry Hiram Ellis and it contains some original furnishings, including a walnut bed shipped around the horn. It offers a splendid setting for the Elliston tasting room.

Tasting notes: The list is balanced, with a mix of whites, reds, sparklers and dessert wines. Choices include Chardonnay, a pair of Pinot Gris renditions, Pinot Blanc, a sparkling wine called California Champagne, Brut rosé, Cabernet Sauvignon, Cabernet Franc, Merlot, Pinot Noir, Captain's Claret (a Bordeaux blend) and a sweet Malvasia Bianca. Prices: **$ to $$$$.**

Westover Vineyards • T$ ✕

34932 Palomares Rd., Castro Valley, CA 94546; (925) 537-3932. (www.westoverwinery.com) Weekends noon to 5, or by appointment; MC/VISA, AMEX. Most varieties tasted free if wine is purchased; modest fee if it isn't. Good selection of books and wine logo items. Picnic area; informal tours.

Westover is housed in an attractive Spanish style complex of red tile roofs, beige stucco and Moorish arch windows. A picnic area occupies a sunny courtyard and mature trees, including some redwoods, complete this alluring creek canyon setting. The atmosphere is equally pleasant inside. The tasting room resembles a casual living room, with a pool table, "foos" ball, a pinball machine and big screen TV. The facility also has a beauty salon and wedding and meeting facilities. Established by Silicon Valley businessman Bill Smyth and his wife Linda, the winery produces about 2,500 cases a year—and growing. Westover and its near neighbor Chouinard are high above the Livermore Valley—so high that they're in the Castro Valley postal zone.

Tasting notes: The Smyths touch most of the classic varietal bases and their wines are uniformly full-flavored and nicely balanced. The list when we last paused included Sauvignon Blanc, several versions of Chardonnay, white Riesling, Petite Sirah and multiple editions of Merlot, Cabernet Sauvignon and Zinfandel, including several late harvest Zins. Prices: *$ to $$$.*

Vintner's choice: "Our estate Chardonnay has a natural grapefruit flavor and our Zinfandel has big body, high alcohol and lots of berry flavor," says Linda.

Chouinard Vineyard and Winery ● T GT ✗

33853 Palomares Rd., Castro Valley, CA 94552; (925) 582-9900. (www.chouinard.com) Weekends and some holidays noon to 5; MC/VISA. Most varieties tasted. Some wine logo items. Shaded picnic area. Tours on request during tasting room hours.

Tucked into a wooded slope and housed in a bright red barn, Chouinard Winery could pose for a Grandma Moses painting. Its pleasant grounds and vineyards are terraced up a shallow ravine. The tasting room is in a cozy loft in the eaves of the red barn winery. Picnic tables rest beneath oaks, maples and redwoods nearby. We'd suggest arriving with a picnic lunch, buying a bottle of wine and spending a couple of hours in this pleasantly wooded mountain retreat.

Architect George Chouinard, his wife Caroline and their sons Rick and Daimian started their vineyards in 1978. They became intrigued with wine after living in France for several years. They opened their tasting room in 1985 and often host theme tastings and other special events, including a popular Music in the Vineyards summer concert series.

Tasting notes: Wines are full-bodied, complex and quite tasty. Our choices included a malolactic Chardonnay with a nutty aroma and nice spicy, buttery taste; and a young Zinfandel with a great raspberry nose and taste. Others on the list are two types of Cabernet Sauvignon, Granny Smith apple wine, a sparkling wine they call California Champagne, an old vine Zinfandel from century-old Lodi vineyards, a fruity Chenin Blanc, a deep flavored Alicante Bouschet and a house red. Prices: *$ to $$$.*

Vintners choice: "Chardonnay and our Granny Smith Apple wine; both are award-winners," says George.

SANTA CLARA VALLEY-MONTEBELLO WINERY TOUR ● One

of California's largest cities now stands where hundreds of acres of vines once flourished. San Jose has topped a million population and its suburbs push far and wide into the Santa Clara Valley, more commonly known as Silicon Valley. Two wineries thrive here, however. Venerable Mirassou remains firmly rooted to the spot where it began more than a century ago. And latecomer Jerry Lohr decided to join the population swell instead of fighting it. He started a winery right in the middle of a San Jose industrial district.

The area's other wineries have found refuge on Montebello Ridge above San Jose, beyond reach of the commotion. Our tour thus takes you from thick civilization to thick forests. (**NOTE:** The two Santa Clara Valley winery tasting rooms are open daily, although some in the mountains have more limited hours.)

Mirassou is the first stop in this urban-mountain winery trek. From the Bayshore Freeway (U.S. 101), pass through the heart of San Jose and take the Capitol Expressway northeast for a couple of blocks. Go right on Aborn Road and follow it past shopping centers and subdivisions to the winery. (If you're continuing from the Livermore Valley tour, head south on I-680. Follow it about a dozen miles until it intersects with U.S. 101 in San Jose, and then go south on 101 just over three miles to Capitol Expressway.)

From Mirassou, return to the Bayshore, go about six miles northwest to Interstate 880, then head southeast, following Santa Cruz signs. After about two miles, exit at The Alameda (State Route 82) and go left under the freeway, following it south. You'll pass through a mile of pleasant older suburbs, and then enter a commercial area. Turn left onto Lenzen Avenue and the **J. Lohr Winery** appears, in a brick building on your right.

Get back to I-880, continue south for just over a mile to the I-280 interchange and follow it right (west) through Cupertino. After about seven miles, take the Foothill Expressway exit and turn left under the freeway, following Foothill Boulevard. Within a mile or so, you'll escape civilization and begin climbing into the Santa Cruz Mountain foothills.

This area offers more winding roads than wines, although it's a pretty drive and the wineries are interesting. Foothill Boulevard becomes Stevens Canyon Road, toiling through brushy slopes toward Stevens Creek Reservoir. Shortly after passing the dam, take a sharp right up Montebello Road, which twists and turns up to **Picchetti Winery.** It's on the historic Picchetti Ranch in the Monte Bello Open Space Reserve. A gravel trailhead parking lot also provides parking for the tasting room.

Continue climbing and spiraling up Montebello Road, enjoying panoramic valley vistas if you dare look. You'll see more trees than vines here, although an occasional vineyard clings to these steep slopes. When it seems that you've climbed halfway to heaven, you see **Ridge Vineyards** crowning the ridge that provided its name. It's one of the most dramatically situated wineries in the country.

Retreat down Montebello to Stevens Canyon Road and turn right. After a couple of miles, fork to the left and upward onto Mount Eden Road. Eden, indeed! Many of the new castle-like "Silicon Valley mansions" of Montebello Ridge are along this route. Turn left up a mountain lane and then left again for **Cooper-Garrod Estate Vineyards.** It's part of a large equestrian complex called Garrod Farms Riding Stables. Back on Mount Eden, follow it to Pierce Road and turn right. Pierce rises steeply and then drops downhill and bumps into Congress Springs Road (Highway 9). Turn right and drive about a mile and a half to **Savannah-Chanel Vineyards,** up a steep, narrow lane to your left. If you were to continue up Congress Springs Road, you'd wind up in Santa Cruz County, whose mountainside wineries we cover in Chapter Nine.

To continue this tour, reverse your route from Savannah-Chanel on Congress Springs Road (which becomes Big Basin Way) and follow it just over three miles into the tree-shrouded, charmingly upscale community of **Saratoga.** En route, you'll pass the **Santa Clara County Arboretum** and **Hakkone Gardens,** both worth a browse. Also, you may want to explore a few Saratoga boutiques and shops before continuing.

Follow Saratoga-Los Gatos Road (still Highway 9) southeast to Los Gatos. Once there, turn right onto University Avenue (at a stoplight, just short of the Highway 17 freeway) and follow it about six blocks until it ends at Main Street. Go left on Main, cross the freeway and quickly turn right onto College Avenue. College winds steeply into wooded hills for about a mile, taking you to the former Novitiate of Los Gatos, on whose grounds resides **Mirassou Champagne Cellars.**

Like Saratoga, Los Gatos is a lushly-wooded foothill town busy with trendy boutiques and restaurants. You may want to explore its **Old Town** Spanish flavored shopping mall.

Mirassou Vineyards • T & T$ GT 🐓

3000 Aborn Rd., San Jose, CA 95135; (888) MIRASSOU or (408) 274-4000. (www.mirassou.com) Monday-Saturday noon to 5, Sunday noon to 4; MC/VISA, AMEX. Most varieties tasted free; library reserves tasted for a small charge. Good wine related gift selection. Tours daily at 2.

If you count in-laws, the Mirassou family traces its California genealogical vines back to 1854, when Pierre Pellier planted grapes in the Santa Clara Valley. Later, his daughter married a Mirassou. Their descendants still make wine on a plot of ground obtained by the second generation of Mirrasous in the late 1800s.

Most of the vines have shifted southward to Monterey County. Only thirteen acres survive here, a small Cabernet vineyard forming a thin green line between the winery and encroaching subdivisions. The venerable winery grounds are stately, with weathered, properly ivy-covered buildings shaded by mature trees. The large and attractive tasting room is housed in one of the venerable winery structures. Inside, you can peek through windows at redwood aging casks.

Tasting notes: We like the way Mirassou conducts tastings. You fetch a large tulip-shaped glass from a wall rack and walk past tables where several wines from a lengthy list are poured. Nearly all popular California varietals are produced by Mirassou. The style is light, crisp and clean. Among our choices were a lightly spicy Chardonnay; a fruity and crisp Monterey Riesling; a spicy and medium bodied Cabernet Sauvignon, excellent for its moderate price; and young Pinot Noirs and Zinfandels, both refreshingly fruity with fine berry aromas. Pricing begins very low and rises into the $30s for the Showcase Chardonnay and Pinot Noir: *$ to $$$$.*

Vintners choice: "Chardonnay, Pinot Noir, Pinot Blanc and Monterey Riesling," says publicity director David Muret. "The cool climate of our Monterey County vineyards brings out the best in these grapes."

J. Lohr Winery • T GT 🐓

1000 Lenzen Ave., San Jose, CA 95126; (408) 288-5057. (www.jlohr.com) Daily 10 to 5; MC/VISA. Most varieties tasted. Good selection of wine logo gift items. Tours weekends at 11 and 2.

Despite its industrial-strength location, Jerry Lohr's urban winery presents an attractive picture. Hedges and bushes grace the narrow space between the sidewalk and the square-shouldered brick winery building. The recently remodeled tasting room is spacious and inviting. Barrels, vats and other winery trappings are just beyond. In one corner, a video cassette recites the J. Lohr story.

That story began in 1974 when Jerry started making wine in this facility, which once housed the Falstaff and Fredericksburg breweries. His tale actually goes back further, to 1966 when he started searching for good vineyard lands. He began planting near Greenfield and other areas of the Salinas Valley and the south central coast. He built a winery near Paso Robles and plans to open a tasting room there. Wine output has grown rapidly, now topping half a million cases a year, with international distribution.

Tasting notes: Lohr wines have won an array of medals, particularly the lush and fruity whites. The extensive list comes in four labels—Estate Wines, Single Vineyard Series, the affordable Cypress series, and Ariel, the country's top selling non-alcoholic wines. Lohr focuses on long-established varietals such as Merlot, Chardonnay, Cabernet Sauvignon, Syrah, Riesling and Zinfandel. Prices: *$$ to $$$.*

Picchetti Winery ● T$ ST ✕

13100 Montebello Rd., Cupertino, CA 95014; (408) 741-1310. (www.picchetti.com) Wednesday-Friday 11 to 3 and weekends 11 to 5; closed Monday-Tuesday; MC/VISA, DISC. Most varieties tasted for a modest fee that applies toward wine purchase. A few wine logo items. Picnic area near tasting room; informal tours.

From urban J. Lohr, the pendulum swings bucolic. Picchetti—formerly Sunrise Winery—occupies weathered stone and wooden buildings at the Picchetti Ranch, where a pioneering family made wine more than a century earlier. Leslie Pantling purchased the winery from Ronald and Rolayne Stortz in 1997 and reinstated the historic name. The oak-shaded rural Americana look likely will remain unchanged, for the Picchetti Ranch is part of the Montebello Ridge Open Space Preserve. The winery operates under a long term lease from the Midpeninsula Regional Open Space District.

The tasting room occupies the top floor of the main winery building, which dates back to 1896. Historic photos and antiques provide a pleasant environment for wine sipping. This ample space is often used for weddings, private parties and such.

Tasting notes: Several versions of Chardonnay, a couple of Merlots and Zinfandels, Cabernet Sauvignon, a pair of sparkling wines and a table wine appropriately called *Vino de Tavola* comprise the Picchetti list. Prices: *$$$ to $$$$.*

Ridge Vineyards ● T

17100 Montebello Rd. (P.O. Box 1810), Cupertino, CA 95015; (408) 867-3233. (www.ridgewine.com) Weekends 11 to 3. Major credit cards. Selected wines tasted. A few wine logo items.

Ridge, indeed. Several Stanford Research Institute scientists discovered and purchases this lofty perch in 1959. They built an earthy yet technologically advanced winery and began producing some of the finest Cabernet Sauvignon in California. Searching for additional acreage for their Cabs, they discovered an ancient Zinfandel vineyard and began producing that as well.

Paul Draper, called by some the state's most intellectual winemaker, joined the crew in the early 1970s. He's still there, intellectually and poetically creating a variety of wines, primarily Zin—perhaps with a bit of Zen.

The Ridge structures are rudimentary, appropriate to this final base camp of the vintners' art. If the winemaking approach here is inward, the view is outward—spectacular and more than panoramic. On a rare clear day, when vehicle exhaust and silicon dust have settled in the valley below, one can see San Francisco's highrises, forty miles away. There's a feeling of Oz about this place. It's like standing in a vineyard in the clouds, peering down at a reality that can't touch you.

Tasting notes: The original list of estate Cabernet, Chardonnay and assorted Zinfandels has been expanded to include limited bottlings of Merlot, Petit Sirah, Carignan, Mourvèdre, Grenache and Syrah. We sipped an incredibly lush and spicy eight-year-old Jimsomare Cabernet, a rich and nutty barrel-fermented Santa Cruz Mountains Chardonnay and a raspberry-rich, mellow and subtly spicy well-aged Geyserville Zinfandel. A peppery ten-year-old Petite Sirah and young yet assertive Dry Creek Syrah completed our day on the mountain. Prices: *$$ to $$$$.*

Cooper-Garrod Estate Vineyards • T

22600 Mount Eden Rd., Saratoga, CA 95070; (408) 867-7116. (www.cgv.com) Wednesday-Friday 1 to 5 and Saturday-Sunday 11 to 5; MC/VISA. Most varieties tasted.

This rambling old ranch and equestrian center dates back to 1893 when David Garrod bought sixty-five acres from the Mount Eden Orchard and Vineyard Company. Four generations later, great-grandson Jan Garrod is still part of the land, serving as vineyard master. George Cooper joined the operation in 1973 after thirty years as a U.S. Army Air Corps and Air Force pilot and an air operations chief. He flew 145 different types of aircraft during his long career. The Cooper-Garrods planted vineyards in the 1970s and released their first wines in 1994, with George Cooper as the winemaker.

The tasting room, like many of the other old ranch buildings, is rustically spartan, with plank floors and a simple tasting counter. Current wine selections are written on a chalkboard. Intermingled with the wine operation is the still active Garrod Farms Riding Stables. Local residents and Silicon Valley flatlanders come to ride along Montebello Ridge trails, and many board their horses here.

Tasting notes: Cooper-Garrod wines have won an impressive array of medals. The lush, subtly spicy Chardonnay won best of show in a San Francisco Bay wine competition; a Cabernet Franc was a gold medal winner in an international tasting; the full-flavored and peppery Cabernet Sauvignon has won gold and silver; and the lush and smooth Cooper-Garrod Claret won gold at the New World Wine Competition. Prices: *$$$ to $$$$.*

Savannah-Chanel Vineyards • T$ GTA ✕ 🍷

23600 Congress Springs Rd., Saratoga, CA 95070; (408) 741-2930. (www.savannah-chanel.com) Daily 11 to 5; MC/VISA. Most wines tasted for a fee. Good selection of wine logo and specialty food items; picnic area. Guided tours by appointment.

Far down from Montebello Ridge although still in a nice wooded setting, Savannah-Chanel occupies a sheltered hollow above Congress Springs Road. Redwoods and other conifers guard this little vineyard valley, reached by a short, tree-canopied drive. Vineyards tumble down a gentle slope and wine is made in a century-old concrete building farther up the hill. Tasting happens in an appealing old wood frame building with rough log rafters, which dates from 1912.

Established by French immigrant Pierre Pourroy in 1892 and closed after Prohibition, the winery is now owned and operated by Michael and Kellie Ballard and named for their two daughters. Its modern history began in 1976 when it was purchased by two local families and reactivated as Congress Springs Winery. It became Mariani winery in 1992 after its purchase by the Delmare and Erickson families who, in turn, sold it to the Ballards.

Tasting notes: The list is brief, led by full-bodied and berry-flavored Zinfandels that have won the notice of wine critics. Others are estate Chardonnay, a big body Cabernet Franc from old vines, and a very fruity Monterey County Riesling. Prices: *$$ to $$$$*.

Mirassou Champagne Cellars • T GT 🐾

300 College Ave. (at the Novitiate of Los Gatos), Los Gatos, CA 95032; (408) 395-3790. (www.mirassou.com) Wednesday-Sunday noon to 5; MC/VISA, AMEX. Good selection of wine logo items. Guided tours at 1:30 and 3:30.

Brother Corte of the Novitiate of Los Gatos produced memorable wines here more than a decade ago, under the Catholic church-owned Novitiate Cellars label. Then officials of this historic 1888 seminary decided to leave the winemaking to others. They leased the property to Mirassou for a sparkling wine facility.

This is a handsome spot, tucked into a mountain shelf, half a mile above Los Gatos. Visitors enter through a formal gate and follow a tree-lined passage to the whitewashed, tile-roofed Colonial Spanish complex. The tasting room, in a bold cut-stone building, is reached via a glowering stone archway right out of an Indiana Jones movie set. However, the airy hospitality room is quite cheerful. Tours take visitors through the ancient winery buildings and pleasantly musty aging caves burrowed into surrounding hills.

Tasting notes: Mirassou produces three sparkling wines, all by *méthode champenoise*. We enjoyed a crisp and dry Blanc de Blancs and Blanc de Noir and a beautifully fruity yet dry Millennium. Some Mirassou still wines also may be sampled and purchased here; see listing above, on page 186. Prices: *$$ to $$$$*.

THE BEST OF THE BUNCH

The best wine buys • Concannon Vineyard, Wente Vineyards Estate Winery, Livermore Valley Cellars and Fenestra Winery in Livermore Valley; and J. Lohr Winery in San Jose.

The most attractive wineries • Wente Visitor Center, Westover Vineyards and Chouinard Winery in Livermore Valley; Ridge Vineyards (for the setting) on Montebello Ridge; and Mirassou Champagne Cellars in Los Gatos.

The most interesting tasting rooms • Concannon Vineyard and Wente Vineyards Estate Winery in Livermore Valley; J. Lohr Winery in San Jose; Savannah-Chanel Vineyards Winery near Saratoga; and Mirassou Champagne Cellars in Los Gatos.

The funkiest tasting rooms • Retzlaff Vineyards, Livermore Valley Cellars and Fenestra Winery in Livermore Valley; and Cooper-Garrad Vineyards on Montebello Ridge.

The best gift shop • Wente Vineyards Estate Winery and Wente Visitor Center in Livermore Valley.

The nicest picnic areas • Retzlaff Vineyards, Concannon Vineyard and Chouinard Winery in Livermore Valley; Ridge Vineyards on Montebello Ridge.

The best tour • Mirassou Champagne Cellars in Los Gatos.

Wine country maps and events

Winery touring maps • Three different winery association maps cover portions of south bay vinelands. *Livermore Valley Wine Country* map and brochure is free at valley wineries or contact the Livermore Valley Winegrowers Association at 1984 Railroad Ave., Suite A, Livermore, CA 94550; (925) 447-9463. *(www.livermorewine.com)*

Wine Tasting in the Santa Clara Valley map includes some of the Montebello Ridge and northern Santa Clara Valley wineries; it's available from vintners or from the Santa Clara Valley Wine Growers Assn., P.O. Box 1192, Morgan Hill, CA 95038; (408) 778-1555. *(www.scvwga.com)*

Wines of the Santa Cruz Mountains map/brochure also includes some of the Montebello Ridge wineries; it's available at wineries and visitors bureaus or contact: Santa Cruz Mountains Winegrowers Assn., 7605 Old Dominion Court, Suite A, Aptos, CA 95003; (831) 479-WINE. *(www.sc-mwa.com)*

Wineland events • Monthly winetasting dinners at Elliston Winery, (925) 862-2377; Wente Winery summer concert series featuring major stars, (800) 95-WENTE; various special events at Concannon Vineyard, (925) 455-7770; Harvest Celebration sponsored by Livermore Valley Winegrowers in September, (925) 447-9463.

BEYOND THE VINEYARDS

While in the Livermore Valley, you might enjoy taking a break at **Del Valle Regional Park** at the end of Arroyo Road. It offers swimming, boating and picnicking. **Pleasanton,** Livermore's next-door neighbor, has a pleasing early American look to its downtown area, with some interesting boutiques. As you work southwestward in your winery quest, **Niles Canyon** has nice spots for picnicking, swimming and bank-sitting. **Mission San José de Guadalupe** in the Warm Springs district of Fremont is certainly worth a visit. The **San Jose-Santa Clara** area has several major attractions, ranging from **Great America** amusement park to museums and missions. Write to the sources at the end of this chapter for details.

If you've come here from the Bay Area and you aren't weary of winding roads, consider returning via the Coast Range's skyline ridge. **Skyline Boulevard** follows the ridgeline all the way to Belmont. There, you can pick up Highway 92 and go east to the Bayshore or west to U.S. Highway 1 and continue into San Francisco. To reach Skyline (Highway 35) take State Route 9 north from Saratoga; it intersects with Route 35 at Saratoga Gap. Views to the east and west are impressive from this remote path high above the densely populated Bay Area.

South Bay attractions

Hakkone Gardens ● *21000 Big Basin Way, Saratoga; (408) 741-4994. Weekdays 10 to 5, weekends 11 to 5; donation requested.* □ Formal Japanese gardens in a fifteen-acre park.

Lawrence Livermore Laboratory Visitors Center ● *Greenville Rd., Livermore; (925) 422-4599. Weekdays 1:30 to 4:30, other days vary; free.* □ Exhibits and slide show concerning the search for new energy sources. Free tours; phone for schedule.

Mission San José de Guadalupe ● *43300 Mission Blvd., Fremont; (510) 657-1797. Daily 10 to 5; free.* □ Mission chapel and museum with artifacts of California's Spanish settlement.

Villa Montalvo ● *Montalvo Road, off State Highway 9 southeast of Saratoga; (408) 961-5800. Weekdays 8 to 5, weekends 9 to 5 October-April; shorter hours the rest of the year. Free.* □ Lush gardens around a Mediterranean villa with an arboretum, art gallery and theater; once the home of wealthy U.S. Senator James D. Phelan.

South Bay information sources

Since South Bay wineries are rather spread out and few lodgings or restaurants are within the vineyard areas, with the exceptions of the deli-café at Stony Ridge Winery, The Restaurant at Wente Visitor Center and Garré Café at Garré Vineyards, listed above. There are, of course, hundreds of restaurants and lodgings in the communities of this thickly populated region. Sources below will happily provide long lists of them.

Livermore Chamber of Commerce, 2157 First St., Livermore, CA 94550; (925) 447-1606. *(www.livermorechamber.org)*

Pleasanton Chamber of Commerce, 777 Peters Ave., Pleasanton, CA 94566; (925) 846-5858.

Los Gatos Chamber of Commerce, P.O. Box 1355 (333 N. Santa Cruz Ave.), CA 95031; (408) 354-9300. *(www.losgatosweb.com)*

San Jose Convention & Visitors Bureau, 333 W. San Carlos St., Suite 1000, San Jose, CA 95110-2720; (408) 295-9600. *(www.sanjose.org)*

Saratoga Chamber of Commerce, 20460 Saratoga-Los Gatos Rd., Saratoga, CA 95070; (408) 867-0753. *(www.saratogachamber.org)*

The blood of the vineyard shall mingle with mine.

— Oliver Wendell Holmes

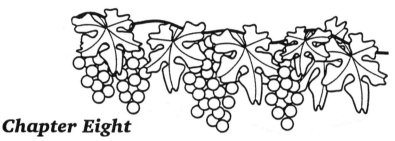

Chapter Eight

SOUTHERN SANTA CLARA
Friendly family wineries in garlic country

Southern Santa Clara Valley ranks with northern Sonoma County as one of our favorite touring areas. The wineries are easy to find, the folks are friendly and the wines are excellent and affordably priced. In fact, the area offers some of the best wine buys in California.

The region's focal point is Gilroy, a town of about 25,000 that's better known for garlic than for wine. Indeed, it produces a lot of both. Community leaders don't mind being kidded about Gilroy's garlicky reputation. In fact, they encourage it; highway signs proclaim the town to be the Garlic Capital of the World. It's a rightful claim, since ninety percent of America's garlic is produced thereabouts. If that statistic doesn't take your breath away, the aroma during the annual Gilroy Garlic Festival will.

"It's the only town in America where you can marinate a steak by hanging it on a clothesline," Will Rogers once quipped.

During the late July festival, citizens present their "scented pearls" in every conceivable format, from garnishes to garlands. Events include a *Tour de Garlique* bicycle run, Garlic Gallop, Garlic Squeeze Barn Dance and—hold your breath for the grand finale—the Great Garlic Cookoff. The *Los Angeles Herald Examiner* once called it the "ultimate summer food fair."

You needn't wait for the festival to immerse yourself in the scented pearl—or the stinking rose, depending on your attitude regarding garlic breath. Three area stores will sell you such savories as garlic-laced relish, mustard, marinade, jam, butter and —good grief!—even garlic ice cream and wine. Two are on U.S. 101 just south of town—Garlic World and The Garlic Shoppé, while the Garlic Festival Store and Gallery is downtown at Monterey and Fifth.

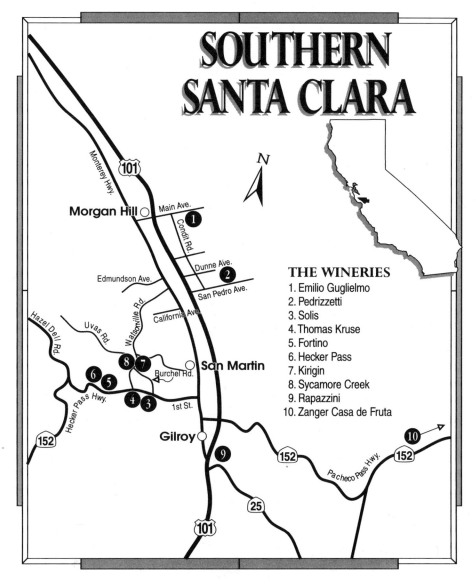

SOUTHERN SANTA CLARA

N

THE WINERIES
1. Emilio Guglielmo
2. Pedrizzetti
3. Solis
4. Thomas Kruse
5. Fortino
6. Hecker Pass
7. Kirigin
8. Sycamore Creek
9. Rapazzini
10. Zanger Casa de Fruta

With all that garlic and all that wine, can Italians be far behind? The list of present and past wineries reads like a Milano phone book: Fortino, Conrotto, Roffinella, Rappazzini, Pedrizzetti and Guglielmo. Names like Kirigin and Kruse, plus Vanni and Wilson of Solis, and Inoue of Sycamore Creek have joined their ranks to create an international brew of winemakers.

Mostly they make red. The sloping hills and sheltering mountains provide the proper soils and warm climate for Zinfandel, Grignolino, Carignane, Petit Sirah, Cabernet and Merlot. You'll find fine whites as well, particularly more full-flavored types such as Chardonnay, Johannisberg Riesling and Sauvignon Blanc.

Wineries of the south Santa Clara region are conveniently packaged. Most stand alongside Hecker Pass Highway west of Gilroy. Others are in the Uvas Valley to the north and near U.S. 101 between Gilroy and Morgan Hill.

Despite their easy access, they're rarely crowded. On a typical day, you'll find few other visitors in the tasting rooms, and the person pouring your wine might be the one who made it. These are mostly family operations, ranging from third-generation vintners of Guglielmo Winery to the latter-day Dave Vanni of Solis.

Neither garlic nor Italians figure in the early history of this area. In 1813, a dour Scotsman named John Cameron went AWOL from a British ship in Monterey Bay and scampered northward. Using his mother's maiden name of Gilroy—presumably to avoid being hauled back to his ship—he befriended the Ortega ranching family, married daughter Clara and settled down. Local historians say he became the first permanent English speaking settler in California. The Ortega-Gilroys planted orchards and raised cattle, gradually forming the hub of a community.

Just up the trail, an Irishman named Martin Murphy acquired a chunk of Rancho Ojo de Agua de la Coche in 1845. In 1882, his granddaughter Diana married wealthy San Franciscan Morgan Hill, and they built a lavish ranch estate. Thus, the town bordering the northern edge of this wine country was named for a gentleman, not a mountain.

Hills do occur in abundance, however. The lower Santa Clara Valley is cradled between the Diablo Range to the east and the Madonna ridge of the Santa Cruz Mountains westward. Highway 152, slicing through this area, spirals over two noted passes—Hecker to the west and Pacheco to the east.

SOUTHERN SANTA CLARA VALLEY WINERY TOUR ● This is

another area you might prefer to tour on weekends, since some of the wineries have limited hours. A good number are open daily, however.

After going through urban San Jose and hilly Montebello Ridge contortions in the previous chapter, this route is simple, and relatively flat. Driving south on U.S. 101, you'll pass by checkerboard agricultural fields, an occasional vineyard and new subdivisions that mark a gradual southward Silicon Valley sprawl. In **Morgan Hill**, take Dunne Road briefly east from the freeway, then swing back north by turning left onto Condit Road. Follow it less than a mile to a stop sign at Main Avenue. Turn right and you'll soon arrive at **Emilio Guglielmo Winery** (pronounced *Goo-YELL-mo*), just across the road from a high school. Obviously, Morgan Hill suburbia has encroached, but vineyards and farm fields still stretch to the east.

Re-trace your route down Main and go south on Condit beyond Dunne Road to San Pedro Avenue, the next cross street. A left turn brings you shortly to **Pedrizzetti Winery.** Return yet again to Condit, continue south to Tennant Avenue and turn right, which gets you back on the freeway. If you want to visit **Casa de Fruta,** with its tasting room, kiddie zoo and extensive gift and wine selection, pick up eastbound Pacheco Pass Highway (Route 152) from downtown Gilroy.

If you like to admire well-tended old downtown areas, take Monterey Street from Morgan Hill to Gilroy instead of the U.S. 101 freeway. Until the freeway was completed several years ago, Monterey Street was Highway 101, carrying its heavy burden of traffic through these two agricultural communities. Now freed from freight trucks and weekend traffic jams, both towns have redeveloped much of Monterey Street. It has been spruced up with landscaped sidewalks, brick crosswalks and street plantings. A few boutiques and antique shops may tempt you to explore.

Once in Gilroy—either via the freeway or Monterey Street—head west on State Route 162. It becomes Hecker Pass Highway, which delivers you to most of the area's wineries. This is one of southern Santa Clara County's nicest drives, passing vineyards, flower and tree nurseries and winding toward forested Madonna ridge, often capped with a soft halo of clouds. However, new subdivisions are beginning to crop up among the vines.

Your first encounter is not a winery but **Goldsmith Seeds,** which presents a spectacular quilt of blooming flowers in spring and summer. Visitors may stroll among its brilliant fields and admire its striking geometric floral displays; take your camera. **Hecker Pass Family Park,** used mostly for scheduled gatherings, is just beyond. Next comes **Western Tree Nursery,** with great forests of potted pines and other trees.

The wineries now start coming thick and fast. You first encounter **Solis Winery** (*SOLE-lees*) on the left. Close by are Sarah's Vineyard (open by appointment only) on the right, and **Thomas Kruse Winery** on the left, opposite the Watsonville Road turnoff. The **Fortino Winery** is just beyond, on the right. The final Hecker Pass facility, appropriately called **Hecker Pass Winery,** is next to Fortino, also on the right.

Backtrack briefly to Watsonville Road, turn left and you'll encounter **Kirigin Cellars** after 2.5 miles; it's on the right, just beyond Day Road. A bit past Kirigin, fork left onto Uvas Road and you'll soon see **Sycamore Creek Vineyards.**

Return now to downtown Gilroy and follow either Monterey Street or U.S. 101 south; they soon blend together. About three miles below town, just short of the Highway 25 Hollister exit, get into a left turn lane for **Rappazzini Winery.** Rappazzini's **Garlic Shoppé** and **Garlic World** are close by.

(**NAVIGATIONAL NOTE:** If you miss the left turn pocket or if the expressway has been upgraded to freeway status, continue on to the Hollister exit, cross east over the freeway, turn north onto a frontage road and you'll see Rappazzini and the garlic shops.)

Emilio Guglielmo Winery ● T GTA ✗ 🏠

1480 E. Main Ave., Morgan Hill, CA 95037; (408) 779-2145. (www.guglielmowinery. com) Weekdays 9 to 5, weekends 10 to 5; major credit cards. Most varieties tasted. Good wine logo and specialty foods selection. Picnic patio near vineyards. Guided tours by appointment.

Italian immigrants Emilio and Emilia Guglielmo began making wines here in 1925 and this handsome facility is the one of the area's oldest wineries. However, 1925 is rather recent in the family's time-line; Guglielmo winemakers have been traced back to the Roman era. The enterprise is presently run by Emilio's son George and his two sons, Gene and Gary, with yet another generation coming along.

WINERY CODES ● *T* = tasting with no fee; *T$* = tasting for a fee; *GT* = guided tours; *GTA* = guided tours by appointment; *ST* = self-guiding or informal tours; ✗ = picnic area; 🏠 = gift shop or a good giftware selection.

WINE PRICES ● *$* = average price under $10 per bottle; *$$* = $10 to $14; *$$$* = $15 to $19; *$$$$* = $20 or more

The Guglielmo's Mediterranean style tasting room-gift shop is an inviting space, with thick tile floors, warm woods and brick trim. Picnic tables sit beside the vineyards on an attractive patio. A new addition is Villa Emile, a hospitality center among the vines, with a concert stage, outdoor wine bar and grassy seating area. It's used for concerts, winemakers dinners and other special events.

Tasting notes: Guglielmo wines, straightforward and full bodied, have won a good share of awards. They cover most of the red, white and blush spectrum. Our favorites were among the Guglielmo Reserve wines—a fruity, nutty flavored Chardonnay with a soft finish; a spicy and full-bodied Zinfandel and a big, peppery and herbal Cabernet Sauvignon. A Grignolino, uncommon as a varietal in California, had a lively berry nose and good spicy-fruity flavor. Others on the list are Sangiovese, Petit Sirah, Merlot and white Riesling. Guglielmo prices are modest, even for its reserves: *$ to $$$.*

Pedrizzetti Winery ● T GTA ✕
1645 San Pedro Ave., Morgan Hill, CA 95037; (408) 779-7389. (www.pedrizzetti.com) Daily 10 to 5 (until 5:30 in summer), major credit cards. Most varieties tasted. Good selection of giftwares and wine logo items. Picnic area; guided tours by appointment.

This small family-run operation dates from 1913, when it was established by Italian immigrant Camillo Colombano. John Pedrizzetti purchased it in 1945, and his son Ed and daughter-in-law Phyllis took over the operation in 1968. The winery is a simple affair, housed in a basic masonry building. A gleaming new Mediterranean style hospitality center was opened recently with an attractive tasting counter and good giftware selection. An adjacent garden patio is used for group barbecues and it's open to casual picnickers. "All you have to do is show up with a basket and I'll throw on a cloth and leave you to a peaceful picnic," says Phyllis.

Tasting notes: Although it's a small operation, Pedrizzetti generates an impressive array of wines, including most of the varietals, several fruit wines, a Sherry, Port, brandy and sparkling wine. We particularly liked a full-bodied, spicy Chardonnay with a nice crisp finish; a smooth and deep-flavored Barbera; a peppery and light but complex Zinfandel; and a Cabernet Sauvignon with a great chili pepper nose and taste and a nice tannic nip. A raspberry wine was delicious; it was like drinking crushed berries. Except for a few reserves, wines are very modestly priced: *$ to $$$$.*

Vintner's choice: "Barbera is our specialty," said Phyllis.

Solis Winery ● T GTA ✕
3920 Hecker Pass Hwy., Gilroy, CA 95020; (888) 411-6457 or (408) 847-6306. (www.soliswinery.com) Wednesday-Sunday 11 to 5; major credit cards. Most varieties tasted. Good giftware selection. Picnic area with vineyard view.

Although it dates from 1917, this winery is one of the more modern and attractive in the area. The current version's roots reach back to 1988 when Watsonville nurseryman Dave Vanni and his wife Valerie purchased part of the vineyards and winery facility. They've since sold their nursery business and devote full time to the winery operation. The original winery was started by the Alfonso Bertero family just before Prohibition, which they somehow managed to survive. Bertero descendants ran it until 1975, then it was operated by a corporation as Summerhill Winery before closing again.

Solis has one of the most appealing tasting rooms in the area. A curved tasting bar is matched by a curving bay window that offers a CinemaScopic view of vineyards and distant forested ridges.

Tasting notes: The Solis list includes moderately priced Chardonnay plus a more expensive reserve version, a delicate and light Muscat, fruity flavored Riesling, light almost rosé-like Carignan, a fuller-flavored Carignane, a Sangiovese blend called *Seducente*, plus three rich and more traditional reds—Zinfandel, Merlot and Cabernet Sauvignon. Prices are quite modest for the quality: *$ to $$$*

Thomas Kruse Winery • T$ ✕

4390 Hecker Pass Hwy., Gilroy, CA 95020; (408) 842-7016. (www.thomaskrusewinery.com) Weekends 12 to 5; no credit cards. Most varieties tasted for a very modest fee, refunded with purchase.

Tom Kruse is regarded as a renaissance man of the wine business. A laconic, philosophical muse, he started the winery in 1971, some years after fleeing the tumult of Chicago. He reactivated a facility originally built in 1910 by the Caesar Roffinella family; it had lain idle since 1946.

His wines and his operation are simple and forthright. Some of his labels are hand-written; one featured a detailed cost breakdown, from grape to foil cap, to suggest that some vintners in the business are charging too much. His laid-back winery is a casual scatter of rudimentary equipment—an old red tractor, plastic jugs and barrels for fermenting, a canoe paddle for stirring. Tastings occur on a plank inside a battered winery structure, or on a barrel head outside if weather permits. "No ill behaved children, bare breasts or large groups of Republicans," advises a sign.

Tasting notes: Kruse produces about 3,000 cases a year, focusing on dry and crisp whites and reds that retain the fruity flavor of the grape. The list is mostly red—Grignolino, Zinfandel, Cabernet Sauvignon, Pinot Noir, Carignane and good old Gilroy Red. Its companion, Gilroy White, and Chardonnay cover the white side of the ledger, plus a bottle-fermented sparkling wine aptly called *Insouciance*. Prices: *$$ to $$$*.

Vintners choice: "Inane question," he responded laconically.

Fortino Winery • T GTA ✕ 🍴

4525 Hecker Pass Hwy., Gilroy, CA 95020; (888) 617-6606 or (408) 842-3305. (www.fortinowinery.com) Daily 10 to 5; MC/VISA, AMEX. Most varieties tasted. Good selection of wine related items and giftwares, plus specialty foods including a Fortino line of sauces and dips, which can be sampled. Guided tours by appointment. Shaded picnic area.

Fortino is the largest, busiest and most versatile of the Hecker Pass wineries. One can buy picnic fare, pick out a bottle of wine or a soft drink, and adjourn to a tree-shaded table beside a vineyard. The hospitality room is an appealing place, with Tiffany style lamps and a long and roomy tasting counter. A new events center is adjacent.

Ernie and Marie Fortino created all of this in less than two decades, after buying the old Cassa Brothers Winery in 1970. Like many of his Italian neighbors, Ernie is an immigrant from the old country, but one of recent vintage. Arriving in 1959, the amiable workaholic began building his version of the American dream, working at other wineries and saving enough money to

The Fortino Winery peeks through a veil of its own vineyards along Hecker Pass Highway west of Gilroy.

buy his own. He and Marie have slowed their paces to enjoy the rewards of their labors. The winery has been turned over to their son Gino and daughter Teri. Gino is the winemaker—as he has been for several years—while Teri manages other aspects of the business. Of course, Ernie and Marie still keep a hand in things—when they aren't dabbling in other activities or traveling.

Tasting notes: The versatile Fortino list ranges from red and white varietals to sparkling wine and cream Sherry. Like his father, winemaker Gino is noted for full-bodied reds, which are among our favorite. And they have won a good share of awards. Among our picks were a rich, spicy and berry-like Petit Syrah; a Cabernet Sauvignon, soft and lush yet with enough tannin to encourage aging; and a fine old vines Zinfandel with a great raspberry nose and taste. Charbono—rarely bottled as a varietal—is outstanding, full flavored and lush. The very inexpensive Fortino Burgundy Reserve is one of our regular daily wines. Of the whites, we liked a lush Chardonnay with a gentle tannic nip and a Sauvignon Blanc with a wonderful floral nose and soft, crisp taste. Prices are modest; only a few premium wines reach toward the twenties: *$ to $$$$.*

Vintners choice: We asked Ernie to pick his favorite from among son Gino's wines. He flashed one of his impish grins and thought for a moment. "They're all good. What can I say?" Gino wouldn't pick one either, although sister Teri favors the "claim to fame" Charbono.

Hecker Pass Winery • T GTA ✕

4605 Hecker Pass Hwy., Gilroy, CA 95020; (408) 842-8755. (www.-scvwga/heckerpass.com) Daily 9 to 5; MC/VISA. Most varieties tasted. Picnic area; guided tours by appointment.

Pardon the pun, but the Fortinos seems to have bottled up the western end of the Gilroy wine country. Ernie's brother Mario and his wife Frances opened their Hecker Pass Winery in 1972, and their son Carlo is now active in the operation. The two Fortino families engage in friendly competition, and both groups are good, solid "back to basics" winemakers.

"Let the wine be wine," Mario once told us. "Chemists have no place in the wine business."

A distinctive redwood and cedar bar is the focal point of the wood paneled tasting room; other décor consists primarily of the more than 100 awards won by the winery. A pleasant Mediterranean style picnic area sits beside the vineyards, near the wooded slopes of Mount Madonna.

Tasting notes: Mario's reds dominate the list, and they're excellent— uniformly spicy and full-bodied; all are 100 percent varietal. The Zinfandel was nicely herbal with a good berry flavor and nippy tannic finish; Carignane had a spicy taste with tannins that were assertive yet not harsh; and Petit Sirah had an appealing herbal-berry flavor. Of the more mellow wines, we liked Mario's Red Velvet, a "secret blend" that was soft, yet full flavored with a gentle finish. Chardonnay, Blanc de Blanc, Merlot, Chianti, cream Sherry and Port complete the list. Prices are very modest: *$ to $$$.*

Kirigin Cellars • T GTA ✕

11550 Watsonville Rd., Gilroy, CA 95020; (408) 847-8827. Daily 10 to 5; MC/VISA. Most varieties tasted. Picnic area. Tours by appointment.

The Gilroy countryside is populated by philosophical winemakers. "Dinner without wine is like a date without kissing," said Nikola Kirigin-Chargin, in his soft middle European accent. Eighty-plus years old, he recently sold his Kirigin Cellars to the Cannon family of Palo Alto. However, as our tasting room hostess explained, "he comes with the sale." Nikola is often at the pleasantly spartan tasting room to greet visitors, when he and his wife Biserka aren't traveling to their native Croatia or other points on the globe.

A good talker, he'll tell you that the wine industry and its writers and judges are too obsessed with the so-called attributes of wine. During the years that he owned the winery, he refused to enter competitions because he thinks judging is silly. "How can someone else judge your taste?"

Nikola left Croatia in disgust after it became Communist Yugoslavia and the government took over his family winery. After working for several vintners in California, he bought the old Uvas Winery in 1976, at an age when most men are contemplating retirement.

The Kirigin-Cannon facility is quite appealing, built around a stylish old country home, with picnic tables under sheltering trees. The property was part of El Rancho Solis, an 1828 Mexican land grant, and the first winery was started here in 1887. Portions of the house date from 1833; it's one of the oldest in the county.

Tasting notes: Out of respect to Nikola, who dislikes winetasting verbosity even more than we do, we'll keep it simple: The list includes Sauvignon Blanc, Chardonnay, Malvasia Bianca among the whites and Pinot Noir, Cabernet Sauvignon and Zinfandels among the reds, plus a basic table wine that's a blend of Cabernet, Pinot Noir and Zinfandel. The tasting room also has an inexpensive Charmant process sparkling wine. Whites are nice and full-bodied, not processed to blandness; reds are lush, tasting like the grapes they came from. Prices are modest for the quality: *$ to $$$.*

Vintners choice: When I asked Nick to pick his favorite wine, he smiled. "Why do you care what I like? You tell me what *you* like!"

Sycamore Creek Vineyards ● T ✗

12775 Uvas Rd., Morgan Hill, CA 95037; (408) 779-4738. (www.sycamorecreekwinery.com) Weekends 11:30 to 5; MC/VISA, AMEX. Most varieties tasted. A few wine related gift items.

This small winery sits in a woodsy hollow, surrounded by vineyards and shaded by an assortment of mature trees. Neat white-painted outbuildings and trim landscaping give it the look of a prosperous, well-maintained old farm. The winery dates back beyond Prohibition, when it was started by the Marchetti family. Later abandoned, it was purchased in 1975 by Terry and Mary Kay Parks and rehabilitated. A Japanese winemaking firm called Morita bought Sycamore Creek from the Parks in 1989, with Masao Inoue as president of the winery.

Tastings occur in a pleasing, country-style hospitality room with plank floors, wormwood walls and views of vines and trees.

Tasting notes: The Japanese like sweet wines and this is reflected in the Sycamore Creek style. Although we prefer our wines dry, we liked the rich honey-like flavor of a semi-sweet Gamay Blanc and a perfumey and tasty Johannisberg Riesling; it was sweet but not sticky. The "Romeo and Juliet" dessert wine was so rich it was like drinking liquid fruit. Sycamore Creek produces dry wines as well. We especially liked a spicy and fruity Sauvignon Blanc and a crisp, light Chardonnay. Several reds—Carignane, Zinfandel, Cabernet Sauvignon and Pinot Noir—compete the list. Prices: *$$ to $$$.*

Rappazzini Winery ● T 🔊

4350 Highway 101 (P.O. Box 247), Gilroy, CA 95020; (408) 842-5649. (www.rappazzini.com) Daily 9 to 6 in summer and 9 to 5 the rest of the year; MC/VISA. Most varieties tasted. Extensive giftware and specialty food selection, with emphasis on garlic products.

It requires a good sense of humor to get serious about garlic, and Jon P. Rappazzini's family has done so. They opened their winery in 1962, and expanded to include a long list of garlic-laced specialty foods. "Mama Rap" Rappazzini has added the spicy pearl to just about everything imaginable: relish, sauces, mustards, mayonnaise, chips, dressings and yes—even chocolate, jelly and ice cream. Several of these items can be sampled at the tasting room and at the adjacent Garlic Shoppé.

Finally, are you ready for garlic wine? After sampling the products above, can you tell the difference? The wine is a French Colombard, which the family has courageously named *Château de Garlic.* It's crisp and subtly fruity with a lingering—*definitely* lingering—finish.

"It goes well with garlic-spiced foods," the tasting room host said with a perfectly straight face.

Tasting notes: Never mind *Château de Garlic*. The Rappazzinis make serious wines, with medals to prove it. The list includes Chenin Blanc, Chardonnay and Pinot Gris among the whites, a blush Zin; and Sirah, Zinfandel, Sangiovese and Ruby Cabernet on the red side. Rappazzini also produces Raspberry Delight, Berry Berry (a grape and berry blend) and Apribella (apricot and peach) fruit wines. Our favorites were a dry, subtly nutty Chardonnay; a Sirah with medium body and spicy finish; and a big Zinfandel, aged to perfection with a lots of berries and spice. Take home *Château de Garlic* for well under $10; other prices are modest as well: *$ to $$$.*

Zanger Vineyards at Casa de Fruta ● T ✕ 📷

6680 Pacheco Pass Highway, Hollister, CA 95023; (408) 842-9316. (www.casadefruta.com) Daily 9 to 8 in summer and 9 to 6 in winter; major credit cards. Most varieties tasted. Large complex with gift shops, restaurants, service station and RV park.

The Zanger family, owners of local orchards since 1908, opened a small fruit stand near the top of Pacheco Pass in the 1940s. From this has grown a huge complex that includes a restaurant, kiddie zoo, narrow gauge train and other rides, several gift galleries, a motel, RV park, service station and—oh, yes—a tasting counter. The wines are made elsewhere.

Tasting notes: Many of the basic varietals are available, bottled for Casa de Fruta, and most are quite tasty. The list includes Johannisberg Riesling, Gewürztraminer, Chenin Blanc, Chardonnay, white Zin, Petit Syrah, Merlot, Cabernet Sauvignon and a couple of sparkling wines. Appropriate to its name, Casa de Fruta also has a large selection of fruit wines, including apricot, blackberry, bing cherry, Santa Rosa plum, raspberry and pomegranate. Prices: *$$ to $$$.*

THE BEST OF THE BUNCH

The best wine buys ● Southern Santa Clara County has some of the least expensive wines in the state. It was difficult to select the most inexpensive, so we didn't. Every winery listed has wines starting around $10 or less.

The most attractive wineries ● Kirigin Cellars and Sycamore Creek.

The most interesting tasting rooms ● Guglielmo Winery, Solis Winery, Fortino Winery, Sycamore Creek Vineyards and Rappazzini Winery.

The funkiest tasting room ● Thomas Kruse Winery.

The best gift shops ● Emilio Guglielmo Winery, Fortino Winery and Rappazzini Winery.

The nicest picnic areas ● Emilio Guglielmo and Kirigin Cellars.

Wine country maps and events

Winery touring map ● *Wine Tasting in the Santa Clara Valley* map is available from vintners or from the Santa Clara Valley Wine Growers Association, P.O. Box 1192, Morgan Hill, CA 95038; (408) 778-1555. *(www.scvwga.com)*

Wineland events ● Spring Wine Festival sponsored by the Santa Clara Valley Winegrowers Association, with tastings, dinner, music and games at various wineries, late April; (408) 778-1555. Gilroy Garlic Festival, mostly garlic but with winery participation, last full weekend of July, (408) 842-1625. Gilroy Passport Kickoff Weekend in mid-October; (408) 778-1555.

BEYOND THE VINEYARDS

Wine is the main draw to this area, along with the seductive aroma of the scented pearl. However, the old historic districts of downtown Gilroy and Morgan Hill are worth pauses. Particularly appealing is the delightful brick and cut stone 1905 **Gilroy City Hall** at Monterey and Sixth, with an ornate façade and fantasyland clock tower. Neighborhoods near downtown Gilroy have some fine old Victorian and early American homes. For a good selection, cruise along Eigleberry Street, a block west of and parallel to Monterey.

Since the southern Santa Clara Valley is cradled between two mountain ranges, forests and their attendant hiking trails, campgrounds and picnic areas are but a short drive away. Pressing beyond the wineries on Highway 152, you'll climb Hecker Pass Highway into pine and redwood country. Near the pass is **Mount Madonna County Park** with beautiful redwood groves, camping, picnicking and hiking trails. It is, incidentally, one of the prettier mountain parks in California, and it's rarely crowded. Just beyond is **Mount Madonna Inn** (see dining listing below), a longtime landmark offering impressive views to the west. From here, you can tumble down to Watsonville and explore the coastal tourist resort communities of Santa Cruz to the north or Monterey and Carmel to the south.

Heading inland on Route 152, you'll climb wooded **Pacheco Pass,** which takes you into the broad San Joaquin Valley. You'll pass **Casa De Fruta** en route. Continue down to **San Luis Reservoir,** with boating, swimming, picnicking and birdwatching.

If you like wilderness areas, head east from Gilroy on Leavesley Road, following signs toward **Henry W. Coe State Park.** It's mostly undeveloped, with hiking trails and primitive camping.

Southern Santa Clara County attractions

Garlic shops • **Garlic World**, 4800 Monterey Hwy. (U.S. 101), Gilroy; (408) 847-2251. Garlic laced specialty foods, garlic souvenirs and a fruit and produce section. The **Garlic Shoppé**, 4350 Highway 101, Gilroy; (408) 848-3646. Similar offerings as Garlic World. **Garlic Festival Store**, 7526 Monterey at Fifth in downtown Gilroy; (408) 842-7081. Garlic souvenirs, containers, garlic-based foods, cookbooks, plus other specialty foods.

Gilroy Historical Museum • *195 W. Fifth Street at Church Street, Gilroy; (408) 848-0470; free. Open Monday, Tuesday, Thursday and Friday 10 to 5, plus the first Saturday of each month from 10 to 2; closed Wednesday and Sunday.* □ Early-day history exhibits in an old Carnegie library building, focusing on agriculture, wine and of course the garlic industry.

Goldsmith Seeds • *2280 Hecker Pass Highway; (408) 847-7333. Weekdays 8 to 5; free.* □ Brilliant floral blooms—some in spectacular patterns—during the May through August blooming season. Self-guided tours and guided group tours by appointment; call for details.

WINE COUNTRY DINING

Harvest Time • ☆☆☆ $$$

□ *7397 Monterey St. (Sixth Street), Gilroy: (408) 842-7575. California-continental; full bar service. Lunch and dinner daily. Major credit cards.* □ Stylish Victorian restaurant tucked into one of downtown's historic buildings.

The changing menu features fresh fare from co-owner Don Christopher's ranch, plus interesting treatments of steak, seafood, chicken and chops.

Mount Madonna Inn ● ☆☆ $$

□ 1285 Hecker Pass Hwy., Watsonville; (408) 724-2275. American; full bar service. Lunch Friday-Sunday; dinner Thursday-Sunday and Sunday brunch. Major credit cards. □ Long popular inn perched atop Hecker Pass, offering faraway views; nights sparkle with the twinkle of a dozen cities. The menu ranges from pastas to assorted steaks, veal, chicken and seafood.

Classico Ristorante ● ☆☆☆ $$

□ 55 W. Fifth St., Gilroy; (408) 848-5008. Italian; wine and beer. Lunch Monday-Saturday; dinner nightly. MC/VISA. □ Appealing restaurant housed in an old brickfront fire station, half a block west of Monterey Street. It's dressed up with antique-modern décor and oak furniture. Entrées include veal Parmagiana, saltimboca, chicken piccata and assorted pastas and pizzas.

Tassos' Old House ● ☆☆☆ $$

□ 383 First St., Gilroy; (408) 847-7527. Eclectic menu; wine and beer. Dinner nightly. Major credit cards. □ Busily decorated early American style restaurant in an old white clapboard house, with an equally busy menu. It dances from chicken Jerusalem and pork tenderloin to New York steak.

VINELAND LODGINGS

PRICE KEY: A two-person room for $35 or less = $; $36 to $50 = $$;
$51 to $75 = $$$; $76 to $100 = $$$$; more than $100 = $$$$$.

Inn of Gilroy ● ☆☆ $$$ to $$$$$

□ 360 Leavesley Rd. (just off freeway), Gilroy, CA 95020; (800) 528-1234 or (408) 848-1467. Major credit cards. □ A 42-unit hotel with TV movies, room phones, refrigerators. Spa, pool and coin laundry; family units.

Casa de Fruta Garden Motel ● ☆☆ $$$ to $$$$

□ 10031 Pacheco Pass Hwy., Hollister, CA 95023; (408) 548-3813. Rates include continental breakfast. MC/VISA. □ Country-style motel with TV, room phones and refrigerators; swimming pool.

Forest Park Inn ● ☆☆☆ $$$ to $$$$$

□ 375 Leavesley Rd., Gilroy, CA 95020; (800) 237-7846 (within California only) or (408) 848-5144. (www.forestparkinn.com) Major credit cards. □ Nicely maintained 123-unit motel with TV movies, room phones with voice mail, refrigerators and balconies. Sauna, spa and pool; family units available.

Comfort Inn ● ☆☆☆ $$$ to $$$$

□ 8292 Murray Ave., Gilroy, CA 95020; (408) 848-3500. Major credit cards. □ Remodeled 66-unit motel with TV movies, refrigerators, microwaves and coffee makers. Pool, sauna, spa and laundry.

Super 8 Motel ● ☆☆ $$ to $$$

□ 8435 San Ysidro (just off freeway), Gilroy, CA 95020; (800) 800-8000 or (408) 848-4108. Major credit cards. □ A 53-unit motel with TV movies and phones; some refrigerators. Continental breakfast. Pool; family units.

Southern Santa Clara Valley information sources

Gilroy Visitors Bureau, 7780 Monterey Rd., Gilroy, CA 95020; (408) 842-6436. (www.gilroyvisitor.org)

Morgan Hill Chamber of Commerce, P.O. Box 786 (25 W. First St.), Morgan Hill, CA 95038-0786; (408) 779-9444. (www.morganhill.org)

*There are two reasons for drinking wine: when you are not thirsty—to pre-
vent it; when you are thirsty—to cure it; prevention is always better than cure.*
— **Lord Duff Cooper**

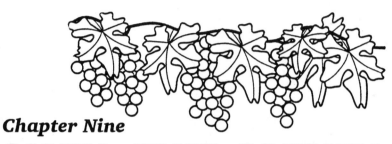

Chapter Nine
SANTA CRUZ COUNTY
Pinot in the pines

Santa Cruz County is one of the neatest small packages in California. In
one small space, it offers miles of lonely beaches, miles of busy beaches,
some remarkably charming little communities, an excellent university, silent
redwood forests and some little jewels of wineries.

Although the county isn't far from the crowded San Francisco Bay Area,
the thick wedge of the Santa Cruz Mountains keeps it relatively isolated.
Fewer than 250,000 people live here and its largest city, Santa Cruz, numbers about 49,000. It's a popular tourist destination, although many visitors
stay on Highway 101 and go shooting past, landing in easier-to-reach Monterey and Carmel.

The two are aquatic neighbors. Santa Cruz occupies the northern curve of
huge Monterey Bay and Monterey has settled in the southern arch. Because
of its sheltered southward position, the Santa Cruz seaside resort is often
fog-free while Monterey is veiled in the mists. Expect the beaches to be
cheek-to-cheek bikinis on a summer weekend. You'd best stay to the high
ground if you want to avoid Coney Island West. Which is just fine, because
the higher reaches of the county are where you'll discover most of the wineries and all of the vineyards.

The sheltering mountains spared this area from much of California's tu-
multuous history. The Spanish, waving their crosses and crossbows, did take
the trouble to establish Mission Santa Cruz in 1791, naming it for the sacred
cross. Being rather isolated, it didn't fare well, despite its access to fertile
river delta croplands just to the south. When Mexico won its independence
from Spain and began closing the California missions a few years later, Santa
Cruz was among the first to go.

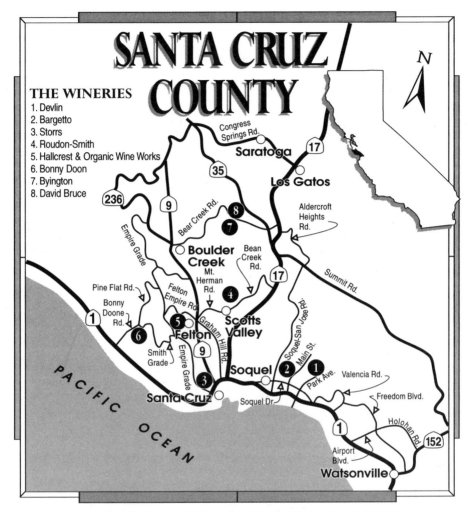

SANTA CRUZ COUNTY

THE WINERIES
1. Devlin
2. Bargetto
3. Storrs
4. Roudon-Smith
5. Hallcrest & Organic Wine Works
6. Bonny Doon
7. Byington
8. David Bruce

N

Congress Springs Rd.
Saratoga
17
35
Los Gatos
236
9
Bear Creek Rd.
8
7
Aldercroft Heights Rd.
Empire Grade
Boulder Creek
Bean Creek Rd.
Mt. Herman Rd.
17
Summit Rd.
Pine Flat Rd.
Felton Empire Rd.
4
Bonny Doone Rd.
1
5
Graham Hill Rd.
Scotts Valley
Soquel-San Jose Rd.
6
Felton
Smith Grade
Empire Grade
9
Soquel
2
1
Main St.
Park Ave.
Valencia Rd.
3
Santa Cruz
Soquel Dr.
Freedom Blvd.
PACIFIC OCEAN
1
Holohan Rd.
152
Airport Blvd.
Watsonville

Americans came during and after the 1849 gold rush and did their best to rid the Santa Cruz Mountains of redwoods. That was the lumber of choice for booming San Francisco to the north. Fortunately, they missed a few and several stands are now preserved in large parks.

When California joined the Union, gringo farmers began clearing the flood plain around present-day Watsonville and vintners sought suitable vineyard sites in the mountains. Commercial winemaking began in 1863 but it never was a major enterprise. All of the county's wineries perished during Prohibition.

One of the first to crop up after Repeal was Bargetto Winery in Soquel. It's alive and well, still run by Bargetto descendants. It had few immediate followers, however. Only three wineries were functioning by the 1960s. Then the wine boom of the '70s encouraged several solitude-seeking entrepreneurs to carve out vineyards in the steep slopes of the Santa Cruz Mountains. These heights offer cool micro-climates suited to Pinot Noir, Cabernet Sauvignon, Chardonnay, Gewürztraminer and Johannisberg Riesling. Today, nearly forty wineries are tucked into these hills, although only a few have tasting rooms that keep regular hours.

Most Santa Cruz area wineries are small and virtually all are family owned, producing only a few thousand cases a year. They probably spill that much at Gallo.

SANTA CRUZ COUNTY WINERY TOUR ● You have to work to tour the county's wineries, since most are scattered among the trees. It's nice work, however, taking you to the coastal retreat of Santa Cruz, then high into its namesake mountains. Further, you'll discover some exceptional wines. If possible, plan this outing for a weekend, since many of the wineries have limited weekday hours.

Since we left you in Gilroy in the last chapter, you may want to come on down by following Hecker Pass over the Mount Madonna ridge to **Watsonville**. To save a few miles after you've topped the pass and reached level ground, watch for a right turn onto Holohan Road at a sign indicating Santa Cruz. This bypasses the main part of Watsonville and hits Highway 1 farther north. You're traveling through the Pajaro River Delta—rich farming country and one of the few level areas in the county.

Pick up Highway 1 in Watsonville and head north past artichoke stands, through Aptos to **Capitola** and **Soquel**. The two small towns flank Highway 1, which is a freeway at this point. Take the Capitola/Park Avenue exit and follow Park Avenue north into the hills. The route quickly clears the suburban edge of Soquel and becomes a narrow lane, climbing steeply into wooded slopes. After less than a mile, swing left, pass through a gate and you'll wind up in someone's yard. Fortunately, it's the **Devlins'** yard, and they operate a winery here.

Come back down Park Avenue—there's no alternative—and take a right onto Soquel Drive at a stoplight, just short of the freeway. Drive north for less than a mile and turn right again onto Main Street at a traffic signal. This takes you to **Bargetto Winery,** just a few blocks up, on the left. Retrace your route on Main Street; cross Soquel Drive and stay aboard until Main ends at Porter Street. Go left and then quickly right and you're back on the freeway. Continue into **Santa Cruz,** staying to the left on Highway 1 at the Freeway 17 interchange. You'll sweep into a wide right-hand cloverleaf, then veer to the left at a sign indicating beaches and Ocean Avenue.

Turn right onto River Street, then after about three blocks, slant right again onto Potrero Street. Within a block, you'll see a light industrial and shopping complex called **The Old Sash Mill.** Take the second right into the facility and you've found **Storrs Winery.**

From here, we offer two choices. If it's Saturday (the only day the next winery is open to the public), or if you'd like a scenic diversion, backtrack to Highway 17 and follow it about three miles north, then take the Mount Hermon Road exit into **Scotts Valley**. This hamlet sits on the edge of the wooded ramparts of the Santa Cruz Mountains. It's a pleasant region, inter-

---

WINERY CODES ● *T* = tasting with no fee; *T$* = tasting for a fee; *GT* = guided tours; *GTA* = guided tours by appointment; *ST* = self-guiding or informal tours; ✗ = picnic area; 🛍 = gift shop or a good giftware selection.

WINE PRICES ● *$* = average price under $10 per bottle; *$$* = $10 to $14; *$$$* = $15 to $19; *$$$$* = $20 or more

laced with winding, redwood-canopied lanes. Don't expect a wilderness, however. Chalet style homes, mountain lodges and RV parks poke through the trees every mile or so, although it's still a far cry from downtown Des Moines. Fork right onto Scotts Valley Road then, after a block, turn left onto Bean Creek Road. A twisting two miles up Bean Creek takes you to **Roudon-Smith Vineyards,** on the left. Watch for the sign, which is quite small. Return to Scotts Valley and follow Mount Hermon Road to **Felton**.

If choose to bypass Scotts Valley and Roudon-Smith, simply follow River Street north into the mountains from Santa Cruz; it becomes State Highway 9 and takes you to Felton. This village of 5,000, scattered among the trees, still shows traces of its 1960s role as a hippie haven. However, boutiques now outnumber health food stores. At a stoplight, turn left onto Felton Empire Road. (If you're coming from Scotts Valley, Mount Hermon Road blends into Felton Empire at that signal.) After a quarter of a mile, you'll see **Hallcrest Vineyards** on your left. To reach the winery, drive through a residential parking area and drop downhill toward a vineyard.

From here, continue west on Felton-Empire, winding steeply upward. This is mostly mountainous woodland, although an occasional small vineyard will remind you of your purpose. After about three miles, you hit a stop sign at Empire Grade. Continue forward onto Ice Cream Grade and follow it 2.5 miles until it dead-ends at Pine Flat Road. You're now in the hamlet of **Bonny Doon,** although you wouldn't know it. It's not a town with a business district, but a collection of homes tucked among the trees. Go left onto Pine Flat and follow it to its junction with Bonny Doon Road. **Bonny Doon Winery** is on your left, opposite the junction.

Our next destination is Boulder Creek. If you have a detailed map, you'll note that several roads wander vaguely in that direction. Some are startlingly steep and winding. For simplicity's sake, we'll return you to Felton and press northward on Highway 9. Once you pass **Ben Lomond** and achieve tree-sheltered **Boulder Creek**, drive through its small business district, then turn right onto Bear Creek Road. After what seems an eternity of winding— actually about eight miles—you'll see the striking château of **Byington Winery** on the right. Half a mile beyond, on the left, is **David Bruce Winery,** terraced into a steep slope.

If you yen now for the flatlands, the quickest escape—albeit a twisting one—is to continue on Bear Creek Road, which winds down to Freeway 17 just south of Los Gatos.

Devlin Wine Cellars ● T ✕

3801 Park Ave. (P.O. Box 728), Soquel, CA 95073; (831) 476-7288. (www.devlinwinecellars.com) Weekends noon to 5; MC/VISA. Most varieties tasted. Some wine logo gift items. Lawn picnic area.

Many California wines win sweepstakes awards, and some have the honor of being served to the President. But few small wineries reach these heights. U.C. Davis grad Chuck Devlin and his wife Cheryl started their winery on this Soquel hilltop in 1978. They've since gathered a remarkable collection of major awards and their wines were among those selected to accompany former President Reagan on his China tour.

The Devlins' facility occupies a lofty hilltop perch. Wines are tasted in a small cottage beside their attractive country home; the winery is just up the hill a bit. The front lawn serves as a picnic area, with a fine view down the valley to Soquel.

Tasting notes: This small winery's Zinfandel had a nice spicy-berry nose, a pronounced raspberry flavor and light tannin finish. An award-winning Merlot was subtly dusky, complex and delicious, with a touch of oak. A Chardonnay had a light floral nose, spicy and crisp flavor with soft tannins. The Devlins also produce a Sauvignon Blanc, Chenin Blanc, Cabernet Sauvignon, Muscat Canelli, Gamay Beaujolais, white Zinfandel and a sparkling wine. Devlin's prices are reasonable for such quality: *$$ to $$$*

Vintners choice: "Merlot and Cabernet; we've won sweepstakes for both," says Chuck.

Bargetto Winery • T GT 📷

3535 Main St., Soquel, CA 95703; (831) 475-2258. (www.bargetto.com) Tasting room also located on Cannery Row in Monterey; see Chapter Ten, page 220. Monday-Saturday 10 to 5, Sunday noon to 5; major credit cards. Most varieties tasted. Good wine logo, gift and wine book selection. Tours daily at 11 and 2.

The Bargetto winery's neat and trim structures appear to occupy a residential area. Step inside the tasting room, however, and you'll discover that the winery's backside borders the attractively wooded bank of Soquel Creek. The buildings shelter a cozy creekside courtyard, often used for art exhibits and sometimes as a tasting area. Visitors enter through a nicely-done gift shop and sales room, then step down to the handsome creek-bank tasting room. It's trimmed in barnwood and decorated with vintage winemaking tools. A large window offers creek views.

Philip and John Bargetto established the winery in 1933; assorted family members including John, Beverly, Tom and Martin run things today.

Tasting notes: The Bargettos earned an early reputation for tasty yet light fruit wines and they still produce them. However, fine medium-bodied varietals are at the forefront of today's list. Our wines of choice were a dry and fruity Gewürztraminer, a spicy and light Chardonnay and a three-year-old Cabernet Sauvignon with a nice spicy-oaky nose and medium rich berry taste. Others on the list include Sauvignon Blanc, Pinot Grigio, Merlot, Pinot Noir and a sparkling Blanc de Noir. Fruit wines are raspberry (our favorite), olallieberry and Mead. A late harvest Riesling dessert wine was so rich it didn't need an accompaniment; it *was* dessert. Prices are modest, with most below the mid-teens: *$ to $$*.

Vintners choice: "Our specialties are Santa Cruz Mountains Chardonnay, Cabernet and our fruit wines," says Beverly Bargetto.

Storrs Winery • T ST

303 Potrero St. (in the Old Sash Mill, #35), Santa Cruz, CA 95060; (831) 458-5030. (www.storrswine.com) Thursday-Monday, noon to 5; major credit cards. Most varieties tasted. Informal tours on request.

Your first impression is that you've found one of those shopping center tasting rooms divorced from the main facility. However, Stephen or Pamela Storrs will happily show you their busy little winery. It's tucked into warehouse space behind the snug tasting room and spilling onto a rear drive. Creatively cluttered, it's a marvel of compactness.

This is a husband-and-wife operation from crush to bottling. Both U.C. Davis graduates with degrees in enology and viticulture, they started their winery in 1988 to create Santa Cruz Mountain varietals. And create they have; the small 5,000-case winery has won an impressive array of awards.

Tasting notes: The Storrs specialize in *les méthodes anciennes,* classic European style winemaking, utilizing barrel fermenting and *sur lie* aging. The result: full-flavored wines with soft touches of oak. They focus on Chardonnays and the selection we tasted was exceptional. Others on the list are a spicy Zinfandel, deep-flavored Merlot and a Petite Sirah with nice spice and hints of tannin. Prices: *$$ to $$$$.*

Vintners choice: "Our Santa Cruz Mountains Chardonnays—filled with aromas of fruit and toasty oak," says Pamela. "We create four different vineyard-designated varieties."

Roudon-Smith Vineyards • T ST ✕

2364 Bean Creek Rd., Santa Cruz, CA 95066; (831) 438-1244. Saturday 11 to 4:30, Sunday by appointment; MC/VISA. Selected wines tasted. Small picnic area; informal tours.

This trim little wooden winery near Scotts Valley is tucked into a slope, encircled by sheltering trees. It's a bit hard to spot because of those trees and because of its small sign, so be watchful. It's probably best to call and get directions. Further, since it's a family operation, it may be closed on some Saturdays. The double-joined name comes from Bob and Annamaria Roudon and Jim and June Smith. They started their small winery elsewhere in 1972 and settled here six years later. The families are now in semi-retirement, producing only about 2,000 cases a year.

Tasting notes: We especially liked the big, spicy reds such as Merlot, Cabernet Sauvignon and Syrah, which the Roudon-Smiths let rest a few years before release. The winery also bottles a modestly priced and very drinkable claret. Of the whites, we tilted toward a nutty-silky Santa Cruz Mountains Estate Chardonnay. Prices: *$$ to $$$.*

Vintners choice: "Estate grown Chardonnay and Syrah from Paso Robles," says Jim Smith.

Hallcrest Vineyards & Organic Wine Works • T GTA ✕

379 Felton Empire Rd., Felton, CA 95018; (800) OWW-WINE or (831) 335-4441. Daily 11 to 5:30; MC/VISA, AMEX. Most varieties tasted. A few giftwares and specialty foods. Nice picnic area with a view of Felton.

The casually arrayed, neat buildings of Hallcrest occupy a wooded basin just beyond Felton. A small vineyard adds authenticity to the setting. The tasting room is a deliberately cute cottage with a schoolhouse-style bell tower. A grassy picnic area is just below; it's shaded by a huge gnarled oak right out of the forest scene from *Snow White.*

Hallcrest's career started in 1941 when it was established by Chaffe Hall. It functioned as Felton-Empire Winery in the late 1970s. Then, John and Lorraine Schumacher and John's sister Shirin bought the facility in 1987 and restored the original name. A U.C. Davis grad, John has been making wines since he fiddled with fermenting fruit from the family orchard as a teenager.

Tasting notes: The winery produces two lines—Hallcrest Vineyards and Organic Wine Works. As you can guess, the latter is made from organically grown grapes, and no sulfites or other preservatives are used in the production. They have a distinctive earthy taste and are quite popular. We sampled a full flavored, herbal Chardonnay, a Fumé Blanc with hints of oak and an excellent big-bodied yet smooth Zinfandel. Others on the organic list are Pinot Noir, Carignane, Cabernet Sauvignon, Merlot and a red blend called *Notre Terre*—appropriate since it means "To our earth." On the Hallcrest side are the usual varietals, all well prepared and quite tasty. Selections include Chardonnay, several Cabernet Sauvignon renditions, Merlot and a Rhône style blend called *Clos de Jeannine*. Prices cover a wide range: **$ to $$$$.**

Bonny Doon Vineyard • T GTA ╳

10 Pine Flat Rd., Bonny Doon; Mailing address: P.O. Box 8376, Santa Cruz, CA 95061; (831) 425-3625. (www.bonnydoonvineyard.com) Daily 11 to 5; MC/VISA, AMEX. Most varieties tasted. Wine logo gift items; picnic area. Guided tours by appointment.

As long as you're making serious wine, you might as well have fun with the names. That appears to be the philosophy of Randall Grahm, owner of Bonny Doon Vineyard. His wines have names such as Big House Red, Cardinal Zin, *Le Cigare Volant, Il Fiasco* and *Il Pescatore,* which goes well with fish. The winery's tasting notes are both erudite and off the wall. For instance, Grahm's Big House Red "is somewhat of a social deviant. An unusual affinity for leather, chains, and confined spaces makes it suspect in most gated communities."

These serious wines with interesting names are tasted in a pleasant wooden cottage at roadside in the Bonny Doon forest. The winery and a scatter of tree-shaded picnic tables are just upslope. The tasting room's best feature—in addition to its wines, of course—is its T-shirt collection. Many memorable Grahm labels have been captured for torso display.

Tasting notes: Behind Grahm's creative labels lurk recognizable wine types such as Charbono, Riesling, Gewürztraminer, Syrah, and Sangiovese. Some are bottled as varietals while the identities of others are buried beneath Grahm's blending and wonderful hyperbole. We found the wines to be excellent for the most part, and if a wine tastes good, it's not important whether the "Freedom of Vinformation Act" requires Grahm to reveal that it's a Sangiovese. Among our favorites were *Il Pescatore* ("We draw ever closer to the platonic ideal of the Fisherman"), a full-flavored La Farfalla Charbono ("...it comports itself with civility"), and of course, Cardinal Zin ("...in perfect harmony with you and your olfactors.") Overall, the prices are all over the court: **$ to $$$$.**

AN INFORMAL TOUR

Byington Winery and Vineyard • T ✕ 📷

21850 Bear Creek Rd., Los Gatos, CA 95030; (831) 354-1111. (www.byington.com) Daily 11 to 5; MC/VISA. Selected wines tasted free; modest fee for limited releases. Giftware selection. View picnic area with barbecue.

Prepare for a surprise. After visiting quaint, prim and funky family wineries of Santa Cruz, you'll be pleasantly startled by the castle-like château of Bill Byington. Tile-roofed and multi-gabled, it's the county's most imposing winery, occupying carefully-groomed grounds in a wooded knoll amidst young vineyards. The tasting room is a high-ceiling, elegant space with tiled floors and arched windows. Views from the winery grounds are awesome, over redwood forests to Monterey Bay and the Pacific. They're yours if you opt for a picnic.

Byington, who established of the West Coast's largest steel treatment plant, bought land here in 1962, began producing wine in 1974, and completed his impressive facility in 1990.

Tasting notes: The Byington list is short and selective: Chardonnay, Gewürztraminer, Merlot, Cabernet Sauvignon, Cabernet Franc and Pinot Noir. Prices: **$$ to $$$$.**

David Bruce Winery • T ✕

21439 Bear Creek Rd., Los Gatos, CA 95030; (831) 354-4212. Weekdays noon to 5 and weekends 11 to 5; MC/VISA. Most varieties tasted. Picnic area on a grassy shelf overlooking the mountains.

Dr. David Bruce, noted for his medal-winning wines and no-nonsense approach to winemaking, has constructed an industrial-looking cinderblock facility bunkered into a hillside and rimmed by vineyards. The tasting room is less businesslike and more appealing—a pleasing space off a terrace on the second floor of the winery, rimmed by a low stone planter wall busy with blooms.

Bruce, a physician, was among the first new-generation Santa Cruz winemakers. He started his hillside facility in 1964 and gradually built it up to its present output of 30,000 cases a year. "My life-long dream has been to concentrate on the wines of the Santa Cruz Mountains," he once told us. "We're on the cool Chardonnay-Pinot Noir side of the hills and we focus with a vengeance on these varietals."

Tasting notes: It is no surprise that Bruce's Chardonnays—silky, lush and toasty—have won numerous medals. And the San Francisco Vintner's Club once selected his beautifully herbal Estate Pinot Noir as the best in America. The balance of his list contains—in addition to numerous Pinot Noir renditions—Grenache, Syrah, Zinfandel, Cabernet Sauvignon and Petite Syrah. Prices: **$$$ to $$$$.**

THE BEST OF THE BUNCH

The best wine buys • Devlin Wine Cellars and Bargetto Winery.

The most attractive winery • Byington Winery.

The most interesting tasting rooms • Bargetto Winery and Byington Winery.

The funkiest tasting rooms • Storrs Winery and Bonny Doon.

The best gift shop • Bargetto Winery, Bonny Doon Vineyard (wine label T-shirts) and Byington Winery.

The nicest picnic areas ● Devlin Wine Cellars, Hallcrest Vineyards, Byington Winery and David Bruce Winery.

The best tour ● Bargetto Winery (guided).

Wineland maps and events

Winery touring map ● *Wines of the Santa Cruz Mountains* map/brochure is available at wineries and visitors bureaus or contact: Santa Cruz Mountains Winegrowers Assn., 7605 Old Dominion Court, Suite A, Aptos, CA 95003; (831) 479-WINE. *(www.scmwa.com)* It covers not only Santa Cruz County but the Santa Cruz Mountains, which extend northward into San Mateo County.

Wineland events ● Santa Cruz Mountains Wine Auction in the spring; Vintners Festival during two weekends in June; Santa Cruz County Fair with participation by many county wineries, in mid-September; and Wine and Roses Benefit Tasting in support of the Pajaro Valley Community Health Trust. For information, call (831) 479-WINE. *(www.scmwa.com)*

BEYOND THE VINEYARDS

It's tempting to suggest that wine is the tip of the tail that wags Santa Cruz County's tourism dog. As we have seen, the area shelters some neat little wineries, although most folks come for the beaches and redwood forests.

Your trek to the wineries has taken you through the county's forested mountains. We'll now suggest a route that exposes its coastal lures. From Highway 1, drive south on River Street through the heart of Santa Cruz. You'll pass **Pacific Garden Mall,** devastated by the 1989 Loma Prieta earthquake and now rebuilt, offering several boutiques and restaurants.

River Street changes to Front Street and takes you to the primary Santa Cruz attractions—the **Municipal Wharf,** the **Beach Boardwalk** and of course, the beach. Head southeastward from here, staying close to the shoreline. Follow Beach Street which turns into Riverside Avenue and swings inland, then turn right onto **East Cliff Drive**. This will keep you tucked close to the shore for the most part. You'll see fine old beachfront homes, lots of sand and seagulls and an occasional sea lion.

With luck, you'll reach **Capitola,** a cute little town of cliff-perched Victorian homes and beachside boutiques. A pedestrian path along Soquel Creek is quite pleasant. Park Avenue will return you to U.S. 1 freeway. From here, with the aid of a local map, you can work southwestward, dipping down to the bayfront where streets permit. An assortment of state and local beach parks invite sunning and surf-sloshing.

If you prefer more beach and less congestion, go west (eventually north) on Highway 1 from the River Street starting point. You might want to divert to the right onto Bay Street and follow signs to the forested campus of the **University of California at Santa Cruz.** Back on Highway 1, continue along the oceanfront, taking time for a stop at **Natural Bridges State Beach.** Other beaches will crop up frequently as you follow this relatively unspoiled coastal stretch toward San Mateo County.

Santa Cruz county attractions

Redwood and other state parks ● **Big Basin Redwoods State Park**, north of Boulder Creek; (831) 338-6132; entrance fee. Camping, hiking and picnicking. **Henry Cowell Redwoods State Park,** off Graham

Hill road near Felton; (831) 335-4598; entrance fee. Camping, hiking, picnicking, restaurant, snack bar and curio shop. **Forest of Nisene Marks**, Aptos Creek Road, Aptos; (831) 335-4598; no fee. Wilderness park with hiking and biking trails. **Wilder Ranch State Park**, 1401 Coast Rd., Santa Cruz; (831) 688-3241; entrance fee. Restored late twentieth century ranch.

Roaring Camp & Big Trees Railroad ● *Graham Hill Road, Felton; (831) 335-4400. Various hours; admission fee.* ☐ Steam train rides through the redwoods; also site of the Felton Covered Bridge.

Santa Cruz Beach Boardwalk ● *At the beachfront; (831) 426-7433 or (831) 423-5590. From 11 a.m. daily in summer, on weekends and holidays only the rest of the year; various closing times. Free admission; fees for rides.* ☐ Nicely restored old fashioned amusement park, one of the few beachfront fun zones left in America.

Santa Cruz Museum of Natural History ● *1305 E. Cliff Dr., Santa Cruz; (831) 429-3773. Tuesday-Sunday 10 to 5; donations requested.* ☐ Exhibits on the natural history of the Santa Cruz area, including native peoples displays and a "touch tide pool."

Seymour Marine Discovery Center ● *At Long Marine Laboratory, 100 Shaffer Rd., Santa Cruz; (831) 459-3800. Call for hours; modest admission fee.* ☐ Aquatic displays, interactive marine life exhibits and tide pool in a new facility operated by the University of California at Santa Cruz.

Santa Cruz County information sources

Santa Cruz Conference and Visitors Council, 701 Front St., Santa Cruz, CA 95060; (800) 833-3494 or (831) 425-1234. *(www.santacruz.org)*

For south county information, contact the **Pajaro Valley/Watsonville Chamber of Commerce**, 444 Main St. (P.O. Box 1748), Watsonville, CA 95076-1748; (831) 724-3900. *(www.pvchamber.com)*

This song of mine
Is a Song of the Vine
To be sung by the glowing embers
Of wayside inns,
When the rain begins
To darken the drear Novembers.
— **Catawba Wine** by Henry Wadsworth Longfellow

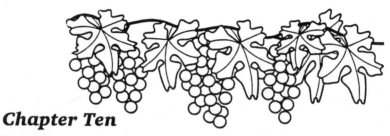

Chapter Ten

MONTEREY COUNTY
Sun-soaked vines in Steinbeck Country

Noted primarily for tourism, Steinbeck novels and golf tournaments, Monterey County offers a vineyard surprise. It contains nearly 30,000 acres of premium wine grapes, more than any other California county except Napa and Sonoma.

They aren't all that evident, however. The visitor will find no great gathering of wineries, and the only concentration of tasting rooms is in that mother of all tourist traps, Cannery Row.

So, where's the grapes? Most are in the cool, flat and wind-brushed Salinas Valley below Salinas. A drive south on Highway 101 won't reveal many vines, although this is one of California's major agricultural areas. Grapes prefer the good drainage offered by slopes, so many of the vineyards are out of sight of the highway, coved into the benchlands of the Gavilan Mountains to the east and the Santa Lucia section of the Coast Range to the west. A few vines also grow in the Carmel Valley, inland from Carmel, although that area is better known for its posh country resorts and riding academies.

Monterey County is rich with the lore of early California. However, it had nothing to do with wine, other than the usual mission grapes stomped by the padres for sacramental sipping. Father Junipero Serra started California's second mission near Carmel in 1770, and it served for decades as headquarters for the twenty-one mission chain. The only record of early grape planting in the county was at Mission Soledad, established in the Salinas Valley in 1791. No trace of those vineyards remain.

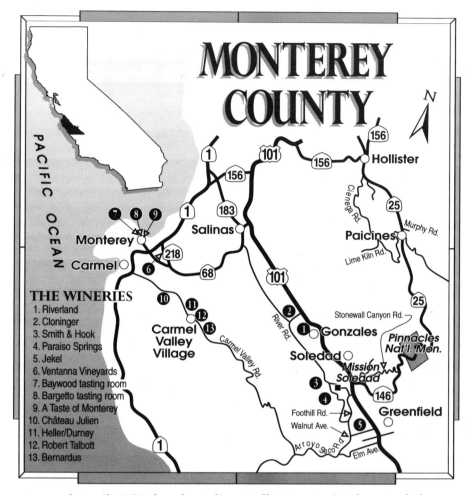

MONTEREY COUNTY

N

PACIFIC OCEAN

Monterey

Carmel

THE WINERIES
1. Riverland
2. Cloninger
3. Smith & Hook
4. Paraiso Springs
5. Jekel
6. Ventanna Vineyards
7. Baywood tasting room
8. Bargetto tasting room
9. A Taste of Monterey
10. Château Julien
11. Heller/Durney
12. Robert Talbott
13. Bernardus

Salinas

Hollister

Cienega Rd.

Murphy Rd.

Paicines

Lime Kiln Rd.

Stonewall Canyon Rd.

Gonzales

Pinnacles Nat'l. Mon.

Soledad

Mission Soledad

Foothill Rd.
Walnut Ave.

Greenfield

Elm Ave.

Arroyo Seco Rd.

River Rd.

Carmel Valley Rd.

Carmel Valley Village

It wasn't until 1960 that the Salinas Valley was seriously regarded as a premium wine producing area. Until then, it was thought to be too dry and windy. Aided by researchers from U.C. Davis, growers solved the wind problem by planting grapes parallel to the prevailing breezes. Drilling proved that the Salinas River had plenty of water, mostly underground.

This is a relatively cool area, kept that way by those winds, so it's ideal for whites, accounting for more than seventy percent of the plantings. Among those that thrive are Chardonnay (the most commonly planted variety), Sauvignon Blanc and Gewürztraminer. Cabernet Sauvignon is the most popular red; Zinfandel, Pinot Noir, Petite Sirah and Merlot are among its companions. Despite its youth, this newcomer to the California wine world has won an impressive number of medals. Monterey County Chardonnays are particularly strong in competitions.

The first vintners were South Bay refugees such as Wente, Mirassou, Alamden and Paul Masson, whose vines were being crowded out by subdivisions. Since they already had elaborate production facilities to the north, they planted grapes here but built no wineries. Monterey Vineyard was the first to build a large winery in the Salinas Valley. It's now operated by Canandaigua Wine Company of New York as Riverland Vineyards.

MONTEREY COUNTY WINERY TOUR ● As we wrote this, only thirteen county vintners had tasting rooms that kept regular hours, and eight of those are disconnecting from the wineries. Most are in Monterey and Carmel, which makes good business sense, since they attract hundreds of thousands of tourists a year—particularly Cannery Row.

Of the tasting rooms still married to their wineries, five are near U.S. Highway 101, south of Salinas. Thus, your tour should begin somewhere on that highway, with your compass set for **Gonzales.**

A winery in Gonzales? Certainly.

Exit the freeway at Gloria Road just south of town, go north on the frontage road (Alta Street) to the impressive California-Mediterranean style **Riverland Vineyards.** Continue to the southern edge of the Gonzales business district, turn left (west) onto Gonzales River Road and head toward the Santa Lucia Mountains. (**NAVIGATIONAL NOTE:** We didn't see a Gonzales River Road sign our last time through, although the turn is near Texaco and Exxon service stations.) After about two and a half miles, the route blends onto River Road, which soon swings to the right; just beyond is **Cloninger Cellars,** on your right. Reverse your route briefly, then go left onto the leg of a T-intersection to stay with River Road. Head south about nine miles and fork to the right onto Foothill Road. Go another couple of miles— some of it on a dirt road—turn right and follow a narrow paved lane about a mile to **Smith & Hook,** cradled among foothill vineyards.

Return to Foothill, turn right then go right again and uphill on Paraiso Springs Road to **Paraiso Springs Vineyards.** From here, follow Paraiso Springs Road east into the flatlands of the Salinas Valley. At a stop sign, swerve to the left onto Arroyo Seco and follow it to U.S. 101 freeway.

If you'd like to visit the ruins of **Mission Soledad,** turn north at that stop sign onto Fort Romney Road. Are you superstitious? It's interesting to note that this was the thirteenth California mission established, one of the least successful and one of the few that fell to complete ruin. Only fragments of adobe walls and a modern-day chapel mark this spot.

Head south on U.S. 101 for about eight miles to **Greenfield.** Ignore the first exit and take the second one, marked Walnut Avenue. Follow Walnut through town and then briefly past vines and veggie fields to **Jekel Vineyard** on your right.

You've now done the Salinas Valley vineyards. Several other tasting rooms are in or near Carmel and Monterey; they're easy to find once you're in the neighborhood. The simplest approach is to drive north on U.S. 101 to **Salinas** and take the Monterey-Salinas Highway (State Route 68) west.

A considerably more challenging and extremely scenic approach is via Arroyo Seco Road from Greenfield. It winds and twists and sometimes bumps through a pretty river canyon, lurching uphill and down. It then links to Carmel Valley Road, which takes you northward on more roller coaster dips,

---

WINERY CODES ● *T* = tasting with no fee; *T$* = tasting for a fee; *GT* = guided tours; *GTA* = guided tours by appointment; *ST* = self-guiding or informal tours; ✕ = picnic area; 🎁 = gift shop or a good giftware selection.

WINE PRICES ● *$* = average price under $10 per bottle; *$$* = $10 to $14; *$$$* = $15 to $19; *$$$$* = $20 or more

kinks and turns into Carmel Valley. The total distance from Greenfield is about forty miles. To begin this trek, as you return from Jekel, turn right on El Camino—Greenfield's main street—, go several blocks south and go right again at the southern edge of town onto Elm Avenue. It soon becomes Arroyo Seco (County Road G-16).

Assuming you choose the more sensible Monterey-Salinas Highway approach—we didn't—you'll encounter the **Ventana Vineyards** tasting room at the junction of routes 68 and 218, about two and a half miles short of Monterey. It's in the northwest corner of that junction, in a tree-sheltered fieldstone complex called the "Old Stone House."

Three other tasting rooms are on Monterey's **Cannery Row**. As you reach Monterey and blend onto the Highway 1 freeway, take the first exit, following signs toward Fisherman's Wharf. Continue past the wharf and its large public parking lot, following signs to Cannery Row. If it's a weekend, get there early. Otherwise, you'll have trouble parking and you'll be lined up five deep at the tasting counters. Our preferred approach is to park in that large lot at Fisherman's Wharf and follow a recreational trail (on a former rail bed) into Cannery Row. It's less than a mile.

If you drive, you'll see **Baywood Cellars** tasting room opposite the large Monterey Plaza Hotel complex on the upper end of Cannery Row. If you're walking, you'll need to leave the rec path and take a cross street down to the "Row." Continue several blocks to a former cannery building on a pier opposite Steinbeck Plaza parking lot, at Cannery Row and Prescott Street. Now busy with souvenir shops and cafes, the building houses the **Bargetto Tasting Room** at street level and **A Taste of Monterey** on an upper level with a great view of Monterey Bay. You may want to continue on down Cannery Row to the outstanding **Monterey Bay Aquarium.**

Return to Highway 1 and head south to Carmel, then go southeast on Carmel Valley Road. After about five miles, you'll see the castle-like **Château Julien** on your right. Continue another four miles into this trendy valley of country clubs, exclusive resorts and stables and you'll encounter the final three tasting rooms. All are in Carmel Valley Village and all are on your left—**Heller/Durney,** then **Robert Talbott** a block beyond at the corner of Pilot Road, and **Bernardus Winery** a few blocks further. The **Carmel Valley Chamber of Commerce** visitor center is between Talbott and Bernardus, also on the left.

Riverland Vineyards ● T ✕ 📷

800 S. Alta St., Gonzales, CA 93926; (831) 675-8838. Wednesday-Sunday 11 to 4; MC/VISA. Most varieties tasted. Wine logo and giftware selection.

Wine sippers of a decade ago will remember this as Monterey Vineyards. It's now part of the Canandaigua Wine Company of New York, which has purchased several major winery operations in California. After being closed to the public for several years, it now hosts tastings under the Mystic Cliffs at Riverland Vineyards label. The California-Mediterranean style structure is rimmed by landscaped grounds where geese glide along placid ponds and picnickers spread their fare on lawn tables. Winetasting is conducted in a handsome Spanish-modern hospitality center.

Tasting notes: Available wines, mostly under the Mystic Cliffs Wine Cellars label, include the more popular and some less common varietals: Chardonnay, Merlot, Pinot Noir, Cabernet Sauvignon, Cabernet Franc, Shiraz, Malbec and Petit Verdot. Prices: *$$ to $$$$.*

Cloninger Cellars • T GTA ✕

1645 River Road, Salinas, CA 93908; (831) 675-9463. (www.usaw-ines.com/cloninger) Monday-Thursday 11 to 4 and Friday-Sunday 11 to 5; major credit cards. Most varieties tasted. A few wine logo items; a couple of picnic tables. Guided tours by appointment.

A weathered ranch yard is home to one of Monterey County's smaller wineries, although this isn't exactly a mom and pop operation. It's presently owned by Joe Boskovich of Boskovich Farms, a major grower of row crops and wine vines. The winery was started in the early 1980s by Loren Cloninger. His Italian-Swiss grandparents came to the Salinas Valley in 1921 and established a dairy farm on this site. The tasting room, opened in the mid-nineties, occupies a simple little cottage, while some of the other outbuildings in this old ranch yard have been converted to winemaking purposes.

Tasting notes: The Cloninger list is small; only three wines were being produced when we last stopped. All are estate grown; mostly on the Santa Lucia benchlands. The offerings were a rich, oak-finished Chardonnay, a full-flavored Pinot Noir with hints of oak and a nice peppery Cabernet Sauvignon from the Carmel Valley. **Prices: $$$ to $$$$.**

Smith & Hook Winery at Hahn Estates • T ST ✕ 🏠

37700 Foothill Rd. (P.O. Drawer C), Soledad, CA 93960; (831) 678-2132. (www.hahnestates.com) Daily 11 to 4; MC/VISA. Most current releases tasted. Good selection of gift and specialty food items; picnic area.

The Smith & Hook tasting room is particularly appealing, housed in a prim clapboard cottage with yellow trim. A deck off the sipping room and a tree-shaded picnic area offer nice views of the Salinas Valley to the east. The ranch-style winery sits in the Santa Lucia benchlands, a refreshing escape from the flatlands of the valley. You'll find no Smiths nor Hooks here today. The winery gets its name from owners of a former horse ranch that occupied this site. The Nicolaus Hahn family established the winery in 1979 and preserved much of the rustic look of the ranch.

Tasting notes: Wines are bottled under the modestly priced Hahn Estates label and the higher priced Smith & Hook brand. The Santa Lucia Highlands are warmer than the valley floor and thus ideal for reds. S&H has won scores of awards for its peppery, medium-bodied Cabernet Sauvignon and Cabernet Franc, among the best Monterey County reds we tasted. We also liked a Merlot, so big and spicy it could have passed for a Cab. Heading the white side of the list is a light yet lush and fruity Chardonnay. Prices: **$$ to $$$$.**

Paraiso Springs Vineyards • T GTA ✕

38060 Paraiso Springs Rd., Soledad, CA 93960; (831) 678-0300. (www.usawines.com/paraiso) Weekdays noon to 4 and weekends 11 to 5; MC/VISA. Most varieties tasted. A few wine logo items.

Like Smith & Hook, steeply-tilted Paraiso Springs offers a fine valley view from its tasting room and picnic area. The appealing sipping parlor, housed in a shingled cottage, has a comfy living room feel, complete with a sofa and a couple of hutches. A few tables and chairs occupy a deck above the vineyards. Richard and Claudia Smith, grape growers in the valley for more than a quarter of a century, opened their winery in the early 1990s. Son Jason helps his dad manage the vineyards and son-in-law David Fleming helps produce and market the wines.

Tasting notes: The Paraiso list is balanced between whites and reds. Among the whites are a Riesling with a subtle pineapple taste, a smooth malolactic fermented Pinot Blanc and a spicy and lush Chardonnay. A fruity and spicy Pinot Noir and a full flavored Syrah comprise the red side. Also available are a rich and subtly sweet late harvest riesling, a late harvest Pinot Noir dessert wine and *Souzao* Port. Prices: *$$ to $$$$.*

Jekel Vineyard • T GTA ✕

40155 Walnut Ave. (P.O. Box 336), Greenfield, CA 93927; (831) 674-5525. (www.usawines.com/jekel) Daily 11 to 4; MC/VISA. Most varieties tasted. Picnic area beneath an arbor; fair selection of wine related items.

A modern metal-sided "winery barn" houses the prosperous looking Jekel winery. The bright, large-windowed tasting room is sheltered by an arbor dripping with wisteria, Inside, an impressive array of medals add to the décor. Several picnic tables are nearby. All of this is accented by carefully tended landscaping. Surrounding vineyards complete this prim picture. William and August Jekel built the winery in 1978, six years after planting their vineyards. It's now owned by a wine group called Gravelstone Vineyard and Sanctuary Estate, which has expanded its vineyards and production.

Tasting notes: Gravelstone Chardonnay, a big award winner for Jekel, had a nice tropical fruit aroma and taste with an herbal accent. The Pinot Noir was full flavored, with lots of berries and a pleasant hint of smokiness. Merlot, Cabernet Sauvignon and Riesling were all nicely crafted wines as well, displaying good varietal character. A crisp and fruity Riesling and rich late harvest Riesling complete the list. Prices: *$$ to $$$$.*

Ventana Vineyards tasting room • T ✕

2999 Monterey-Salinas Highway, Suite 2, Monterey, CA 93940; (800) BEST-VIN or (831) 372-7415. (www.ventanawines.com) Daily 11 to 5; MC/VISA. Most varieties tasted. Sheltered picnic deck.

Some years ago, former Vietnam fighter pilot J. Douglas Meador decided he wanted to go into the wine business. He cleared and planted a 400-acre vineyard in gravelly soil along the Arroyo Seco River, between Soledad and Greenfield. In 1978, when he began making his wines, perhaps even he was amazed. According to a winery source, Ventana has won more awards than any other single vineyard winery in America. You can taste these wines in a handsome hospitality center in a rough-stone, vine covered complex called "the Old Stone House" just east of Monterey.

Tasting notes: Most premium whites appear on Doug's list, along with Cabernet Sauvignon, Syrah and a couple of dessert wines. His flagship Sauvignon Blanc was excellent, fruity and spicier than most Chardonnays; his barrel-fermented malolactic Chardonnay was—predictably—spicier still. Of the reds, we liked a rich, peppery young Cabernet Sauvignon accented with a typical Bordeaux blend of Cabernet Franc and Merlot; and a Pinot Noir Reserve rich with berries. Prices are modest for such award winners: *$ to $$$.*

Vintners choice: "Sauvignon Blanc, Chardonnay and Riesling," said a winery source.

Baywood Cellars tasting room • T 📦

381 Cannery Row, Suite C, Monterey, CA 93940; (831) 645-9035. (www.baywood-cellars.com) Daily 11 to 8; major credit cards. Most varieties tasted for a modest fee. Good selection of giftwares and wine logo items.

This storefront facility offers samples of the efforts of John and James Cotta, third generation vintners from the Monterey area. They've been growing grapes and producing wines in this region since 1986, initially bottling their products under the Las Viñas label. James manages the vineyards and brother John makes the wines. Their vines and winery, obviously not along Cannery Row, are elsewhere in Monterey County.

Grandfather Joe Cotta, Sr., established Cotta Properties in 1925, growing grapes and assorted produce. This is not a small operation. James and John, with their father Joe Cotta, Jr., farm more that 2,000 acres of vineyards throughout California. Their Baywood Cellars produces more than 300,000 cases of wine a year.

Tasting notes: The Baywood list offers lots of choices—whites, reds, dessert wines and sparkling wines. Of the whites, we liked a spicy and fruity Gewürztraminer. The Monterey Pinot Noir aged in French oak won our vote among the reds. Late harvest Symphony topped the dessert wine list and we liked the crisp dryness of a Napa Valley Brut, obviously not locally made. Other wines include Chardonnay, Merlot, Zinfandel, Syrah, Vintage Port and Napa Valley Blanc de Noir. Prices: *$$$ to $$$$.*

Bargetto Winery tasting room • T 🎁

700 Cannery Row, Monterey, CA 93940; (831) 373-4053. (www.bargetto.com) Daily 10 to 6; MC/VISA. Most varieties tasted. Extensive wine logo, giftware, specialty foods and souvenir selection.

Bargetto's tasting room is on the ground floor of a former cannery building, which also houses A Taste of Monterey (below). It offers a large gift selection, and a particularly good choice of specialty food items and cookware.

Tasting notes: See listing in the previous chapter, on page 208.

A Taste of Monterey • T 🎁

700 Cannery Row, Monterey, CA 93940; (831) 646-5446. (www.tastemonterey.com) Daily 11 to 6. Modest fee for tasting select wines, which are changed weekly. Extensive wine logo, giftware and souvenir selection.

This is a multiple winery tasting facility, representing more than thirty-five Monterey and Santa Cruz county vintners. Once the Paul Masson wine tasting room, it occupies one of Cannery Row's best perches. On the second floor of an old cannery, reaching over the water on pilings, it commands a striking Monterey Bay view. One can sip wine samples or purchase glasses of wine and snacks and relax in chairs before a window-wall on the bay. The gift area rivals the other Cannery Row curio shops in its selection of specialty foods, giftwares and tourist doodads. Portions of the former Paul Masson Wine Museum survive and other elements have been added. Exhibits include photos, graphics and film s about thewine industry.

Tasting notes: With more than thirty-five wineries and as many as three hundred different wines tasted on a rotating basis, we've not attempted specific comments. It's all rather pot luck, depending on which wineries are taking their turn, which is part of the fun of visiting this huge tasting room.

Château Julien Wine Estate • T GTA

8940 Carmel Valley Rd. (P.O. Box 221775), Carmel, CA 93923; (831) 624-2600. (www.chateaujulien.com) Weekdays 8:30 to 5, weekends 11 to 5; MC/VISA, AMEX. Most varieties tasted. Wine oriented giftwares. Guided tours at 10:30 and 2:30 weekdays and 12:30 and 2:30 weekends; reservations requested.

If King Arthur had yearned to make wine instead of fussing about Lancelot, he might have created Château Julien, a modern fairy castle set in affluent Carmel Valley. This Camelot is complete with a tower, but presumably no Repunzel resides therein. The tasting room is properly Arthurian, with a carved tasting table—not round but more or less oval—arched windows and a crackling fireplace. A modern winery is sheltered within the castle, which can be explored by reservation, followed by a tasting intelligently conducted by the tour host. All of this opulence was conceived in 1983 by a corporation with a name no less modest than its creation—Great American Wineries, Inc. It later was sold to Bob and Patty Brower, who operate it as a family winery.

Tasting notes: The list of medals is considerably longer than the roster of wines. Varietals are Chardonnay, Merlot, Cabernet Sauvignon, Sauvignon Blanc, Gewürztraminer and Johannisberg Riesling. They're full-bodied creations, often made *sur lie* to add to their complexity. We favored a young and spicy barrel fermented Chardonnay, a dry yet fruity *sur lie* Semillon and a soft, complex Merlot. A cream Sherry was nutty and sensuously lush. Prices: *$$ to $$$$*.

Vintners choice: "Chardonnay, Merlot and Cabernet Sauvignon, consistent gold and silver medal winners," says a winery spokesperson.

Heller Estate/Durney Vineyards • T 🏮

69 W. Carmel Valley Rd., Carmel Valley, CA 93924; (800) 625-VINO or (831) 659-6220. (www.durneywines.com) Weekdays 11 to 5 and weekends 10 to 5; MC/VISA. Most varieties tasted. Nice selection of giftwares.

An attractive salmon-colored building houses the tasting room for Heller Estate/Durney Vineyards. The vines and winery are elsewhere in the Carmel Valley. A cherry little garden with a free-form statue called "The Dancers" by internationally known sculptor Toby Heller is just outside the cottage style tasting room. You'll see that statue again inside—on the wine labels. Another focal point here is an elaborately carved wooden table that serves as the tasting bar.

The late William Durney and his wife Dorothy of Los Angeles planted some of Carmel Valley's first vineyards in 1968 and started their winery in 1976. It was they who helped establish the Carmel Valley appelation in 1983. The operation was sold to a group of European investors in 1994.

Tasting notes: The Durney Vineyards list features Chenin Blanc, a couple of Chardonnays, several versions of Cabernet Sauvignon and Pinot Noir, plus a rich late harvest Riesling. Prices: *$$ to $$$$*.

Robert Talbott Vineyards • T ✕ 🏮

53 W. Carmel Valley Rd. (P.O. Box 49), Carmel Valley, CA 93924; (831) 659-3500. (www.usawines.com/talbott) Thursday-Sunday 11 to 5; MC/VISA. Most varieties tasted for a small fee; logo glass included for a slightly larger price. Nice selection of giftwares; adjacent picnic area.

An elaborately landscaped garden and tree-shaded picnic patio mark the tasting room of Robert Talbott Vineyards. Opened in 1999, it occupies a handsome stone building in the heart of Carmel Valley Village. The winery itself was started in 1982. Obviously well-received, the wines have found their way to a White House dinner. The winery's creators come from rather a different direction. In 1950, Robert and Audrey Talbott migrated from New York to Carmel, where they established what was to become one of America's leading neckwear companies. They followed with a series of retail shops, then added a line of men's shirts and other accessories. The operation, with Audrey as its president, is still based on the Monterey Peninsula.

Tasting notes: From a varietal standpoint, Talbott's list is quite brief—Chardonnay and Pinot Noir. However, winetasters will find quite a few renditions of these classic wines, and those we tasted were excellent. We counted—but did not taster—fifteen bottlings of Chardonnay and four of Pinot Noir. Although prices range beyond $50, some of the Chards and Pinots are in the teens: *$$ to $$$$.*

Bernardus Winery • T
5 W. Carmel Valley Rd. (P.O. Box 1800), Carmel Valley, CA 93924; (800) 223-2533 or (831) 659-1900. (www.bernardus.com) Daily 11 to 5; MC/VISA. Select wines tasted for a modest fee, which applies toward purchase. A few giftware items.

Of the three Carmel Valley Village tasting rooms, this is the only one that comes with a winery attached. It occupies a square masonry building with lattice trim. The tasting room is in one end, inside a bougainvillea-splashed entryway. It's an attractive space, with wood beam ceilings and a nice display of giftwares—mostly wine logo clothing. Dutchman Ben Pon came to this area and determined that the warm Carmel Valley was an ideal place to plant classic Bordeaux grape varieties. He started his operation more than a decade ago and opened this Carmel Valley Village tasting room and winery in the mid-nineties.

Tasting notes: The Bernardus flagship is Marinus, a full-flavored Bordeaux-style blend of Cabernet Sauvignon, Merlot, Cabernet Franc and Petite Verdot. The winery also makes a surprisingly hearty rosé from Cabernet grapes called Saignee de Marinus. Others on the list are a lush and toasty Chardonnay, a light and fruity Semillon, Sauvignon Blanc, Pinot Gris, Merlot and the Rhône varietal Marsanne. Prices: *$$ to $$$$.*

THE BEST OF THE BUNCH

The best wine buys • Smith & Hook and Ventana Vineyards.

The most attractive wineries • Jekel Vineyard and Château Julien.

The most interesting tasting rooms • Riverland Vineyard, Smith & Hook and Ventana Vineyards.

The best gift shops • Bargetto Winery tasting room in Monterey.

The nicest picnic areas • Smith & Hook Winery, Jekel Vineyard and Robert Talbott Vineyards.

The best tour • Château Julien Wine Estate.

Wine country maps and events

Winery touring guide • *Monterey Wine Country* map and guide is available at most member wineries, or contact: Monterey County Vintners and Growers Assn., P.O. Box 1793, Monterey, CA 93942-1793; (831) 375-9400. *(www.montereywines.org)*

Wineland events • Winemakers' Celebration in mid-August, involving more than twenty-five Monterey County vintners; and the Great Wine Escape Weekend in mid-November, with bus tours, tastings, winemaker dinners and other activities. For information on either event, call (831) 375-9400.

BEYOND THE VINEYARDS

From a visitor standpoint, Monterey and Santa Cruz counties have much in common. Both have namesake cities bordering on huge, crescent shaped Monterey Bay and both are major tourist draws. The **Monterey Peninsula** is a playland for the rich, who tee off at Pebble Beach, gallop their horses on the trails of **Carmel Valley** and play tennis at luxury resorts. The wanna-be-rich shop the boutiques of **Carmel**, prowl **Fishermans Wharf** and **Cannery Row** in Monterey and hang out, scantily clad, at assorted beaches.

The more esoteric seek solitude on stormy strands and in the wilds of **Los Padres National Forest** to the south, particularly in the coastal area with that mystical name, **Big Sur**. (Utter the phrase and you can almost see Liz Taylor in *The Sandpiper*, scuffing along the beach, eyes downcast.)

Monterey County attractions

Mission Nuestra Señora de la Soledad ● *Fort Romni Road, Soledad; (831) 678-2586. Wednesday-Monday 10 to 4; donations requested.* ☐ Fragments of original mission walls and a newer chapel with a museum.

Mission San Carlos Borromeo del Rio Carmelo ● *3080 Rio Rd., Carmel; (831) 624-3600. Monday-Saturday 9:30 to 7:30, Sundays and holidays 10:30 to 7:30 June through Labor Day; closes at 4:30 the rest of the year.* ☐ Beautifully preserved former headquarters of the California missions, with a museum, chapel, courtyard and history exhibits.

Monterey Bay Aquarium ● *886 Cannery Row, Monterey; (800) 756-3737 in California, or (831) 648-4888. Daily 9:30 to 6 Memorial Day to Labor Day and 10 to 6 the rest of the year; admission charge.* ☐ One of America's leading aquariums with more than twenty habitat exhibits and tide pools.

Monterey State Historic Park ● *20 Custom House Plaza, Monterey; (831) 649-7118. Daily 10 to 5 Memorial Day through Labor Day and 10 to 4 the rest of the year. Admission charge, covers all exhibits and museums.* ☐ A collection of historic structures tracing Monterey's history as the Spanish, then Mexican capital of California.

Point Lobos State Reserve ● *Four miles south of Carmel off Highway 1; (831) 624-4909. Daily 9 to 6:30 Memorial Day through Labor Day; 9 to 5 the rest of the year; modest admission charge.* ☐ Wildlife preserve on a beautiful seacoast peninsula with beaches, picnicking and hiking.

The Seventeen-Mile Drive ● *Pacific Grove to Carmel; (831) 625-8426 or (831) 624-6669. Toll charge.* ☐ This famous drive takes visitors through the green and blue seacoast ramparts of the Monterey Peninsula's scenic tip, past famous golf courses, trendy villages and mansions.

Monterey County information sources

Few lodgings and restaurants are near Monterey's wineries. For a comprehensive compendium of what to do and see, where to play, eat and sleep, get a copy of the *Monterey Peninsula Visitors Guide* from the **Monterey County Visitors & Convention Bureau,** P.O. Box 1770, Monterey, CA 93942; (888) 221-1010 or (831) 649-1770. Also check with the **Carmel Valley Chamber of Commerce,** 13 W. Carmel Valley Rd., Carmel Valley, CA 93924; (831) 659-4000. (*www.monterey.com* is the website for both Monterey and Carmel.)

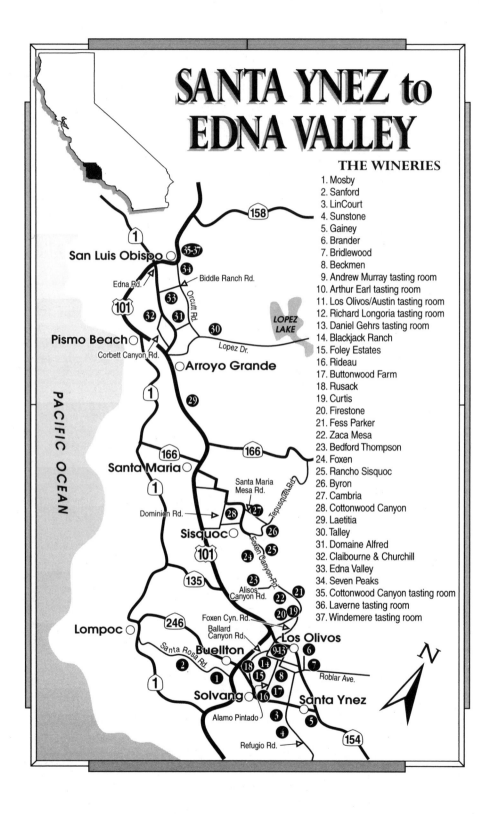

SANTA YNEZ to EDNA VALLEY

THE WINERIES

1. Mosby
2. Sanford
3. LinCourt
4. Sunstone
5. Gainey
6. Brander
7. Bridlewood
8. Beckmen
9. Andrew Murray tasting room
10. Arthur Earl tasting room
11. Los Olivos/Austin tasting room
12. Richard Longoria tasting room
13. Daniel Gehrs tasting room
14. Blackjack Ranch
15. Foley Estates
16. Rideau
17. Buttonwood Farm
18. Rusack
19. Curtis
20. Firestone
21. Fess Parker
22. Zaca Mesa
23. Bedford Thompson
24. Foxen
25. Rancho Sisquoc
26. Byron
27. Cambria
28. Cottonwood Canyon
29. Laetitia
30. Talley
31. Domaine Alfred
32. Claibourne & Churchill
33. Edna Valley
34. Seven Peaks
35. Cottonwood Canyon tasting room
36. Laverne tasting room
37. Windemere tasting room

San Luis Obispo

Edna Rd.

Biddle Ranch Rd.

Orcutt Rd.

LOPEZ LAKE

Lopez Dr.

Pismo Beach

Corbett Canyon Rd.

Arroyo Grande

PACIFIC OCEAN

Santa Maria

Santa Maria Mesa Rd.

Tepusquet Rd.

Dominion Rd.

Sisquoc

Foxen Canyon Rd.

Alisos Canyon Rd.

Lompoc

Santa Rosa Rd.

Foxen Cyn. Rd.

Ballard Canyon Rd.

Buellton

Los Olivos

Roblar Ave.

Solvang

Santa Ynez

Alamo Pintado

Refugio Rd.

Drink no longer water but use a little wine for thy stomach's sake.
— First Timothy 5:23

Chapter Eleven

SOUTH CENTRAL COAST
Santa Barbara and San Luis Obispo counties

Since the outside world discovered the south central coast and its wineries a couple of decades ago, its popularity has snowballed. In vineyard acreage and new wineries, it's the fastest growing wineland in America.

The winegrowing regions of San Luis Obispo and Santa Barbara counties, which had only a handful of wineries two decades ago, now have more than 125. And nearly a hundred of these have tasting rooms, making it one of the most versatile wine-tasting areas in California.

This "discovery" came about in the late 1970s when growers from the Napa Valley and Sonoma began buying grapes from south central coast growers. Many of these growers, seeing wines from their vines winning all sorts of medals, started opening their own wineries. About the same time, several large Napa-Sonoma producers began buying or planting vineyards here, and some even opened branch wineries in the area.

Several years ago, Al Nerelli of Pesenti—one of the area's first wineries—summed it up quite effectively. We'd commented to him that many locally made wines were now rivaling those from Napa.

"Whaddya mean, our wines are as good as the Napa Valley's?" he growled. It was his gruff way of agreeing with me. "Hell, we *are* the Napa Valley!"

I looked at him curiously, not yet aware of the south central coast's Napa-Sonoma invasion.

"They've bought up half the damned area," he continued. "Bob Mondavi and those people. You drink Napa Valley wine, and it's a good bet you're drinkin' south coast wine!"

Of course, he was right on target. "Those people" from Napa, Sonoma and other north coast wineries have discovered a vineland equal to their own. Robert Mondavi, Kendall-Jackson, the huge Wine World conglomerate and others have bought generously into Santa Barbara and San Luis Obispo counties.

Local folks have known for years what outsiders have now discovered: The south central coast provides ideal conditions for premium wine grapes. This is hill country, seamed by rough ridges that cradle river valleys leading to the sea. Cooling breezes and morning fogs temper the summer sun, creating a proper grape-growing climate. Chardonnay, Merlot, Cabernet Sauvignon and Zinfandel do exceptionally well here.

GEOGRAPHIC NOTE: As we researched the original edition of this book more than a decade ago, some San Luis Obispo and Santa Barbara county winery folks said this chapter should be called "Central Coast." This is the geographic term used locally, and this region is part of the Central Coast AVA or Approved Viticultural Area. However, the Central Coast AVA is much broader, extending all the way north to the Livermore Valley and southern Santa Clara County. The region covered by this chapter occupies only the southern half of the huge Central Coast AVA. Further, this area is twice as close to Los Angeles as it is to San Francisco. "South central coast" is a better geographic term.

The wineries in these two counties have drawn an interesting mix of personalities—from veteran winemakers to entrepreneurs to change-of-life second career people. Among these personalities are a former TV star, a onetime Miss America, the son of one of America's largest tire makers, the owners of a chain of Mexican restaurants, the creator of a cardroom game, a baseball scout and a former Indianapolis 500 racer. Some started making their wines with lots of money and the most modern equipment that it could buy. Others began by floating loans on their homes and crushing their first grapes in garbage cans with baseball bats.

Four vineyard areas

The vines and wineries are focused in four areas, two in each of the counties. Santa Barbara's winelands are in the Santa Ynez Valley around Solvang and Buellton and in the Santa Maria Valley, east of the town by that name. Although most of the wineries are in the Santa Ynez Valley, most of the county's more than 10,000 vineyard acres are on the Santa Maria flood plain. San Luis Obispo County's vinelands are concentrated in the Edna and Arroyo Grande valleys inland from Arroyo Grande, and the Templeton-Paso Robles-Estrella River Valley area.

Whites thrive in the cooler Santa Ynez, Santa Maria and Edna-Arroyo Grande regions while reds become big and bold in the summer heat of the Paso Robles area.

Compared with Sonoma and Napa, the south central coast became a major premium wine producer almost overnight. Among wineries open to visitors, only Pesenti and York Mountain date back more than twenty-five years. Most of the others have emerged since the late 1970s and new ones are blooming rapidly. This is particularly true in the Paso Robles region, where nearly forty new wineries have opened in recent years.

All of this adds up to good tasting and uncrowded touring for the visitor. Although not tightly bunched like those in the Sonoma-Napa areas, the wineries are easily reached and regional vintners' associations offer free maps.

The facilities range from elegant to funky and they're tucked into some of the prettiest valleys and rolling hill country in California. This is a classic slice of the oak-chaparral woodland climate zone.

Manmade attractions abound as well. The Pacific coast provides an abundance of recreation, from clam digging in Pismo to sunning off Santa Barbara. Los Padres National Forest lures hikers and reservoirs lure boaters. The region's five missions—Santa Barbara, Santa Inez, La Purísima Concepcion, San Luis Obispo and San Miguel—are havens of California history.

SANTA BARBARA COUNTY

Despite the youth of the county's wine industry, vines go deeply into Santa Barbara County's historic roots. The first cuttings likely were planted shortly after the founding of Mission Santa Barbara in 1786. Other vines followed with the establishment of Mission Santa Inez in 1804 in the Santa Ynez Valley.

Rancher Don Jose de Ortega predates even the missions; he arrived in 1769 and developed the largest rancho in the county. During the late 1700s, he planted extensive vineyards and sold wine to his neighbors and to folks in the emerging pueblo of Santa Barbara.

The Santa Ynez Valley had hundreds of acres of vines and several wineries until Prohibition shut them down. They weren't re-established after Repeal. Following an extended dry spell, the first major vineyards were planted by Richard Sanford in 1971, followed by Leonard Firestone and his son Brooks in 1974. Members of the huge tire and rubber family, the Firestones decided they'd rather make wine than whitewalls.

The Santa Barbara coastline is curiously shaped, taking a sharp right-angle turn at Point Conception to face south instead of west. This invites a west-to-east Pacific air flow that moderates the summer sun, providing proper temperatures for Chardonnay, Riesling, Merlot and other cool-weather grapes. The Santa Ynez Valley now has nearly twenty-five wineries; more than half of them host visitors.

However, more people come to see the deliberately cute Danish village of Solvang than to tour wineries. A group of Danes arrived in 1910 to establish a colony and school beside Mission Santa Inez. The name of their hamlet is Danish for "Sunny Field." Since World War II, this collection of Scandinavian architecture has grown into one of the largest theme villages in America. Cross-timbered buildings abound and windmills creak in the wind, pumping nothing but atmosphere. Scores of shops sell import giftwares, restaurants serve *aebleskivers* and *smörgasbord*, and gas lamps flicker images of old Copenhagen.

The valley also is home to thoroughbred farms and elegant ranch estates with château-like mansions behind expansive lawns and neat white painted fences. Many of these shelter lifestyles of the rich and famous. Luminaries

---

WINERY CODES ● *T* = tasting with no fee; *T$* = tasting for a fee; *GT* = guided tours; *GTA* = guided tours by appointment; *ST* = self-guiding or informal tours; ✕ = picnic area; ⌂ = gift shop or a good giftware selection.

WINE PRICES ● *$* = average price under $10 per bottle; *$$* = $10 to $14; *$$$* = $15 to $19; *$$$$* = $20 or more

A demonstration plot at Gainey Vineyard in the Santa Ynez Valley exhibits grape varieties and trellis styles. A couple of visitors discuss some of the finer points of Semillon.

such as Ronald and Nancy Reagan, Bo Derek and Mike Nichols own ranches and horse farms here. Michael Jackson's Neverland and Fess Parker's estate are just down the road from one another. The Parker spread, however, is not a hideaway but a working winery open to the public. Some of the area's wineries are quite elaborate, reflecting the overall opulence of this valley. This also is reflected in some of the valley's wine prices, which rival those of the Napa Valley estates. On the other hand, many wineries here are quite modest, with prices to match.

SANTA YNEZ VALLEY WINERY TOUR ● Begin not in Solvang but in **Buellton,** a neat and prim little town four miles west on Highway 101. Its primary presence is Anderson's, a large restaurant and gift shop. It dates back to 1924 when Juliette Anderson came up with a pretty tasty recipe for split pea soup. Anderson billboards, with Sweet-Pea and Ha-Pea splitting peas, are familiar sights throughout the state. A cellar tasting room offers samples of sweet fruit wines for small fee.

From Anderson's, head south on the town's wide Avenue of the Flags, which blends into Santa Rosa Road after a mile. As it swings sharply to the right, continue straight ahead into **Mosby Winery**, which is within sight of the freeway. About four miles beyond is **Sanford Winery**, on the left.

Now backtrack to Buellton and follow State Highway 246 to and through **Solvang.** Go about two miles beyond town and turn right onto Refugio

Road at a traffic signal. **LinCourt Winery** soon appears on your right. Continue another quarter of a mile and you'll see the handsome Spanish adobe style **Sunstone Winery**, also on the right, just short of the Santa Ynez River bridge. Return to Highway 246 and continue east. You'll pass through a small swatch of the Santa Ynez Indian reservation, home to the **Chumash Casino**. It offers the usual Indian gaming lures; (800) 728-9997. Just beyond is **The Gainey Vineyard** on your right, about half a mile short of the highway 246-154 junction.

Swing left onto State Highway 154 and drive about 3.5 miles to Roblar Avenue. Turn right and quickly left, following signs to **The Brander Vineyard.** Now, put it in reverse and go east on Roblar (without crossing Highway 154) about a mile to the handsome **Bridlewood Winery.** Retrace your route on Roblar, cross Highway 154 and then continue straight ahead as Roblar veers the right. Follow signs and curving vineyard lanes to **Beckmen Vineyards**. To get back to Roblar, turn left just outside the lane that led to Beckmen, go a short distance to a stop sign and turn left again.

Follow Roblar into the Victorian style town of **Los Olivos**, blending onto Grand Avenue. This tiny and tidy town contains a startling concentration of tasting rooms. Occupying assorted old storefronts and cottages, they form a winetasters' row along Grand Avenue, starting at the "flagpole corner" of Alamo Pintado Avenue. In addition to several winery-specific tasting parlors, you can pause at **Los Olivos Tasting Room and Wine Shop**, which offers sips—for a fee—from area wineries that have no tasting rooms. It's open daily 11 to 5:30; (805) 688-7406; MC/VISA. The various sipping parlors—all in a row on the left side of Grand Avenue—are **Andrew Murray Vineyards,** the aforementioned Los Olivos Tasting Room, **Arthur Earl Winery, Los Olivos Vintners, Richard Longoria Wines** and **Daniel Gehrs Wines.**

The next several wineries are along Alamo Pintado *Road*, not to be confused with Alamo Pintado *Avenue*, which is the main cross street in downtown Los Olivos. To get there, go west from the flagpole on Alamo Pintado *Avenue* for a couple of blocks, cross a bridge and turn left onto Santa Barbara Avenue. After about a mile, Santa Barbara becomes—at a stop sign—Alamo Pintado *Road*. Got that?

Your first winery, just over a mile from Los Olivos, is **Blackjack Ranch Vineyards** on an upslope to your right. Less than a mile beyond, just past a stop sign, is **Foley Estates** on your right. Just below on the left is **Rideau Vineyard,** set back off the road and reached by an evergreen-lined lane. Continue briefly on Alamo Pintado and you'll encounter **Buttonwood Farm Winery,** also on your left. A short distance beyond is State Highway 246 and a right turn puts you back in Solvang. You're probably ready to hit some gift shops and then graze through a *smörgasbord* in one of the town's many Danish restaurants.

Mosby Winery • T$ ST ⚔

9496 Santa Rosa Rd. (P.O. Box 1849), Buellton, CA 93427; (805) 688-2415. (www.mosbywines.com) Daily 10 to 4. Most varieties except grappa tasted for a small fee; MC/VISA, DISC. Some wine related gift items; a few picnic tables near the tasting room.

The Mosby Winery occupies an old red barn with an attractive little tasting room tucked into one end. A restored 1853 adobe home will transport you—metaphysically, at least—far from the freeway rumbling nearby. The adobe's occupants Bill and Jeri Mosby started Vega Vineyards here in 1979, then decided to use their family name in 1985. The wine business is quite a departure from Bill's earlier endeavors. A native of Klamath Falls, Oregon, he attended Oregon State University and was twice the Pacific Coast wrestling champion. He attended dental school and began making wines as a hobby before going from dentistry to full time winemaking. Dentistry didn't qualify him for his present occupation. He earned a food science and enology degree from U.C. Davis.

Tasting notes: The list is distinctly Cal-Italian, including medal winning Pinot Grigio, Dolcetto, Nebbiolo and Sangiovese, small lots of Teroldego and Primitivo, plus some quite fine Chardonnays. (Serious students of Zin will know that Primitivo is a clonal twin and thus ancestor to Zinfandel.) Several powerful Italian brandies—Grappa, *Distillato di Prugne Selvaggie* and *Aqua di Lampone* (raspberry)—are sold, although not tasted, at the winery. Wine prices: *$$ to $$$$.*

Sanford Winery ● T ✕

7250 Santa Rosa Rd., Buellton, CA 93427; (805) 688-3300. Daily 11 to 4; MC/VISA, AMEX. Most varieties tasted. Picnic area beside a creek.

This mid-sized winery occupies a bucolic creek hollow, just uphill from Santa Rosa Road. Scattered winery buildings are deliberately rustic; some were fashioned of scrap lumber from dairy barns that once stood here. The tasting room is distinctively funky, with weathered wood siding and a twig-roofed *ramada* out front. Books about wine and other subjects share shelf space with some impressive winetasting awards. A pot-bellied stove and comfortable chairs occupy one area of the room and a sleeping pooch usually occupies the doorway. Richard and Thekla Sanford planted some of the valley's first grapes in 1971. They began making wine ten years later in San Luis Obispo County before moving to this part of the Santa Ynez Valley in 1983.

Tasting notes: The Sanfords' wines frequently gain *grand prix*, sweepstakes awards and platinum medals. The list is short and excellent—a flowery, crisp Sauvignon Blanc; nutty-spicy and complex Chardonnay; and a soft, lush and low tannin Pinot Noir. Prices: *$$ to $$$$.*

Vintners choice: "Our Chardonnay and Pinot Noir have both received international awards," boasts the winery's Shelley Smith.

LinCourt Vineyards ● T ST ✕

343 N. Refugio Rd., Santa Ynez, CA 93460; (805) 688-8381. (www.lincourtvineyards.com) Daily 10 to 5; MC/VISA. Most varieties tasted. Wine related items and specialty foods. Sheltered picnic area; self-guiding tours.

Founded in 1979 as Santa Ynez Valley Winery by Doug and Candace Scott, this small facility was purchased in 1996 by the Foley family, owners of Foley Estates Vineyard; see below. The curious name comes from the Foleys' two daughters, Linda and Courtney. The winery occupies the site—and one of the cow barns—of a former dairy. Signs identify varietal vines that fan out below the neat gray tasting room. Picnic tables on the vineyard-view porch offer an inviting rest stop.

Tasting notes: All LinCourt wines are aged in French barrels, giving them a distinctive but subtle oak flavor. The brief list, balanced between whites and reds, includes a couple of buttery and toasty Chardonnays, a crisp and floral Viognier, a Pinot Noir with lots of berries and that soft hint of oak, a full-flavored and peppery Syrah and an assertive yet soft and berry-like

Cabernet Sauvignon. Prices are moderate when compared with most other Santa Ynez Valley wines: **$$ to $$$$**.

Sunstone Vineyards and Winery ● T$ GTA ✕

125 Refugio Rd., Santa Ynez, CA 93460; (800) 313-WINE or (805) 688-WINE. (www.sunstonewinery.com) Daily 10 to 4; MC/VISA, AMEX. Most varieties tasted for a modest fee, which includes the glass. A few wine logo items; courtyard picnic area; tours of wine caves by appointment.

Fred and Linda Rice have created one of the valley's most striking wineries on the banks of the Santa Maria River. It was completed in 1994 on land purchased in 1989, yet it appears to be a couple of centuries old. The appealing facility has been fashioned as an early French country estate, complete with adobe walls and a courtyard of hard-packed earth. Gnarled oaks, around which the winery was built, add to the sense of antiquity. Rough tiles form the floor of the tasting room and much of the attached winery has been bunkered into a low hill. Step into the earthen aging cellars and again you're transported back a pair of centuries. Even the pleasantly musty aroma is convincing. Out front, picnic tables in the courtyard offer views of the river and surrounding hilly countryside.

Tasting notes: Winemaker Blair Fox likes to keep things basic, thus producing complex, full-flavored wines with minimal filtering. Organic grapes are used whenever possible. The result is pleasingly herbal wines with pronounced varietal flavors. From the brief list, we sampled a fruity and soft Chardonnay, an exceptional Merlot with a great herbal-spicy nose and taste, a big and complex yet soft Syrah, and an outstanding Cabernet Sauvignon that was mellow and yet had enough tannin to encourage aging. A recent arrival is a fruity and almost tropical flavored Viognier. Prices: **$$$ to $$$$**.

Vintners choice: "Merlot, Syrah and Viognier" said Fox, a winemaker of few words.

The Gainey Vineyard ● T$ GT ✕

3950 E. Highway 246 (P.O. Box 910), Santa Ynez, CA 93460. Daily 10 to 5; MC/VISA. Modest fee for tasting current releases, which includes a souvenir glass. Picnic tables in a vineyard garden. Guided tours daily at 11, 1, 2 and 3.

The winding, pepper tree-lined drive, the carefully landscaped Spanish style winery and its gleaming high-tech equipment speak of moneyed elegance. Wine columnist Robert Lawrence Balzer once called Gainey "one of the most beautiful wineries in the world." It also offers an excellent educational tour, starting with a small demonstration vineyard exhibiting various grape varietals and different styles of trellising. From there, visitors pass through the high tech winery, then return to the refined tasting room—furnished with French antiques—for a personally conducted tasting.

The Daniel Gainey family, owners of a 2,000-acre Arabian horse ranch, created this refined facility in 1984. Presumably, their investment has been returned, for their wines are winning a goodly share of awards.

Tasting notes: The Sauvignon Blanc was clean, crisp and wonderfully fruity. Chardonnay was spicy-nutty and lush with hints of oak. A Cabernet was full-bodied with strong tannins and a pleasant oak touch, suitable for laying away. Overall, the Gainey wines are excellent. Prices: **$$ to $$$$**.

Vintners choice: "They're all great but our limited selection Pinot Noir is exceptional," exudes the winery's Karen Owens.

The Brander Vineyard ● T ✗

2401 Refugio Rd. (P.O. Box 92), Los Olivos, CA 93441; (800) 970-9979 or (805) 688-2455. (www.brander.com) Daily 10 to 5; MC/VISA, AMEX. Most varieties tasted. Some wine related gift items; small picnic area.

C. Frederick "Fred" Brander began planting grapes in 1975, then he made his first wine—a Sauvignon Blanc—at a neighbor's winery. It won a gold medal at the Los Angeles County Fair—the first ever won by a Santa Barbara County vintner—and Fred knew he was on the right track. One of the Santa Ynez Valley's first wineries, it now produces about 9,000 cases of estate wines a year. In addition to the Brander label, the winery has a second line called Domaine Santa Barbara, featuring Burgunian style wines from vines grown in the county.

The complex includes an Italianate château that houses the spacious tasting room and—in bucolic contrast—a weathered barn as the main winery.

Tasting notes: Brander's wines are excellent, exhibiting strong varietal character and still winning medals. Sauvignon Blanc is still the flagship wine, produced in several tasty versions. Fred also makes a smooth and fruity Semillon, a couple of fine Chardonnays, Pinot Gris, Pinot Noir, Cabernet Franc and a non-wimpy pink wine made from Grignolino grapes called *Bouillabaisse Rosé.* Prices: *$$ to $$$.*

Bridlewood Winery ● T$ ✗ ⛩

3555 Roblar Ave., Santa Ynez, CA 93460; (800) 467-4100 or (805) 688-9000. (www.bridlewoodwinery.com) Daily 10 to 5; MC/VISA. Most wines tasted for a fee, which includes a souvenir glass; also wines sold by the glass. Tasteful selection of giftwares and specialty foods; picnic tables on landscaped patios.

A tree-shaded lane leads through vineyards to the most elegant winery complex in the Santa Ynez Valley. The winery and visitor center—too elegant to be called a mere tasting room—have a distinctive California mission look, with beige stucco walls, red tile roof and even a *campanile* or bell tower. The look is no accident and this property wasn't always a winery. It was an Arabian horse ranch and equestrian rehabilitation center, established in the 1970s by the Elam family and styled after Mission San Diego, which was a family favorite.

The 105-acre estate was acquired in the 1990s by Cory Holbrook, who had made his mark as a wholesale florist in Medford, Oregon. He opened the visitor facility to the public in 1999. It's a handsome affair, surrounded by landscaped gardens, lawns, pools and grassy picnic areas.

Tasting notes: The Bridlewood focus is on Chardonnay, Pinot Noir, Sauvignon Blanc, Syrah and other Rhône varietals. Among our choices were a dark and spicy Mourvèdre, a full-flavored Viognier rich with fruit, a Paso Robles Zinfandel with lots of berries and light wood, and a rich Syrah aged in American oak. Although Bridlewood produces serious wines, some display a sense of humor. Ranger Red, a blend of Zinfandel and Grenache, is a good everyday drinking wine. Saddlesore Rosé is an assertive pink made from Zinfandel and Syrah. Prices are quite modest for all of this elegance: *$ to $$$.*

Beckmen Vineyards ● T ✗

2670 Ontiveros Rd. (P.O. Box 542), Los Olivos, CA 93441; (805) 688-8664. (www.beckmenvineyards.com) Daily 10 to 4; MC/VISA. Most varieties tasted. Small selection of giftwares. Pleasant picnic area by a pond.

This inviting vineyard-rimmed winery is built around a tree-shaded ranch yard with a pool and rose gardens. It was established in 1985 by David and Margy Houtz, then purchased by Tom and Judy Beckmen in 1994. He arrived in the wine business by a rather curious route. As founder of Roland Corporation US, he pioneered electronic music, including computer-generated melodies. He and his wife—who also has a musical background—focus on Rhône style wines. Their son Steve, detoured from a planned archaeology career, is the vineyardist.

The winery occupies a redwood barn, where the Beckmens produce about 3,000 cases a year. The family pours selections in an airy cottage tasting room with an atrium ceiling.

Tasting notes: The list is small, topped by a pair of full flavored Chardonnays. The rest of the wines are hearty reds—a nicely balanced Merlot, a medium bodied propriety blend of Cabernet Franc and Merlot called *Atelier*, a spicy and dark Nebbiolo and a hearty Cabernet Sauvignon with a hint of oak. The list finishes with a fruity Muscat Canelli with a hint of sweetness. Prices: *$$ to $$$$.*

Andrew Murray Vineyards tasting room ● T$

2901-A Grand Ave. (P.O. Box 718), Los Olivos, CA 93441; (805) 693-9644. Daily except Tuesday, 11 to 6; MC/VISA. Most varieties tasted for a fee. Good selection of gift items.

The Murray operation might be described as a son-and-father enterprise. James Murray and his wife Fran sold their chain of Los Angeles-area Mexican restaurants in the mid-1990s and "retired" to the Santa Ynez Valley to establish a winery with their winemaker son Andrew. True restaurateurs, the parents are avid cooks and both their catered parties and their son's wines have been written up in publications such as *Bon Appetít* and *Gourmet* Magazine.

Tasting notes: Andrew focuses his efforts almost entirely on Rhône varietals. His list consists of a fruity and lush Viogner; a perfumy Marsanne and Roussanne blend called *Cuvée de l'Avenir*; another proprietary blend of Marsanne, Roussanne and Viogner called *Enchanté*, a full-bodied Syrah with touches of Carignane and Grenache; a Syrah, Grenache and Mourvèdre bend called *Espérance*; and a full-bodied Hillside Reserve Syrah. Prices: *$$$ to $$$$.*

Arthur Earl Winery tasting room ● T$

2921 Grand Ave., Los Olivos, CA 93441; (800) 646-EARL or (805) 693-177. (www.arthurearlwinery.com) Daily 11 to 6; MC/VISA. Most wines tasted for a fee; includes logo glass. Small giftware selection.

This small Santa Ynez two-family winery produces about 2,500 cases a year at their nearby vineyards. Two family? That's right; the Arthur and the Earl families started the winery a few years ago, and presumably could have named it the Earl Arthur Winery. Either way, it has won a sizable collection of medals.

Tasting notes: The winery is following the current trend toward lesser known varietals from the Rhône Valley and Italy. We sampled a French Roussanne with a nice tropical fruit flavor; a rich, berry-like Nebbiolo from Italy's Piedmont area; and a crisp, clean Pinot Grigio. Others on the list include the more familiar Grenache, Merlot and Cabernet Sauvignon. Prices: *$$ to $$$.*

Los Olivos Vintners/Austin Cellars • T 📷

2923 Grand Ave. (P.O. Box 636), Los Olivos, CA 93441-0636; (800) 824-8584 or (805) 688-9665. (www.losolivosvintners.com) Daily 11 to 6; MC/VISA, AMEX. Most varieties tasted. Good selection of wine related items and specialty foods.

Established in 1983 by Tony Austin, the fourth-generation son of a Sonoma Winemaker, Austin Cellars was purchased in 1992 by a corporation headed by Arthur and Nancy White. Initially, they commuted from the East Coast, where Art was in the computer business. How did the Whites, three thousand miles away, learn about Tony's winery? Nancy is a native of Santa Barbara and they were already fans of Austin wines. Why not, they reasoned, capture the source? Wines are tasted in the pleasant environment of a refurbished turn-of-the-century cottage.

Tasting notes: Wines are marketed under both the Los Olivos and Austin Cellars brands; the former being higher end and the latter designed for "everyday drinking." We sampled the Austin line, which continues the winery's tradition of producing tasty, inexpensive wines with good varietal flavor and nice herbal touches. The Chardonnays are rich and full bodied with vanilla hints of oak and Sauvignon Blanc is pleasingly light and fruity. A medium bodied Pinot Noir and a Cabernet with lots of berry flavor comprise the red list. The Los Olivos Vintner labels include Chardonnay, Merlot, sweet Muscat and Merlot Port. Prices: *$ to $$$.*

Richard Longoria Wines • T$ ✕ 📷

2935 Grand Ave., Los Olivos, CA 93441; (805) 688-0305. (www.longoriawine.com) Monday, Wednesday-Thursday noon to 4:30; Friday-Sunday 11 to 4:30; closed Tuesday. Modest fee for tasting. Good giftware selection; adjacent picnic area.

Rich Longoria has been making wines for others in the Santa Ynez Valley since the 1970s. He and his wife Diana established their own small winery in 1982, and now produce about 5,000 cases a year. They opened their tasting room on Grand Avenue in 1998. It's housed in a funky old pressed-tin building with a landscaped patio garden to one side.

Tasting notes: Longoria's list is brief and traditional, focusing on long-established French varietals. Drawn from various areas of the south central coast and all exhibiting strong varietal characteristics, his wines are expertly crafted and not inexpensive. The list consists of Chardonnay, Pinot Noir, Cabernet Franc, Merlot and Syrah. Prices: *$$$$*

Daniel Gehrs Wines • T 📷

2939 Grand Ave. (P.O. Box 344), Los Olivos, CA 93441; (805) 693-9686. (www.dgwines.com) MC/VISA. Most wines tasted. Extensive selection of giftware items.

Veteran vintner Gehrs has made wine for several other California wineries since the 1970s, then he started his own label in the Santa Ynez Valley in 1991. However, busy Dan continued making wine for nearby Zaca Mesa from 1993 until 1997. Now his own boss, he still finds time to act as a consultant and winemaker for several other valley wineries and grape growers. His tasting room occupies the rustically cute old Heather Cottage along winetasters' row in downtown Los Olivos. Its several rooms are decked out with an interesting assortment of wine logo items and giftwares.

Tasting notes: The Gehrs list represents a brief cross section of currently fashionable wines, ranging from French classics to some of the newer types. The wines, all with strong varietal character, include Pinot Blanc, Sauvignon Blanc, a Grenache-Syrah blend, Barbera, Pinot Noir, Cabernet Sauvignon, Cabernet Franc, black Muscat and a rich Fireside Port.

Blackjack Ranch Vineyard & Winery • T ✗

2205 Alamo Pintado Rd., Solvang, CA 93463; (805) 686-9922. (www.blackjackranch.com) Daily 11 to 5 in summer, Friday-Sunday 11 to 5 the rest of the year; MC/VISA. Select varietals tasted. Small selection of gift items; view picnic area.

Established in 1998 by Roger Wisted, this winery occupies a barnboard structure on an upslope above the vineyards. The deliberately rustic tasting room, built of wood salvaged from old barn buildings, offers a view of those vineyards. The tasting counter, made of wood from the old Solvang Bowling Alley, has barstools, so tasting here is an unhurried event. The adjacent wine cellar offers a "Hall of Fame" display of classic wines from California.

Like Tom Beckmen (above), Wisted came into the wine business from a rather curious direction. Since an old law in the California code prohibited the playing of "21" or blackjack, he devised and patented a 22-point game called California Blackjack, which could be played legally. Starting in 1990, he licensed the game to scores of casinos and cardrooms, and from his profits, he purchased an old ranch and created this winery. He opened his tasting room and released his first wines in 2000.

Tasting notes: The list focuses on buttery, full-flavored Chardonnays, and a reserve was a recent gold medal winner at the Orange County Fair. Other wines are berry-flavored and medium bodied Pinot Noir, an outstanding Bordeaux blend called *Harmonie*, and a rather hearty rosé called *Vin Gris*, made from Mourvèdre grapes. The everyday wine—not really inexpensive—is *La Mas Rouge* (Farmhouse Red), made from Mourvèdre and Syrah grapes. Prices: *$$ to $$$$.*

Foley Estates Vineyard & Winery • T$ ✗ 📷

1711 Alamo Pintado Rd., Solvang, CA 93463; (805) 688-8554. Daily 10 to 5; MC/VISA. Most varieties tasted for a fee, which includes the logo glass. Wine related gift items; picnic deck with vineyard view.

Foley Estates is a handsome winery, housed in a weathered red barn tucked beneath giant oaks above hillside vineyards. A picnic deck off the tasting room offers valley views. The facility has gone through several ownerships in recent decades. Fashioned from an old dairy barn, it was established as one of the Santa Ynez Valley's first wineries in 1978 by Dr. J. Campbell Carey and his wife Mary Louise. In 1987, they sold it to Brooks and Kate Firestone of the nearby Firestone Vineyard. The Firestones then sold it in 1997 to William Foley, whose business holdings have included the Carl's, Jr., hamburger chain and a pair of title companies.

The tasting room occupies a cute yellow and white trimmed cottage. An exceptionally appealing picnic deck sits just outside, shaded by giant oak trees. The view down through the vineyards is a rural joy.

Tasting notes: Two whites, Chardonnay and Sauvignon Blanc, were fruit-filled and perfectly balanced. The brief list also features a La Cuesta Vineyard Merlot with wonderful berry taste and hints of oak; and a La Cuesta Cabernet Sauvignon aged eighteen months in French oak, with deep color, great complexity and a nice peppery undertone. Other than the mid-teens Sauvignon Blanc, prices are not inexpensive, with some climbing toward $40. Prices: **$$ to $$$$.**

Rideau Vineyard ● T$ ✕ 📷

1562 Alamo Pintado Rd., Solvang, CA 93464; (805) 688-0717. (www.rideauvineyard.com) Daily 11 to 4:30; MC/VISA. Tasting fee includes logo glass. Nice giftware selection; picnic areas on shaded lawns.

For years, this valley had been a weekend retreat for New Orleans native and successful southern California businesswoman Iris Rideau. She purchased part of the historic Pintado Ranch with the intention of restoring its 1884 adobe ranch house during her spare time. Instead, she wound up developing a winery, which has become a full-time pursuit. The ranch has now become a vineyard and the Alamo Pintado Adobe is now an attractively rustic tasting room. Early California furnishings give it special appeal. Outside, the adobe is surrounded by green lawns and ancient oaks, under which picnic tables reside.

Tasting notes: Rideau's winemaker Jim Rutherford crafts his wines mostly from hand-harvested Rhône varietals. Among them are a Syrah and Mourvèdre blend called *Chateauneuf Cuvée* with a great bouquet and taste; a reserve Viognier with a nice full-of-fruit flavor; and a soft, full flavored, malolactic fermented Viognier. Others on the list include Chardonnay, Syrah, Nebbiolo and an inexpensive Vin Blanc made from Chenin Blanc, Viognier and White Riesling. Prices cover a wide range: **$ to $$$$.**

Buttonwood Farm Winery and Vineyard ● T$ ✕ 📷

1500 Alamo Pintado Rd. (P.O. Box 1007), Solvang, CA 93464; (805) 688-3032. (www.buttonwoodwinery.com) Daily 11 to 5; MC/VISA, AMEX. Most varieties tasted for a modest fee, which includes the glass. A few wine logo items, specialty foods and good selection of organically grown produce. Single picnic table near the tasting room.

PICKNICKING AMONG THE VINES

A neat and prim gray cottage houses the Buttonwood tasting room. The winery itself is up the hill a bit. This tidy facility represents an interesting transition for owner Betty Williams. A New Orleans native, she obtained a law degree from the University of Southern California, taught school and then retired and came here to raise raised thoroughbreds. She decided to shift to wines in the late 1980s and planted her first vineyards, along with several organic garden plots. The tasting room opened in 1992, originally combined with a produce mart. Now in her eighties, she still keeps busy on her ranch-turned-winery while finding time for community activities. Her son-in-law Bret Davenport assists in the operation, serving as winery president.

Tasting notes: Although not completely organic, the Buttonwood wines are mostly from pesticide-free grapes. They're made in the French style—earthy and herbal. One of the more interesting offerings is a Rhône varietal rarely bottled in California. It's light and slightly herbal, with a subtle floral finish—a great sunny day wine with light foods. Others on the list are a lush and herbal Sauvignon Blanc that could almost pass for a Chardonnay; a soft and spicy Merlot; a light yet mouth-filling Cabernet Franc; and a big, dark and peppery four-year-old Cabernet Sauvignon. Prices: *$ to $$$*.

FOXEN CANYON-SANTA MARIA WINERY TOUR ● Foxen Canyon is an exceptionally scenic area that extends northwest from Solvang and blends into the broad Santa Maria Valley. From downtown, head north at a traffic light on Atterdag Road. It soon becomes Chalk Hill Road, which shortly ends at Ballard Canyon Road. Turn right onto Ballard Canyon and follow its twisting course two miles to **Rusack Vineyards** on an upslope to your left. You've not yet reached Foxen Canyon, although we've placed Rusack on this route for navigational purposes. Continue on Ballard Canyon Road's winding and scenic course for a couple of miles more then spiral down to the edge of Los Olivos. When Ballard Canyon Road reaches Highway 154, turn left across the highway and you're on the scenic although often bumpy Foxen Canyon Road. A sign says you're on the Foxen Canyon wine trail.

Continue about four miles to Zaca Station Road and you'll see **Curtis Winery** across the road and just to your left. A brief drive left on Zaca Station then leads to **Firestone Vineyard,** up a hill on your right. Return to Foxen and follow it a mile or so to the striking **Fess Parker Winery** on the right; a short distance beyond is **Zaca Mesa Winery** on the left. Less than a mile beyond Zaca Mesa, turn left onto Alisos Canyon Road and follow it 4.5 miles to **Bedford Thompson Winery.**

Return to Foxen Canyon Road and press onward; you'll soon leave rough-hewn Foxen Canyon and enter the broad **Santa Maria Valley.** As the terrain begins to soften, watch for **Foxen Vineyard** on the left. Then continue into the valley, take a sharp right turn (just beyond an old twin steeple hilltop chapel) and follow a narrow road to **Rancho Sisquoc Winery.** From here, continue along Foxen Canyon for a mile, turn right onto Tepusquet Road and follow its gravelly course across the usually dry Santa Maria River to **Byron Vineyard and Winery.**

From Byron, retrace your route briefly on Tepusquet Road, then veer to the right away from the river crossing, which puts you on Santa Maria Mesa Road. Follow it less than a mile to **Cambria Winery and Vineyard,** uphill to your right at the end of Chardonnay Lane. Continue northwest for a few miles on Santa Maria Mesa, go left onto Foxen Canyon Road, then turn right after a mile onto Orcutt Gary Road. You'll shortly hit a stop sign at Old Dominion Road; go right for a quarter of a mile to **Cottonwood Canyon Vineyard** on the right. Continue on Old Dominion and you'll soon hit a stop sign and blend back onto Foxen Canyon. Now well paved and smooth, passing through fertile farmlands, it swings to the west and blends into Betteravia Road, which returns you to U.S. 101 in **Santa Maria.** Head north across the Santa Maria River and you're in San Luis Obispo County.

Rusack Vineyards • T$ ✗ 📦

1819 Ballard Canyon Rd., Solvang, CA 93463; (805) 688-1278. Daily 11 to 5; MC/VISA. Most wines tasted for a fee, includes souvenir glass. Some giftwares and deli foods; view picnic area.

This attractive winery, owned by Geoff and Allison Rusack, is bunkered into a ridge above tilted vineyards. Retiring from earlier careers—he was a Santa Monica attorney and she was a Hollywood script writer—they bought the Ballard Canyon Winery in 1992. They opened the tasting room in 1997. The picnic area below the roomy cottage style tasting room is one of the most appealing in California. Picnic tables rest beneath gnarled oaks, some on a deck and some on lawns. All have fine views of the sloping vineyards and distant ridges.

Tasting notes: The brief Rusack list consists mostly of traditional French varietals. Best of the lot were a pair of Chardonnays, one from the Santa Ynez Valley and another drawn from several Santa Barbara County vineyards. Both had lots of fruit with that slightly nutty taste typical of a well-made Chard. Others were a full-flavored Pinot Noir, a fine Cabernet Sauvignon with deep color, a crisp and dry Riesling that recently won a double gold and a rich Muscat Canelli. Prices: *$$ to $$$$.*

Curtis Winery • T$ ✗ 📦

5249 Foxen Canyon Rd. (P.O. Box 244), Los Olivos, CA 93441-0244; (805) 686-8790. (www.curtiswinery.com) Daily 10 to 5. Most varieties tasted for a fee, includes logo glass. Nice selection of clothing and other giftwares; attractive picnic deck.

When the Firestones sold Carey Cellars to the Foley family in 1997, they purchased an old art gallery and surrounding lands to create yet another winery. Like Carey Cellars, the new winery is primarily the realm of Kate Firestone, seeking to make her own mark in the wine business. The gallery has been shaped into a quite handsome tasting room, adjacent to the winemaking complex. All of this sits in a pretty landscaped glen shaded by ancient oaks. A focal point here is an ancient tractor, presumably not used by Kate to till her new vineyards, although she does have a reputation for her hands-on approach. The new winery also puts her closer to her husband's facility, just down the road. In fact, the two are linked by a half-mile hiking trail though vale and vineyard.

The winery's name honors a family ancestor, noted journalist William Elroy Curtis.

Tasting notes: While her husband Brooks offers the more traditional French varietals, Kate has focused on the currently popular Rhône types. Her sort list includes a fruity Rhône blend called Heritage Blanc, a lush and rich

Viognier, a Rhône style Heritage rosé, a soft and fruity blend of five Rhône reds called Heritage California, and excellent Syrah and Viognier. Some of her prices are quite modest: *$ to $$$$.*

Firestone Vineyard • T$ GT ✕ 📷

5000 Zaca Station Rd. (P.O. Box 244), Los Olivos, CA 93441; (805) 688-3940. (www.firestonewine.com) Daily 10 to 4; MC/VISA. Most wines tasted for a fee, includes logo glass. Selection of gift items; courtyard picnic area. Tours start at a quarter past the hour from 10:15 to 3:15.

In 1972, Brooks Firestone focused the wine world's attention on the Santa Ynez Valley when he and his father Leonard planted one of the first post-Prohibition vineyards in the county. The Firestones' present winery, an intriguing complexity of rooflines, is a large brown presence on an oak-studded knoll overlooking the vineyards. Detailed and comprehensive tours through this facility provide views of a gallery of stainless steel tanks and a cellar filled with French and American oak barrels. Participants are then given a personal tasting in an attractive tile floor tasting room overlooking the vineyards and the Santa Ynez Mountains.

Tasting notes: The list includes Chardonnay, Sauvignon Blanc, Johannisberg Riesling, Gewürztraminer, Cabernet Franc, Cabernet Franc rosé, Cabernet Sauvignon, Merlot, Zinfandel, Sauvignon Blanc and Syrah. The rosé is one of the few pinks we like—rich and full of flavor. The Chardonnay, Central Coast Riesling and Sauvignon Blanc all displayed a nice crisp fruitiness with light acid. A Cabernet and Merlot were full flavored yet soft, with gentle finishes. Prices: *$ to $$$.*

Fess Parker Winery • T$ GT ✕ 📷

6200 Foxen Canyon Rd. (P.O. Box 908), Los Olivos, CA 93441; (805) 688-1545. (www.fessparker.com) Daily 10 to 5; MC/VISA. Most varieties tasted for a modest fee. Tours daily at 11, 1 and 3.

Television's Daniel Boone and Davy Crockett didn't swap his coonskin cap for a corkscrew. He's made the two work together at the most opulent winery on the south central coast. Fess Parker's wholesome TV image carries into his real life; he's a down-to-earth family man who shed the trappings of Hollywood decades ago to return to the soil. He's also as down-home astute as the TV heroes he played. Early in his career, he began investing his Hollywood earnings in land, and he owns a couple of cattle ranches.

He and his wife Marcy became interested in winemaking after visiting Napa's Silverado Vineyards, which was established by Lillian Disney, Walt's widow. It was Disney who started Parker's TV career by starring the tall Texan in *Davy Crockett: Indian Fighter*. In 1987, the Parkers bought their first vineyard land in the Santa Ynez Valley, where they'd been living since 1958. The first Fess Parker wines, complete with the coonskin cap on the label, were released in 1989.

The strikingly handsome winery and tasting room is suggestive of a huge pitched-roofed French château outside and an elegant hunting lodge within. This is a family operation, with Parker—now 70-plus—as the mover, shaker and marketer. His son Eli is the winemaker, while wife Marcy and daughter Ashley help run the day-to-day operation. Fess doesn't hesitate using his TV hero image to promote his wines and yes, you can buy coonskin caps in the tasting room.

Tasting notes: Although Fess admits he's no wine expert, his son has learned the craft well, aided by consulting winemaker Jed Steele, who brought fame and awards to the Kendall-Jackson winery. We tasted a couple of fine, buttery and herbal Chardonnays; and a complex and full flavored American Tradition Reserve Syrah, rated very highly by wine critics. The rather extensive list also includes Viognier, a red blend called *Mélange du Rhône*, Chenin Blanc, Pinot Blanc, Sauvignon Blanc, a light blend of Dolcetto and other reds, Meritage and a barrel-fermented sparkling wine called Marcella's Blanc de Blanc. Prices: *$$ to $$$$.*

Zaca Mesa Winery ● T ✗

6905 Foxen Canyon Rd. (P.O. Box 899), Los Olivos, CA 93441; (800) 350-7972, ext. 308. (www.zacamesa.com) Daily 10 to 4; MC/VISA, AMEX. Most varieties tasted. Good selection of wine related giftwares and specialty foods. Tours every hour on the half hour from 10:30 to 2:30.

Zaca Mesa's appealing cedar-sided barn of a winery sits in a hollow off Foxen Canyon Road. Here, the view is primarily inward. The building's elongated U-shape forms three sides of a courtyard; sheltering oaks provide the fourth. One can picnic at tables tucked under a roof overhang. A large, appealing hospitality room occupies one end of the winery. We settled before an oversized walnut banquet table to work through the list of six to eight wines.

Owned by John C. Cushman III, Zaca Mesa is one of the area's earlier wineries, dating from 1978; the first vineyards were planted in 1972.

Tasting notes: All wines are estate produced and vineyard designated. Two Chardonnays showed markedly different styles, although both were excellent. The Zaca Vineyards Chardonnay was fruity, fresh and crisp while the Chapel Vineyard Chardonnay was more complex, nutty and buttery. Currently, the winery is focusing on several Rhône varietals, including Syrah, Grenache, Mourvèdre and Viognier. Prices: *$ to $$$$.*

Vintners choice: "Vineyard designated Chardonnays and Rhône varietals," says Zaca's Jim Fiolek. "They're our focus varietals."

Bedford Thompson Winery & Vineyard ● T ✗

9303 Alisos Canyon Rd. (P.O. Box 507), Los Alamos, CA 93440-0507; (805) 344-2107. (www.bedfordthompsonwinery.com) Daily 10 to 5; MC/VISA. Most wines tasted; a few picnic tables near the tasting room.

Bedford Thompson isn't a person; it's two people who have combined their talents to make fine wines. Young, lanky David Thompson grows the grapes and Stefan Bedford, an area vintner for twenty years and formerly with nearby Rancho Sisquoc, makes the wine. They started their partnership in 1994, and now produce about a thousand cases a year.

Its obvious that they're more concerned about producing good wines than creating an attractive environment for tasting the results. The tasting room occupies an extremely rustic, bare-floored ranch cottage beneath old oaks. The tasting counter consists of a slab over a row of wine barrels. A curiously large collection of picnic tables sit out front. The tiny winery doesn't attract large numbers of picnickers, however. Thompson is quite interested in the performing arts and often invites friends out to present summer plays and concerts. A few cassette tapes and CDs of their efforts are available in the tasting rooms.

Tasting notes: Ignore the funky environment and concentrate on the wines. They're among the best and most reasonably priced in the area, and you don't have to buy a souvenir glass. Spiciness seems to be an overall characteristic in Bedford Thompson wines. The Gewürztraminer had a great flowery nose, yet a crisply dry taste; the Pinot Gris was nice and spicy. Our favorite—although we normally lean toward reds—was a malolactic fermented Chardonnay with great fruit flavor with spicy undertones. Others on the Bedford Thompson list were smooth and full flavored Syrah and Cabernet Franc. Prices: *$$ to $$$*.

Foxen Vineyard • ✕
7200 Foxen Canyon Rd., Santa Maria, CA 93454; (805) 937-4251. Friday-Monday noon to 4; MC/VISA. Modest tasting fee; small picnic area.

This rustic winery is tucked among the oaks and vineyards, with a small tasting counter tucked among barrels and tanks. The facility occupies the site of Rancho Tinaquaic, and the winery is housed in a two-century-old barn. It was established in 1987 by a pair of longtime local citizens, Dick Doré and Bill Wathen. Sixth generation valley resident Doré grew up on this ranch, then left to pursue a banking career and later moved to France, where he became intrigued with wine. He moved his family back to the ranch in the 1970s and, after meeting Bill Wathen, started the winery. Wathen, a native of San Luis Obispo, was graduated from Cal Poly with a degree in fruit science. He worked as a vineyardist for several California wineries before joining with Doré in the Foxen partnership.

Tasting notes: A modest fee offers access to the Doré-Wathen list of traditional varietals—Chardonnay, Viognier, Chenin Blanc, Syrah, Merlot, Pinot Noir and Cabernets Sauvignon and Franc. Prices: *$$ to $$$*.

Rancho Sisquoc • T ✕
6600 Foxen Canyon Road, Santa Maria, CA 93454; (805) 934-4332. (www.ranchosisquoc.com) Daily 10 to 4; MC/VISA. Most varieties tasted. Picnic tables on a lawn area.

The long lane into Rancho Sisquoc delivers you to a large, neatly maintained farmyard, the work center of a 38,000 acre cattle ranch and winery. As you approach the winery, note the historic San Ramon Chapel, which also adorns the wine labels. The tasting room is easy to spot—a somewhat weathered brown shed that stands in contrast to the prim white farm buildings. San Franciscans James and Betty Flood purchased the ranch in 1952 and opened their ruggedly handsome, hidden-away winery to the public in 1977. The surrounding ranch was established as a Mexican land grant in 1852.

Tasting notes: Most Sisquoc wines are aged in wood, giving even the whites a nice complexity. Barrel-fermented Sauvignon Blanc and Chardonnay were delicious, with nice spicy-fruity flavors. A Sylvaner, uncommon in this area, was crisp yet fruity rich. Merlot and Cabernet Sauvignon had powerful peppery bouquets and flavors; both were big wines suitable for putting away. Others on the list are lightly sweet Riesling and full flavored Merlot with a nice touch of oak. Prices: *$$ to $$$$*.

Byron Vineyard & Winery • T GT ✕
5230 Tepusquet Rd., Santa Maria, CA 93454; (805) 937-7288. Daily 10 to 4; major credit cards. (www.byronwines.com) Wine related gift items and picnic fare. Picnic tables overlooking Tepusquet River. Guided tours on request.

Byron represents Robert Mondavi's entry into the south central coast wine area. However, founder and managing partner Byron Ken Brown still runs the operation and makes the wine. Byron Vineyard was established by Brown and several partners in 1984, and later purchased by the Mondavi family.

The winery is among the most dramatically situated in the county. Surrounded on three sides by vines, it perches on the wooded rim of a small ravine. Tepusquet Creek rustles beneath the trees, fifty or so feet below. It's an appealing facility, a stylish wood sided barn with vague Spanish-Oriental lines. The tasting room, tucked under a balcony at one end, is done in knotty pine. A landscaped picnic area on the edge of the ravine is a great spot for a lunch break.

Tasting notes: Byron's list offers an interesting mix of wines; all show strong varietal character and most have been medal winners. The list includes Pinot Gris, two fine Chardonnays, and several versions of big, full flavored and deeply purple Pinot Noirs. Prices: *$$ to $$$$.*

Vintners choice: The focus is on premium Burgundian varietals—Chardonnay and Pinot Noir, according to a winery source.

Cambria Vineyard & Winery • T ✕

5475 Chardonnay Lane, Santa Maria, CA 3454; (805) 937-8091. (www.cambriawine.com) Weekends 10 to 5; MC/VISA. Most varieties tasted. A few wine logo items. Picnic tables with a grand valley view.

Cambria is an imposing operation with a forest of stainless steel tanks bunkered into a steep vineyard slope. The adjacent winery is in an industrial-strength cinderblock building. The tasting room occupies one end, identified by a cheerful grape motif stained glass window that adds a flash of color to this otherwise businesslike environment. If the complex is industrially severe, the setting is stunning. Anyone who works here or comes up to sip wine will be treated to a grand sweeping view of the gently rolling Santa Maria Valley far below.

The facility is part of the historic Rancho Tepusquet, a Mexican land grant dating from 1838. Growers planted some of the area's first grapes here in the 1970s, selling their fruit to various vintners, including Kendall-Jackson. In 1987, K-J's Jess Jackson assembled some other investors, bought several of the vineyards and later created this imposing winery.

Tasting notes: The wine list is rather small, focusing on varietals that do best in this rather cool climate. They include Chardonnay, Viognier, Syrah, Sangiovese and Pinot Noir. Prices: *$$ to $$$$.*

Cottonwood Canyon Vineyards • T$ ✕

3940 Old Dominion Rd., Santa Maria; (mailing address: P.O. Box 3459, San Luis Obispo, CA 93403-3459); (805) 937-9063. (www.cottonwoodcanyon.com) Daily 10:30 to 5:30; MC/VISA, AMEX. Most varieties tasted for a modest fee, which includes glass. A few wine logo gift items; small picnic area. A second tasting room is near the San Luis Obispo airport; see page 248.

San Luis Obispo winemaker Norman Beko bought seventy-eight acres of land in the Santa Maria Valley in 1988, and planted Chardonnay and Pinot Noir to produce estate wines. He built his no-nonsense metal sided winery in 1995, then had caves dug into the adjacent slopes for aging cellars. The winery perches on a shelf above a vineyard valley, and a landscaped picnic area offers views of the valley and a distant mountain ridge. The winery building shares space with a small tasting room and a hospitality center, where Norman often hosts special events. He hopes eventually to expand his operation, possibly with a restaurant and bed & breakfast inn.

Tasting notes: Norman focuses primarily on Chardonnays; several are usually available for tasting. They're lush, herbal and buttery. Some were fruity while others exhibit vanilla accents from barrel finishing. The Pinot Noir had a big berry flavor with a soft, complex finish and a slight tannic nip—a typical Burgundian style. On our last visit, we took away a bottle of light, unassuming Bistro Cabernet, which the tasting room host said was a good pizza wine. A phone call to Dominos Pizza from our motel room that night proved that he was right. Prices: *$$ to $$$$.*

SAN LUIS OBISPO COUNTY

With a wider climate range than those Santa Barbara County, San Luis Obispo County vineyards produce hearty reds as well as whites. The Edna-Arroyo Grande valley area, open to Pacific breezes, is noted for its premium whites and full-flavored Pinot Noir. The Paso Robles-Templeton-San Miguel area is sheltered by the Coast Range, providing warmer climates for outstanding Zinfandel and Cabernet.

Edna-Arroyo Grande valleys

The vintners of Edna Valley and Arroyo Grande Valley are new kids on the block. This area northeast of Arroyo Grande shelters eight wineries with the oldest dating back to the 1980s; the first vines were planted here in 1972. Pacific breezes provide natural summer air conditioning that's ideal for Chardonnay and Pinot Noir. Six vintners offer their products for sampling in the valley, while another three wineries have tasting rooms near the San Luis Obispo airport.

EDNA-SAN LUIS OPISPO WINERY TOUR ● This tour begins just east of Arroyo Grande and winds up in a San Luis Obispo industrial area near the airport. Picking up from the end of the Foxen Canyon-Santa Maria River Valley tour, drive about fourteen miles north of **Santa Maria** on U.S. 101. Just south of Arroyo Grande, you'll see the modern **Laetitia Winery** sprouting among hillside vineyards on your right, reached by a short uphill lane. Continue north on U.S. 101, take the Grand Avenue exit and drive east into the old fashioned business district of **Arroyo Grande**. You might want to pause and browse through the shops tucked behind false front and brick façades in the prim, well-maintained downtown area.

Heading east from town, you'll go through several street name changes, although it's easy to stay your course by following signs toward **Lopez Lake**. The route eventually becomes Lopez Drive. Clearing the Arroyo Grande suburbs, you'll enter bucolic **Edna Valley**, rimmed with softly contoured hills. They're green velvet in spring and French-bread beige in summer and fall. An occasional vineyard climbs toward the low horizon. After a few miles on Lopez Drive, just past its junction with Orcutt Road, you'll encounter **Talley Vineyards,** up a rise to your left. Retrace your route briefly on Lopez Drive and turn right (north) onto Orcutt Road. Follow it about three miles to the small **Domaine Alfred** (formerly Chamisal) on your left. Backtrack less than a mile to Tiffany Ranch Road and turn right, following it a mile past opulent country estates and ranches to Corbett Canyon

Road. Turn right and go north past the large Corbett Canyon Vineyards, which no longer hosts visitors. Continue about two miles to Carpenter Canyon Road (Highway 227) and go right; you'll immediately encounter **Claiborne & Churchill Vintners** on your left. Continue north on Carpenter Canyon (which becomes Edna Road) and turn right onto Biddle Ranch Road, following it a short distance to the large **Edna Valley Vineyard** complex on the right. Continue across the Valley on Biddle Ranch Road to Orcutt Road and turn left. You'll soon encounter **Seven Peaks Winery** with a tasting room in a cute yellow schoolhouse.

We must, with some reluctance, remove you from this pretty land of peaks and valleys, since the final three tasting rooms are—good grief!—in an industrial area. Expect to see freight trucks and forklifts; not vineyards. Continue northwest on Orcutt Road a couple of miles, heading into the industrial edge of San Luis Obispo. Turn left onto Tank Farm Road and follow it briefly to a traffic light at Broad Street (Highway 227). If it's a weekend and you haven't visited **Cottonwood Canyon Vineyard**—which was the last stop on our previous tour—you can taste some of its wines at the main winery, which is near San Luis Obispo County airport. To get there, cross Broad Street on Tank Farm, passing just above the airport, turn left (south) on Santa Fe Road for a couple of blocks and go right into a parking area adjacent to several industrial buildings. Look for the small "Cottonwood Canyon tasting room" sign. The winery/tasting room is at the rear of the parking area, in a dull gray concrete building behind a blue-clad chain link fence.

If you've done Cottonwood and/or this isn't a weekend (the only time the airport tasting room is open), turn right onto Broad Street instead of crossing it, and watch on your right for small Capitolio Way; it comes up within a couple of blocks. Go right for a block and then left onto Sacramento Street. The two final tasting rooms and their industrial strength wineries are right on the corner, in side-by-side buildings—**Laverne Vineyards** and **Windemere.** From here, return to Broad Street and go right; you'll soon be in the heart of San Luis Obispo, a vibrant old town that's well worth exploring.

Laetitia Winery ● *T & T$ GTA* ✕ 🍶

453 Tower Grove Dr., Arroyo Grande, CA 93420; (888) 809-VINE or (805) 481-1763. (www.laetitiawine.com) Daily 11 to 6 in spring and summer and 11 to 5 in fall and winter; major credit cards. Up to six wines tasted for no fee; modest fee for reserve wines, tasted Friday through Sunday. Good selection of specialty foods and giftwares; picnic area. Guided tours by appointment.

This handsome winery complex rimmed by its own vineyards occupies a hillside just above Highway 101, providing grand views of the Pacific. Laetitia is an impressive facility, with French château-style buildings and a tile-floored, cathedral ceiling tasting room. It was established in 1982 as Maison Deutz, a French-American venture to produce sparkling wines. Under new American ownership, Laetitia specializes in full flavored Burgundian style varietals. The curious name, incidentally, is Latin for happiness. A chamber off the attractive tasting room often features exhibits of local artists.

The large 1,850-acre wine estate provides a variety of microclimates suited to the nurturing of Pinot Noir, Chardonnay and Pinot Blanc. The winery also produces sparkling wine by the classic *méthode champenoise* process. Laetitia uses what company officials call a "team winemaking approach." It combines the talents of French consultants with American winemakers, led by Bilo Zarif, to create its Burgundian style wines.

Tasting notes: Laetitia's list of French style varietals consists of moderately priced estate Pinot Noir, Chardonnay and Pinot Blanc, plus premium versions of these wines at higher prices. The non-reserve wines we tasted were quite good, including a crispy fruity Sauvignon Blanc, a soft and full-flavored Pinot Noir and a smooth Zinfandel with a hint of oak. Wines from Barnwood Vineyards of the Santa Barbara Highlands viticultural area also are available for sampling here. Prices: *$$ to $$$$.*

Talley Vineyards • T ✕ 🏠

3031 Lopez Dr., Arroyo Grande, CA 93420; (805) 489-0446. (www.tally-vineyards.com) Daily 10:30 to 4:30; MC/VISA. Most varieties tasted. Wine logo gift items and specialty foods. Picnic tables in a gazebo and on a lawn near the tasting room.

A square-shouldered, two-story brown farmhouse first catches your eye. It stands, almost arrogantly, above the surrounding landscape, without need of shielding vegetation. Curiously, the foreground fields sprout not grapevines but bell peppers. The imposing structure is the 1863 El Rincon Adobe, impeccably restored and housing Talley's tasting room and offices. Originally, it was headquarters of a 4,000-acre rancho. El Rincon is a mini-museum as well as a tasting facility. An exhibit room has been furnished with Spanish and early American antiques.

The Talley family has owned this land for three generations. The winery dates back to the late 1980s when Don and Rosemary and their son Brian began producing a select list of wines.

Tasting notes: We sipped an excellent Chardonnay, full of buttery fruit, with a hint of oak; and a soft and fruity Sauvignon Blanc; both were barrel-aged. Among the Talley reds are a soft Italian varietal called Dolcetto, a fine barrel-aged and unfiltered Pinot Noir and a soft and flavorful Zinfandel laced with Sangiovese and Nebbiolo. An inexpensive Bishop's Peak Cuvée is a flavorful blend of Zinfandel and Syrah. Prices: *$ to $$$$.*

Vintner's Choice: "Our Chardonnay and Pinot Noir, both from the family vineyards," said a voice from the tasting room.

Domaine Alfred • T ✕

7525 Orcutt Rd., San Luis Obispo, CA 93401; (805) 541-WINE. (www.domainealfred.com) Friday-Sunday 10 to 5. Most varieties tasted. A few picnic tables nearby.

Originally established as Chamisal Winery, this simple masonry facility closed it doors after the death of founder Norman Gross. Silicon Valley electronics entrepreneur Terry Speizer bought the winery in 1994 and replanted the Chamisal vineyards the following year. Since his expertise was electronics, he brought in Pacific Vineyards president Jim Efird as viticulturist and Steven Dooley Wines president Steven Ross as his enologist. They produced their first Domaine Alfred wines in 1998.

Tasting notes: The winery produces Chardonnay, Pinot Noir and Syrah, mostly from new vines in the adjacent Chamisal Vineyards. Prices: *$$ to $$$.*

Claiborne & Churchill Vintners • T ST ✕

2649 Carpenter Canyon Rd., San Luis Obispo, CA 93401; (805) 544-4066. (www.Claibornechurchill.com) Daily 11 to 5; MC/VISA, AMEX. Most varieties tasted. A few wine logo items.

The Claiborne and Churchill winery can be forgiven for looking like a lopsided barn. It's one of the most organically energy efficient building in these parts and the first commercial building in America made from stacked bales of rice straw. The big bad wolf can't huff and puff and blow it down because it's sealed with stucco. And it maintains ideal temperatures for aging and storing wine—winter and summer. Step inside this curious structure and sidle up to the tasting bar, which occupies one end of the winery. Tours are quite casual here. Fetch your sample of wine and wander—glass in hand— among the aisles of wine barrels, admiring giftwares that have been placed about on assorted tables and shelves.

All of this reflects the eclectic tastes and unusual personalities of the owners, Claiborne (call him Clay) Thompson and his wife Frederika Churchill Thompson. A kid from Little Rock, Clay obtained an advanced degree in Scandinavian studies from Harvard and taught at the University of Michigan. There, he met Frederika, a German language lecturer. Deciding to flee the academic scene, they married and came to California, where he initially worked for minimum wages as a "cellar rat" at nearby Edna Valley Vineyard. The pair save their money, bought vineyard land in 1983 and opened the tasting room in 1995.

Tasting notes: Well, of course the winery offers an everyday drinking wine called Straw Bale White. Other interesting wines on the list are a curiously dry and tasty Muscat, a Gewürztraminer with lots of floral aroma and a crisp taste; and a fine barrel-fermented Chardonnay with a nice oak background. The lone red entry is a light Pinot Noir with lots of fruit. Prices are rather modest for the quality: *$$ to $$$.*

Edna Valley Vineyard • T GT ✕ 📷

2585 Biddle Ranch Rd., San Luis Obispo, CA 93401; (805) 544-9594. Daily 10 to 5; MC/VISA, AMEX. Most varieties tasted. Guided tours hourly weekends from 11 to 3; weekdays by appointment. Picnic area.

A dramatically modern hospitality center, named in honor of Edna Valley Vineyard founder Jack Niven is the centerpiece for one of the area's more successful wineries. Stand at the long tasting counter and you're rewarded with picture window views of the vineyards and several of the volcanic spires called Seven Peaks that rim Edna Valley. The spacious Jack Niven Hospitality Center also offers a fine assortment of giftwares, specialty foods and wine-related items, including a good collection of books on wine. Outside, picnic tables on landscaped grounds invite further lingering to enjoy the valley views.

Nearby are the cellars where this mid-sized winery's 58,000-case production matures. Periodic guided tours will get you there. The winery is operated as a partnership between Paragon Vineyard, the valley's largest grower, and Chalone Wine Group, which also owns Chalone Vineyard, Acacia Winery and Carmenet Vineyard, and co-owns Seven Peaks. The Niven family, the primary stockholders, became involved in the local wine scene after selling their Purity food store chain. Jack's son James is head of Paragon and Edna Valley Vineyards.

Tasting notes: The Paragon Vineyard Chardonnay topped our tasting list; it was buttery, spicy and crisp. Pinot Gris, lightest of the whites, was crisp and refreshing with nice fruit tones. The Pinot Noir was lush and complex, while the Cabernet Sauvignon and Viognier were wonderfully fruity. Prices: *$ to $$$.*

Seven Peaks ● T ✕ 🎁

5828 Orcutt Rd., San Luis Obispo, CA 93401; (805) 781-0777. (www.7peaks.com) Daily 10 to 5; MC/VISA. Nice selection of wine-theme giftwares; picnic area.

Seven Peaks has one of the cutest tasting rooms in the land. It's housed in the cheerful yellow clapboard Independence schoolhouse where local kids hit the books from 1909 until 1954. A county historical landmark, the one-room school has been carefully refurbished and now offers—not books and teachers' dirty looks—but an attractive tasting counter, a good selection of giftwares and a few deli items. This cheery complex also has the most comfortable picnic facility in the land—wrought iron tables with upholstered lounge chairs. The winery is named for the seven volcanic peaks or *morros* that form a dramatic backdrop to Edna Valley. Most of them are visible from here on a good day.

The facility was founded in 1996 as a joint venture between the Niven family and Southcorp Wines of Australia. Southcorp is Australia's leading vineyard owner and the Nivens are longtime south central coast grape growers. In this joint venture, the Nivens provide the grapes and Southcorp makes the wine.

Tasting notes: When Southcorp bought into this venture, it sent one of its winemakers along. Australian Ian Shepherd has created a select list of excellent, full-bodied varietals. Among them are a pair of fine Chardonnays with lots of fruit, including an Edna Valley Reserve that won a recent double gold and best of region; a dark and spicy Pinot Noir with a subtle oak background; a very berry Merlot; a deep purple and herbal Shiraz; and a silky and spicy Cabernet Sauvignon. Prices are quite reasonable for the quality of these wines: *$$ to $$$$.*

Cottonwood Canyon tasting room ● T$

4330 Santa Fe Rd., San Luis Obispo, CA 93401; (805) 549-WINE. Weekends only, 11 to 5; MC/VISA, AMEX. (www.cottonwoodcanyon.com) Most varieties tasted for a small fee.

The main production facility of Cottonwood is in an industrial park near San Luis Obispo Airport, and it offers a small tasting facility, handy for folks from the nearby city. Far more appealing is the rural vineyard site in the Santa Maria River Valley. See page 242 for details and tasting notes.

Laverne Vineyards ● T

3490 Sacramento Dr., Unit E, San Luis Obispo, CA 93401; (805) 547-0616. (www.usawines.com/laverne) Saturday and Sunday noon to 4. Most varieties tasted.

This small winery, established by Peter and Therese Cron, occupies an industrial building near San Luis Obispo County Airport. Peter and son Donald are the winemakers.

Tasting notes: Laverne produces limited quantities of Chardonnay, Cabernet Sauvignon and Pinot Noir, drawing from various south central coast vineyards. Prices: *$$$ to $$$$.*

Windemere/Cathy MacGregor Wines ● T

3482 Sacramento Dr., Unit E, San Luis Obispo, CA 93401; (805) 542-0133. (www.windemerewinery.com) Thursday-Tuesday 11:30 to 5; MC/VISA. Most varieties tasted for a very small fee; includes logo glass.

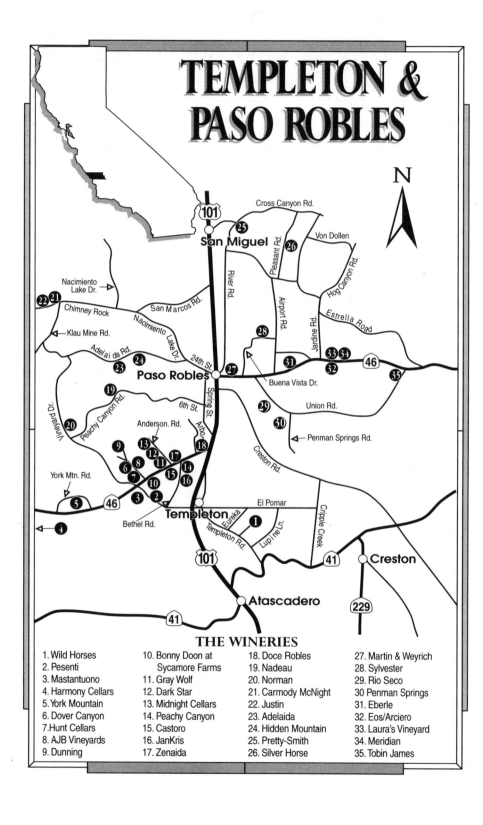

TEMPLETON & PASO ROBLES

N

Cross Canyon Rd.
101
25
San Miguel
Von Dollen
26
Pleasant Rd.
Hog Canyon Rd.
Nacimiento Lake Dr.
22 21
Chimney Rock
San Marcos Rd.
River Rd.
Airport Rd.
Jardine Rd.
Estrella Road
Klau Mine Rd.
Nacimiento Lake Dr.
Adelaida Rd.
28
24th St.
33 34
46
23 24
Paso Robles
27
31
32
35
Buena Vista Dr.
19
Spring St.
6th St.
Union Rd.
Vineyard Dr.
20
Peachy Canyon Rd.
Anderson. Rd.
29
30
Penman Springs Rd.
9 13
Arbor
18
Creston Rd.
6 8 12 11 17
York Mtn. Rd.
7 10 15 14
5 46 3 2 16
El Pomar
4
Templeton
Eureka
1
Bethel Rd.
Templeton Rd.
Lupine Ln.
Cripple Creek
101
41
Creston
Atascadero
229
41

THE WINERIES

1. Wild Horses	10. Bonny Doon at	18. Doce Robles	27. Martin & Weyrich
2. Pesenti	Sycamore Farms	19. Nadeau	28. Sylvester
3. Mastantuono	11. Gray Wolf	20. Norman	29. Rio Seco
4. Harmony Cellars	12. Dark Star	21. Carmody McNight	30. Penman Springs
5. York Mountain	13. Midnight Cellars	22. Justin	31. Eberle
6. Dover Canyon	14. Peachy Canyon	23. Adelaida	32. Eos/Arciero
7. Hunt Cellars	15. Castoro	24. Hidden Mountain	33. Laura's Vineyard
8. AJB Vineyards	16. JanKris	25. Pretty-Smith	34. Meridian
9. Dunning	17. Zenaida	26. Silver Horse	35. Tobin James

One of California's first—and certainly most active woman winemakers—Cathy MacGregor was graduated from U.C. Davis with an enology degree in 1977. For several years, she worked for assorted Napa and Sonoma vintners. Then, deciding she'd rather make money for herself than for someone else, she established Windemere in 1985, naming it for her ancestral village in Scotland. She draws some of her best grapes from MacGregor Vineyard, owned not by Cathy but by her father, who settled in the Edna Valley in the early 1970s after a career as a space engineer. "I always get first pick of his grapes," she grinned.

Her aging cellars and tasting counter—complete with barstools—occupy a warehouse building. It's likely that either she or her assistant, Mark Yeager, will do the pouring. He's been a wine enthusiast since he was fourteen, when he pushed boxes around in a Los Angeles wine shop.

Tasting notes: Two things are evident when you taste Windemere wines—the skill of this lady winemaker and the low overhead of her operation. The wines were uniformly excellent and remarkably inexpensive. We tasted three outstanding Chardonnays—her specialty, two Cabernets with great varietal flavor and a fine everyday sippin' wine called Rustic Red, which is a blend of Zinfandel and Barbara. The finale—and the only wine to push the price range to "$$$$," was one of the best Zinfandels we've ever tasted. It had awesome flavor and a great spicy finish. Prices: *$$ to $$$$.*

Paso Robles and environs

In contrast to the Edna and Arroyo Grande region, the Paso Robles area has a long history in the wine business. And we aren't just referring to the usual practice of Spanish padres sticking cuttings into the ground.

Indeed, founders of Mission San Miguel Archangel north of Paso Robles *did* plant vines around 1797. In 1882, Andrew York established the York Mountain winery, followed by Adolph Siot's winery in 1890, which was purchased by the Rotta family in 1907. Both survived Prohibition, and York survives to this day under new ownership. Another old-timer is Pesenti Winery, started by Frank Pesenti in 1934 and now owned by the Turley wine enterprise of the Napa Valley.

This area contains the most wineries on the south central coast. In fact, it's the fastest growing wine region in the entire state—not in vineyard acreage but in individual wineries. More than a dozen new ones have cropped up in the last few years, bringing the total count to nearly thirty, and most have tasting rooms. Wineries are grouped around Templeton, near San Miguel and east and west of Paso Robles.

This is primarily red wine country, and vintners produce outstanding Zinfandel, Pinot Noir and Cabernet. White wine enthusiasts needn't stay away; award-winning Chardonnay and exceptional Sauvignon Blanc is created here as well. The region's somewhat scattered wineries are in three areas, so we'll divide it into a trio of tours.

TEMPLETON-PASO ROBLES WINERY TOUR ● This tour has become much more complex than it was when we wrote the first edition of this book, since wineries here are proliferating like spring daffodils. The first segment is a loop, taking you west from Templeton to the Pacific Ocean and then back along State Highway 46 toward U.S. 101. In this segment, you'll

be galloping off in all directions to visit new wineries on country lanes leading into vineyard-clad hills from Highway 46.

The tour begins with an appropriately named route. From the Vineyard Drive interchange on U.S. 101, go east briefly to rustic little **Templeton.** It's a handsome town of 2,000 folks that has preserved its distinctive old west look. Brick and false front buildings house restaurants, trendy shops and galleries. For a peek, turn left at a traffic signal and cruise along Main Street. Then return to Vineyard Drive, go left (east) across the Salinas River Bridge and take a quick right onto Templeton Road. After two miles, a sign directs you to the left up a narrow lane to **Wild Horse Winery.** Now, return to Templeton, cross over the freeway on Vineyard Drive and head west. You'll pass upscale horse farms and fancy country homes similar to those in the Santa Ynez Valley. Some of California's finest breeding stables are hereabouts. You'll pass vinelands as well. About three miles from the freeway, **Pesenti Winery** appears on your right and then the château-shaped **Mastantuono Winery** is on the left. It's near the point where Vineyard blends into Highway 46.

Now, settle back for a twenty-mile drive on Route 46, through a parade of picturesque country images. You'll pass a pleasing mix of meadows, pasturelands, clumps of oaks and madrones. Stay alert and you can catch an occasional glimpse of the distant Pacific. Vineyards appear now and again to remind you that this is wine country. Forested hills of the Lucia mountains of the Coast Range cradle this area, marking the horizon on every side. Then you'll1 quickly break free of the rolling hills and hurry downhill to green headlands above the Pacific.

At Highway 1, turn left and drive about a mile to a tiny nest of rustic charm called **Harmony**. Once a busy dairy complex, this 130-year old hamlet tucked into a green hollow now boasts a population of 18. The weathered buildings—all five of them—are occupied by artists, boutiques and one good restaurant (listed below). The tasting room for **Harmony Cellars** occupies a hill overlooking the town.

Retrace your route on Highway 46; after about twelve miles, turn left at York Mountain Road to visit **York Mountain Winery.** Continue eastward on York Mountain since it loops back to the highway. When you reach the Vineyard Avenue intersection, turn left opposite Mastantuono Winery and drive north 1.3 miles to **Dover Canyon Winery**; it's on your right, up a tree-lined lane and behind a walnut orchard. Return to Highway 46 and continue heading west—but only briefly.

Cider Creek on your left, not a winery but a country style bakery and specialty foods place, is worth a stop. Particularly if you have a weakness for apple crumb cake or fresh pies. The cute little barn style place also offers cider tasting. It's open daily 8 to 5; (805) 238-4144. (www.cidercreek.com)

About a mile below, on your left at the corner of Oakdale Road is **Hunt Cellars.** Take a hard left here, then fork to the right onto Las Tablas. You'll shortly see **AJB Vineyards** above a tilted vineyard to your right, at the corner of Township Road. Continue up twisting, narrow Las Tablas Road about a mile, fork right onto Niderer Road and follow it 1.4 miles beneath a gorgeous canopy of moss-draped oaks, then turn left at a sign indicating **Dunning Vineyards.** It sits beneath its own oak umbrella at the end of a narrow dirt lane. Return to Highway 46, turn east and you'll soon see **Sycamore Farms** on the right. This isn't a winery but a large herb and specialty foods outlet in a well-tended old farm complex, with a **Bonny Doon Vineyard** tasting room. Just beyond is **Grey Wolf Cellars** tasting room in a little farmhouse on the left.

Press eastward briefly on Highway 46, then go left on Anderson Road for side-by-side wineries, **Dark Star** and **Midnight Cellars.** Despite the moody similarity of their names, they have no connection. Return to the main route and you'll soon encounter a cluster of three wineries at Highway 46 and Bethel Road. **Peachy Canyon Winery** occupies a restored Victorian school at the junction. A short distance up Bethel are **Castoro Cellars** in the vineyards off to the right and **JanKris Winery** in an attractive ranch yard on the left.

Return to Highway 46 and go a brief distance to **Zenaida Cellars** on your left. Just beyond, turn left onto Twelve Oaks Lane and follow it to **Doce Robles Winery.** Pressing eastward on Highway 46, you'll soon hit U.S. 101 between Templeton and Paso Robles. If you plan to blend into the next tour, turn left onto Vine Street just short of the freeway. Follow it north about six blocks and go left onto Sixth Street.

Wild Horse Winery ● T$ ✕

1437 Wild Horse Winery Court (P.O. Box 910), Templeton, CA 93465; (805) 434-2541. (www.wildhorsewinery.com) Daily 11 to 5; MC/VISA. Choice of five wines from the current list. Small, busy assortment of wine logo gift items; attractive courtyard picnic area.

A narrow lane delivers you to an appealing collection of white tile-roofed buildings rimmed by new vineyards and trimmed by carefully manicured landscaping. A picnic area occupies a courtyard accented by a gurgling fountain. The tasting room is a bright and cheery space with Spanish tile floors and open beam ceilings. The overall impression at Wild Horse is prosperity, well maintained.

Winery owner Ken Volk's beginnings were a bit more plebeian. While a student at Cal Poly in San Luis Obispo, he used a baseball bat and a trash can to crush some grapes from the campus vineyard. He hasn't missed many vintages since. He'd intended to become an orchard manager, but the idea of making wine fascinated him. He began "working the industry" in 1981 and produced his first commercial crush in 1983. His marriage in 1986 to chef and cooking instructor Tricia Tartaglione produced a perfect pairing of wine and food enthusiasts, and they often sponsor epicurean events at the winery.

Tasting notes: Two dozen wines occupy the Wild Horse list. Our chosen five were a lush and buttery Chardonnay, a great buy for its mid-teen price; *Valdiguie,* a light Gamay style wine, almost like an assertive rosé; Pinot Noir with a light nose yet big flavor; a middleweight Zinfandel with a soft finish; and a spicy and pleasantly tannic Barbera. Others on the list are Malvasia Bianca, Sauvignon Blanc, Pinot Grigio, Pinot Blanc, Muscat Canelli, Syrah, Malbec, Merlot and Cabernet Sauvignon, plus Rainforest red and white, whose proceeds go to conservation causes. Prices: ***$$ to $$$$.***

Pesenti Winery ● T GTA 📷

2900 Vineyard Dr., Templeton, CA 93465; (805) 434-1030. Daily 9 to 5. Most varieties tasted. Extensive giftware and wine logo selection.

Pesenti is one of the oldest wineries in the south central coast, started just after Repeal. However, you may not recognize the old place during your next visit. It recently was purchased by Helen Turley's wine enterprises from the

Napa Valley and was undergoing a complete overhaul when we last passed. Since the Turley operation in Napa is quite upscale, we'll assume that the 44-item Pesenti wine list will shrink. Don't look for the jug wines, hard cider and fruit wines that once drew the faithful to this venerable institution.

The winery's history began in 1923 when Italian immigrants Frank and Caterina Pesenti began growing grapes here, right in the middle of Prohibition. They somehow survived and opened their winery in 1934. Their son Victor, daughter Sylvia and her husband Al Nerelli ran the winery from the 1940s until its recent sale. Although the new owners are may change the winery's direction, some of the Pesenti-Nerelli legend remains. Several family members are staying as winery employees.

Mastantuono Winery ● *T* ✕ 📷

100 Oak View Rd. (Route 2), Templeton, CA 93465; (805) 238-0676. Daily 10 to 6; MC/VISA, DISC. Most varieties tasted. Extensive selection of gift-wares, stemware and deli foods. Picnic area.

Step inside Pasquale Mastantuono's tasting room and you may expect to see jolly knights thumping their flagons on the bar, demanding refills. From afar, the place looks like a cross between a château and castle. From within, it might be a Bavarian hunting lodge, with game trophies glaring from their wall mounts.

"*Italian* hunting lodge," corrected the gregarious founder of this place. Between sips of wine as robust as their creator, we get the Pasquale Mastantuono story. "I started a furniture business in L.A. With these hands; tool box and the whole thing. I wanted to make a million so I could retire at 39. So that's what I did."

With an exaggerated sweep of his left hand, he gestured around the tasting room. "*This* is my retirement. This is fun!"

Pat started having fun in 1976 when he began making wine commercially. His Italian forbearers had been doing it for three generations, so he figures it was in his genes. Actually, he says he doesn't make wine; he only guides it along.

"The wine is made in the vineyard," he said, in refreshing contradiction to the modern school of test tube winemakers.

Tasting notes: Mastantuono's philosophy practically jumps from the glass. His reds are dry-farmed, unfined and unfiltered. The Zinfandels run a tasty gamut from light and berry-like to powerful and robust. A six-year-old Zin, aged three years in oak, was one of the best we've tasted and the Chardonnays were crisp and spicy with hints of wood. Also on the list were Sauvignon Blanc, white Zinfandel, Sangiovese, a couple of Barberas, Nebbiolo, Muscat Canelli, a sparkling wine, California Port and—leave it to Mastantuono—a tequila wine called San Luis Agave. Prices: *$ to $$$$.*

Vintners choice: The license plate on Pat's flashy boat-tailed vintage Auburn sports car displayed out front says it: "ZINMAN 1."

Harmony Cellars ● *T* ✕ 📷

Harmony Valley Road (P.O. Box 2502), Harmony, CA 93435; (805) 927-1625. Daily 10 to 5; MC/VISA. Most varieties tasted. Wine logo and specialty food items; view picnic area.

This small family-owned winery is tucked into a hillside with a splendid view of the tiny hamlet of Harmony and the rolling headlands of the Pacific Coast. The tasting room, once in Harmony, has moved up to the winery, where sippers can enjoy that great view. The site also includes a picnic area with access to that vista.

Tasting notes: Winemaker Chuck Mulligan likes a lot of fruit in his wine. The Chardonnay and Johannisberg Riesling displayed pronounced varietal character, strong on berries, light on wood, with a crisp acid finish. The Pinot Noir was pleasantly herbal with a spicy nose and a good taste of berries, while the Cabernet was lighter and herbaceous. Prices: *$ to $$$$*.

Vintners choice: Mulligan's favorite is his buttery and oaky Chardonnay, which has won numerous medals, including a recent double gold at the California State Fair.

York Mountain Winery ● T ST ✕ ▯

York Mountain Road (Route 2, Box 191), Templeton, CA 93465; (805) 238-3925. (www.yorkmountainwinery.com) Daily 10 to 5; MC/VISA. Most varieties tasted. Good giftware selection, books and specialty foods. Tours by appointment, or one can peek into the winery.

York Mountain is aging gracefully. The venerable winery occupies an early American farmyard fringed by trees and vineyards high on the flanks of the Santa Lucias. The vine-entwined tasting room has the look of an old general store, with a wide selection of gifts, specialty foods and books. It's one of wineland's more intriguing tasting rooms, with a beamed ceiling, craggy stone fireplace and a 1910 New Era motorcycle parked along one wall. As far as we could determine, York Mountain is the oldest surviving winery in all of southern California, dating from 1882, when it was established by Andrew York. Present owner Max Goldman bought it from the York family in 1970.

Tasting notes: York's busy list ranges from red and white jug wines and classic varietals to a sparkling wine and dry Sherry. The Zinfandel, Pinot Noir and Cabernet Sauvignon were hearty and full-bodied with a strong taste of the grape. Chardonnay, the only varietal white, was crisp and light. Sherry, made from Chenin Blanc and French Colombard, was properly nutty. Prices: *$ to $$$$*.

Vintners choice: "Pinot Noir," said Goldman simply.

Dover Canyon Winery ● T

4520 Vineyard Dr., Paso Robles, CA 93446; (805) 237-0101. (www.dovercanyon.com) Friday-Sunday 11 to 5; MC/VISA. Most varieties tasted free; wine logo glasses may be purchased.

A walnut orchard—not a vineyard—slopes down from this pleasantly rustic farm style winery complex. Owner-winemaker Dan Panico buys most of his grapes, although he has planted Zinfandel vines on a slope behind his hilltop farm. A fifteen-year veteran of the Paso Robles wine industry, he opened this operation in 1997 by purchasing several acres of the old Rancho Paso de Robles. He lives in the restored 1921 farmhouse, and the simple tasting room occupies an adjacent Dutch style barn. An avid conservationist, he employs organic farming methods, plants native flora to preserve wildlife habitats and recycles everything—even computers with blown hard drives.

Tasting notes: Dan is among the south central coast's "Rhône rangers," producing both red and white Rhône varietals. The whites on his list are a fruity Viognier Reserve, a lush and spicy Chardonnay, and Sunshine, a slightly sweet blend of Chard and Viognier. The reds are a smoky and full flavored unfiltered Merlot, a peppery Zinfandel, a more complex and oak-aged

Cujo Zinfandel and Renegade Red, a smooth blend of Cabernet Sauvignon, Zinfandel and Merlot. Prices: *$$ to $$$$.*

Hunt Cellars ● T ✕

2875 Oakdale Rd., Paso Robles, CA 93446; (877) 677-1600 or (805) 237-1600. (www.huntwinecellars.com) Daily 10:30 to 5:30; MC/VISA. Most varieties tasted. Picnic deck adjacent to the tasting room.

This tasting room in a prim cottage sends mixed messages. A tethered balloon out front—the kind you see at RE/MAX real estate offices—is labeled: "KILLER WINES!" While this borders on tacky, the tasting room itself is quite nice and the wines are very elegant. Some, in fact, have achieved near perfect scores in jusging. However, their prices may bend your budget; some range to $50 and beyond.

All of this—the prim cottage, the big bright balloon and the outstanding wines—are the work of a remarkable individual. If you aren't familiar with David Hunt's name, you've heard of his firm—First Alert security systems. This son of a poor South Carolina family also is an accomplished pianist, songwriter and singer, one of the early developers of the voice mail concept and a computer expert. He has accomplished all of this while slowly losing his vision, the victim of an an ailment called retinitis pigmentosa. Now almost totally blind, he can no longer see the winery and tasting room that he had built, nor the vineyards he planted. Still, he supervises the winemaking by taste and feel, and visitors may encounter him at one of the two pianos in the tasting room, hammering away with the skill of an Elton John.

Tasting notes: Hunt's wines are excellent and pricey, ranging from the mid-teens into the high twenties, with a splendid Opus style wine called Rhapsody in Red fetching $50 a bottle. His least expensive wine, a mid-teen Sauvignon Blanc, was soft and lush, surprisingly good for this modest varietal. The rest of the wines—all more than $20—are a lush and silky Moonlight Sonata Chardonnay, an intense and spicy Sangiovese; an outstandingly spicy Zinfandel, a full-flavored Merlot, a lush and peppery Cabernet Sauvignon and an herbal Syrah. Prices: *$$ to $$$$.*

AJB Vineyards ● T$

3280 Township Rd., Paso Robles, CA 93446; (805) 239-9432. Weekends noon to 5; MC/VISA. Most varieties tasted for a very modest fee.

This attractive complex sits above a vineyard, with a handsomely restored gabled barn and matching house that were once part of a Mennonite community. Southern California dentist Alfonso John Berardo bought the facility in the early 1990s, intending to retire. He started growing grapes to stay active and soon found himself in the winery business. The first vineyards were planted with Viognier and Syrah in 1993. Additional plantings came later and the winery and tasting room were opened in late 1999. John makes his wines with the assistance of neighbor Dan Panico of Dover Canyon Winery

The simple tasting room occupies a small woodframe building adjacent to the century-old farmhouse, where the family lives. Not far away is Hilltop Hacienda, a two-bedroom country home with a pool and spa, which visitors can rent.

Tasting notes: The AJB label consists of various vintages of excellent and expensive Viognier, Nebbiolo, Sangiovese and Syrah. All are estate grown. Prices: *$$$$.*

Dunning Vineyards • T ✗

1953 Niderer Rd., Paso Robles, CA 93446; (805) 238-4763. (www.dunningvineyards.com) MC/VISA. Weekends 11 to 5. Most varieties tasted. Shaded picnic area.

The Dunning winery occupies one of the most scenic and tucked-away corners of the Paso Robles wine country. It rests beneath a gorgeous canopy of oaks at the end of a half-mile-long dirt lane. The winery complex occupies blue and white clapboard ranch buildings that date back to the turn of the last century. The tiny tasting room is in a shingled cottage, with a slab thrown across barrels for a serving counter. The only adornments—quite pleasant—are paintings done by Al Dunning, an uncle of the winery owners.

Malibu natives Robert and Jo-Ann Dunning experimented with home winemaking for fifteen years before starting their commercial winery. Dunning Vineyards occupies an eighty-acre ranch that had been purchased by Robert's family in 1960. He planted vineyards here in 1991 and opened the winery in 1994. The Dunnings children John and Barbara help with the operation.

Tasting notes: The Dunning list is brief—a fruity and spicy Chardonnay, an excellent Select Ranches Zinfandel, a smooth and deep flavored Merlot and a spicy Cabernet Sauvignon with nice hints of oak. The "house wine" is literally that—*Vin de Casa*, a busy blend of Cabernet Sauvignon, Zinfandel, Nebbiolo, Barbera and Petit Verdot. Prices: **$$$ to $$$$.**

Bonny Doon tasting room at Sycamore Farms • T$ ✗ 🐦

2485 Highway 46 West (P.O. Box 49-A), Paso Robles, CA 93446; (805) 239-5614. (www.bonnydoonvineyard.com) Open daily; hours vary with the seasons. Major credit cards. Most varieties tasted for a small fee that includes glass. Extensive wine logo and giftware selection; picnic area.

Sycamore Farms is a large produce, specialty foods and giftwares outlet in an old fashioned farm complex, complete with friendly critters in corrals. Bonny Doon Vineyard of Santa Cruz, noted for its fine wine blends and hilariously campy labels, started a tasting facility here in 1994. If you haven't or don't plan to visit the winery in the Santa Cruz Mountains, this provides an opportunity to sample *Le Cigare Volant, Ca' del Solo* Big House Red and Cardinal Zin. And yes, the wines are serious. For specifics, see the Bonny Doon listing in Chapter Nine, page 210. Sycamore Farms also sells an array of specialty foods, cookbooks, gardening books and American folk crafts.

Grey Wolf Cellars • T ✗

2174 W. Highway 46, Paso Robles, CA 93446; (805) 237-0771. Daily 11 to 5:30; MC/VISA. Most varieties tasted. Small picnic area; a few wine logo and gift items.

Joe and Shirlene Barton discovered the wine business by a rather circuitous route. Native Californians, they moved to the ski town of Steamboat Springs, Colorado. There, they developed an interest in premium wines and, returning to California, they established a small winery in partnership with local vineyard manager Gary Porter in 1994. The Bartons started with a small tasting room east of Paso Robles. Later, they moved it to a renovated a fifty-year-old farm cottage on west Highway 46. Joe Barton died in 1998, although his wife Shirlene and their son Joseph, Jr., continue the family enterprise. He's the winemaker and she runs the business end.

Their farmhouse tasting room is fashioned as a comfy old fashioned living room with early American furnishings and family photos on the walls. Visitors can expect to be greeted by a pair of excessively friendly dogs, who likely will follow them into the tasting room.

Tasting notes: The Grey Wolf list is quite fine. Our favorite was the least expensive—a full flavored "ZinfulCab" with sixty percent Cabernet and forty percent Zinfandel. Chardonnay, the Bartons' only white, was properly lush and smooth with a hint of oak. The Zinfandel had a deep, spicy fruit flavor and crisp finish, and the Merlot was soft and complex with low acid. On the reserve list were a full-flavored Family Meritage of Cabernet Sauvignon, Cabernet Franc and Merlot; an excellent Reserve Chardonnay; and Alpha Cab, an outstanding Cabernet Sauvignon with thirty months on oak. Prices are very modest for the quality: *$$ to $$$$.*

Dark Star Cellars • T

2985 Anderson Rd., Paso Robles, CA 93446; (805) 237-2389. (www.dark-starcellars.com) Friday-Sunday 11 to 6; MC/VISA. Most varieties tasted.

Is it time for wine? Definitely so at Dark Star. The walls of an overwise austere tasting room are covered with more than a hundred clocks of all sorts and shapes. Owner-winemaker Norm Benson collects timepieces for his International Tacky Wall Clock Wall of Fame, often swapping a bottle of wine for an interesting timepiece. However, competition's getting tough, the tasting room host told us. Just any old wall clock won't earn you a bottle of wine.

Norm, who's father was a longtime a veteran of the beverage business, established the winery in 1994 to create deeply colored "stellar" red wines, and thus the name Dark Star. As a winemaker, he believes in obtaining good grapes and letting the wines produce themselves, while giving them "gentle guidance."

Tasting notes: Benson's philosophy is reflected in his full bodied, deep colored wines. He makes a single white—a full-flavored Chardonnay. The rest are hearty reds: A Merlot with deep color and flavor; a spicy Zinfandel; a 100 percent Syrah with classic varietal character; a Cabernet Sauvignon with a great chili pepper nose and hint of oak in the taste; and his own proprietary blend called *Ricordati*, with Cabernets Sauvignon and Franc and Merlot. He made it as a tribute to his father; the name means "always remember." Prices: *$$$ to $$$$.*

Midnight Cellars • T$

2925 Anderson Rd., Paso Robles, CA 93446; (805) 239-8904. Daily 10 to 5:30; MC/VISA. Most varieties tasted for a modest fee.

This modern mid-sized operation, bunkered against a brushy hillside, was established in 1995 by the Hartenberger family from Chicago. Bob and Mary Jane are major stockholders and their sons Rich and Mike, and Rich's wife Michelle run the operation. None have vintners' backgrounds. Bob is a retired patent attorney, Mike was in sales, Rich was in marketing and Michelle had a science background. The family simply decided to get into the wine business after frequent vacation trips to California winelands. By pooling their respective talents, they've established a successful winery, with the two brothers as the winemakers.

Tasting notes: A white and a pink appear on a rather short list—a full flavored and spicy Chardonnay and the ubiquitous white Zinfandel. Representing the reds are a big flavored, medium body Full Moon Zinfandel, a fruity and spicy Merlot a Cabernet Sauvignon with a nice oaky touch, and *Mare Nectarus*, a rich and smooth Bordeaux blend.

Peachy Canyon Winery ● T & T$ ✕

1480 N. Bethel Rd., Templeton, CA 93465; (800) 315-7908 or (805) 239-1918. (www.peachycanyonwinery.com) Daily Weekends 11 to 5; MC/VISA. Most varieties tasted free; modest fee for tasting some reserves. Giftwares and wine logo items; picnic area.

The Peachy Canyon tasting room no longer occupies its namesake chasm. It recently was moved from the winery in the hills west of Paso Robles to the 1886 Bethel Schoolhouse building on Bethel Road. Earlier, this charming white clapboard structure was home to Live Oak Winery. The tasting room occupies a splendid space with polished tile floors, antique furnishings and an inviting fireplace. Ancient oaks and landscaped gardens accent the yard, with vineyards just beyond.

Former school teachers Doug and Nancy Beckett dabbled in real estate and co-owned a chain of liquor stores in the San Diego area, then moved to Paso Robles in 1981. He worked for another vintner, then started Tobias Vineyards with partner Pat Wheeler. In 1988, after the partnership was dissolved, the Becketts established their Peachy Canyon label. The winery now involves sons Jacob and Joshua.

Tasting notes: The Becketts produce outstanding Zinfandels. *Bon Appetit* once rated a Peachy Canyon Zin as one of the best in America. Available selections when we last tasted included a very berry Incredible Red Zinfandel, a medium bodied Paso Robles Zinfandel and a dark and powerful Westside Zin. Other wines on the list are a crisp and fruity Chardonnay, a medium-bodied Sangiovese, a dark and complex Cabernet Sauvignon, and an intense Merlot that was suitable for aging. Several reserve Zins and a Zinfandel Port are available for tasting at a small fee. Prices: *$$ to $$$$.*

Castoro Cellars ● T$ ✕ 📷

1315 N. Bethel Rd., Templeton, CA 93465; (800) DAM-FINE or (805) 238-0725. Daily 11 to 5:30; MC/VISA, AMEX. Most varieties tasted for a modest fee, which includes a logo glass. Good selection of wine related giftware and specialty food items. Picnic area nearby.

Castoro Cellars was established in 1983 by Niels and Bimmer Udsen. Initially, they were partnered with John and Dawn Hawley, who provided the tasting room. Then in 1994, the Udsens moved their operation to its present site at the old El Paso de Robles Winery. However, you'll not think of it as "old." It has been handsomely renovated into a Spanish mission style complex reached by a colonnade walkway. Picnic tables occupy a lawn area. The tasting room interior is even more impressive—a grand open space with a cathedral ceiling held up by huge trusses. A fireplace, tile floor and replica of a Loire Valley tapestry of winemaking complete this appealing setting.

The Udsen family winery produces about 22,000 cases a year, which they immodestly call "Damned fine wine!" Most varieties are available at the tasting room.

Tasting notes: The Castoro Fumé Blanc, one of the few produced on the south central coast, was crisp and light with a nice acidic finish. A light touch of oak accented the Chardonnay. Of the reds, the Pinot Noir was full and complex yet soft. The Zinfandel nicely spicy with a typical raspberry flavor. A pretty cranberry-colored Gamay Nouveau had a light strawberry taste. Cabernet Sauvignon, a rich late harvest Zinfandel, white Zin and Muscat Canelli complete the list. Prices: *$ to $$$*.

Vintners choice: "What we're really known for is our reds, especially our Zin and Cab" commented winemaker Niels.

JanKris Vineyard ● *T* ✕ ⬛

Bethel Road (Route 2, Box 40), Templeton, CA 93465; (805) 434-0319. Daily 10 to 5:30; MC/VISA, AMEX. Most varieties tasted. Picnic area; wine logo and specialty food items.

JanKris occupies an elegantly restored 120-year-old gray and white Victorian farm house. It's part of a ranch complex that includes a barn-turned-winery, corrals with livestock and surrounding pasturelands and vineyards. This facility once was home to Farview Farms Winery. The present facility was started by Paula and Mark Gendron in 1991. They named it for their daughters January and Kristin, who were too young to drink what's behind the JanKris label. The Gendrons closed the winery after a few years, then recently reopened it—at the request of their daughters, who had attained drinking age and wanted to get serious about the winery business. The facility produces about 1,400 cases a year.

Tasting notes: "Fruity and soft" describes the JanKris wine style, although some of the reds are rather assertive. We particularly liked a smooth, mouth-filling Chardonnay. The Zinfandel was complex and full of berries, and the Merlot was soft and fruity, yet with enough tannin to suggest aging. Others on the list are a Merlot-Zinfandel blend called Merzin, Cabernet Sauvignon, Riesling, white Zinfandel and a sweet late harvest Zinfandel. Prices are among the least expensive on the south central coast: *$ to $$*.

Zenaida Cellars ● *T* ✕ ⬛

1550 Highway 46, Paso Robles, CA 93446; (805) 227-0382. (www.zenaidacellars.com) Daily 11 to 5; MC/VISA. Select varieties tasted. Nice selection of gift and wine logo items. Vineyard-view picnic area.

This handsome tile-roofed mission style winery, started in 1998, sits beneath the shade of century-old oaks. An inviting picnic area overlooks the vineyards. The mission theme carries into the tasting room, with its glossy tile floors, Spanish arches and polished woods. Although the winery is new, its founder Eric Ogorsolka is a longtime area resident. He majored in biology at Cal Poly in San Luis Obispo, worked as a state fisheries biologist and dabbled in other professions before getting into the wine business. He started as a home winemaker, bottling grapes from the family vineyard, then he launched the Zenaida Cellars label in 1998.

Tasting notes: The Zenaida wines, all with strong varietal characteristics, include Chardonnay, Pinot Noir, Merlot, Cabernet Sauvignon, Zinfandel, Syrah, Cabernet Franc and Sangiovese. Prices: *$$ to $$$$*.

Doce Robles Winery ● *T* ✕

2023 Twelve Oaks Dr., Paso Robles, CA 93446; (805) 227-4766 or (805) 227-6860. Daily 10 to 5; MC/VISA, AMEX. Most varieties tasted. A few giftwares and a small picnic area.

Whoever said the best wines are made in the vineyards could have been thinking of Jim Jacobsen. Although relatively new to the Paso Robles area, he's a third-generation grape grower from the Selma area of the San Joaquin

Valley. There, he and his wife Maribeth grew grapes for both wine and raisins. Then, lured by their tastebuds, they purchased forty acres here in 1996. Jim produces about 2,000 cases a year and the wines, nurtured by his grape-growing expertise, are uniformly excellent.

The spacious, big-windowed tasting room and adjacent winery occupy an old oak-shaded ranch complex surrounded by vineyards. Expect to be greeted by a pair of friendly farm dogs as you head for your tasting experience. And unless you flunked high school Spanish, you know that *Doce Robles* means Twelve Oaks.

Tasting notes: The Jacobsens produce some of the best wines we've tasted, and prices are reasonable for the quality, starting in the middle teens. Our samplings included an outstanding Merlot with a great berry taste, a spicy medium-weight Zinfandel with a crisp finish, a lush and spicy Syrah, and an absolutely gorgeous Barbera that was full-flavored with an awesome berry taste. Others on the list are Chardonnay, a late harvest Zinfandel and *Robles Rojos*, a blend of Cabernets Sauvignon and Franc and Merlot. And unless you *really* flunked Spanish, you know that *Robles Rojos* is red oaks. Prices: *$$$ to $$$$.*

WEST PASO ROBLES WINERY TOUR ● Several wineries with tasting rooms are scattered in the Santa Lucia Range west of Paso Robles and south of the twin reservoirs of San Antonio and Nacimiento. Some are so remote that they call themselves "The Far Out Wineries of Paso Robles," and they've issued a brochure to help folks find them. Actually, none of the wineries are all that difficult to locate and the scenery is splendid in this area. Narrow lanes wind through thickly wooded foothills, passing beneath moss-draped oaks. Vineyards appear as occasional patchworks, terraced up steep slopes and mounded over high ridges. (**NOTE:** This tour is best done on a weekend since some of the wineries have limited hours.)

The route begins and ends in Paso Robles. Follow Spring Street (which is the main drag, paralleling Highway 101) to Sixth Street and turn west. (Or reach Sixth from the end of the previous tour; see above on page 251.) Go through a couple of stop signs, then swing right onto Olive and left onto Pacific. This soon becomes Peachy Canyon Road, which takes you on a twisting course through this wooded foothill wine country. The first wineries you'll encounter are—well—really far out.

Once you reach Peachy Canyon Road, about four and a half twisting and scenic miles will deliver you to **Nadeau Family Vintners,** down in a pretty little glen to your right. Continue another five and a half miles on snake-coiling Peachy Canyon to Vineyard Drive; turn right and you'll shortly see the Romanesque **Norman Vineyards** on your right. Continue north on Vineyard Drive about three miles until it ends at Adelaida Road. Turn left, then go right at a stop sign onto Chimney Rock Road. Follow this about three and a half miles to **Carmody McNight Estate** on your right. Just beyond, also on the right, is the imposing **Justin Winery.** From Justin, retrace your path back to Adelaida Road and follow it east just under four miles to **Adelaida Cellars** on your right. Continue half a mile on curving Adelaida Road, then turn right and follow a narrow lane about a mile up and over a steep hill and down to a winery that lives up to its name, **Hidden Mountain Ranch.** Continue eastward on Adelaida until it blends into Nacimiento Lake Drive, which takes you quickly back to Paso Robles.

Nadeau Family Vintners • T ✕

3860 Peachy Canyon Rd., Paso Robles, CA 93446; (805) 239-3574. Weekends noon to 5:30 or until dusk; MC/VISA. Most varieties tasted; picnic deck.

This new winery occupies a charming old ranch complex in a sheltered glen, with vineyards climbing up the surrounding hills. A picnic area with umbrella tables, which shares a deck with a stemmer-crusher, offers nice views of those vineyards. The rudimentary tasting room, where wines are sipped from a slab resting on wine barrels, does double duty as the winery's lab. If the tasting room is closed, a sign says: *Door locked? Thirsty? Ring bell.*

Robert and Patrice Nadeau established their winery in 1997, planting mostly Zinfandel the hilly vineyards that surround them. They produce about 1,600 cases a year.

Tasting notes: Robert makes his wines the old fashioned way—by obtaining good fruit and letting nature do its work. "Our job, simply, is not to goof it up!" he says. The results are some fine wines with strong varietal character. His list includes Zinfandel, RVR (a Rhône varietal blend), Syrah, Mourvèdre, Grenache, Cabernet Sauvignon, Petit Sirah and Outback, a blend of Cabernet and Shiraz.

Norman Vineyards • T GTA ✕

7450 Vineyard Dr., Paso Robles, CA 93446; (805) 237-0138. (www.normanvineyards.com) Daily 11 to 5; major credit cards. Most varieties tasted. Some wine logo items; view picnic deck.

Norman emerges as a stucco and masonry Romanesque structure with columns and curved roof lines, bunkered into a hillside and surrounded by woods, vines and lawns. It's of the more attractive of the west Paso Robles wineries. The tasting room is as comfortable as a living room, with overstuffed furniture and exposed beam ceilings with dangling fans. A picnic terrace offers an exceptional view of surrounding hills and vineyards.

The winery is the work of Art and Lei Norman, native Californians who planted their first vines on this scenic slope way back in 1971. They were among the south central coast's first modern vintners. Art, who had been fiddling with fermentation since he was a teenager, used a tractor shed as the first winery. Today's imposing Italianate facility room was completed more than two decades later.

Tasting notes: The Normans believe in letting nature produce their wines, minimizing the use of pesticides and fertilizers. The results are evident in their clean, straightforward taste. The Chardonnay was light and crisp and almost flinty, while the Cabernet Sauvignon was light yet full flavored. The new release "Monster" Zinfandel was the best of the lot, with a big spicy nose, full berry taste and soft tannic finish. Others on the list are Meritage No Nonsense Red, Sauvignon Blanc, white Zinfandel, Pinot noir, Barbera, Cabernet Franc, Merlot and a rich late harvest Zinfandel. Prices are modest for the quality: *$ to $$$$.*

Carmody McNight Estate Wines • T$ ✕ 📷

11240 Chimney Rock Rd., Paso Robles, CA 93446; (800) 282-0730 or (805) 238-9392. Daily 10 to 5; MC/VISA. Most varieties tasted for a fee. Artwork and giftwares; picnic area.

Tasteful elegance is written into the landscaped grounds, mirrored fountain pond and prim buildings of this country estate. It's the handiwork of two very interesting people—movie actor-producer and artist Gary Carmody Conway and former Miss America Marian McNight Conway. Their entry into the wine business reads like a blend of Miss America fairy tale and adventure movie plot. During her year as Miss America, South Carolina native Marian went on several tours of Europe and fell in love—not yet with Gary—but with the fine wines of France. About thirty years ago, after they were married, Gary was being flown over the west Paso Robles area in search of a site for a mountain hideaway. As they passed over a particularly attractive spot, the chopper lost power and crashed. Gary, the real estate agent and the pilot emerged unscathed and Gary announced: "This is a great spot! I'll take it!"

For years, it remained their mountain hideaway, then they opened a winery in 1989, initially calling it Silver Canyon. As their vineyards grew, they began producing only estate wines and changed the name to Carmody McNight Estate. Their daughter Kathleen helps make the wine and runs the business end. The tastefully appointed tasting room also serves as a gallery, displaying Conway's oils and pastels.

Tasting notes: The Carmody McNight list features a full flavored Chardonnay with hints of oak; a rich tasting Cabernet Sauvignon, a softer Cabernet Franc and a deep ruby and full flavored Merlot. Proprietary wines are *Cadenza*, a mix of Merlot and Cabernets Sauvignon and Franc; and Art of the Vineyards, a Cabernet Sauvignon and Merlot blend. Two dessert wines complete the list—a late harvest Cabernet Franc and a Port style Cabernet Sauvignon. Prices: *$$ to $$$$.*

Justin Vineyards and Winery ● T GTA ✕
11680 Chimney Rock Rd., Paso Robles, CA 93446; (805) 238-6932. (www.justinwine.com) Daily 10 to 5; major credit cards. Most current releases tasted. Garden picnic area; guided tours by appointment.

What's this? A French château in the Santa Lucia wilds? This grand symbol of affluence rises in striking contrast to its bucolic surroundings. Architecture of the multi-gabled wooden winery appears to be a mix between French manor house and a California seacoast hideaway. It's rimmed by formal English gardens, with picnic tables beneath an arbor. The tasting room features thick ceiling beams, rough terrazzo floors, an iron chandelier dangling above a glass-topped tasting table, a grand piano and walls of—uh—simulated marble. The winery complex also has a bed and breakfast, the Just Inn and Deborah's Room restaurant, listed below.

All of this elegance is the work of Justin and Deborah Baldwin, who bought seventy-two acres in 1981 to create an estate vineyard. They began producing small, hand-crafted lots of wine in 1987.

Tasting notes: Justin's wines, which win numerous medals, often sell out. The Chardonnay was a crisp, flinty Burgundian style and the Sauvignon Blanc provides a nice balance of light fruit and gentle acid. The Meritage, labeled *Isosceles*, was lush and berry like, with a pleasant nip of tannin. Others on the select list are Merlot, Cabernet Franc, Cabernet Sauvignon, Syrah, a Cal-Ital blend of Sangiovese and Nebbiolo, Orange Muscat and a rich Port style wine called Obtuse. Prices: *$$ to $$$$.*

Adelaida Cellars ● T$ 🏮
5805 Adelaida Rd., Paso Robles, CA 93446; (800) 676-1232 or (805) 239-8980. (www.adelaida.com) Daily 11 to 5; MC/VISA. Most varieties sampled for a modest fee, which includes the glass. A few giftwares and wine logo items.

The Adelaida tasting room occupies a great open space at one end of a pleasantly cavernous winery. It's corralled by a low wall of barrels and wine boxes, which are hung with artwork and draped with wine logo T-shirts. Soft music issues from unseen speakers. The Adelaida grounds, tucked into a wooded glen among vineyards, are invitingly landscaped.

The Adelaida Cellars label was started in 1981 by John and Andreé Munch, who came to this area from quite different backgrounds. He grew up on a banana plantation in Central America and she was raised in a hamlet in the French Alps. In 1990, they formed a joint venture with Don and Elizabeth Van Steenwyck, who own this ranch property on Adelaida Road. The emphasis was switched from the Van Steenwycks' walnuts and almonds to the Munch's wines.

Tasting notes: The winery produces excellent reds. The Zinfandel was round and lush and full of berries and the Cabernet was spicy and complex, with tannin to invite aging. The Chardonnay was fine as well, with great nutty flavor and a soft, lush finish. A dry Riesling, Pinot Noir and Cabernet Sauvignon complete the brief list. Prices: *$$$ to $$$$.*

Hidden Mountain Ranch ● T

2750 Hidden Mountain Rd., Paso Robles, CA 93446; (805) 238-7143. Weekends 11 to 5; MC/VISA. Most varieties tasted.

This appealing winery in a pocket canyon with spectacular mountain views was established in the 1970s as Hoffman Mountain Ranch by Stanley Hoffman, a Beverly Hills cardiologist. Producing wines made under the guidance of Beaulieu Vineyard's legendary Andre Tchelistcheff, the winery became known by its initials—HMR. In 1997, three families from the San Francisco Bay Area—David and Audrey McHenry, Jean and Heidi Changala and Randy and Georgia Vignola—acquired the winery. Without having to change its initials, they renamed it Hidden Mountain Ranch. David McHenry is the winemaker.

The HMR tasting room is among the area's more attractive, occupying a little dark wood cottage trimmed with flower beds and window boxes. An L-shaped counter is laid across wine barrels in the deliberately rustic tasting room; ceiling fans whisper quietly from above.

Tasting notes Our HMR samplings included a couple of fine full bodied Chardonnays with nutty undertones, a smooth Merlot with a hint of oak, and an outstanding Zinfandel from the half-century-old Dante Dusi Vineyards. Others on the list are Cabernet Sauvignon, Muscat Canelli, a sweet late harvest Muscat and *Dos Viñas*, a blend of Syrah and Zinfandel.

SAN MIGUEL-ESTRELLA RIVER VALLEY WINERY TOUR ●

The Estrella River Valley is shallow and softly contoured, not as striking as the Peachy Canyon-Adelaida area with its steep oak-thatched hills and tilted meadows and vineyards. You will be rewarded, however, with fine wines and some impressive looking wineries.

To sample your first wine in this area, head north from Paso Robles on U.S. 101 about nine miles to **San Miguel,** an historic if scruffy hamlet that's home to the wonderfully weathered **Mission San Miguel.** Take the first San Miguel turnoff and follow Main Street briefly north to the mission. To reach **Pretty-Smith Vineyards and Winery,** follow Main Street another half mile north and turn right onto River Road. It crosses a narrow bridge, climbs into vineyard benchlands above town and shortly reaches the winery, uphill to your left. Continue briefly north on River Road to Cross Canyon Road, go right and follow it about four miles to Pleasant Road and turn south. **Silver Horse Vineyards** will appear shortly on your left, up a slender lane.

Return to Paso Robles and take the eastbound Highway 46 exit, indicating Fresno and Bakersfield. The next winery comes up within half a mile— **Martin & Weyrich** on your left at Buena Vista Drive. From here, continue north on Buena Vista about three miles, through several rural ninety-degree turns. As the road swings eastward, the **Sylvester Winery** appears on your left. Continue on Buena Vista for a mile to a stop sign at Airport Road, turn right (south) and follow it back to Highway 46.

Go west briefly on the highway, take the next left and then another quick left to get onto Union Road. After two miles, you'll encounter small **Rio Seco Vineyard** on your right. Continue a short distance to Penman Springs Road, turn right and then another right will take you up a ridge to **Penman Springs Vineyard**. Return to Highway 46, continue eastward and the remaining Estrella River Valley wineries will present themselves without further search. Just over half a mile west of the Airport Road Junction, **Eberle Winery** is on the left, elegant **Eos Estate Winery** soon appears on the right and the simple tasting room of **Laura's Vineyard** is directly across the highway. After a short drive, you'll see **Meridian Vineyards** on the left. A mile or so beyond, turn right from Route 46 onto the eastern end of Union Road for **Tobin James.**

Pretty-Smith Vineyards & Winery ● T ✕ 📷

13350 N. River Rd. (P.O. Box 3407), San Miguel, CA 93451; (805) 467-3104. (www.prettysmith.com) Friday-Monday 10 to 5; MC/VISA. Most wines available for tasting. Fair selection of wine logo and gift items.

Until late 2000, this attractive winery perched atop a benchland above San Miguel functioned as Mission View Estate, which had been established in 1979. Then Canadian-born computer executives and home winemakers Lisa Pretty and Victor Smith purchased the winery and several acres of vines. Lisa, a high tech marketing specialist, decided to use the symbol of Kokopelli, the mischievous Pueblo Indian spirit, as their logo. "He's noted for providing abundance and fertility and that's what we're accomplishing here," she said.

The winery and adjacent tasting room occupy rustically handsome wood-sided buildings. Visitors can sip wines at a long counter inside the spaciously attractive tasting room, then perhaps adjourn for a picnic on the adjacent deck. Both tasting room and picnic deck offer pleasant views of the region's rolling vinelands.

Tasting notes: When we last passed, the new owners were still selling off its stock of Mission View wines, although Pretty-Smith wines with their Kokopelli label may be available by the time you arrive. Since the new owners are drawing from the surrounding vineyards, choices may be similar to Mission View offerings, which included Fumé Blanc, Chardonnay, Cabernet Franc, Merlot, Cabernet Sauvignon and Zinfandel. Prices: *$ to $$$.*

Silver Horse Vineyards ● T ✕

2995 Pleasant Rd. (P.O. Box 2010), Paso Robles, CA 93447-2010; (805) 467-WINE. Friday-Sunday 11 to 5; MC/VISA. Most varieties tasted. A few wine logo and specialty food items; picnic patio near a pond.

Occupying a knoll above the vineyards, the Silver Horse tasting room offers pleasing rural views from its large windows. The tasting bar consists of planks laid across wine barrels—a nice touch. The grounds and adjacent horse farm are tidily kept, and the complex is reached by a narrow lane rimmed by pasturelands and vines.

This 3,000-case winery was established in 1989 by Rich and Kristen Simons when they purchased a horse ranch with a two-year-old vineyard. They were absentee grape growers for several years, commuting from their home in Del Mar above San Diego. In 1992, they decided to go into the wine business, using a converted airplane hanger on the property as their winery. Another couple with a fascination for wine, Jim and Suzanne Kroener, purchased an interest in the winery in 1997.

Tasting notes: The list is brief and quite good. A Zinfandel, in fact, was excellent—peppery nose, lush herbal taste and a nice smooth finish. A five-year-old Cabernet Sauvignon was spicy and herbal, with a bit of oak; and the Chardonnay was medium-soft and fruity with a hint of wood. Also on the list are a white Zinfandel and Pinot Noir. Prices: **$$ to $$$.**

Martin & Weyrich ● T ✕ 📷

Highway 46 at Buena Vista Drive (P.O. Box 7003), Paso Robles, CA 93447; (805) 238-2520. (www.martinweyrich.com) Daily 10 to 5; major credit cards. Most varieties tasted. Specialty coffee drinks for a fee. Extensive selection of gift items, books, specialty foods and wine accessories; view picnic patio.

This winery was started in 1981 by Irish brothers Nick and Tom Martin to specialize in Italian wines. In 1998, they sold the winery to their sister Mary and her husband hotelier David Weyrich. Thus, the Martin name remains in the winery title. The wine list still reflects the Italian vines planted earlier by the brothers—Nebbiolo, Sangiovese and Pinot Grigio. If the vines haven't changed much, the tasting room has. Weyrich has built an impressive mustard-colored Tuscan style structure with a red tile roof. Within is an extensive selection of giftwares, plus facilities for monthly winemakers dinners, prepared by Erich Koberl, the chef at Weyrich's Carlton Hotel in nearby Atascadero. Summer concerts are held in an amphitheater among the vineyards.

Tasting notes: Since a good Cab or Chard isn't hard to find in the south central coast, we were particularly interested in winery's Italian entrées. Pinot Grigio is a light and fruity white, a pleasant sipping wine. Nebbiolo is a crisp, tannin-rich red with a nice berry flavor. The Sangiovese is another lively red with a pleasantly spicy taste. Weyrich also offers several fine Zinfandels and—to stretch a point—they can be considered Italian, since Zin is a DNA twin to Italy's Primitivo. One of the winery's most popular offerings is *Muscato Allegro* made from Muscat Canelli grapes; it's fruity rich and pleasantly effervescent. Prices: **$$ to $$$$.** A *Grappa di Nebbiolo* and *Grappa di Moscato* are around $30; they aren't available for tasting.

Sylvester Winery ● T ✕

5115 Buena Vista Dr., Paso Robles, CA 93446; (800) 891-6055 or (805) 227-4000. (www.) Daily 11 to 5; MC/VISA, AMEX. Most varieties tasted; some wine related gift items and large deli with specialty foods; picnic area.

The focal point of this new winery is three handsomely restored 1950s Pullman "Streamliner" Santa Fe Railroad cars, which are open to visitors. They are the trademark of Austrian businessman Sylvester Feichtinger, since one of his many successful enterprises is a railcar restaurant in the Los Angeles area. He also has pistachio orchards and owns a firm that produces deli items. Feichtinger purchased the 430-acre Rancho Robles farm in the 1960s, began planting vineyards in 1982 and opened his winery in 1995.

Tasting notes: The short list includes Chardonnay, Cabernet Sauvignon and Merlot, plus some interesting and very drinkable Italian varietals. Prices: *$$ to $$$.*

Rio Seco Vineyard ● T ✗ 📷

4925 Union Rd., Paso Robles, CA 93446; (805) 460-WINE. (www.riosecovineyard.com) Friday-Sunday 11 to 5:30; MC/VISA. A few giftware items; small picnic area.

This appealing little winery is housed in an old fashioned red barn with white trim. The rustically comfortable tasting room is open to the winery, and a few gift items are displayed on barrel heads. Rio Seco was established in 1999 by a couple with interesting athletic backgrounds. Tom Hinkle was a catcher with a Detroit Tigers farm team, then he went on to coach high school and college baseball. He's now a scout with the Toronto Blue Jays and has discovered such stars as Randy Johnson and Mark Gardiner. His wife Carol was a gymnast in the 1971 NCAA Nationals and a longtime physical education and dance teacher at a local high school. She's also active in community theater. Their small winery produces about a thousand cases a year.

Tasting notes: The current list includes a pair of whites and three reds. The Pinot Blanc was soft and buttery, almost like a Chardonnay; and a blend of Viognier and Orange Muscat had a nice floral aroma and crisp taste. The reds are a fruity medium bodied Pinot Noir, a hearty Cabernet Sauvignon suitable for aging and a nice Zinfandel drawn from several vintages. A rich late harvest Zinfandel dessert wine completes the list. Prices: *$$$ to $$$$.*

Penman Springs Vineyard ● T ✗ 📷

1985 Penman Springs Rd., Paso Robles, CA 93446; (805) 237-7959 or (805) 237-8960. (www.penmanspringsvineyard.com) Friday-Sunday 11 to 5:30; MC/VISA. Most wines tasted. Some giftwares and specialty foods.

This well-kept ranch style winery occupies a benchland with views of the gently rolling Estrella River Valley. A couple of farm dogs named Rowdy and Curley may greet you as you head for the small, neat tasting room.

Penman Springs has gone through several proprietors since its establishment in 1981, and is now owned by businessman Carl McCasland and his wife Beth. They arrived on the scene in 1996. The original owner, former fireman Tom Baron, sold the winery to Gary Porter and Joseph Barton, who renamed it Grey Wolf Cellars. The Bartons later moved Grey Wolf to a spot along Highway 46; see above on page 255. McCasland was an executive with a corrugated box company before deciding to move his wife and their two teenage daughters to the wine country. He's a self-taught winemaker, "reading every book on wine I could get my hands on, and taking every class offered."

Tasting notes: When we last past, McCasland was offering just four wines, although he's planted additional varietals to expand his list. On the white side were a spicy and subtly sweet Muscat Blanc, and a barrel fermented toasty Chardonnay. The reds were a rich Merlot with enough of a tannin bite to suggest aging, and a classic peppery Cabernet Sauvignon with soft acid. Prices: *$ to $$$.*

Eberle Winery • T GT ✕ ☗

P.O. Box 2459 (Highway 46 East), Paso Robles, CA 93447; (805) 238-9607. (www.eberlewinery.com) Daily 10 to 5, until 6 in summer; MC/VISA. Most varieties tasted. Good selection of giftwares and books. Picnic tables on a view deck; guided tours daily.

This attractive cedar winery sits on a rise above its own vines, commanding a wide-angle view of the shallow river valley. The tasting room suggests a nicely furnished modern home with beamed ceilings, fabric walls and a fireplace. Formal landscaping completes a pleasant setting. W. Gary Eberle established the winery in 1982. A "pioneer" in this young area, he studied winemaking at U.C. Davis and settled here in 1973, working initially with Estrella River Vineyards. He was named Central Coast Winemaker of the Year in 1990. The much traveled young wine pioneer was a doctoral student in enology at U.C. Davis and a defensive tackle for Penn State; he has the barrel chest to prove it.

Tasting notes: The Eberle wines we tasted were uniformly excellent. The Chardonnay was crisp, buttery and spicy, while the Cabernets were light yet lush with a peppery nose and nicely complex flavor. Zinfandel was powerful and fruity; peppery with strong tannic accents, it will improve with aging. For chuckles, Gary has created a rosé from a blend of Cabernet, Zinfandel, Muscat Canelli and Chardonnay. This is no wimpy rosé; think of it as a blush wine with the heart of a defensive tackle. A recent edition is Viognier, which had a nice herbal nose and taste—kind of a cross between a Chardonnay and Sauvignon Blanc. Prices: *$ to $$$.*

Eos Estate Winery at Arciero Vineyards • T ST ✕ ☗

Highway 46 at Jardine Road (P.O. Box 1287), Paso Robles, CA 93447; (800) 429-WINE or (805) 239-2562. (www.arcierowinery.com) Daily 10 to 5 (until 6 on summer weekends); MC/VISA, AMEX. Select varieties tasted. Extensive gift, wineware and deli selection. Self-guided tours; racing car display.

This is how you build a family winery if you happen to be a family of millionaires. Visually, Eos Estate is one of America's great wine châteaux—a study in tile-roofed elegance set into a vineyard slope. It's modeled after the Benedictine monastery in Montecassino, Italy. A juniper-lined drive, extensive lawns, lavish landscaping and umbrella picnic tables create a setting of moneyed country refinement. The high ceiling tasting room is accented with glossy tile, chandeliers and a fireplace. A horseshoe-shaped tasting counter is its focal point. Excellent graphics take you on a self-guiding tour through the winery. Bunkered into the hillside, it rivals the luxury of the tasting room, with carved oaken doors, a brass chandelier in the entry and carpeted corridors. View windows allow peeks into the winery operations.

Brothers Frank and Phil Arciero immigrated from Italy in the 1930s, eventually their fortunes in southern California construction and ran a stable of racing cars as a pastime. Frank, in fact, competed in the Indianapolis 500. Some of their cars, including an Indy Super Vee driven by Phil Hill, Dan Gurney and Al Unser, are displayed in the tasting room. The Arciero forbearers had made wine in Italy "for centuries," so the brothers decided to continue the tradition, buying 160 acres in 1982 to start their winery.

Tasting notes: The wines are uniformly upscale yet modestly priced. The Chardonnay was full bodied and nutty, with a nice hint of oak. Chenin Blanc was fruity and sweet; good if you like sweeter whites. Cabernet Sauvignon, Zinfandel and Petite Sirah were full flavored and robust, suitable for immediate sipping or putting down. Also on the list are Merlot, Nebbiolo and Sangiovese. Prices: *$ to $$$.*

Laura's Vineyard ● *T* ✕ 📷

5620 Highway 46 East, Paso Robles, CA 93447; (805) 238-6300; mailing address: P.O. Box 304, San Miguel, CA 93451. Daily 10 to 6; MC/VISA. Most varieties tasted. Fair selection of giftwares, specialty foods and wine logo items. Shaded picnic area.

Who says you can't turn a doublewide into an appealing wine tasting rooms? Perched on a knoll above the vineyards, this space is a busy blend of assorted gift items, good wines and cheerful décor. The winery was started in 1977 by Cliff Giacobine, longtime local winemaker and formerly a principle at Estrella River Winery. He sold Laura's Vineyard in 1996 to Patrick O'Dell. Who was Laura? A remarkable lady and mother of two Estrella Valley vintners—Cliff and his half-brother Gary Eberle. The current Laura in residence at the winery is a large, fluffy calico cat, who obviously has the run of the tasting room.

Tasting notes: The Cabernet was excellent—well balanced, soft and lush; and the Chardonnay was smooth and spicy, the result of sleeping in both American and French oak. Cabernet Franc, blended with a bit of Petite Sirah and Cabernet Sauvignon, displayed a spicy, herbal flavor. We were even convinced to try a nip of white Zinfandel, which had a touch of Muscat to bring up the flavor. It wasn't bad. Others on the list are Semillon, Zinfandel, Syrah and Merlot. Prices are very fair for the quality: *$ to $$$.*

Meridian Vineyards ● *T* ✕ 📷

7000 Highway 46 East (P.O. Box 3289), Paso Robles, CA 93447; (805) 237-6000. (www.meridianvineyards.com) Daily 10 to 5; MC/VISA. Most varieties tasted. Wine related gift items. Picnic area near winery.

Starting from a small but well-financed base, Meridian has emerged as a major Paso Robles wine estate. Nestlé's Wine World division built this facility, which crests a hill with a fish-eye view of its own vineyards. It's an impressive affair—a large U-shaped complex with stone facing, a landscaped courtyard and other amenities. An herb garden and picnic area invite visitors to linger. Most of its grapes are drawn from three vineyards owned by Meridian in Santa Barbara County; others are maturing right at the winery's doorstep. The facility was started in 1988 and the tasting room opened in 1990, with other embellishments added later.

Tasting notes: The winery likes to focus on central coast grapes. Both the Santa Barbara County and Edna Valley Chardonnays were excellent, fruity and toasty with crisp finishes and hints of oak. The Pinot Noir had a berry-like nose and taste; light in body and mouth-filling. Paso Robles Syrah was big, oaky and peppery; excellent if you like assertive wines. The Cabernet Sauvignon was softer, complex and spicy with a light tannin finish. Others on the list include Sauvignon Blanc, Merlot, Zinfandel, Gewürztraminer and a slightly sweet Cabernet Blanc. Prices: *$$ to $$$$.*

Tobin James Cellars ● *T GTA* ✕ 📷

8950 Union Rd., Paso Robles, CA 93446; (805) 239-2204. Daily 10 to 6; MC/VISA. Most varieties tasted. Good selection of wine logo items; picnic area. Guided tours by appointment.

You don't often hear the expression "Belly up to the bar boys," in the wine country, yet it's appropriate at this Western style winery. And what a great bar it is—an elaborately carved structure more than a century old, complete with a mirrored backbar. Tobin found it in an old saloon in Overton, Missouri—back there in Jesse James country. In fact, there's a couple of James Gang posters in his tasting room—stuck on the walls near the farm implements. In the background, you may hear Clint Black whining a country tune.

Are you *sure* we're in the wine country?

If you think all this is improbable, how about an eighteen-year-old Cincinnati kid with no money deciding that he wanted to own a winery, and then actually doing it? This unlikely chain of events started when Tobin James Shumrick—working in a wine shop in Cincinatti—met Gary Eberle, then a partner and winemaker at Estrella River Winery. Tobin offered to follow Gary back to Paso Robles and work for no pay. Less than fifteen years later, working hard, having fun and often laboring for free just to learn, Tobin had his own winery. He opened his cellars with its old Western saloon motif in 1994. Why the Western look?

"We wanted a place where people could feel comfortable," Tobin told us. "Sometimes, the wine industry takes itself too seriously."

Tasting notes: Tobin *is* serious about making wine, particularly big and hearty reds—and "the medals just keep rockin' in," he said. A James Gang Reserve, big, lush and spicy was as good as Zinfandel gets. The Sure Fire Zinfandel was almost as great—spicy and peppery with a raspberry taste. The Blue Sky Cabernet Sauvignon was complex and full of berry flavor, big enough to face off any entrée. Barrel fermented Sundance Chardonnay was lush, silky and toasty. Perhaps the best buy is an inexpensive blend of Gamay, Syrah and Mourvèdre that's soft, herbal and complex. It's called *Château le Cacheflo*. We said he was serious about *making* wines, not about naming them. Prices: *$$ to $$$$*.

Vintners choice: "My favorite? Whatever we have the most of."

THE BEST OF THE BUNCH

The best wine buys ● Bridlewood Winery, Los Olivos Vintners (Austin Cellars brands) and Buttonwood Farms in Santa Ynez Valley; Tally Vineyards in Edna Valley and Windemere in San Luis Obispo; Pesenti Winery and Jan-Kris Winery in the west Paso Robles area; and Arciero Winery and Tobin James in the Estrella River Valley.

The most attractive wineries ● Bridlewood Winery, The Gainey Vineyard and Sunstone in Santa Ynez Valley; Fess Parker Winery in Foxen Canyon; Corbett Canyon Vineyards in Edna Valley; Justin Winery east of Paso Robles; and Arciero Winery in the Estrella River Valley.

The most interesting tasting rooms ● Sanford Winery east of Buellton; Bridlewood Winery, Gainey Vineyard, Sunstone Winery and Rideau Vineyard in Santa Ynez Valley; Curtis Winery and Fess Parker Winery in Foxen Canyon; Jack Niven Hospitality Center at the Edna Valley Vineyard and the "schoolhouse tasting room" of Seven Peaks winery in the Edna Valley; Mastantuono Winery, Castoro Cellars and Hope Farms in the Templeton area; Carmody McNight Estates, Norman Vineyards, Adelaida Cellars and Hidden Mountain Ranch west of Paso Robles; and Martin & Weyrich Winery, Laura's Vineyard and Arciero Winery in the Estrella River Valley.

The funkiest tasting rooms • Bedford Thompson in the Foxen Canyon area, Claiborne & Churchill in the Edna Valley, Windemere in a San Luis Obispo industrial park and Tobin James in the Estrella River Valley.

The best gift shops • Bridlewood Winery, Daniel Gehrs Los Olivos tasting room and Buttonwood Farm (with its wine, produce and specialty foods blend) in the Santa Ynez Valley; Jack Niven Hospitality Center at Edna Valley Vineyards; Mastantuono Winery, York Mountain Winery, Hope Farms and Martin & Weyrich Winery in the Templeton area; and Arciero Winery in the Estrella River Valley.

The nicest picnic areas • Bridlewood Winery, Foley Estates, Rusack and Firestone Vineyard in Santa Ynez Valley; Byron Winery and Cambria Winery in the Santa Maria Valley; Harmony Cellars above Harmony; JanKris Vineyard in the Templeton area; Norman Vineyards and Justin Cellars west of Paso Robles; and Arciero Winery in the Estrella River Valley.

The best guided tours • The Gainey Vineyard in Santa Ynez Valley and Firestone Vineyard in Foxen Canyon.

Wine country maps and events

Santa Barbara County Wineries, available at area wineries or from the Santa Barbara County Vintners' Association, P.O. Box 1558, Santa Ynez, CA 93460-1558; (805) 688-0881. *(www.sbcountywines.com)*

Wineries of the Edna Valley and Arroyo Grande Valley, is available at area wineries or from: Edna Valley Arroyo Grande Valley Vintners, P.O. Box 159, Arroyo Grande, CA 93420; (805) 541-5868. *(www.ednavalley.com or www.thegrid.net/vintners)*

Wine Tasting in Paso Robles, is available at area wineries or from: Paso Robles Vintners and Growers Association, P.O. Box 324, Paso Robles, CA 93447; (805) 239-8463. *(www.pasowine.com)*

The Far Out Vineyards of Paso Robles, is available at ten participating wineries west of the town.

Wineland events • **Santa Barbara County**: Vintners' Festival with barrel tastings and other events in late April, and A Celebration of the Harvest featuring tastings, food and entertainment in Santa Ynez Valley in mid-October; both sponsored by the Santa Barbara County Vintners' Association; (800) 218-0881 or (805) 688-0881. Danish Days in Solvang includes some winery events, September; (800) 468-6765.

San Luis Obispo County: Zinfandel Festival with Paso Robles area wineries the third weekend of March; (800) 406-4040 or (805) 238-0506. Paso Robles Wine Festival, third weekend of May; (800) 406-4040 or (805) 238-0506. Central Coast Winetasting Classic, San Luis Bay Inn, Avila Beach, July; (805) 544-5229 or (805) 543-1323. Central Coast Wine Festival, Mission Plaza, San Luis Obispo, September; (805) 543-1323. Harvest Wine Affair, third weekend in October in Paso Robles, (800) 406-4040 or (805) 238-0506. Individual wineries also sponsor events throughout the year.

BEYOND THE VINEYARDS

The south central coast was a popular tourist area before the first Pesenti squeezed his first grape, and certainly before the new crop of high-tech wineries arrived. Without all those tasting rooms, tens of thousands still would come to prowl through the missions, poke about Solvang's shops and toast themselves on Pacific beaches. Just over the ridge, architecturally gorgeous tile-roofed Santa Barbara is one of California's major tourist lures.

Starting from **Solvang**, we'll suggest driving tours that will carry you to the area's touristic highlights. First, you'll likely want to go "shop-about" in Solvang, stuff your little faces with Danish pastries, ride the horse-drawn streetcar and perhaps catch a play at the **Festival Theater.** A repertory group performs summer-long in this outdoor playhouse. **Elverhoj Museum** in a Scandinavian style building at 1624 Elverhoy Way (Second Street) recalls Solvang's Danish heritage and the **Hans Christian Andersen Museum** above the Book Loft on Mission Drive has exhibits concerning the legendary storyteller. You'll also want to investigate the museum and ancient adobe halls of **Mission Santa Inez.**

From Solvang, head south on Alisal Road, which coils through some of Santa Ynez Valley's prettiest oak woodlands. Pause at lushly wooded **Nojoqui Falls County Park** for a short hike to the waterfalls, which may or may not be falling, depending on the season. Continue on Alisal Road to U.S. 101; you can follow it south to **Gaviota State Beach** and on to alluring **Santa Barbara**, or head north to **Buellton** of pea soup fame.

We'll focus on the northern route, which is closer to the vinelands. From Buellton, take State Highway 246 west to **La Purísima Mission State Historic Park** near Lompoc. It's the most authentically restored of California's twenty-one missions, having been rebuilt as a WPA project during the Depression. The Lompoc area also is famous for its glittering Technicolor **flower fields** in spring and early summer.

From Lompoc, head north on one of America's most scenic byways, State Highway 1. It will take you to the wide sandy beaches of **Oceano, Grover City** and clam-famous **Pismo Beach**. At the Grover City-Oceano section of **Pismo State Beach,** you can drive right along the surf, just like they do in the TV commercials—if your car has the proper tires. Be careful you don't get stuck; ask the ranger at the gate if the sand's firm enough for your vehicle.

Highway 1 rejoins U.S. 101 in Pismo, but avoid that and follow the ocean-front drive through **Shell Beach** to wonderfully funky old **Avila Beach.** It's a resort town right out of the Thirties with tiny stucco cottages and a beach walk. Just beyond, weathered **Port San Luis Pier** is host to a good seafood restaurant (listed below), a fish market, uncounted seagulls and an occasional visiting sea lion.

Return to U.S. 101 and explore tidy and well-kept old **San Luis Obispo.** Its visitor offerings include **Mission San Luis Obispo;** several boutiques, restaurants and antique shops in SLO's tidy downtown area, just below the mission. Nearby is the comely campus of **California Polytechnic State University,** or simply Cal Poly. (Noted for its agricultural courses, it's sometimes unkindly called "Cow Piley.")

From SLO, take State Highway 1 northwest to **Morro Bay**, a seaside charmer with dome-shaped **Morro Rock** as its centerpiece. Two state parks, **Morro Bay** and **Montaña de Oro**, preserve slices of rocky beaches, windy headlands and lush forests. Driving north on Highway 1, you'll skim the rough hewn coastline and pass **Harmony**, the dairy town turned art colony. From here, you can continue north to aquatically rustic **Cambria**. Just beyond is **Hearst San Simeon State Historical Monument**, the lavish castle-home of the late newspaper baron William Randolph Hearst.

Santa Ynez Valley attractions

Elverhoj Museum • *1624 Elverhoy Way, Solvang; (805) 686-1211. Wednesday-Sunday 1 to 4; free.* □ This small museum focuses on Solvang's Scandinavian heritage.

Hans Christian Andersen Museum • *Above the Book Loft and Coffee House, 1680 Mission Dr., Solvang; (805) 688-2052. Open daily from 9, various closing hours.* □ Exhibits concerning the life of storyteller Hans Christian Andersen, plus vintage books for display and sale.

La Purísima Mission State Historic Park • *Lompoc; (805) 733-3713. Daily 9 to 5; modest admission charge.* □ A faithful WPA reconstruction of an early California mission. Workers used the same tools as those originally employed by the Indians.

Mission Santa Inez • *1760 Mission Dr., Solvang; (805) 688-4815. Daily 9 to 7 in summer and 9 to 5 the rest of the year.* □ Restored early California mission; self-guiding tour and museum.

Santa Ynez Valley Historical Society Museum and Carriage House • *3596 Sagunto St., Santa Ynez; (805) 688-7889. Museum open Friday-Sunday 1 to 4 and carriage house Tuesday-Saturday 10 to 4 and Sunday 1-4.* □ Exhibits on local history and the Chumash Indians, plus large horse-drawn vehicle collection.

San Luis Obispo County attractions

Mission San Luis Obispo • *Chorro and Monterey streets, San Luis Obispo; (805) 543-6850. Daily 9 to 5 in summer and 9 to 4 the rest of the year; donations appreciated.* □ Restored early California mission in the heart of downtown; self-guiding tours, museum.

Mission San Miguel Arcangel • *775 Mission St., San Miguel; (805) 467-3256. Daily 9:30 to 4; donations appreciated.* □ Attractively weathered mission and museum; self-guiding tours.

San Luis Obispo County Historical Museum • *696 Monterey St., San Luis Obispo; (805) 543-0638. Wednesday-Sunday 10 to 4; donations appreciated.* □ Historical exhibits in restored Carnegie Library.

Santa Maria Valley Historical Museum • *616 S. Broadway, Santa Maria; (805) 922-3130. Tuesday-Saturday noon to 5; free.* □ Exhibits tracing the Santa Maria Valley history from the Chumash Indians to the present.

WINE COUNTRY DINING

PRICE KEY: Dinner entrée with soup or salad, without drinks or dessert for under $10 = $; $10 to $14 = $$; $15 to $25 = $$$; over $25 = $$$$.

Santa Barbara County

A.J. Spurs • ☆☆☆ $$$

□ *350 E. Hwy. 246 (just east of the freeway), Buellton; (805) 686-1655. Western barbecue-style fare; full bar service. Dinner nightly. MC/VISA, AMEX.* □ Housed in an oversized log cabin, abrim with Old Western atmosphere, contrived but nicely done. Cowboy curios, game trophies and geegaws to study while you chew. The menu is as Western as John Wayne's drawl—barbecued steaks, ribs and chicken, served with soup, salsa and tequila beans. Live music Friday and Saturday.

Bit O' Denmark ● ☆☆ $$

□ 473 Alisal Rd. (Mission Drive), Solvang; (805) 688-5426. Danish-American; full bar. Breakfast through dinner daily. Major credit cards. □ Popular Danish restaurant featuring breakfasts with a variety of pancakes; a full smörgasbord for lunch and dinner, plus frikadeller (meatballs with sweet and sour red cabbage). Local wines and international beers.

Cold Spring Tavern ● ☆☆☆ $$$

□ 5995 Stagecoach Rd. (half an hour uphill from Solvang on Highway 154), Santa Barbara; (805) 967-0066. American; full bar service. Lunch daily; dinner nightly; breakfast weekends only. Reservations essential on weekends; MC/VISA. □ Century-old stage stop tucked into the bottom of a ravine, in a setting that's at once dramatic, romantic and rustic. Wagon wheel chandeliers, kerosene lamps and the like. Varied menu with large portions—steak, pasta, chops, venison, rabbit and chicken.

The Hitching Post ● ☆☆ $$$

□ 406 E. Hwy 246 (half mile east of the freeway), Buellton; (805) 688-0676. Western barbecue; full bar service. Dinner nightly. MC/VISA. □ Long established, locally popular place featuring barbecue specialties—steak, baby back pork ribs, grilled quail, chicken or duck and seafood. Décor is rustic rural American.

The Little Mermaid ● ☆☆ $$

□ 1546 Mission Dr. (Fourth), Solvang; (805) 688-6141. Danish-American; wine and beer. Lunch and dinner daily. MC/VISA, AMEX. □ Cute Scandinavian-style café featuring puffy round breakfast pancakes called aebleskivers. The "skiver-maker" works in full view, observable from within or without the restaurant. Danish and American lunches and dinners.

Massimi's Ristorante ● ☆☆ $$$

□ Alamo Pintado Avenue near Grand Avenue, Los Olivos; (805) 688-0027. Italian; wine and beer. Lunch and dinner Tuesday-Saturday. MC/VISA, AMEX. □ Pleasingly decorated Italian chef-owned restaurant in an old pressed tin building in downtown Los Olivos. The mostly Italian menu features fresh pastas, Osso Buco, chicken marsalla and piccata, fresh seafood, veal and in-house desserts.

Mattei's Tavern ● ☆☆☆ $$

□ Highway 154 (Grand Avenue), Los Olivos; (805) 688-4820. American; full bar service. Dinner nightly; reservations advised on weekends; MC/VISA. □ An 1886 stage stop, refurbished and furnished with antiques and western America artifacts. Menu ranges from prime rib and steaks to fresh seafood and pastas.

Moellekrohn ● ☆☆ $$

□ 435 Alisal Rd., Solvang; (805) 688-4555. Danish-American; wine and beer. Lunch and dinner daily. Major credit cards. □ Another of Solvang's Danish restaurants, serving a complete smörgasbord dinners, plus Danish sausage and meatball entrées, and open faced sandwiches for lunch.

Mustard Seed ● ☆☆ $$

□ 1655 Mission (First), Solvang; (805) 688-1318. American rural; no alcohol. Breakfast & lunch daily; dinner Tuesday-Saturday. MC/VISA. □ American country restaurant in a Danish style cottage, featuring rural fare such as breaded veal cutlets, sautéed beef liver and southern fried chicken.

Pea Soup Andersen's ● ☆☆ $$

□ 376 Avenue of the Flags, Buellton; (805) 688-5581. American; full bar service. Lunch through dinner daily. MC/VISA. □ Historic restaurant started in 1924, based on Juliette Andersen's recipe for split pea soup. It's still the most interesting thing on the menu, which features steaks, chops and pot roast. Complex includes gift shops, fruit wine tasting and a mini-museum offering a quick study of Andersen family history.

Royal Scandia Restaurant ● ☆☆ $$$

□ 420 Alisal Rd. (downtown), Solvang; (805) 688-8000. American-continental; full bar service. Lunch through dinner daily. Major credit cards. □ Danish-style restaurant with Scandinavian entrées, plus other European and American fare. Buffet breakfast daily; brunch on Sunday. Scandinavian interior with open beam cathedral ceiling; outdoor patio.

The Viking Garden ● ☆☆ $

□ 446-C Alisal Rd. (Copenhagen), Solvang; (805) 688-1250. Danish, German, American and Mexican; wine and beer. Breakfast through dinner daily. MC/VISA. □ Small restaurant that looks more Italian than Danish, with red checkered tablecloths. The menu is eclectic and inexpensive, and includes "early bird" Danish dinners such as breaded pork patties and red cabbage, and smoked pork chops with sauerkraut and potato pancakes. Indoor and outdoor dining.

San Luis Obispo County

A.J. Spurs ● ☆☆☆ $$$

□ 508 Main St., Templeton; (805) 434-2700. Western barbecue; full bar service. Dinner nightly. Major credit cards. □ See description under Santa Barbara County.

Apple Farm ● ☆☆☆ $$ to $$$

□ 2015 Monterey St. (near U.S. 101), San Luis Obispo; (805) 544-6100. American; full bar service. Breakfast through dinner daily. MC/VISA. □ Country cute family restaurant featuring homestyle fare such as roast turkey, pan fried trout, chicken & dumplings and country pot roast. Elaborate down home décor and large country crafts gift selection.

Chelsea Book and Café ● ☆ $

□ Spring and Sixth streets (Valley Oak Plaza), Paso Robles; (805) 237-2464. Light fare; no alcohol. Breakfast through dinner Monday-Saturday; lunch through early evening Sunday. MC/VISA. □ Attractive bookstore-café with comfortable couch seating amidst book shelves. Simple menu features salads, sandwiches and specialty coffees; oatmeal cookies are a popular item.

Deborah's Room ● ☆☆☆☆ $$$$

□ At Justin Winery Hospitality Centre, 11680 Chimney Rock Rd., Paso Robles; (805) 237-4150. (www.justinwine) American regional; prix fixe dinners featuring Justin wines. Dinner nightly; advance reservations required. Major credit cards. □ Opulent "French country" dining room at the winery. Daily changing regional menu is matched to current and older vintages of Justin wines. Wine pairing menus feature current releases and barrel tastings.

Hot Springs Grill ● ☆☆☆ $$

□ At the Paso Robles Inn, 1103 Spring St. (Eleventh Street), Paso Robles; (805) 238-2660. American; full bar service. Lunch through dinner daily. Major credit cards. □ Turn-of-the-century dining room in Paso Robles' landmark multi-gabled brick hotel. The menu offers babyback ribs, fresh fish, chicken marsala, jumbo prawns over linguine and several steaks, with a focus on local wines. Veranda dining; live music on weekends.

Ian McPhee's Grill ● ☆☆☆ $$$

☐ *416 Main Street (between Fourth and Fifth), Templeton; (805) 434-3204. American; full bar service. Breakfast and lunch Monday-Saturday, dinner nightly and Sunday brunch. Major credit cards.* ☐ Appealing old style restaurant with a contemporary menu—rosemary chicken breast, oak-grilled sirloin, Asia spiced rack of lamb and broiled honey mustard salmon. The look is early Americana with cane back chairs, coffered ceiling and old style bar.

Joshua's Restaurant and Vineyards ● ☆☆☆ $$$

☐ *Thirteenth and Vine streets, Paso Robles; (805) 238-7515. American; full bar service. Lunch Monday-Friday; Sunday brunch; dinner Monday-Sunday. MC/VISA, AMEX.* ☐ Very appealing restaurant, fashioned into a century old Catholic church building; spacious interior with the original stained glass. Menu focuses on steaks, sweetbreads, prime rib, chicken, baby back ribs, seafood and pastas. Periodic "Meet the Winemaker Dinners," with five courses and five local wines. Live entertainment Friday and Saturday nights.

Mission Grill ● ☆☆ $$

☐ *1023 Chorro St. (beside the mission), San Luis Obispo; (805) 547-5544. Southwestern; full bar service. Lunch and dinner daily. Major credit cards.* ☐ Handsome restaurant in an old brick building, overlooking San Luis Creek and Mission San Luis Obispo; some creek view and patio tables. Open kitchen with Southwestern menu features several Santa Fe style entrées plus enchiladas, burritos and such.

Old Harmony Pasta Factory and Saloon ● ☆☆ $$

☐ *Two Old Creamery Rd., Harmony; (805) 927-5882. Italian-Californian; wine and beer. Lunch in the saloon daily; dinner nightly; Sunday brunch. Reservations advised; MC/VISA, AMEX.* ☐ Cute old place done in rural Americana, in the old Harmony creamery complex. Italian menu with assorted home made pastas, pork and chicken dishes, plus seafood with California accents. Outdoor dining.

Olde Port Inn ● ☆☆☆ $$$

☐ *Port San Luis Pier; (805) 595-2515. American, mostly seafood; full bar service. Lunch and dinner daily. Reservations essential on weekends; MC/VISA.* ☐ Cheerfully rustic fish house perched on the Port San Luis Pier with views of sand, sea and headlands. Daily seafood specials are fresh, often just off one of the restaurant's boats. The spicy *bouillabaisse* is excellent.

WINELAND LODGINGS

PRICE KEY: A two-person room for $35 or less = $; $36 to $50 = $$;
$51 to $75 = $$$; $76 to $100 = $$$$; more than $100 = $$$$$.

Santa Barbara County

Chimney Sweep Inn at Tivoli ● ☆☆☆ $$$$ to $$$$$

☐ *1564 Copenhagen Dr. (Atterdag Avenue), Solvang, CA 93463; (800) 266-1484 or (805) 688-0559. (www.chimneysweepinn.com) Rates include continental breakfast. Major credit cards.* ☐ Nicely appointed Danish style inn with fifty rooms and suites and six cottages. TV, phones, refrigerators and coffee makers; some units with fireplaces; spa.

Country Inn and Suites ● ☆☆☆ $$$$ to $$$$$

❑ *1455 Mission Dr., Solvang, CA 93463; (805) 688-2018. Rates include breakfast. Major credit cards.* ❑ Danish-style 82-room lodge with TV, phones and refrigerators; swimming pool.

Meadowlark Motel ● ☆☆ $$ to $$$$$

❑ *2644 Mission Dr. (near Refugio Road), Solvang, CA 93463; (800) 344-9792 or (805) 688-4631. (www.meadowlarkinnsolvang.com) Rates include continental breakfast. Major credit cards.* ❑ A nineteen-room inn on two acres just east of Solvang; TV, phones; pool; nicely landscaped grounds. Kitchen units available.

Svendsgaard's Lodge ● ☆☆ $$$ to $$$$$

❑ *1711 Mission Dr. (Alisal Road), Solvang, CA 93463; (800) 733-8757 or (805) 688-3277. Major credit cards.* ❑ Danish-style 48-room motel with TV, room phones; free continental breakfast, swimming pool.

Solvang Royal Scandinavian Inn ● ☆☆☆ $$$$$

❑ *400 Alisal Rd. (P.O. Box 30), Solvang, CA 93464; (800) 624-5572 or (805) 688-8000. Major credit cards.* ❑ Attractive newly remodeled resort; 133 rooms with TV movies and phones. Pool, spa, fitness room, fireplace in lobby. **Royal Scandia restaurant** serves breakfast through dinner daily; California-continental with Danish specialties; full bar service and extensive local wine list.

Bed & breakfast inn

The Ballard Inn ● ☆☆☆☆ $$$$$

❑ *2436 Baseline (Alamo Pintado Road), Ballard, CA 93463; (800) 638-BINN or (805) 688-7770. Fifteen rooms with private baths; full breakfast. MC/VISA.* ❑ Comfortably elegant Victorian inn furnished with antiques. Individually decorated rooms; some with fireplaces. Full cooked-to-order breakfast, afternoon wine with *hors d'oeuvres.*

San Luis Obispo County

San Luis Obispo, Santa Maria, Morro Bay and Pismo Beach have dozens of motels. Our list here covers only communities next door to the vineyards: Paso Robles, Arroyo Grande and Templeton.

Adelaide Inn ● ☆☆ $$$ to $$$$

❑ *1215 Ysabel Ave. (Highway 46 exit), Paso Robles, CA 93446; (800) 549-PASO (California) or (805) 238-2770. Major credit cards.* ❑ Nicely-appointed 67-unit motel; TV movies, video rentals, phones, radios and refrigerators. Heated pool; laundry. Suites available.

Best Western Black Oak Motor Lodge ● ☆☆☆ $$$ to $$$$

❑ *1135 24th St. (Highway 46 exit), Paso Robles, CA 93446; (800) 528-1234 or (805) 238-4740. Major credit cards.* ❑ A 110-unit motel with TV, radios, phones and refrigerators. Swimming and wading pools, spa, sauna, coin laundry. **Margie's Diner** serves American fare; breakfast through dinner; full bar service.

Best Western Casa Grande Inn ● ☆☆☆ $$$$ to $$$$$

❑ *850 Oak Park Rd. (Oak Park exit), Arroyo Grande, CA 93420; (800) 528-1234 or (805) 481-7398. Major credit cards. Rates include breakfast.* ❑ A 113-unit motel with TV movies and phones; some rooms with refrigerators; some efficiency units. Pool, spa, sauna, game room, small exercise room, coin laundry. Kitchenettes and suites available. Adjacent **restaurant** serves breakfast through diner; full bar service.

Econo Lodge ● ☆☆ $$$ to $$$$$
☐ *611 El Camino Real (Halcyon Road exit), Arroyo Grande, CA 93420; (805) 489-9300. Rates include continental breakfast. Major credit cards.* ☐ A forty-unit motel with TV, room phones; pool.

Los Padres Motel ● ☆☆ $$ to $$$
☐ *1575 Monterey St., San Luis Obispo, CA 93401; (800) 543-5090 or (805) 543-5017. Major credit cards. Rates include breakfast snack.* ☐ Prim, clean and cute motel just south of the north U.S. 101 interchange and within walking distance of downtown; TV movies, phones and refrigerators.

Madonna Inn ● ☆☆☆ $$$$ to $$$$$
☐ *100 Madonna Rd., San Luis Obispo, CA 93405; (800) 543-9666 or (805) 543-3000. Major credit cards.* ☐ Legendary for its whimsical, gaudy architecture, the inn has 109 rooms, all decorated differently. Many travelers stop just to check out the architecture in the lobby, restaurant and even the restrooms. Rooms have TV, phones and flashy décor. Suites available. **Dining room** and **coffee shop** serve breakfast through dinner; American fare; full bar services.

Paso Robles Inn ● ☆☆☆ $$$$$
☐ *1103 Spring St. (Eleventh Street), Paso Robles, CA 93446; (800) 676-1713 or (805) 238-2660. (www.pasoroblesinn.com) Major credit cards.* ☐ Historic inn dating from 1891 and recently renovated. Attractively furnished rooms with phones, refrigerators and coffee makers; some with fireplaces and therapy spas fed by hot springs. Pool and spa; elaborate landscaping. **Hot Springs Grill** listed above.

Bed & breakfast inns

Arbor Inn ● ☆☆☆☆ $$$$$
☐ *2175 Arbor Rd., Paso Robles, CA 93446; (805) 227-4673. Eight rooms with private baths; full or continental breakfast. Major credit cards.* ☐ Beautiful multi-gabled inn with rooms furnished in English antiques. Appealing common areas and nicely landscaped grounds; late afternoon snacks with wine.

Arroyo Village Inn Bed & Breakfast ● ☆☆☆ $$$$$
☐ *407 El Camino Real (Brisco or Halcyon exits), Arroyo Grande, CA 94320; (800) 563-7762. (www.arroyovillageinn.com) Seven rooms with private baths; full breakfast. Major credit cards.* ☐ Luxuriously replicated Victorian farmhouse with early American country décor, featuring Laura Ashley prints and antiques. Garden theme rooms have sitting areas and TV; some have spa tubs, VCRs and CD players. Complimentary wine, tea and cordials; evening desserts.

Just Inn ● ☆☆☆☆ $$$$$
☐ *At Justin Winery Hospitality Centre, 11680 Chimney Rock Rd., Paso Robles, CA 93446; (805) 238-6932. (www.justinwine) Three suites with private baths and full breakfast. Price discount for Justin Wine Society members (membership is free). Major credit cards.* ☐ Opulent French château style inn with luxuriously furnished three-room suites with decks; overstuffed tapestry-covered furniture, down comforters, ceiling murals and marble bathrooms with hydro-tubs. Full breakfast, evening wine; pool, spa and bicycles.

South central coast information sources

Arroyo Grande Chamber of Commerce, 800-A W. Branch St., Arroyo Grande, CA 93420-1999; (805) 489-1488.

Paso Robles Chamber of Commerce, 1225 Park St., Paso Robles, CA 93446-2234; (805) 238-0506. *(www.pasorobleschamber.com)*

San Luis Obispo Chamber of Commerce, 1039 Chorro St., San Luis Obispo, CA 93401; (805) 781-2777. *(www.visitslo.com)*

Santa Maria Valley Visitor & Convention Bureau, 614 S. Broadway, Santa Maria, CA 93454-5111; (805) 925-2403. *(www.santamaria.com)*

Solvang Chamber of Commerce, P.O. Box 70 (1511 Mission Dr.), Solvang, CA 93463; (805) 688-3317. *(www.solvangusa.com)*

WINE TASTING IS SERIOUS BUSINESS

EL DORADO & AMADOR COUNTIES

Coloma

Lotus

Cold Springs Rd.

Gold Hill Rd.

Mosquito Rd.

Union Ridge

Hassler

North Canyon

Carson Rd.

Camino

Broadway

Placerville

Newton Rd.

Pleasant Valley Rd.

Pleasant Valley

Diamond Springs

Cedar Ravine Rd.

Bucks Bar Rd.

Leisure Ln.

Sly Park Rd.

Somerset

Grizzly Flat Rd.

Perry Creek Rd.

Mt. Aukum Rd.

Fair Play Rd.

Slug Gulch Rd.

N

Mt. Aukum

Omo Ranch Rd.

Shenandoah Rd.

Ostrom Rd.

Plymouth

Fiddletown Rd.

Fiddletown

THE WINERIES

1. Gold Hill
2. Venezio
3. Boeger
4. Lava Cap
5. Madroña
6. Coulson Eldorado
7. Jodar
8. Sierra Vista
9. Firefall
10. Granite Springs
11. Single Leaf
12. Van der Vijver
13. Fitzpatrick
14. Oakstone
15. Perry Creek
16. Windwalker Farm
17. Charles B Mitchell
18. Latcham
19. Young's Vineyard
20. Monteviña
21. Villa Toscano
22. Nine Gables
23. Domaine de la Terre Rouge
24. TKC Vineyards
25. Karly Winery
26. Story Winery
27. Renwood
28. Shenandoah
29. Amador Foothill
30. Deaver
31. Charles Spinetta
32. Dobre Zemlja
33. Sobon Estate
34. Rabbit Hill

I wonder often what the Vintners buy
One half so precious as the stuff they sell?
— The Rubaiyat of Omar Khayyam

Chapter Twelve

THE GOLD COUNTRY
Bottled bullion from the Sierra foothills

No region looms larger in the history of California than the foothills of the Sierra Nevada. Here, the discovery of gold in 1848 catapulted a remote Mexican outpost into the most populous and prosperous state in the Union.

This also was the one of California's first major wine producing areas. There were, after all, a lot of thirsty miners in those hills! When the gold ran out in the late 1800s, most of the people ran out, too, and wineries began closing. Prohibition finished off all save one. Today, the wineries and the people are coming back, and this region of the Sierra Nevada foothills called the "Gold Country" is one of California's most diverse and scenic winelands.

The Sierra foothills wine country is focused in three counties in the heart of the Gold Country—El Dorado, Amador and Calaveras. Early Spanish miners called this region *La Veta Madre*. We know it by the more familiar "Mother Lode."

During the rush to riches, towns germinated overnight, then they faded as the gold was depleted. In the fading, they left a treasure trove of sturdy brick buildings, grand balconied hotels and Victorian homes. These now house antique and curio shops, museums and bed & breakfast inns. The area has more state historic parks than any other region of California. All of this yesterday lore is set in scenic foothills of oak clusters, pine forests and tawny meadows.

Vineyards are scattered about the Mother Lode, draped over ridges, terraced up steep slopes and tucked into hidden canyons. They merge with woodlands, pastures and an occasional Christmas tree farm to create a rumpled patchwork quilt. Sierra foothills tasting rooms are inviting places, often

279

in intriguing settings. Some are in log or rough stone cellars dating back to the gold rush. Others are in modern structures perched on high knolls, offering panoramas of the hilly countryside.

Since most of the wineries are small, your tasting room host may be the winemaker-owner or a family member. Many of these friendly family wineries also offer snacks or samples of specialty foods; some elaborate spreads amount to virtual free lunches. And because these wineries aren't overwhelmed by visitors, most do not charge for tasting.

As further incentive to visit this region, the wines are excellent, winning a goodly share of medals, and they're inexpensive compared with the better known Napa and Sonoma regions. This is primarily red wine territory. The area's Zinfandels are legendary, and account for more than half the total vineyard acreage. Sierra foothills reds are typically robust, spicy and full-flavored, without a lot of filtering and fining. They're straightforward and hearty, like the people who settled this land. Some excellent whites are made here as well, in the higher, cooler elevations.

There is no best season to tour the Gold Country's wine country, although we favor fall, when both vineyards and hardwood groves add golden hues to this predominately green terrain. In winter, one can sip a bit of Zin after hitting the ski slopes a few miles above the vineyards. In spring and summer, these mountains and their running streams lure hikers, campers, whitewater enthusiasts and fisherfolk. Dams, thrown across rivers to form reservoirs and quench flatlanders' thirst, draw the boating set.

Free-flowing streams

Those streams ran unchecked for millions of years, leaching gold from the great granite *massif* of the Sierra Nevada—Spanish for snowy peaks. As they reached the foothills, the streams slowed their flow, depositing their valuable cargo in gravelly beds.

On January 24, 1848, an itinerant carpenter named James Wilson Marshall had the dumb luck to find a bit of this gold in the tailrace of a sawmill. He'd been hired by John Sutter, a flamboyant Swiss entrepreneur, to build the mill on the American River. Sutter had conned 50,000 acres of land from officials of Mexican California, and he needed lumber to create a new empire. Checking his tailrace after a rainstorm one morning, Marshall saw something glitter. He bent down and picked up two tiny nuggets, about "half the size and of the shape of a pea." The rest is epic.

Although many of the adventurers drawn by Marshall's discovery struck it rich, most found nothing but frustration. Many moved down into the valley to start farms and to finish building the hastily assembled cities of San Francisco, Stockton and Sacramento. A few, mostly Italians, stayed in these sun-warmed hills and planted grapes. They figured their brethren still laboring in the mines would work up a mighty thirst. Soon, thousands of acres of vines thrived in the foothills. By the 1880s, a hundred wineries were operating.

They were never very large and all except one was closed, either by dwindling population as the gold ran out, by phylloxera or by Prohibition. Only D'Agostini Winery (now Sobon Estate) survived. It was founded in 1856 by Adam Uhlinger who, like Sutter, was Swiss.

In the 1970s, U.C. Davis researchers found that the soil and terrain in some of the foothill areas provided ideal conditions for Zinfandel. Hot summer afternoons, cool alpine nights and tough granite soil produce high-sugar, high-acid grapes that ripen late, sometime between deer season and the first rains. Growers began planting new vineyards or resurrecting old ones, selling their grapes to vintners in Napa and Sonoma. Observers noted that many award-winning Zins bore curious names like Amador, Grandpère and Fiddletown. Soon, a new gold rush began in these hills—quieter this time, and from a different direction. Between 1970 and the turn of the last century, the number of wineries increased from one to more than fifty.

Amador County is the region's best known wine producing area because of its Zinfandel reputation. Most of its vineyards and wineries are concentrated in the Shenandoah Valley east of Plymouth. The counties above and below Amador are gaining in vinicultural stature, as well.

El Dorado County to the north has some of the world's highest vineyards, approaching 3,000 feet. These elevations offer suitable climate for Chardonnay, Sauvignon Blanc, Cabernet Sauvignon, Merlot and other cool-weather types. El Dorado's wineries are focused in two areas—the Apple Hill region north of Placerville, and the Somerset-Fairplay area to the south. Calaveras County, just below Amador, is the Gold Country's newest wine region, boasting several hundred acres of grapes and nearly a dozen wineries with tasting rooms. Most are around Murphys, uphill from Angels Camp.

We'll divide our Gold Country tour into its three major wine producing counties. Assuming that you plan to approach them one at a time, we'll suggest the most logical routes from the San Francisco Bay Area. Some wineries in this region have limited hours, so plan accordingly. Some of these, however, will offer tastings and informal tours on weekdays if you call ahead.

EL DORADO COUNTY WINERY TOUR ● If you've ever been lured

by the cool scenery and hot dice of south shore Lake Tahoe, you've passed this way, driving eastward on U.S. Highway 50. Let the dice cool this time and get off in Placerville, where the dry Central Valley begins to rumpling the Sierra foothills.

The freeway ends in this former mining town and then resumes about a mile further up. You might like to detour through the old downtown area. Main Street, paralleling U.S. 50, offers an interesting mix of brick front, cut stone, Art Deco and modern store fronts. They house assorted shops, boutiques, cafés and antique stores. Check the beautifully restored **Cary House** hotel, on the right as you enter town. (See listing below on page 314.) Also worth a look is the Greek federalist style **El Dorado County Courthouse** at the upper end of the historic district.

Apple Hill, home to most of El Dorado County's apple orchards and many of its wineries, is east of Placerville, immediately north of U.S. 50. During autumn, tens of thousands of visitors swarm over ribboned country lanes to buy apples, home baked pies and other apple goodies from dozens of fruit stands, packing sheds and seasonal café-bake shops. Some of these shops operate the year-around. This is exceptionally pretty country. It's a patchwork of orchards, vineyards and evergreens—both Christmas tree farms and forests *au natural.* Clusters of cottonwoods and poplars provide dazzling bursts of yellow. Weekdays are best for an autumn visit to Apple Hill, since both the fruit stands and the tasting rooms can be rather crowded on weekends. Most of the Apple Hill wineries are open daily. On the other hand, most of the Somerset-Fairplay wineries are open only on weekends.

Before heading for Apple Hill, you might want to take a side trip north from Placerville to visit a couple of often overlooked wineries. The route also takes you to Coloma, where you can explore the site that triggered the great California gold rush. (**NOTE:** The two wineries—Gold Hill and Venezio—aren't open daily, so check the listings below before you go.)

Begin by heading north from Placerville on Highway 49. You can pick it up from downtown (Spring Street) or by turning north from Highway 50 at a traffic signal. After four and a half miles, turn left onto Gold Hill Road, follow it through appealing wooded countryside for a mile and a half, then turn right at a stop sign onto Cold Springs Road. After a couple of miles, you'll see some vines and then **Gold Hill Vineyard** on your right. A short distance from Gold Hill, the road drops steeply into **Marshall Gold Discovery State Historic Park** in Coloma. You've rejoined Highway 49 at this point; continue north past Coloma about four miles and watch for **Venezio Winery & Vineyard** on your right.

From Venezio, follow Highway 49 back through Coloma to Placerville and head east a short distance on U.S. 50. Just beyond the Broadway interchange, take the Schnell School Road exit and go left under the freeway. Follow it briefly uphill, then go right on Carson Road, headed into the pine trees and Apple Hill country.

You'll encounter your first winery within a quarter of a mile—**Boeger,** sitting down in a pretty little hollow to your left. Continue about a mile up Carson Road, turn left onto Union Ridge Road at Abel's Apple Acres, then take a quick right onto Hassler Road. Follow it briefly to Fruitridge Road and **Lava Cap Winery** on the right. From Lava Cap, cross Hassler Road, heading east on Fruitridge. You'll soon pass the **U.S. Forest Service Placerville Tree Nursery** with its great swatches of tree seedlings. Fruitridge soon bumps into North Canyon Road; go right and you'll return to Carson Road. Pressing northward for a mile, turn left onto High Hill Road and follow signs through a large—and often busy—apple orchard complex to **Madroña Vineyards**.

Press northward on Carson Road for another mile or so and you'll see **Coulson Eldorado Winery** on your right, about a quarter of a mile past a U.S. 50 freeway interchange. Continue briefly on Carson Road into the cute little town of **Camino** and watch on your right for the tasting room of **Jodar Winery.** It's housed in the old woodframe Camino Hotel. From here, backtrack briefly to Snows Road and head south, passing under U.S. 50 freeway (there's no interchange here). A twisting, three-mile downhill spiral gets you to Newtown Road. Go left and follow it to Pleasant Valley Road and go left again. Drive a bit over half a mile and turn right up Leisure Lane in downtown Pleasant Valley. Two upward miles will take you to **Sierra Vista Winery,** occupying a knoll with an impressive view of the Sierra Nevada. This is one of the few foothill perches where you see the great granite ridge itself, since foothill mountains generally block your view.

WINERY CODES ● *T* = tasting with no fee; *T$* = tasting for a fee; *GT* = guided tours; *GTA* = guided tours by appointment; *ST* = self-guiding or informal tours; ✕ = picnic area; 🎁 = gift shop or a good giftware selection.

WINE PRICES ● *$* = average price under $10 per bottle; *$$* = $10 to $14; *$$$* = $15 to $19; *$$$$* = $20 or more

Retreat from these heights, continue half a mile east on Pleasant Valley Road and turn right onto Mount Aukum Road. Follow it three and a half miles to a stop sign at the tiny hamlet of **Somerset**. Just beyond is **Firefall Vineyards** tasting room, on your left. Press southward for about three miles on Mount Aukum, heading for a cluster of wineries surrounding a wooded hamlet with a great name left over from the rush to riches—**Fairplay**. (It's often written as two words.) Turn left onto Fairplay Road and drive a mile and a half to the turnoff for **Granite Springs Winery,** up a narrow lane on your left. Just beyond, up another narrow lane is **Single Leaf Vineyards**, on the right. Almost opposite Single Leaf, on the left, is **Van der Vijver Estate Winery.**

About a mile beyond, **Fitzpatrick Winery** occupies a bluff with an awesome vineyard and mountain view. A short distance past Fitzpatrick, in the hamlet of **Fairplay,** make a hard left onto Perry Creek Road. After about half a mile, turn right onto a lane with a great name—Slug Gulch Road—and follow it briefly to **Oakstone Winery.** Return to Perry Creek Road and drive just over a mile to its namesake winery, the imposing **Perry Creek Vineyards.** Immediately beyond is **Windwalker Vineyards**, also on your right. Now, retrace your route to Fairplay, turn left onto Fairplay Road and follow it briefly to **Charles B Mitchell Vineyards,** up a lane to your left. Just beyond, Fairplay bumps into Omo Ranch Road; turn right and within about three miles, **Latcham Vineyards** appears on your left, tucked behind its own vines.

This ends the El Dorado segment. If you continue west on Omo Ranch Road and follow it to Mount Aukum Road, you'll wind up in the Shenandoah Valley, home to most Amador County wineries.

Gold Hill Vineyard & Brewery ● T ✗

5660 Vineyard Lane (off Cold Springs Road), Placerville, CA 95667; (530) 626-6522. (www.goldhillvineyard.com) Thursday-Sunday 10 to 5; MC/VISA. Most varieties tasted free; small fee for beer tasting. A few wine logo items; view picnic tables on a deck overlooking the vineyards.

Occupying a spectacular setting above the American River Canyon, Gold Hill is one of the few wineries in the nation where visitors can sip either wine or beer or both. The Hank Battjes family began making wine from their hilly fifty-acre vineyard in 1980, initially as a part-time venture. An electrical engineer with GTE, he retired in 1989 to devote full time to his new profession. The family built an imposing, oak-shaded tasting room with a picnic deck offering grand views of this grand countryside.

In 2000, Battjes tasted some home-brewed beer made by a friend, Jim Gowan. He was so impressed with the beer that he invited Gowan to set up a brewery in the winery complex. Gowan took courses from the American Brewers Guild Academy and now produces about 200 kegs of beer a year.

A pleasing byproduct of this operation is excellent fresh bread, made from the same full-flavored, earthy grains used in beer production. A tray of still-warmed bread often appears at the tasting counter. Visitors can buy a fresh loaf to take home, or adjourn to the picnic deck for a bread or beer and wine repast.

Tasting notes: On the wine side of the tasting room, visitors can sip typical varietals such as Barbera, Syrah, Merlot, Cabernet Sauvignon, Cabernet Franc, Chardonnay, Johannisberg Riesling and a curiously sweet "white

Cabernet." Our chosen wines were a nutty, full-flavored Chardonnay; a spicy and earthy Syrah; a Merlot with good fruit and subtle hints of oak; and a rich and smooth table wine made from Cabernet Sauvignon, Barbera and Sangiovese. Prices: *$$ to $$$$.* On the sudsy side, *brewmeister* Gowan pours hearty hand-crafted beers for a small tasting fee.

Venezio Winery & Vineyard ● T ✕

5821 Highway 49, Coloma, CA 95679; (530) 885-WINE. (www.venezio.com) Wednesday-Sunday 11 to 5; MC/VISA. Most varieties tasted; a few wine logo items and specialty foods. Picnic area beside the tasting room.

The small vineyard in front of the tasting room suggests that most of this winery's grapes come from elsewhere. So does winery owner Jack Venezio. The stocky, powerfully built winemaker originally had a small vinting operation in the nearby—and oddly named—town of Cool. In 1997, he purchased 120 acres near the south fork of the American River, where he built his winery and tasting room. His son Val and daughter-in-law Gina have joined the firm, with Val serving as winemaker. They still "outsource" most of their wine grapes for their annual production of about 3,500 cases, although they plan additional plantings on their land.

The Venezio tasting room is inviting and cheerful. A focal point is a set of beautifully wood-carved *bas relief* winemaking panels behind the tasting counter.

Tasting notes The list is relatively short and quite good, focusing primarily on reds. However, we felt that the lone white—a lush, barrel-aged Chardonnay—was one of Venezio's better wines. Of the reds, we tried a soft and gently spicy Zinfandel, a smooth Cabernet Sauvignon with light oak, and a fine Venezio Table Red comprised of ninety percent Zinfandel and ten percent Cabernet. A Venezio Port was rich and full-flavored without being cloying. The winery's prices are quite modest, starting at less than $10 for the table wine; *$ to $$$.*

Boeger Winery ● T $ T$ ST ✕

1709 Carson Rd., Placerville, CA 95667; (530) 622-8094. (www.boegerwinery.com) Daily 10 to 5; MC/VISA. Most varieties tasted free; modest fee for tasting reserves, which includes a logo glass. Some wine oriented gift items. Casual tours on request; attractive picnic facilities.

This rustic ranch style winery has two links to the past. Although the present facility dates from 1972, it was established on the site of the Fossati-Lombardo Winery, hearkening back to the 1870s. Also, founder Greg Boeger is the grandson of Anton Nichelini, who started the still-operating Nichelini Winery high above the Napa Valley in 1890. The Boegers and Nichelinis still share close ties, swapping grapes and probably stories of the old days. For a time, Greg served as the Nichelini winemaker.

The tasting room is in a rough-cut stone structure that housed the original Fossati-Lombardo facility. It's listed on the National Register of Historic Places as one of America's oldest winery structures. The family lived upstairs and stomped the grapes there; juice flowed down through wooden chutes to fermenting vats in the cellar. Those chutes are still in place, hanging above the tasting counter.

Pear trees, vines and flowers share the busy farmyard with winery buildings. Several picnic tables are tucked into assorted shady spots; some are on a terrace above a pond.

Tasting notes: Boeger produces a Chardonnay, Sauvignon Blanc, Muscat Canelli, white Riesling, Zinfandel, Barbera, Merlot, Cabernet Sauvignon, Cabernet Franc and Syrah. The winery also bottles several proprietary blends including a table wine with a great name—Hangtown Red. Our favorites were a nutty-fruity Chardonnay; Walker Zinfandel with a great peppery taste; and that Hangtown Red, a merger of Cab, Barbera and Petite Sirah. Reserve wines include Sangiovese, a Spanish varietal called Tempranillo, red Meritage and *Migliôre*. Prices: *$$ to $$$*; higher for reserves.

Vintners choice: Greg's wife Sue read them off: "Merlot, Cabernet Sauvignon, Barbera and Cabernet Franc. Our elevation, climate and soil are excellent for the reds."

Lava Cap Winery ● T GTA & ST ✗

2221 Fruitridge Rd., Placerville, CA 95667; (800) 475-0175 or (530) 621-0175. (www.lavacap.com) Daily 11 to 5; MC/VISA. Most varieties tasted. Some wine logo items. Picnic deck; casual peek into the winery; guided tours by appointment.

Housed in a rustic yet modern barn-like structure, Lava Cap Winery sits among its own vineyards in the heart of Apple Hill. The curious name comes from the cap of volcanic ash and lava that once covered the area's gold-bearing quartz. David Jones, who opened the winery in 1987, taught at U.C. Berkeley; not surprisingly, geology is a favorite subject. He and his wife Jeanne are primarily weekend vintners; their sons pretty much run things. Tom is the winemaker and Charlie tends the vineyards.

Tastings happen in a pleasant redwood paneled room. One set of windows opens into the winery and another looks over vineyards, orchards and the distant American River Canyon. That same view can be enjoyed from a picnic deck just off the tasting room.

Tasting notes: Wines are estate bottled and the overall style is soft and lush, with lots of fruit. A Chardonnay reserve was outstanding, full flavored with subtle spice; the Fumé Blanc had a nice herbal nose that carried into the crisp, fruity flavor; and a young Zinfandel exhibited nice berries, spice and a light finish. Barbera, Merlot, Syrah, a couple of Cabernets Sauvignon, Petite Sirah and a sweet, fruity Muscat Canelli dessert wine complete the list. Prices: *$$ to $$$$*.

Vintners choice: "Our Chardonnays are coming on strong and we've won lots of medals with our Sauvignon Blanc," said Dave.

Madroña Vineyards ● T & T$ ST ✗

High Hill Road (P.O. Box 454), Camino, CA 95709; (800) 230-7662 or (530) 644-5948. (www.madrona-wines.com) Daily 11 to 5; MC/VISA. Most varieties tasted free; a modest fee for reserve wines. A few wine logo items. Casual tours by request. Picnic tables in a surrounding glen.

Madroña occupies a shady retreat beneath the cinnamon-barked trees that inspire its name. Vineyards and orchards are just beyond. The neat wood-sided winery looks deceptively small from the front; it's a two-story affair built into a downslope behind the tasting room. Several picnic tables are tucked beneath the madrones, black oaks and pines.

Dick and Leslie Bush planted vines in a section of the High Hill apple ranch in 1973, then opened their winery seven years later. Like those at neighboring Lava Cap, their wines are all estate bottled.

Tasting notes: Madroña produces excellent wines for rather modest prices. We sipped a Chardonnay with great fruit and a crisp finish, a lush Gewürztraminer, an outstanding Zinfandel with fine spice and berries, a pleasantly peppery Cabernet Franc, medium-bodied Cabernet Sauvignon, and a really fine and spicy proprietary wine called *La Tinta*, a blend of Zinfandel, Syrah and Cabernet Franc. Others on the list are a Riesling and dry Riesling, Merlot, Syrah and a rich late harvest Riesling, Prices: *$$ to $$$$.*

Coulson Eldorado Winery • T GTA

3550 Carson Road, Camino, CA 95709; (530) 644-2854. (www.coulson-winery.com) Daily 11 to 5; MC/VISA, AMEX. Most wines tasted. Tours of the adjacent winery available by advance arrangement.

This small operation is housed in a basic, metal-sided shed that was built in 1927 as an apple and pear processing facility. A winery, installed here in 1972, went through a couple of owners before retired chemical engineer Edgar Coulson leased the property in 1995. His Coulson Eldorado Winery isn't his first winemaking enterprise, however. He'd been a home winemaker for more than a decade before turning his hobby into a profession. He's obviously learned his craft well, for his wines are frequent gold medal winners. He also is owner of the Eldo Wine Lab, which performs lab test for other wineries in the county.

The Coulson tasting room is a simple affair, occupying part of a strip mall storefront on the highway, not far from the winery. While it's not particularly impressive, the wines poured therein certainly are.

Tasting notes: Coulson focuses on Rhône, Bordeaux and Italian varietals, producing mostly reds. The single white, a Chardonnay, was rather light but nicely fruity and spicy. Among the reds, we liked a fine Von Huene vineyard Cabernet Sauvignon; a rich and spicy Cabernet Franc; an inky, high-alcohol let-it-age Zinfandel; and a soft and fruity Vintner's Select, which is a Rhône blend of Grenache, Syrah and Mourvèdre. Others on the list are Syrah, a Cabernet Franc-Cabernet Sauvignon blend, Sangiovese, and a Mourvèdre proprietary blend called *Mataro*.

Jodar Vineyards & Winery • T

Tasting room in the Camino Hotel at 4103 Carson Rd. (P.O. Box 1197), Camino CA 95709-1197; (530) 621-0324 or (530) 644-3474. (www.jodar-winery.com) Friday-Sunday, 11 to 5. Most wines tasted; a few gift items.

The Jodar winery is tucked high in the mountains above Apple Hill and its tasting room once was a challenge to reach. The sipping parlor has since been moved to Camino's historic downtown hotel. In a cozy, cheerful space, visitors can tilt against a tasting counter and sample Jodar's small but excellent list. Byron and Sherril Jodar and Byron's brother Vaughn opened their winery in 1992, and their production has increased significantly, to 3,000 cases a year. They own forty acres on a mountain ridge on the edge of El Dorado National Forest, where they grow premium grapes on steeply terraced vineyards. Three different careers are represented by the team. Byron was a geologist employed by the federal government, Sherril is an accountant and Vaughn is a public health worker. They aren't amateurs, however; they've been making wine at home for twenty-five years.

Tasting notes: All Jodar wines are estate grown, and production is a hands-on affair. As a result, their short list has won an impressive number of gold medals. We tasted a three-year old Cabernet Sauvignon with big body and good fruit; a lush and buttery Chardonnay with tropical flavors; and a spicy Zinfandel with lots of berry flavor and a good tannin nip. We finished with a rich, chocolaty Port made from Cabernet grapes. A dish of walnuts and chocolate bits, sitting invitingly on the tasting counter, made a nice accompaniment. The Jodars also produce a tasty and inexpensive American River Red. Overall, prices are quite modest for the quality: **$$ to $$$.**

Sierra Vista Winery • T GTA ✕

In Pleasant Valley at the end of Leisure Lane; mailing address: 4560 Cabernet Way, Placerville, CA 95667; (530) 622-7221. (www.sierravistawinery.com) Daily 10 to 5; major credit cards. Most varieties tasted. Some wine logo gift items. Tours by appointment. Picnic area with a spectacular view.

Visitors who make the uptilted drive to Sierra Vista are rewarded with fine views of the Crystal Range of the Sierra Nevada. The dramatic peaks are visible from the winery and picnic area, and they grace the wine labels. This lofty ridge—rimmed in vineyards—is one of California's most dramatic winery perches, and one of the highest, at 2,900 feet. John and Barbara MacCready were among the first of El Dorado's modern-day vintners, buying their property in 1972 and starting the winery five years later. They've since shed their respective careers as a university professor and computer programmer to devote full time to vinting. They've built a simple, attractive wood-sided winery from their own pines, and increased their output from a handful of cases to 9,000 a year.

Tasting notes: Sierra Vista has been a leader in developing Rhône varietals. Among its plantings are Syrah, Grenache, Roussanne (a southern French white), Mourvèdre and Viognier. *Fleur de Montagne* is a Rhône style blend and Lynelle, named for daughters Lynette and Michelle, is a Provence style blend. The winery also produces excellent Cabernet Sauvignon, Chardonnay, Fumé Blanc and Zinfandel. Prices: **$ to $$$.**

Vintners choice: "Since we're Rhône rangers, we tend to favor Syrah, Mourvèdre and Viognier," says Barbara.

Firefall Vineyards • T ✕

5951 Mount Aukum Rd., Somerset, CA 95684; (530) 626-5432. (www.firefallvineyards.com) Weekends 11 to 5; MC/VISA. Most varieties tasted. Small picnic area shaded by a canvas canopy.

Former Los Gatos residents Laurie and Robert Jones planted their vines in the 1991, crushed their first grapes in 1994 and opened a small, attractive roadside cottage tasting room in 2000. Although they came from different backgrounds—he ran a manufacturing firm and she was in marketing—they aren't strangers to the wine business. Three generations of Robert's family have grown grapes in San Joaquin Valley, and both he and Laurie studied viticulture and wine making at U.C. Davis.

The winery's distinctive name comes from the fiery cloud-laced sunsets common to the California Gold Country. And speaking of pretty sunsets, their story reads like a romance novel. The pair met while they were taking a wine appreciation course at U.C. Davis. As a mutual wedding present, they planted seven acres of new vines—Syrah—in one of their vineyards.

Tasting notes: The small list offered three wines when we last visited—a crisp, berry-like *Rosato di Sangiovese*; Sangiovese with a fruity nose and smooth berry flavor; and estate grown Syrah, the most assertive of the trio with lots of berries and a nippy tannin finish. Prices: **$$ to $$$.**

Granite Springs Winery ● T ST ✕

5050 Granite Springs Winery Rd., Somerset, CA 95684; (800) 638-6041 or (530) 620-6395. (www.granitesprings.com) Daily 11 to 5; major credit cards. Most varieties tasted. A few wine logo items; shaded picnic area near a pond. Informal tours on request.

The basic bungalow tasting room and simple, barn like winery belie Granite Springs' success. It's one of America's most award-winning wineries. Not only have its wines been served in the White House, but its Chenin Blanc was poured as the official reception wine there for several years. The tasting room offers visitors one of the most elaborate snack spreads of any California winery. One could build a complete lunch from the offerings of soup, dips, sliced meats and cheeses, bread and crackers, with candy bars for dessert.

Les and Lynne Russell planted their vines in a stubborn granite slope in 1981, then they blasted away additional granite to plant their winery against a hillside. After Lynne passed away in 1994, Les sold the winery to neighboring winegrower Frank Latcham, who had been using the Russell's facilities to make his wines. Both Granite Springs and Latcham Vineyards wines are now produced here, although Latcham maintains a separate tasting room; see below. Under the guiding hand of the Russells and now the Latchams, Granite Springs wines have won more than a hundred medals. They hang by the cluster, like golden grapes, from the beams of the tasting room.

Tasting notes: Although a couple of whites appear on the lengthy list, this is a serious red wine venue, particularly noted for its Zinfandels. Often, a separate tasting counter is set up, where visitors can select from a "hot sheet" of newly released reds. We tasted two outstanding Zins—a just-out-of-the-barrel estate wine with a pleasingly floral nose and flavor; and a *La Falda Zin* that was soft, yet rich, with classic foothill spices. Meanwhile back at the main counter, we sipped a stainless steel-fermented fruity and rich Chardonnay, a curiously effervescent Zinfandel, a full flavored Cabernet Sauvignon with a light pepper finish, and a soft and mouth-filling Petite Sirah with spicy tones. Others on the list are a tasty and inexpensive Sierra Reserve Red; a couple of Merlots; black Muscat; and vintage Port made from a blend of Merlot, Cabernet Sauvignon and Petite Sirah grapes. Prices: *$ to $$$$*.

Single Leaf Vineyards ● T ST ✕

7480 Fairplay Rd., Somerset, CA 95684; (888) ONE-LEAF or (530) 620-3545. Tasting 11 to 5, Friday-Sunday from January through August and Wednesday-Sunday the rest of the year; MC/VISA. Most varieties tasted. A few wine logo items; view picnic area. Self guiding tours.

This small winery occupies an attractive redwood structure on a slope among the trees and vineyards. Picnic tables on a concrete deck offer a nice view of the valley. Single Leaf was established in 1993 by Scott and Pam Miller of Carson City, Nevada. They'd been farming the area since 1988. The Millers bring interesting backgrounds to the wine business. Scott, a biologist by profession, was administrator for the Nevada State Museum in Carson City and Pam was a marketing specialist. And the winery's unusual name? The source is a bit esoteric. The single-leaf piñon is the Nevada state tree and Scott, stepping out of his house one day, saw a single oak leaf on the ground. That leaf now resides on the winery label.

Tasting notes: This is Zinfandel country and it's a specialty of the Single Leaf house; the Zins are hardy and spicy. Others on the list are a full-flavored, buttery Chardonnay; an earthy and complex Merlot; a classic Bordeaux blend of Cabernet Sauvignon, Cabernet Franc, Merlot, and Malbec; and a table wine blend of Zin and Cab called Signature Red. Prices are quite reasonable for the quality: *$ to $$$.*

Vintner's choice: "We're best known for our reds and we pride ourselves in producing robust Zinfandels," said Scott.

Van der Vijver Estate • T ✕ 🍷

1451 Fairplay Rd. (P.O. Box 564), Fairplay, CA 95684; (530) 620-3210. Wednesday-Sunday 11 to 5; MC/VISA. Most varieties offered for tasting.

Netherlands natives Robert and Shannon van der Vijver opened their charmingly cute oak and pine shaded tasting room in 1999. They'd produced their first wines two years earlier. Although the winery complex has a classic Western farmyard look, the accents are definitely Dutch. The prim tasting room's small gift selection includes brightly colored wooden shoes and Delft china. Outside, more wooden shoes are tacked to the neat stained wood farmyard fences. The Van der Vijvers sell about 3,500 cases a year, made by a Dutch winemaker who likes to sip Heinekens beer as he works.

Tasting notes: The list consists of a flowery, lush Chardonnay that recently won a double gold; a fine Cabernet Sauvignon with medium body and a great chili pepper taste with touches of oak; an excellent, spicy Zinfandel; and a house red called Mellow Yellow, which is a blend of Sangiovese, Cabernet Franc and Zinfandel. No, the wine isn't yellow; it's named for an impressionistic painting on the tasting room wall. Prices: *$$ to $$$$.*

Fitzpatrick Winery and Lodge • T ST ✕

7740 Fairplay Road, Fairplay, CA 95684; (800) 245-9166 or (530) 620-3248. (www.fitzpatrickwinery.com) Weekends 11 to 5; major credit cards. Most varieties tasted. Picnic deck with valley view. Plowman lunch served in the lodge on weekends. Rooms available; see listing below on page 315.

A combined lodge and winery, Fitzpatrick occupies a high bluff with a stellar view of the surrounding hills. It's an imposing structure of heavy logs, with a rustic tasting room. A picnic deck offers vistas of vineyards and an occasional Christmas tree farm. Well-kept and tidy, with lawns and landscaping, it's among the more appealing of the Sierra foothill wineries.

Brian and Diane Fitzpatrick began their operation on Fairplay Road in 1980 near their Famine's End nursery. It was the first winery in the Fairplay area. Later, they moved two miles uphill to build—mostly by hand—their impressive tasting room and lodge, which looks like it was spirited away from Yosemite Valley. The winemaking operation is a few hundred feet away.

Tasting notes: The list is typical of hearty Gold Country wines—a spicy and full-flavored Cabernet Sauvignon; a light and crisp Chardonnay; an herbal Sauvignon Blanc; and a spicy, raspberry flavored Zinfandel. Prices: *$$ to $$$.*

Vintners choice: "We specialize in wines made from organically grown grapes," says winemaker Brian, declining to pick a favorite child.

Oakstone Winery • T ✕ 🍷

6440 Slug Gulch Rd., Somerset, CA 95684; (877) OAK-STONE or (530) 620-5303. (www.oakestone-winery.com) Wednesday-Sunday 11 to 5; major credit cards. Most varieties tasted. Picnic tables near the tasting room. Small selection of giftwares and specialty foods.

An attractive oversized cottage houses this new winery and tasting room which—perhaps fortunately—is not called Slug Gulch Cellars. Owners John and Susan Smith named it for a nearby 400-year-old oak tree growing from a granite outcropping. The roomy tasting parlor has two sipping counters—an imposing one-piece oak plank where most of the wines are poured, and a smaller "reds only" counter where one might find John offering sips of his Cabernet Sauvignon. Dips with bread and crackers are available at both.

Winemaker John has an advanced degree in analytical chemistry and Susan teaches at West Valley College in Saratoga. Although relatively new to the commercial wine industry, they had been making wine at home since 1972. They started their Oakstone operation in 1997, a year before he retired as an executive with the LifeScan division of Johnson & Johnson. A wall plaque in the tasting room—presented at his retirement—has a great cartoon captioned: "It means taking a hefty pay cut, but I've decided to accept the position of god of wine."

Tasting notes: John specializes in reds although his list includes several whites including a surprisingly good apple wine. No, this isn't sweet apple cider; it's a pleasantly dry and crisp wine made from a blend of three different juices. Also on the white side of the list are a full flavored Viognier and a fruity Chardonnay with a tiny hint of sweetness in the nose and taste. The reds include a light unfiltered Zinfandel with a pleasantly earthy taste; a Sangiovese with lots of berries and a crisp finish; an outstandingly lush and spicy Syrah; a soft, full-flavored Merlot; and a very spicy Cabernet Sauvignon. Oakstone also produces a red Meritage and a Merlot Port. Prices are quite reasonable for the quality; *$ to $$$.*

Perry Creek Vineyards • T ✕ 🏠

7400 Perry Creek Rd. (P.O. Box 304), Somerset, CA 95684; (800) 880-4026 or (530) 620-5175. (www.perrycreek.com) Tasting 11 to 5, weekends only January through October and Wednesday-Sunday in November and December. Major credit cards. Most varieties tasted. Good specialty foods and wine oriented gift selection. Patio picnic facilities; antique car collection.

One of the most striking of El Dorado County's wineries, this tile roof mission style complex occupies an upslope among the trees. Colonnade arches, patios, hand carved doors and a friendly fountain help transport the visitor from the Sierra foothills to a Spanish villa. The handsome tile floor tasting room with blonde wood furnishings complete this appealing picture. An unexpected bonus for visitors is a small collection of classic cars, a hobby of owners Mike and Alice Chazen, who completed this imposing showplace in 1991.

"They say you can make a small fortune in the wine business, as long as you start with a large fortune," mused wealthy garment importer Chazen. He and his wife are the accidental tourists of the Gold County wine industry. They were driving from Beverly Hills to Reno, taking the back roads so they could relax, when they saw a "for sale" sign on a piece of pastureland. They impulsively bought this 155-acre tract, planning to build a cabin as an escape from the rat race of international trading. Instead, a few months and a considerable sum of money later, they were owners of an opulent new winery. A New Yorker who moved to Beverly Hills after "doing very well" contracting for the overseas manufacture of mens' sweaters, he has now forsaken both cities for the laid back Levi lifestyle of the foothills.

The multi-layered look of the Gold Country's wine country—old vines, distant hills and a peaceful pond. This scene is in the Shenandoah Valley.

Tasting notes: The Perry Creek label covers the classic varietals and the facility has won many medals under the hand of Nancy Steel, one of California's few woman winemakers. Among our favorites were a full-flavored Chardonnay with a nice crisp finish, a soft and big flavored Viognier, a properly spicy Zinfandel, and a big and peppery Cabernet Sauvignon. Others on the list are Muscat Canelli, Sangiovese, Syrah, Merlot, Cabernet Franc, a pair of proprietary wines called *Mistelle Blanc* and *Mistelle Rouge* and a Port. Prices: *$$ to $$$*.

Windwalker Vineyards • T ST ✗

7360 Perry Creek Rd., Somerset, CA 95684; (530) 620-4054. (www.wind-walkervineyard.com) Wednesday-Sunday 11 to 5 or by appointment; MC/VISA. Most varieties tasted. A few wine logo items. Informal tours on request.

Perry Creek's next door neighbors also are accidental vintners. Arnie and Paige Gilpin were vacationing in nearby Arnold in 1992 when they saw a "winery for sale" add in the local newspaper. Why did they decide to buy it? Because their son Rich happened to be a graduate of U.C. Davis with a degree in Enology. He had worked at other wineries for seven years and the idea of being the winemaker for his own family was obviously appealing. It is indeed an all-family venture; Rich's wife Siri handles marketing and sales.

The winery's name and impressionistic horse logo come from previous owners Gaylene and Ken Bailey of Sacramento, who had a combined winery and Arabian horse ranch here. The horses are gone and the Gilpins are brightening up this attractive ranch style complex with new lawns and a gazebo. The winery and matching house are of Pennsylvania Dutch architecture. A picnic deck sits under sheltering oaks, offering views of vines and the valley below.

Tasting notes: The Gilpins suffer the happy fate of having many of their wines sold out; several were unavailable when we last visited. We were able to taste a flowery Sauvignon Blanc, a rich and nicely acidic Chardonnay, an excellent Zinfandel with great berries and classic foothill spice, a full-flavored Merlot and a Cabernet Sauvignon with a nicely spicy flavor. Others on the list—when they're not sold out—include Viognier, Orange Muscat, Barbera and Sangiovese. Prices: *$ to $$$.*

Charles B Mitchell Vineyards ● T GT ✗

8221 Stoney Creek Rd., Fairplay, CA 95684; (800) 704-WINE or (530) 620-3467. Daily 11 to 5:30; MC/VISA, AMEX. Most varieties tasted. Wine logo items and specialty foods. Large lawn picnic area under oaks; tours by request. Bed & breakfast inn adjacent.

This small winery and its vineyards are tucked into an upslope among oaks, blackberry vines, sheep pastures and other things rural. Expect to be greeted by an occasional squirrel and scolded by a Steller Jay as you prowl about or picnic on its pleasantly wooded grounds. The tasting room occupies a cheerful little cottage with white trim and the sipping counter is a simple affair, laid across barrel heads and wine racks. However, a comic wooden statue of an early-day pilot—complete with silk scarf—and a couple of splendid examples of hand-carved European furniture suggest that the winery owner isn't as bucolic as the setting.

In 1994, Charles B Mitchell, wine broker and columnist, amateur pilot and admitted Mammoth Lakes ski bum, purchased this small winery, which had been established in 1981 by Vernon and Marcia Gerwer. He hired U.C. Davis graduate Mark Foster as a consultant, took some Davis courses himself, bought the best grapes he could find and started making wines. His first releases began winning gold medals, and the wines continue to do so.

"As a winemaker, I'm more of a philosopher than a technician and it seems to be paying off. Wine is more art than science."

Tasting notes: The list includes a good selection of quite inexpensive varietals and moderately priced dessert wines. Among the whites are Sauvignon Blanc; barrel-fermented Chardonnay with hints of oak; light and flowery Riesling; soft Zinfandel, Merlot and Cabernet Sauvignon; a blend of Beaujolais and Chianti called *Monsieur Omo*, and *Côtes du Cosumnes*, a Rhône style red; and a rich Port. Among the reserves are a light Viognier; rich Pinot Noir with touches of oak; barrel-aged Cabernet Franc; full-bodied Napa Valley Zinfandel and Grand Reserve, a proprietary Bordeaux blend. Prices: *$ to $$$$.*

Latcham Vineyards ● T ST ✗

2860 Omo Ranch Rd. (P.O. Box 80), Mount Aukum, CA 95656; (800) 750-5591 or (530) 620-6642. (www.latcham.com) Daily 11 to 5; major credit cards. Most varieties tasted. A few wine logo items and specialty foods. Informal tours; picnic areas.

A courtliness in his manner tells you that Frank Latcham, pushing eighty, isn't an ordinary sodbuster. He's a retired San Francisco attorney, fulfilling an urge to get closer to the land. He and his wife Patty bought this land in

1980 and opened their winery ten years later. Although he still does consulting with his old firm, Frank likes to roll up his sleeves and get involved in the wine business. The Latchams' son and daughter-in-law, Jon and Joyce, complete the cast of this family operation. Several years ago, Frank purchased Granite Springs Winery, where all of his wines are produced. Visitors often find him at either winery, pouring wines and discussing the grape crop.

Like Granite Springs, the roomy Latcham tasting room offers two sipping venues, one for the primary wine list and another for special reds, where tasters can choose from a hot pink "hot sheet."

Tasting notes: Latcham produces most of the classic varietals, which have won more than a hundred medals and ribbons. After sipping a creamy and soft Chardonnay, we grabbed a hot sheet and headed for the red table, where we sampled some outstanding spicy and full-bodied Zinfandels. These were among the best we've tasted in California and —deservedly so— Latcham's Zins are more expensive than his Cabernets. Other wines on the two lists include Muscat Canelli, a perfectly decent table wine called Goldrush Red, several Cabernets Sauvignon, Cabernet Franc, Barbera and a classic Port made with traditional Portuguese grapes. Prices: *$ to $$$$*.

AMADOR COUNTY WINERY TOUR • The Shenandoah Valley, home to most of Amador's wineries, is one of the few relatively level areas in the foothills. We did say "relatively;" it gently pitches and rolls like a green ocean of vineyards, pasturelands and oak groves. The valley was settled in the 1850s by folks seeking farm and ranch land, not gold. Many Shenandoah settlers were "Downeasters" and Southerners (thus, the valley's name). There's still an eastern American air about its neat farms and occasional red barns.

If you continue westward from Frank Latcham's place, you'll wind up in the back end of this valley. However, after all of those El Dorado tasting rooms, you've probably saved Amador for a different trip. The logical access is from Highway 49, in the small hamlet of **Plymouth**.

Approaching either from the north or south, turn eastward at a sign indicating the Shenandoah Valley, opposite Plymouth's main street. After a few hundred yards, fork left onto Shenandoah Road. The right hand fork leads to Fiddletown, home to some noted vineyards and one tasting room, which we'll catch at the end of this tour. Your first winery, **Young's Vineyard,** arrives quickly, on your right. Just beyond, turn right onto Shenandoah School Road and follow it two miles to the imposing **Monteviña** winery complex on the right. Return to Shenandoah Road, turn right and follow it about two-thirds of a mile to the imposing **Villa Toscano,** on your right. Continue briefly on Shenandoah for the turnoff to **Nine Gables Vineyard,** also on the right. The complex is reached by following a narrow lane past an old farmhouse to a striking new country home; the tasting room is just beyond.

Just up from Nine Gables, turn left onto Dickson Road and follow it about a quarter of a mile to **Domaine de la Terra Rouge**. Return to Shenandoah, continue northeast about a quarter of a mile and turn left onto Bell Road. A long lane leading to **TKC Vineyards** comes up almost immediately. After less than half a mile, watch for a sign directing you to the left to **Karly Winery,** reached by a pleasantly winding drive through vineyards and pasturelands. Continue on Bell road until it ends, then turn left and follow a fragmented bit of pavement about half a mile to **Story Winery.**

Return to Shenandoah Road, turn left and go about a mile before turning left again onto Steiner Road. About a mile up Steiner, several wineries are grouped together, almost within walking distance of one another—**Renwood/Santino** on the left at Steiner and Upton Road, and then **Shenandoah Vineyards** and **Amador Foothill Winery**, both uphill and above the vineyards to your right. Just beyond is **Deaver Vineyards** and then **Charles Spinetta Winery and Wildlife Gallery** down in a hollow; both are on the left. Almost immediately beyond Spinetta, follow a half-mile lane over hill and down dale to **Dobra Zemlja** winery.

Continue up Steiner Road, which curves back to Shenandoah Road after less than a mile, then go northeast about two miles to **Sobon Estate,** on the right. Finally, reverse yourself about a mile on Shenandoah, turn left (southeast) onto Ostrom Road and follow its twisting, scenic course just over a mile to **Rabbit Hill Winery,** on your left. Continue on Ostrom to the tiny and rustic old town of Fiddletown, then head west on Fiddletown Road, which takes you back to Plymouth.

OTHER AMADOR WINERIES

Three Amador County wineries outside the Shenandoah Valley are worth a visit if you're in the area. **Clos du Lac Cellars** is on Highway 88, the main route from the San Joaquin Valley to Amador County; open Wednesday-Sunday 10 to 4; (209) 274-2238; (www.closdulac.com) It's on the left, just beyond the Jackson Valley Road junction below **Ione**. If you return to Ione and head north on Route 124, then turn left onto Willow Creek Road, you'll encounter **Argonaut Winery** on your left; open weekends 11 to 5:30; (209) 245-5567. For **Sutter Ridge Vineyards,** head south from Plymouth on Highway 49 and turn left onto Ridge Road between **Sutter Creek** and **Jackson**; it's open Friday-Sunday 11 to 4; (209) 267-1316.

Young's Vineyard • T ST ✕

10120 Shenandoah Rd., Plymouth, CA 95669; (209) 245-3005. Weekends 10 to 5 or by appointment; MC/VISA. Most varieties tasted. A few wine logo items; casual tours. Picnic area by a duck pond.

Established in 1979 as Kenworthy Vineyards, this winery was reopened in 1995 by the Young family—Steven, his wife Annette and Steve's father Stell. Dad, a former military test pilot and head of the California National Guard, is the winemaker and Annette helps run the business end of things. Steve, who travels abroad for a company that makes specialty tools for nuclear and industrial plants, lends an occasional hand. (Steve and Annette met on one of his trips to Europe.) Yet another family member, Steve's sister Sharon, runs the tasting room and paints the distinctive labels for their wines.

The family has spruced up the once weather-worn Kenworthy Ranch, refacing and painting the buildings and repairing an ancient Chinese-built rock wall that rims a duck pond and picnic area.

Tasting notes: Stell likes to handcraft his wines, evident in the strong varietal character of the estate Cabernet Sauvignon and Zinfandel. They're aged in French oak to add complexity. Muscat Canelli completes the short list. Prices: *$$ to $$$$*.

Monteviña Winery • T ✕

20680 Shenandoah School Rd., Plymouth, CA 95669; (209) 245-6942. (www.montevina.com) Daily 11 to 4:30; MC/VISA. Most varieties tasted. Good selection of wine logo items. Large, landscaped picnic area.

Bob Trinchero of Napa Valley's Sutter Home Winery, who started the white Zinfandel craze three decades ago, was among the first to call attention to Sierra foothill grapes. He won scores of awards with his hearty Amador County Zinfandels in the 1970s. It seemed logical, then, to move closer to the source, so he bought Monteviña Winery in 1988. He operates it as a separate entity.

Monteviña was among the first of the post-Prohibition Gold Country facilities, established in 1970. Trinchero recently constructed an imposing new multi-gabled wood-sided winery building to house his growing output. It's rather a handsome structure—dark wood with burgundy trim and a stonework base. The original cathedral ceiling tasting room, decorated with artwork and photos, still occupies an adjacent Spanish-California style structure. Flower beds, lawns and a picnic area beneath a shady arbor complete this pleasant scene.

Tasting notes: Although many of Monteviña's wines are on the light side, they've won their share of medals. And they're among the least expensive in the Gold Country. A long list includes several Italian varietals, plus a few Zinfandels. Among our favorites were a dry and crisp Pinot Grigio, a fruity and rich *Nebbiolo Rosato* blush (better than Trinchero's trademark white Zin), and three spicy Zins, each better than the first—a medium bodied "basic Zin," School House Zin with a touch of Barbera and Petit Sirah, and a big and spicy *Terra d'Oro* Zin. Other Monteviña wines include Fumé Blanc, Sangiovese, Syrah and Barbera, plus Italian reds called Brioso, Montanero and Refosco. A particularly good buy is *Cucina Mista*, a sturdy jug wine comprised of "whatever's left over" among the reds. Prices: *$ to $$*.

Villa Toscano • T ✗ 🍷

1600 Shenandoah Rd. (P.O. Box 1029), Plymouth, CA 95669; (209) 245-3800. (www.villatoscano.com) Daily 10 to 5; major credit cards. Most wines tasted. Extensive giftware and specialty foods selection; elaborate courtyard picnic area.

The most stylish complex in the Shenandoah Valley, Villa Toscano is a vision of Italy, with its yellow stucco winery topped by red tile roofs. It's no accident; owners Erika and Jerry Wright, while not Italian, had traveled through Tuscany frequently and wanted to bring a vision of Italy's winelands to America. The two southern California land developers bought a horse ranch here in the mid-1990s, began planting vineyards and opened their winery in 2000. The grounds are elaborately landscaped, with flower gardens, pools, fountains and an attractive picnic area with wrought iron tables and chairs. The luxuriant look carries into the tasting room with its tile floors, carved woods and marble accents. Tables brim with tasteful giftwares and specialty foods.

Tasting notes: The wines we tasted were uniformly excellent and—except for a couple of whites—moderately pricey. A pair of Semillons were dry and crisp with touches of oak. The reds all displayed classic varietal character with lots of fruit, complex flavors and deep colors. Our favorite—not the most expensive on the list—was a Sangiovese with spicy flavor and a subtle tannin finish. Others, all worthy of anyone's wine list, were a rich Zinfandel with typical Gold Country spices, a flavorful Syrah with a curiously earthy aroma, and a classic Cabernet Sauvignon with a great chili pepper nose and taste. Prices: *$$ to $$$$*.

Nine Gables Vineyard & Winery ● T ✕

10778 Shenandoah Rd., Plymouth, CA 95669; (209) 245-3949. Thursday-Sunday 10 to 5; MC/VISA. Most wines tasted. Small picnic area.

Home winemakers for more than twenty-five years, Jerry and Pam Notestine turned their hobby into a profession when they opened their winery and tasting room just before the Millennium. They built an attractive nine-gabled home—thus the winery name—among their vineyards, with a small tasting room in a matching cottage nearby. Their son Ryan helps manage the operation and he usually runs the tasting room. However, the wines were so popular after their first release that they ran out, so Ryan was able to close the tasting room for the winter and concentrate on other winery business. If this good fortune continues, you may see a "sold out" sign. The best time to catch their wines is in the spring; most new releases come out in February or March.

The Notestines, who lived in Carmichael near Sacramento, bring varied backgrounds in to the wine business. He was a property appraiser and probate referee and she runs a hair salon in Sacramento. In 1989, they bought five acres of vineyards—including some ancient Mission grapes—then opened the winery a decade later.

Tasting notes: The Mission grapes may be the most interesting on the Notestines' list, at least from an historical perspective. This vine was brought to California by early Spanish padres, although it's rarely used to make wine these days because the juice is rather bland. However, the Notestines' vines are so old and the grapes so mature that Jerry was able to produce an award-winning wine by adding a bit of Barbera to give it more intensity. How does it taste? We can't say; it was one of several wines that had run out by the time we got there. The wines we *were* able to taste were soft and full-flavored with light tannins, which is the Notestine style. The Sangiovese, Merlot, Zinfandel and Cabernet Sauvignon were quite fine. Others on the list are Syrah, Barbera, Barbera Port, Mission claret and Mission Sherry. Prices: **$$$ to $$$$.**

Domaine de la Terre Rouge ● T ✕ 🏠

10801 Dixon Rd., Plymouth; (209) 245-3117. Mailing address: P.O. Box 41, Fiddletown, CA 95629. Friday-Sunday 11 to 4; MC/VISA. Selected varieties tasted. Small selection of wine logo items; shaded picnic area out front.

"The Estate of the Red Earth" isn't nearly as imposing as its name. It's housed in an industrial-strength building with a small tasting room tucked among the aging wines. But never mind that; Domaine de la Terre Rouge produces some of the best and most reasonably priced wines in the Gold Country. And the Sacramento *Bee* once voted this place as "the friendliest tasting room in California." This is the domaine of two friendly folks, Bill and Jane O'Riordan Easton, who operated a wine shop and bistro in Berkeley. They bought some vineyards near Fiddletown in the late 1980s and opened their winery in the mid-1990s. Jane also is a noted gourmet cook and author of *Rhône Appétit,* a cookbook with recipes geared to Rhône wines.

Tasting notes: Considering Jane's cookbook title, it's no surprise that the winery focuses on Rhônes. They're issued under the Terre Rouge label while other varietals are marketed under the Easton label. Our favorites were an Easton Zinfandel with a great spicy nose and flavor, priced in the low teens and one of the best Zin buys in the state; a crisp and fruity white blend labeled Easton Natoma, with Sauvignon Blanc, Semillon and Viognier; and extremely soft and pleasant Terra Rouge Mourvèdre; and a spicy, full flavored year-old Terra Rouge Syrah. Several other Easton Zinfandels are on the list, along with Terre Rouge Muscat Blanc, Roussanne and several Syrahs. Prices: **$$ to $$$$.**

TKC Vineyards • T
11001 Valley Drive, Plymouth, CA 95669; (888) 637-2356 or (209) 245-6428. Saturday 11 to 5 and Sunday 1 to 5, or by appointment; major credit cards. Most wines tasted.

This small winery dates from 1981 when Harold and Monica Nuffert started buying and crushing grapes to make "big, non-wimpy reds." To assure a reliable source, they began planting their own Cabernet and Mourvèdre grapes in 1994. The operation is small, with an annual output of 1,500 cases. Tastings occur in a simple space at one end of their modest winery.

Harold came to the wine business by way of the aerospace industry. After years as an engineer, he decided that the business was suffering from "technology stagnation," so he sought a new and different kind of challenge and one that was more creative than technological—making wines.

Tasting notes: Only three varietals occupy the TKC list—Cabernet Sauvignon, Mourvèdre and Zinfandel. They are indeed non-wimpy, full bodied with lots of fruit and enough tannin to age for eight to ten years. Prices: **$$ to $$$$.**

Karly Winery • T GTA ✕
11076 Bell Rd., Plymouth, CA 95669; (209) 245-3922. Daily noon to 4; MC/VISA. (www.karlywines.com) Most varieties tasted. Some wine logo gift items. Snacks served with wine samples. Small picnic area; guided tours by appointment.

You may go to Karly for the wines, but you may return for *her* snacks. Lawrence (Buck) Cobb makes full-bodied wines, and his wife Karly serves oven-warm bread and bits of cheese to weekend tasters. This happens in a neat tasting room that's also a kitchen, which is certainly appropriate. A full set of appliances is installed behind the counter. The winery is a modern metal structure, bunkered unobtrusively into a slope, surrounded by vineyards. The Cobbs were drawn to this area to escape from the corporate rat race in 1980. Earlier, Buck served as an Air Force fighter pilot in Korea, and he now flies a high performance stunt plane.

Tasting notes: Buck likes a touch of oak in his wines; we found them to be quite tasty. Our picks were a silky Roussanne with a bit of wood; a soft yet spicy and full-bodied three-year-old Zinfandel and a *big* two-year-old Zin that should be kept around for a bit. Others on the list are Syrah, Sauvignon Blanc, Mourvèdre, Grenache, the requisite white Zinfandel and a tasty sweet Orange Muscat. Prices: **$$ to $$$$.**

Story Winery • T GTA ✕
10525 Bell Rd., Plymouth, CA 95669; (209) 245-6208. (www.zin.com) Weekdays noon to 4, weekends 11 to 5; MC/VISA, DISC. Select varieties tasted. Picnic area with valley view; tours by appointment.

Following a narrow lane past ancient gnarled vines toward Story, you don't realize that you're approaching a crest with a striking view. The old farmyard winery sits on the rim of the Consumnes River Canyon, with a sweeping vista of vineyards, oak clusters and pine forests. The tasting room in a weathered barnboard cottage perches on this knoll, beside a casually kept lawn. Picnic tables entice one to linger for the view.

Founded early in the 1970s by the late Eugene Story and now owned by Bruce and Jan Tichenor, this is one of the foothills' oldest wineries. In classic Gold Country fashion, it focuses heavily on Zinfandel, since Eugene had the good fortune to find a ranch with some old vines still in place.

Tasting notes: Several Zins occupy the list and a tasting consists of a vertical sampling of wines ranging from light fruity to big and boisterous. Others on the list are a light and fruity estate Chenin Blanc, white Zinfandel and a dessert wine made from old Mission vines. Prices: *$ to $$$.*

Renwood/Santino Winery • T & T$ ⚔ 🏮

12225 Steiner Rd., Plymouth, CA 95669; (800) 348-8466 or (209) 245-6979. (www.renwood.com) Daily 11 to 4:30; major credit cards. Select varieties tasted free; modest fee for reserve wines. Good selection of giftwares and specialty food items. Grassy, shaded picnic areas.

Folks who haven't visited the former Santino Winery lately will find several changes. Scott Harvey, who had been Santino's winemaker since it was started by Matt and Nancy Santino in 1979, purchased the winery in partnership with Boston stockbroker Robert L. Smerling in 1993. Scott has since left and is now with Folie à Deux Winery in the Napa Valley. He owns the Shenandoah Valley's legendary 125-year-old Grandpère Zinfandel vineyard, and some of his grapes still find their way into Renwood's finest wines. Although there are no more Santinos at the winery, the label survives on the Rhônes, Chardonnays and Merlots.

The other changes are physical—additional vineyard plantings and an enlarged and brightened tasting room in a California-Spanish tile roofed building, with an appealing lawn area and shaded picnic area out front.

Tasting notes: Zin's the name of the Renwood game, although the better ones have become quite pricey, rivaling and sometimes exceeding the cost of a good single-malt Scotch. Renwood's Grandpère remains one of California's grandest Zins, lush with fruit, deep with spice and color and—good grief!—costing nearly $50. The winery does produce more affordable and very tasty Zins. Among those we sampled—on the free side of the tasting sheet—were a soft and peppery Renwood Old Vine and a light and oak-tinted Renwood Grandmère. We also tasted a pleasantly light, lush and inexpensive Santino Sauvignon Blanc and Santino Chardonnay; a fruity Santino Viognier with a hint of sweetness; and a full-flavored Santino Syrah. Prices range widely: *$$ to $$$$.*

Shenandoah Vineyards • T ⚔

12300 Steiner Rd., Plymouth, CA 95669; (209) 245-4455. (www.sobon-wine.com) Daily 10 to 5; MC/VISA. Most varieties tasted. Some wine logo items and art gallery; small picnic area.

Leon and Shirley Sobon claim to be risk-takers, although their timing appears to be good. When the aircraft industry slowed in 1977, he left his engineering job at the Lockheed research lab in Palo Alto, bought a piece of land with a handsome fieldstone house and started Shenandoah Vineyards. Three years later, they sold a chunk to Ben Zeitman (who started Amador Foothill Winery) at a tidy profit. Their wines have caught on quickly, winning numerous awards; their production has leaped from a few cases to 35,000. In 1989, they bought the defunct D'Agostini Winery, one of California's oldest and turned it into Sobon Estate, a satellite winery and site of the Shenandoah Valley Museum (see below).

Shenandoah is an appealing complex, with a modern fieldstone winery fashioned to match the house. The tasting room is a delight—part rustic with log beam ceilings, and part art gallery, with rotating exhibits among barrels of aging wines.

Tasting notes: The Shenandoah list is predominately red, typical for Amador, although the winery produces an excellent full-bodied Sauvignon Blanc. Our favorite reds included a rich and mellow Zingiovese (obviously a Zinfandel Sangiovese blend), a spicy Zinfandel Reserve and a three-year-old mellow and tasty Cabernet Sauvignon. The list also includes Barbera, Sangiovese, and Rhône varietals such as Syrah, Viognier and Roussanne. Prices are quite moderate: *$ to $$$.*

Amador Foothill Winery • T ST ✕

12500 Steiner Rd., Plymouth, CA 95669; (209) 245-6307. (www.amador-foothill.com) Friday-Sunday and most Monday holidays noon to 5; MC/VISA. Most varieties tasted. Casual winery tours. Picnic area with valley and mountain views.

When we wrote *The Best of the Gold Country* several years ago, we conducted a blind tasting among knowledgeable friends to pick the region's best Zinfandel and white Zinfandel. To our surprise and Ben Zeitman's pleasure, his Amador Foothill wines won both. Ben and his wife Katie Quinn's Zins also win in arenas much more prestigious than ours.

A former NASA chemist, Ben started the winery in 1980. Then in 1986, he had the good sense to marry Katie, who brought with her a master's degree in Enology from U.C. Davis. The winery is simple but on the leading edge of technology—a glossy white passive solar structure equipped with the best of the winemaking art and science. All of this is visible from the tasting counter, on a gallery above the main part of the winery. A tour thus consists of looking over your shoulder, glass in hand.

Tasting notes: Zinfandel, of course, dominates the list and it has won many of the awards that decorate the walls. The Clockspring Vineyard and Ferrero Vineyard Zins were excellent; drinkable now and full-bodied enough for aging. The list also includes Sangiovese, a crisp and dry rosé of Sangiovese, barrel-fermented Semillon, Fumé Blanc, Carignane and Syrah. Prices: *$ to $$$.*

Deaver Vineyards • T ✕ 🏺

12455 Steiner Rd., Plymouth, CA 95669; (209) 245-4099. Daily 11 to 5; major credit cards. (www.deavervineyard.com) Most wines tasted; good selection of giftwares, books and specialty foods. Picnic area near a lake.

This contemporary winery complex traces its roots back to the gold rush—in a sense. John Davis came to California in search of gold in 1850. Finding none, he became a cooper in the foothill wine country and some of his barrels still exist at Sobon Estate. He adopted young Kenneth Deaver, and members of the Deaver family has been in the valley ever since. The present generation began making wine in 1985 and opened a sales outlet in 1988. The Deavers completed a handsome new winery and tasting room in 1994, with the equally attractive Amador Harvest Inn adjacent. (See "Wineland lodgings" below, on page 315.)

The tasting room is an appealing space, bright and airy, with tile floors and oak wood trim. Samples from an extensive selection of specialty foods are offered, along with sips of wine. Outside, well-tended lawns and a picnic area border a lake, where several affable ducks have taken up residence.

Tasting notes: The list is brief and quite good. We sampled a soft, fruity Chardonnay; crisp and spicy Zinfandel with medium body; and a late harvest Zinfandel so rich that it could have passed for a Port. Others on the list are white Zin and white and red table wines. Prices are modest: *$ to $$.*

Charles Spinetta Winery and Wildlife Gallery • T ✕ 🎨

12557 Steiner Rd., Plymouth, CA 95669; (209) 245-3384. (www.charlesspinettawinery.com) Weekdays 8 to 4 and weekends 10 to 4:30; MC/VISA. Selected wines tasted, plus wines by the glass a modest fee. Wine logo items and extensive wildlife art collection and frame shop. Large picnic area.

This square-shouldered masonry block building, rather austere from without, is a surprise package within. Visitors step into a huge, high-ceiling tasting room with an L-shaped counter. Wildlife scenes fill the redwood paneled walls and scores more occupy a mezzanine gallery above. Bronzes and other sculptures complete the collection. It's all for sale and generally affordable, since most are prints of works by leading artists. Another element of the facility, unique to the wine country, is a picture framing shop.

The operation is an all-family affair. Charles, whose background is forestry management, bought the vineyards in 1979 and completed the winery-gallery a decade later. Wife Laura runs the frame shop and has framed the more than 400 prints on the walls. Son Jim manages the vineyards, Tony is into marketing and Michael, the youngest, has joined the operation. Not surprisingly, there's always a Spinetta on hand to greet visitors.

Tasting notes: Spinetta's Zins were our favorites, unfiltered and full-flavored. We tasted a mellow nine-year-old Eschen Vineyard entry from eighty-year-old vines and a lighter five-year-old Amador Zinfandel. Zinetta is a rich appetizer wine with big flavors of berries and cherries. Also on the list are white Zinfandel, Heritage Red table wine, sweet and dry Chenin Blancs, Chardonnay, Barbera, Primitivo, a sweet Muscat Canelli and a rich, ice-wine style Frost Chenin Blanc. Prices: *$ to $$$.*

Vintner's Choice: The winery's top three varietals are Zinfandel, Primitivo and Barbera, says Spinetta.

Dobra Zemlja • T ✕

12505 Steiner Rd., Plymouth, CA 95669; (209) 245-3183. Daily 9 to 5; MC/VISA. Most wines tasted. Attractive picnic area.

Dobra Zemlja isn't some strange kind of new wine, nor is it the winemaker's name. It means "the good earth" in Croatian and that's just what Croatia-born Milan Matulich and his wife Victoria have found at an old homestead-turned-winery. A sturdy old barn houses the winery and one end—bunkered against a hill—has been gunnited to create a cave-like tasting room. Thick, 400-pound wooden doors swing so easily that they almost take you with them as you enter the "cavern." With drop lamps to light a simple tasting counter, artwork on the walls and casks of wine sleeping in the nearby shadows, this is one of the more sensuous tasting rooms in California. Outside, picnic tables occupy a pretty green lawn shaded by slender eucalyptus trees. A droopy-eyed, tawny dog named Pilot sometimes rises from his nap to greet visitors. It's an altogether pleasing environment.

Back inside, the cheerful couple serves excellent wines—mostly Rhônes—to their guests. And one feels more like a guest than a visitor here. She's the chatty one; he warms the room with an engaging grin and talk about his wine. A former electronics technician and longtime home winemaker, Milan opened the winery in 1997. He produces about 1,300 cases a year while Victoria runs the business end.

Tasting notes: All wines are estate grown and uniformly excellent with big, complex flavors. The list is brief, although the tasting ritual mixed with lively conversation may take some time. We started with a rich and fruity Viognier, then moved quickly to the serious reds—a Zinfandel with great spice and berry flavor, an equally spicy Syrah and a peppery and full flavored Sangiovese. Prices are moderate for the quality: *$$ to $$$$.*

Vintners choice: Asked to pick his favorite wine, Milan ran a hand through his bushy shock of gray hair. "That's like asking which fruit I like best. I like them all." He admitted that his Syrah was quite good, with an unusual spicy flavor that's more typical of foothill Zinfandels. "It's become an Amador wine," he concluded.

Sobon Estate ● T ✕ 📷

14430 Shenandoah Rd. (mailing address: 12300 Steiner Rd.), Plymouth, CA 95669; (209) 245-6554. (www.sobonwines.com) Daily 9:30 to 5; MC/VISA. Most varieties tasted. Good giftware selection, deli and picnic fare. Self-guiding tour of the Shenandoah Valley Museum. Shaded picnic area.

D'Agostini winery—California's fourth oldest—is in good hands. Since buying the facility in 1989, Leon and Shirley Sobon have installed the Shenandoah Valley Museum in the main cellar, thus preserving this state historical landmark. Exhibits focus on the gold rush, Shenandoah Valley pioneers and early farming and wine production. It also captures that wonderful musty-grapy old library smell typical of ancient wineries. The large tasting room, in another of the old buildings, fits the historic theme, with heavy ceiling beams and barnwood paneling. It offers one of the better selections of gift and specialty food items of the foothill wineries.

Tasting notes: Many Sobon Estate wines use grapes from the old D'Agostini vineyards, although they're produced mostly at the family's Shenandoah facility. Selections vary, depending on availability. Our favorites on our last visit were a tasty herbal Zinfandel and a Cabernet Sauvignon with a big chili pepper nose and herbal-berry flavor. Others on the list include Rhône varietals such as Syrah, Viognier and Roussanne. Prices: *$ to $$$.*

Rabbit Hill ● T ✕

21220 Ostrom Rd., Fiddletown, CA 95629; (209) 245-5568. Weekends 11:30 to 4:30; major credit cards. Most varieties tasted.

Although some of Amador County's best vineyards thrive near the tiny hamlet of Fiddletown, the area didn't have a winery until Joseph and Jennifer Caesar started their small facility in 1999. An Oklahoma native who's half Pawnee, Joseph gained much of his winemaking interest through his wife's side of the family. Jennifer, a longtime Gold Country resident, is the sister of Scott Harvey, owner of Amador's legendary Grandpère Zinfandel vineyard. Joseph learned many of his skills from Scott. Incidentally, Rabbit Hill isn't named for a local landmark or vineyard. "I just like rabbits," Jennifer said with a grin.

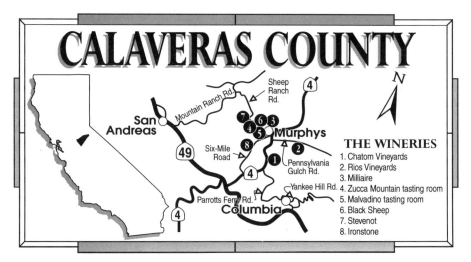

CALAVERAS COUNTY

Sheep Ranch Rd.

San Andreas

Mountain Ranch Rd.

Murphys

Six-Mile Road

Pennsylvania Gulch Rd.

Yankee Hill Rd.

Parrotts Ferry Rd.

Columbia

N

THE WINERIES

1. Chatom Vineyards
2. Rios Vineyards
3. Milliaire
4. Zucca Mountain tasting room
5. Malvadino tasting room
6. Black Sheep
7. Stevenot
8. Ironstone

The Caesars do about a thousand cases a year, preferring to hand craft small lots of select varietals. Their simple tasting room occupies a trim little burgundy and white cottage, with a couple of oak-shaded picnic tables out front. The winery functions in a nearby Pennsylvania Dutch style barn.

Tasting notes: The list is short and definitely not sweet. Winemaker Joseph makes crisp, full-flavored wines with lots of complexity. We sipped a dry, lush barrel-fermented Chardonnay; a remarkably complex and fruity Sauvignon Blanc; a soft, complex and spicy Zinfandel from century-old vines; and Grand Hare Barbera, the best of the lot with huge flavors and a nice tannic finish. Prices: *$$$ to $$$$.*

CALAVERAS COUNTY WINERY TOUR ● The southernmost wine
country in the Gold Country also is the newest. Of Calaveras County's ten tasting rooms, six opened in the decade of the Nineties. Most are in or near the appealing old mining town of Murphys.

As you tour this southern reach of the Gold Country's wine country, you will be rewarded with considerable variety, from funky tasting rooms to modern wineries with aging caves. You will note, as you explore, that the area abounds with other attractions as well, from limestone caverns to restored mining towns and gold rush museums.

The most direct route to Murphys is via State Highway 4 from **Stockton**. You can pick it up from Interstate 5 or U.S. 99 and follow it through **Angels Camp**. Another approach, used by many Bay Area visitors, is via I-580 to I-205 past **Tracy**, then State Highway 120 through **Manteca.** Follow signs to and through **Sonora** on Highway 49, then drive seventeen miles north to Angels Camp and turn right onto Route 4.

For a more scenic variation, fork to the right onto Parrotts Ferry Road about four miles north of Sonora; this takes you to **Columbia State Historic Park,** the Gold Country's most visited attraction. Beyond this restored mining town, Parrotts Ferry spirals down to the Stanislaus River Canyon, now filled with New Melones Reservoir. You'll cross the big pond and enter Calaveras County, climb out of the canyon, pass the **Moaning Cavern** limestone cave, then hit a stop sign at Route 4. Go right toward Murphys, about four miles up the highway.

Using any of these approaches, you'll encounter the first wine sipping stop before you reach Murphys—the stylish winery and tasting room of **Chatom Vineyards** on your right, near the hamlet of **Douglas Flat**. Continue a couple of miles to Murphys and turn right onto Pennsylvania Gulch Road. A winding one-mile drive into pleasant oak woodlands takes you to **Rios Winery.**

Return to Highway 4, go east for a few hundred feet and follow signs (a left and a quick right) into the business district of **Murphys.** Shaded by huge locust and elm trees, it's one of the Sierra foothills' more charming towns, with a nice collection of old brick and false front stores, plus the largest concentration of tasting rooms in the Gold Country. As you approach downtown on Main Street, watch for **Milliaire** (*millie-AIR*) winery on your right. It's easy to spot, since it's housed in a former service station. Continue a few blocks into the historic heart of Murphys and watch for a sign on your left to the cellar-dwelling **Zucca Mountain Vineyards**. It's tasting room near the corner of Main and Algiers streets. Just beyond on Algiers is **Malvadino Vineyards** tasting room, occupying a small cottage.

Continue beyond the business district to **Black Sheep Vintners,** in a weathered structure on your right at Main and Murphys Grade. Now, backtrack briefly on Main and turn left onto Sheep Ranch Road at the Olde Timers Museum. (Look for a black and orange Mercer Caverns sign.) This lane seems too narrow to be a serious road, but it quickly takes you out of town, into pine and oak woodlands. Considerable twisting and turning will deliver you to **Mercer Caverns,** another limestone cave attraction. The road then swings right and spirals down into a hideaway canyon, green with pines and vines, home to **Stevenot Winery.**

Return to Main Street and head southwest on Algiers beside the venerable Murphys Hotel. It takes you past the neat little city park and soon ends at a stop sign, where you turn right onto Six Mile Road. After a mile of oaks and pasturelands, you'll see **Ironstone Vineyards** on your right, just beyond Hay Station Ranch. From here, reverse your route to get back to Murphys, or continue down Six Mile Road and you'll hit Highway 4, headed for Angels Camp.

Before or after your Calaveras winery tour, you may want to take time to explore Murphys' shops and boutiques, as well as next-door Columbia State Historic Park. Columbia is a restored 1851 mining town with time-worn but carefully preserved buildings housing gift and curio shops, restaurants and gold rush hotels. The only traffic on Main Street is an occasional stagecoach or string of horses, hauling grinning tourists.

Chatom Vineyards ● T ✕ 📷

1969 E. Highway 4, Douglas Flat; mailing address: P.O. Box 2730, Murphys, CA 95247; (800) 435-8852 or (209) 736-6500. (www.chatomvineyards.com) Daily 11 to 4:30; major credit cards. Most varieties tasted. Good gift shop and specialty foods selection. Landscaped picnic area under arbor.

Gay Callan, daughter of a long line of growers and ranchers, planted vineyards in a sheltered valley near Calaveras County's San Andreas in 1981. She started making wines five years later. After winning a number of awards, she "went public," opening a striking new winery and tasting room on the highway to Murphys in 1991. Seven years later, she shifted the rest of her winery operation to this site from San Andreas.

The winery, part masonry and part weathered wood, is something of a blend between French country and early American railroad station, which is more appealing than it sounds. The tasting room is light and cheerful, trimmed with oak and artwork. A picnic area is particularly inviting, with bentwood lounges as well as tables. It's sheltered by a sturdy arbor which, as the seasons pass, is becoming entwined with vines.

Tasting notes: Light, fruity and crisp are proper adjectives for the Chatom wine list. It includes Sauvignon Blanc, Chardonnay, Merlot, a Sangiovese-Cabernet blend called *Gitano*, Syrah, Zinfandel, Cabernet Sauvignon and a semi-sweet Semillon. Our favorites were a rich and nutty Chardonnay, a Zinfandel with classic Gold Country spiciness, a light yet full-flavored Syrah and a Cabernet Sauvignon with a subtle chili pepper flavor. And there's more to taste here than wine; Chatom offers a selection of interesting dips accompanied by bread, crackers and cheese. Wine prices: *$ to $$$*.

Rios Vineyards & Winery ● T ✕

1154 Pennsylvania Gulch Rd. (P.O. Box 1526), Murphys, CA 95247; (209) 728-1020. Weekends 10 to 5; no credit cards. Most varieties tasted. Pleasant picnic area on lawn beside a lake.

Established in 1985 as Indian Rock Vineyard by Boyd Thompson and his son Scott, this bucolic winery was acquired in 1998 by Jose J. Rios. He's a San Joaquin Valley grape grower and head of Rios Farm Services, Inc. He remodeled and reopened the tasting room in late 1999 and planted an additional thirty acres of vines the following year.

The vineyards and winery occupy an idyllic spot among pines and vines beside a small lake. This is the site of Table Mountain Ranch, established in 1855 as one of the first ranches in the California Gold Country. It was purchased in 1889 by Mrs. Ethel Willard Adams, and it was operated as a dairy farm until 1940. The simple tasting room is in the original dairy barn. As you drive into this farmyard-turned-winery complex, expect to be greeted by an excessively friendly golden Labrador called Indiana.

Tasting notes: The Rios' short lists consists of a light, crisp and fruity Chardonnay; a light and yet peppery Zinfandel; an equally spicy Merlot and a full-flavored Cabernet Sauvignon. Prices: *$$$ to $$$$*.

Milliaire Vineyard Selections ● T

276 Main St. (P.O. Box 1554), Murphys, CA 95247; (209) 728-1658. (www.milliairewinery.com) Daily 11 to 5; MC/VISA. Most varieties tasted. A few wine logo items.

"Fill 'er up" takes on a new meaning when you visit Milliaire. It may be America's only winery operating in a former service station. The overhang that once sheltered Flying A gas pumps is still in place, although the pumps themselves are gone. "We'd love to find one of those old gravity feed gas pumps for color," Liz Millier mused.

The ancient little building began as a carriage house, then served as a livery stable and service station before assuming its new role. The tasting room, with a simple plank over a barrel head, occupies the store portion of the station, where you once paid for your gas and picked out a new set of wiper blades. Wine ages in the former garage, where grease racks once stood.

Steve and Liz Millier started their winery in 1983 and moved to their unique quarters in 1990. *Milliaire*, derived from Steve's family name, means "milestone" in French. A Fresno State University grad, he served as winemaker at David Bruce Winery in the Santa Cruz Mountains, then locally at Stevenot, Ironstone and half a dozen other wineries. Then he decided it was finally time to put his own labels on his wine. He produces about 3,000 cases a year. Liz runs the business end and is active in local affairs.

Tasting notes: Milliaire reflects the big, spicy character of Gold Country wines. We liked all the varietals—a fruity and herbal Sauvignon Blanc; spicy and buttery Chardonnay; Zinfandel with a great herbal-berry flavor; a full-bodied, oak finished Cabernet Sauvignon; and a spicy Merlot. Three dessert wines were rich but not yucky sweet—a late harvest Zinfandel, Orange Muscat and Zinfandel Port. Prices are moderate: *$ to $$$.*

Zucca Mountain Vineyards tasting room • T

431 E. Algiers St., Murphys, CA 95247; 728-1623. (www.zucca-wines.com) Weekends 11 to 5; MC/VISA. Most varieties tasted. A few wine logo items.

Carol Patterson Zucca spent most of her adult life teaching university and high school students. She then retired from teaching but certainly not from life. With help from her family, she turned a home winemaking hobby into a second career. In the mid-1990s, they planted vineyards on a peninsula on nearby New Melones Reservoir. Later, they opened a tiny tasting room in the rustic cellar in one of Murphys' weathered downtown buildings.

Tasting notes: Our favorite on Carol's list was a lush, full-flavored Chardonnay. A Syrah and Merlot both were full flavored with subtle hints of oak. Two blush wines, Summer Sangiovese and *Nebbiolo Nuovo*, were light and fruity, and a bit more assertive than rosé. Bits of bread and crackers are offered between tastes, and one can consummate sipping with something unique for a tasting room—warm chocolate fondue ladled over vanilla wafers. Wine prices: *$$ to $$$$.*

Malvadino Vineyards tasting room • T

457-C Algiers St., Murphys, CA 95247; (209) 728-9030. Daily 11 to 5; MC/VISA. Most varieties tasted. A few wine-oriented giftwares.

Like his tasting room neighbor Carol Zucca, soft-spoken silver-haired Rocco J. Malvini found retirement to be too passive. After a career in the construction trades, he and his family planted vines in the foothill hamlet of Mountain Ranch, then opened a prim, homestyle tasting room in a small cottage in Murphys in 1996.

"I came here to retire twenty-five years ago, then started growing grapes to keep busy." He isn't entirely new to the wine industry, however. His family operated vineyards back in Italy. He apparently has inherited their skills, for his young winery has won a fair number of medals.

Tasting notes: Rocco is one of the few vintners making wine from the Mission grape brought by early California padres. He produces a light, blush style wine good for everyday drinking. More assertive is his spicy and crisp Fiddletown Zinfandel and a medium bodied Calavares Cabernet Sauvignon. Others on the list are a light and fruity Nebbiolo and a crisp and lush Sierra Foothills Chardonnay. Prices: *$$ to $$$.*

Black Sheep Vintners • T ST

Main Street at Murphys Grade (P.O. Box 1851), Murphys, CA 95247; (209) 728-2157. (www.blacksheepwinery.com) Weekends noon to 5 or by appointment weekdays; major credit cards. Most varieties tasted. A few wine logo and gift items. Informal tours.

Black Sheep *looks* like a Gold Country winery. It occupies a weather-textured wooden building with a rusting corrugated roof, at the far end of Murphys' gold rush era Main Street. Inside, rough-cut posts hold up the ceiling. Tasting room doors open right in to the cellar, filled with tiers of sleeping wines. A collection of sheep figurines, given by friends to honor the winery name, clutters a shelf behind the rustic tasting bar. Dave and Jan Olson bought the old Chispa Cellars in the mid-1980s. They'd been farming near the hamlet of Sheepranch in the hills above Murphys, so they decided to use a woolly reference for their winery name. Jan describes Dave as a home winemaker who "got out of control."

Tasting notes: Black Sheep Zinfandel is one of the standards—typically spicy with big berry flavors. Other wines we sampled were equally tasty—a Cabernet Sauvignon with lots of berries and a touch of oak and tannin at the end; and a crisp, fruity Semillon. To honor nearby Angels Camp's annual frog-jumping celebration, the Olsons created the "True Frogs Lily Pad White" label. It's a lightly sweet wine with a great label—two grinning croakers enjoying a lily pad picnic. Prices are moderate: *$ to $$$*.

Vintners choice: "Our Zinfandel—very peppery with nice berry flavors," says Jan. "It's our hallmark wine, and a gold medal winner."

Stevenot Winery • T ST ✕ 📷

2690 Santo Domingo Rd., Murphys, CA 95247; (209) 728-3436. (www.stevenotwinery.com) Daily 10 to 5; MC/VISA, DISC. Most varieties tasted. Good wine related gift selection and picnic fare. Arbor picnic area; tours on request.

Sitting at the bottom of a deep draw, walled by pines and limestone slopes, Stevenot occupies one of the California wine country's prettiest settings. This scene is further enhanced by the "Alaska House," a sod roofed log cabin that seems to have sprouted from the earth in centuries past. It once served as the tasting room but it became "too small and too rustic for the modern age," said our winery hostess. Tasting is now conducted in the former living room of the original Stevenot home, beside an imposing stone fireplace. Nearby, a vine-entwined picnic arbor and lawn invite visitors to linger. Old ranch buildings sheltering modern winery equipment and several acres of vineyards complete this idyllic setting.

The first Stevenots came to the Sierra foothills seeking gold in 1849 and stayed on as ranchers and farmers. Fifth-generation Barden started planting vineyards on the historic Shaw Ranch in 1974 and turned the hay barn into a winery in 1977. Newer facilities have been added. It's the county's oldest winery and the largest in the foothills, producing about 40,000 cases a year.

Tasting notes: Stevenot wines have won many awards for their spicy, fruity foothills style. We particularly liked a full-flavored and nutty Chardonnay, an outstanding herbal Sangiovese, a soft Cabernet Franc with a crisp finish, an inky-rich and complex Syrah, and Tempranillo, a full-flavored Spanish red. Others on the list are Merlot, a couple of Zinfandels, sweet Muscat Canelli and Orange Muscat, plus an alarmingly rich McGuigan Tawny Port imported from Australia. Prices: *$ to $$$*.

Ironstone Vineyards • T ✕ 📷

1894 Six Mile Road (P.O. Box 2263), Murphys, CA 95247; (209) 728-1251. (www.ironstonevineyards.com) Daily 10 to 5; MC/VISA. A choice of six wines tasted. Large deli and extensive wine logo giftware selection. Tours of winery caverns daily at 11:30, 1:30 and 3:30. Shaded picnic area, plus tables inside tasting room and on a winery deck.

Fitted into a gentle slope, shaded by ancient oaks and rimmed by terraced landscaping, Ironstone is easily the most attractive winery in the Gold Country, and one of the most appealing in the entire state. This elaborate multi-tiered facility rivals the most opulent wine estates of the Napa Valley. It also can draw crowds comparable to those in the Napa Valley, so it's best visited on weekdays.

The winery's focal point is an imposing twin-gabled stone and wood structure with a tasting room, deli and visitor facility above and winery below. A massive four-way fieldstone fireplace with a barbecue for special cooking events commands one end of the vaulted-ceiling tasting room. Old farm implements and trophy heads decorate display balconies. Deli and wine purchases can be fashioned into lunch, and visitors can eat at tables inside, on an outside deck or at a picnic area. A terraced, grassy amphitheater is the scene of frequent concerts and other special events. Although the winery isn't old enough to have much of a history, it features a Heritage Museum and Gallery that focuses on the California gold rush. Its most imposing exhibit is the world's largest chunk of crystallized leaf gold. This 44-pound specimen, housed in a stone vault, was unearthed at the nearby Jamestown mine several years ago.

John Kautz, a successful Lodi grower and vintner, began planting vines near Murphys' historic Hay Station Ranch in 1988. He then had tunnels bored into a slope as his first "buildings" and aging cellars in 1991. Tours take visitors through these caves and to an underground spring that was discovered during the "mining."

Tasting notes: Ironstone wines are very modestly priced, considering their elegant surroundings. Among our sippings were a soft and light Chardonnay, an excellent spicy and full-flavored Merlot, a rich Shiraz with a spicy back-of-the-palate finish, a Cabernet Franc with a huge berry taste, and a light yet peppery Zinfandel. Symphony Obsession is a semi-dry sipping wine with an apple-flower petal nose and taste. The winery also produces Port, Meritage, sparkling brut, grape and apple brandy and Italian style grappa. Prices: *$$ to $$$$.*

THE BEST OF THE BUNCH

The best wine buys ● Sierra foothills vintners consistently offer some of California's best premium wine buys. Some of the better prices are at Venezio Winery & Vineyard, Sierra Vista Winery, Granite Springs, Single Leaf Vineyards and Oakstone in El Dorado County; Monteviña Winery, Domaine de la Terre Rouge, Storey Winery, Amador Foothill Winery, Deaver Vineyards and Sobon Estate in Amador County; and Milliaire Vineyard Selections, Black Sheep Vintners and Stevenot Winery in Calaveras County.

The most attractive wineries ● Monteviña Winery and Perry Creek Vineyards in El Dorado County; Renwood Winery and Sobon Estate (with its museum) in Amador County; Chatom Vineyards, Ironstone Vineyards and Stevenot Winery (for its setting) in Calaveras County.

The most interesting tasting rooms ● Boeger Winery, Gold Hill Winery (for its view), Fitzpatrick Winery, Perry Creek Vineyards and Charles B Mitchell Vineyards in El Dorado County; Renwood Winery, Charles

Spinetta Winery, Shenandoah Vineyards, Sobon Estate, Deaver Vineyards and Dobra Zemlja in Amador County; Ironstone Vineyards and Stevenot Winery in Calaveras County.

The funkiest tasting rooms ● Story Winery in Amador County; Rios Winery, Milliaire Winery, Black Sheep Vintners and Zucca Mountain Vineyards in Calaveras County.

The best gift shops ● Perry Creek Vineyards in El Dorado County, Charles Spinetta Winery and Wildlife Gallery, Deaver Vineyards and Sobon Estate in Amador County; Stevenot Winery and Ironstone Vineyards in Calaveras County.

The nicest picnic areas ● Boeger Winery, Madroña Vineyards, Sierra Vista Winery, Fitzpatrick Winery and Charles B Mitchell Vineyards in El Dorado County; Monteviña Winery and Story Winery in Amador County; Chatom Vineyards, Ironstone Vineyards and Stevenot in Calaveras County.

The best tours ● Sobon Estate (self-guiding tour of winery museum) in Amador County; and Ironstone Vineyards (guided tour of wine caves) in Calaveras County.

Wineland maps and events

Winery touring maps ● These map-brochures cover the Gold Country's three major wine producing regions:

El Dorado Wine Country Tour, El Dorado Vintners Association, P.O. Box 1614, Placerville, CA 95667; (800) 306-3956. *(www.eldoradowines.org)*

Amador County Wine Country, Amador Vintners Assn., c/o the Amador County Chamber of Commerce, P.O. Box 596, Jackson, CA 95642; (209) 223-0350. *(www.amadorwine.com)*

Calaveras Wine Country, Calaveras Wine Association, P.O. Box 2492, Murphys, CA 95247; (800) 225-3764 or (209) 736-6722. *(www.calaveraswines.org)*

Wineland events ● A Taste of Amador in February, with wine and food event at Amador County vintners; (800) 400-0305 or (209) 223-0350. El Dorado Wine Passport, last weekend of March and first weekend of April; (800) 306-3956 or (530) 446-6562. Sierra Showcase of Wine with auction and tasting, early May, Amador County Fairgrounds in Plymouth; (209) 267-5978, extension 50 or (209) 245-6921. Amador County Grape Growers Wine Festival in June, Amador County Fairgrounds; (209) 245-6119, Fairplay Wine Festival, June; (530) 245-3467. El Dorado County Harvest Faire, September; (530) 621-5885. El Dorado County Wine Appreciation Week with barbecue, music, tours and tasting; (800) 306-3956. Calaveras Passport Weekend the third weekend of June and Calaveras Grape Stomp, first Saturday in October; (800) 225-3764 or (209) 736-6722.

The Amador County Fair in Plymouth in late July; (209) 245-6921; and El Dorado County Fair, August, (530) 621-5885 feature local wine displays.

BEYOND THE VINEYARDS

Like Monterey and Santa Cruz, the Sierra foothills are more famous for tourism than for wineries—although those citadels of Zinfandel are quickly gaining note. The favored route for exploring the Sierra foothills is Highway 49, named in honor of the peak year of the gold rush. Call the "Golden Chain," it meanders for 310 miles through the full length of the Sierra Nevada mining area, from Vinton in the north to Oakhurst in the south. It's a popular vacationers' route; some folks spend days wandering its serpentine course. As we have noted, only its central area offers functioning wineries. Using each of the three wine producing areas as a base, we'll suggest some driving tours that take you past other mid-Sierra foothill attractions.

El Dorado County

Placerville was so rowdy in its early days that it was first called Hangtown in honor of the chosen form of discipline. Later, more sedate citizens changed the name. After exploring its lures, you can continue east on U.S. Highway 50 to south shore **Lake Tahoe** with its famous glitter—coming both from the lake and its surrounding casinos. This was the route of the **Pony Express** and markers chart its progress through the Sierra Nevada.

If you follow the twisting course of State Highway 193 fifteen miles north of Placerville, you'll encounter **Georgetown,** one of the best-preserved of the old mining towns. An eight-mile winding drive northwest on Highway 49 will take you to **Marshall Gold Discovery State Historic Park in Coloma**. Beyond, you'll travel through the ruggedly imposing **American River Canyon** and arrive in **Auburn,** which has a funkily attractive Old Town section, now surrounded by in sprawling suburbia.

Amador County

Little remains of Plymouth's glory days, although **Drytown, Amador City** and **Sutter Creek,** south on Highway 49, have preserved much of their yesterday charm. They're noted for boutiques and antique shops and they offer several bed and breakfast inns, handy stops for Shenandoah Valley wine country visitors.

Sutter Creek-Volcano Road heading northeast from Sutter Creek leads through one of the prettiest creek valleys in the foothills, ending at the rustic mining town of **Volcano.** Just above is **Daffodil Hill,** where acres of daffodils blossom every spring; call (209) 223-0608 for bloom times. Nearby is **Indian Grinding Rock State Park,** preserving the history of the area's earliest residents.

Calaveras-Tuolumne counties

Several historic hamlets draw visitors to Calaveras County, most notably **San Andreas,** where stage coach bandit Black Bart was jailed, and **Angels Camp,** made famous by Mark Twain's frog-jumping yarn. Both have historic districts with the requisite boutiques and antique stores. You already know that an uphill drive on Highway 4 takes you to the wine country around Murphys. Stay on the highway and you'll reach the high Sierra and the famous **Bear Valley** summer and winter resort. On the way, you'll pass **Calaveras Big Trees State Park,** whose giant sequoia groves are definitely worth a stop.

Neighboring Tuolumne County brims with gold rush lore, most notably **Columbia State Historic Park.** Just south on Highway 49, **Sonora** and **Jamestown** are treasure-troves of early California architecture and memorabilia. Much of downtown Sonora has been renovated, with boutiques and restaurants occupying ancient storefronts. **Railtown 1897 State Historic Park** is "Jimtown's" premier attraction. A drive north from Sonora takes you to the piney wood hamlets of **Twain Harte** and **Pinecrest,** popular Sierra retreats.

Drive east from Jamestown on Highway 49, blend onto Route 120, and you'll climb up to the neat old mining town of **Groveland** and then to the Sierra Nevada's most famous attraction, **Yosemite National Park.**

Gold Country attractions
El Dorado County

Apple Hill • *For a guide map, contact Apple Hill Growers, Inc., P.O. Box 494, Camino, CA 95709; (530) 644-7692.* ☐ Nearly fifty Apple Hill growers offer direct-to-consumer products, particularly apple goodies, between Labor Day and Thanksgiving. A few remain open the year-around.

El Dorado County Historical Museum • *100 Placerville Dr., Placerville; (530) 621-5865. Wednesday-Saturday 10 to 4, Sunday noon to 4. Free, donations appreciated.* ☐ Artifacts of early-day Hangtown and El Dorado County.

Gold Bug Park and Mine • *549 Main St., Placerville; (530) 642-5232. Daily noon to 4, March to mid-April; daily 10 to 4, mid-April through October; weekends only, noon to 4 in November; closed during December; modest fee.* ☐ Gold mine, stamp mill and other mining artifacts.

Marshall Gold Discovery State Historic Park • *Coloma; (530) 622-3470. Museum open daily 10 to 4:30, Memorial Day through Labor Day; 11 to 5 the rest of the year; day use fee.* ☐ Historical buildings and exhibits, reconstruction of Sutter's Mill, where James Marshall first found gold.

Amador County

Amador County Museum • *225 Church St., Jackson; (209) 223-6386. Wednesday-Sunday 10 to 4; modest admission charge.* ☐ Relics of early Amador County; mine exhibit and mining gear.

Chaw'se Indian Grinding Rock State Historic Park • *14881 Pine Grove-Volcano Rd., Pine Grove; (209) 296-7488. Museum open weekdays 11 to 3 and weekends 10 to 4; day use fee for park.* ☐ Reconstructed Miwok village, museum and huge Indian grinding rock; campgrounds.

Knight Foundry • *81 Eureka St., Sutter Creek; (209) 267-0201. One hour tours on weekends from 10 to 4 for a modest fee.* ☐ America's only surviving water-powered iron works and machine shop, established in 1872 and now a museum. Call for schedule of periodic "iron pours."

Monteverde General Store • *3 Randolph St., Sutter Creek; (209) 267-1344. Weekends 10 to 3.* ☐ Old fashioned general store that operated from 1898 until 1971; now a living history museum with yesterday furnishings and merchandise.

Calaveras & Tuolumne counties

Angels Camp Museum • *753 S. Main St., Angels Camp; (209) 736-2963. Open 10 to 3, daily in summer and Wednesday-Sunday the rest of the year; modest admission charge.* ☐ Historic relics and old farming and gold-mining equipment.

Calaveras County Museum and Archives • *30 N. Main St., San Andreas; (209) 754-3918. Daily 10 to 4; modest admission charge.* ☐ Pioneer museum in old Hall of Records building; original Black Bart jail cell out back.

Cave tours • Three limestone caverns are near Calaveras County's wine country: California Caverns at Cave City above San Andreas and Moaning Cavern near Murphys, both (209) 736-2708; and Mercer Caverns above Stevenot Winery, (209) 728-2101. *(www.caverntours.com)* Admission charge at each.

Columbia State Historic Park • *Parrotts Ferry Road, Columbia; (209) 532-4301 or (209) 536-1672. (www.sierra.parks.state.ca.us) Most museums and shops open 10 to 5 daily; free.* □ Restored gold mining town that once was the gem of the Mother Lode. Stage coach rides, horseback rides, gold panning, Hidden Treasure Mine tour, costumed docent tours; hotels, restaurants (see below).

Old Timers Museum • *470 Main Street at Sheep Ranch Road, Murphys; (209) 728-1160. Friday-Sunday 11 to 4; small admission charge.* □ Early-day mining relics and reconstructed blacksmith shop, plus a humorous "E. Clampus Vitus Wall of Comparative Ovations."

Railtown 1897 State Historic Park • *Fifth Avenue, Jamestown; (209) 984-3953 or (916) 445-6645 for recorded information. Gift shop and roundhouse open daily 9:30 to 4:30, free admission.* □ Old time steam trains, roundhouse and rail memorabilia. Train rides April-October on weekends hourly from 11 to 3, Saturday only in November; fee charged. Special excursions also available.

Tuolumne County Museum and History Center • *158 W. Bradford Ave., Sonora; (209) 532-1317. Monday-Friday 10 to 4, Saturday 10 to 3:30, closed Sunday; donations accepted.* □ Gold rush and pioneer relics, old jail cells, gold nugget exhibit.

WINE COUNTRY DINING

PRICE KEY: Dinner entrée with soup or salad, without drinks or dessert for under $10 = $; $10 to $14 = $$; $15 to $25 = $$$; over $25 = $$$$.

El Dorado County

Cable House Restaurant • ☆☆ **$$**

□ *4110 Carson Rd., Camino; (530) 644-1818. American; no alcohol. Breakfast through mid-afternoon daily. MC/VISA.* □ Small café tucked into a wood frame cottage, serving hefty breakfasts and "cookhouse lunches" of fried chicken or steak, plus sandwiches. Woodsy interior with walls hung with whipsaws and other lumbering gear. The restaurant's name comes from a suspension cable carriage that once hauled lumber across the American River gorge.

Hangtown Grille • ☆☆ **$$**

□ *432 Main St., Placerville; (530) 626-4431. American; wine and beer. Breakfast through dinner daily. MC/VISA.* □ Early American style café tucked into one of Placerville's old brick buildings, with wainscotting, tulip lamps and café curtains. The menu offers babyback ribs, barbecued pork tenderloin, chicken breasts and assorted steaks, plus several health oriented dishes.

La Casa Grande • ☆☆ **$$**

□ *251 Main St. (at Spring, just off Highway 50), Placerville; (530) 626-5454. Mexican-American; full bar service. Lunch through dinner daily. Major credit cards.* □ Family-style Mexican café housed in a pair of 1896 storefronts in the historic area of Placerville. Large *Latino* menu has typical tortilla-wrapped fare, specials such as enchilada verde, chicken chimichangas and roast pork in molé sauce, plus several American dishes.

Mel's of Placerville ● ☆☆ $ to $$

□ *Main at Sacramento streets, Placerville; (530) 626-8072. American; wine and beer. Breakfast through dinner daily. MC/VISA, AMEX.* □ Remarkably cute nostalgic diner descended from the Mel's chain that started in 1947. Classic "American graffiti" look with black and white tile, chrome rimmed counter stools and Wurlitzer style jukeboxes that are actually CD players. The menu is typical as well, featuring chicken fried steak, 'burgers, shakes and such.

Powell Brothers Steamer Company ● ☆☆☆ $$

□ *425 Main St., Placerville; (530) 626-1091. Seafood; full bar service. Lunch through dinner daily. MC/VISA.* □ Lively place with a brick-walled "old wharf atmosphere" in one of downtown Placerville's store fronts. The menu features oysters on the half shell, *cioppino,* scampi, chowders and similar seafood fare. Extensive Gold Country wine list.

Amador County

Bar-T-Bar ● ☆☆ $$

□ *Highway 49 (just south of town), Plymouth; (209) 245-3729. American; full bar service. Lunch through dinner daily and Sunday brunch. MC/VISA* □ A likable roadhouse that dishes up hearty fare at modest prices; steak, seafood, ribs and chops dinners include soup and salad, potatoes or rice and hot bread. American country décor with warm wood paneling, ceiling fans and maple furnishings. Amador County wines featured.

Bellotti Inn ● ☆☆ $$

□ *53 Main St., Sutter Creek; (209) 267-5211. Italian-American; full bar service. Lunch through dinner daily except Tuesday. MC/VISA.* □ Gold rush era restaurant in an 1858 hotel with attractive although spartan nineteenth century décor. Usual pastas plus specials such as breast of chicken Parmesan, calamari steak and some American steak and prime rib dishes.

Caffé Via d'Oro ● ☆☆☆ $$

□ *26 Main St., Sutter Creek; (209) 267-0535. American-Italian; wine and beer. Lunch and dinner daily except Tuesday. MC/VISA, DISC.* □ Occupying one of Sutter Creek's historic storefronts and offering an assortment of pizzas, calzones, pastas and American dishes such as grilled pork medallions, steak and seafood. It has the proper yesterday look with high ceilings, oiled wood floors and wooden booths lit by old fashioned bowl lamps.

Imperial Hotel Restaurant ● ☆☆☆ $$$

□ *Main Street, Amador City; (209) 267-9172. (www.imperialamador.com) American and continental; full bar service. Dinner Tuesday-Sunday. Major credit cards.* □ Attractive old style restaurant in an 1879 brick Gold Country hotel. High backed fabric chairs, ceiling fans and white nappery in a cozy dining room. The changing menu features a tasty mix of American *nouveau* and more classic continental dishes. Oasis Bar adjacent to the dining room.

Sutter Creek Palace ● ☆☆☆ $$$

□ *76 Main St., Sutter Creek; (209) 267-1300. Continental; full bar service. Lunch and dinner daily except Thursday. Reservations suggested on weekends; major credit cards.* □ Sutter Creek's most attractive restaurant; a study in Victorian elegance, housed in an 1884 building that began life, appropriately, as a restaurant and saloon. Entreés include a mix of Italian fare such as calamari amondine, scampi, chicken marsala and American New York steak, pork tenderloin and fresh seafood. Good local wine list.

Zinfandels at Sutter Creek ● ☆☆☆☆ $$$

□ *51 Hanford St. (Highway 49), Sutter Creek; (209) 267-5008. American nouveau with Asian accents; wine and beer. Dinner Thursday-Sunday. Reservations suggested on weekends. Major credit cards.* □ Highly regarded restaurant housed in a cozy country-style cottage. Small, frequently changing menu features tasty and creatively labeled fare such as "Fruit of the Sea" (assorted fresh seafoods), "A thousand wise dragons" (charbroiled steak with hoisen sauce), and "Try it on for size" (boneless chicken breast topped with mushrooms, onions and smoked cheese. Noted for excellent deserts and large wine list, including more than twenty Zinfandels.

Calaveras-Tuolumne counties

City Hotel Restaurant ● ☆☆☆☆ $$$$

□ *Main Street (Jackson), Columbia State Historic Park; (209) 532-1479. American nouveau; full bar service. Dinner nightly; Sunday brunch. Reservations essential on weekends; MC/VISA, AMEX.* □ Splendid Victorian dining room in a restored gold rush hotel (listed below); considered by many as the Sierra foothills' finest restaurant. Entrées on the ever-changing menu may include grilled salmon filet, ribeye steak, ranch venison, rack of lamb or old fashioned liver and onions. Good foothills wine list.

Columbia House Restaurant ● ☆☆ $ to $$

□ *Main and State streets, Columbia State Historic Park; (209) 532-5134. American; wine and beer. Breakfast to midafternoon weekdays, to late afternoon weekends; closed Tuesday. MC/VISA.* □ Hearty breakfasts plus lunches of sandwiches, sirloin steak, chicken breasts and pasties (a meat pie specialty of Cornish miners). The restaurant's roots date back to 1850. Country décor with wainscotting, print wallpaper and quilt panels.

Lickskillet Café ● ☆☆ $$

□ *11256 State St., Columbia; (209) 536-9599. Eclectic menu; wine and beer. Lunch and dinner daily in summer and Wednesday-Sunday the rest of the year. Major credit cards.* □ Cute early American style café, despite its unfortunate name. Fare is international, ranging from salmon piccata and rosemary roasted chicken to duck noodles and barbecued pork. Extensive foothills wine list. Outdoor tables on a porch and lawn.

Murphys Grille ● ☆☆ $$$

□ *380 Main St., Murphys; (209) 728-8800. American-continental; wine and beer. Lunch through dinner daily. Major credit cards.* □ Appealing café tucked into one of Murphys' historic buildings, with an inviting sun porch out front. Eclectic fare ranges from squash ravioli and pan roasted chicken to beef Wellington and osso bucco. Good local wine selection.

Murphys Hotel Restaurant ● ☆☆☆ $$$

□ *457 Main St. (Algiers Street), Murphys; (209) 728-3444. (www.murphyshotel.com) American-continental; full bar service. Lunch through dinner daily. Major credit cards.* □ Victorian style restaurant in 1856 hotel (listing below), featuring fare such as steaks, prime rib, pastas and seafood, with homemade desserts and a good selection of Amador wines. Elaborate period décor includes hurricane ceiling lamps, pioneer photos and relics.

Peppermint Stick ● ☆☆ $

□ *454 Main St. (downtown), Murphys; (209) 728-3570. American; no alcohol. Lunch through late afternoon Monday-Friday; mid-morning through dinner Saturday; noon through late afternoon Sunday. MC/VISA.* □ Cute old fashioned fountain in a century-old building, with white wrought iron chairs and folk art décor. Light lunch and dinner fare, including unusual "miners chili" and "old timers beef stew" served in a hollowed-out bread loaf. Slurp the soup and eat the bowl.

WINELAND LODGINGS
PRICE KEY: A two-person room for $35 or less = $; $36 to $50 = $$; $51 to $75 = $$$; $76 to $100 = $$$$; more than $100 = $$$$$.

El Dorado County

Best Western Placerville Inn ● ☆☆☆ $$$ to $$$$

□ *6850 Greenleaf Dr. (Highway 50 at Missouri Flat), Placerville, CA 95667; (800) 854-9100 or (530) 622-9100. (www.rimcorp.com) Major credit cards.* □ Attractive 105-room motel with Southwest décor. TV movies and phones; some fireplaces. Pool and spa.

Cary House Hotel ● ☆☆☆ $$$$ to $$$$$

□ *300 Main St., Placerville, CA 95667; (800) 537-8438 or (530) 622-4271. (www.caryhouse.com) Major credit cards. Rates include continental breakfast.* □ Beautifully restored 1857 hotel in the Placerville historic district, with an opulently decorated lobby and period furnished rooms. Some suites and kitchenettes available.

Gold Trail Motor Lodge ● ☆ $$ to $$$

□ *1970 Broadway (Point View), Placerville, CA 95667; (530) 622-2906. Major credit cards.* □ A 32-room motel on landscaped grounds TV and room phones; some room refrigerators and hair dryers. Pool and picnic area.

Mother Lode Motel ● ☆ $$ to $$$

□ *1940 Broadway (Point View), Placerville, CA 95667; (530) 622-0895. Major credit cards.* □ A 21-unit motel with pool, lawn area. Rooms have TV movies and phones; some refrigerators.

Bed & breakfast inns

Camino Hotel Bed & Breakfast ● ☆☆ $$$ to $$$$

□ *4103 Carson Rd. (P.O. Box 1197), Camino, CA 95709-1197; (800) 200-7740 or (530) 644-7740. (www.caminohotel.com) Nine rooms; some private and some share baths; full breakfast.* □ Nicely restored former loggers barracks with early American décor. Simple and comfortable furnishings; large parlor warmed by a pellet stove. Close to Camino shops and Apple Hill. Jodar Winery tasting room on ground floor; see page 286 above.

Chichester-McKee House Bed & Breakfast ● ☆☆☆ $$$$ to $$$$$

□ *800 Spring St., Placerville, CA 95667; (800) 831-4008 or (530) 626-1882. Four rooms with private baths; full breakfast. Major credit cards.* □ Nicely furnished 1892 Queen Anne Victorian home with Victorian, American and country antiques. Conservatory, landscaped garden, porch with old fashioned swing, fireplaces in parlor and lobby. Elaborate breakfasts are served in an attractive Victorian dining room.

Fitzpatrick Lodge ● ☆☆ $$$

☐ *7740 Fairplay Road, Somerset, CA 95684; (530) 620-3248. Five rooms with private baths; full breakfast. Major credit cards.* ☐ Handsome log chalet with hilltop view of mountains and valleys; part of Fitzpatrick Winery. Comfortable country-style furnishings; all rooms with view decks. Chalet style sitting room with fireplace; afternoon wine and snacks.

Seven-Up Bar Guest Ranch ● ☆☆☆ $$$$ to $$$$$

☐ *P.O. Box 304 (8060 Fairplay Rd.), Somerset, CA 95684; (800) 394-1680 or (530) 620-5450. (www.perrycreek.com) Six units with private baths; ranch style breakfast. MC/VISA, DISC.* ☐ A 1930s dude ranch owned by Alice and Michael Chazen of Perry Creek Vineyards and spruced up as a Western-style B&B. Log cabins with contemporary Western furnishings. Activities include hiking, fishing and treks to a Native American archeological site.

Amador County

Gold Quartz Inn ● ☆☆☆ $$$$ to $$$$$

☐ *15 Bryson Dr., Sutter Creek, CA 95685; (800) 752-8738 or (209) 267-9155. Rates include full breakfast and afternoon tea. MC/VISA, AMEX.* ☐ Nicely maintained 24-room Queen Anne style inn. Rooms furnished in period décor with American and Victorian antiques; TV, phones, sitting porches and private entrances.

Imperial Hotel ● ☆☆☆ $$$$ to $$$$$

☐ *14202 Highway 49 (P.O. Box 195), Amador City, CA 95601; (209) 267-9172. (www.imperialamador.com) Rates include full breakfast. Major credit cards.* ☐ Nicely restored brick 1879 hotel; six individually decorated rooms with period furnishings and modern private baths. **Restaurant** and bar listed above.

Shenandoah Inn ● ☆☆☆ $$$ to $$$$$

☐ *17674 Village Dr., Plymouth, CA 95669; (800) 542-4549 or (209) 245-4491. Rates include continental breakfast. Major credit cards.* ☐ Attractive Spanish style inn with forty-seven rooms; TV movies, phones, in-room coffee. Pool, spa, landscaped grounds. Suites available. Near turnoff to Shenandoah Valley wine country.

Bed & breakfast inns

Amador Harvest Inn ● ☆☆☆ $$$$ to $$$$$

☐ *12455 Steiner Rd. (Shenandoah Valley), Plymouth, CA 95669; (209) 245-5512. Four rooms with private baths; full breakfast and afternoon snacks. Major credit cards.* ☐ Beautifully restored farm house adjacent to Deaver Vineyards tasting room, with views of vineyard and a lake. Victorian and early American décor; comfortable living room with fireplace. Near Shenandoah Valley wineries.

Eureka Street Inn ● ☆☆☆ $$$$$

☐ *55 Eureka St., Sutter Creek, CA 95685; (800) 399-2389 or (209) 267-5500. (www.eurekastreetinn.com) Six rooms with private baths; full breakfast. Major credit cards.* ☐ Handsomely appointed two-story 1914 Craftsman bungalow tucked between Sutter Creek's historic Main Street and Knight Foundry. Rooms individually furnished with vintage European or early American themes; gas stoves or fireplaces.

Sutter Creek Inn ● ☆☆☆ $$$ to $$$$$

□ 75 Main St. (P.O. Box 385), Sutter Creek, CA 95685; (209) 267-5606. (www.suttercreekinn.com) Eighteen rooms with private baths; full breakfast. MC/VISA. □ Handsome Gold Country inn fashioned from an 1850s Greek revival house. Individually decorated rooms feature antique and contemporary furnishings; some have fireplaces. Landscaped garden with hammocks; shops and restaurants nearby.

The Foxes ● ☆☆☆☆ $$$$$

□ 77 Main St. (P.O. Box 159), Sutter Creek, CA 95685; (209) 267-5882. (www.foxesinn.com) Six rooms, all with private baths; full breakfast. MC/VISA, DISC. □ Beautifully appointed B&B in a renovated early day merchant's home. Period furnishings with fox decorator theme; radio/tape players in rooms, some with TV. Landscaped grounds, gardens and covered porches. Downtown, near shops and restaurants.

The Hanford House ● ☆☆☆ $$$$ to $$$$$

□ 61 Hanford St. (P.O. Box 1450), Sutter Creek, CA 95685; (530) 267-0747. (www.hanfordhouse.com) Nine rooms and suites, all with private baths; expanded buffet breakfast. MC/VISA, DISC. □ A stylish B&B fashioned around a 1920s home. Eight of the units have fireplaces. Large parlor, sun deck and landscaped patio; conference facilities.

The Heirloom Bed & Breakfast Inn ● ☆☆☆ $$$$

□ 214 Shakeley Lane (Preston Avenue), Ione, CA 95640; (209) 274-4468. Five rooms with private baths; full breakfast. Major credit cards. □ An 1863 antebellum brick mansion listed as a Native Sons of the Golden West "Dedicated Historical Site." Rooms done in American and Victorian antiques and art works; three with fireplaces or wood burning stoves. Convenient to Ione-area wineries.

Indian Creek Bed & Breakfast ● ☆☆ $$$$$

□ 21950 Highway 49, Plymouth, CA 95669; (800) 24-CREEK or (209) 245-4648. (www.indiancreek.com) Four rooms with private baths; full breakfast. MC/VISA, DISC. □ An elegant, carefully restored 1932 log lodge on ten wooded acres, once owned by a millionaire Hollywood producer. Handsome polished log living room with stone fireplace, native American style rugs and comfy furniture; sun room, outdoor decks and a Western style bar.

Mine House Inn ● ☆☆☆ $$$$ to $$$$$

□ 14125 Highway 49 (P.O. Box 245), Amador City, CA 95601; (800) 646-3473 or (209) 267-5900. Eight rooms and five suites, all with private baths; full. MC/VISA. □ Attractive bed & breakfast inn fashioned from an 1880 mining office building, overlooking Amador City and the Keystone mine headframe. Eight rooms in the historic building, with suites in a nearby 1930s style structure and a newly constructed Victorian. Waterfall, pool and spa.

Calaveras-Tuolumne

City Hotel and Fallon Hotel ● ☆☆☆☆ $$$ to $$$$$

□ P.O. Box 1870, Columbia, CA 95310; (800) 532-1479 or (209) 532-1479. (www.cityhotel.com) Rates include continental breakfast. MC/VISA, AMEX. □ Impeccably restored gold rush hotels in the heart of Columbia State Park. Furnished in the style of the 1860s and 1870s. Wainscoting, print wallpaper, Victorian and American antiques; service staff in period dress. Some half-baths and shared showers. **City Hotel Restaurant** listed above.

Columbia Gem Motel ● ☆ $$$ to $$$$$
□ *22131 Parrotts Ferry Rd. (P.O. Box 874), Columbia, CA 95310; (209) 532-4508. (www.columbiagem.com) MC/VISA.* □ Cute and well-kept old fashioned motor lodge with twelve units in cottages, plus a motel wing. TV, in-room coffee; some units have refrigerators and microwaves. Near Columbia State Historic Park.

Murphys Hotel ● ☆☆☆ $$$$
□ *457 Main St. (P.O. 329), Murphys, CA 95247; (800) 532-7684 or (209) 728-3444. (www.murphyshotel.com) MC/VISA, AMEX.* □ National historic landmark hotel, handsomely refurbished in Victorian style. The Presidential Suite, where Ulysses S. Grant once slept, is particularly opulent. Nine rooms in the 1856 hotel have share baths; twenty rooms in adjacent lodge wing have TV, phones and private baths.

The Redbud Inn ● ☆☆☆ $$$$ to $$$$$
□ *402 Main St. (P.O. Box 716), Murphys, CA 95247; (209) 728-8533. MC/VISA.* □ Attractive inn housed in one of downtown Murphys' historic buildings. Twelve rooms and a suite; most with balconies, spa tubs and wood stoves or fireplaces. In the Miner's Exchange shopping center.

Bed & breakfast inns
Dunbar House, 1880 ● ☆☆☆ $$$$$
□ *271 Jones St., Murphys, CA 95247; (800) 692-6006 or (209) 728-2897. Five rooms with private baths; full breakfast. MC/VISA, AMEX.* □ Imposing Italianate style bed & breakfast inn furnished with country and Victorian antiques. Rooms have wood-burning stoves and refrigerators with a bottle of local wine. Two-room suite with spa tub. Afternoon refreshments; country-style gardens.

The Harlan House ● ☆☆☆ $$$$ to $$$$$
□ *22890 School House St. (P.O. Box 686), Columbia, CA 95310; (209) 533-4862. Three rooms, plus a cozy cellar suite, all with private baths; full breakfast. Major credit cards.* □ Handsome two-story Victorian style bed & breakfast inn, perched on a slope above Columbia State Historic Park. Nicely appointed rooms feature a mix of Victorian and American antiques. Shady porch and garden patio. Free shuttle to Columbia airport.

Gold Country information sources
Amador County Chamber of Commerce, P.O. Box 596, Jackson, CA 95642; (209) 223-0350. *(www.amadorcountychamber.com)*

Calaveras Visitors Bureau, P.O. Box 637 (1211 S. Main St.), Angels Camp, CA 95222; (800) 225-3764 or (209) 736-0049. *(www.visitcalaveras.org)*

El Dorado County Chamber of Commerce, 542 Main St., Placerville, CA 95667; (800) 457-6279 or (530) 621-5885. *(www.eldoradocounty.org)*

Sutter Creek Visitor Center, 80 11-A Randolph St. (P.O. Box 1234), Sutter Creek, CA 95685; (800) 400-0305 or (209) 267-1344. *(www.suttercreek.org)*

Tuolumne County Visitors Bureau, 542 W. Stockton Rd., (P.O. Box 4020), Sonora, CA 95370; (800) 446-1333 or (209) 533-4420. *(www.thegreatunfenced.com)*

Our pale day is sinking into twilight,
And if we sip the wine, we find dreams coming soon upon us
Out of the imminent night.
— **Grapes** by D.H. Lawrence

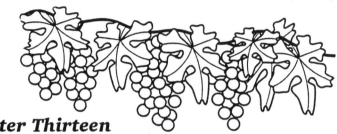

Chapter Thirteen
TEMECULA VALLEY
Chardonnay in a Southland suburb

During California's formative years, its population was centered in the north central area, drawn by the discovery of gold in the Sierra Nevada foothills. Wine production, however, began in the south, since that's where most of the mission vineyards were located. The state's first commercial planters were drawn to southern California as well.

Today, of course, conditions are reversed. Most of the people live in the south and most of the premium wine production is in the north central area. In fact, the Southland's only major vineyard area is quite new.

Pioneer planters such as Jean-Louis Vignes and William Wolfskill made Los Angeles the center of the state's commercial wine industry in the 1830s. Later, a utopian colony of Germans planted tens of thousands of vines in Anaheim, not far from the land now ruled by a senior citizen mouse named Mickey. Urban growth pushed the vines eastward from Los Angeles and Anaheim toward Cucamonga, where a dozen or so wineries functioned from the 1930s until the 1960s. New population surges and the popularity of orange groves put the squeeze on the grapes again and they shifted southward.

In the 1970s, a new home was found for Southern California's wine country—the Temecula Valley between Riverside and San Diego. Although a few wineries are scattered elsewhere about the Southland, Temecula offers the only concentration of vineyards and vintners. It's in southern Riverside County, about fifteen air miles from the Pacific, close enough to benefit from temperate ocean air.

Those cooling breezes, morning fogs and a 1,300-foot elevation provide suitable climate for premium whites. Chardonnay and Sauvignon Blanc are the most popular, and we found some excellent examples here. Some reds

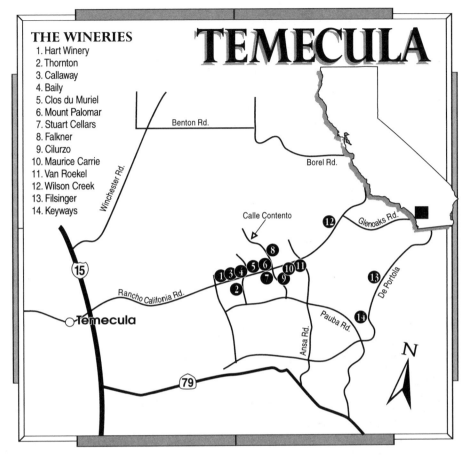

THE WINERIES
1. Hart Winery
2. Thornton
3. Callaway
4. Baily
5. Clos du Muriel
6. Mount Palomar
7. Stuart Cellars
8. Falkner
9. Cilurzo
10. Maurice Carrie
11. Van Roekel
12. Wilson Creek
13. Filsinger
14. Keyways

TEMECULA

Benton Rd.

Borel Rd.

Winchester Rd.

Calle Contento

Glenoaks Rd.

Rancho California Rd.

De Portola

Temecula

Ansa Rd.

Pauba Rd.

N

also do quite well, and growers are beginning to make room for Cabernet, Merlot and Zinfandel. Several wineries are featuring some Italian varietals, such as Viognier, Moscato and Nebbiolo.

Temecula's vineyards aren't exactly removed from the Southland's population sprawl. In thirty years, the town has rocketed from a quiet cowboy hamlet into a semi-planned community of more than 30,000. One sees a virtual explosion of planned residential areas, shopping centers and business parks. This is one of California's fastest-growing regions.

However, the vines are in a protected agricultural zone, to the east of the mushrooming city. There, they share dry, sandy hillocks with avocado and citrus groves, fancy horse ranches and a remarkable tally of luxurious country estates. The area's architectural look—apparently by some silent dictate—is Spanish Southwest. From business parks to ranch mansions to shopping centers to winery tasting rooms, the rule is beige stucco, pink tile and Spanish arches, with salmon and turquoise accents. The effect is quite pleasing.

Temecula began as a genuine cowtown, laid out in 1884 to serve the commercial needs of the huge Vail Ranch, which occupied most of the valley. The town consisted of the Longbranch Saloon, the Stables Bar, a folksy restaurant called the Swing Inn, and a couple of stores. Real cowboys and Indians, most of whom were employed on the ranch, strolled about the streets. Passersby called the place quaint. The name is quaint, too. "Temecula" is a native word for "Valley of Joy."

In the late 1960s, it became just that, at least for land speculators. The ranch was sold to Kaiser Development Company, and the planned community of Rancho California began taking form. The die was cast for the pink tile and turquoise Temecula of today. As the community grew eastward, Old Town sought refuge in boutiques and antiques. It survives as a touristy Western style shopping and dining area, complete with boardwalks and piped-in country music. Worth a look is an historic transportation mural at a public parking area at Front Street and Sixth.

Vineyard growth has nearly out-paced the spread of tile roofs. The Temecula wine industry emerged in less time than it takes a newborn infant to reach drinking age. Only one winery, Calloway, existed in 1974; twenty-one years later, there were a dozen. The first vineyard was planted in 1967 by Vincenzo Cilurzo, who started his winery in 1978. Nearly 5,000 acres of vines now thrive in the shallow valley. Still, some winemakers import additional grapes from other areas. Most seek juice from the south central coast, since that's the nearest major wine producing neighbor.

TEMECULA VALLEY WINERY TOUR ● The area offers a pleasing assortment of more than a dozen wineries and tasting rooms, from family funky to corporate opulent. Most are clustered along Rancho California Road east of Temecula. All wineries save one charge for tasting and some offer logo glasses for their fee, so you'll likely come away with a nicely mismatched set.

Winery touring is relatively simple. Approaching Temecula on Interstate 15, take the Rancho California exit and head toward the sunrise. The first two miles will carry you through shopping centers and monotonously attractive tile-roofed housing tracts. After passing subdivisions with wine-cute names like Chardonnay Hills, you'll enter real Chardonnay country. The transition is rather abrupt, since new homes have been built right up to the edge of the agricultural reserve.

Small **Hart Winery** is on your left, up a narrow lane; the imposing **Thornton Winery**—the most elegant complex in the valley—is just beyond, on the right. Practically across the road is **Callaway Coastal Winery.** Just beyond is **Baily Winery** tasting room on your left, at Rancho California and La Serena. A short distance further on Rancho California, you'll encounter **Clos du Muriel**, and then **Mount Palomar Winery** and **Stuart Cellars,** whose driveways are directly opposite one another.

Next, turn left onto Calle Contento and you'll find **Falkner Winery,** at the end of a country lane. Now, reverse yourself on Calle Contento, cross Rancho California and you'll encounter **Cilurzo Winery** (*chee-LURE-so*), about a fourth of a mile up, on your left. Return to Rancho California, turn right and you'll quickly see the fanciful **Maurice Carrie Winery** on the right, just beyond Calle Contento, followed almost immediately by **Van**

WINERY CODES ● *T* = tasting with no fee; *T$* = tasting for a fee; *GT* = guided tours; *GTA* = guided tours by appointment; *ST* = self-guiding or informal tours; ✗ = picnic area; 🏠 = gift shop or a good giftware selection.

WINE PRICES ● $ = average price under $10 per bottle; *$$* = $10 to $14; *$$$* = $15 to $19; *$$$$* = $20 or more

Roekel Vineyards & Winery, also on the right. Continue east on Rancho California; shortly after you pass Anza Road, you'll encounter **Wilson Creek Winery** on your left.

The remaining two wineries require a short looping drive around the valley, providing an excuse to admire some of the opulent estates perched on the knolls. From Wilson Creek, continue briefly to Glenoaks Road, turn right and follow it just under three miles to a stop sign at De Portola and go right again. After two miles, you'll see the small Spanish-style tasting room of **Filsinger Vineyards and Winery**, on your right. Another two miles takes you to **Keyways Vineyard,** also on the right and also Spanish style.

To get back to Temecula, continue past Keyways briefly to Anza Road, turn right, follow it to Rancho California Road and go left toward I-15.

Hart Winery ● T$ ✗

41300 Avenida Biona (P.O. Box 956), Temecula, CA 92593; (909) 676-6300. Daily 9 to 4:30; MC/VISA, AMEX. Most varieties tasted for a modest fee, which includes a wine logo glass. A few wine related items. Small picnic area.

This small barnboard winery started as a weekend venture by Travis (Joe) Hart, who taught school weekdays in Carlsbad, a coastal town northwest of here. He planted vineyards in 1974 and built his winery six years later. Assisted by son Bill, Joe makes wines in small lots with an emphasis on reds, particularly Mediterranean varietals, which are suited to the local climate. The tasting room is a small, cozy place where you may be hosted by one Hart or the other while sipping their sturdy, tasty wines.

"Dad's a seat-of-the-pants winemaker, mostly self-taught," Bill once told us. "He started out making wine as a hobby, then took a few courses at the university at Davis."

Tasting notes: The Harts Cabernet Franc displayed a spicy varietal character and the barrel fermented Fumé Blanc had a properly smoky flavor. The Harts also do a full bodied yet mellow and exceedingly tasty Merlot, Viognier, Grenache Rosé, Syrah, Barbera, Mourvèdre, Zinfandel, a Grenache-Syrah blend and an Aleatico dessert wine. Prices: **$$ to $$$$**.

Vintner's Choice: "While our Fumé Blanc and Merlot are perennial favorites, our Syrah, Grenache Rosé and Viogner have become our best sellers," said Bill.

Thornton Winery ● T$ GT 🍷

32575 Rancho California Rd. (P.O. Box 9008), Temecula, CA 92591; (909) 699-0099. Gift shop open daily 10 to 5; Champagne Bar tasting room daily 11 to 5; MC/VISA. Fee for tasting; wines also sold by the glass. Tours weekends at 12, 2 and 4. Extensive giftware selection. Café Champagne adjacent; see listing under "Wine country dining" on page 330.

The Thornton champagnery and winery is one of the more opulent of the Temecula Valley facilities. It's a French style château done in textured stone and brick, built around a courtyard and fountain. An herb garden—which is occasionally plucked to enhance the fare in the restaurant—greets visitors as they enter the complex. On weekends, you can join tours followed by a sit-down tasting of four sparkling wines. During the week, tastings are conducted in the stylish Champagne Bar, which adjoins a large gift shop. You can buy wine by the glass or bottle here, along with some interesting appetizers, and adjourn to indoor or outdoor tables.

In the aging cellars of California's wineries, tomorrow's wines sleep to soften their tannins and absorb a touch of oak. Although wineries have modernized, they still use the ancient ritual of wood to finish many of their wines.

John and Martha Culbertson began making wine at their home in nearby Fallbrook in 1981. They opened this Temecula facility in 1988 as the Culbertson Winery, producing *méthode champenoise* sparkling wines. Their partners, the Thornton family, bought them out in 1993, renamed the facility and added a line of still wines to its list.

Tasting notes: The Brut Reserve had a nice herbal nose and taste with a soft yet crisp finish. Blanc de Noir is a gentle pink wine, dry with a very berry taste. Both were nicely complex for sparkling wines. Of the table wines, we tasted a Thornton Viognier and Cabernet-Merlot blend. The Viognier was crisp yet mellow and the Cab-Merlot blend was smooth and pleasant, with a hint of oak. Others among the table wines are Aleatico, Côte Red, Syrah and a rather hearty Old Vine Zinfandel. Prices: *$$$ to $$$$.*

Vintner's Choice: A winery spokesperson insists that the sparkling wines are on a par with dry French Champagnes, and who's to argue? They've been among the state's most award winning sparkling wines.

Callaway Coastal Winery • T$ GT ✕ 📷

32720 Rancho California Rd., Temecula, CA 92589; (909) 676-4001. (www.callawaycoastal.com) Daily 10:30 to 5; MC/VISA, AMEX. Four varieties tasted for a fee, which includes the glass. Arbor picnic area. Extensive gift, wine logo, deli and specialty foods selection. Attractive tasting patio and picnic area. Tours weekdays at 11, 1 and 3, and weekends hourly from 11 to 4. Vineyard Terrace Café listed on page 331.

Callaway is the oldest and largest of Temecula's wineries, with an output of more than 250,000 cases. Founded in 1969 by Ely Callaway, the winery is currently owned by Allied Domecq Spirits and Wines. The hundreds of thousands of cases emerge from a facility that resembles a light industrial park, crowning one of the valley's sandy hillocks. The large tasting room and gift shop are more attractive, with vine-covered exterior walls and big windows offering pleasing valley views. A tasting patio is particularly appealing, and picnic tables are sheltered under vine-entwined arbors.

Tasting notes: Our favorite was Callaway Coastal Chardonnay, aged on its yeast cells to give it a hearty, spicy flavor. The Viognier had a pleasantly complex fruity flavor. Our favorite was Sauvignon Blanc, with a nice pepper-herbal aroma and taste and a soft finish. Others on the list are Pinot Gris, Chenin Blanc and Muscat Canelli among the whites; and Nebbiolo, Dolcetto, Merlot and Cabernet Sauvignon among the reds. Prices: **$ to $$$$.**

Baily Vineyard and Winery • T$ ✕

33440 La Serena, Temecula, CA 92589; (909) 676-WINE. Daily 10 to 5; MC/VISA. Five samples tasted for a moderate fee, including a logo glass. Fair selection of giftwares.

Phil and Carol Baily opened their winery in late 1990 on Pauba Road in the southeast reaches of Temecula Valley. Then to spare their visitors the bumpy drive along the dirt passage to the winery, they built this new facility in the winter of 1998. Surrounded by young vines, the sturdy cut stone facility has a vaguely Roman look, with an attractive tasting room. The Bailys also operate a restaurant in Temecula; see below, on page 330.

Tasting notes: The brief Baily list consists of Chardonnay, a Sauvignon Blanc-Semillon blend called *Montage*, Riesling, Cabernet Blanc, Rosé of Cabernet Franc, a light Cabernet Sauvignon an a non-vintage sparkling wine. We preferred the fruity, nutty Chardonnay with a nice crisp finish; the *Montage*, with its interesting herbal-dusky flavor; and a spicy, complex and dry Mothers' Vineyard Riesling. Prices: **$ to $$$.**

Vintners choice: "Our two styles of Riesling—dry and off-dry, and our Montage," says Carol Baily.

Clos du Muriel Vineyards and Winery • T$ ST ✕

33410 Rancho California Rd., Temecula, CA 92390; (909) 676-5400. Daily 10 to 5; major credit cards. Current releases sampled for a fee. Small picnic area. Informal tours. Wine related gift items.

Earlier Temecula Valley visitors will remember this as the Piconi facility, opened in 1982 by Dr. John Piconi. Then, in a game of musical wineries, it was taken over in the early 1990s by Clos du Muriel, which originally had a winery and tasting room on nearby Calle Contento. That facility was, in turn, purchased by the Baily winery people and some other investors, and reopened as Temecula Crest. It was sold recently and is now Falkner Winery.

The Clos du Muriel winery is a simple Spanish style affair, occupying a high ridge with 360-degree views of the valley. One gets a quickie tour while in the small tasting room, for it's perched above the winery's stainless steel and wooden tanks. Outside, a small picnic area sits in the shade of the tile-roofed building.

Tasting notes: Clos du Muriel offers a couple of fine reds even though the Temecula Valley is primarily white wine country. The Merlot was rich and full-bodied and the Cabernet was soft to the palate with just a hint of wood. Of the whites, the Chardonnay was dry with pleasing touches of spice and fruit, while the Viognier was soft and crisp, with hints of fruit. Prices: *$$ to $$$.*

Mount Palomar Winery • T$ ✕ ⬛

33820 Rancho California Rd., Temecula, CA 92591; (800) 854-5177 or (909) 676-5047. (www.mountpalomar.com) Daily 10 to 4; MC/VISA. Choice of six tastes for a modest fee. Good selection of giftwares and specialty foods. The full-service Mediterranean Deli offers light entrées and assorted deli items Thursday through Sunday. View picnic area and an outdoor dining patio.

One of Temecula's earliest wineries, Palomar was established by John Poole; it has won an impressive number of awards since its creation in the 1970s. It's an attractive place, tucked into a little pocket behind a hill, out of sight of the busy Rancho California corridor. A multi-gabled Spanish façade hides the business-like winery, and picnic tables have been placed under just about every available tree. The tasting room is done up in white stucco and barn board—a nice effect.

Tasting notes: Palomar specializes in Italian and Rhône style wines, and we found most to be full bodied with nice herbal undertones. Particularly appealing among the whites was an aromatic, almost perfumy *Castelletto Cortese*, which has scored very high in tastings. The Viognier was typically fruity with a touch of spice. Among the reds are Sangiovese, Trovato, and a hearty Meritage style blend of Cabernet Sauvignon, Cabernet Franc and Merlot. Palomar also bottles several dessert wines, including a Sherry and Port. Prices: *$ to $$$$.*

Stuart Cellars • T$ ✕ ⬛

33515 Rancho California Rd., Temecula, CA 92591; (888) 260-0870 or (909) 676-6414. (www.stuartcellars.com) Daily 10 to 5; MC/VISA. A small tasting fee includes a logo glass. A few wine-focused gift items; picnic area.

Marshall Stuart and his wife opened their small, nicely landscaped winery and tasting room on a hill beside their home in 1998. The winery, surrounded by the promise of new vines, occupies a barnboard structure with an attractive picnic area adjacent. Sitting on a rise above the highway, both the winery and picnic area have views of the surrounding Temecula Valley. From the small tasting room, once can glimpse into the adjacent aging cellars, where the Stuarts' wines rest in wood and steel.

Tasting notes: The Stuart list is short and uniformly tasty. Among the whites, we tilted toward a Chardonnay with a classic nutty flavor, and a Viognier that displayed the floral, crisp characteristics of a Sauvignon Blanc. Of the reds, the Zinfandel was one of the best we tasted in the Temecula Valley, full flavored with a nice berry aroma. Another significant red is the proprietary *Tatria*, a Bordeaux-style blend of Cabernet Sauvignon, Cabernet Franc and Merlot, with a smooth, full flavor and hint of oak. Stuart also produces an interesting pinkish *Callista* blend of Viognier, Granache Rosé, Chardonnay and Sauvignon Blanc; a soft and sweet Muscat; and a deeply rich Zinfandel Port. Prices: *$$ to $$$.*

Falkner Winery • T$ GTA 🎁

40620 Calle Contento, Temecula, CA 92591; (909) 676-8231. (www.temeculawines.org) Weekdays noon to 5 and weekends 10 to 5; MC/VISA. Five wines tasted for a modest fee, which includes the glass. Fair selection of wine logo and gift items. Picnic area; group tours available by appointment.

This facility started as Britton Cellars in 1984, then it was the home of Clos du Muriel before that operation moved westward. It was then purchased by the Baily family and some investing friends and christened as Temecula Crest. After a recent sale, it has yet a new name—Falkner Winery, purchased in 2000 by Ray and Loretta Falkner, who produce about 4,500 cases a year. The structure is one of the valley's most appealing spaces, inside and out. It's a large designer barn, accented by Bacchus scenes in leaded glass windows. The interior is a great open space of huge laminated beams and winery paraphernalia. The tasting room and gift shop blend into one end, with no partitions to clutter the open feeling. Gift items are scattered about on barrel heads, drawing browsers into the winery. To shop is to tour.

Tasting notes: The Falkners' short list is balanced between whites and reds, with a single dessert wine, a fruity Muscat Blanc. We particularly liked the lush, nutty and spicy Chardonnay. Other whites are a dry and fruity Sauvignon Blanc and a slightly sweet Riesling. The best of the reds was a lushly smooth Merlot, followed closely by a Cabernet Sauvignon that displayed classic peppery flavor with a hint of wood. A Nebbiolo and an everyday wine called Rancho Red complete the list. Prices: *$ to $$$.*

Cilurzo Vineyard and Winery • T ST ✕ 🎁

41220 Calle Contento (P.O. Box 775), Temecula, CA 92592; (909) 676-5250. Daily 10 to 5; MC/VISA. Six samples for a very small fee. Giftwares and a good selection of specialty foods and picnic fare. Self-guiding tours; hilltop picnic area above the winery.

Vincenzo and Audrey Cilurzo are the senior members of the relatively new group of Temecula vintners. They planted their vines in 1967 and have raised both grapes and children here. This is a world apart from the glitter of Hollywood, where Vince worked for decades as a highly respected lighting director. He has an Oscar to prove his skills, and the tasting room walls are papered with photos of stars who've been placed in his limelights. In true Hollywood fashion, he and Audrey met on the set of the Roy Rogers show.

The rambling winery, tasting room and gift shop run together in a pleasantly inviting scatter. Visitors are encouraged to follow a self-guiding tour for one-on-one encounters with filters, vats and barrels.

Tasting notes: Tastings are conducted in a sit-down classroom environment. The Cilurzos produce some of the best reds in the valley—unfiltered, with big body and complex flavors. We liked a lush, herbal Merlot with a soft finish; a peppery medium bodied Cab with a nice tannic nip; and—of the whites—a fine Viognier, full flavored and busy with fruit. Others on the list include Sauvignon Blanc, a nice barrel-fermented Chardonnay reserve, Chenin Blanc, Muscat Canelli, a rich late harvest Petit Syrah and a sweet Zinfandel rosé. Prices: *$ to $$$.*

Maurice Carrie Winery • T ✗ ⬛

34225 Rancho California Rd., Temecula, CA 92591; (909) 676-1711. Daily 10 to 5; major credit cards. Most wines tasted. Extensive giftware and specialty food assortment. Picnic area and children's playground.

The Maurice Carrie complex is both imposing and cheerful, an intriguing mix of French country manor and upscale American farm architecture, with an old-fashioned windmill for good measure. A gazebo, rose garden, picnic areas and even a kiddie land complete this inviting picture. The cheery tasting room is accented with beam ceilings, French windows and café curtains.

It's a safe bet that Gordon and Maurice Carrie Van Roekel are the only vintners who entered to this profession on roller skates. They retired to the valley in 1984 after successful careers as skating rink operators, then they soon became bored. They bought a vineyard in 1985 and completed their elaborate winery and hospitality center two years later.

Tasting notes: The white list includes two types of Chardonnay, a soft and fruity Chenin Blanc, a crisp and dry Sauvignon Blanc, a blend called Heather's Mist and a sweet Muscat Canelli. On the red side of the ledger are a mellow and dry Cabernet Sauvignon, a light *nouveau* Pinot Noir, a soft and drinkable Merlot and Cody's Crush, a light Gamay-style blend. The winery also produces several rosés and a sparkling wine. Prices: *$ to $$$.*

Van Roekel Winery and Vineyards • T$ ✗ ⬛

34567 Rancho California Rd., Temecula, CA 92591; (909) 699-6961. Daily 10 to 5; major credit cards. Separate modest tasting fees for reds and whites; both include a souvenir glass. Extensive gift selection and a good choice of deli items. Hilltop picnic area with a valley view.

Not satisfied with being solo vintners in the Temecula Valley, Maurice and Carrie Van Roekel purchased several next-door acres in 1988 and created a second winery bearing their Dutch family name. Appropriately, a scale model windmill marks the entrance to the facility, although the large tasting room has more the look of an oversized Spanish cottage. If you like to shop, Van Roekel is your stop, since the tasting room offers an extensive wine logo and giftware selection, and another gift shop called the Yankee Cottage stands near the entrance to the complex.

Tasting notes: This is one of the few wineries we've encountered with a two-tiered tasting program. Six of the reds—which are the Van Roekels' best wines—can be tasted for a moderate fee, while a flight of whites can be sipped for even less. Overall, the reds are the finest in the Temecula Valley. We sipped happily through a medium-bodied Zinfandel with a hint of wood, an outstanding full-flavored old vines Grenache (*not* a rosé!), a deeply flavored Merlot, and a soft and pleasantly tame Cabernet Sauvignon. We ended with an excellent proprietary wine called *Chaleur*, with a berry-fruit bouquet and intense flavor; it's a blend of Syrah and Petit Syrah. The short white flight includes Viognier, Pinot Blanc and Chardonnay. The Van Roekels' also produce several blush wines and a late harvest Zinfandel dessert wine called *Allegria*. Prices: *$ to $$$.*

Wilson Creek Winery • T$ ✗ ⬛

35960 Rancho California Rd., Temecula, CA 92592; (909) 693-WINE. (www.temeculawines.org) Daily 10 to 5; major credit cards. A modest tasting fee includes a logo glass. Some gift items; picnic area adjacent.

Wine and weddings is the theme of Wilson Creek, a small winery opened in 1998. It occupies a handsome two-story Spanish style building. The expansive, well-tended grounds often are the site of "Wine Country Weddings." The rather spacious tasting room offers a fair selection of wine logo items. The winery was established as a "retirement project" by Gerry and Rosie Wilson. They had purchased a twenty-acre vineyard in 1969. It's now a family enterprise involving their son Bill and daughter Libby and their spouses.

Tasting Notes: The Wilsons list eight wines, five of which are available for tasting. Perhaps the best of the lot is a buttery-spicy Reserve Chardonnay. Also available are less complex Chardonnay, a deep purple and full-flavored Mourvèdre, a light tannin Cabernet Sauvignon and a sparkling wine called Almond Champagne. Also on the list, not offered for tasting when we stopped by, are a Rhône blend called *Miramonte*, Green Hungarian (rarely bottled as a varietal these days) and Grand Cuvée Champagne. Prices: *$$$ to $$$$*.

Filsinger Vineyards ● T$ GTA ✗

39050 De Portola Rd., Temecula, CA 92592; (909) 302-6363. (www.filsingerwines.com) Friday 11 to 4 and weekends 10 to 5; MC/VISA, AMEX. Five wines sampled for a very small fee. A few wine logo gift items; attractive picnic gazebo.

The Filsingers' cottage-style tasting room is one of the coziest in the valley. It's an inviting Spanish colonial space with ceramic tile floors, a carved tasting counter and lazily-turning ceiling fans. A nearby picnic area is equally appealing, housed within a large gazebo. The plain, business-like winery is a discreet distance away. This pleasant enclave is the handiwork of physician Bill Filsinger and his wife Kathy. In fact, they built much of it with their own hands. They planted vines in 1972 and started making wine eight years later. Son Eric now has a hand in things as well, as assistant winemaker.

Tasting notes: Dr. Filsinger's wines are full-flavored and complex, with the medals to prove it. He makes one of the valley's few Gewürztraminers and it's properly herbal and rich. Others we liked were a piquant, fruity and crisp Chardonnay; a spicy buttery Fumé Blanc; and a fine medium-bodied Cabernet Sauvignon, aged in American Oak. The good doctor also produces a white Zinfandel that we actually liked. The addition of small amounts of Gewürztraminer, Muscat and Cabernet give it a complexity rarely found in this infamous Sunday picnic wine. Three *méthode champenoise* sparkling wines can be tasted for a small charge. Overall, prices are modest: *$ to $$$*.

Keyways Winery & Vineyard ● T$ ✗

37338 De Portola Rd., Temecula, CA 92592; (909) 302-7888. Daily 10 to 5; MC/VISA. Most varieties tasted for a moderate fee. Some wine related gift items. Exhibit of Americana antiques; small picnic area.

This medium-sized Spanish-style facility is an interesting blend of winery, tasting room, art gallery and American folk museum. Two old fashioned jukeboxes flank the tasting counter, and a pot-bellied stove, antique kitchenware and a copper-topped tasting bar contribute to this American Gothic image. From an art gallery loft, one can peer into a cellaring facility; wines are made elsewhere.

Carl Key is one of those people who has a problem with retirement. After succeeding rather handsomely in the restaurant and liquor business, he built an elegant Spanish style mansion in this valley. Getting restless, be began growing grapes and producing wines in the 1980s, then he opened this facility in 1990. "I keep retiring, but it never seems to work out," he grinned.

Tasting notes: Light and soft describes the Keyways style. Prices are soft as well, starting below $10. The short list includes a mellow and fruity Sauvignon Blanc, a lush and spicy Chardonnay, a surprisingly fruity and tasty white Zinfandel that's more assertive than most Zin pinks, a Cabernet Sauvignon with a good chili pepper nose and taste and hints of wood, and a spicy medium bodied Zinfandel. Prices: *$ to $$$.*

THE BEST OF THE BUNCH

The best wine buys ● Mount Palomar Winery, Falkner Winery, Baily Winery, Clos du Muriel, Maurice Carrie Winery, Filsinger Vineyards and Keyways Winery & Vineyard.

The most attractive wineries ● Thornton Winery, Maurice Carrie Winery, Falkner Winery, Wilson Creek and Filsinger.

The most interesting tasting rooms ● Cilurzo Vineyard & Winery, Falkner Winery, Van Roekel Winery, Filsinger Vineyards and Keyways Winery & Vineyard.

The best gift shops ● Thornton Winery, Callaway Vineyard & Winery, Mount Palomar Winery, Maurice Carrie Winery, Van Roekel Winery and Falkner Winery.

The nicest picnic areas ● Callaway Vineyard & Winery, Mount Palomar Winery, Stuart Cellars, Maurice Carrie Winery, Wilson Creek and Filsinger Vineyards.

The best tours ● Thornton Winery (guided tour with wine tasting) and Cilurzo Vineyard & Winery (self-guided).

Wineland maps and events

Winery touring map ● *Temecula Valley Wine Country* is available at area wineries or contact: Temecula Valley Vintners Association, P.O. Box 1601, Temecula, CA 92593-1601; (800) 801-WINE or (909) 699-3626. *(www.temeculawines.org)* Also the centerfold of the *Temecula Valley Visitors Guide* has a winery map, with a description of the wineries. It's produced by the Temecula Valley Chamber of Commerce; see below.

Wineland events ● Winter Barrel Tasting in early February, Vintners Festival in May, Spring Passport Tasting with paired wine and foods in mid-May, Temecula Valley Wine Auction Labor Day Weekend, and Harvest Barrel Tasting the third weekend in November. For information on all of the above, call (800) 801-WINE. Individual wineries also sponsor events. Thornton Winery is particularly active, with a summer and fall concert series, wine dinners and other activities; call (909) 699-3021.

BEYOND THE VINEYARDS

What lies beyond Temecula's vineyards is the whole of Southern California, one of America's leading vacation destinations. An hour's drive south on I-15 gets you to **San Diego,** where you can soak in the sun at the beaches, visit California's first mission, its oldest park with a fine collection of museums, and the state's finest zoo. An hour and a half north delivers you to the **Anaheim-Los Angeles** area.

Temecula's immediate surrounds provide a few vineyard distractions as well. **Murietta Hot Springs** just to the north is a family resort offering mud and mineral baths. **Lake Skinner** county park, immediately northeast of the vineyards, has water sports, fishing and camping. **Lake Elsinore** to the northwest, off I-15, and **Lake Perris,** north off State Highway 215, are major water sports areas with shoreside resorts. Beyond Elsinore, State Route 74 wanders through the oaks, pines, campsites and hiking trails of **Cleveland National Forest.** It ends at the Pacific, just beyond **San Juan Capistrano,** home to the mission of the swallows.

A more direct route to *El Pacifico's* beaches is State Highway 76, reached via I-15 about twelve miles south of Temecula. The approach takes you through the wooded **San Luis River Valley,** past **Mission San Luis Rey** to the coastal towns of **Oceanside** and **Carlsbad.** Both have extensive public beaches and Carlsbad is home to the famed **La Costa** resort.

If you head inland on Highway 76, you'll encounter **San Antonio de Pala,** the only California mission still fulfilling its original role—serving native people. It's on the Pala Indian reservation. Beyond is **Palomar Mountain State Park** and the famed **Palomar Observatory**.

Temecula area attractions

Bike tours • **Gravity Activated Sports** offers downhill rides from Mount Palomar and wine country bicycle tours; (800) 985-4427. *(www.ga-sports.com)*

Pala Mission • *Off Route 76 in Pala; (760) 742-1600. Tuesday-Sunday 10 to 4 April through October and 10 to 3 the rest of the year. Mission admittance is free, small charge for museum.* □ Nicely restored mission still serving native people, with early California relics and mineral exhibit.

Palomar Observatory museum and gallery • *In Palomar Mountain State Park; (760) 742-2119; free. Astronomy museum and Hale 200-inch telescope visitors gallery open daily 9 to 4; gift shop open daily in summer and weekends only the rest of the year.* □ World's second largest telescope (after a newer 236-inch Russian lens) plus a visitor center with exhibits on the heavens and recent astronomical discoveries.

Temecula Valley Museum • *28314 Mercedes Street in Old Town Temecula; (909) 676-0021. Tuesday-Saturday 10 to 5, Sunday and holidays 1 to 5, closed Monday; donations requested.* □ Attractive museum in Sam Hicks Park, with historic exhibits of Temecula's Indian, Spanish and American ranching days. Displays include storefront mockups and Vail Ranch artifacts.

WINE COUNTRY DINING

Most Temecula restaurants are grouped in two areas—Old Town and the Rancho California Town Center just east of the freeway interchange. We list three in Old Town—The Bank, Rosa's Cantina and Swing Inn; and three in Town Center—Baily Wine Country Café, the Claimjumper and Hunan Garden. Two more are out in the wine country—Café Champagne and Vineyard Terrace Café.

Baily Wine Country Café • ☆☆☆ $$

□ *27644 Ynez Road (Town Center); (909) 694-6887. American nouveau; good local wine list, plus a variety of domestic and imported beers. Lunch and dinner daily. Reservations recommended Friday and Saturday nights. Major credit cards.* ☐ An appealing café with white nappery and modernistic wrought iron grape clusters on the walls. The fare is American regional, with interestingly spiced treatments of seafood, chicken, steaks and chops on a frequently changing menu. Outdoor dining patio.

The Bank of Mexican Food ● ☆ $

☐ *28645 Front Street (Main street); (909) 676-6760. Mexican; wine and beer. Lunch and dinner daily. Major credit cards.* ☐ This "bank" is a basic smashed beans and rice place in an interesting setting—the 1912 Temecula Bank building. It once was called "The Pawn Shop" by its rancher board of directors. The high ceiling dining room is brightened by Mexican artifacts; there's patio dining area adjacent.

Café Champagne ● ☆☆☆ $$$

☐ *At Thornton Winery, 32575 Rancho California Rd.; (909) 699-0088. American regional; extensive local wine list. Lunch and dinner daily. Reservations essential for weekend lunches; MC/VISA.* ☐ This stylishly modern restaurant features dishes designed to match Temecula Valley wines, such as cioppino, Pacific prawns and rack of lamb. Herbs are plucked from a nearby garden to season this *nouveau* fare. Food is served indoors or on an attractive patio with vineyard views.

The Claimjumper ● ☆☆☆ $$

☐ *29370 Rancho California Rd. (Town Center); (909) 694-6887. (www.claimjumper.com) American; full bar service. Lunch through late dinner daily. Reservations accepted; recommended Friday and Saturday nights. Major credit cards.* ☐ New but made to look old, it's a cleverly fashioned Western style restaurant with brick interior walls, simulated Tiffany glass and pressed tin ceilings. Rural American menu ranges from hickory smoked prime ribs to assorted chickens and chops. Large beer selection.

Hunan Garden ● ☆ $

☐ *27536 Ynez Road (toward the rear of Temecula Town Center); (909) 699-5709. Chinese; wine and beer. Lunch and dinner daily. Major credit cards.* ☐ Small, prim and simply decorated storefront café offers an extensive menu of mild Cantonese and spicier Szechuan and Mandarin fare. It features a very inexpensive luncheon buffet.

Rosa's Cantina ● ☆ $

☐ *28636 Front St. (Main); (909) 695-2428. Mexican; wine and beer. Lunch and dinner daily on weekdays and breakfast through dinner weekends. Major credit cards.* ☐ This cheerful, recently remodeled Mexican diner is dressed up with *faux* adobe and bright Hispanic doodads. Patio dining is appealing on a sunny afternoon or warm evening. While not gourmet, the food is priced right; many entrées are well under $10.

Swing Inn ● ☆ $$

☐ *28676 Front St. (Third); (909) 676-2321. Rural American; wine and beer. Early breakfast through dinner daily. Major credit cards.* ☐ The sign says "World famous" and it is if Temecula is your world. Swing Inn has been getting up with the roosters and feeding folks breakfast, dinner and supper for nearly a century. It's an authentic slice of the Old West, updated with 1950s Formica. The menu lists steaks, chops, chickens and even chicken fried steak, with generous portions and cheap prices.

Vineyard Terrace Café ● ☆☆ $$

☐ *At Callaway Winery, 32720 Rancho California Rd., (909) 308-6661. American; wine. Lunch Thursday-Sunday and dinner Friday-Saturday. MC/VISA.* ☐ The most appealing thing about this simple café is its view of rolling vinelands. Patrons can sit in an open, canvas-roofed dining room or at umbrella tables on a landscaped, terraced patio. The fare ranges from pastas and salmon to beef tenderloin and tri-tip; fresh baked bread is a specialty.

WINELAND LODGINGS

PRICE KEY: A two-person room for $35 or less = $; $36 to $50 = $$; $51 to $75 = $$$; $76 to $100 = $$$$; more than $100 = $$$$$.

Best Western Country Inn ● ☆☆☆ $$$ to $$$$$

☐ *27706 Jefferson Ave. (at I-15 Winchester exit), Temecula, CA 92590; (800) 528-1234 or (909) 676-7378. Major credit cards.* ☐ A 74-unit motel with TV movies, room phones and refrigerators; some in-room spas. Pool, outdoor spa, fireplace; microwaves available.

Best Western Guest House Inn ● ☆☆ $$$$$

☐ *41873 Moreno Rd., Temecula, CA 92591; (909) 676-5700. Major credit cards.* ☐ Well-kept 24-room motel with TV movies and phones. Pool and spa; restaurant adjacent.

Embassy Suites ● ☆☆☆ $$$$$

☐ *29345 Rancho California Rd. (at the I-15 interchange), Temecula, CA 92591; (800) 362-2779 or (909) 676-5656. Major credit cards.* ☐ Attractive resort complex with pool, spa and other amenities. All two-room suites; 176 units with TV movies, VCRs, phones, microwaves and refrigerators. Complimentary evening beverages. **Restaurant** serves breakfast through dinner; full bar service.

Temecula Creek Inn ● ☆☆☆☆ $$$$$

☐ *44501 Rainbow Canyon Rd. (Highway 79), Temecula, CA 92592; (800) 962-7335 or (909) 694-1000. Major credit cards.* ☐ Appealing Southwest theme resort with 27-hole golf course, tennis courts, pool and spa. Eighty-four rooms with TV, phones, safes, honor bars, refrigerators and balconies or patios. **Temet Grill** serves breakfast through dinner; full bar service.

Bed & breakfast inn

Loma Vista Bed & Breakfast ● ☆☆☆☆ $$$$$

☐ *33350 La Serena Way (off Rancho California), Temecula, CA 92591; (909) 676-7047. Six rooms, all with private baths; champagne breakfast. MC/VISA.* ☐ Handsome Spanish mission style inn on a bluff overlooking the Temecula Valley vinelands. Rated a "Top Ten Inn" by the publication *INNovations*. Rooms nicely done in early American and California style.

Temecula area information source

Temecula Valley Chamber of Commerce, 27450 Ynez Rd., Suite 124, Temecula, CA 92590; (909) 676-5090. The chamber operates a visitor center at 28464 Old Town Front St. *(www.temecula.org)*

Wine is really quite simple. Like art or music, the more you know about it, the more you can enjoy it, but you certainly don't need to know any five-syllable words for that. — **Plain Talk About Fine Wine by Justin Meyer**

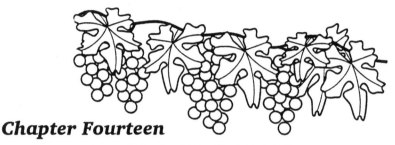

Chapter Fourteen

AFTERTHOUGHTS
Serving & storing tips; a winetalk lexicon

We end this book with a few items of useful information. As we said at the beginning, wine is neither an enigma or something to be revered. It is merely a tasty and relaxing beverage best enjoyed with food—and sometimes on a hot August afternoon with nothing at all, if it's white or maybe even pink and properly chilled.

Thus, our rules have to do with practicality, not with mysticism. We begin with the basics: serving and storing wine.

Pulling the cork on food & wine rules

Wine is the only adult beverage created primarily to be consumed with food—with the exception of iced-down beer at a Texas chili cook-off. It is therefore helpful to determine which works with what. For many of us, wine *is* food, as much a part of the evening meal as the meat and veggies.

Unfortunately, some wine writers and winery brochures complicate a simple issue with a lot of specific rules about wine and food combinations. One suggestion, for instance, is that Zinfandel should be served with game. But Zinfandel can range from a light and soft young wine to bold, high-tannin, industrial strength stuff from century-old vines. And what about white wine with fish? A Chenin Blanc can be fruity and lush with a touch of sweetness, or dry and crisp. Do you really want sweet, fruity wine with filét of sole?

So, you wonder as you wander through this wilderness of wines, what rules *does* one follow. The rules are simple. Both of them.

CONQUERING WINE LIST PANIC

You and your archrival, Watercooler Willie, are being considered for that vice presidency slot. Your boss invites you and your wife out to dinner; you just *know* he's testing your social graces. He's a wine aficionado but you wouldn't know a Cabernet from a cantaloupe. A guy with a spoon hanging from his vest hands your boss the wine list and—*omygawd*—he passes it over to you! It flashes through your mind that you have four choices:

1. Hand it back.

2. Smile naively at the *sommelier* and say: "It's difficult to pick from such a wonderful selection. What would *you* suggest?"

3. Order white Zinfandel.

4. Go for it.

You didn't become manager of the Vertical Flange Department through timidity, so you decide to go for it.

Here are the five essential steps to bluffing your way through a wine list:

1. Thumb—casually—to the California wine section. It's easier to pronounce Zinfandel than *Côtes de Provence Sociéte Civile des Domaines Ott Frères.*

2. Remember that, as a general rule, white wines are more suitable with subtly-flavored foods such as poached fish or mildly-seasoned fowl. The flavor of heartier reds will stand up to red meats, highly-spiced dishes and just about anything Italian, up to and including Gina Lolabrigida.

3. Poll your table to see what's been ordered. If it's a mix of fish and red meat, go for a light red such as a young Merlot, or for a more complex white like aged Chardonnay. Resist the temptation to order rosé. Make major points by suggesting that the Chardonnay shouldn't be *too* cold, lest it mask that wonderful spicy aroma. Or be Joe Cool and order a sparkling wine—to celebrate your coming promotion? (If it's from California, don't call it Champagne.)

4. When the wine arrives, the waiter or *sommelier* will unplug the thing and hand you the cork. F'gawdsake, don't sniff it! Check its little bottom to see if it's damp (meaning it was properly stored), then place it on the table.

5. Now, here's where you nail down that vice presidency. Swirl the wine vigorously, keeping the base of the glass on the table so you don't shower the boss. (If you ordered a sparkling wine, you *don't* swirl it, of course.) Then sniff the wine with one long, dramatic inhalation, purse your lips thoughtfully and—don't sip it!* Nod knowingly to the waiter and tell him it's fine.

*If it's a bad wine, you can tell by the smell—a pungent vinegary or sour aroma. You should refuse a wine only if it's spoiled; not because you chose poorly and don't care for it. Besides, it's really cool just to sniff the wine without taking a sip.

1. Match the wine to the strength of the food. Bold wines are best with highly-spiced meat and pasta dishes; delicate wines work well with mildly flavored dishes. The idea is to balance the two, so the flavor of one doesn't overwhelm the taste of the other. Generally speaking—and only generally— red wines are more robust than whites so under most circumstances, reds go well with meats, stews and other full flavored dishes, while whites work best with seafood and light poultry.

2. If both spicy and subtly flavored dishes are being served (he ordered pepper steak, she's having scallops), try a light yet lively wine. This is where rosés, sparkling wines and young reds are useful.

Serving temperatures

Here's a rule that may be *too* simple: Experts tell us to serve white wines chilled and reds at room temperature. But chilling can muffle the bouquet and flavor of a lush and spicy, barrel-fermented Chardonnay. At room temperature—particularly if it's August in Las Vegas—a delicate young red may lose its fresh berry taste. Our rules? We serve crisp whites, rosés and sparkling wines at about 50 degrees, full bodied whites and some young reds at 55 to 60, and heartier reds around 65 degrees.

The story on storing wine

So you've really gotten into this thing and you want to build your own wine cellar. But suppose you don't have a basement? Maybe your house is on a concrete slab, or you live in a twelfth floor condo. You could spend a few thousand dollars on a temperature and humidity controlled wine mausoleum, which will certainly impress your friends. Or you could use that money to send your kids to college, and still create a safe place for your wines.

Bottles should be stored on their sides to keep the corks moist. They should be in a dark, cool place with little day-to-day temperature fluctuation. Extreme changes cause expansion and contraction, pushing wine out through the cork and drawing in air. Remember, wine plus air equals expensive vinegar. A dark closet on the north side of the house will provide proper protection for your precious wine caché. If your house is on a raised foundation with a crawl space, tuck those puppies down there. An old refrigerator or freezer can serve as a good, inexpensive wine vault. Don't plug it in! You just want to take advantage of its insulation, which will mute temperature changes.

It's wise to peel the lead foil caps off the bottles, so you can keep an eye on the corks. If you see wine seeping along the cork's side, you'd better schedule that bottle for tonight's dinner.

Bringing them home: Protecting your investment

It's not difficult to protect your wines at home, since it's an environment you can control. However, getting newly purchased wines home in good health may be a challenge. You may be touring the wine country on a hot August day and—while you sampled wines in a cool cellar—the greenhouse effect elevated the temperature in your car to 130 degrees. Putting your newly purchased bottles in your car is like putting them in an oven.

When you go shopping among the vinelands on a summer day, take a cooler along so you can moderate their temperature changes. Remember, it's sudden and extreme changes that can damage a wine. If you've flown in and are renting a car, pick up one of those inexpensive styrofoam coolers. Also, keep your wine in the vehicle's trunk. Because of that greenhouse business, it's cooler than the passenger compartment. And—oh yes—don't set it in the area of the trunk that's over the tailpipe.

If you're flying home, make your new wine purchase part of your carry-on luggage. After all, what's more precious—a suitcase full of wrinkled shirts or six bottles of awesome Zinfandel? Most wineries can provide handy six-pack carriers and you can slip a couple of them under your seat. Wine bottles of course are fragile, and the wine within shouldn't be subjected to unpredictable temperatures and pressure changes in a cargo compartment. If you must check it, ask the winery tasting room folks if they have styrofoam "over-shippers" which come in six and twelve bottle sizes.

If you've gotten carried away and purchased several cases, most wineries will offer to ship them. Unfortunately, most states have restrictive laws that forbid wine shipments, and the U.S. Postal Service refuses to touch the stuff. UPS will ship to states that permit incoming wine. And some shippers can be discreet about restrictive state laws.

What price wine?

Someone—probably me—once said that a good bottle of wine shouldn't cost more than a good bottle of Scotch. Wine is less complicated to produce, and it's taxed at a much lower rate. So why are $50 Chardonnays, $60 Cabernets and $125 *Louis Jadot Chevalier-Montrachet Les Demoiselles* on the market? Because people will pay for them. We don't question their motives, but guidebook authors—even clever ones—can't afford such extravagance.

If you follow winetasting results, you'll often note little similarity between quality and price. We regularly discover fine wines for under $15, and often for under $10. Only by sampling a variety can you determine which is best for you and your budget. That's one of the great advantages of wine country tasting. Come to think of it, isn't that why you bought this book?

The great house wine heist

Do you often order house wine because you're dining alone or your partner doesn't drink, and you don't want a full bottle? You probably aren't getting your money's worth, particularly if you desire two glasses to get through a meal. House wine is the single greatest profit item of many restaurants.

Perhaps the place pours one of the better jug varietals—an August Sebastiani or Fetzer. These aren't bad wines, but the restaurant probably paid $5 to $8 wholesale, and it's nicking you $5 to $6 a glass. A 1.5-liter bottle contains 52 ounces, from which the establishment can get nearly nine six-ounce servings. Multiply that by $5 and you've got $45. Not a bad return on the restaurant's investment, but a lousy bargain for you. And if it's pouring Grace L. Furguson Modesto Red and charging $5 a pop—try not to think about it.

You're better served, literally, by ordering half bottles if the restaurant offers them. That gives you about two and a half glasses of decent wine. If the restaurant sells premium wines by the glass, they may be a better buy than the overpriced jug stuff, although by-the-glass varietals often are overpriced.

In California and a few other civilized states, the law allows you to take unfinished wine home, so go for a regular bottle and ask for a brown paper doggie bag. Full bottles generally are marked up three to five times over wholesale. That's still rather steep, and we think restaurants in general charge too much for their wine. But it's better than the eight to ten-fold mark-up on a jug. And you'll be getting a better quality wine.

A WINETALK LEXICON

As in most professions and avocations, wine world participants and enthusiasts have their own language. What follows is a glossary of vintners' and wine enthusiasts' shop talk.

Acid — The grape's tartaric and malic acid that give a wine its crisp after-taste.

Appellation — No, it's not a West Virginia coal miner. The term describes a legally defined grape growing area in the winelands of the world. In America, it's called an Approved Viticultural Area (AVA) and it's administered—gawd knows why—by the Bureau of Alcohol, Tobacco and Firearms—the same outfit that shot up Waco. For an American label to bear an appellation designation, eighty-five percent of its grapes must come from that area, and the wine must be "fermented, manufactured and finished" there. Dry Creek, Carneros, Chalk Hill and Shenandoah Valley are typical California appellations. The first winegrowing designations started in France decades ago, called *Appellation d'Origine Contrôlée* (AOC). It dictates the types of grapes that can be grown in each area as well as how it is labeled. American AVA rules don't address grape types.

Aperitif (*a-PERI-teef*) — A drink taken before a meal as an appetizer; often a full flavored but dry wine like vermouth or dry Sherry.

Aroma — The smell of the grape from which the wine was made.

Balance — A catch-all term describing a wine in which nothing is out of balance: not too acidic, not too sweet, not too high in tannin.

Berry — To a vineyardist, grapes are berries; berry-like describes the flavor of the fruit in wine.

Big — No, it's not a large bottle. "Big" in winetalk refers to a wine with strong, complex flavor, full bodied and often high in alcohol. Tasters use the expression "big nose" to describe a wine with a strong aroma and bouquet.

Binning — Storing wine away, or "putting it down" for aging.

Blush — A term to describe a pink wine made from red grapes, usually Grenache, Zinfandel, Cabernet Sauvignon or Pinot Noir.

Body — The fullness of a wine, sometimes—but not always—referring to the viscosity or alcoholic content. A thin and watery wine lacks body.

Bordeaux (*bor-DOE*) — A large area of France that produces some of the world's finest red wines, usually blends of Cabernet Sauvignon, Merlot, Cabernet Franc, Malbec, Petit Verdot and Carmenere.

Botrytis cinerea (*bo-TREET-is sin-AIR-e-ah*) — A mold that wrinkles ripening grapes, causing a concentration of sugar and flavor that produces a rich, full-bodied wine. Called "noble mold" by romantics and "noble rot" by cynical romantics.

Bottle sick — The condition of a wine immediately after bottling, when it has been filtered, shaken and otherwise abused. The condition passes after the bottle has rested a few weeks.

Bouquet — The often complex smell of wine that comes from fermenting and aging, as opposed to aroma, which is the smell of the fruit.

Breathing — The practice of letting a wine stand open so it absorbs oxygen, supposedly to enhance its aroma and taste. Experts disagree on its usefulness, but it's a harmless gesture to let your wine catch its breath.

Brilliant — Not a measure of the winemaker's cleverness, but the clarity of the wine. All good wines should be brilliant. So should a good winemaker, for that matter.

Brix — The measure of sugar content in a grape, which will determine its alcoholic level upon fermentation.

Brut (*brute*) — One of the driest of champagnes.

Bulk process — Cheap method of making sparkling wine by fermenting it in large sealed tanks to capture the bubbles.

Cap — Layer of skins, pulp and other grape solids that floats to the top of a fermenting vat of grape juice. The winemaker "punches it down" or pumps the wine over itself to keep it broken up.

Cave (*Kahv*) — French for cellar, as in wine cellar; "Cava" in Spanish.

Chai — French word for a small building, usually above ground, for aging wine in small oak barrels. Some California wineries now use the term.

Champagne — Specifically, it refers to a sparkling wine produced in France's Champagne district although some countries—notably ours—use the term to describe any effervescent wine. The use of the French term is becoming less common here, however.

Character — Term used to describe the good qualities of a wine. A poor wine, like a poor citizen, "lacks character."

Charmat (*SHAR-mahn*) — French term for bulk process champagne-making; named for the Frenchman who developed it.

Château — Not necessarily a house or mansion; "château" is commonly used in France to describe a particular winery operation.

Claret — Usually refers to a Bordeaux in England, but used to describe just about any red wine in the rest of the world.

Coarse — A full-bodied wine, but with ragged edges and perhaps a harsh aftertaste; no finesse.

Cooperage — Wooden wine containers—barrels, vats and such.

Corky — A wine that has been invaded by a disintegrating cork, giving it a bad flavor.

Crush — It's often used as a noun in winetalk, referring to the harvest and subsequent crushing of wine grapes. "We had a good crush this year," a winegrower might say.

Cuvée (*Coo-VAY*) — A specific blend of wine, as in the "cuvée" used for a champagne. Also a vat or tank used for blending or fermenting wine.

Demijon — A large and rather squat wine bottle, sometimes covered with wicker.

Demi-sec — Sparkling wine with rather high residual sugar content; sweeter than sec.

Disgorging — Removing sediment that has settled in the neck of a bottle of sparkling wine; most of it is trapped in a small plastic *bidule*, placed there for that purpose

Dosage (*Do-SAJ*) — The mix of sugar syrup, wine, brandy or other product added to sparkling wine to make it less dry.

Dry — Crisp and not sweet or sour. In winetalk, it has nothing to do with lack of wetness.

Enology — Winemaking science; one who makes wine is an enologist. Classic spelling is *oenology*.

Estate bottled — A wine in which all the grapes came from the vintner's "estate" or vineyards.

Fermentation — The reason for all this—the wine industry, winery touring, this book in your hand. It's the process of converting the sugar in grape juice into alcohol and carbon dioxide by the addition of yeast.

Fining — Clarifying wine to remove the solids, usually by adding an agent such as egg white that collects them.

Finish — The aftertaste of a wine, created primarily by the acid. A crisp, properly balanced wine will have a "long, lingering finish." A thin, wimpy one won't.

Flowery — The aroma of a wine more akin to blossoms than to grapes.

Fortified — A wine whose alcoholic content has been increased by the addition of brandy or other high-alcohol beverage.

Fruity — The flavor of a wine that comes from the grape.

Generic — A wine of no particular pedigree. In America and many other wine producing countries, Burgundy, Chablis and Chianti are generic names; in France and Italy, they are specific regions that produce a specific type of wine.

Grapey — A wine that tastes too much like grape juice (think of Welsh's). The grape taste should be subtle and is often described, particularly in reds, as berry-like.

Grassy — A subtle grass-like flavor, sometimes found in reds; sort of herbal without the herbs. Not necessarily unpleasant.

Green — A wine not ready to drink; too young; harsh and raw tasting.

Haut (*oh* or *auh*) — French for "high" or "upper," referring to wine producing regions. Haut-Sauternes is a general term applied to a sweet white wine from upper Sauternes; the name has no bearing on quality.

Hock — Generic term for white wine, usually used in England.

Horizontal tasting — No, it doesn't mean you've sampled too many wines. It's a comparative tasting of the same wine type from different vineyards. Vertical tasting is sampling the same wine from different vintages.

Jerez (*hair-eth*) — A city and a wine producing region of Spain; the birthplace of Sherry.

Jeroboam — Wine jug holding the equivalent of six .75 liter bottles.

Late harvest — A wine made from grapes left on the vine until their sugar content is unusually high. It produces a full-bodied, high-alcohol wine—and sometimes a very sweet one if the fermentation is interrupted to leave some residual sugar.

Lees — Dead yeast cells and other sediment cast off by a young wine as it ages.

Magnum — A container twice the size of a normal wine bottle.

Maceration — A method of softening red wines after fermentation by letting them sit with their skins and seeds in sealed tanks for several weeks.

Malolactic fermentation — A secondary fermentation that occurs in wine, converting malic acid into milder lactic acid and carbon dioxide. This action, often occurring in reds, helps reduce their youthful harshness to create a softer, more complex wine.

May wine — Sweet white wine, sometimes flavored with leaves or herbs; of German origin.

Meritage — A term adopted by several California wineries to designate red or white premium wines blended from classic French grape varieties. Red Meritage seems to be more common. A winery must join the Meritage Association and meet strict blending criteria in order to use the label. Many California wineries do similar blends—particularly reds—without calling the wine Meritage.

Méthode champenoise (*me-thoad sham-pen-WAH*) — The classic French method of making sparkling wine, in which it is produced and aged in the same bottle.

Methusalem — King-sized glass wine container, holding the equivalent of eight ordinary bottles.

Micro-climate — Specific climatic conditions in a small area—a sheltered valley or exposed knoll—that make it ideal for a particular grape.

Must — The liquid of crushed grapes, en route to becoming wine.

Nature — The driest of sparkling wines; in other words, one that is natural, supposedly with no sweetener added, although a very light *dosage* usually is.

Negociant — A winery that owns no vineyards, but buys grapes from selected growers. Advantages are that it permits flexibility and—if the firm's wines are selling well—rapid expansion.

Noble grapes — The term, given somewhat arbitrarily, to the Cabernet Sauvignon of Bordeaux, Pinot Noir and Chardonnay of Burgundy and Riesling of Germany.

Nose — The aroma and bouquet of a wine.

Oakey — Wine with a strong flavor of the wood in which it was aged.

Off — Slang taster's term, meaning that a wine is "off base"; not "on."

Off-dry — A wonderfully silly winetaster's redundancy for slightly sweet.

Ordinaire (*or-dee-nair*) — French for ordinary. *Vin ordinaire* is a basic table wine; in America, a jug wine.

Oxidized — A wine that has been exposed to air, and is starting to become vinegary.

Phylloxera (*fill-LOX-er-ah*) — Nasty little plant louse, 1/25th of an inch long, which destroys grapevines by attacking their roots. It raised havoc in America late in the nineteenth century and destroyed seventy-five percent of France's wine crop. The scourge was stopped by grafting European varietals onto phylloxera-resistant native American root stock. However, it's back on the attack in some California vineyards.

Proof — The measurement of alcohol by volume, in which the proof number, for some odd reason, represents half the alcohol content. A hundred-proof whisky is half alcohol. The term isn't used in winemaking; its measure is "percentage of alcohol"—by volume, not by weight.

Proprietary wine — Special name given to a wine by the proprietor, usually reflecting place names or some pet fetish. They're almost always blends. "Riverside Farms White" or "Workhorse Red" are examples.

Pulp — A grape's fleshy part.

Punch down — The process of breaking up the thick layer of solids that float to the top when a wine, particularly a red, is fermenting.

Racking — Clarifying a wine by drawing off the clear liquid from one cask or vat to another, leaving the lees and sediment that has settled to the bottom.

Residual sugar — The sugar that remains in a wine to give it sweetness, usually measured by percentage. In table wines, fermentation is stopped by lowering the temperature to kill the yeast cells, thus leaving residual sugar. In dessert wines, brandy is added, which pickles the yeast.

Riddling — Periodically turning and gently bumping champagne bottles to work the sediments into the neck. It can be done by hand or with automatic riddling racks.

Sack — Elizabethan term for Sherry; thus "Dry Sack."

Schloss — "Castle" in Germany, synonymous with France's "château" in describing a winery.

Sec — French for dry (not sweet), yet it describes a sweeter style of Champagne—and yes, it doesn't make sense.

Secondary fermentation — Creating a sparkling wine by injecting sugar and yeast into a still wine and keeping it sealed (in the bottle or other closed container) so the carbon dioxide bubbles can't escape. Sometimes, a secondary fermentation begins by accident because a wine is bottled with some surviving yeast and residual sugar. That, in fact, is how Champagne was accidentally discovered three centuries ago by French monk Dom Pérignon. He blurted something out about "tasting stars." Probably after he'd emptied the bottle.

Sekt — German for sparkling wine.

Set — The appearance of berries after a vine has finished flowering.

Soft — A wine lacking harshness or rough edges.

Solera — The process of blending wines of different ages but the same type to achieve a consistency of style. This practice is commonly used to produce Sherries. *Solera* refers not to the sun; it comes from *suelo*, the Spanish word for "floor," since the wines usually are blended from tiers of barrels, from top to bottom.

Stemmy — An unpleasant veggie flavor to wine, as if stems were left in during fermentation.

Still wine — Any wine that isn't sparkling.

Sulfuring — Sterilizing wine casks or barrels to kill harmful bacteria, and dusting vines with sulfur to eliminate fungus.

Sur lie aging — The technique of letting white wines rest on their yeast lees (and sometimes other solids) for months, causing the release of amino acids, esters and other compounds. This adds to the wine's complexity.

Tannin — Organic acid found in most plant matter. In wine, it comes primarily from the skins and seeds of grapes. Reds are higher in tannin because they're usually fermented with their skins. Tannin adds complexity, and an acidic "bite" to wine. Aging mellows these tannins while leaving the full, complex flavor. Don't be alarmed, but tannic acid is used to treat leather, thus the word "tan."

Tartar — Those sparkly little crystals you may see on the underside of a cork are tartaric acid, which occurs naturally in wine and settles out during aging. If the wine is stored upside down, which it should be, the crystals settle onto the cork. Don't worry; they're harmless.

Tirage (*tee-RAJ*) — French word with three definitions: 1. The sugar-syrup yeast mixture added to still wine (*liqueur de tirage*) to begin secondary fermentation; 2. Drawing off wine, usually from a barrel into a bottle; 3. *En tirage* indicates bottles stacked for aging.

Vermouth — Yes, that stuff that adds zing to your martini is a wine. Vermouth originated in Germany and is flavored with assorted herbs and spices. The word comes from *wermut* or wormwood, whose flowers are used to add aroma. Both sweet and dry Vermouths are produced in California. In Europe, sweet Vermouth is usually made in Italy and dry Vermouth is associated with France.

Vertical tasting — Sampling several wines of the same variety from different vintages, usually from the same winery. Horizontal tasting is sampling the same variety of wines from different wineries.

Viniculture — The science of growing grapes for wine production.

Vintage — The year in which grapes of a particular wine were harvested. In California, a wine bottle can be "vintage dated" only if ninety-five percent of the grapes therein were harvested in that year. The harvest itself is sometimes called the "vintage."

Viticulture — The science of grape-growing in general.

Vineyard designated wine — A varietal named for the vineyard where the grapes were grown; ninety-five percent of the grapes must be from there.

Vitis labrusca — The American grape, found growing wild and used unsuccessfully in early attempts at winemaking. Its rootstock, however, proved resistant to deadly phylloxera, so it became the base for many premium grapes, both in Europe and America.

Vitis vinifera — The source of most premium grapes; the vine grew wild in Asia Minor and likely was one of mankind's first cultivated crops. The Crusaders probably brought cuttings back to Europe.

INDEX: Primary listings indicated by *bold face italics*

A BIT ABOUT THE AUTHORS

Don and Betty Martin have written more than twenty guidebooks on travel and wine, mostly under their *DISCOVERGUIDES* and Pine Cone Press banners. When not tending to their publishing company in Las Vegas, they explore America and the world beyond, seeking new places and new experiences for their readers. Both are members of the Society of American Travel Writers. They are gold medal winners in the Best Guidebook category of the annual Lowell Thomas Travel Journalism Awards, North America's most prestigious travel writing competition.

Don, who provides most of the adjectives, has been a journalist since he was sixteen, when classmates elected him editor of his high school newspaper. (No one else wanted the job.) After school, he left his small family farm in Idaho, wandered about the country a bit, and then joined the Marine Corps. He was assigned as a military correspondent in the Orient and at bases in California. Back in civvies, he worked as a reporter, sports writer and editor for several West Coast newspapers, then he became associate editor of a San Francisco-based travel magazine. He left to establish Pine Cone Press, Inc., and now devotes his time to writing, travel and—for some odd reason—collecting squirrel and chipmunk artifacts. He has been a serious wine sipper for more than four decades and has written numerous wine articles for newspapers and magazines.

Betty, a Chinese-American whose varied credentials have included a doctorate in pharmacy and a real estate broker's license, does much of the research, editing and photography for their books. She also has written travel articles for assorted newspapers and magazines and sold photos through a New York stock agency. Exhibiting a scholarly interest in wine, she has taken courses through the hospitality management program of Columbia (California) College and the Napa Valley Wine Library Association. Even though she has an excellent palate, she's not much of a wine drinker—thus leaving more Zinfandel for Don. When she isn't helping Don run *DISCOVERGUIDES* she wanders the globe—with or without him. Her travels have taken her from Cuba to Antarctica.

Remarkably useful DISCOVERGUIDES
By Don & Betty Martin

Critics praise the "jaunty prose" and "beautiful editing" of travel, wine and relocation guides by authors Don and Betty Martin. They are recent winners of a gold medal for best guidebook of the year in the annual Lowell Thomas Travel Writing Competition. Their DISCOVERGUIDES are available at bookstores throughout the United States and Canada, or you can order them on line at **www.amazon.com, bn.com** or **borders.com.**

ARIZONA DISCOVERY GUIDE

This guide covers attractions, scenic drives, hikes and walks, dining, lodgings and campgrounds in the Grand Canyon State. A "Snowbird" section helps retirees plan their Arizona winters.   — **408 pages; $15.95**

ARIZONA IN YOUR FUTURE

It's a complete relocation guide for job-seekers, retirees and "Snowbirds" planning a move to Arizona. It provides essential data on dozens of cities, from recreation to medical facilities.   — **272 pages; $15.95**

THE BEST OF DENVER AND THE ROCKIES

Discover the very finest of the Mile High City, from its Ten Best attractions, museums and parks to its leading restaurants and lodgings, and then explore attractions of the nearby Rockies.   — **256 pages; $16.95**

THE BEST OF THE WINE COUNTRY

Where to taste wine in California? More than 350 wineries are featured, along with nearby restaurants, lodging and attractions. Special sections offer tips on storing and serving wine.   — **348 pages; $16.95**

CALIFORNIA-NEVADA ROADS LESS TRAVELED

This is a "Discovery guide to places less crowded." It directs travelers to interesting yet uncrowded attractions, hideaway resorts, scenic campgrounds, interesting cafes and other discoveries.   — **336 pages; $15.95**

LAS VEGAS: THE BEST OF GLITTER CITY

This impertinent insiders' guide explores the world's greatest party town, with expanded "Ten Best" lists of casino resorts, restaurants, attractions, buffets, shows and much more!   — **296 pages; $15.95**

NEVADA DISCOVERY GUIDE

This comprehensive travel guide covers all of the Silver State, with a special focus on the gaming centers of Las Vegas, Reno-Tahoe and Laughlin. A special section advises readers how to "Beat the odds," with casino gambling tips.   — **416 pages; $15.95**

NEVADA IN YOUR FUTURE

It's a complete relocation guide to the Silver State, with useful information for job-seekers, businesses, retirees and winter "Snowbirds." A special section discusses incorporating in Nevada. — *292 pages; $16.95*

NEW MEXICO DISCOVERY GUIDE

This useful guide takes travelers from Santa Fe and Taos to busy Albuquerque, Carlsbad Caverns and beyond. — *384 pages; $16.95*

OREGON DISCOVERY GUIDE

From wilderness coasts to the Cascades to urban Portland, this book guides motorists and RVers throughout the state. —*448 pages; $17.95*

SAN DIEGO: THE BEST OF SUNSHINE CITY

Winner of a Lowell Thomas gold medal for best travel guide, this lively and whimsical book picks the finest of sunny San Diego, featuring its Ten Best attractions, restaurants and much more. —*248 pages; $15.95*

SEATTLE: THE BEST OF EMERALD CITY

This upbeat and opinionated book steers visitors to the very best of Emerald City and the rest of Western Washington. —*236 pages; $15.95*

THE ULTIMATE WINE BOOK

This great little book covers the subject in three major areas—Wine and Heath, Wine Appreciation and Wine with Food. And it does so with good humor, poking harmless fun at wine critics —*194 pages; $10.95*

UTAH DISCOVERY GUIDE

It's a remarkably useful driving guide covering every corner of the Beehive State, from its splendid canyonlands to Salt Lake City to the "Jurassic Parkway" of dinosaur country. —*360 pages; $13.95*

WASHINGTON DISCOVERY GUIDE

This handy book steers motorists and RVers from the Olympic Peninsula to Seattle to the Cascades and beyond. —*464 pages; $17.95*

DISCOVERGUIDES ARE AVAILABLE AT BOOKSTORES EVERYWHERE

If your store doesn't have a title in stock, tell the clerk it can be ordered from any major distributor, such as Publishers Groups West, Ingram or Baker & Taylor. And you can buy our books on-line from *www.amazon.com, bn.com* and *borders.com.*

TRADE BOOK BUYERS

DISCOVERGUIDES are available through
PUBLISHERS GROUP WEST — (800) 788-3123